ENTREPRENEURSHIP

ENTREPRENEURSHIP

David Stokes
Nick Wilson
Martha Mador

SOUTH-WESTERN
CENGAGE Learning

Australia • Brazil • Japan • Korea • Mexico • Singapore • Spain • United Kingdom • United States

SOUTH-WESTERN
CENGAGE Learning™

Entrepreneurship

David Stokes, Nick Wilson and Martha Mador

Publishing Director: Linden Harris

Publisher: Tom Rennie

Development Editor: Jennifer Seth

Editorial Assistant: Charlotte Green

Content Project Editor: Oliver Jones and Adam Paddon

Head of Manufacturing: Jane Glendening

Senior Production Controller: Paul Herbert

Marketing Manager: Amanda Cheung

Typesetter: MPS Limited, A Macmillan Company

Cover design: Adam Renvoize

Text design: Design Deluxe, Bath, UK

For product information and technology assistance, contact **emea.info@cengage.com**.

For permission to use material from this text or product, and for permission queries, email **clsuk.permissions@cengage.com**.

The Author has asserted the right under the Copyright, Designs and Patents Act 1988 to be identified as Author of this Work.

British Library Cataloguing-in-Publication Data
A catalogue record for this book is available from the British Library.

ISBN: 978-1-4080-0745-7

Cengage Learning EMEA
Cheriton House, North Way, Andover, Hampshire, SP10 5BE, United Kingdom

Cengage Learning products are represented in Canada by Nelson Education Ltd.

For your lifelong learning solutions, visit **www.cengage.co.uk**

Purchase your next print book, e-book or e-chapter at **www.CengageBrain.com**

Printed in Singapore
1 2 3 4 5 6 7 8 9 10 – 12 11 10

Dedicated to Charles Stokes, Philip Wilson and Ray Crotty

BRIEF TABLE OF CONTENTS

CONTENTS

PREFACE

IN SEARCH OF ENTREPRENEURSHIP

This book goes 'in search of entrepreneurship'. It seeks to present both theory and practice, aiming to clarify the underpinning theoretical concepts as well as to demonstrate the practical applications of how entrepreneurship does – or doesn't – work.

We investigate entrepreneurship from three particular perspectives, dividing the book into three Parts to reflect each one:

■ **Part 1, In search of entrepreneurship**, explores entrepreneurship as a *process* that identifies opportunities and seeks to make something of value from them. This process involves other well-known concepts such as creativity, innovation and social capital. It is a process that has become vital to the economies of the world in a variety of contexts that span the private and public sectors of small, large and not-for-profit organisations. It begins with an idea that grows into a new venture and finishes when the enterprise closes after a relatively successful or unsuccessful existence.

■ **Part 2, In search of the entrepreneur**, looks for the entrepreneur as a *person*, attempting to find out who they are and what they do by investigating their attributes, skills and behaviours. Concluding that entrepreneurs are both born *and* made, it assesses key areas for personal entrepreneurial development such as self-efficacy and networking. It explores how entrepreneurs do things that set them apart in key areas including managing creativity, recognising opportunities, leveraging resources, decision-making, dealing with risk and planning.

■ **Part 3, In search of enterprise value**, investigates how entrepreneurs create *value* through the development of an entrepreneurial venture. It devotes a chapter to each of five key areas that have particular potential to add value to any enterprise: market position and customer base; knowledge and intellectual property; the development of an entrepreneurial team; viable business models and processes; and cash flow and financial management.

As you read through this book you will discover more about the nature of entrepreneurship, its importance in society and its reliance on our individual creative potential. We have ensured that each chapter gives lots of examples of how entrepreneurship unfolds in a wide range of contexts. These are not just success stories but also feature mistakes and failures as entrepreneurs specialise in learning from experience – bad as well as good. Many examples are embedded within each chapter, but at the end of each Part we have added three more cases (nine in total) contributed by guest authors from around the world.

We hope this will guide your own entrepreneurial journey and inspire you to an entrepreneurial future.

David Stokes, Nick Wilson and Martha Mador

ABOUT THE AUTHORS

Dr David Stokes combines an academic with a practical involvement in entrepreneurship. He is Director of Entrepreneurship, Kingston University and a director of an electronics manufacturing company that he co-founded. Following education at Oriel College, Oxford and the City University Business School, his management career has been with large and small enterprises in the private and public sectors. As director of WestFocus, a consortium of seven universities, he has responsibility for the development of entrepreneurship education amongst students and staff of all disciplines. He is Chair of the Higher Education Entrepreneurship Group of the South East Development Agency that includes 23 universities. He has published widely and is co-author of other popular text books including Small Business Management and Entrepreneurship, 6th Edition, and Marketing: a Brief Introduction both published by Cengage Learning.

Dr Nick Wilson is Senior Lecturer in Cultural and Creative Industries at the Centre for Cultural, Media & Creative Industries Research at King's College London. He was previously Principal Lecturer in Entrepreneurship and Small Business at Kingston University, and Course Director of the Programme of Master's courses in the Creative Industries & the Creative Economy. He studied music at Clare College, Cambridge and went on to train as a singer at the Royal College of Music, London and the Hochschule der Künste, Berlin, before moving into music management, working for a leading artist management and concert promotions company. After completing his MBA, he joined the Small Business Research Centre, Kingston University, as a researcher and lecturer, subsequently completing his doctoral thesis on the emergence of the early music performance labour market in the UK. He has undertaken a wide range of research and consultancy projects focusing on entrepreneurship and the creative industries. His current research interests include exploring the boundaries of the creative economy, the relationship between creativity and entrepreneurship, the need for a new discipline of social creativity, and the role of multi-disciplinary learning in creativity, arts, entrepreneurship and management. With David Stokes, he is co-author of Small Business Management and Entrepreneurship, 6th Edition published by Cengage Learning.

Dr Martha Mador is Head of Enterprise Education at Kingston University, London. Her background encompasses marketing roles in new media companies, programme development and direction at Kingston Business School, and entrepreneurship promotion across London and the South-East of England. Educated in Toronto and the UK, Martha holds degrees from Trinity College University of Toronto, Cranfield School of Management, and Henley Management College. Through the WestFocus collaboration, Martha has developed a programme of extra-curricular entrepreneurship activities designed to develop and meet the aspirations of students across the 7 universities. She is responsible for the cross-university development of in-curriculum and extra-curricular entrepreneurship education at Kingston University. Martha's business interests focus on consultancy and management development work in the private and public sectors.

ACKNOWLEDGEMENTS

Thanks to all the entrepreneurs and student entrepreneurs whose experiences helped to fill this book. Particular thanks to the Kingston University Entrepreneurship Centre (KUEC), WestFocus and HEEG teams including:

Alan Fitzgerald	Chris Rye	Nadia Zernina
Alison McGregor	Hsin Chen	Neil Lockwood
Anna Faulkner	Ingrid Stafford	Richard Sant
Cassie Talfourd-Rich	Jenny Ilsley	Tony Greenwood
Charise Rawlinson	Julie Powell	Yuliana Topazly

In addition to the dozens of international academics who answered online surveys at the start of this project, the publisher would particularly like to thank the following academics for supplying detailed feedback on the proposal and manuscript which has helped inform the development of this new textbook:

Mary Bragg, London Metropolitan University
Dermot Breslin, University of Sheffield
Tony Douglas, Napier University
Paul Ferri, University of the West of Scotland
Margaret Fletcher, University of Glasgow
Karl Lester, University of Cumbria
John Lewis, University of Glasgow
Kate Pascoe, University of Northampton
Andreas Rauch, RSM Erasmus University Rotterdam
Retha Scheepers, University of Stellenbosch
David Taylor, Manchester Metropolitan University
Louise Tetting, Umeå University
Christian Viertel, International University in Geneva

We would also like to thank the international range of academics who kindly supplied case studies that appear throughout this textbook where credited:

Torben Bager, University of Southern Denmark
Steve Barnes, University Campus Suffolk
Chris Birch, Thames Valley University
Dermot Breslin, University of Sheffield
Mike Clements, Staffordshire University
Jun Li, University of Essex
Fernando Lourenço, Manchester Metropolitan University
Suna Løwe Nielsen, University of Southern Denmark
Retha Scheepers, University of Stellenbosch
S.H.J. van den Hoogen, Tilburg University

INTEGRATIVE CASE STUDIES

WALK-THROUGH TOUR

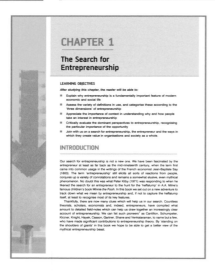

Learning Objectives appear at the start of every chapter to help you monitor your understanding and progress through the chapter

Preview Cases appear at the start and end of each chapter to frame your learning within a real-world context

Entrepreneurship in Action appear throughout every chapter to provide real-world illustrations of the surrounding theory

When Things Go Wrong some of the best insights into enterprise can be found in failed ventures and these unique examples provide you with a realistic understanding of modern enterprise

Summary each chapter ends with a comprehensive summary that provides a thorough re-cap of the key issues in each chapter, helping you to assess your understanding and revise key content

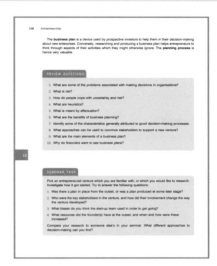

Review Questions and Seminar Tasks are provided at the end of each chapter to help reinforce and test your knowledge and understanding, and provide a basis for group discussions and activities

References and Further Reading comprehensive references at the end of each chapter allow you to explore the subject further, while annotated further reading acts as a starting point for projects and assignments

Integrative Cases have been contributed by international academics to help consolidate learning by bringing together all of the themes and concepts discussed throughout the textbook

ABOUT THE WEBSITE

Visit the *Entrepreneurship* companion website at www.cengage.co.uk/stokeswilsonmador to find valuable teaching and learning material including:

For Students
Website Links
Case Study Updates
Multiple-Choice Questions
Additional Tutorial Activities

For Lecturers
Downloadable Instructor's Manual
PowerPoint Slides
Additional Case Material
Additional Tutorial Activities

ENTREPRENEURSHIP

Part 1

IN SEARCH OF ENTREPRENEURSHIP

Going in Search of Entrepreneurship

Like most students, Jasmine and Jake were short of money so when they saw a poster for a competition advertising prizes of £1000 they were naturally interested. The problem was that they knew little about the subject of the competition – entrepreneurship.

'Prizes will be awarded to students demonstrating their entrepreneurship potential by successfully completing an entrepreneurial project', Jake read out.

'What do they mean by "entrepreneurship"?' asked Jasmine.

'Coming up with an invention?' suggested Jake.

'Or maybe persuading investors to back it.' Jasmine took a closer look at the small print. 'No it says that you have to come up with an idea for a social enterprise in a team of two or more people.'

'I didn't know enterprise could be social. Maybe we should ask a few other people about entrepreneurship if we are going to have a serious chance of winning any prizes', said Jake.

So they began to ask around about entrepreneurship.

Jake emailed the professor of entrepreneurship at the University. He sent back seven different definitions of entrepreneurship and a list of journal articles to read.

'It says entrepreneurship is about moving resources from an area where they are relatively undervalued to an area where they have greater value', summarised Jake. 'Any idea what that means?'

Jasmine quizzed her father, who ran his own business. 'Entrepreneurship is about discovering an opportunity and doing something about it', he said.

Jake asked a friend who worked for a bank. 'Our manager says that entrepreneurship is about three things if it is to succeed: innovation, innovation and innovation. But our business customers tell me it's more than just that', she said.

Jasmine telephoned her local Member of Parliament who said that entrepreneurship was at the heart of the economy and would provide the new growth to get the country moving forward again.

Jake discussed entrepreneurship with the owner of a cafe he frequented. He found his reply the most intriguing of all. 'It's about keeping going even when everything goes pear-shaped, until one day something goes right. So you could say it's about failing in order to succeed.'

If Jasmine and Jake asked you to tell them what entrepreneurship was about, what would you say?

Learning Objectives and Structure of Part 1

Like Jasmine and Jake, this section of the book goes in search of entrepreneurship. It investigates the meaning of the term 'entrepreneurship' and various aspects that make it a distinctive process in our society. It considers why it has become such an important phenomenon in the global economy and in many different aspects of our lives. It emphasises the dynamic nature of entrepreneurship that changes over time.

By the end of Part 1, the reader should be able to:

■ Define what entrepreneurship is all about

■ Assess the properties and constituent parts of the entrepreneurship process

■ Understand the key role of the creative process and innovation

■ Evaluate the importance of entrepreneurship in global economies

■ Understand the various different contexts in which entrepreneurship can take place

■ Analyse the life cycles of entrepreneurship from enterprise creation to closure and exit.

There are six chapters that focus on these learning objectives:

Chapter 1   The search for entrepreneurship

Chapter 2   The properties of entrepreneurship

Chapter 3   Entrepreneurship and innovation

Chapter 4   Entrepreneurship and the economy

Chapter 5   Entrepreneurship in context

Chapter 6   The life cycle of entrepreneurship

CHAPTER 1

The Search for Entrepreneurship

LEARNING OBJECTIVES

After studying this chapter, the reader will be able to:

- Explain why entrepreneurship is a fundamentally important feature of modern economic and social life
- Assess the variety of definitions in use, and categorise these according to the 'three dimensions' of entrepreneurship
- Appreciate the importance of context in understanding why and how people take an interest in entrepreneurship
- Critically evaluate the dominant perspectives to entrepreneurship, recognising the particular importance of the opportunity
- Join with us on a search for entrepreneurship, the entrepreneur and the ways in which they create value in organisations and society as a whole.

INTRODUCTION

Our search for entrepreneurship is not a new one. We have been fascinated by the entrepreneur at least as far back as the mid-nineteenth century, when the term first came into common usage in the writings of the French economist Jean-Baptiste Say (1803). The term 'entrepreneurship' still elicits all sorts of reactions from people, conjures up a variety of connotations and remains a somewhat elusive, even mythical phenomenon. No doubt this was what Peter Kilby (1971) was responding to when he likened the search for an entrepreneur to the hunt for the 'heffalump' in A.A. Milne's famous children's book *Winnie the Pooh*. In this book we set out on a new adventure to track down what we mean by entrepreneurship and, if not to capture the heffalump itself, at least to recognise most of its key features.

Thankfully, there are now many clues which will help us in our search. Countless theorists, scholars, economists and, indeed, entrepreneurs, have compiled what amount to detailed field-notes which can help us draw together an increasingly clear account of entrepreneurship. We can list such pioneers[1] as Cantillon, Schumpeter, Kirzner, Knight, Hayek, Casson, Gartner, Shane and Venkataraman, to name but a few, who have made significant contributions to entrepreneurship theory. By 'standing on the shoulders of giants' in this book we hope to be able to get a better view of the mythical entrepreneurship beast.

PREVIEW CASE

The sweet taste of entrepreneurship

When Craig Sams and Jo Fairley decided to launch an organic chocolate bar in 1991, they brainstormed a suitable brand name in their Notting Hill pad. Remembering childhood confectionery brands such as Callard & Bowser, Barker & Dobson and Charbonnel & Walker, they decided an ampersand would give it class. 'Green' hit the organic button, while 'Black' highlighted the darkness created by the high cocoa content. In ten minutes, the couple had created Green & Black's, now a £100m brand with a range of confectionery, hot drinks, ice cream and snacks sold around the world.

Why were Craig and Jo able to create a brand in ten minutes whereas marketing departments typically take many weeks over a brand creation process?

See the Case study 'Sweet taste of entrepreneurship' at the end of the chapter for more about Green & Black's.

COURTESY OF GREEN AND BLACK'S

Source: Sams, C. and Fairley, J. (2009) The Story of Green & Black's: How two entrepreneurs turned an ethical idea into a business success. (Random House, London)

We probably all believe we would recognise an 'entrepreneur' if we met one – yet if asked to describe the properties of this particular type of individual, we might find the task much harder. The modern-day media treatment of the entrepreneur tends to produce something of an iconic image – a cross between Richard Branson, Alan Sugar, Donald Trump and Anita Roddick. Television programmes like *The Dragon's Den* and *The Apprentice* often present a ruthlessness that the audience can both love and hate. On the one hand, we might admire an individual's capacity to be single-minded and devoted to the task of winning a deal or investment; on the other hand, we might shudder at the apparent insensitivity required to make this happen.

Entrepreneurial qualities

This is how one commentator[2] summarised the qualities needed for successful entrepreneurship. Do you agree with them all?

1   A high level of drive and energy.

2   Enough self-confidence to take carefully calculated risk.

3   A clear idea of money as a way of keeping score and as a means of generating more money.

4   The ability to get other people to work with you and for you productively.

5   High but realistic and achievable goals.

6   Belief that you can control your own destiny.

1

7 Readiness to learn from your own mistakes and failures.

8 A long-term vision of the future of your business.

9 Intense competitive urge, with self-imposed standards.

Despite the interest, there still remains considerable confusion over exactly what is involved in entrepreneurship. To address this and make a contribution to our overall understanding of this fascinating and important phenomenon, we start by reviewing in more detail some of the definitions put forward.

1.1   DEFINITIONAL MAYHEM

1.1.1 The Three Dimensions of Entrepreneurship

Entrepreneurship is seen as a fundamentally important part of modern economic and social life. Entrepreneurs play a key role in our societies. So what exactly is entrepreneurship and what sets entrepreneurs apart from other managers?

Key features of entrepreneurship definitions

There are at least eight different features which regularly feature in definitions of entrepreneurship:[3]

1 The *environment* within which entrepreneurship occurs.

2 The *people* engaged in entrepreneurship.

3 *Entrepreneurial behaviours* displayed by entrepreneurs.

4 The *creation of organisations* by entrepreneurs.

5 *Opportunities* identified and exploited.

6 *Innovation*, whether incremental, radical and/or transformative.

7 Assuming *risk*, at personal, organisational and even societal levels.

8 *Adding value* for the entrepreneur and society.

Which of these features do you think would be of most interest to:

■ *Entrepreneurship educators?*

■ *Entrepreneurship policy-makers?*

■ *Young entrepreneurs?*

■ *Corporates?*

■ *Venture capitalists?*

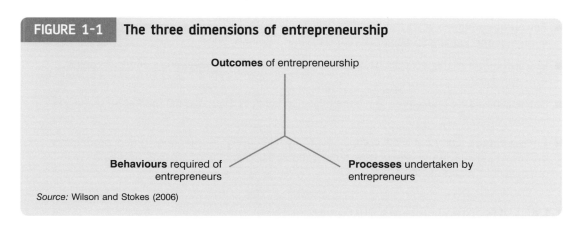

FIGURE 1-1 **The three dimensions of entrepreneurship**

Outcomes of entrepreneurship

Behaviours required of
entrepreneurs

Processes undertaken by
entrepreneurs

Source: Wilson and Stokes (2006)

As there are many different definitions of entrepreneurship we can usefully categorise them according to three main 'dimensions of entrepreneurship', which focus attention on **behaviours**, **processes** and **outcomes** (see Figure 1-1).

1.1.2 Entrepreneurship as Process

These definitions all focus in the first instance on the process of entrepreneurship – what is involved and why it matters to individuals, organisations and society as a whole. For example:

■ **Entrepreneurship** is 'the process of creating something new of value by devoting the necessary time and effort, assuming the accompanying financial, psychic and social risks, and receiving the resulting rewards of monetary and personal satisfaction and independence' (Hisrich and Peters, 2002).

■ **Entrepreneurship** is 'the process by which individuals – either on their own or inside organisations – pursue opportunities without regard to the resources they currently control' (Stevenson and Jarillo, 1990).

The *process* dimension has often centred on the development of a new business or innovation strategy and the writing of a business plan, activities that are sometimes viewed as surrogate for the entrepreneurship process itself. This confuses the micro level 'agential' processes of entrepreneurial activities, that is the nuts and bolts practices carried out by individual entrepreneurs with the 'structural' process at the level of societal change.

1.1.3 Entrepreneurship as Behaviours

These definitions are concerned to highlight the role of particular individuals (whom we call entrepreneurs) with specific behaviours which set them apart from others. For example:

■ **Entrepreneurship** is 'the manifest ablity and willingness of individuals, on their own, in teams, within and outside existing organisations, to: perceive and create new economic opportunities (new products, new production methods, new organisational schemes and new product–market combinations) and to introduce their ideas in the market, in the face of uncertainty and other obstacles, by making decisions on location, form and the use of resources and institutions' (Wennekers and Thurik, 1999).

1

- **Entrepreneurship** is 'a way of thinking, reasoning and acting that is opportunity based, holistic in approach and leadership balanced' (Timmons and Spinelli, 2004).

- **Entrepreneurs** are 'specialists who use judgment to deal with novel and complex problems' (Casson, 1982).

- **Entrepreneurship** consists of 'the competitive behaviours that drive the market process' (Kirzner, 1973).

- **Entrepreneurs** 'carry out "new combinations" by such things as introducing new products or processes, identifying new export markets or sources of supply, or creating new types of organisation' (Schumpeter, 1934).

1.1.4 Entrepreneurship as Outcomes

These definitions focus on the results of entrepreneurship (as a process or set of behaviours). Outcomes are usually understood in terms of new products and services, innovation, new ventures and/ or the creation of value for society. For example:

- **Entrepreneurship** is 'the introduction of new economic activity that leads to change in the market place' (Simon in Sarasvathy, 1999).

- **Entrepreneurship** is 'the creation of new organisations' (Gartner, 1988).

- **Entrepreneurship** 'results in the creation, enhancement, realisation and renewal of value not just for the owners but for all participants and stakeholders' (Timmons and Spinelli, 2004).

There is clearly a good deal of overlap in many of these definitions, as their authors themselves often suggest. Whilst Gartner (1988), for example, focuses on the creation of a new organisation as the outcome of entrepreneurship, he also stresses the importance of studying the behaviours required to achieve this outcome.

1.1.5 A Summary of Definitions

As we discuss later in this chapter, there is increasing awareness of the importance of *all* three dimensions. Entrepreneurship is understood in terms of the synthesis of behaviours, processes and outcomes – or the behaviours undertaken in the processes of discovery and exploitation of ideas for new business ventures (Davidsson, 2003: 47). Elsewhere,[4] we define entrepreneurship as a societal phenomenon or process of change, comprising the following three behavioural components:

1 The identification, evaluation and exploitation of an opportunity.

2 The management of a new or transformed organisation so as to facilitate the production and consumption of new goods and services.

3 The creation of value through the successful exploitation of a new idea (i.e. innovation).

We can now summarise what we know about entrepreneurship so far:

- We know that entrepreneurship is a phenomenon that affects peoples and societies – it is a creative process of social and organisational change (the focus of Part 1 of this book).

- We know that entrepreneurship involves the introduction of new products, services and markets (as well as new organisations).

1

- We know that entrepreneurship depends upon individuals with particular skills, attributes and behaviours – whom we call entrepreneurs (the focus of Part 2 of this book).

- We also know a good deal about how entrepreneurs create value (this will form the focus of Part 3 of this book).

1.2   ENTREPRENEURSHIP – A QUESTION OF CONTEXT

1.2.1 The Diversity of the Entrepreneurial Context

Definitions of entrepreneurship are dependent on *whose* perspective is being considered. Low and Macmillan (1988) discuss the *focus* of entrepreneurship analysis (i.e. the specific phenomena that should be investigated), the *level of analysis* (ranging from individual, group, organisation, industry and society), and the *time frame*. Elsewhere, the Cambridge economist Tony Lawson (1997) suggests that our particular *vantage point* has a significant bearing on how we perceive any object of study.

Whilst entrepreneurship is usually associated with the world of business, the context for entrepreneurship is highly differentiated, and there are all sorts of different and specialised accounts which focus on variables as diverse as gender, family and ethnicity (Carter and Dylan-Jones, 2000); industry sectors such as technology-based firms (Oakey, 1994); green entrepreneurship and the development of 'ecopreneurship' (Schaper, 2002); and cultural entrepreneurship

Integrative Case Link
Read more about how entrepreneurs are inspired to take up opportunities for the benefit of their community in Case Study 3 at the end of Part 1.

ENTREPRENEURSHIP IN ACTION

The importance of context – Tukiso Mokoena at the Branson School of Entrepreneurship[5]

'My name is Tukiso. I've always had a passion for African development, poverty eradication, wealth creation and distribution. For me, education is a means of empowerment. You empower individuals to positively contribute to society. Growing up, education was an afterthought for me. I really didn't like the system I was forced to study under. But things changed when I got a mentor and a bursary to finish my matriculation at a private school. It's through that grant that I ended up at CIDA (a business and leadership university with

the Branson School of Entrepreneurship). Great emphasis is placed on the personal development of individuals through emotional intelligence and creativity. CIDA is a vehicle that will help me fulfil my vision of becoming an entrepreneur. I want to empower my community and transform the economy of South Africa. I'm currently involved in the South African leg of *The Apprentice* as part of the creative team. It doesn't matter who you are or where you come from, if you put your mind to it, you can achieve the impossible. Impossible is nothing.'

Reproduced with permission from The Cida Foundation: www.cidafoundation.org

WHEN THINGS GO WRONG

Rhee Nami faces a culture clash

The Korean born designer and illustrator Rhee Nami worked for 13 years in America before returning to her native Korea in order to set up her own publishing venture. During this time she broadened her skills and contacts and developed her creativity in many ways, benefiting from the exposure to US media and culture. Full of enthusiasm, she arrived back in Korea in 1994 and launched her new magazine – *EVE*. It was quickly apparent, however, that Korean culture was more conservative than Rhee had become accustomed to in America. *EVE* never took off. Rhee was not deterred by this failure, however, and soon she had set up a small design and publishing studio, producing mini books which could be given as gifts. These mini books took Korea by storm. Rhee was involved in all aspects of the book production, including writing, illustrating, designing and manufacturing. Rhee's new enterprise 'Studio Baf' soon gained an enviable reputation for their highly creative products, which are now sold worldwide.

Source: From a case-study prepared by Seung Hee Ko, London, 2009.

(Leadbeater and Oakley, 1999; Fillis and McAuley, 2000; Brindley, 2000; Ellmeier, 2003; Wilson and Stokes, 2005). We can also point to a growing interest in international entrepreneurship in the sense of understanding the different economic and socio-cultural conditions that impact entrepreneurship as it is carried out across the world (see, for example, Bannock, 2005; Begley and Tan, 2001) in an increasingly competitive environment.

In this section we consider entrepreneurship from the vantage point of governments, corporate businesses, small and medium-sized businesses, economists, researchers and educationalists, as well as entrepreneurs and 'nascent' entrepreneurs.

1.2.2 The Context of Government

The basic premise of many (though not all) governments is that entrepreneurship is a source of potential benefit for society as a whole. If entrepreneurship generates wealth and jobs, it is a good news story, and one that can and should be supported. Typically, policy support for entrepreneurship at this level is equated with (1) stimulating the setting up of new businesses, and (2) encouraging more innovative businesses which will have the potential to grow at a fast rate.

Entrepreneurship in South Africa – The Apprentice Nation?[6]

In a bid to tackle South Africa's persistent unemployment rate (at least 35 per cent), entrepreneurship has become a key part of the evolving post-apartheid curriculum. Students can't necessarily count on getting good jobs when they graduate, so they're being taught to create their own work. Equipping schoolchildren with entrepreneurial skills emerged as a key means of combating South Africa's unemployment problems. There remain significant problems, however, not least in reinforcing an entrepreneurial culture. While politicians and sporting heroes receive much adulation, most South Africans have little appreciation of what it takes to build a successful business.

However, this is slowly changing as a result of increased media coverage. The TV series '*The Apprentice*' has been credited with doing much to raise the awareness regarding the value of entrepreneurship.

The OECD's Entrepreneurship Framework sets out the potential societal and economic impact of entrepreneurship, distinguishing between entrepreneurial 'determinants', 'entrepreneurial performance' and 'impact' (see Figure 1-2). Policy interest in entrepreneurship (and subsequent performance measurement) can be profiled against the potential for job creation, economic growth and poverty reduction. Each of these areas, in turn, relate to performance in respect of firms, employment and wealth. Key determinants of entrepreneurship within a given country include the regulatory framework, research and development (R&D) and technology, entrepreneurial capabilities, culture, access to finance and market conditions.

FIGURE 1-2 Framework for European indicators

Determinants						Entrepreneurial performance	Impact
Regulatory framework	R&D and technology	Entrepreneurial capabilities	Culture	Access to finance	Market conditions	Firms	Job creation
Administrative burdens for entry	R&D investment	Training and experience of entrepreneurs	Risk attitude in society	Access to debt financing	Anti-trust laws		
Administrative burdens for growth	University/ industry interface	Business and entrepreneurship education (skills)	Attitudes towards entrepreneurs	Business angels	Competition	Employment	Economic growth
Bankruptcy regulations	Technological cooperation between firms	Entrepreneurship infrastructure	Desire for business ownership	Access to VC	Access to the domestic market	Wealth	Poverty reduction
Safety, health and environmental regulations	Technology diffusion	Immigration	Entrepreneurship education (mindset)	Access to other types of equity	Access to foreign markets		
Product regulation	Broadband access			Stock markets	Degree of public involvement		
Labour market regulation	Patent system; standards				Public procurement		
Court and legal framework							
Social and health security							
Income taxes; wealth/bequest taxes							
Business and capital taxes							

Source: OECD/EUROSTAT

1

In March 2008, the UK Prime Minister outlined his vision of building 'the strongest entrepreneurial culture that the world has ever seen'. He went on to articulate this culture in terms of encouraging 'young people to realize and unlock their talents so that their potential is realized to the full' (BERR, 2008: 10), and 'to be enterprising, whether expressed through starting or growing a business' (BERR, 2008: 22).

It is interesting to note how policy-makers appear to refer to 'enterprise' and 'entrepreneurship' as if they are interchangeable. Actually, as we shall explore, there are important differences between enterprising and entrepreneurial individuals. Put simply, in order to be entrepreneurial you need to act in an enterprising way. Entrepreneurship requires being enterprising in a particular context – where innovative new products and/or services are produced.

Entrepreneurs and entrepreneurship[7]

■ Entrepreneurs are those persons (business owners) who seek to generate value, through the creation or expansion of economic activity, by identifying and exploiting new products, processes or markets.

■ Entrepreneurial activity is the enterprising human action in pursuit of the generation of value, through the creation or expansion of economic activity, by identifying and exploiting new products, processes or markets.

■ Entrepreneurship is the phenomenon associated with entrepreneurial activity.

Innovative new products and services are produced in a wide range of contexts. At a fundamental level, however, we can distinguish between large established firms, or 'corporates', and the small and medium-sized enterprises which make up the bulk of enterprise activity in most countries.

1.2.3 The Context of Commerce

Large Companies   In a corporate context, entrepreneurship is associated positively with innovation and growth. It may also be associated negatively with a group of people who, frankly, are difficult to manage. There is an obvious dilemma for large organisations here. On the one hand, the imperative to innovate, in order to keep ahead of the competition, demands employees who can bring this innovation about. On the other hand, such people (sometimes referred to as 'intrapreneurs' or 'corporate entrepreneurs') are often seen as mavericks and troublesome by the management.

Corporate perspectives on entrepreneurs[8]

Here are some of the opinions expressed by corporate leaders in a recent focus group on 'entrepreneurs in the corporate workplace':

'These people tend to have a lot of bad attributes but also some brilliant ones ... '
'Entrepreneurs are very high maintenance people ... they get angry and upset, so they go and step over the mark ... life is actually easier if you get rid of them ... I'm not sure if this is the "right" solution for the business!'

The writer Adam Morgan has suggested that having a more 'maverick' approach to business is a good thing. He suggests that being a 'pirate' can be more fun than 'joining the navy'.

Small and Medium-Sized Enterprises (SMEs) We tend to use the terms 'entrepreneur' and 'small business manager' interchangeably. Many small business owners would think of themselves as entrepreneurs (and vice versa). In this book we take the view that there is a clear distinction between those individuals who are enterprising enough to set up their own business (small business managers) and those (entrepreneurs) who introduce a new and innovative product or service to the market.

The 'super-normal' entrepreneur[9]

The entrepreneur must be someone special because he has to be able to break through the resistance to change that exists in any society. Most people are unable to do this; they can only handle what is familiar to them. The entrepreneur, on the other hand, has the strength and the courage to challenge the accepted ways of doing things and to sweep aside the forces of tradition . . . There are naturally very few people who can do this, according to Schumpeter, since they have to have 'super-normal qualities of intellect and will'.

How would *you* summarise the difference between an entrepreneur and a small business manager?

1.2.4 The Context of the Economists

Despite being introduced into the language of economic theory and discourse in the nineteenth century (by Jean Baptiste Say), the role of the entrepreneur has remained on the fringes of economic theory for many generations of economists. Indeed, many economic theories have left the entrepreneur out of the picture altogether. The work of the Austrian economist, Joseph Schumpeter in the 1930s and 1940s is significant for focusing attention on the role of the entrepreneur in introducing *innovation*. As we shall see, it is this approach which has had probably the most significant bearing on how we understand entrepreneurship today.

Where did all the entrepreneurs go?

The British economist Mark Casson has blamed the 'simplifying assumptions' of economists, including the idea that we all have access to 'perfect information', as one of the main reasons why the term 'entrepreneur' virtually disappeared from the economics literature by the end of the nineteenth century. In short, this left no role for the entrepreneur.

   Fortunately, economists have dropped this assumption of perfect information, meaning that the entrepreneur's judgement is once more central to models of economic activity and behaviour. As Casson observes, judgement is a capacity for making a successful decision when no obviously correct model or decision rule is available or when relevant data is unreliable or incomplete. Entrepreneurs are specialists who use judgement to deal with novel and complex problems.

Source: http://www.econlib.org/library/Enc/Entrepreneurship.html

---

1.2.5 The Context of Researchers and Educationalists

There remains a very live debate concerning the nature of entrepreneurship and whether there is such a thing as a distinctive field of study (Phan, 2004). Whilst some aspects of this debate may be 'academic' in the sense that entrepreneurs themselves are unlikely to spend too much of their time worrying about whether or not *they* are an entrepreneur, this continued focus on the need to legitimise the study of entrepreneurship remains a hot topic in countless journal articles and books. The tremendous interest in

1

entrepreneurship education, from secondary school through to MBAs and executive training programmes, also makes a strong case for clarity of perspective.

It is worth reflecting that the number of UK-based programmes in enterprise or entrepreneurship grew from just 8 in 2001 to 56 in 2007 and 94 in 2009 (according to UCAS figures[10]). Many degrees now include some kind of entrepreneurship-related module, as universities embed entrepreneurship and employability skills within the curriculum. In the UK, The National Council for Graduate Entrepreneurship (NCGE) has been established to stimulate graduate start-ups and to narrow the gap in graduate start-up rates between the UK (7 per cent) and the US (12 per cent). Evidence that entrepreneurship education does help grow graduate start-up rates has helped to increase extra-curricular content and support.

Enterprise, entrepreneurship and innovation

■ 'The *enterprise* concept focuses upon the development of the "Enterprising person and Entrepreneurial Mindset". The former constitutes a set of personal skills, attributes, behavioural and motivational capacities which can be used in any context (social, work, leisure).'

■ 'The *entrepreneurial* concept focuses upon the application of enterprising skills in the context of setting up a new venture, developing/growing an existing venture and designing an entrepreneurial organisation.'

■ 'The *innovation* concept is the product of enterprise and entrepreneurship. Innovation is defined as creating and exploiting opportunities for new ways of doing things resulting in better products and services, systems and ways of managing people and organisations.'

Source: http://www.ncge.com/home.php, The National Council for Graduate Entrepreneurship

---

1.2.6 The Context of Entrepreneurs and Nascent Entrepreneurs

There is widespread agreement that entrepreneurs display particular behaviours, skills and attributes, which mark them out from other types of individuals. Naturally, if there is indeed a connection between entrepreneurs and successful high-growth businesses, there are many who have a vested interest in selecting would-be or 'nascent' entrepreneurs to lead future enterprise development.

The nascent entrepreneur

The nascent entrepreneur is defined as someone who initiates serious activities that are intended to culminate in a viable business start-up. There are many programmes designed to encourage individuals to do this. For example the **Young Enterprise Programme** (see www.young-enterprise.org.uk) aims to inspire and equip young people to learn and succeed through enterprise. Their vision is that all young people will have the opportunity to gain personal experience of how business works, understand the role it plays in providing employment and creating prosperity, and be inspired to improve their own prospects, and the competitiveness of the nation. **The Prince's Trust** (see http://www.princes-trust.org.uk/) helps young people through training, skill building, business loans, grants, personal development and study support outside school. **Students in Free Enterprise** (see www.sife.org) is a non-profit organisation educating people on concepts like market economics, entrepreneurship, and business ethics through educational outreach projects.

Source: Reynolds, P. (1994) Reducing barriers to understanding new firm gestation: Prevalence and success of nascent entrepreneurs. Paper presented at the meeting of the Academy of Management, Dallas, TX.

Although there are psychometric tests that attempt to screen for the entrepreneurs of tomorrow, it is unlikely that these will prove to be reliable indicators of who will become successful. It is precisely the capacity of human beings to develop their personalities, to learn and absorb new knowledge and to act unpredictably that makes entrepreneurship such a fascinating phenomenon to study in the first place. Having said this, however, it may be possible to measure changes in a person's *attitudes* towards entrepreneurship.

Whereas psychometric tests aim to measure personality traits or tendencies such as the General Enterprise Tendency Test (Caird, 1991), an alternative theoretical approach is provided by attitude theory. Attitude theory is perhaps a better theoretical model because the psychological personality theories on which psychometrics is based, are inappropriate to the study of entrepreneurship, which is a dynamic process involving behaviours and attitudes, rather than a set of traits (McLine *et al.*, 2000).

Attitudes are shaped by social context and have the advantage of being more accessible to research investigation than are underlying personality traits. Attitudes are also closer to actual behaviours than traits. The conceptual development of the attitude scale centres on entrepreneurial cognition, or the *mental processes* of the entrepreneur, rather than on a particular set of personality traits. The focus of measurement is not on the 'creativity' or the 'leadership' traits of an entrepreneur, but rather on the entrepreneur's attitudes towards using 'creativity' and so on.

An attitude scale, designed to measure changes in attitudes towards entrepreneurship, has been developed for young people aged 16–18 at the Small Business Research Centre (SBRC), Kingston University (Athayde, 2009; Athayde and Hart, 2008). The scale is called the Attitudes To Enterprise (ATE) Test. Enterprise potential in young people was conceptualised for the tool as a constellation of attitudes, in young people, associated with key dimensions of enterprising individuals. Altogether, five attitudes were included:

1 Attitudes towards creativity (beliefs about the importance of creativity and personal assessment of creativity, e.g. 'How creative am I?').

2 Attitudes to personal control over future career (internal, e.g. 'I am in control'; or external, e.g. 'others are in control').

3 Attitudes towards achievement in project work (seeing things through, taking pride in project work).

4 Attitudes towards using intuition in problem-solving (preferring informality to formality; coping with uncertainty, being prepared to take risks in problem-solving).

5 Attitudes to leading others: fellow students and friends (bringing people together, achieving consensus, persuading others).

Early findings have shown that participation in an enterprise programme can positively influence young peoples' enterprise potential and attitudes to entrepreneurship.[11]

ENTREPRENEURSHIP IN ACTION

Entrepreneur's tips – John Caudwell

John Caudwell set up the mobile phones group that includes the Phones 4U retail chain in 1987. In 2006 he sold it for £1.4 billion, making £1.2 billion personally.

'The one bit of advice that I would always give to people before they start a business is: to examine whether they have the six skills that you need to be really successful. They are: ambition, drive, resilience, passion, commercial intellect and leadership'.

Source: http://www.ft.com/reports/entrepreneur2006

1

Against this backdrop of different interests, we can point to the development of a number of dominant perspectives on entrepreneurship (Cope, 2005). These give rise to separate debate and encourage rhetoric which might at best be described as ambiguous, and, more critically for those studying it, potentially confusing. These perspectives reflect the three dimensions of entrepreneurship, already introduced, as well as the particular vantage point of those involved. In this next section we introduce the functional, personality, behavioural and dynamic learning perspectives, as well as approaches which focus on new venture creation and the discovery, evaluation and exploitation of opportunities.

1.3.1 The Functional Perspective

As we have seen, early theories of entrepreneurship originate in the field of economics. The primary objective was to define the 'entrepreneurial function' (Casson, 1982), which one might think of as encapsulating activities (and behaviours) characteristic of entrepreneurship. This *functional* perspective leads with a conceptualisation of the entrepreneur's interaction with his or her environment. In other words, it is interested to understand what the entrepreneur actually does.

What do entrepreneurs do?

'The critical ingredient is getting off your butt and doing something. It's as simple as that. A lot of people have ideas, but there are few who decide to do something about them now. Not tomorrow. Not next week. But today. The true entrepreneur is a doer, not a dreamer' – *Nolan Bushnell, founder of Atari and the video games industry*

Like Nolan Bushnell, entrepreneurs seem to have a preference for action. But what is it that they actually do?

Can you outline what an entrepreneur does?

© ROGER RESSMEYER/CORBIS

Nolan Bushnell in his workshop.

1.3.2 The Personality Perspective

More recently, the focus shifted to the entrepreneur, with research aimed at identifying so-called 'entrepreneurial traits'. This *personality* perspective takes the premise that certain individuals possess a distinctive range of personality characteristics which are sufficiently stable and enduring to predispose them to entrepreneurial activity (including such characteristics as a high need for achievement, internal locus of control, risk-taking and self-efficacy). This trait-based perspective has been subject to heavy criticism (see Gartner, 1988). Much of this criticism has been focused on the static nature of this approach to understanding entrepreneurs, giving little or no room for the individuals concerned to develop, learn and change as they undertake their entrepreneurial activities. Interest in entrepreneurial personality remains strong, however, with some commentators holding that there is such a thing as 'the entrepreneurial personality', which is both socially constructed and reliant upon a set of consistent behaviours, skills and competencies (see Chell, 2008).

Change and be changed

'An entrepreneur tends to bite off a little more than he can chew hoping he'll quickly learn how to chew it' – *Roy Ash, co-founder of Litton Industries*

Entrepreneurs are 'change agents' in that they make changes happen. In doing so, many like Roy Ash claim that they learn along the way and in some ways change themselves.

How have you changed in your life?

Are you the same person you were when you left school, started a degree programme, or got your first job?

What personality traits do you have which would be helpful for entrepreneurship?

In his paper 'Towards the Entrepreneurial University', Allan Gibb (2005) replaces the 'dominant model of the entrepreneur', which he describes as a 'Frankensteinian' (p. 17) creation born out of corporate business concerns, with an 'alternate' model that has entrepreneurial values at its heart. These values are associated with 'the ways of doing things, organising things, feeling things, communicating things, understanding and thinking things, and learning things' (p. 19). They include such values as a strong sense of independence; strong sense of ownership; belief that rewards come with own effort; belief in being able to make things happen.[12]

Gibb's entrepreneurial values

Here is a list of some key values associated with the entrepreneur:

- strong sense of independence

- distrust of bureaucracy and its values

- self-made/self-belief

- strong sense of ownership

- belief that rewards come with own effort

- hard work brings its rewards

- belief can make things happen

- strong action orientation

- belief in informal arrangements

- strong belief in the value of know-how and trust

- strong belief in freedom to take action

- belief in the individual and community not the state.

Source: NCGE Benchmark Template, 2008

1.3.3 The Behavioural Perspective

Partly as a response to the criticisms voiced above, entrepreneurship theorists have developed a more comprehensive model that is focused on a process-based view of new venture creation (see Gartner,

1

1985). The 'inherently futile' (Low and Macmillan, 1988: 148) task of identifying the entrepreneurial personality has given way to a perspective that sees personality characteristics being ancillary to behaviour (Cope, 2005). This research focuses on what entrepreneurs *do* rather than who they *are* (Gartner, 1988). The principal aim of this perspective is, then, to explain 'the functions, activities, and actions associated with the perceiving of opportunities and the creation of organisations to pursue them' (Bygrave and Hofer, 1991: 14).

When it comes to educating and training people for entrepreneurship, the focus on entrepreneurial *behaviours* is very much in the ascendancy, as this sense of self-discovery and behavioural independence sits very comfortably with popular notions of what being entrepreneurial, or enterprising, is all about. It endorses the view of 'peoplism' – that the most important driver of value creation is the enterprise and creativity of individuals, 'assets which only the individuals themselves can own' (Horne, 2000: 10). It also resonates with the proactive, risk-taking image of the entrepreneur that has established the centre ground in our public consciousness. Interestingly, fear of failure still represents the single largest barrier to entrepreneurship for men and women in the UK (Harding, 2005: 11), suggesting that non-entrepreneurs are more passive, and risk adverse.

Entrepreneur's tips – Matthew Riley
(Founder of Daisy and Ernst & Young Entrepreneur of the Year 2007)

1 Use your time wisely – set realistic timescales.

2 Surround yourself with a management team of people you can trust to do a job.

3 Don't create an unnecessary hierarchy. A flat level management model means you will get results from all staff, who feel valued.

4 Don't linger on decision-making – resolve outstanding actions as soon as possible.

5 Act on your instinct – if you don't think it feels right then it generally isn't.

6 Make sure your figures stack up – ensure your ideas make good financial sense.

7 Keep abreast of changes across the whole of your business, maintaining a top level view.

8 Stay agile and alert – stay on top of the changes and adapt to them.

9 Execute a plan and ensure it is delivered to the standards you originally envisaged.

10 Concentrate on the finer details as these usually are the first to draw scrutiny.

Founded in 2001, Daisy is now one of the leading providers of communications technology to small businesses.

Source: Interview in Growing Business: http://www.growingbusiness.co.uk/06959143452042111293/matthew-riley.html Viewed on 19 July 2008

Gibb's entrepreneurial behaviours

More entrepreneurial behaviours, as highlighted by Allan Gibb, might include the following:

■ opportunity-seeking

■ initiative-taking

- ownership of a development

- commitment to see things through

- personal locus of control (autonomy)

- intuitive decision-making with limited information

- networking capacity

- strategic thinking

- negotiation capacity

- selling/persuasive capacity

- achievement orientation

- incremental risk-taking

Source: NCGE Benchmark Template, 2008

1.3.4 The Dynamic Learning Perspective

Whilst the behavioural perspective has the advantage of joining up entrepreneurial behaviours with influences from the environment, there remain concerns that this perspective fails to take into account the ability of entrepreneurs to learn and adapt once the business is established (Cope, 2005). The *dynamic learning* perspective goes beyond the start-up phase to consider the complex ways in which entrepreneurs learn to adapt as their enterprises grow. This perspective has important implications for the role of entrepreneurship in established and larger firms, in particular.

Gibb's generic entrepreneurship competencies

Entrepreneurs have to be good at the following:

- finding an idea

- appraising an idea

- seeing problems as opportunities

- identifying the key people to be influenced in any development

- building the know-how

- learning from relationships

- assessing business development needs

- knowing where to look for answers

- improving emotional self-awareness, managing and reading emotions and handling relationships

- constantly seeing themselves and their business through the eyes of stakeholders and particularly customers

Source: NCGE Benchmark Template, 2008

1

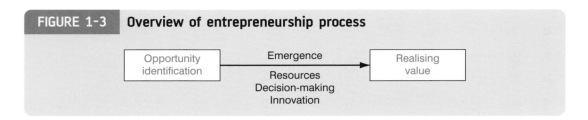

FIGURE 1-3   Overview of entrepreneurship process

1.3.5 Entrepreneurship as New Venture Creation (Setting up New Businesses)

In the past 20 years or so we have seen something of a polarisation into those theories that consider how, by whom, and with what effects opportunities to create future goods and services are *discovered*, *evaluated and exploited* (see Shane and Venkataraman, 2000), and those which focus on the creation of new organisations (Gartner, 1988). Whilst many people still associate entrepreneurship with setting up a new business, we would argue that new venture creation is, in effect, a contingent outcome of entrepreneurship. In other words, you don't have to start a business to be entrepreneurial. It may well be necessary to start a business – but this is certainly not the primary goal of entrepreneurship. This is clearly an important distinction to make, not least because so much entrepreneurship education now focuses on new venture creation and the writing of business plans, rather than the discovery, evaluation and exploitation of opportunities.

1.3.6 Entrepreneurship as Opportunity Identification, Evaluation and Exploitation

As we have seen, entrepreneurship involves a transformative process of social and market change that creates value for individuals and for society. This process can take place in a wide variety of contexts, but follows a simple formula – with the progression from *opportunity identification* through to *realising value* (see Figure 1-3).

   This value can take many forms – personal wealth, family security, social inclusion, or perhaps cultural and aesthetic pleasure. Most modern definitions of entrepreneurship usually entail some aspect of this process.

WHEN THINGS GO WRONG

Looking for something really 'big', the serial entrepreneur Chris Fogg once stumbled across an opportunity to trade second-hand jumbo jets. He recalls it was probably something of a mistake since at the time he didn't know his flaps from his ailerons. Having at least a basic knowledge of the product or service and the market into which it will sell is essential, he notes, with hindsight. Chris ended up selling seven planes, but this was one venture that never really 'took off'.

   (More of Chris Fogg's entrepreneurial ventures are revealed in the case study at the end of Chapter 6.)

1.4   THE SEARCH FOR ENTREPRENEURSHIP – THE PERSPECTIVE TAKEN IN THIS BOOK

Our search has already provided many clues as to the nature and importance of entrepreneurship for individuals, organisations and for society in general. In finishing the last section with a focus on the 'opportunity', we have arrived at probably the single most important concept associated with this phenomenon. Our particular perspective on entrepreneurship will emerge more clearly throughout this book. However, it follows closely the view that entrepreneurship involves the discovery, evaluation and exploitation of opportunities – or what we can think of as 'opportunity recognition'. In the next chapter we outline in more detail who and what is involved in this process, and we also explain the relationship between the key concepts of creativity, opportunity, innovation and entrepreneurship, which are often used loosely or interchangeably.

One of the difficulties we have with basing entrepreneurship around the concept of the 'opportunity' is that we need to determine more clearly whether it exists independently of the entrepreneur – as if waiting to be discovered – or whether it is in some way created by the individual who 'discovers' it. As our search for entrepreneurship continues in Chapter 2 we present our own emergent model of entrepreneurship which deals with this problem and acknowledges the key stages of creativity, opportunity recognition and innovation, all within the competitive and transformational market context.

1.5   SUMMARY AND ACTIVITIES

The purpose of this opening chapter has been to outline the importance of entrepreneurship as a **social and economic process** that **creates value** for many different people in a wide variety of contexts. We assess and discuss the huge variety of **definitions** put forward, and suggest that these can usefully be categorised according to three dimensions:

- **processes** undertaken by entrepreneurs

- **behaviours** required of entrepreneurs

- **outcomes** of entrepreneurship.

It is acknowledged that current perspectives on entrepreneurship tend to **synthesise** ideas relating to all three dimensions. The search for entrepreneurship is to a large extent dependent on the particular **vantage point** of those doing the searching – whether this is at a societal level (as in the case of national and international governments), organisational level (whether in large or small firms), or at the level of the individual (including the entrepreneur or 'would-be' nascent entrepreneur).

The chapter then outlines six perspectives on entrepreneurship which introduce key theoretical approaches that have been used to consider this phenomenon. Our search for entrepreneurship includes a focus on the **entrepreneurial function** – what entrepreneurs actually do. It explores the **entrepreneurial personality** and what makes an entrepreneur 'tick'. It looks at the characteristic **behaviours** of those involved in the entrepreneurship process and recognises the importance of **learning** at both a personal and organisational level. Finally, we suggest that two main perspectives have come to dominate our thinking – either entrepreneurship as **new venture creation** (setting up new businesses), or entrepreneurship as **opportunity identification**, **evaluation and exploitation**. In this book we focus largely on the role of the opportunity and the importance of **opportunity recognition**.

1

REVIEW QUESTIONS

1 Why do you think entrepreneurship matters – and for whom?

2 Why do you think there are so many definitions of entrepreneurship?

3 What is meant by vantage point?
 a getting ahead of everyone else
 b your particular perspective
 c a growing market.

4 What do the 'three dimensions' of entrepreneurship refer to?

5 The functional perspective of entrepreneurship is concerned with what difference entrepreneurship makes and what those involved actually do. True or False?

6 It is generally agreed that we cannot predict entrepreneurship from personality traits alone – why is this?

7 Can you explain what is involved in the behavioural perspective of entrepreneurship?

8 Entrepreneurship is always about setting up a new organisation. True or False?

9 Are opportunities discovered or created?

10 Outline what you understand by the opportunity recognition perspective of entrepreneurship.

SEMINAR TASK

This is a group exercise (1hr)

Begin by writing down the names of countries from across the world, chosen at random. Put these into a hat (or any other convenient container if you don't have a hat to hand). Then, divide the whole group into small teams. Each team picks out the name of a country. You are given ten minutes to put yourselves in the place of this country's government and construct an entrepreneurship policy that suits their country's particular needs. When this time is up, each group presents their case.

   This works well, of course, in an international group. Alternatively, the exercise can be prepared by handing out short briefing notes about selected countries' current economic and social welfare beforehand. You might also wish to have two teams per country – one as the government and one as representing the interests of entrepreneurs. The task is helpful for sensitising everyone to the importance of understanding entrepreneurship in context.

Preview case continued

The sweet taste of entrepreneurship

Craig Sams, co-founder of Green & Black's.

It would be fair to say that Craig Sams has 'form'. Long before he co-founded Green & Black's, he had opened the first macrobiotic restaurant in the UK. He and his brother had also set up 'Whole Earth', a company dedicated to organic, no added sugar foods. Brought up on a farm in Nebraska, Sams describes himself as a 'product of the land he was born on', and describes his parents as 'natural-living pioneers'. His father suffered from a stress-related digestive disorder, and it was as a result of a diet imposed by a Japanese doctor based in Hollywood that the family got used to brown rice and wholeweat bread. In hindsight, this was to have a considerable impact on Craig's future direction and interest in health foods.

By the time Sams was a freshman at college he had developed some strong entrepreneurial credentials. He got a small business going selling peanut butter and jelly sandwiches to other students in the dormitory. As he recalls, it was a distraction from his studies, but he learned a few key principles of small business that you can only get by 'doing it'. More

businesses followed, and by February 1967 Sams was running a busy macrobiotic restaurant, just off Notting Hill Gate in London. His heart was well and truly in promoting healthy food, and when an opportunity for a larger restaurant appeared, he grabbed it. In 1969 Sams and his brother Gregory opened Ceres Britain's first natural foods shop, followed by the Harmony Foods range of products. Further expansion followed, as the brothers took over the former eel and pie shop next door. Crucially, as Sams recalls, the business thrived on innovation. More accurately perhaps 'innovation provided the fingernails by which we held on as the business surrendered territory after territory. It was not enough to be the first with brown rice, miso, wholemeal sourdough breads, brewed soya sauces such as shoyu and tamari, aduki beans, natural peanut butter, no sugar added jams, organic baked beans and carbonated fruit-juice drinks. There was always someone bigger and stronger who waited until an innovative line got big enough, then did whatever it took to capture the market.' This was a crucial lesson for Sams which has informed his approach to entrepreneurial ventures and decision-making subsequently.

You could say that the birth of Sams' adventure with chocolate happened by accident – as is so often the case with entrepreneurial ventures. It all started with a shipment of organic peanuts which failed a quality control test. The seven weeks it took for a replacement container to arrive from Paraguay was too long for the main customer Tesco. In the search for a more reliable peanut supplier, Sams heard about growers of certified organic products in the highlands of south-west Togo. One of these products was cacao beans, and his contact in the region arranged a sample bar to be made from them. Craig remembers having to restrain himself from eating the whole bar because he wanted his partner Jo to taste it when she got home. For her part, when she did get to taste it,

1

it made a lasting impression 'as this square of dark chocolate melted on my tongue, I knew my hunt for chocolate heaven was over'. As a journalist, Jo also knew that being 70 per cent cocoa solids as compared with 50 per cent which was the highest percentage on the UK market at the time, was a newsworthy story-line. But there was a problem. Sams' business under the Whole Earth brand went by the credo of 'no added sugar'. Launching a new choc-olate bar was difficult to reconcile with this strong company line. Fairley remembers nag-ging Sams until he agreed to 'go for it', but only on condition that Jo did the marketing and PR and found the initial £20,000 for the opening stock. Later that year Fairley bought the first consignment of 2000 cases, together they launched Green & Black's, and the phenom-enon of organic chocolate was born.

Many adventures and successes followed. However, cash-flow problems and a natural disaster in the form of Hurricane Iris dealt Green & Black's some heavy blows over the coming years. But none were knock-out punches. As Sams notes 'it's the passion and drive that entrepreneurs pour into their busi-nesses that makes them grow'. Green &

Black's did grow, finally being bought by Cadbury's in 2005, with Sams remaining as President of the company. In response to the question of whether he and Fairley still feel any connection with the brand, Sams states 'it is exactly like asking parents "Do you still feel any connection to your child, now he or she has grown up and gone away to university?" A business is like a baby.'

Questions

1 Which feature of Sam's background do you consider most influential in his subsequent career as an entrepreneur? Why is this?

2 Assess how Fairley and Sams took the decision to start up the business. How important do you think was market research?

3 Entrepreneurship involves creating value through undertaking innovation in the marketplace. (A) What was innovative about Green & Black's? (B) What types of value were created in this business?

Source: Sams, C. and Fairley, J. (2009) The Story of Green & Black's: How two entrepreneurs turned an ethical idea into a business success. (Random House, London)

1.6   NOTES, REFERENCES AND FURTHER READING

Notes and Further Information

1. See references for key works of these pioneers.

2. Timmons, J.A. (1979) Careful self analysis and team assessment can aid entrepreneurs, *Harvard Business Review,* 57 (6): 198–206.

3. Stearns, T.M. and Hills, G. (1996) Entrepreneurship and new firm development: A definitional introduction. *Journal of Business Research*, 36, 1–4. See also Busenitz *et al.* (2003) who provide an interesting unified framework for thinking about these features in terms of the intersections between opportunities, individuals and teams, and mode of organising, all within the context of wider environments for entrepreneurship.

4. Stokes, D. and Wilson, N. (2006) *Small Business Management and Entrepreneurship*, 5th Edition, London: Thomson, p. 32.

5. The CIDA Foundation (Branson School of Entrepreneurship) at: http://www.cidafoundation.org/student-testimonials.html.

6. Centre for Innovation and Entrepreneurship, University of Cape Town (2007) A Review of Literature and Studies Conducted on the Youth in the Western Cape, Cape Town, available at http://www.gsb.uct.ac.za/gsbwebb/

userfiles/ReviewofLiteratureReport12June2007.pdf; and see GEM South African Report 2006 available at: http://www.gemconsortium.org/document.aspx?id=558.

7. Ahmad N. and Hoffman A. (2007) A framework for addressing and measuring entrepreneurship. *Entrepreneurship Indicators Steering Group*, OECD, Paris, available at: http://www.oecd.org/dataoecd/21/51/39629644.pdf.

8. Kingston University Entrepreneurship Centre for Cripps Sears and Morgan, A. (2004) *The Pirate Inside: Building a Challenger Brand Culture Within Yourself and Your Organisations*, London: Wiley & Sons.

9. Swedberg, R. (1991) *Joseph A. Schumpeter: His Life and Work*, Cambridge: Polity Press, p. 35.

10. Source: UCAS. Figures for 2009 obtained using a search for 'business entrepreneurship' at http://search.ucas.com accessed on 27 April 2009.

11. The test is being revised for use in the context of enterprise education in universities.

12. For a full list see Gibb (2005: 40).

References

Ahmad N. and Hoffman A. (2007) A framework for addressing and measuring entrepreneurship. *Entrepreneurship Indicators Steering Group*, OECD, Paris, available at: http://www.oecd.org/dataoecd/21/51/39629644.pdf.

Athayde, R. (2009) Measuring enterprise potential in young people, *Entrepreneurship Theory and Practice,* March, 481–500.

Athayde, R. and Hart, M. (2008) An Empirical Investigation of the Impact of Enterprise Education in Schools. Third European Conference on Entrepreneurship and Innovation, University of Winchester, September.

Bannock, G. (2005) *The economics and management of small business: An international perspective*, Routledge: London.

Begley, T.M. and Tan, W. (2001) The socio-cultural environment for entrepreneurship: a comparison between East Asian and Anglo-Saxon countries. *Journal of International Business Studies,* Washington, Sept, 32 (3).

BERR. (2008) *Enterprise: Unlocking the UK's Talent*, Strategy document, Department for Business Enterprise & Regulatory Reform. Available at http://www.berr.gov.uk/bbf/enterprise-smes/enterprise-framework/index.html.

Brindley, P. (2000) *New Musical Entrepreneurs*, London: IPPR.

Busenitz, L.W., West III, G.P., Shepherd, D., Nelson, T., Chandler, G.N. and Zacharakis, A. (2003) Entrepreneurship research in emergence: Past trends and future directions. *Journal of Management*, 29 (3), 297.

Bygrave, W. and Hofer, C.W. (1991) Theorising about entrepreneurship, *Entrepreneurship Theory and Practice*, 15 (4), 13–22.

Caird, S. (1991) Testing enterprise tendency in occupational groups. *British Journal of Management*, *12*, 177–186.

Cantillon, R. (1730) *Essai sur la Nature du Commerce in Général*, (ed, trans.) H. Higgs (1959), Frank Cass and Co: London.

Carter, S. and Dylan-Jones, D. (2000) *Enterprise and Small Business: Principles, Practice and Policy*, London: FT Prentice Hall.

Casson, M.C. (1982) *The Entrepreneur: An Economic Theory*, London: Martin Robertson.

Centre for Innovation and Entrepreneurship, University of Cape Town (2007) *A Review of Literature and Studies Conducted on the Youth in the Western Cape*, Cape Town, available at http://www.gsb.uct.ac.za/gsbwebb/userfiles/ReviewofLiteratureReport12June2007.pdf; and see GEM South African Report 2006 available at: http://www.gemconsortium.org/document.aspx?id=558.

Chell, E. (2008) *The Entrepreneurial Personality*, 2nd edn. London: Routledge.

Cope, J. (2005) Toward a dynamic learning perspective of entrepreneurship, *Entrepreneurship Theory and Practice*, July: 373–397.

Davidsson, P. (2003) The domain of entrepreneurship research: Some suggestions, in J. Katz & S. Shepherd *Advances in Entrepreneurship, Firm Emergence and Growth* (eds), Oxford: Elsevier/JAI Press, 6: 15–372.

Ellmeier, A. (2003) Cultural entrepreneurialism: On the changing relationship between the arts, culture and employment, *The International Journal of Cultural Policy*, 9 (1): 3–16.

Fillis, I. and McAuley, A. (2000) Modelling and measuring creativity at the interface, *Journal of Marketing Theory and Practice*, 8 (2): 8–17.

1

Gartner, W.B. (1985) A framework for describing and classifying the phenomenon of new venture creation, *Academy of Management Review*, 10 (4), 696–706.

Gartner, W.B. (1988) 'Who is an entrepreneur' is the wrong question, *American Small Business Journal*, Spring, 11–31.

Gartner, W.B. (2001) Is there an elephant in entrepreneurship? Blind assumptions in theory development, *Entrepreneurship Theory and Practice*, 25 (4).

Gibb, A.A. (2005) Towards the Entrepreneurial University Entrepreneurship Education as a Lever for Change, *National Council for Graduate Entrepreneurship Policy Paper 3*, available at http://www.ncge.org.uk/downloads/policy/Towards_the_Entrepreneurial_University.pdf.

Harding, R. (2005) *Global Entrepreneurship Monitor UK 2004 Report*, London: GEM.

Hayek, F.A. von. (1945) The use of knowledge in society, *American Economic Review*, 35 (4): 519–530.

Hisrich, R.D. and Peters, M.P. (2002) *Entrepreneurship,* Fifth edition, London: McGraw-Hill.

Horne, M. (2000) *Enterprise Learning*, London: Demos and the Academy of Enterprise.

Kilby, P. (1971) *Entrepreneurship and Economic Development*, New York: Free Press.

Kirzner, I. (1973) *Competition and Entrepreneurship*, Chicago: University of Chicago Press.

Knight, F. (1921) *Risk, Uncertainty and Profit*, New York: Hougthon Mifflin.

Lawson, T. (1997) *Economics & Reality*, London: Routledge.

Leadbeater, C. and Oakley, K. (1999) *The Independents: Britain's New Cultural Entrepreneurs,* London: Demos.

Low, M. and Macmillan, I. (1988) Entrepreneurship: Past research and future challenges, *Journal of Management*, 35: 139–161.

McCline, R.L., Bhat, S., and Baj, P. (2000) Opportunity recognition: An exploratory investigation of a component of the entrepreneurial process in the context of the health care industry, *Entrepreneurship Theory and Practice*, 25: 81–144.

NCGE (2008) National Council for Graduate Entrepreneurship Website: http://www.ncge.org.uk/index.php.

Oakey, R. (1994) *New Technology-Based Firms in the 1990s*, London: Paul Chapman.

Phan, P.H. (2004) Entrepreneurship theory: Possibilities and future directions, *Journal of Business Venturing*, 19: 617–620.

Reynolds, P. (1994) Reducing barriers to understanding new firm gestation: prevalence and success of nascent entrepreneurs. Paper presented at the meeting of the Academy of Management, Dallas, TX.

Sarasvathy, S. (1999) Seminar on research perspectives in entrepreneurship, *Journal of Business Venturing*, 15: 1–57.

Say, J.B. (1803) *A treatise on political economy, or the production, distribution and consumption of wealth* (trans, eds C.R. Prinsep and C.C. Biddle), Philadelphia: John Grigg.

Schaper, M. (2002) 'The essence of ecopreneurship', in M. Schaper (ed.), *Environmental Entrepreneurship: Greener Management International (GMI),* 38, Sheffield: Greenleaf.

Schumpeter, J.A. (1934) *The Theory of Economic Development: An Inquiry into Profits, Capital, Credit, Interest and the Business Cycle,* tr. R. Opie, Cambridge, MA: Harvard University Press.

Shane, S. and Venkataraman, S. (2000) The promise of entrepreneurship as a field of research, *Academy of Management Review,* 25 (1), 217–226.

Stearns, T.M. and Hills, G. (1996) Entrepreneurship and new firm development: A definitional introduction, *Journal of Business Research*, 36: 1–4.

Stevenson, H.H. and Jarillo, J.C. (1990) A paradigm of entrepreneurship: Entrepreneurial management, *Strategic Management Journal: Special Edition Corporate Entrepreneurship*, 11: 17–27.

Stokes, D. and Wilson, N. (2006) *Small Business Management and Entrepreneurship*, 5th edition, London: Thomson.

Swedberg, R. (1991) *Joseph A. Schumpeter: His Life and Work*, Cambridge: Polity Press.

Timmons, J.A. (1979) Careful self analysis and team assessment can aid entrepreneurs, *Harvard Business Review,* 57 (6): 198–206.

Timmons, J.A. and Spinelli, S. (2004) *New Venture Creation Entrepreneurship for the 21st Century,* 6th edn. McGraw-Hill.

Wennekers, S. and Thurik, R. (1999) Linking entrepreneurship and economic growth, *Small Business Economics*, August, 13 (1): 27–55.

Wilson, N. and Stokes, D. (2005) Managing creativity and innovation: The challenge for cultural entrepreneurs, *Journal of Small Business and Enterprise Development*, 12 (3): 366–378.

Wilson, N. and Stokes, D. (2006) Entrepreneurship education: The road less travelled, Working Paper, Birmingham: National Council for Graduate Entrepreneurship (NCGE).

Recommended Further Reading

There are some excellent overviews of the theoretical background to entrepreneurship and the development of our understanding of the phenomenon in a global context. Amongst these, we would recommend checking your library for the comprehensive editions published by Sage, which include:

Blackburn, R. and Brush, C.G. (2008) *Small Business and Entrepreneurship*, London: Sage Publications (5 volume set).

McNaughton, R.B. and Bell, J.D. (2009) *Entrepreneurship and Globalization*, London: Sage Publications (5 volume set).

Scott Shane's general theory of entrepreneurship provides a helpful account of what he refers to as the 'individual-opportunity nexus':

Shane, S. (2003) *A General Theory of Entrepreneurship*, Cheltenham: Edward Elgar Publishing.

For those wishing to research entrepreneurship further, we would also recommend:

Casson, M., Yeung, B., Basu, A. and Wadeson, N. (eds) (2008) *The Oxford Handbook of Entrepreneurship*, Oxford: Oxford University Press.

CHAPTER 2

The Properties of Entrepreneurship

LEARNING OBJECTIVES

After studying this chapter, the reader will be able to:

- Understand that entrepreneurship is an emergent phenomenon – the whole is greater than the sum of the parts

- Recognise that entrepreneurship depends upon our creative potential – a distinctively human characteristic that we all possess

- Account for the difference between creativity, innovation, opportunity and entrepreneurship, and be able to explain how they are related

- Assess the fundamental importance of opportunity recognition within the process of entrepreneurship

- Describe the key processes undertaken by the entrepreneur, including spotting opportunities, networking, resource recombination, decision-making, and organisation of tasks.

INTRODUCTION

In Chapter 1 we began our search for entrepreneurship and explored the many definitions and perspectives that help us to understand this phenomenon. We also highlighted the significance of the *opportunity* to our understanding of entrepreneurship. In this chapter we pursue the dominant perspective that sees entrepreneurship as 'opportunity identification, evaluation and exploitation', presenting a theoretical model that seeks to clarify key terms and explain the relationship between them (see Figure 2-1). As such, we look at our capacity as human beings to:

- fulfil our creative potential and discover new things

- engage in entrepreneurial projects, involving specific practices such as spotting opportunities, recombining resources, and organising tasks

- be driven by many different motivations, including extrinsic financial reward and intrinsic goals, such as the satisfaction from just seeing the project through

- recognise the opportunity, before it is taken to market

- distinguish innovation from invention and/or creativity.

2

A desire named Streetcar[1]

Andrew Valentine and Brett Akker launched their self-service pay-as-you-go car company *Streetcar* in 2004. In many ways, Streetcar sits halfway between car ownership and car rental. Customers can book a car online or over the phone 24 hours a day 7 days a week. The cars are parked in a dense network across the city, each one within a few minutes of the next location. This means that as a Streetcar member, you don't have to travel halfway across town to go to a car rental depot. From modest beginnings, but after several years of structured planning, Streetcar now has over 50,000 members sharing a fleet of over 1000 cars, based in 850 locations in 6 UK cities. The company aims to have around 250,000 members by the end of 2012.

Over several years, Andrew and Brett proactively searched for an 'opportunity' for their new venture. What do you think were the main challenges facing the two founders once they had identified the potential of this business idea?

Reproduced with permission from Andrew Valentine (Andrew.Valentine@streetcar.co.uk)

| **FIGURE 2-1** | **Key features of the entrepreneurship process** |

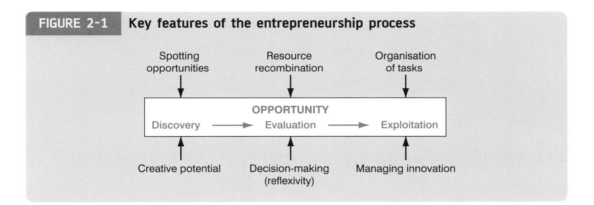

2.1   CONCEPTUALISING ENTREPRENEURSHIP

As a first step in building our conceptual model of entrepreneurship, we need to make crucial conceptual distinctions between:

- entrepreneurship and the entrepreneur;

- creativity and innovation; and

- creativity and the entrepreneurial opportunity.

Why definitions matter. . .

Who is doing what?

- *Can you list five entrepreneurs, creatives, managers, innovators?*

2

Who is doing what ... when?

■ *Can you explain the difference between creativity, opportunity identification, innovation?*

How do we know who is doing what ... when?

■ *Can you give five examples of creativity and another five opportunities?*

How would you describe each of the people listed below? Use only one of the following labels to best describe each one: 1. Entrepreneur 2. Innovator 3. Creative.

    Tip: if you've never heard of some of them, try doing a bit of research on the Internet to find out more. Let this research take you on your own journey of creative discovery. You never know what you might come up with ...

Gugliemo Marconi	Florence Nightingale
Thomas Edison	Marie Curie
Isambard Brunel	Francis Bacon
Leonardo da Vinci	Anita Roddick
Ludwig van Beethoven	James Dyson
James Watt	Narayana Murthy
Albert Einstein	Jamie Oliver
Akio Morita	Elvis Presley
Pablo Picasso	Bob Geldof

What do you think are the key differences between the three terms 'entrepreneur', 'innovator' and 'creative'?

2.1.1 The Difference Between Entrepreneurship and the Entrepreneur

Entrepreneurship and *entrepreneur* are used interchangeably and they are, of course, necessarily related concepts. However, as we indicated in discussing the 'three dimensions' of entrepreneurship in Chapter 1, they are also concerned with fundamentally different aspects of a phenomenon. When we talk about *entrepreneurs* we are usually interested in their particular *behaviours*, attributes and skills.[2] When we talk about *entrepreneurship* we have a *process* in mind – a process which involves specific *outcomes* relating to the introduction of new economic activity.

Human beings have behaviours, attributes and skills which can be developed through learning, that is entrepreneurial education. You are probably reading this book, after all, because you are looking to learn about entrepreneurship and develop your own behaviours, attributes and skills accordingly. However, entrepreneurship – as 'the identification, evaluation and exploitation of an entrepreneurial opportunity' (Shane, 2003), for example – involves both *agential* actions and social *structures*.[3] Agency refers to the capacity of individual humans to act independently and to make their own free choices. Structure refers to those factors such as class, religion, gender and ethnicity, which seem to limit or enable the opportunities that individuals have.

There has been a tendency to explain entrepreneurship in terms of the potential of individuals to act freely and be 'entrepreneurial'. This agential view is sometimes referred to as a *voluntaristic* perspective. It contrasts with much of the research on small business and entrepreneurship which is more *deterministic* in nature (i.e. associated with a structural view), and emphasises the role of social structures and institutions in influencing what individual entrepreneurs can and can't do. Entrepreneurship involves individuals, groups of individuals, organisations, industries and society as a whole. As a social process it cannot be reduced to human behaviour, cognitive processes or decision-making alone.

To the extent that entrepreneurship involves the production of new and innovative products and services and the creation of value for those involved, it is clear that we need to understand who and what is involved in bringing about 'new' and 'innovative' things. In short, we need to take a closer look at the concepts of creativity and innovation.

2.1.2 The Difference Between Creativity and Innovation

All too often, creativity and innovation are used to mean the same thing (i.e. something new or different). However, there is a growing body of research that clearly differentiates between the two.

A question of creativity

There are estimated to be just over 6.68 billion people living in the world. Based on current estimates, this is expected to grow to nearly 9 billion by the year 2042. *What proportion of these people would you describe as creative (a) now, and (b) in the year 2042?*

Tip: Ask yourself how many people are definitely not creative. What would this mean if true?

Notwithstanding the many different definitions applied to the term creativity, there is general agreement that it depends upon two central characteristics which are rooted in a Western philosophical tradition (Bilton, 2007). The first of these is difference or novelty. The second characteristic is individual talent or vision which is expressed through creative individuals. We are all very familiar with this way of looking at creativity – after all, we tend to associate creativity with especially talented musicians, actors, film-makers, authors, scientists (even entrepreneurs, perhaps). According to this line of thinking – which is characteristic of most of the business management and related entrepreneurship literature – creativity can be understood as the generation of new ideas (Cox, 2005) or as the 'ideation' component of innovation (West and Farr, 1990). Whilst creativity is all about coming up with the good ideas in the first place, innovation is 'the successful exploitation' of these new ideas (DTI, 2003) (see Figure 2-2). This perspective is reversed in much of the writing on the subject from the fields of psychology and the arts (which hold a different vantage point). Here, creativity is seen as both novel and *valuable*. Innovation is more concerned with any change often as a result of some technological advance.

2.1.3 Putting Creativity at the Heart of Entrepreneurship

Creativity is not just a useful or desirable component of entrepreneurship, but it is in fact a central feature of this phenomenon. Without creativity (in the sense of generating new and valuable ideas) there would not be any entrepreneurship. In every case, therefore, the conceptual starting point for entrepreneurship must be our individual creative potential. As sentient human beings we are *all* capable of generating new and potentially valuable ideas.

Everyday usage of these terms has given rise to some misperceptions of what they actually mean (see Figure 2-3). Creativity is associated with certain individuals (e.g. Mozart, Einstein, Picasso) who bring something new to the world. The entrepreneur is also seen as a special individual, but someone who delivers *economic* value, that is they normally make money for themselves or for others. Innovation tends to be understood more at the level of products/services, organisations or society, and we refer to

2

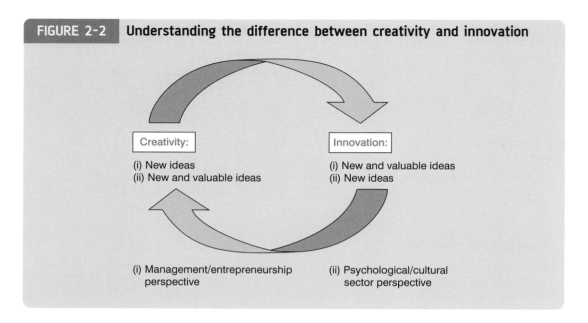

FIGURE 2-2   Understanding the difference between creativity and innovation

Creativity:
(i) New ideas
(ii) New and valuable ideas

Innovation:
(i) New and valuable ideas
(ii) New ideas

(i) Management/entrepreneurship
perspective

(ii) Psychological/cultural
sector perspective

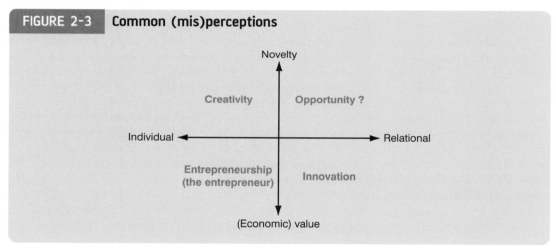

FIGURE 2-3   Common (mis)perceptions

Novelty

Creativity

Opportunity ?

Individual ◄─────────────► Relational

Entrepreneurship
(the entrepreneur)

Innovation

(Economic) value

something as innovative when it is not just 'new' but also economically valuable, that is it sells well. The opportunity is a little harder to pin down, but seems to be something that is new and will have an impact across a range of people either in an organisation, a market or society as a whole.

2.1.4 The Difference Between Creativity and the Opportunity

If creativity involves the creation of something both novel and valuable it begs the question of who decides whether or not anything is in fact 'creative'. For it would seem that we have to be able to *recognise* creativity in order for it to exist.[4] Whilst we don't have to get overly concerned with the philosophical arguments for and against this point of view here, it does focus attention on the process of recognising creativity. As we will discuss in more detail in the course of this chapter, entrepreneurship depends upon

ENTREPRENEURSHIP IN ACTION

Spotting the opportunity[5]

Opportunities can arise in the most unlikely of places. For Sheri Schmelzer, the inspiration for her entrepreneurial breakthrough came when playing at home with her three children in the basement of their Boulder, Colorado home. The family had 12 pairs of Crocs™ shoes between them. On this particular day, they decided to decorate the shoes by fitting clay and rhinestone charms into the holes of the Crocs. Keeping it in the family, it was husband, Rich, who recognised the creativity and the potential to develop an accessory brand of colourful snap-on products specifically suited to these types of shoe.

The family set to work in producing a small range of products which they named jibbitz, after Sheri's nickname 'flibberty-jibbit'. They shared the early designs with family and friends, taking the plunge to open up the company website on their weeding anniversary in 2005. Within the first 12 months, sales reached over 8 million, and jibbitz were being sold in thousands of stores worldwide.

Can you think of any examples of entrepreneurship that didn't involve someone coming up with at least one new and valuable idea?

recognising creativity. Indeed this is probably the most important factor in distinguishing between creativity in general, where new and valuable discoveries are made, and what entrepreneurship theorists have termed the opportunity, which is the *ex ante* (before the event) recognition of creativity.

$$\boxed{\text{Opportunity recognition}} \quad = \quad \boxed{\begin{array}{c}\text{Recognising creativity}\\ (\textit{before} \text{ it is shown to be}\\ \text{novel and valuable})\end{array}}$$

Whilst we define creativity as being both novel and valuable, we distinguish the opportunity as normally being both novel and *economically* valuable.[6] Creativity does not have to be recognised in order to exist – but we *do* have to recognise an opportunity.

ENTREPRENEURSHIP IN ACTION

Spotting a smashing opportunity

The four founders of Smash & Grab Glass Recycling Ltd (two senior managers in the financial sector, one in engineering and one patent attorney), identified an opportunity in glass recycling. They spotted that wine bars, pubs, restaurants and other licensed retail establishments generate huge volumes of glass every day, which have to be collected by large non-eco-friendly trucks. Since the glass bottles are empty, much of what is carried by the lorries is air. By crushing the glass first (in a compact patented glass crusher) the clients could get much more glass into each load.

Most of us have probably spent enough time in pubs, wine bars and restaurants to have spotted this opportunity ourselves. However, even if the idea had occurred to us it may well have gone no further, since actually designing and making a compact glass crusher probably needs a level of engineering expertise that most of us don't possess.

Ask yourself was it one of the managers, or the need for more efficient transport of empty bottles that first sparked off this idea?

Source: http://www.startups.co.uk/6678842908746372717/smash-and-grab-glass-recycling.html and www.smashgrab.co.uk

2.2 THE EMERGENT NATURE OF ENTREPRENEURSHIP

One of the reasons that scholars have found it so difficult to pin down entrepreneurship is because it is an 'emergent phenomenon' or the whole is greater than the sum of the parts. To help understand what we mean by this, consider some of the good things in life. For example, we appreciate good food and great music but we cannot readily describe what makes it attractive to us in terms of specific features alone because there is something greater than the individual elements – their emergent nature. All of us have probably experienced what it is like trying to make a delicious recipe from a great cookbook. We use the same ingredients as the Michelin star chef; we follow the same processes and timings; but somehow the result just doesn't taste as good as when they are in charge. However much we break down a great piece of music into its component parts – the structure, chords, instrumentation, vocal lines, stylistic origins – we cannot explain how it makes us feel, or what makes it 'great' in terms of these separate parts alone. It is the same with entrepreneurship.

A useful way of thinking of the entrepreneurship 'whole' is that it is made up of a number of separate layers (just like an onion). Starting in the middle we can examine each of the layers in turn until we reach the outer layer. We can explain entrepreneurship in terms of the separate successive layers, whilst noting that the whole is greater than the sum of the parts (see Figure 2-4).

- The innermost layer is our *creative potential*. This is our ability to make discoveries about the world around us. We all have this ability – though clearly some people are better than others when it comes to coming up with (novel and valuable) ideas.

- The next layer up is the *entrepreneurial project* – where we can first identify the opportunity, following a hunch, a feeling or an intuition. At its most basic we can think of this project as involving 'an end that is desired, however tentatively or nebulously, and also some notion, however imprecise, of the course of action through which to accomplish it' (Archer, 2003: 6). In other words, it is at this point that we reflect on the idea(s) floating around our subconscious and bring them into a conscious part of our thinking. We begin to map out the idea in earnest and start to develop some kind of strategy for how we will achieve it – though we probably haven't got as far as formal business planning or feasibility analysis.

- The next layer is probably the most important of all – *opportunity recognition*. This is where we recognise that we have a potentially valuable and new idea. It is on the basis of this recognition that we take the decision to follow through with our strategy, or revise it in such a way so as to be able to implement it successfully. Note how easy it is for entrepreneurship to stall at this point – we might come up with great ideas but do nothing to follow through. It is within this layer that the competitive context of market exchange becomes crucial. Since those involved must make decisions about market entry and resource recombination *before* committing their capital (financial, human and otherwise), it is vital to determine whether the proposed product or service is indeed novel and economically valuable. This involves our careful judgement and decision-making, as well as appropriate recombination of resources.

- With our new products and/or services now being exchanged successfully in the market (i.e. people are buying them) we have reached the stage called *innovation* (in effect a *post hoc* recognition of creativity – i.e. after the event). It is not enough just to have proved the concept; we now need to deliver the new products and services on a scale that will bring us a sustainable economic value (i.e. financial reward).

- Appropriating this economic value, either for ourselves or for others we want to benefit from it, is then the final stage in the entrepreneurial journey. We have now reached the final emergent layer of entrepreneurship.

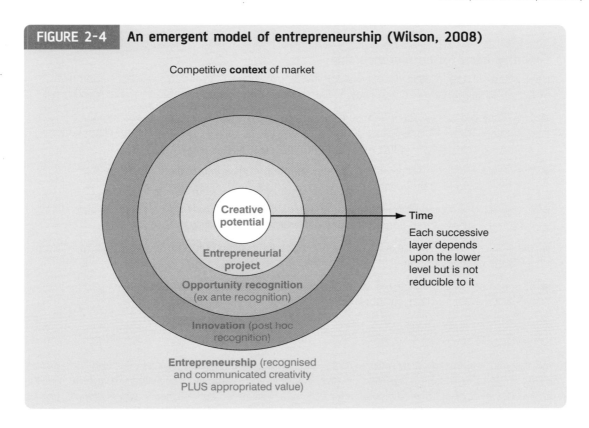

FIGURE 2-4   **An emergent model of entrepreneurship (Wilson, 2008)**

2.2.1 An Emergent Definition of Entrepreneurship

In the light of this model we can add to the definitions discussed in Chapter 1 and present our own – which synthesises each of the three dimensions of entrepreneurship:

■ **Entrepreneurship** is the emergent process of recognising and communicating creativity such that the resulting economic value can be appropriated by those involved.

Apart from offering some clarification as to the nature of the relationship between creativity and entrepreneurship, which tends to be left rather unclear, this conceptualisation of entrepreneurship also has the benefit of being able to distinguish between the key concepts of creativity, innovation, opportunity and entrepreneurship.

We now look at each of these emergent layers of entrepreneurship in more detail.

2.3   ENTREPRENEURSHIP AND OUR CREATIVE POTENTIAL

In discussing this emergent model of entrepreneurship we have suggested that a good starting point is the individual's creative potential. (Actually, we might note that we can always go further back to explain what happened before the situation that we currently find ourselves in. After all, nothing comes out of nothing.)

Cognitive basis for entrepreneurship

Baron and Shane (2008) have outlined the importance of taking a cognitive approach to understanding entrepreneurship. They outline the following cognitive features of entrepreneurship:

- The more experience people have in a given field, the more likely they are to identify opportunities in it. This depends upon the most basic cognitive system for storing information – known as memory (including working; long-term; procedural memory).

- We create cognitive frameworks that help us interpret new information and relate it to information we already possess.

- An example is prototypes – idealised representations of the most typical member of a category – which are important for idea generation and creativity.

- We also rely on simple rules known as heuristics for making complex decisions in a rapid and relatively effortless manner.

- Various heuristics (such as the optimistic bias, planning fallacy, confirmation bias) end up in us making the wrong decision, however.

Source: Baron and Shane (2008) Chapter 3, 66–74

We discuss 'sources of opportunity' in more detail in relation to the literature on innovation in Chapter 3. We also focus on developing our own creative potential and managing creativity in Chapter 8. For the moment, however, we draw particular attention to a feature of entrepreneurs which should not be overlooked. This is their tendency to act in line with their imagination. Whilst we are all imaginative, to a greater or lesser degree, it is the particular capacity to *act* on an unaffirmed proposition that sets the entrepreneur apart.[7]

ENTREPRENEURSHIP IN ACTION

Acting in line with imagination

For many people today, having a food allergy of some kind is a reality of life. Most sufferers have to bear with the difficulty of finding suitable foods, particularly when eating out. For Emma Killilea, however, her frustration at discovering she suffered from a serious food allergy, led to setting up her own award-winning business. Delicious Alchemy provides a range of breads, cakes, and desserts to hotels and restaurants, specifically catering for food allergies. As Emma says 'When I was 28 I found out I had a wheat allergy. I couldn't buy nice food even in the supermarket, so I had to start making everything for myself. There was very little in the way of ready meals I could have, so I had to get back into cooking. I started researching and found out 10 per cent of the population suffers from a food allergy and thought I could do something. So I started baking and experimenting.'

The key lesson from this example is that Emma acted in line with her imagination. Many of us might have the 'idea' of setting up a similar company, but not all of us follow this through. In Emma's case, she won £15,000 worth of start-up capital through various awards, including the UK national student entrepreneur (UK SECK award).

Source: http://www.startups.co.uk/6678842908643110776/delicious-alchemy.html

2.4   ENTREPRENEURIAL PROJECTS AND IDENTIFYING THE OPPORTUNITY

Even in the case of most world-beating entrepreneurial ventures, the entrepreneurial project usually starts in a fairly modest form. Very probably the entrepreneurial project is little more than a hunch, an irritation or a gut-feeling to begin with. Just as our feelings and our intuition play a vital role in creativity in other contexts (see Robinson, 2001), so they do in the formation of the entrepreneurial project. Within our emergent model of entrepreneurship we distinguish between this entrepreneurial project and opportunity recognition. This is important because in effect we are drawing attention to the pivotal role of our feelings and intuition in terms of spotting or identifying the opportunity in the first place. It is only when we have done this that we undertake a more cognitive and usually more rational and deliberate evaluation of the idea to see whether we think it is both new and valuable, that is we recognise opportunity.

Much of the literature on how an entrepreneur identifies an opportunity suggests that they must first of all be 'alert to the opportunity' (Kirzner, 1973). Entrepreneurs have their eyes and ears open. More than this, they are *actively* seeking new ideas that have the potential to be real opportunities in the marketplace. This places emphasis on the entrepreneur as 'seeker'. We can contrast this with an alternative mode of entrepreneurship behaviour, where it would be more accurate to describe the entrepreneur as 'finder' – as someone who through their experimentation has come across the opportunity. Within this approach, the pursuit of an opportunity is an iterative process, which might lead

ENTREPRENEURSHIP IN ACTION

Launching a designer boutique: KAPDAA

Young entrepreneur Nishant Parekh was commissioned to design and brand a new clothes boutique in India. He had the idea to develop a concept store that would stand out from the crowd, and which could showcase the latest designs and reinforce a strong brand image. The first thing he noticed when going round the workshop was that there was a lot of waste materials that weren't being put to good use. In particular, there were yards of spare cloth. Inspiration struck, and Nishant realised that the boutique's *raison d'être* centred on the use, look and feel of cloth. From this initial thought, Nishant was able to both brand the boutique – calling it KAPDAA which in most Indian languages means 'cloth' – and conceive of a design concept in which spare cloth could be incorporated in all aspects of the boutique store's operations. With the support of the company's design team, KAPDAA then began fashioning visiting cards, bags, invitation cards for the launch, the ceiling and part of the floor, and even the accounts book out of cloth. Sustainable, practical, fashionable, the new cloth concept worked perfectly with the boutique's image and promised a bright future for those working for the small enterprise.

Saras Sarasvathy has put forward an 'effectuation' theory of entrepreneurship (Sarasvathy, 2001) which emphasises the tendency for entrepreneurs to work with what they've got, rather than look for new things and people to develop entrepreneurial opportunities. A helpful way of thinking about this is to use the metaphor of the cook in a small family restaurant. Either she can dream up a delicious menu and then go out and buy the ingredients from the local supermarket; or she can create a recipe from what she already has in the fridge and the store cupboard. This latter approach seems to be the one that Nishant preferred in this example.

Ask yourself what you have in your creative 'fridge'. How might you turn these ingredients into an exciting entrepreneurial dish?

Reproduced with permission from Nishant Parekh.

2

Seeking Crocs

When Scott Seamans and Duke Hanson were sailing through the Caribbean and noticed how useful it would be to have a non-slip and durable sailing shoe that was similar to a running shoe, they could have just binned the idea then and there. What marks them out as entrepreneurs is that they followed through with their idea, managed to source a manufacturer that had developed a lightweight, slip and odour resistant resin material, and founded what was to become the world's fastest growing shoe company – Crocs™.

Crocs on sale

Source: Crocs™ website http://www.crocs.com/company/viewed 20 April 2009

off in any particular direction because of whom you talk to, what you read in the newspaper or who takes an interest in your idea.[8]

Galenson (2008) has outlined these same two behaviourial patterns in the context of artistic creativity. He contrasts the 'seeker' artist, whose conceptual innovations are motivated by the desire to communicate specific ideas or emotions, with the 'finder', whose experimental innovations are primarily motivated by aesthetic criteria and who sees painting 'as a process of searching, in which they aim to discover the image in the course of making paintings' (p. 4). At the very least, we must be careful not to characterise the entrepreneur as solely a proactive seeker of new goods and services. For some, the opportunity may appear unannounced, or through a long process of experimentation perhaps within a specific sector.

Finding Crocs

To use an appropriate analogy one might suggest that the founders of Crocs™ shoes literally stumbled across more success than they could have hoped for. Whilst their original shoe was intended as a boating/outdoor shoe because of the particular slip-resistant, non-marking properties of the sole, the Croc was to become an all-purpose shoe for comfort and fashion, as well as function. The success of the shoe across so many markets indicates that the scope of innovation in this case goes much further than what was initially planned.

2.5   ENTREPRENEURSHIP AND RECOGNISING OPPORTUNITY

In our conceptual model of entrepreneurship we suggest that the next emergent layer of the 'onion' is *opportunity recognition*. This is where the entrepreneur recognises creativity in the form of an opportunity, prior to it actually being legitimised through exchange (i.e. the new product or service has not been tested in the market yet). There are two distinctive features of this process:

1 cognitive and rational decision-making and judgement; and

2 resource recombination.

It is no longer enough just to have a hunch or a feeling about an idea. At this point in the entrepreneurship process the entrepreneur is making vital decisions about their *goals* (what they want to achieve) and the *methods* they will use to achieve them. As Shane (2003: 6) describes it, they 'use new means–ends frameworks to recombine resources to generate profit'.

2.5.1 Judgement and Decision-Making

An entrepreneur can never know with absolute certainty before the event that their proposition or project will be affirmed (e.g. that a new product or service such as a new type of shoe will sell profitably). Much of the debate about entrepreneurship, particularly amongst Austrian economists (see Vaughn, 1994) has therefore focused on the subjectivity of knowledge and strategic decision-making.

In this conceptual model, the environment for acting entrepreneurially is the opposite of the virtual world of many computer games, where the hero amasses points (information) as discreet (objective) packages, so as to win the game. In real life, the entrepreneur wins the game by making an entrepreneurial appraisal (Salerno, 1999), which is based on the entrepreneur's prior knowledge (Shane, 2000) and the mental framework he applies to the process of evaluation (Penrose, 1959; Lachmann, 1986). As we saw in Chapter 1, the entrepreneur is, therefore, something of a specialist who uses their judgement to deal with novel and complex problems (Casson, 1982).

The paradox of opportunity recognition

When entrepreneurs exploit opportunities, they transfer information to others about what the opportunity is and how to pursue it. Although this imitation might initially legitimate an opportunity, it also generates competition that exhausts the discrepancy to the point where the incentive to act no longer exists (Schumpeter, 1934; Shane and Venkataraman, 2000; Eckhardt and Shane, 2003). In a market context, therefore, the very act of recognising the opportunity generates potential competition. This can make it difficult for the entrepreneur to know (a) who to tell about their opportunity; and (b) when to tell them. Whilst some advise talking freely with people about your entrepreneurial ideas, there is another school of thought which suggests secrecy is the best policy.

Simon Woodroffe, founder of Yo! Sushi and Yotel says 'Unless its patentable … then what I've always done is stood up and told everybody. What happens is when you talk about ideas it creates an energy actually that stops your competitors, but also that gets you going and wanting to do it.'[9]

© YO! SUSHI BLUEWATER, WWW.YOSUSHI.COM

A Yo! Sushi restaurant

2.5.2 Resource Recombination

According to Schumpeter, someone is an entrepreneur only when they are putting together a new combination of resources (see Swedberg, 1991: 34). Resources, as key factors of production, can take many forms, including raw materials, money (financial capital), skills and employees (human capital), and the relations required to engage successfully in market exchange (social capital). Entrepreneurship requires appraising resources and deploying them to new uses (Foss and Ishikawa, 2006). Indeed, particular attention has been drawn to the role of entrepreneurship in creating new strategic resources, through, for example, the combination and recombination of existing resources (Schumpeter, 1934; Nelson and Winter, 1982). The entrepreneurial practice of (re)combining resources (usually requiring their exchange) is seen as an important property of entrepreneurship.

The issue of explaining how the *future* contribution of resources (i.e. what Shane refers to as the belief in 'yielding a profit') is actually determined by those agents undertaking their recombination (i.e. recognising creativity in this context), is central to our understanding of entrepreneurship. We discuss further how resources are recombined and leveraged in Chapter 10.

2.6   ENTREPRENEURSHIP AND INNOVATION

Returning now to our emergent model of entrepreneurship, we have arrived at the outer ring, where innovation is shown to have taken place. To recap, innovation is the *post hoc* recognition of creativity. The opportunity has now been proved through market exchange as being both new and economically valuable.

There could be a world of difference between selling one new product or service and being 'successful' in this context. The goals of the entrepreneur are key here in terms of laying down the criteria for success. Whilst it is often assumed that entrepreneurs are solely driven by financial and other external rewards (so-called extrinsic motivation), there is plenty of evidence to suggest that this is not always the case. Intrinsic motivation – the love of doing something for its own sake – can be a very strong motivator for many entrepreneurs, especially if they are working in an area where they have years of in-depth knowledge and experience, or where they are developing a hobby, perhaps. Research suggests that entrepreneurs are often driven by the need for achievement (McClelland, 1961), and this may well override any rewards actually received (financial or otherwise).

Over and above issues of motivation, entrepreneurs will need the right mix of management skills in order to sustain the level of business required, often in a changing market context, and to appropriate the value involved. Two sets of skills, discussed in the following sections, are needed:

1   those relating to the *qualification* of goods and services; and

2   those required in the *organisation of tasks*.

2.6.1   Entrepreneurship and Qualification

In order for a *new* product to be sold in the market it has to be judged by the prospective consumer in comparison with other goods for quality, price and other criteria. This process is known as 'qualification' (Callon, 1998) and it has two distinct aspects:

■ First, the producer (i.e. the entrepreneur) has to stabilise the product so that it is ready for sale. For example, if you were to consider selling a house, you need to clean it up, make those repairs that you've been meaning to do for years, but somehow never got round to, and have the estate agent come round to take pictures and make measurements. This process is essentially stabilising the house as a 'good' which can be sold. After all, you may have added a loft conversion or changed all the carpets since the last time that the house was put up for sale. The same process applies to any new product or service that has taken a journey from 'just an idea', a blueprint, or a prototype through to the final good. Whilst we typically think of entrepreneurs as change agents and 'creative destructors' we might also remember that part of their role is to standardise and stabilise new goods so that they can be exchanged successfully and normally over a relatively long period of time.

■ Second, in order for the consumer to buy a new good of some kind, they must 'detach' themselves from an existing product and 'attach' themselves to the new one. For example, before the consumer makes the switch to a new iPod to play their music, they may need to detach themselves from the trusted CD player that they've relied on for the past few years. This is partly a psychological process requiring the consumer's active decision-making. Anything the entrepreneur can do to make this process easier, such as explaining very clearly what the benefits will be, is to their advantage.

2.6.2 Organisation of Tasks

In order to achieve their goals, entrepreneurs have to be experts in the coordination of different people and processes (see Becker and Murphy, 1992: 1144). In an age of extraordinary change and technological developments, we might then think of entrepreneurs as specialists at coordinating the activities of other specialists. We might also suggest that their role (as both transformers and stabilisers) is becoming ever more important. Indeed, the ability to recognise and to communicate creativity and to appropriate the value from it (i.e. entrepreneurship), particularly in a massively expanding world of digitalised 'free' content, will surely become the single most important skill-set for developed economies across the world, if it isn't already.

WHEN THINGS GO WRONG

Entrepreneurs' mistakes – anything but a red letter day

By 2001, Rachel Elnaugh's business Red Letter Days was generating £1 million profit on £10 million turnover. She recalls that she first knew Red Letter Days was in trouble on 20 December 2002. The business went into administration in 2005. In her words, she wishes that in hindsight she had just kept the business running at that level rather than being greedy and trying to go for gold. She also felt that she allowed the board to become too big and unwieldy (at one point the company had eight Directors, costing over £1million a year). Rachel says, small teams are far better – this after signing authority to a CEO who 'wasted' £4 million on exceptional one-off costs related to systems and infrastructure. Rachel is keen to point out the lessons of what went wrong with Red Letter Days. In particular she notes that when you start out a business you can easily control everything because you are close to every function. The problem starts when you need to delegate authority.

We might contrast this with the views of other well known entrepreneurs. Alan Sugar when speaking about Richard Branson said 'He has a way of not getting involved in detail – he recruits lieutenants who understand it. I could tell you where the last bolt in my company is; what room, which drawer. It's not clever, but it's something I do.' Duncan Bannatyne, founder of the Bannatyne Group of hotels, leisure and fitness centres with turnover of £90 million said 'I would say one of my main strengths is a great ability to delegate and to be able to motivate people to work for me.' There is clearly no one way of getting the right balance when it comes to delegating.

Source: Interview in Growing Business online, http://www.growingbusiness.co.uk/06959143452236932465/rachel-elnaugh. html, viewed 19 July 2008. For more information about Rachel Elnaugh see her website www.rachelelnaugh.com. Alan Sugar quote taken from Growing Business online: http://www.growingbusiness.co.uk/06959143455189354217/sir-alan-sugar.html, viewed 19 July 2008. Duncan Bannatyne quote taken from Growing Business online: http://www.growingbusiness.co.uk/06959143453358504609/duncan-bannatyne.html, viewed 19 July 2008.

2

2.7 SUMMARY AND ACTIVITIES

The process of entrepreneurship has a number of key properties:

- **Creative potential**   We all have the capacity to discover new things and this creative potential is the starting point for entrepreneurship. Creativity is not just a useful or desirable feature of entrepreneurship, but it is a central requirement of the phenomenon.

- **Opportunity identification**   Being alert to new discoveries, in the form of responding to hunches, feelings and intuitions, is not enough on its own. We need to use our judgement and decision-making to assess whether our entrepreneurial projects are based on true opportunities, and whether they will be both novel and valuable. It is only in recognising the opportunity that the entrepreneur takes the vital next step in terms of recombining and deploying resources to create value.

- **Opportunity recognition**   Having introduced some form of change, the entrepreneur then has to stabilise, or standardise the features of the new good so that it can be compared against other existing goods and exchanged at the right price. This requires specialist organisational skills and the ability to get the right team in place, with the right equipment and appropriate funding.

- **Innovation**   It is only when the entrepreneur has successfully introduced the new product or service into the marketplace that it can be recognised as an innovation.

- **Value appropriation**   Once the project has produced value for the entrepreneur and/or society the entrepreneurship process is complete.

Although we need to be aware of each of these 'layers' of entrepreneurship, we cannot reduce our explanation of the phenomenon to them alone. Throughout, entrepreneurship is an **emergent process** in that the whole is greater than the sum of the parts. This leads to an alternative, but synthesising, definition of entrepreneurship as *the emergent process of recognising and communicating creativity such that the resulting economic value can be appropriated by those involved*.

This chapter highlights the varied motivations, goals and methods of entrepreneurs. We should be careful not to characterise entrepreneurs as always interested in making money. Similarly, we draw attention to the important role entrepreneurs play in standardising and stabilising new goods for exchange. Entrepreneurship is about **transformation**, but it is also about **standardising** processes, procedures and new goods, so that they can be successfully exchanged to **create value**.

REVIEW QUESTIONS

1 Write down three examples of creative people. What characteristics do they share?

2 To what extent do you share these characteristics?

3 Explain what the difference is between a 'finder' and a 'seeker' in the context of entrepreneurship.

4 Entrepreneurship is always dependent upon being alert to opportunities. True or False?

5 'Opportunities are found not created'. To what extent would you agree with this statement?

6 Entrepreneurs tend to be driven by extrinsic motivation not intrinsic motivation. Do you agree?

7 List the types of resources that might be recombined in the process of entrepreneurship.

8 Which of the following does the process of qualification involve:
  a transforming products
  b stabilising products
  c making sure products don't change.

9 Entrepreneurs are often described as being very skilled in organising tasks. What sort of tasks do you think are the most important?

10 Entrepreneurship is an emergent phenomenon. What does this mean?

SEMINAR TASK

In small groups, spend ten minutes listing as many new products as you can (i.e. introduced in the last five years). Swap the lists, and then each group will write down what hunches and feelings they think would have first initiated an 'entrepreneurial project' in each case. After another ten minutes share your ideas, and encourage a broader discussion about how these hunches and feelings were followed through.

Preview case continued

A desire named Streetcar[10]

In 2004 Andrew Valentine and university friend Brett Akker launched their new venture Street-car. The real birth of the business can be traced back four years earlier to a hot evening in Cape Town where Andrew was living at the time. After a couple of drinks too many in a downtown bar, they decided it would be a good idea to start a business together. In 2002, now back in London, the two friends started meeting up a couple of times a week to discuss potential opportunities. During this period Andrew and Brett were holding down good jobs in large companies; but they both felt a great frustration with their work in terms of how slowly a large company moves and the length of time it was going to take before they were able to get any real responsibility for business decisions.

Looking back, Andrew reflects on the path to Streetcar being somewhat unusual. The two friends undertook a structured process of identifying and evaluating opportunities, and considering options across a very wide range of industries. Over the course of 2002 and 2003 they explored literally hundreds of different business ideas in manufacturing, retailing, trading and business services. Each business they looked at was assessed against a core set of criteria:

■ *Could their skills be put to good use in this business?*

■ *Is the business scalable? Can it be grown into a large business?*

■ *Is it saleable? – neither Andrew nor Brett thought there was any point in slogging away at a business for five or ten years if there wasn't any value in it at the end.*

■ *How much investment would be required? A company requiring £10 million to launch was going to be pretty tough.*

■ *How risky would it be?*

▶

2

Andrew and Brett didn't stumble across their entrepreneurial opportunity. They actively sought it out through a structured research process. But for nearly two years, every business idea they looked at failed against at least one of their criteria. Then in June 2003 Andrew read about a business operating a commercial car club in the US. 'When I read about it, my initial reaction was wow…what a brilliant idea. This must be huge in London'. But Andrew and Brett were amazed to find that there were no existing commercial operators. Worryingly though, there were some semi-commercial operators and they appeared to be making crunching losses! Still, the more the two friends looked into it, the more they felt this idea was worth further research. There were two vitally important questions they needed to answer before they could take that decision to go ahead:

1 *Is there a market for this product?*

2 *Can we make it work financially?*

It was clear that they couldn't answer these questions without enlisting the support and help of friends. This was the first time, but certainly not the last that they 'took some liberties' with their friends' goodwill. Andrew recalls 'This is a key skill in launching a new enterprise – gently persuading your friends and family to do things for you, for free!' They asked a friend who worked for an FMCG company [Fast Moving Consumer Goods] to run a series of customer focus groups. As they couldn't afford to rent a professional focus group venue or pay for participants they used Andrew's house, got together a group of friends as 'subjects' and gave them pizza and cheap red wine. Everyone in the focus group got the concept of Streetcar immediately. There were lots of questions and a few criticisms, but by the end of the evening all of the people there, without exception, said that they would join up to this type of service.

Andrew and Brett ran a second focus group, and then a third. Each group came back with the same message 'yes, they would use this service'. So, the two friends were convinced there was demand. They then put together some very basic financial models. They were forced to guesstimate quite a worrying number of things, but spent a lot of time reverse engineering the financials of several other companies abroad which had released financial information into the public domain.

The first analysis showed that the business would achieve profitability when they reached 100 cars. For this they would need around £450,000 in cash and asset financing facilities to run a pilot project. Andrew and Brett sat back and asked 'OK, so are we going to go ahead with this?' Remember, both were fully employed in sensible corporate jobs with company cars, pension schemes, medical insurance and decent career prospects. Balanced against this, they were looking to start a brand new company in an industry sector in which they had absolutely no experience and where the only existing UK operators were growing very slowly and making very big losses. But, on the plus side, neither of them had the responsibilities of a wife or family. They were both at the stage in their careers where if Streetcar failed they would probably be able to find a job again relatively quickly. They'd also done six months of research, and Andrew and Brett felt that they had learned more about business in those six months than they had in the previous seven years of corporate life put together.

So, one Sunday evening, after a long day of looking at the financial projections, Andrew and Brett ran out of reasons not to launch. In a nutshell, their logic was 'If we don't do it now, with this business idea, we'll never do it'. The next morning, they handed in their notices to their employers, and a few months later, launched Streetcar.

►

Questions

1   Question 1: What information did Andrew
    and Brett have to establish whether or not
    this venture would be successful? Was this
    information freely available to all?

2   Question 2: Describe what aspects of
    creativity are important in this story of
    Streetcar's development. How did Andrew
    and Brett recognise the creativity involved?

3   Question 3: Assess the level of a) creativity,
    and b) innovation involved in this new
    venture. To what extent would you say this
    was typical of all entrepreneurial ventures?

Reproduced with permission from Andrew Valentine (Andrew
.Valentine@streetcar.co.uk)

2.8   NOTES, REFERENCES AND FURTHER READING

Notes and Further Information

1. Streetcar's website: http://www.streetcar.co.uk/media.aspx.

2. For a helpful summary of these skills, see Gibb, 2005: 37.

3. A helpful definition of social structure is 'the connections among agents causally affecting their actions and in turn causally affected by them' (Porpora, 1998).

4. Martin (2007) has put forward a strong argument for showing how this is not the case. Creativity is defined as 'the human potential, power or capacity to make discoveries about the pre-existing potentials and powers of the world' … the 'actualising of a potential or the revealing of a power, or combinations of both' … either 'for the first time in history' … or 'for the first time to the individual or individuals concerned'. (pp. 3–4).

5. More details about jibbitz, now wholly owned by Crocs™ can be found at the company's website – www1.jibbitz.com.

6. Increasingly we talk of acting entrepreneurially in a non-market context. Whilst the primary objective may not be to produce economic value this remains an important part of what constitutes an opportunity as opposed to creativity *per se*.

7. Scruton (1997) states that 'propositions may be affirmed; but they may also be entertained without affirming them'.

8. See Sarasvathy (2001) on effectuation theory – which discusses this aspect of entrepreneurship in some depth.

9. Simon Woodroffe, founder of Yo! Sushi talks about his entrepreneurial journey on the DTI's Living Innovation website. See http://www.innovation.gov.uk/living_innovation/broadband/living_innovation/index.asp.

10. See note 1.

References

Archer, M.S. (2003) *Structure, Agency and the Internal Conversation*. Cambridge: Cambridge University Press.

Baron, R.A. and Shane, S.A. (2008) *Entrepreneurship: A Process Perspective*, Mason, OH: Thomson South-Western.

Becker, G.S. and Murphy, K.M. (1992) The division of labour, coordination costs, and knowledge, *The Quarterly Journal of Economics*, November, 107 (4).

Bilton, C. (2007) *Management and Creativity*, Oxford: Blackwell Publishing.

Callon, M. (ed.) (1998) *The Laws of the Markets*, Oxford: Blackwell.

Casson, M.C. (1982) *The Entrepreneur: An Economic Theory*, London: Martin Robertson.

Cox, G. (2005) *Cox Review of Creativity in Business*, HM Treasury, at http://www.hm-treasury.gov.uk/independent_reviews/cox_review/coxreview_index.cfm.

DTI (2003) *Innovation Report: Competing in the Global Economy: The Innovation Challenge*, London: DTI, December.

Eckhardt, J.T. and Shane, S.A. (2003) Opportunities and entrepreneurship, *Journal of Management*, 29 (3): 333–349.

2

Foss, N.J. and Ishikawa, I. (2006) Towards a dynamic resource-based view: Insights from Austrian capital and entrepreneurship theory, *Centre for Strategic Management and Globalization Working Paper 6*, April: available at www.cbs.dk/smg.

Galenson. D. (2008) *Old Masters and Young Geniuses: The Two Life Cycles of Artistic Creativity*, Princeton: Princeton University Press.

Gibb, A.A. (2005) Towards the Entrepreneurial University Entrepreneurship Education as a Lever for Change, *National Council for Graduate Entrepreneurship Policy Paper 3*, available at http://www.ncge.org.uk/downloads/policy/Towards_the_Entrepreneurial_University.pdf.

Kirzner, I. (1973) *Competition and Entrepreneurship*, Chicago: University of Chicago Press.

Lachmann, L.M. (1986) *The Market as an Economic Process*, Oxford: Basil Blackwell.

Martin, L. (2007) An augmented conceptual framework for creativity studies. In *Unpublished doctoral thesis*, Department of Organisation, Work and Technology, Lancaster University.

McClelland, D. (1961) *The Achieving Society*, Princeton, NJ: Van Nostrand.

Nelson, R. and Winter, S. (1982) *An Evolutionary Theory of Economic Change*, Cambridge, MA: The Belknap Press.

Penrose, E. T. (1959) *The theory of the growth of the firm*, Oxford: Oxford University Press.

Porpora, D. V. (1998) Four concepts of social structure, in M. Archer, R. Bhaskar, A. Collier, T. Lawson, and A. Norrie (eds) *Critical Realism Essential Readings*, London: Routledge, pp. 339–355.

Robinson, K. (2001) *Out of Our Minds: Learning to Be Creative*, London: Capstone.

Salerno, J. (1999) The place of Mises's Human Action in the development of modern economic thought, *Quarterly Journal of Austrian Economics,* 2: 35–65.

Sarasvathy, S.D. (2001) Causation and effectuation: Toward a theoretical shift from economic inevitability to entrepreneurial contingency, *Academy of Management Review*, 26 (2): 243–288.

Schumpeter, J.A. (1934) *The Theory of Economic Development: An Inquiry into Profits, Capital, Credit, Interest and the Business Cycle*, tr. R. Opie, Cambridge, MA: Harvard University Press.

Scruton, R. (1997) *The Aesthetics of Music*, Oxford: Clarendon Press.

Shane, S. (2000) Prior knowledge and the discovery of entrepreneurial opportunities, *Organisation Science*, 11 (4): 448–469.

Shane, S. (2003) *A General Theory of Entrepreneurship: The Individual-Opportunity Nexus*, Cheltenham: Edward Elgar.

Shane, S. and Venkataraman, S. (2000) The promise of entrepreneurship as a field of research, *Academy of Management Review,* 25 (1), 217–226.

Swedberg, R. (1991) *Joseph A. Schumpeter: His Life and Work*, Cambridge: Polity Press.

Vaughn, K.I. (1994) *Austrian Economics in America: the Migration of a Tradition*, Cambridge: Cambridge University Press.

West, M.A. and Farr, J.L. (1990) *Innovation and Creativity at Work*, London: Wiley.

Wilson, N. (2008) Whose creativity is it anyway? A critical realist evaluation of managing creativity in the creative economy, Paper for the Fourth Art of Management and Organisation Conference, Banff, September.

Recommended Further Reading
....

Research into entrepreneurship has flourished over recent years. Given so much scholarly activity, many published papers and books from many different disciplinary perspectives, it is helpful to get an overview of the state of research. Zoltan Acs and David Audretsch have edited an excellent collection from leading entrepreneurship researchers which is available in one volume:

Acs, Z. and Audretsch, D. (2005) *Handbook of Entrepreneurship Research: An Interdisciplinary Survey and Introduction*, London: Springer.

The entrepreneurship theorist Saras Sarasvathy has written a thought-provoking paper which 'encourages us to throw away our obsession with dividing the world into entrepreneurs and nonentrepreneurs':

Sarasvathy, S. (2004) The questions we ask and the questions we care about: reformulating some problems in entrepreneurship research, *Journal of Business Venturing*, 19 (5), 707–717.

CHAPTER 3

Entrepreneurship and Innovation

LEARNING OBJECTIVES

After studying this chapter, the reader will be able to:

- Understand the importance of innovation to individuals, organisations and society
- Assess the relevance of innovation to entrepreneurship
- Be aware of some key innovation policy issues and debates
- Critically evaluate how innovation is managed in an organisational context
- Recognise barriers to innovation and how these can be overcome.

INTRODUCTION

The opening two chapters began our search for entrepreneurship and introduced a conceptual model of entrepreneurship as an emergent process. Whilst the terms creativity and innovation are often used interchangeably, we can distinguish innovation as a *post hoc* recognition of creativity. In other words, innovation is the successful exploitation of a new idea (DTI, 2003). Focusing directly on innovation in this chapter, we consider the journey from new idea through to market exchange, and present some of the leading thinking on how this journey is undertaken successfully. Typically, this involves the introduction of some new technology and we investigate the relationship between technology and business success. We also ask whether innovation is really so important, or whether imitation might be a safer and as rewarding business strategy.

A further key focus for this chapter concerns the distinction often made between individual creativity and the necessarily relational or 'dynamic' aspect of innovation. Whilst the UK government's definition of creativity rests on 'individual creativity' (see DCMS, 1998), innovation is generally considered to require interaction between individuals who bring with them different but complementary skills, experience and qualifications.

PREVIEW CASE

The magic of mushrooms: Jan Rutgers Science (JRS)

Jan Rutgers has a passion for basidiomycetes – fungi and mushrooms to you and me. As a natural products chemist working for some of the big firms in natural product discovery, Jan became interested in the potential of mushrooms to produce organic compounds that could be turned into commercial products, such as antibiotics, fungicides, biofuels and potential treatments for disease. He embarked on doctorate level research focused on fermenting certain types of bioactive compound from tropical fungi. In the case study at the end of this chapter, we tell the extraordinary story of what happened next, revealing the highs and lows of scientific innovation, journeys to the Ecuadorian rain forest and the very real challenges of commercialisation.

Imagine you had just discovered a new species of plant growing in your garden that had curative properties for those suffering from the common cold. How might you go about bringing this potentially innovative discovery to market? What challenges might you face?

Source: Interview with Jan Rutgers, November 2008.

WHEN THINGS GO WRONG

Three cautionary tales

1 Alexander Graham Bell suggested that his new invention (the telephone) might be useful for calling ahead to the next town to tell them a telegram was coming. In hindsight, this seems an extraordinary lapse in judgement. Just what would he have made of the iPhone?

2 Joseph Swan in England developed a light bulb at the same time as Edison in the USA. Swan produced a superior light bulb (Edison recognised this by buying up his patents), for which others developed a market. There is surely a lesson about the difference between invention and innovation here.

3 The marketing philosophy of Sir Clive Sinclair's C5 electric car was based on the same principles as his earlier innovations of turning technologically advanced but expensive products into something which could be afforded by mass markets. However, he misjudged the market and the C5 was a financial disaster, forcing Sinclair to sell off his computer assets to Amstrad. Taking the right decisions is at the heart of innovation.

© HULTON-DEUTSCH COLLECTION/CORBIS

The Sinclair C5

Source: Virgin media, at http://www.virginmedia.com/money/features/business-blunders.php?ssid=2

3.1   WHAT IS INNOVATION?

The term innovation comes from the Latin *innovare* meaning 'to make something new'. Modern-day understanding is that innovation is a process of turning ideas into new opportunities for value creation and putting these into widely used practice. Roberts defines innovation as the successful commercial implementation and exploitation of a new idea or invention (Roberts, 1988). Innovation is the process of taking new ideas effectively and profitably through to satisfied customers.

As a much-loved buzz-word of managers, *innovation* sounds good. Everyone feels as if they should be doing it – even if they are unsure about what precisely *it* is.

INNOVATION PERSPECTIVES

Innovation and creative ideas

All innovation begins with creative ideas...We define innovation as the successful implementation of creative ideas within an organisation. In this view, creativity by individuals and teams is a starting point for innovation; the first is necessary but not sufficient condition for the second.
(Amabile *et al.*, 1996)

Innovation and entrepreneurs

Innovation is the specific tool of entrepreneurs, the means by which they exploit change as an opportunity for a different business or service. It is capable of being presented as a discipline, capable of being learned, capable of being practiced.
(Drucker, 1985)

Innovation and competitive advantage

Companies achieve competitive advantage through acts of innovation. They approach innovation in its broadest sense, including both new technologies and new ways of doing things.
(Porter, 1990)

Innovation and creativity

Innovation is the *post hoc* recognition of creativity, involving a new and valuable discovery of some kind. In other words, innovation can only be said to have taken place after the event. It is an outcome phenomenon.
(Wilson, 2008)

It may be helpful to define what innovation is *not*, rather than what it is:

- Innovation is *not* the same as invention. It is perfectly possible to come up with an invention that no-one ever actually uses or gains any benefit from.

- Innovation is *not* just about new products and/or services. It can also involve new organisational forms, strategies, processes and more besides.

- Innovation does *not* require wholly original ideas. A good new idea is very often two old ideas meeting for the first time.

- Innovation is *not* always the result of one-off inspiration. Often innovation is the result or the outcome of many years of patient work and planning.

- Innovation is *not* the same as creativity. Whereas creativity involves the discovery of something new and valuable, innovation can only be determined after the event, when its novelty and value have become manifest.

3.2   TYPES OF INNOVATION

Joseph Schumpeter was the first economist who clearly identified innovation as an outcome of entrepreneurship (Schumpeter, 1934). Early on in his career, Schumpeter argued that an entrepreneur disrupts markets and causes new ones to be formed in circular flows. The 'true' entrepreneur causes a radical change that is discontinuous with the previous flows by obtaining and using information caused by these 'tides of creative destruction'. There are periods when uncertainty and resistance are substantial, but eventually standardisation or acceptance occurs as the innovation is diffused. Although Schumpeter changed his views in later life to a somewhat different position, he remains influential to this day in conceptualising innovation.

We probably think of innovation first and foremost in terms of those products and services which are released onto the market and appear to be genuinely 'new'. Very often these innovations have the potential to *transform* the marketplace, or at least have a *radical* impact on existing competitors. But there are many different possible innovation outcomes. New ideas come in many shapes and sizes. A new idea applied to the work-place might make some minor difference to daily routines (the scheduling of a weekly team-meeting, for example) – an *incremental process* innovation – or it might radically affect the nature of the organisation and the industry it competes in (e.g. as in the example of Amazon and the book trade). We can think of innovation as happening across a wide continuum – from incremental to transformational – and within a very wide set of contexts – including product, service and process innovation (see Figure 3-1).

From a strategic point of view, firms seek to innovate so as to be able to compete successfully in their industry. This can involve undertaking incremental product, service and/or process innovations, or it might be focused on achieving transformational innovation, where the very rules of the competition are changed in the firm's favour (as in the example of the first telephone insurance service in the UK – Direct Line, introduced in 1985).

Other types of innovation include *technological*, *organisational* and *strategic* innovation. The latter two categories occur in both the organisational behaviour and strategic management literatures applied to large firms and are increasingly associated with corporate entrepreneurship in firms in mature or maturing industries.

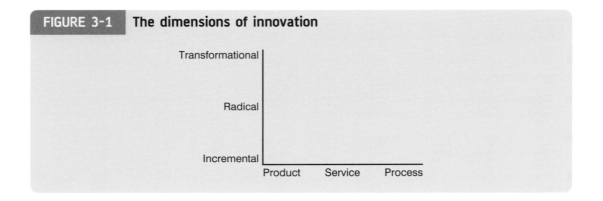

FIGURE 3-1   **The dimensions of innovation**

ENTREPRENEURSHIP IN ACTION

Making the right call

It used to be the case that insurance was something you bought from slick, fast-talking, door-to-door insurance salesmen. Things changed for ever in April 1985, when the first telephone insurance service in the UK was launched by the entrepreneur Peter Wood. 'Direct Line' has subsequently grown rapidly, from 63 employees when it set up, to 10,000, offering a range of personal finance products to more than 10 million customers across the UK and Europe. Wood himself gained a legendary reputation (and remuneration to match). Today, a Direct Line policy is sold every 10 seconds and the company receives over 22 million telephone calls a year. At the heart of the business model, therefore, is the operational capacity to deal with huge quantities of enquiries quickly and efficiently.

Peter Wood, founder of Direct Line in 1985, left in 1997 and has founded six more businesses since then.

Source: Directline, at http://www.directline.com/about_us/history.htm

Schumpeter describes the main types of entrepreneurial behaviour or innovation in the second chapter of his *The Theory of Economic Development* (1934):

1 Introducing a new good

2 Introducing a new method of production

3 Opening a new market

4 Conquering a new source of raw materials

5 Reorganising an industry in a new way.

3.3   WHY DO BUSINESSES NEED TO INNOVATE?

There are three fundamental reasons why innovation is considered critical for companies and countries in the twenty-first century (DTI, 2003):

1 Trade liberalisation and globalised markets mean that developed Western countries increasingly compete against other countries with much lower labour costs and well-educated labour forces. To provide some examples, wages in China may be as little as 5 per cent of those in the UK; labour costs in Korea are just over half UK levels, and the proportion of graduates in the working age population is almost identical.

2 Breakthroughs in scientific understanding and technology are changing our world faster than ever before. Opportunities for innovation are springing up through developments in information and communications technologies (ICT), new materials, biotechnology, new fuels and nanotechnology. These, in turn, are creating many opportunities for entrepreneurial businesses to gain competitive advantage through exploiting innovation opportunities.

3 The extraordinary growth of global communications (the 24 hours, 7 days of the week media phenomenon), means that consumer tastes are also changing faster, as new fashions, ideas and products spread across the world almost instantaneously.

3.4   GLOBAL INNOVATION POLICY

Innovation policy is commonly defined as 'a set of policy actions to raise the quantity and efficiency of innovation activities whereby innovation activities refer to the creation, adaptation and adoption of new or improved products, processes or services'.[1] So-called 'third generation' innovation policy is increasingly cross-cutting (i.e. horizontal), therefore linking in with other policies on research, education, training and health.[2] It is not enough to have a single innovation policy, but this needs to integrate with policies relating to all sorts of other societal issues. We can see the importance of this 'joined up' thinking particularly in the context of the global recession that hit the world in 2008. Countries the world over recognise the importance of innovative products and services as a means to boost national competitiveness and growth, and to provide a means of kick-starting their economies in order to provide new wealth and job opportunities at a time of great need.

3.4.1 Innovation in Europe

Innovation is not seen as an optional extra but as a 'must have' in Europe. Indeed, as the European Commission[3] has indicated, if Europe is to maintain its competitive position it has to innovate. Furthermore, this is not just innovation in science or technology-based industries, but in less obvious contexts for change (e.g. the ceramics industry in Spain). Indeed, as one recent report (NESTA, 2007) puts it, 'Innovation policy should encompass science and technology policy and not the other way round'. The European Union has published extensively on the need to 'become a truly knowledge-based and innovation-friendly society where innovation is not feared by the public but welcomed' (Commission of the European Communities, 2006: 3). It has outlined nine strategic priorities for how innovation should be encouraged and supported (see Table 3-1).[4]

Within Europe there are now extensive and detailed data available on individual countries' comparative innovation performance. This is known as the European Innovation Scorecard.[5] In line with the Lisbon Agenda,[6] the EU has set an ambitious target of raising investment in R&D to 3 per cent of GDP by 2010 (of which two-thirds will come from the private sector). This is unlikely to be achieved across the board (not least because R&D spending tends to get cut back at times of economic

TABLE 3-1	Nine strategic priorities for European innovation

1 Ensuring an effective IPR framework

2 Creating a proactive standard–setting policy

3 Making public procurement work for innovation

4 Launching Joint Technology Initiatives

5 Boosting innovation and growth in lead markets

6 Enhancing closer cooperation between higher education, research and business

7 Helping innovation in regions

8 Developing a policy approach to innovation in services and to non-technological innovation; and

9 Enabling risk capital markets.

difficulty), but it sets an important benchmark against which other countries are comparing themselves. For example, the South African government committed itself to raise national spending on R&D to 1 per cent of GDP by the year 2008/9 (clearly someway short of the OECD average). This would put South Africa in the same league as countries such as Brazil, New Zealand and Spain.[7]

3.4.2 Innovation in South Africa

In South Africa, as in other countries of the world, innovation policy is regarded as having the potential to make an important contribution towards promoting and achieving key national objectives. South Africa's national system of innovation[8] has the potential to:

■ improve and sustain the quality of life of all South Africans

■ develop human resources for science and technology

■ build the South African economy

■ strengthen the country's competitiveness in the international sphere.

A key issue for South Africa is the building of a skilled workforce who can provide the human capital required to undertake innovation. It is important to remember, of course, that R&D is not just about the financial and technological investment into innovation but also about the individuals involved having appropriate skills and expertise.[9]

If you read the who's who of famous inventors from history, most have one thing in common – they are predominantly men, from Leonardo da Vinci to Tim Berners-Lee. A South African woman is trying to change that by empowering women to develop innovative projects. She created an investment vehicle, Wiphold in 1994 that has two aims: to empower women through investment and to take the stock market to South Africa's black population.

Integrative Case Link
Read more about Gloria's innovative work at the frontiers of the financial services market in Case Study 4 at the end of Part 2, 'Gloria Serobe: Empowering women in South African society'.

3.4.3 Innovation in South Korea

South Korea came into being in 1948, following the partition of Korea into two parts. Reconstruction started in 1951, with attention given to an effective national educational system and land reform. Subsequent economic health largely depended upon manufactured exports and state intervention (Eriksson, 2005: 5). Between 1962 and 1997 South Korea achieved an annual growth rate of nearly 8 per cent, which some commentators regard to be 'the greatest development success in history' (Ibid.: 16). However, the majority of modern technologies were acquired from abroad, with South Korea adopting a restrictive policy towards inward investment until the mid-1980s. There was a lack of well-trained scientists and inadequate university research. In 1988, the military regime was replaced by a democratically elected government. The financial crisis of the late 1990s had a major impact on South Korea, along with most of East and Southeastern Asia. In 2001 the Science and Technology Framework Law was enacted and brought about several important changes in science, technology and innovation policy in Korea. The law places emphasis on the coordination of national science and technology and R&D policies and investments.

The government has also initiated new programmes to promote technology transfer, diffusion and commercialisation of new technologies. South Korea is now committed to lifting the nation's technological capability to the level of the G-7 countries by 2020 (Ibid.: 23).

3.5 NATIONAL SYSTEMS OF INNOVATION

3

From the examples above we can see that every country has a different endowment of national resources and capabilities. These, in turn, affect the type of industries in which the country engages. The national system of innovation in which a firm is embedded has a major influence on its innovation strategy. Business firms are strongly influenced in their choice of technological strategies by the conditions existing in their home countries. This has a bearing on the sectoral specialisation we might observe in any one country. There are also very different aggregate levels of financial resources targeted at research and development, suggesting very different contexts for innovation in different countries.

From the preceding discussion it will be clear that these factors disguise complex relationships between the economic, social and environmental conditions that characterise any one country. At the heart of these relationships is the interaction between physical appliances and human ways of doing things – otherwise known as technology.

3.5.1 Technology and Innovation

We easily get carried away by the phrase 'new technology' and immediately think of this as something beyond our control – but, of course, technology needs human input. Technology can either be purely *hi-tech* (i.e. carried out by machines / software) or *low-tech* (involving a change in the pattern of human behaviour).

> **CERN and the benefits of partnership**
>
> On 21 October 2008, the Large Hadron Collider,[10] the world's largest and most complex scientific instrument, was inaugurated. The world's biggest particle accelerator is expected to produce more than 15 million Gigabytes of data each year. The computing power needed to deal with this requires the services of more than 140 computer centres in 33 countries. Famous brands such as HP, Intel and Oracle are all involved in a partnership to develop a grid computing infrastructure like no other ever seen before. In short, the partnership of scientists, hardware and software is changing the way science is done.
>
> *Source:* http://public.web.cern.ch/public/ on 1 November 2008

Technologies can be shared among industries, universities, governments and other institutions so as to ensure that scientific and technological developments are accessible to a wide range of users. This *technology transfer* can then help to facilitate the wider exploitation of technology into new products, processes, applications, materials and services.

A key issue for organisations is how they might marry their technological innovation strategy, involving the research and development of new products, services and processes, with their market strategy of ensuring they enter the market at the right time. For example, it may well be that Microsoft has already developed a new operating system that surpasses the benefits and features of Windows XP or Vista. However, since there are so many current and potential customers for XP and Vista already, it would be strategically risky, to say the least, to introduce a new competitor too early.[11]

One of the interesting tensions faced by those managers who actively engage in promoting innovation in their business is that between planning and opportunism. Research on business growth has identified the central importance of developing the right strategies for the business, which in turn are based on organisational objectives. A 'deliberate' strategy would seem at odds with the notion of 'emergent' or opportunistic strategy that embraced new ideas and fostered innovation (Mintzberg and Waters, 1985). A successful innovation strategy would appear to have to be both deliberate and emergent, which makes it quite a trick to pull off.

In an attempt to conceptualise the links between type of business activity and the nature and direction of innovation, researchers have put forward the notion of *technological trajectory*. This recognises the sense of path dependency that contextualises all business activity. Once a path has been selected and established, it develops a momentum of its own which, in turn, enforces the direction towards which 'problem-solving activity' moves (see Dosi, 1982 and Nelson and Winter, 1982). A much-cited example of path dependency is the QWERTY computer keyboard. Whilst various keyboard lay-outs have been shown to be ergonomically more efficient than the traditional set-up, it is impossible to introduce an alternative approach because, quite simply, we all use the QWERTY keyboard and have learned to type according to this.

3

Knowing when it pays to talk technical

Stuart Fisk is well-versed in technology having graduated in chemical engineering and worked for the likes of Intel Corporation and Kingston Technology. In co-founding the data storage company Data SolutionZ, he became the lead player on the commercial side of the business. As he recalls, however, in the early days, he was wary of taking his very creative co-founder and the inventor of the data storage technology along with him to key meetings.

> 'It was quite simple. He was a technical guy. My concern was that he probably gave the impression of somebody who was lost in technical nirvana, and I didn't want our potential customers to think that we were a load of geeks'.

However, Stuart's co-founder eventually challenged him to take him along to vital business development meetings. So, for the next meeting, which happened to be with one of the leading PC retail giants, the two of them went along together. It was clear from the start, recalls Stuart, that the computer retailer liked the product and saw the market potential. However, there was also mounting scepticism during the meeting that this product couldn't easily be integrated within their PCs. It was at this point that the inventor who had been silent up until now spoke up. There then followed a technical discussion during which the inventor became more and more animated. Stuart recalls thinking 'he's going to blow it . . . ' But it was far from it. He had won the respect of the technical guys and before long, a deal was struck. The PC retailer became the small start-up's largest global customer. Only a handful of years later Data SolutionZ was acquired in a leveraged buy-out for $45 million. The co-founders and some venture capitalists made considerable sums of money. And Stuart had learned a valuable lesson. Never underestimate the value of technical knowledge if applied in the appropriate context.

Source: Interview with Stuart Fisk, November 2008

3.6   MANAGING INNOVATION

There is something of a paradox in the notion of 'managing' innovation. By its very nature, innovation requires change. Being open to the possibility of change appears to run counter to a planned approach. Having a deliberate approach towards innovation must be tempered by an opportunistic approach that can deal with emergence. This tension becomes all too real in times of economic downturn, when very often it is companies' research and development budgets which are cut first. It is difficult to maintain a medium- to long-term view when you have to manage very real difficulties of paying bills and covering costs today.

Economic downturn hits the pharmaceutical industry

The pharmaceutical industry depends upon innovation for both its medium- and long-term future. The impact of the global economic downturn is likely to be quite devastating, especially for the smaller company and contract research organisations. Although R&D spending has tripled in the past ten years or so, output has gone down considerably, and in the wake of the recession, it is set to reduce still further. For the larger pharma firms, this might involve less work being outsourced, whilst for the smaller pharmaceutical and biotech firms, outsourcing might halt altogether. Investment in biotech start-ups has typically relied on venture capital. Unfortunately, private equity providers are few and far between as the credit crunch deepens. The outsourcing 'hubs' like India and China are beginning to lose their attractiveness, as the big players look to other emerging locations such as the Philippines, Eastern Europe, Central and South America and other South Asian countries. As a backdrop to all of this, however, pharma companies are only too aware of the need for innovative new products. Some $60 billion will be off patent protection by 2012, leaving many businesses looking for new income streams to make up for previously secure revenues.

What percentage of annual sales income do you think most large pharmaceutical companies spend on R&D? How does this compare with other industry sectors, such as property and construction; energy; entertainment?

Source: Sylvia Miriyam Findlay, Frost & Sullivan, http://www.frost.com/prod/servlet/market-insight-top.pag?Src=RSS&do cid= 155855105.

3.6.1 Where Does Innovation Come From?

As we have seen, the innovation process begins with new ideas. Whether these are flashes of inspiration or carefully crafted responses to years of dedicated thinking, they are the source of all innovation. It is helpful to understand a little more about where new ideas come from, not least because the innovation process is managed proactively in many firms. Peter Drucker (1985) listed seven sources of opportunity:

1 **The unexpected** – world events, including natural disasters, acts of terrorism and wars, have all given rise to innovative new products and services including security devices and rescue equipment.

2 **The incongruous** – medical scientists have often found that their search for a cure or treatment to condition *A* leads to a new cure and treatment for *B*, *C* or *D*. In other words, what they thought was going to happen was trumped by some altogether different and surprising finding.

3 **Process need** – a key problem for glass manufacturers is to be able to make sheets of glass that are without any imperfections which would limit the material's strength and reliability. The first successful application of float-glass, where glass is produced by floating molten glass on a bed of molten tin, was introduced in the mid-1950s by the UK Pilkington Brothers.

4 **Industry and market structures** – the print industry has undergone seismic change over the past 20–30 years. The advent of digital technology has revolutionised the job of the printer, and the opportunities for High Street print shops.

5 **Demographics** – the current world average lifespan is 66 years, which compares with 30–40 in the early twentieth century, 20–30 in medieval Britain, classical Greece and Rome, and just 18 in the Bronze age. As people live older, so there are more opportunities for businesses serving the needs of older people (nursing homes, care for the elderly, insurance products and so on).

6 **Changes in perception** – the world is waking up to its responsibilities to manage the planet and its resources. Global warming and climate change present enormous challenges to humankind. They also present a myriad of opportunities to those prepared to be early adopters of energy-conserving and sustainable innovations.

7 **New knowledge** – perhaps the least common source of innovation is the application of genuinely new knowledge. Blue skies research on the Genome Project, and, more recently, the Large Hadron Collider, hold the promise of innovative processes, products and services.

It will be apparent from the above examples that innovation is very often something that emerges out of an individual's particular needs. *End-user innovation* describes where an agent (person or company) develops an innovation for their own (personal or in-house) use because existing products do not meet their needs (see von Hippel, 1994, or read about the early life of the Internet or Google.com). We can contrast this with linear models of innovation, such as *manufacturer innovation*, where those involved innovate in order to sell the innovation. Whether innovation is mainly *supply-pushed* (based on new technological possibilities) or *demand-led* (based on social needs and market requirements) is an issue of considerable debate.[12]

3.6.2 The Innovation Management Process

The innovation management process can be loosely divided into the following four stages (see also Figure 3-2):

> **Stage 1**   involves scanning the environment for relevant signals indicating threats and opportunities for change.

> **Stage 2**   involves deciding which of these signals to respond to, based on a strategic view of how the enterprise can best develop.

> **Stage 3**   involves acquiring the resources to enable the response. This might be as a result of R&D or acquiring key resources from elsewhere (e.g. via technology transfer).

> **Stage 4**   involves implementing the project, developing both the technology and the market in order to respond effectively.

In practice, we might suggest a fifth phase is just as vital, namely reflection on the success (or failure) of each of the four stages in order to learn how to manage the process better. This is an iterative process. The ability to respond to changing circumstances and changing needs is vital. Whilst there are those who claim to have seen the 'credit crunch' banking crisis, which began in 2007, coming, the vast majority of businesses found themselves having to respond to a major economic downturn that they simply weren't prepared for. The ability to innovate successfully depends, in part, on the organisation's *absorptive capacity*. Even where it does spot a viable business opportunity, an organisation can only exploit this opportunity if it has the capacity to deal with the extra commitment or new direction required.

The linear nature of the diagram in Figure 3-2 disguises the complexity and serendipity of innovation in the real world. As Charles Leadbeater has observed, 'the process of innovation (is) lengthy, interactive and social; many people with different talents, skills and resources have (to) come together' (Leadbeater, 2003).

3

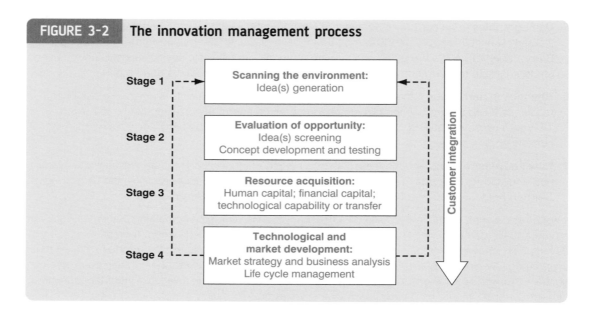

FIGURE 3-2   **The innovation management process**

Stage 1 → **Scanning the environment:**
Idea(s) generation

Stage 2 → **Evaluation of opportunity:**
Idea(s) screening
Concept development and testing

Stage 3 → **Resource acquisition:**
Human capital; financial capital;
technological capability or transfer

Stage 4 → **Technological and market development:**
Market strategy and business analysis
Life cycle management

Customer integration

The iconic Danish toy maker LEGO has developed a particular approach to the management of innovation which they apply to all aspects of their business.[13] Design for Business (D4B) maps how a project is conceived, assessed and developed with design as a key stakeholder. The following approaches to innovation are used in the model:

■ **No change** – a product or process is currently fit for purpose.

■ **Adjust** – minor changes are used to update products or modify processes in order to improve performance.

■ **Reconfigure** – existing techniques and parameters are put together in a new way in order to better meet existing business and customer needs.

© 2009 THE LEGO GROUP

■ **Redefine** – an entirely new approach (and product) is introduced.

LEGO has developed a wide range of tools to help all those involved work through the D4B process. This includes bespoke pamphlets and templates which can be used to monitor and record progress, as well as other developments relating to shared language and the use of 3D modelling.

3.7   BARRIERS TO INNOVATION

In practice, innovation is far from being an easy option for either a new or established firm to take. There are a range of internal and external barriers to innovation, depending upon the particular industry, size of enterprise, reward structure and motivation of those involved.

3.7.1 **The Importance of Context**

Innovation is highly context- and sector-specific. The development of new exploration techniques is vital in oil production, for example, whilst a very different type of innovation is required in order to build modular accommodation systems in the construction industry, or rehabilitation programmes for offenders. Innovation processes differ greatly from sector to sector. The Organisation for Economic Co-operation and Development, for example draws attention to the following types of differences (OECD, 2005):

■ innovation development (e.g. R&D in high-technology sectors)

■ rate of technological change (e.g. adoption of knowledge and technology)

■ linkages and access to knowledge (dependent upon a region's stock of human capital, innovation centres, science parks, universities)

■ organisational structures (including absorptive capacity)

■ institutional factors (e.g. regulations and intellectual property rights).

Typically, innovation has been linked with science-based industries rather than other less 'hard-nosed' contexts such as the arts, culture, sport, leisure, tourism and education. In fact, science-based innovation takes place in just 6 per cent of the UK economy (NESTA, 2007: 4). A great deal of innovation remains hidden from view, not being captured in traditional indicators such as investments in R&D or patents awarded. NESTA (2007: 5) have put forward four types of 'hidden innovation':

Type 1: Innovation that can be measured by traditional indicators, but which is currently excluded (e.g. the development of new technologies in oil exploration).

Type II: Innovation without a major scientific and technological basis, such as innovation in business models or organisational structures (e.g. the development of new contractual relationships between major construction suppliers and clients).

Type III: Innovation created from novel combinations of existing technologies and processes (e.g. how banks have integrated their various back office IT systems to deliver innovative customer services such as Internet banking).

Type IV: Small-scale, local innovations that take place 'under the radar' (e.g. the everyday innovation that occurs throughout society).

A potential barrier to innovation is, therefore, the tendency to overlook the potential for it to take place in areas one might not expect to find it.

The working dynamics of innovation are not something which can easily be abstracted into a conceptual model, to be carried round like an innovation 'tool-kit'. Context matters. Innovation in the car industry is very different from that in the prison service. However, this is not to say that the one can't learn from the other. Indeed, one of the strong underlying arguments of this book is that a creative and entrepreneurial approach to our economy demands collaboration, divergent thinking, and the ability to broker technology from different worlds and from across separate disciplines (see also Hargardon, 2003).

Networks and collaboration are fundamental to innovation. It is certainly over-simplistic to suggest that innovation moves in a linear fashion from 'laboratory to marketplace' within a single organisation or business. Collaborations between businesses and their suppliers, contractors and clients or customers generate the majority of innovations. Very often they involve a complex and interactive process, which

3

Kingston Technology Corporation — Making the right decisions

Chinese and Taiwanese immigrants, John Tu and David Sun founded their first business together in 1982. Camintonn Corporation was a manufacturer of enhancement products for DEC (Digital Equipment Corporation) systems. The company, which first ran out of Tu's garage, grew quickly, and by 1986 the co-founders had sold it to AST Research for $6 million. In hindsight, it would have been easy for the two friends to have put their feet up and cashed in on their business successes. In fact, Tu and Sun invested much of their profits on the stock market, but then suffered badly when it crashed in 1987. Although they lost nearly everything, they spotted an opportunity to recoup their losses, designing what was to become the industry standard Single In-Line Memory Module (SIMM). Kingston Technology Corporation was founded in 1987, but at this stage it wasn't at all clear that there was a particularly big or sustainable market for memory products. Tu, in particular, remained sceptical that the company would outlast its fifth birthday. It wasn't all plain sailing, as Tu recalls. 'David and I, we once incurred a debt of US$1 million in the early days. So, we might well have become people sitting on the streets too.' As it was, he was to be proved very wrong. In fact, the company made over $12 million in sales in the first year and it has grown ever since. It is now a $5 billion company, the biggest supplier of memory in the world, and has also been ranked at the fastest growing privately held company in America.

When asked as to what they attribute their success, David Sun notes 'John is a person who is good at communicating, enjoys communicating, and places a lot of importance on communicating'. 'The "Kingston Secret" is the sharing and communicating John engages in' says Sun. Of course, this is perhaps to underplay the importance of the co-founders technical skills which got them into the business in the first place.

What attributes do you think were critical to the subsequent success of Kingston Technology? Is technical knowledge more important than commercial knowledge?

Sources: http://www.fundinguniverse.com/company-histories/Kingston-Technology-Corporation-Company-History.html accessed April 28 2009. Kingston Technology President John Tu, *How the 'Good Boss' Changed 150 Children's Lives*, by Jimmy Hsiung, published on 28 March 2007; http://www.cw.com.tw/english/article/368060.jsp available at http://www.kingston.com/anz/press/2007/local_media/KingstonTechnologyPresidentJohnTu.pdf accessed on 28 April 2009

may well throw up surprises – sometimes in the form of unexpected new products and services (see Drucker's list above).

3.7.2 The Importance of Size

Where once larger firms were considered the sole engine of innovative activity, it is increasingly recognised that smaller firms play an important role in innovation in many industries. There are differences between small and large firms that impact on their innovation potential and capacity which are summarised in Table 3-2.

A key fact is that smaller firms contribute more innovations than larger firms however they are measured (Audretsch, 1995).

TABLE 3-2	Innovation in small and large firms – a comparison	
Small firms	**Large firms**	
Usually have to find inputs for the innovation process outside the firm, overcoming resource constraints and putting the emphasis on certain types of management capabilities to facilitate the innovation process.	Have an advantage in capital intensive, concentrated industries where substantial resources and converging technologies are present.	
Have more limited networks than larger firms and so may find it harder to diffuse their innovations.	Have the potential to generate their own ideas for innovation through their own internal research and development departments (Audretsch and Vivarelli, 1996; Piergiovanni et al., 1997).	
Have the advantage of being more flexible, informal, and responsive to change.	Can rely on economies of scale and scope to help innovations to spread out (diffuse) across their markets and industries.	
Have the advantage in emerging industries with high levels of innovation (Acs and Audretsch, 1990) and in those industries where individual creativity is at a premium (e.g. creative industries).	Can diversify their financial risks across different business units and product lines.	

3.7.3 The Innovation Life Cycle

Over and above the particular sector the business is operating in, its size, and the prevailing national system of innovation, the nature or 'dynamic' of innovation has been shown to be related to industry life-cycle. The barriers to innovation for young firms operating in new technology industries are clearly quite different from those for established firms in more mature markets. The Abernathy-Utterback model (Utterback, 1994) describes the changing rates of product and process innovation at different life cycle stages (see Figure 3-3).

In the *fluid phase* many enterprises (often SMEs) compete with different designs, hoping that their solution could be the next big business. So it was that when the car was first invented in the late nineteenth century, a host of initial (and quite different) designs for the car were introduced on the emerging market.

In the following *transition phase* various different designs tend to converge. At this point the market sorts out product alternatives, and the volume of sales increases. By the end of this transition phase a dominant design emerges. In the case of car manufacture, when Ford entered the industry in around 1910 there were already more than 500 car-making companies in the US.

In the *distinct phase* the dominant design is established, and large companies move in, drawing on their potential advantage in terms of financial leverage and economies of scale. This may well result in smaller players being squeezed out of the market altogether.

Windows of opportunity for innovation are becoming shorter. Product and service life cycles become ever shorter requiring rapid responses from organisations if they are to keep up. In addition, many technologies are large-scale and converging, sometimes called technology fusion. Even large firms are unable to undertake the tasks on their own, and there is an increasing trend towards collaboration and technology clusters, rather than vertical integration in which one firm operates across the whole of the value chain.

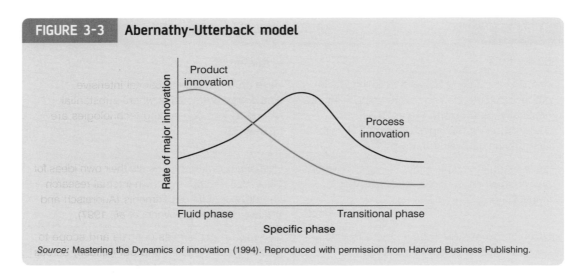

FIGURE 3-3   **Abernathy-Utterback model**

Source: Mastering the Dynamics of innovation (1994). Reproduced with permission from Harvard Business Publishing.

3.7.4 The Importance of Motivation (and Rewards)

For all that we can focus attention on the identification and exploitation of an opportunity, it is as well to remember that innovation is very much a human process, where individual motivations play a central role. In the case of the lone inventor or the creative entrepreneur, motivation is very often wrapped up in a love for the particular product, process or industry concerned. Economists have referred to this type of motivation as *intrinsic* (Frey and Pommerehne, 1989), contrasting it with *extrinsic* motivation, where financial reward is the explicit objective. A key problem for larger firms is to ensure that entrepreneurial staff are sufficiently motivated and rewarded to become involved in the innovation process in the first place. As shown in Figure 3-4, innovation will not flourish without the appropriate opportunity, resources and motivation in place.

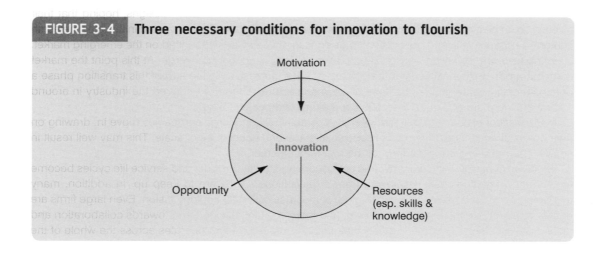

FIGURE 3-4   **Three necessary conditions for innovation to flourish**

A range of internal factors has been identified as affecting the rate of inventiveness of organisations in the private sector (Tidd *et al.*, 1997). These in turn influence the rate of innovation displayed by such organisations:

■ The relationship between the innovation strategy and the overall strategic management process (e.g. the degree to which innovation is a formal goal).

■ The rewards that encourage behaviour likely to foster innovation. In fact, many reward and incentive schemes are aimed at measuring the bottom line and are short-term rewards unlikely to encourage innovation.

■ Fostering a climate that is friendly towards innovation within the organisation. As the organisation becomes more established it becomes increasingly complex and the culture more entrenched. Inimical culture and reward system are two of the greatest barriers to successful innovation.

3.8   INNOVATION AND ENTREPRENEURSHIP

In Chapter 2 we introduced the emergent properties of entrepreneurship, which result in innovation and the appropriation of value for those involved. A key issue for entrepreneurs is how they can ensure that ownership of the innovation is not lost in the implementation process itself, or in subsequent diffusion. Intellectual property strategy is often fundamental to this. Owning a patent or copyright, for example, could make all the difference between business success and failure. We discuss the impact of intellectual property rights in more detail in Chapter 12 in the context of a discussion of the creation and protection of knowledge.

3.8.1 Innovation, Stabilisation and Imitation

Although innovation is closely linked to novelty, new things and new ways of doing things, it is not just about change and transformation. Though the entrepreneur must be skilled in generating new ideas and introducing them into the market, a big part of innovation is the ability to stabilise processes and market conditions in order to allow customers and clients to buy the products or services over a sustained period of time.

The essence of innovation is the successful exploitation of a new idea. It is clearly important to remember that the process of entrepreneurship requires *both* the skills to transform an existing market and to standardise a new product, service or process. This should prompt us to think again about whether or not entrepreneurship is dependent upon particular individuals (who we call entrepreneurs) or whether, in fact, it is dependent upon the dynamic interaction between individuals with complementary skills. We discuss this in more detail in Chapter 13 on the entrepreneurial team.

Two further issues arise in considering how fundamental a change an innovation is required to deliver:

■ *Is innovation always the best response to changing market conditions?*
   At the heart of this issue is the concept of *value*. Value is subjective. Whilst innovation may offer value in one area, it may detract in another. For example, a local plumber was recently overheard complaining 'the problem with boilers these day is that they've got just *too much* innovation … what's the point of re-inventing the wheel?' Better is not always best. A computer-designed boiler is smaller, quieter, more efficient and more environmentally friendly. However, it is often much more difficult to put right if something goes wrong. It is not designed for a plumber's hands to get in to

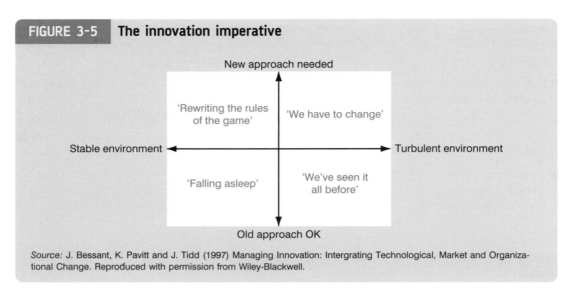

FIGURE 3-5 **The innovation imperative**

Source: J. Bessant, K. Pavitt and J. Tidd (1997) Managing Innovation: Intergrating Technological, Market and Organizational Change. Reproduced with permission from Wiley-Blackwell.

the pipe work and replace faulty parts. Perhaps it is also not as sustainable as at first we might be led to believe.

■ *Is it better to lead or follow? Innovate or imitate?*

According to the Abernathy-Utterback model and the concept of technological trajectory introduced earlier, organisations respond differently according to the maturity of the market, whist being constrained by the path dependent nature of their history, resources, skills and technological capabilities. Tidd *et al.* (2005) have put forward four types of business challenge which are identified in Figure 3-5. Clearly the danger for those organisations who consider their old response to be 'OK' is that they fall into the so-called competency trap, where what has worked up until now probably won't work in the future.

A major or minor role played by the large music firms?

With the benefit of hindsight it is easy to be critical of the large music industry companies, the so-called 'majors', for their inability to grapple with the opportunities (and the threats) presented by the digital revolution. For whilst the likes of EMI, Universal, Sony and BMG continued with their traditional business model, supplying CDs to the High Street, a leading computer company (Apple) rewrote the rules of the game and introduced i-Tunes, innovating both the hardware and the software solutions that could take the distribution of music a giant leap forward. At the end of the 1990s, the music majors were accused of burying their heads in the sand, too worried that the digital age encouraged illegal copying and piracy, rather than innovating their way out of their difficulties. To some extent they have been playing 'catch up' ever since. No doubt there will be other step changes to the way in which we purchase and then listen to music. It remains to be seen whether the majors will play a major or minor role in the changes to come.

Innovation may require a depth of commitment in terms of resources and investment that is simply too risky or beyond the means of many SMEs. There can be a lot to be said for allowing other organisations to invest in innovative technologies, new products and services, and then, when the new technology is becoming available, pursue a strategy of imitation rather than innovation.

3.9   SUMMARY AND ACTIVITIES

In this chapter we have taken a more detailed look at the role of **innovation** in the process of entrepreneurship. Innovation is defined in terms of the successful exploitation of a new idea and the *post hoc* **recognition of creativity**, involving a valuable discovery of some kind. There are many different types of innovation, ranging from **incremental** innovation, involving minor revisions and improvements to existing ways of doing things, to **transformational** innovation, where the rules of the game are changed altogether.

Innovation is increasingly *important* to organisations and nation states because of:

■ **global competition** but large differences in the cost base of manufacturing between countries;

■ **new technologies** making more innovations possible; and

■ **fast pace of changing** consumer tastes and desires.

Nations, as well as companies, have **innovation policies** because of their perceived importance. The national **resources and capabilities** of a country will help determine its innovation strategy and industrial specialisation. There is also a link between type of business activity and the direction of innovation, or **technological trajectory** that generates a momentum of its own which is difficult to change (e.g. the QWERTY keyboard).

According to Drucker (1985) there are **seven sources of innovation**: the unexpected; the incongruous; process need; industry and market structures; demographics; changes in perception; and new knowledge.

The innovation management process consists of four stages:

■ scanning the environment and ideas generation,

■ evaluation of opportunity,

■ resource acquisition,

■ technological and market development.

Key **internal and external barriers** to innovation include: business sector; size of organisation; innovation life cycle; motivation and reward.

Innovation strategies are not all about doing something new. There is a need to systematise and standardise innovative products in order to make them market ready. At times, the best strategic choice is to imitate rather than innovate.

REVIEW QUESTIONS

1   Define what is generally meant by innovation.

2   List five different types of innovation.

3   Discuss the main reasons enterprises need to innovate.

4   Explain what is meant by national system of innovation.

5   What factors need to be considered when setting national innovation policy?

6 Describe seven different sources of innovation (with examples).

7 Explain the four stages of the innovation management process.

8 What are the main *external* barriers to innovation?

9 What are the main *internal* barriers to innovation?

10 Give reasons for why an enterprise should imitate rather than innovate.

SEMINAR TASK

A useful seminar task is to consider the different types of technological trajectories which are associated with particular industries and contexts. As a starting point, use the following template to think about key issues. You can then discuss your ideas in small teams before opening this up for debate across the whole class.

	Supplier-dominated	Scale-intensive	Information-intensive	Science-based	Specialised suppliers	Creative and expressive
Representative industries						
Primary source(s) of technology						
Primary tasks of technology strategy						

Preview case continued

The magic of mushrooms: Jan Rutgers Science (JRS)

Jan Rutgers founded his company, Jan Rutgers Science BV (JRS), in 2005. By this time he already had 12 years of experience as a natural products chemist behind him. It would not be overstating the case to say that Jan has a passion for fungi, and he was able to turn this passion into more than just a hobby when invited to join a small research group travelling out to the Ecuadorian rain forest to collect samples to bring back for analysis. From this and other trips, Jan and his colleagues have been able to gather a huge collection of fungi and mushrooms – to date, over 2000.

At the heart of the 'discovery' of new and useful organic compounds is a special proprietary process of fermentation. This allows the subsequent extraction of complex bioactive compounds, many of which are new to science. The fermentation process has evolved over the years, and involves some rather unusual applications, which now represent core competencies (and trade secrets) for JRS.

Though this may all sound a world away from the hardcore business of entrepreneurship and innovation, in fact the potential in this kind of discovery is enormous. As Jan notes, 'if we find something it is the largest deal-making area in the pharmaceutical sector'. The potential rewards are very high indeed. But, so too are the risks – years of expensive lab work with very little to show for it. Even when discoveries are made, Jan explains that it might not be easy to commercialise these. A wide range of challenges need to be overcome first.

▶

Expect the unexpected

Jan's research began as an exploration of the role of chemical stimulators on producing fungi, rather than as a means of fermenting and then extracting complex compounds with potentially health-giving benefits. It was only when his experiments 'went wrong' that the true potential of the fermentation process he had pioneered revealed itself. One is reminded of Alexander Fleming's 'accidental discovery' of penicillin. As Fleming himself noted, 'When I woke up just after dawn on September 28, 1928, I certainly didn't plan to revolutionize all medicine by discovering the world's first antibiotic, or bacteria killer . . . but I guess that was exactly what I did' (Haven, K.F. (1994) *Marvels of Science*, London: Libraries Unlimited, p. 182).

Secure and protect your intellectual property

Having discovered some likely antibiotics, Jan, together now with his two full-time colleagues, set about trying to persuade several virtual healthcare companies to invest in the research, with the intention of licensing the discovery on to a pharmaceutical company. However, it soon became clear to Jan and his team that they were going to find it difficult to secure and protect their most precious resource – their knowledge (intellectual property) of the fermentation process. It was one thing to come up with an original technology, but quite another to protect this and prevent others from copying.

Convincing sceptical investors and others

Jan recalls the challenge of deal-breaking with bigger pharmaceutical companies where, on the one hand, it was necessary to demonstrate the potential of the process without actually giving away the trade secrets of what the process involved, on the other. In addition, Jan advises that when it comes to the negotiation process it is vital to have a credible adviser on your side, and preferably one who has experience of negotiating deals successfully.

Leveraging resources

As all entrepreneurs know, getting as much as possible for as little as possible – the so-called 'parsimonious path to entrepreneurship' – is a must. JRS could not afford to pay its legal advisers to begin with, so negotiated a payment based on a successful deal being struck. No deal, no fee. The company benefited enormously by laying its hands on lab equipment that was otherwise about to be confined to the skip. Through Jan's contacts he was able to salvage €300,000 worth of equipment during the start-up phase. Furthermore, the fledgling company set up its first laboratory in a Netherlands-based university, benefiting from this location even more when it was able to secure the services of a resident professor as business angel investor. The company was also awarded a modest grant from the Dutch government.

Recognise essential ingredients for success

Finally, Jan observes that there are at least two *essential* ingredients in the potential success of JRS. First, there is a great market need. New drugs are needed to deal with many medical and health issues, but also because pharmaceutical companies will not survive without these innovations. Secondly, underlying the company's development is the passion and motivation of Jan and his colleagues for what they do. Although they might be stereotyped as a 'bunch of geeks' by those not involved in the scientific process, the enthusiasm that he expresses for his mushrooms and fungi is as tangible as that expressed by any designer, musician, architect or film-maker for their works of art.

Questions:

1 *Why is innovation important to (a) the pharmaceutical industry; (b) JRS; and (c) Jan Rutgers?*

2 *Do you think national and international innovation policies have any influence or bearing on the activities of JRS? Discuss.*

3 *How would you assess the way in which innovation is managed in JRS?*

Source: Interview with Jan Rutgers, November 2008.

3.10   NOTES, REFERENCES AND FURTHER READING

Notes and Further Information

1. Technopolis Group (2008) *Sectoral Innovation Systems: The Policy Landscape in the EU25*, February, Europe INNOVA, p. 1.

2. Ibid., p. 2.

3. Source: European Commission: http://ec.europa.eu/enterprise/innovation/index_en.htm.

4. Information note from the Commission Services: Progress Report (March 2008) on the Broad-based innovation strategy, available at http://ec.europa.eu/enterprise/innovation/doc/bbi_strategy_progress_report_march_2008.pdf.

5. The latest report can be found at http://www.proinno-europe.eu/.

6. When European leaders met at a summit in Lisbon in March 2000 they set the European Union the goal of becoming 'the most dynamic and competitive knowledge-based economy in the world' by 2010.

7. Source: NACI (2007) Annual Report 2006/7, NACI, p. 8.

8. Source: NACI, at http://www.naci.org.za/.

9. Human Capital and the South African Knowledge Base, 2007, quoted in NACI (2007) Annual Report 2006/7.

10. CERN (http://lhc.web.cern.ch/lhc/).

11. See Burgelman, R., Christensen, C. and Wheelwright, S. (2003) *Strategic Management of Technology and Innovation*, London: McGraw-Hill/Irwin.

12. There is an extensive literature on models of innovation. Roy Rothwell's (1992) work on the coupling model of innovation (later referred to as 'research, design and development') is well worth reading.

13. See the Design Council's case study on LEGO at http://www.designcouncil.org.uk/Documents/About%20design/managing_design/pdf/PDF%20Design%20at%20LEGO.pdf. LEGO and the LEGO logo are trademarks of the LEGO Group, here used with special permission.

References

Acs, Z.J. and Audretsch, D.B. (1990) *Innovation and Small Firms*, Cambridge MA: MIT Press.

Amabile, T., Conti, R., Coon, H., Lazenby, J. and Herron, M. (1996) Assessing the work environment for creativity, *Academy of Management Review*, 39 (5): 1154–1184.

Audretsch, D.B. (1995) *Innovation and Industry Evolution*, Cambridge, MA: MIT Press.

Audretsch, D.B. and Vivarelli, M. (1996) Firm size and R&D spillover: Evidence from Italy, *Small Business Economics*, 8: 249–258.

Cabinet Office (2003) *Innovation in the Public Sector*, Strategy Unit, London, October.

Commission of the European Communities (2006) *Putting knowledge into practice: A Broad-based Innovation Strategy for the EU*, CEC.

DCMS (1998) Creative Industries Mapping Document, London: Department for Culture, Media and Sport.

Dosi, G. (1982) Technological paradigms and technological trajectories: A suggested interpretation of the determinants and directions of technical change, *Research Policy*, 11: 147–162.

Drucker, P.F. (1985) *Innovation and Entrepreneurship*, London: Heinemann.

DTI (1996) *Innovation the Best Practice*, London: Department for Trade and Industry.

DTI. (2003) *Innovation Report: Competing in the Global Economy: The Innovation Challenge*, DTI, London, December.

Eriksson, S. (2005) *Innovation policies in South Korea & Taiwan*, VINNOVA Analysis, July.

Frey, B. and Pommerehne, W. (1989) *Muses and Markets*, Oxford: Blackwell.

Hargadon, A. (2003) *How Breakthroughs Happen: Technology Brokering and the Pursuit of Innovation*, Cambridge, MA: Harvard Business School Press.

Leadbeater, C. (2003) *The Man in the Caravan and Other Stories*, Improvement and Development Agency, London.

Mintzberg, H. and Waters, J.A. (1985) Of strategies, deliberate and emergent, *Strategic Management Journal*, 6: 257–272.

NACI (2007) NACI Annual Report 2006/7, NACI.

Nelson, R.R. and Winter, S.G. (1982) *An Evolutionary Theory of Economic Change*, Cambridge, MA: Harvard University Press.

NESTA (2007) *Hidden Innovation: How Innovation Happens in Six 'Low Innovation' Sectors*, Research Report, June, NESTA, London. Available at: http://www.nesta.org.uk/assets/Uploads/pdf/Research-Report/hidden_innovation_report_NESTA.pdf.

OECD (2005) *The Oslo Manual: Guidelines for Collecting and Interpreting Innovation Data. Third edition.* Available at: http://213.253.134.43/oecd/pdfs/browseit/9205111E.PDF

Piergiovanni, R.E., Santarelli, E. and Vivarelli, M. (1997) From which source do small firms derive their innovative inputs? Some evidence from Italian industry, *Review of Industrial Organisation*, 12 (2): 243–258.

Porter, M. (1990) *The Competitive Advantage of Nations*, London: Macmillan.

Roberts, E.B. (1988) What we've learned: managing invention and innovation, *Research and Technology Management,* January–February: 11–29.

Rothwell, R. (1992) Successful industrial innovation: Critical success factors for the 1990s, *R&D Management*, 22 (3): 221–239.

Schumpeter, J.A. (1934) *The Theory of Economic Development: An Inquiry into Profits, Capital, Credit, Interest and the Business Cycle*, tr. R. Opie, Cambridge, MA: Harvard University Press.

Tidd, J., Bessant, J. and Pavitt, K. (1997) *Managing Innovation*, Chichester: J. Wiley.

Tidd, J., Bessant, J. and Pavitt, K. (2005) *Managing Innovation* website at http://www.managing-innovation.com/innovation/cda/index.php.

Utterback, J. (1994) *Mastering the Dynamics of Innovation*, Boston: Harvard Business School Press.

von Hippel, E. (1994) *The Sources of Innovation*, New York: Oxford University Press.

Wilson, N. (2008) Whose creativity is it anyway? A critical realist evaluation of managing creativity in the creative economy, Paper for the Fourth Art of Management and Organisation Conference, Banff, September.

Recommended Further Reading

There is a very large literature relating to the subject of innovation and its management. A very good starting point is with Tidd, Bessant and Pavitt's *Managing Innovation* book. They also have an excellent website (see References). You may also find it helpful to review the research and working paper series available at the University of Sussex's Science and Technology Policy Research Unit (SPRU). Visit their website at http://www.sussex.ac.uk/spru/.

In the UK, the National Endowment for Science, Technology and the Arts (NESTA) produce some very helpful research publications. Refer to the NESTA website for further details.

CHAPTER 4

Entrepreneurship and the Economy

LEARNING OBJECTIVES

After studying this chapter, the reader will be able to:

- Evaluate the integral relationship between entrepreneurship and the economy
- Distinguish between the main forms of economic system
- Assess the underlying economic conditions necessary for economic development
- Evaluate the role of small business in the economy, and appreciate why this has changed
- Compare the state of entrepreneurship in developed, transition and developing economies.

INTRODUCTION

In Chapter 3 we saw how innovation systems and technological trajectories affected the kind of entrepreneurial activity which might be possible in a given national context. It was noted that entrepreneurship is affected by the social, cultural, environmental, political and economic conditions which characterise the world around us. Our focus in this chapter is specifically on the relationship between the process of entrepreneurship, resulting in the introduction of new economic activity, and the particular economic conditions which enable and constrain this process. This is important, since entrepreneurship is now widely recognised as the 'engine of economic and social development throughout the world' (Audretsch and Thurik, 2006: 24).

In researching this book, we have drawn on many scholarly articles and books on entrepreneurship which were written at specific points in time, stretching over the last 150 years or so. The particular vantage point of the author matters. After all, we can never escape the temporal context in which we write. It is worth highlighting, therefore, that much has changed in the world economy since the period this book was first commissioned (in 2007). No doubt there are many economic surprises in store in the future as well. When things are 'going well' we might be relatively unaware of macroeconomic factors affecting entrepreneurship; but when times get difficult, the economy really does matter. In the words attributed to a former president of the United States of America – 'It's the economy, stupid!'[1]

PREVIEW CASE

Tata – Driving home advantage

In 2008 the Indian automobile company Tata launched the Nano, which it described as the world's least expensive production car. Against the odds, the company appeared to have managed what other Western car manufacturers had failed to bring off – a desirable family car that is potentially affordable for the millions of citizens of India and other developing nations.

What do you think are (a) the advantages and (b) the disadvantages for Tata in being located in India?

4

Macro and micro-economic factors

Macro-economic factors are those which affect the performance and structure of a national or regional economy as a whole. Macro-economists study such indicators as gross domestic product (GDP), price indices and unemployment rates. For example, the European Central Bank sets base interest rates for borrowing money in the euro zone – a macro-economic decision.

Micro-economic factors are those relating to the decision-making process of individuals, households and firms when dealing with limited resources. Micro-economists study how decisions and behaviours might affect the supply and demand for goods and services. For example, a European entrepreneur decides if the returns on an investment in new equipment justify the costs, including the latest interest rates on finance – a micro-economic decision.

The relationship between the economy and entrepreneurship is central to our individual and social welfare. Entrepreneurship is held to be one of the principal mechanisms that can help to turn around recession. For example, under-used assets, such as manufacturing equipment or plant, may be sold on by failing businesses, providing others an unusual opportunity to acquire key resources at lower cost than usual. Alternatively, job losses might lead to teams of highly educated and skilled individuals starting up their own businesses together in the absence of other opportunities for employment (this is so-called *necessity* entrepreneurship, which we discuss further below).

ENTREPRENEURSHIP IN ACTION

From Woolworths to Wellworths

A former manager of the famous UK retail company Woolworths, which closed all its 815 stores in 2008 as a result of the global recession, took the opportunity to re-open one store under a new name and separate ownership. Claire Robertson, a former 'Saturday girl', recruited 20 of her former Woolworths staff to join the new venture in Dorchester, England. With financial backing secured from the landlord, the new company plans to take advantage of the prime location and the publicity surrounding this 'good news story' in otherwise gloomy economic times.

Claire Robertson outside Wellworths in Dorchester.

Entrepreneurial activity is enabled when the right kind of economic conditions are in place. We discuss the nature of these conditions in the course of this chapter, highlighting differences associated with particular economic systems (e.g. transition vs. market economies), and levels of overall economic maturity (e.g. factor-based economies through to innovation-driven economies).

4.1   THE ECONOMY – A BRIEF INTRODUCTION

Before investigating the impact of the economy on entrepreneurship, we need to understand some basic economic concepts. The meaning of the Greek word *economy* is literally 'one who manages a household'. It is associated with the means by which we look after our basic needs (i.e. our shelter, food and clothing). Ancient economies were based on subsistence farming. For most peoples, the exchange of goods and services to fulfil their needs took place through social relationships, rather than through what we would now recognise in terms of market exchange. However, there were also traders who bartered for goods in the marketplace.

As the exchange of goods and services became more frequent and widespread we see the emergence of *economic systems* within given regions or nations. An economic system essentially involves the production, distribution and consumption of goods and services between the individuals, households and institutions which together comprise a given society. A wide range of different systems have developed over time, although capitalist, socialist, planned, and mixed economy systems are most well-known today.

Capitalism – still the dominant economic system?

Capitalism has been the dominant economic system since the end of the late eighteenth and early nineteenth centuries. As people started dividing up their work, not directly meeting their own needs but relying on others to do this for them in return for something, we can begin to see the emergence of modern day capitalism and reliance on the commoditisation of products and services.

Capitalism is characterised by the private ownership, control and production of wealth. An underlying tenet of this economic system is that the economy should be left alone with minimal interference from the state. However, this 'laissez-faire' approach does not exist in its pure form in practice. Since all developed economies rely to some extent on a mix of publicly as well as privately owned enterprise we refer to 'mixed economies' instead.

The year 2009 has been characterised by a very significant level of intervention by governments in the financial and other markets. In Germany, for example, the Chancellor Angela Merkel has increased the state's influence in the market, buying holdings in banks (e.g. a 25 per cent share in Frankfurt-based Commerzbank) and bailing out individual industries and companies. This represented the biggest economic stimulus programme in German postwar history, leading some to question whether Germany is turning into a planned economy.[2]

Different economic systems carry with them different underlying beliefs concerning the production and distribution of wealth, and how these might be in tension with one another. As far back as ancient Athens, when private property rights were first established, the economic and political effects of private ownership were recognised as potentially problematic. The dilemma of efficiency vs. equality was considered unavoidable (Bitros and Karayiannis, 2006: 14). Citizens in ancient Athens believed that profit and wealth seeking activities performed a useful operation and that a moderately unequal distribution of wealth would promote the work efforts of individuals. Crucially, these generally accepted

ENTREPRENEURSHIP IN ACTION

'Enterprise of the Indies' – An unexpected discovery

When Christopher Columbus set out to find a westward sea passage to the Orient he had no idea that he would discover a New World. This unintentional discovery would change the course of history. Columbus's journey nearly didn't happen. His first attempts to seek the funding from Portuguese, French and English courts failed. Displaying entrepreneurial belief, he finally persuaded King Ferdinand and Queen Isabella of Spain to sponsor his expedition. On 3 August 1492, Columbus and his fleet of three ships set sail across the Atlantic. Ten weeks later they set foot on an island that was later to become known as the Bahamas.

4

principles, as well as the maximisation of 'individuality' and 'happiness', as taught by the Sophists, provided the minimum necessary conditions for the early emergence and development of entrepreneurship.

The economy during the Middle Ages was still primarily driven by subsistence. However, the medieval period was also the time when a truly global economy began to take root with explorers such as Marco Polo (1254–1324) and Christopher Columbus (1451–1506) making discoveries that would lead to worldwide trading. There was also the first colonisation, which itself led to a heightened role for intermediaries (a type of 'arbitrage entrepreneur') working as brokers between private merchants and the public interest. Between the sixteenth and eighteenth centuries, the economy was characterised by *mercantilism* which saw ruling governments play an increasingly protectionist role, encouraging exports and discouraging imports. In turn this led to many European wars and fuelled European imperialism.

Until the seventeenth century, economic stagnation was the natural order of the day, with economic growth at the miniscule rate of about 0.1 per cent per annum (McCraw, 1997). The first period of strong economic growth was when the *industrial revolution* replaced the former era of mercantilism (in the late eighteenth century and early nineteenth century). The distinguishing feature of this revolution was the ability of industrialists to mass produce. Goods and services that had formerly been produced only for the specific needs of those involved, or local communities, now could be produced for the benefit of people across nations, continents and, indeed, the world. The economy now fully embraced national and international interests, rather than interests of individuals or small groups.

4.2   ENTREPRENEURSHIP AND THE MARKET

Central to all economic activity is the exchange between a buyer and a seller. In focusing on the relationship between entrepreneurship and the economy, we need to consider the context for this exchange – which we refer to as the *market*. The historical origin of the market is to be found in the marketplaces which lie at the heart of small communities, towns and cities. Despite being the central institution that underlies neoclassical economics there is surprisingly little discussion of the market in the literature on economics (see North, 1977; Rosenbaum, 2000), or sociology (Callon, 1998). From its physical origins as a central meeting place, the market has come to denote the abstract mechanisms whereby supply and demand confront each other 'in search of a compromise' (Callon, 1998: 52). Orthodox economic theory maintains that 'in a market society, the allocation of resources[3] is the outcome of millions of independent decisions made by consumers and producers all acting through the mechanism of the market' (Lipsey, 1968: 71). There is a danger that this perspective implies that those involved (buyers and sellers) are denied the freedom to take strategic decisions concerning the exchange of economic objects. This deterministic viewpoint sits uncomfortably with much of the literature on entrepreneurship, and particularly the role of entrepreneurs in making decisions about market entry.

4.2.1 Entrepreneurs and the Market

Three of the best known treatments of entrepreneurship (Knight, 1921; Kirzner, 1973; and Schumpeter, 1934) all take what we might think of as market-centred approaches – though with very important conceptual distinctions. Knight's work considers market information and uncertainty. Kirzner also explains entrepreneurship in terms of decision-making and the market interaction, focusing more overtly on the entrepreneurial dynamic that drives the economy through a market process towards equilibrium (i.e. where economic forces such as demand and supply are balanced). For Schumpeter, this entrepreneurial dynamic creates disequilibria (not equilibria). In other words, entrepreneurs disrupt the status quo and the general flow of things – constantly seeking to take advantage of the pricing system to gain a competitive position. Whereas Kirzner's entrepreneurs respond to changing information, Schumpeter's are responsible for the information changing in the first place. This is an important distinction and underlies a long-standing tension between the Kirznerian/Austrian conception that entrepreneurial dynamics drive the economy through a market process towards equilibrium, and the Schumpeterian conception that entrepreneurial dynamics create disequilibria.

The model of entrepreneurship presented in Chapter 2 places both the market and the entrepreneur at the centre of things. By highlighting how entrepreneurs must make decisions about market entry and resource recombination before committing their capital (i.e *ex ante* decisions about the future value of their investments) we are drawing attention to the market-making role of entrepreneurs (see also Casson, 2003).

Market exchange can take a variety of forms and takes place in some very contrasting contexts. The buyer or seller may be an individual, a firm or a government, for example. The motivation for exchange may be private wealth accumulation or the development of social value (i.e. not necessarily a private for-profit venture). Whilst we think of market exchange as necessarily involving money, there are other forms of possible transaction (e.g. those based on bartering).

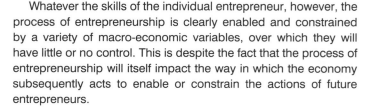

Integrative Case Link
You can read about the impact of country-specific factors on entrepreneurial activity in Case Study 2 at the end of Part 1.

Whatever the skills of the individual entrepreneur, however, the process of entrepreneurship is clearly enabled and constrained by a variety of macro-economic variables, over which they will have little or no control. This is despite the fact that the process of entrepreneurship will itself impact the way in which the economy subsequently acts to enable or constrain the actions of future entrepreneurs.

4.3 THE NATURE OF THE RELATIONSHIP BETWEEN ENTREPRENEURSHIP AND THE ECONOMY

There is something of the chicken and egg about our evaluation of the impact of entrepreneurship on the economy. The conditions for entrepreneurship are in some way themselves the product of earlier entrepreneurial activities. As we have seen, the prevailing economic conditions in a country will have a significant impact on the level of entrepreneurship. Entrepreneurs drive innovation, which speeds up structural changes in the economy, forcing other organisations to try to compete.

In making connections between entrepreneurship and economic development attention is drawn to the role of the entrepreneurship process in fostering the wealth and health that comes from economic prosperity. Whilst it would be desirable to establish some basic causal principles which would help us (and especially those responsible for policy in governments) to provide the right conditions for economic development, we need to exercise some caution here. Our very interaction with the world around us changes our environment – as is becoming only too clear in the context of the environment and global warming. As such, there is no single formula or recipe for achieving economic prosperity, nor will there ever be. Nevertheless, we can highlight a range of key economic conditions which play a central role.

4.3.1 Economic Development Life Cycle

The contribution of entrepreneurship to an economy depends to some extent on the particular phase of its economic development (Wennekers et al., 2005; Gries and Naude, 2008). Over the past couple of decades researchers have developed increasingly sophisticated models for analysing the state of economic development and level of entrepreneurship in particular countries. One of the most important research projects in this area is the Global Entrepreneurship Monitor Programme.[4] In this report the authors follow Porter, Sachs and McArthur (2002) in distinguishing between factor-driven countries, efficiency-driven countries and innovation-driven countries.

Examples of different economic development life cycles

Factor-driven economies
Angola, Bolivia, Bosnia and Herzegovina*, Colombia*, Ecuador*, Egypt, India, Iran*
Efficiency-driven economies
Argentina, Brazil, Chile, Croatia**, Dominican Republic, Hungary**, Jamaica, Latvia, Macedonia, Mexico, Peru, Romania, Russia, Serbia, South Africa, Turkey, Uruguay
Innovation-driven economies
Belgium, Denmark, Finland, France, Germany, Greece, Iceland, Ireland, Israel, Italy, Japan, Republic of Korea, Netherlands, Norway, Slovenia, Spain, United Kingdom, United States
* Transition country: from factor-driven to efficiency-driven
** Transition country: from efficiency-driven to innovation-driven

Source: Bosma et al, 2008: 4 Permission to reproduce this material from the GEM 2008 Global Report, which appears here, has been kindly granted by the copyright holders. The GEM is an international consortium and this report has been produced from data collected in 43 countries in 2008. Our thanks go to the authors, national teams, researchers, funding bodies and other contributors who have made this possible. Please note that the classification used here is adopted from the World Economic Forum's 'Global Competitiveness Report'

Typically, countries with low levels of economic development are reliant on the exploitation of land, with a large agricultural sector providing for the population. As extractive industries start to develop (e.g. mining, oil and gas and related industrial activity), economic growth is triggered, alongside the migration of surplus labour to work in these sectors. The resulting over-supply of labour (i.e. more people than there are jobs) feeds subsistence entrepreneurship in regional locations, as opportunities are created to make a living through self-employment (Bosma et al., 2008: 8).

As this economic development spreads, we see increasing industrialisation and the build-up of scale manufacturing and commerce, where organisations are seeking to maximise returns through higher productivity and economies of scale. This describes what is referred to as 'efficiency-driven' economies. Here we typically see niches opening up in industrial supply chains, providing further opportunities for entrepreneurial new ventures and small businesses.

In the third phase of economic development (innovation-phase) we might typically expect to see an expanding service-sector catering to the ever more sophisticated needs of an increasingly affluent population. The expectations of both producers and consumers rise, alongside the increase in knowledge-generating institutions. This is a potentially supportive environment for genuinely innovative behaviour where entrepreneurs are looking for opportunities to challenge the established key-players in the economy (see Schumpeter, 1934 on 'creative destruction').

4.3.2 Economic Conditions that Support Entrepreneurship

There are clearly a wide range of underlying conditions that will impact the prevalence and success of entrepreneurial ventures and their subsequent impact on national prosperity. The model presented in Figure 4-1 outlines some of the key factors.

Social Cultural and Political Context To begin with, there is a foundation level of national infrastructure and institutional context which provides a framework for possible entrepreneurial activity. This includes the provision of basic utilities, roads and transport connections, as well as telecommunications. It also includes basic levels of healthcare, and primary education in which first levels of reading and writing are attained. Without these in place the chances of developing new enterprises and job growth become greatly reduced.

It would be wrong to characterise a country with a relatively low level of economic development as being devoid of entrepreneurship. Indeed, the level of *necessity-driven* self-employment (where individuals undertake entrepreneurial projects because they have either few or no other options is particularly high at low levels of economic development (see Bosma *et al.*, 2008)). As the economy develops, this level of necessity-driven entrepreneurship gradually gives way to *opportunity-driven* entrepreneurial activity (where individuals spot an opportunity for a new enterprise). This is known as the 'U-curve' hypothesis (see Wennekers, Van Stel, Thurik and Reynolds, 2005).

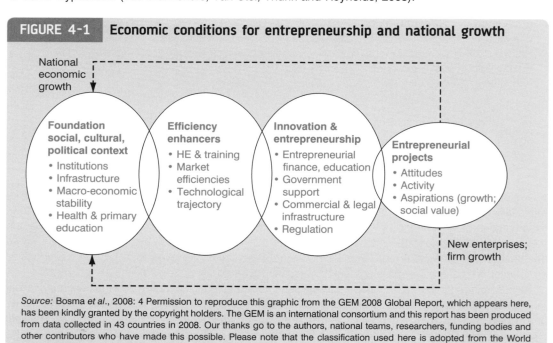

FIGURE 4-1 | **Economic conditions for entrepreneurship and national growth**

Source: Bosma *et al.*, 2008: 4 Permission to reproduce this graphic from the GEM 2008 Global Report, which appears here, has been kindly granted by the copyright holders. The GEM is an international consortium and this report has been produced from data collected in 43 countries in 2008. Our thanks go to the authors, national teams, researchers, funding bodies and other contributors who have made this possible. Please note that the classification used here is adopted from the World Economic Forum's 'Global Competitiveness Report'.

Efficiency Enhancers Over and above these basic foundation-level conditions, we can then outline a set of factors which enhance (and constrain) the level of efficiency in economic markets. Skills and knowledge are essential resources for economic development, and so the level and quality of higher education and training is crucial. Finance is another key resource which demands the presence of effective and efficient capital markets. At a time of 'credit crunch' where banks have reduced lending to small businesses and entrepreneurial ventures, it is all too easy to see the impact of an inefficient capital market on the potential for entrepreneurship. As we saw in the previous chapter, a country's stock of natural resources and its associated technological capabilities (its 'technological trajectory') also plays a pivotal role in the subsequent entrepreneurial activity undertaken.

Innovation and Entrepreneurship Notwithstanding these more general conditions for economic activity, researchers have identified a set of additional factors which are more explicitly linked to the development of entrepreneurial ventures, job growth and national prosperity.

■ The first of these concerns the provision of entrepreneurial finance – in other words, finance that is needed to develop the high growth enterprise, where jobs and wealth are created. Typically this finance involves a higher degree of risk than most banks are prepared to consider. Rich individuals known as business angels, as well as companies dedicated to provide large sums of risk capital, known as venture capitalists, are the main providers of this finance (see Chapter 15 for more details).

■ In addition, we have seen an explosion in interest over the past decade in entrepreneurship education. Arguably there exists a far greater awareness of the challenges, conditions and context of entrepreneurship which of itself will have an impact on individuals' propensity to act entrepreneurially in the future. This book, of course, has been written in order to make a contribution to this developing landscape.

■ Thirdly, we can point to specific policies which are targeted at encouraging and enabling enterprise and entrepreneurship (see for example the UK government's policy 'Unlocking the UK's talent', BERR, 2008).

■ Closely allied to such policy initiatives include the concern to ensure an environment where there is the legal and commercial underpinning, as well as the 'light touch' of regulation to provide the confidence and framework for entrepreneurial projects to flourish.

Entrepreneurial Projects Whatever the conditions in place, however, there is no entrepreneurship at all without some individuals taking the decision to actually do something. The entrepreneurial project was introduced in our emergent model of entrepreneurship (see Figure 2-4). In recent years, attention has focused on the importance of a society's attitude towards entrepreneurship as a key determinant of the level of entrepreneurial activity. The general attitude of a population towards the concept of entrepreneurship, taking risk, recognising opportunities, knowing entrepreneurs personally, attaching high status to entrepreneurs, and possessing the skills required to create successful start-ups are all seen to have a major bearing on actual levels of entrepreneurship. Clearly, the role of entrepreneurship education is important in this respect. It is also interesting to note the tremendous growth in interest in entrepreneurship in the popular media. Television programmes such as *The Apprentice* and *Dragons' Den* have done much to popularise entrepreneurship, even if they exaggerate some aspects of entrepreneurial behaviour at the expense of others.

The level of entrepreneurial activity in any given country is not easily measured. In the GEM study, entrepreneurial activity is defined as the new venture start-up rate, adjusted for the churning effect of business closures, initiated by educated entrepreneurs and launched because of opportunity motivations (Bosma *et al.*, 2008). This measure can be criticised as it does focus on new venture start-up rather than

4

An incongruous consequence of the Celtic Tiger boom

Danny Breslin founded his own porcelain giftware company in 1985. The market for Donegal China's giftware was based on the taste for porcelain and ceramics which could be displayed in glass cases in peoples' front rooms. However, as a consequence of the economic boom years in the 1990s, more and more skilled workers returned to Ireland, bringing with them new tastes and perspectives that were quite different from those of their parents. These modern consumers no longer chose the traditional porcelain and crystal giftware, preferring more contemporary and functional gifts. As Danny Breslin recalled, he 'saw the writing on the wall'. His entrepreneurial venture was sold to his former employer, Belleek China, in 2000.

Integrative Case Link
For more about Danny's entrepreneurial journey, see Case Study 7 at the end of Part 3.

on the introduction of innovation in the form of products and services. Clearly there is a difference in aspiration between setting up a lifestyle enterprise, perhaps as a sole trader cleaning windows, and launching a growth-oriented new media company that aims to compete with the likes of Google. Nor does GEM measure levels of entrepreneurial activity in large and established organisations.

4.4   THE ROLE OF SMALL FIRMS IN THE ECONOMY

Economists have shown that capital (money) and labour (skills) are not sufficient of themselves to stimulate growth. Many now agree that the vital determining factor in economic growth is knowledge. It would be easy to assume that large firms have the advantage when it comes to producing and capitalising upon knowledge. They are in a better position than most small businesses in terms of paying for R&D (research and development), human capital (employing skilled staff) and patenting inventions (protecting their intellectual property). However, whilst the factors of capital and unskilled labour are sources of competitive advantage in an economy characterised by large-scale production (the so-called 'managed economy'), an entrepreneurial economy built upon the production of knowledge and capacity to engage in and generate entrepreneurial activity depends upon the small organisation.

Prior to the 1970s it was generally considered that large firms were the dominant force in the economy. For over a century, business and management interest focused increasingly on the large and established corporation as the driver of economic development, not the small business. In the UK, the Bolton Report of 1971 made the case for the contribution of small and medium-sized enterprises to the national economy and the 'inevitable' demise of small firms began to reverse itself (see Blau, 1987; Evans and Leighton, 1989). It is now generally acknowledged that small and new enterprises play a very important role in the entrepreneurial economy, more so than in the managed economy where large firms dominate through their competitive advantage. Given that 99.8 per cent of the UK's 4.3 million businesses are small or medium-sized enterprises, it is not surprising that interest in SMEs from a policy and educational perspective remains high.

The following six factors have been important in the growing importance of the small business (Brock and Evans, 1989):

1 **Technological change**   The importance of scale economies in manufacturing is reduced by technological changes and advances.

2 **Globalisation**   Increased globalisation and the accompanying international competition contributes to market volatility, opening up opportunities for the new entrant.

3 **Flexible specialisation**   With a labour market characterised by greater participation of women, immigrants, young and old workers, and with the considerable premium placed on flexibility (flexible specialisation), the relative adaptability and flexibility of the small enterprise comes into its own.

4 **Consumption**   Demand for new goods and services moves away from standardised and mass-produced goods towards tailor-made products. This is beneficial to small producers working in niche markets.

5 **Deregulation**   With deregulation and privatisation, small firms can enter markets that were previously inaccessible or protected.

6 **Innovation**   As large-scale production in high-wage countries is reduced, it is replaced by innovative activities in the economy that promote entrepreneurship.

The rise of the small business

Why not try this useful mnemonic to remember the key theories for the increase in importance of small businesses:

The	–	Technological change
Giant	–	Globalisation
Firm	–	Flexible specialisation
Can't	–	Consumption
Dance	–	Deregulation
Inside	–	Innovation

It would be misleading, however, to suggest a wholly polarised view of the business terrain in which small firms have little or nothing to do with their larger counterparts. The entrepreneurial economy is characterised in part by the nature of the complex relationships that exist between small and large firms.

4.5 COMPARING NATIONAL ECONOMIC CONDITIONS FOR ENTREPRENEURSHIP

Underlying the discussion of the relationship between entrepreneurship and the economy is the premise that a nation's competitive position can be enhanced by both the appropriate policy interventions and by the actions of individual entrepreneurs. Interest in entrepreneurship has fuelled research that seeks to measure and then compare the level of economic development within a given country or region, and link this to the level of entrepreneurial activity observed.

A conceptual model of economic development can be visualised as a diamond-shape with four key indicators (as presented in Figure 4-2).

Economic freedom is defined as 'the absolute right of property ownership, fully realized freedom of movement for labor, capital, and goods, and an absolute absence of coercion or constraint of economic liberty beyond the extent necessary for citizens to protect and maintain liberty itself' (Bosma *et al.,* 2008: 37). The Index of Economic Freedom (IEF) was created by *The Wall Street Journal* and The Heritage

4

ENTREPRENEURSHIP IN ACTION

Vodacom Community Services

South Africa's largest cellular phone company, Vodacom, works with the South African government and with entrepreneur-owned and operated phone shops to provide telecommunications services in under-serviced, disadvantaged communities. They have developed an innovative business model which allows telecommunication services to be delivered in townships well below the commercial rates. In keeping with the objectives of successful social enterprise, the programme now covers its costs with revenue from sales.

The emphasis in the Community Services model is to empower local entrepreneurs to own and operate the phone shops within a franchise model. Entrepreneurs pre-pay Vodacom for calls on their phones at rates that retain one-third of calling revenue for themselves. The Community Services programme currently partners with 1800 entrepreneurs who operate over 4400 phone shops at sites throughout South Africa. Whilst there is little risk of bankruptcy for phone shop owners given the requirement to pre-pay for services, profits are dependent upon the entrepreneurial management skills of the owner. This includes the capacity of the entrepreneurs to spot opportunities for locating the shops where market interest will be maximised; networking to ensure local people and other business owners take up the service; innovating in marketing their business; and leveraging resources – in this case through working with this corporate under government support, gaining vital business support and training in the process.

Source: Reck, J. and Wood, B. (2003) What works: Vodacom's Community Services Phoneshops, World Resources Institute, available at http://www.digitaldividend.org/pdf/vodacom.pdf

---

FIGURE 4-2   The economic development diamond

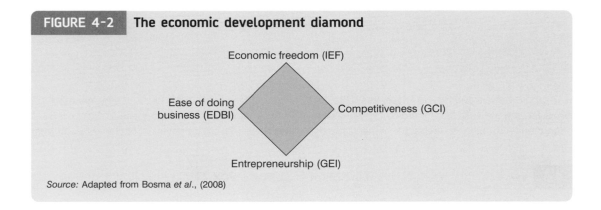

Source: Adapted from Bosma *et al.*, (2008)

Foundation. It is constructed using ten economic measures taken from the World Bank, IMF and the Economist Intelligence Unit.

Global competitiveness 'assesses the ability of countries to provide high levels of prosperity to their citizens' (Bosma *et al.,* 2008: 37). The Global Competitiveness Index (GCI) is an annual report by the World Economic Forum, covering about 131 countries. It reviews how productively a country uses available resources. The Index is made up of about 90 variables, two-thirds of which come from the Executive Opinion Survey and one-third from publicly available data sources such as the United Nations.

Ease of doing business refers to the level of regulations in place in a given economic region or country and the extent to which these are both appropriate and appropriately managed. The Ease of

Doing Business Index (EDBI) was created by the World Bank to measure the simplicity of regulations for businesses and the level of protection of property rights.

Entrepreneurial activity is the fourth index making up the economic development diamond. There are many measures of entrepreneurship currently being developed. Of these, the Global Entrepreneurship Index (GEI) uses 19 variables from GEM and 32 in total (Acs and Szerb, 2008). These give 14 indicators and three sub-indices that measure entrepreneurial activity, entrepreneurial aspiration and entrepreneurial attitudes (Bosma *et al.*, 2008: 38).

4.5.1 National Economic Growth Rates

It is one thing to set up a new business but quite another to launch a new venture that will go on to be a large firm of the future. Research suggests that comparatively few entrepreneurs expect to develop scalable businesses. Indeed, only 8 per cent of all start-up attempts expected to create 20 or more jobs (Bosma *et al.*, 2008: 31). However, the picture varies from country to country. Some European countries, notably Belgium, Germany and France, consistently have the lowest rates of entrepreneurial activity levels. The GEM study suggests that China's nascent and new entrepreneurs appear to be the most growth-oriented, with nearly 20 per cent of them anticipating high growth (Bosma *et al.*, 2008: 33).

We now look in more detail at the relationship between entrepreneurship and the economy in the context of some developed, transition and developing economies.

4.5.2 Entrepreneurship in the US

It is fascinating to reflect on how fortunes (literally) change over just a matter of days. In the summer of 2007 it seemed as if the US economy was in very good shape. There had been a doubling of productivity growth compared to the preceding two decades. This success was accredited to the 'continued transformation of the U.S. economy toward a more entrepreneurial form of capitalism', where 'new firms play an unusually central role in developing and commercializing the radical technologies that provide the underpinnings to whole new ways of doing things and enjoying life' (Kauffman Foundation, 2007).

By late 2008 the US economy was reeling from the subprime mortgage crisis and the wider meltdown of the financial sector and subsequent global recession. Interestingly, in a survey carried out by the Kauffman Foundation in late 2008, it was found that most American voters (circa 70 per cent) view entrepreneurship as key to solving the US economic crisis.[5] However, this contrasted sharply with the finding that the vast majority of these people are reluctant to start businesses themselves (only 26 per cent said that they would actually consider starting a business in the next five years).

4.5.3 Entrepreneurship in Germany

When it comes to evaluating entrepreneurship performance across Europe we can usefully make some broad generalisations which compare and contrast on the basis of national style and approach. For example, commentators refer to the new Spanish capitalist model; the Italian model of industrial districts; the innovation-based growth of the Scandinavian model and so on. The German economy from 1870s onwards has been described as 'coordinated', 'organised' or 'cooperative capitalism' (Berghoff, 2006). This type of economy is characterised by the following four criteria:

1 A close relationship between private businesses and state authorities (with subsidies in time of need). This type of relationship is sometimes referred to as Keynesian, after the twentieth-century British economist John Maynard Keynes, who advocated active policy responses by the public sector.

2 A highly developed system of lobbying organisations. Membership of the Chambers of Commerce was and remains compulsory.

3 Businesses display a strong propensity to avoid competition, practising collusive forms of cooperation, or setting up cartels (e.g. in the coal, iron and steel sectors in the early twentieth century).

4 Banks play a major role, especially in terms of mediating cooperative behaviours, with financiers often holding multiple interlocking directorships of other companies.

This background of cooperative capitalism may have contributed to a relatively low level of entrepreneurial activity, with Germany ranking 34 out of 42 countries included in terms of nascent entrepreneurship in the GEM 2006 survey. This also masks considerable variation in the lower level of entrepreneurship undertaken in the former East Germany (1.7 per cent) as compared with the West (2.9 per cent) (Sternberg et al., 2006). Commentators highlight the technological specialisation of the German model, whereby activity is concentrated around technologically advanced sectors – such as engineering, chemicals and motor vehicles (ERAWATCH, 2007).

Cooperation proves costly

The merging of the Stuttgart-based automobile company Daimler-Benz and the American car giant Chrysler Corporation in 1998 was intended to produce a trans-Atlantic automotive powerhouse. Both companies had seen extraordinary sales and growth since their humble beginnings in 1880s and 1925 respectively. However, the strategic move proved disastrous and Chrysler was sold back to a New York private equity firm specialising in troubled firms in 2007. With the subsequent economic downturn, Daimler's full year profits in 2008 fell 65 per cent from the previous year. Meanwhile, Chrysler received a $4 billion loan by the US government at the end of 2008, requesting a further $5 billion in order to allow it to avoid filing for bankruptcy and shutting down all operations permanently.

4.5.4 Entrepreneurship in France

It has often been suggested by its own citizens that France is a country lacking in the spirit of enterprise, with few entrepreneurs (Bonin, 2006). Certainly, the French have a mentality that is attached to corporatism that implies regulations, wage status, and sectoral privileges. However, the perspective of France as somehow un-entrepreneurial is unfair at best, and ignores the fact that the corporate world is heavily dependent upon the enterprising spirit of industrialists (Bonin, 2006: 65).

The French model of entrepreneurship is founded on a relatively high-level skills-base. Engineers, designers and technicians play a key technological, cultural and aesthetic role in the national economy. Entrepreneurship reaches its apex in 'high-intellect' activities, like the luxury sectors dedicated to the equipment and the care of people and towards equipment engineering.

French economic growth has been marked by a strong predisposition towards those sectors that depend strongly on short demand cycles, such as consumer goods, and public works, exposing it to the fluctuating competitive commercial environment. This would appear to be in marked opposition to Germany, for example, which tends more towards capital equipment. This reliance on the vagaries of the economic environment, contributes to the 'hide and seek' nature of French entrepreneurship. As commentator Hubert Bonin puts it, it is the 'come-and-go nature of French entrepreneurship that has so often caused people to doubt its very existence and made them run to the government to ask it to engender debates on ways of resuscitating it' (Bonin, 2006: 88).

ENTREPRENEURSHIP IN ACTION

Augustin and the 'Code du Travail'

Augustin Paluel-Marmont runs Michel et Augustin, a manufacturer of cookies (petits sablés ronds et bons) and yoghurt drinks, which was founded in 2005 in Paris. Although the firm only had seven staff in its early days, Augustin explains that he had to employ a full-time head of human resources who spent much of his days running around Paris trying to deal with the legal and regulatory paper-work associated with the nine-volume, several thousand page *Code du Travail*.

Augustin notes 'Your first hire must be a human resources manager, or you're dead in the water.'

Michel et Augustin yoghurt drinks on sale in Paris.

Assess the level of state regulation and 'red tape' in your country. To what extent do you think this puts off 'would-be' entrepreneurs from setting up their own enterprises?

Source: *Business Week*, 14 August 2006, http://www.businessweek.com/magazine/content/06_33/b3997064.htm accessed 3 May 2009

4.5.5 Entrepreneurship in Italy

Up until about 30 years ago, the general perception amongst the Italian population was that entrepreneurs freeloaded public resources, exploited workers and evaded taxes. In other words, they were generally self-interested and greedy, operating often at other people's expense (Amatori and Colli, 2006). During the 1970s, after two decades of steady growth, Italy found itself on the verge of total collapse. There was post oil shock inflation of nearly 20 per cent, and unemployment of 8 per cent. The 'old' view of Italy's industrial and social structure, based upon the dualism between the rich and developed North-western regions and a relatively backward South began to be replaced with a new perspective stressing the dynamism of entrepreneurship with peasant origins, especially within the North-eastern and Central regions of the country (Amatori and Colli, 2006: 138). This led to an 'economic miracle' built around individual production units grouped in geographically concentrated clusters – known as 'industrial districts'.

According to Becattini (1989), the economist who first built a theoretical framework to describe the term, the *industrial district* is essentially a territorial system of small and medium-sized firms producing a group of commodities whose manufacturing processes can be split into different phases (Amatori and Colli, 2006: 139). An important feature of the industrial district was the sense in which the firms' activities relied upon an embedded and complex social structure, largely dependent upon local traditions and trading practices, and bonds of trust between individuals. This has led to a specific form of 'diffuse entrepreneurship' in Italy which has benefited from refined craftsmanship, a strong tradition of cosmopolitan trade, and an ethic of hard work in the countryside (see Porter, 1990). A good example is the well-known fashion brand Benetton, founded by the Benetton family in 1965, which during the 1970s developed a highly networked business model in and around Treviso (see Chapter 9 for more discussion of this famous entrepreneurial venture).

4

Key economic factors affecting entrepreneurship

Interest rates – how expensive is borrowing? An interest rate of 1 per cent (European Central Bank fixed rate at the time of writing) makes a sizeable difference both for individuals and for companies, when compared with interest rates of nearly 4 per cent six months earlier.

Credit crunch – how available are loans or overdrafts? The current financial climate has seen a dramatic fall in the availability of credit, which threatens the survival of many small (and large) businesses.

Inflation – how much is my money worth? Inflation refers to the rise in the general level of prices of goods and services in an economy over time. It can be seen as a loss in the real value of money. As prices rise, so each unit of currency buys fewer goods and services. At the time of writing (early 2009), inflation in Zimbabwe, for example, had passed 516 quintillion per cent, with prices doubling every 1.3 days.

Exchange rates – how expensive is it to export/import? The foreign exchange rate between two currencies states how much one currency is worth in terms of the other. Although a 'weak pound', for example, should mean that British exports are more affordable – good news for UK manufacturers – this is being more than offset by sharply deteriorating domestic demand in key export markets, such as the eurozone and the US.

Gross domestic product (GDP) – what is the value of all the output produced in a nation in the course of one year? GDP is dependent on a wide range of factors. Broadly speaking, however, it depends upon levels of consumption, investment, government spending, as well as exports and imports.

4.6   ENTREPRENEURSHIP IN TRANSITION ECONOMIES

Since the fall of the Berlin Wall in 1989 the former Soviet Union and countries of central and Eastern Europe have been engaged in an epic transformation of their political and economic systems, on an unprecedented scale. The transition being undertaken implies a process of transformation towards a target stage – namely a market economy. However, it is important to realise that this may not be the explicit objective of all those states regarded to have 'transition economies'. For example, Belarus doesn't appear to be showing any desire to form a market economy (Smallbone and Welter, 2009: 11). It may be more appropriate, therefore, to refer to transition economies where formally centrally planned economies have introduced sufficient changes to allow private businesses to exist.

4.6.1 Key Features of a Transition Economy

There are considered to be three main changes which are necessary for 'transition' (Smallbone and Welter, 2009: 12):

■ The first is a shift in the dominant form of ownership from public to private;

■ Secondly, there needs to be a liberalisation of markets and a removal of price controls; and

■ Thirdly, supportive market institutions, including intellectual and physical property rights, banks, and business support need to be created. Under central planning, banks were often little more than accounting agencies without an active role in the financial transactions of enterprises. Most banks in countries such as Ukraine and Belarus, lack a willingness to finance small businesses. This is reinforced by a lack of experience and know-how.

Fundamental to all of these changes is an adequate legal and regulatory structure which is comprised of appropriate laws covering property, bankruptcy, contracts, commercial activities and taxes. Low public-sector salaries, lack of education and training opportunities for those working in enforcement institutions can often be problematic. In addition, frequent changes in tax regulations and commercial laws make life difficult for the small business owner. In countries where market reforms have been slow or only partially implemented it is likely that there will be an inadequate institutional environment for the development of small businesses.

4.6.2 Entrepreneurship in Former Soviet Union and Eastern Europe

Drawing towards the third decade after transformation began (1989/90) there is considerable variation between countries in terms of the extent to which an environment conducive to entrepreneurship has been created. East Germany, where effectively West Germany's institutional framework was simply extended, can be contrasted first with all other socialist economies outside the former Soviet Union, where some form of market-based system had existed in the inter-war period, and secondly with the newly independent states (NIS), where the challenge facing policy-makers was perhaps the greatest (Smallbone and Welter, 2009).

Table 4-1 maps the progress in transition in selected countries. Poland and Estonia have seen at least three-quarters of GDP being contributed by the private sector, and a minimum score of 3 is achieved on all of the selected indicators. In Russia and Ukraine there is a significant majority of GDP generated from the private sector, although progress and market reforms remain more patchy. Finally, in Belarus, private sector development is restricted and market reform is stalled.

TABLE 4-1 Progress in transition in selected countries (based on EBRD indicators 2005)					
	Russia	**Belarus**	**Ukraine**	**Poland**	**Estonia**
Pop. mid-2005 (m)	144.9	9.8	47.3	38.2	1.4
Private sector share of GDP	65%	25%	65%	75%	80%
Large-scale privatisation	3	1	3	3+	4
Small-scale privatisation	4	2+	4	4+	4+
Governance and enterprise restructuring	2+	1	2	4+	4+
Price liberalisation	4	3−	4	4+	4+
Trade and foreign exchange system	3+	2+	3+	4+	4+
Competition policy	2+	2	2+	3	3−
Banking reform and interest rate liberalisation	2+	2−	3−	4−	4
Infrastructure reform	3−	1+	2	3+	3+

Source: EBRD (2005:4) Smallbone and Welter, p. 21
Note: The measurement scale used for the indicators ranges from 1 (little or no change from a rigid centrally planned economy) to 4+, which represents the standards of an industrialised market economy. Reproduced with permission.

The role of entrepreneurship in the transformation process highlights the key impact of SMEs for job generation. It could be suggested that the nature of the relationship between the transformation of the economy and entrepreneurship is a recursive one. The development of a business-owning class and a positively supported SME sector play an important role in reorienting public awareness.

4.7   ENTREPRENEURSHIP IN DEVELOPING MARKETS

Following on from the previous section we now turn attention to the role of entrepreneurship in developing markets. Particular interest has focused on the emerging markets in countries such as China and India (which together with Brazil and Russia form the BRIC grouping), Eastern Europe, much of Southeast Asia, and countries in Africa and Latin America, where there is rapid growth and industrialisation.

4.7.1 Entrepreneurship in China

Following Mao Zedong's ascent to power in 1949, China became an ideologically Marxist country, actively suppressing capitalist activities for decades. Entrepreneurship was not something that could be openly practised, and yet the desire to 'be one's own boss' is as strong in China as elsewhere. The proverb 'It is better to be a chicken's head than a phoenix's tail' puts it rather well (Liao and Sohmen, 2001).

China's existing market economy was gradually transformed into a socialist economy. Agriculture and industry began to be collectivised and nationalised. The private sector had all but disappeared by 1956. The state enjoyed a monopoly over production and distribution, promising the 'Iron Rice Bowl' of lifetime employment. After the Cultural Revolution the scope for entrepreneurial activity increased, such that by 1987 there was a surge towards the private sector, with the number of private enterprises growing by 93 per cent in that year alone.

Entrepreneurship in China took many forms. Three main types have been identified (see Liao and Sohmen, 2001):

Type 1: Before reform and through the 1980s there was a good deal of small-scale enterprise activity such as street vending and businesses known as *getihu*. Those involved, often from poorer backgrounds, tended towards entrepreneurial activity (perhaps more accurately described as necessity self-employment in this case).

Type 2: We can contrast this first group of necessity entrepreneurship with the more highly educated individuals who chose to set up larger businesses in the late 1980s and after. These businesses, known as *siying qiye*, included restaurants, manufacturing and transportation firms.

Type 3: The third type involved individuals who were largely foreign-educated and who now had returned to China to start businesses. These have been affectionately referred to as the 'sea-turtles' – individuals who spend significant time abroad and then come back to China to 'lay eggs', that is, start new ventures.

All three types of entrepreneur have faced considerable difficulties in running their businesses. Chinese government policy has had a track record of considerable volatility. With insecure property rights, for example, it is difficult for any entrepreneur to know just 'where they stand'. There is also a raft of unpublished (*neibu*) regulations which are operated at multiple levels, whether by local, provincial or central government. Notwithstanding the regulatory environment, gaining access to key resources, especially funding, labour and technology, could be very challenging. It would be easy to describe the turbulent past and the various macro-economic conditions characterised here as acting as a constraint to entrepreneurial behaviour in China. However, in the light of more recent events, one has to exercise some caution about this viewpoint. Entrepreneurs are now thriving and opportunities are abundant in times of change, or chaos and uncertainty. Entrepreneurship is now recognised as an integral element in China's economic advancement. Successful entrepreneurs are now upheld as role models and idols. China is seen as essentially being tied with the US and well ahead of Europe, Singapore and Hong Kong, in terms of measurable entrepreneurial activity (see Reynolds, Bygrave and Autio, 2004).

4.7.2 Entrepreneurship in India

The environment for entrepreneurial activity in India has changed substantially since Independence in 1947. From being a government-dominated economy in the immediate post-independence years, the culture has shifted to encourage a blossoming of new and private entrepreneurial ventures. The remedy for India's vicious cycle of poverty before independence was rapid industrialisation of the economy. The hope was that development of the industrial sector would 'trickle down' to the other sectors, bringing all-round development and alleviating India's poverty. This was a type of Fabian socialism, which aimed not to destroy capitalism but merely to mitigate the social injustices it caused (see Bagchi and Pal, 2003). As such, the Industrial Policy Resolution of 1948 envisaged the role of the government as a pioneer in entrepreneurial activities in India, with, unusually, only a limited role to be played by the private sector. The intention was to socialise public sector profits through distributive policies that would prevent their concentration in only a handful of capitalists. The government's faith in the public sector continued through the following decade, with public sector control extending far and wide, including the famous 'industrial licensing system', where would-be entrepreneurs had to seek approval from the Ministry of Industries prior to making an investment. There was rapid growth in industrial production during the period 1956–65, but this growth could not be sustained.

The basic framework of the industrial policies remained much the same until 1991. By that stage it was clear that there were (at least) three main factors contributing to the failure to bring about entrepreneurship development in India (Bagchi and Pal, 2003). These were:

1 extensive bureaucratic controls over production, investment and trade;

2 inward looking policies for trade and foreign investment; and

3 a very large public sector.

The New Industrial Policy of 1991 sought to remedy this state of affairs, through, for example, abolishing the industrial licensing system, easing of entry requirements for foreign direct investment; encouraging private investment in sectors of the economy previously reserved for the public sector.

Entrepreneurs in India have now become folk heroes. The founder of Infosys, for example, Narayana Murthy, is often compared to Microsoft's founder Bill Gates. Property rights for nascent entrepreneurs are not fully secure, but the protection regime is certainly far stronger than that experienced in China. India's capital markets are also benefiting from these institutions. India is poised to capture more foreign direct investment (FDI) than ever before. New Delhi is also welcoming back the diaspora, which includes many very highly skilled knowledge workers. In the light of recent events in terms of the global recession, where major developed countries' governments have been 'interfering' with the invisible hand of the market economy – bailing out banks, building societies, car companies and others – it is particularly interesting to reflect on this alternative direction.

4.7.3 Drawing Comparisons

The fact that India is increasingly building from the ground up as opposed to China's top-down approach reflects their contrasting political heritage. India is founded on democratic principles, and China is not. China's state owned enterprises (SOEs) are still strongly protected at the expense of private sector entrepreneurs. China has enjoyed the fruits of foreign direct investment (FDI), but India, in comparison, is something of a laggard. However, some commentators have suggested that China's export-led manufacturing boom is largely a creation of foreign direct investment, which effectively serves as a substitute for domestic entrepreneurship (see Huang and Khanna, 2003).

The Indian diaspora was, until recently, resented for its success and seemed unwilling to invest back home. India then provided a more nurturing environment for its home-grown entrepreneurs, which has led to some companies which compete internationally. Furthermore, many of these competitor firms operate in cutting edge, knowledge-based industries – e.g. software companies Infosys and Wipro. These emerging economies appear to be poised to make a huge impression on not just their own citizens but on the people and entrepreneurial ventures of the world.

4.8   ENTREPRENEURSHIP OUTSIDE OF THE MARKET CONTEXT

Not all entrepreneurial behaviour happens within a market context. We can contrast the public market place of the 'formal economy' with the 'informal economy' where economic activity is not taxed or indeed recognised as occurring by the government, or its legislative arms. It would be wrong to think of the informal economy as only happening in relatively undeveloped countries, or at times of political and social upheaval (such as that following the fall of the Berlin Wall). There is, no doubt, informal economic activity happening in all countries. The capacity for individuals to act entrepreneurially, spotting opportunities, and arranging transactions between buyers and sellers, appears to be a deeply pervasive and ubiquitous human characteristic.

4.9   SUMMARY AND ACTIVITIES

Entrepreneurship has a vital role to play in the development and maintenance of **economic prosperity**. Our interest in the **economy** (how we look after our basic needs) is closely related to our interest in entrepreneurship. The production, distribution and consumption of goods and services in a given society comprise what is termed an **economic system**. There are many different types of such system, and despite the considerable economic shocks that are arising at a time of global recession, **capitalism** remains the dominant form.

Central to the capitalist system is a tension between efficiency and equality. The profit and wealth seeking activities of some individual entrepreneurs may potentially come at the expense of others in the **marketplace**. Whilst there is no one formula for achieving economic prosperity, capitalism's 'moderately unequal distribution' is considered to promote work efforts of individuals in general.

Entrepreneurial activity is enabled when the right kind of **economic conditions** are in place for individuals to undertake **entrepreneurial projects**. As countries move from **factor-driven** economies through **efficiency-driven** to **innovation-driven** economies they are likely to require and then benefit from specific **innovation and entrepreneurship** enablers – such as entrepreneurial finance and education, government support, appropriate commercial and legal infrastructure and effective regulation. The **economic development diamond** was introduced to help explain how we might measure entrepreneurial activity in different countries.

With modern economies depending heavily upon **knowledge**, we have seen the increasingly important role played by the **small and medium-sized enterprise** (SME) in the economy. At the heart of all enterprises (large or small) are the individual entrepreneurs whose **aspirations, attitudes and activities** determine the level of entrepreneurship in any given society. It was noted that most small business owners don't set out to **grow** their companies.

Although it is easy to characterise European entrepreneurship as distinct from, say, US or Indian sub-continent entrepreneurship, the major developed Western economies display distinct characteristics in their own right, such as Germany's **cooperative capitalism**, or Italy's **industrial districts**. Since the fall of the Berlin Wall in 1989, particular opportunities (and challenges) have faced those countries with **transition economies**. Not all of the post-socialist countries have the aspiration to develop market economies. We can contrast this, however, with the likes of China and India whose **emerging markets** are challenging for supremacy on the global stage. Here, the role of the entrepreneur will be a crucial and decisive one.

4

REVIEW QUESTIONS

1 What is the literal meaning of the word economy?

2 How many different economic systems can you think of?

3 Name five economic conditions which enable entrepreneurial activity.

4 What do macro-economists study?

5 Is South Africa currently a factor-driven, efficiency-driven or innovation-driven economy?

6 Give six reasons for the increase in importance of small businesses in developed economies.

7 According to the GEM 2008 study, what percentage of start-ups expect to create 20 new jobs or more?

   a) 2%   b) 8%   c) 16%

8 Explain what is meant by the term 'transition economy'.

9 Which countries make up the BRIC grouping?

10 Explain why foreign direct investment may not always be beneficial.

SEMINAR TASK

Imagine that you were developing a new type of affordable mobile phone that would bring video, music, GPS and reliable communication to everyone, regardless of location and income – the so-called 'people's phone'. Working in small teams, outline the advantages and disadvantages of setting up your operations in China. Draw up a table to illustrate your findings, and present an overview to the rest of the seminar group, indicating whether you would go ahead in China or elsewhere (and if so, where?).

4

Preview case continued

Tata – Driving home advantage

The Tata Nano

The origins of Tata Motors, now India's largest automobile company, go back to the nineteenth century and the road to independence from the British Empire. Jamshetji Tata 'the father of Indian industry' was the founder of the family firm which started off with interests in cloth mills and hotels. No doubt he would be amazed by the fortunes of the company today, embracing such diverse interests as energy, software, communications, salt, chemicals, steel (Corus), tea (Tetley), and not least, cars and commercial vehicles.

Tata Motors' first production car, in collaboration with Daimler Benz AG was rolled out in 1954. It is now India's largest passenger automobile and commercial vehicle manufacturing company, and the world's twentieth largest (in 2006). The company has capitalised upon its strategic advantages over other car manufacturers, including the fact that labour costs represent 8–9 per cent of sales as against 30–35 per cent of sales in developed countries. The company also has forged strong links with machine tools and metal sectors in India and abroad.

'The People's Car' (the Tata Nano) was launched in 2008, as the cheapest new car ever made (equivalent of £1300 – the same price as the DVD player in the Lexus). Tata cut costs by minimising on components, particularly steel, and taking advantage of India's low production costs. It has placed considerable emphasis on

developing its engineering capabilities, employing over 2500 engineers and scientists at its Engineering Research Centre. The engineering team first came up with a solution that had bars instead of doors and plastic flaps to keep out the monsoon rains. However, this was the catalyst to build a proper car. At first, many were sceptical (including Germany's Bosch, which makes the computer at the heart of the vehicle). However, before long many of the suppliers were working at their part of the car. Despite the fact that the prices of raw materials have increased over the past four years or so (e.g. steel's price doubled) all suppliers were forced to cut costs.

As Tata prepares for the launch in India it has entered into an agreement with the country's largest state-sector bank, State Bank of India, which will provide loans to prospective owners to help make the new car more affordable. Would-be buyers, even in the remotest of Indian villages, will have to pay $6 for a booking form (which will be available from the Tata group's extensive existing retail outlets) and then make an initial payment of $60. The bank loan will cover the rest. The company plans additional marketing of the new car through sale of Nano phones, key chains, caps and T-shirts.

Tata Motors puts its success down to a deep understanding of economic stimuli and customer needs, as well as leading edge R&D (Tata website, 9 February 2009). Chief Executive Ravi Kant recalls that 'the innovation wasn't in technology, it was in a mindset change'. The story of the Nano reflects an emerging nation that is ambitious and poised to challenge developed economies through the reach of its entrepreneurial aspirations and activities.

Discussion questions

1 *What specific underlying economic conditions have enabled Tata to develop the Nano in India?*

2 *In general, do you think a country's economy represents more of a constraint or an enablement to entrepreneurial behaviour? Discuss your answer in relation to Ravi*

▶

Kant's observation about the nature of innovation.

Sources:

i) BusinessWeek.com, 'Tata: Making the Nano more affordable, 24 March 2009, available at http://www. businessweek.com/globalbiz/content/mar2009/ gb20090324_801474.htm viewed on 29 March 2009

ii) Tata Motors website – http://www.tatamotors.com/ our_world/profile.php

iii) Autocar, 'A history of Tata', 26 March 2008, available at http://www.autocar.co.uk/News/NewsArticle/AllCars/ 231882/ viewed on 29 March 2009

4.10   NOTES, REFERENCES AND FURTHER READING

Notes and Further Information

1. This phrase was widely used during Bill Clinton's successful 1992 presidential campaign against George H.W. Bush.

2. See http://www.spiegel.de/international/business/0,1518,602632,00.html.

3. Most of the problems considered by economists arise out of the use of scarce resources to satisfy human wants. These resources, which together constitute the factors of production, can be broken down into three main groupings – land, labour and capital.

4. GEM is run by a not-for-profit academic research consortium. For more details see GEM's website at http://www. gemconsortium.org/. For a glossary of the main terms used and an understanding of the methodology applied, see Bosma *et al.*, 2008: 13.

5. Source: *Wall Street Journal*, 2 October 2008: http://blogs.wsj.com/independentstreet/2008/10/02/can-entrepreneurs-rescue-the-us-economy/.

References

Acs, Z.J. and Szerb, L. (2008) *Gearing Up to Measure Entrepreneurship in a Global Economy*, Mimeo, Faculty of Business and Economics, University of Pecs.

Amatori, F. and Colli, A. (2006) Models of entrepreneurship in a latecomer country: Italy, in *Country Studies in Entrepreneurship: A Historical Perspective* (eds Y. Cassis and I. Pepelasis Minoglou), Basingstoke: Palgrave Macmillan, pp. 129–148.

Audretsch, D.B. and Thurik, A.R. (2001) What is new about the new economy: Sources of growth in the managed and entrepreneurial economies, *Industrial and Corporate Change*, 19: 795–821.

Audretsch, D.B. and Thurik, A.R. (2006) A model of the entrepreneurial economy, in *Modern Perspectives on Entrepreneurship* (ed. A.E. Burke), London: Senate Hall, pp. 23–46.

Bagchi, S. and Pal, D. (2003) Entrepreneurship and Indian economy: Role of government policies in entrepreneurship development, Working Paper, Jadavpur University, available at http://papers.ssrn.com/sol3/papers.cfm?abstract_id=858044.

Becattini, G. (1989) Riflessioni sul distretto industriale marshallioano come concetto socio-economico, *Stato e Mercato*, XXV.

Berghoff, H. (2006) Entrepreneurship under 'cooperative capitalism': The German case, in *Country Studies in Entrepreneurship: A Historical Perspective* (eds Y. Cassis and I. Pepelasis Minoglou), Basingstoke: Palgrave Macmillan, pp. 98–128.

BERR (2008) *Enterprise: Unlocking the UK's Talent*, Strategy document, Department for Business Enterprise & Regulatory Reform, 2008, available at http://www.berr.gov.uk/bbf/enterprise-smes/enterprise-framework/index.html.

Bitros, G.C. and Karayiannis, D. (2006) The liberating power of entrepreneurship in ancient Athens, in Cassis, Y. and Pepelasis Minoglou, I. (eds) *Country Studies in Entrepreneurship: A historical perspective*, Basingstoke: Palgrave Macmillan, pp. 11–24.

Blau, D. (1987) A time-series analysis of self-employment in the United States, *Journal of Political Economy*, 95 (3): 445–467.

Bonin, H. (2006) A short history of entrepreneurship in France (From 1780 up to today), in *Country Studies in Entrepreneurship: A Historical Perspective* (eds Y. Cassis and I. Pepelasis Minoglou), Basingstoke: Palgrave Macmillan, pp. 65–97.

Bosma, N., Acs, Z.J., Autio, E., Coduras, A. and Levie, J. (2008) *Global Entrepreneurship Monitor 2008 Executive Report*, Babson College, Universidad del Desarrollo, London Business School, available at http://www.gemconsortium.org/download/1233669410187/GEM_Global_08.pdf.

Brock, W.A. and Evans, D.S. (1989) Small business economics, *Small Business Economics*, 1(1): 7–20.

Callon, M. (ed) (1998) *The Laws of the Markets*, Oxford: Blackwell.

Casson, M. (2003) *The Entrepreneur: An Economic Theory*, second edition (first edition 1982), Cheltenham: Edward Elgar.

ERAWATCH (2007) *Country Specialisation Report – Germany*, European Communities, available at: http://cordis.europa.eu/erawatch/ accessed on 28 March 2009.

Evans, D. and Leighton, L.S. (1989) The determinants of changes in U.S. self-employment, 1968-1987, *Small Business Economics*, 1 (2): 111–119.

Gries, T. and Naude, W. (2008) Entrepreneurship and Structural Economic Transformation, *UNU-Wider Research Papers*, Helsinki.

Huang, Y. and Khanna, T. (2003) Can India overtake China? *Foreign Policy*, July/August, available at http://www.foreignpolicy.com/Ning/archive/archive/137/13.PDF viewed on 29 March 2009.

Jorgenson, D.W. (2001) Information technology and the U.S. economy, *American Economic Review*, 91 (1): 1–32.

Kauffman Foundation (2007) *On the Road to an Entrepreneurial Economy. A Research and Policy Guide*, Ewing Marion Kauffman Foundation, July, available at: http://www.kauffman.org/pdf/entrepreneurial_roadmap_2.pdf.

Kirzner, I.M. (1973) *Competition and Entrepreneurship*, Chicago: University of Chicago Press.

Knight, F. (1921) *Risk, Uncertainty and Profit*. London School of Economics and Political Science, London. Reissued 1965, New York: Harper & Row.

Liao, D. and Sohmen, P. (2001) The development of modern entrepreneurship in China, *Stanford Journal of East Asian Affairs*, Spring (1): 27–30.

Lipsey, R.G. (1968) *An Introduction to Positive Economics*, London: Weidenfeld and Nicolson.

McCraw, T.K. (ed.) (1997) *Creating Modern Capitalism*, Cambridge, Mass: Harvard University Press.

North, D.C. (1977) Markets and other allocation systems in history: The challenge of Karl Polanyi, *Journal of European Economic History*, 6: 703–716.

Porter, M.E. (1990) *The Competitive Advantage of Nations*, Free Press, New York.

Porter, M.E., Sachs, J.J. and McArthur, J. (2002) Executive Summary: Competitiveness and Stages of Economic Development, in *The Global Competitiveness Report 2001–2002* (eds Porter, M, Sachs, J., Cornelius, P.K., McArthur, J.W. and Schwab, K.), New York: Oxford University Press, pp. 16–25.

Reynolds, P.D., Bygrave, W.D. and Autio, E. (2004) *GEM 2003 Global Report*, GEM.

Rosenbaum, E.F. (2000) What is a market? On the methodology of a contested concept, *Review of Social Economy*, 58(4): December, 455–482.

Schumpeter, J.A. (1934) *The Theory of Economic Development*, Cambridge, MA: Harvard University Press.

Smallbone, D. and Welter, F. (2009) *Entrepreneurship and Small Business Development in Post-Socialist Economies*, London: Routledge.

Sternberg, R., Brixy, U. and Hundt, C. (2006) *Laenderbericht Deutschland 2006*, GEM.

Wennekers, A.R.M., van Stel, A., Thurik, A.R. and Reynolds, P.D. (2005) Nascent entrepreneurship and the level of economic development, *Small Business Economics*, 24 (3): 293–309.

Recommended Further Reading

A core text that discusses the challenges of integrating ideas on entrepreneurship with economic development theories is:

Leff, N.H. (1979) Entrepreneurship and economic development: The problem revisited, *Journal of Economic Literature*, 17: 46–64.

More recent contributions to this relationship include:

Acs, Z.J. and Storey, D.J. (2004) Entrepreneurship and economic development, *Regional Studies*, 38 (8): 871–877.

Bygrave, W. and Minniti, M. (2000) The social dynamics of entrepreneurship, *Entrepreneurship Theory and Practice*, 24 (3): 25–36.

George, G. and Zahra, S. A. (2002) Culture and its consequence for entrepreneurship, *Entrepreneurship Theory and Practice*, Summer: 5–8.

Harper, D.A. (2003) *Foundations of Entrepreneurship and Economic development*, London: Routledge.

Reynolds, P.D., Bosma, N.S., Autio, E., Hunt, S., De Bono, N., Servais, I., Lopez-Garcia, P. and Chin, N. (2005) Global Entrepreneurship Monitor: Data collection design and implementation, 1998–2003, *Small Business Economics*, 24 (3): 205–231.

CHAPTER 5

Entrepreneurship in Context

LEARNING OBJECTIVES

After studying this chapter, the reader will be able to:

- Understand the significance of the different contexts in which entrepreneurship operates
- Evaluate the corporate entrepreneurial environment
- Evaluate the context of social enterprises
- Evaluate the public sector entrepreneurial environment
- Analyse the global reach of entrepreneurship.

INTRODUCTION

Entrepreneurship tends to be linked with two contexts in particular:

- the start-up and management of small enterprises; and
- private sector ventures targeted to make a profit.

Entrepreneurship is not limited to these fields only and in this chapter we explore the many other contexts in which it can flourish. In particular we will examine:

- large as well as small businesses;
- social as well as for-profit enterprise;
- public as well as private sector organisations;
- international as well as local communities of entrepreneurs.

PREVIEW CASE

The Maverick

Ricardo Semler took over his father's marine pump manufacturing company in Sao Paulo, Brazil in 1982 when he was just 21 years old. Twenty years later, he had succeeded in growing Semco from $4 million to over $200 million turnover by developing an innovative product range including dishwashers and air conditioning units. Success came from transforming a traditional manufacturing company through entrepreneurial internal management practices. His methods have proven successful but few have tried to copy him even though he has written about it and lectured around the world. He recognised his status as a different kind of entrepreneur when he entitled his autobiography 'Maverick!'[1]

Why does a successful entrepreneur who innovated in an established large company label himself as a maverick?

Find out more in the case study 'The Maverick who turned his company upside down' at the end of the chapter.

5.1 CORPORATE ENTREPRENEURSHIP

5.1.1 The Foundations of Corporate Entrepreneurship – or 'Intrapreneurship'

'Entrepreneur' is a title that is sometimes given automatically to the owner-manager of a small business. When leaders of large companies are acknowledged as 'entrepreneurs' (such as Bill Gates, Richard Branson and Anita Roddick), it is usually because they themselves have built the business from scratch as a new venture. However, small business owners are not always entrepreneurs and large corporations often employ entrepreneurial staff (Rieple and Vyarkarnam, 1994). Historically, entrepreneurs may have seemed out of place in large companies. The development of mass manufacturing techniques relied on meticulous planning to improve efficiencies and lower costs. Planners could ensure manufacturing processes were repeated many times in the same way to produce the necessary economies of scale. Entrepreneurs by definition encourage change which tends to disrupt carefully planned efficiencies so that their role in large companies was perceived to be limited.

A number of factors, including the decline of the manufacturing sector and growth of service industries, led to a change in emphasis signalled in 1976 by Norman Macrae (1976: 42) who foresaw that 'methods of operation in business are going to change radically in the next few decades, in a direction opposite to that which most businessmen and nearly all politicians expect'. His survey – 'the coming entrepreneurial revolution' – claimed that the world was probably drawing to the end of the era of large corporations, because it was nonsense to have hierarchical managements sitting in offices trying to arrange how 'brainworkers' (who in future would be most workers) could best use their imaginations. Big businesses have survived, although there are fewer of them, but this prediction was partly accurate in that they have done so mainly by acting more like smaller enterprises.

Today, many large organisations deliberately try to remain entrepreneurial by encouraging managers to innovate and some have succeeded in sustaining entrepreneurial tendencies longer than many smaller firms. This has been made even more necessary by the intensity of global competition and the speed of technological change (Ramachandran et al., 2006). Because the word entrepreneur has been so linked to small business, the term *intrapreneur* was coined to describe someone who behaves in an entrepreneurial fashion in a larger organisation. Intrapreneurship, or corporate entrepreneurship in an existing business structure, has been further encouraged by developments such as downsizing and delegation of powers to smaller, strategic business units.

Large organisations need intrapreneurs for two main reasons:

■ First, to improve the performance of the core business through innovative developments and modifications to existing products and processes; and

■ Secondly, to guard against market obsolescence through the creation of new ventures (Gautam and Verma, 1997).

Thus, corporate entrepreneurship represents the company's efforts at renewal through innovation and new business development through venturing. It allows existing firms to revitalise by providing an antidote to fossilisation (Burns, 2008). Although entrepreneurship and intrapreneurship share many common characteristics, entrepreneurship is 'developmental' whilst intrapreneurship is 'restorative' (Kirby, 2003: 300). Entrepreneurs develop new ventures from scratch; intrapreneurs aim to restore innovation and counter stagnation in an existing organisation, which often involves overcoming a corporate culture that resists change and avoids risk. Intrapreneurs do not necessarily appear unbidden in an organisation – it requires entrepreneurial leaders to encourage and foster them in an existing organisation. Entrepreneurial leadership is therefore the ability to encourage an entrepreneurial culture within a larger organisation so that it continues to seek opportunities and encourage innovation and to adopt new ways of doing business (Burns, 2005).

5.1.2 Encouraging Corporate Entrepreneurship

A number of conditions need to exist in the firm to support corporate entrepreneurship or to motivate entrepreneurial behaviour (Marvel *et al.*, 2007). In particular, entrepreneurship needs enthusiastic staff who are motivated to champion entrepreneurial initiatives. These are not easy to identify, recruit and retain. Hisrich and Peters (1995: 542) cite 13 factors that encourage a 'climate for intrapreneurship':

■ Sufficient resources are invested in research and development (R&D) so that the organisation operates at the cutting edge in its particular technology;

■ New ideas are encouraged and supported even if they seem at odds with short-term profits;

■ Experimentation through trial and error is encouraged;

■ Failures are allowed even though this may run counter to the traditional career path in large companies;

■ No parameters are laid down for potential developments as this can inhibit creativity;

■ The necessary resources in terms of time and money are made available;

■ They are also readily accessible and not subject to lengthy approval processes;

■ Multi-skilled teams from a variety of backgrounds are encouraged;

■ Long time horizons for evaluating success are established;

■ Intrapreneurs are encouraged to come forward voluntarily – they cannot be forced;

■ An appropriate reward system is in place offering financial gains, promotions and other recognition. Equity in a new venture is often the best incentive;

■ Sponsors and champions are available within the organisation to encourage and mentor would-be intrapreneurs;

■ Support of top management is a vital ingredient without which an intrapreneurial environment is unlikely to succeed.

A key measure of how far this culture of entrepreneurship has permeated an organisation is the *intensity* of entrepreneurial activity. Some organisations may develop a small number of innovations with high

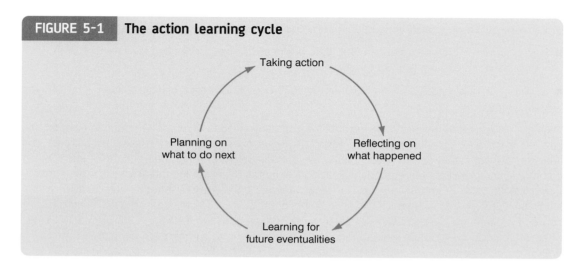

FIGURE 5-1   The action learning cycle

impact; others may manage more entrepreneurial activities but of less significance. The aim of a truly entrepreneurial organisation is to do both, exhibiting a high intensity of entrepreneurial outcomes both in terms of significance and frequency (Morris and Kuratko, 2002).

In order to do this, an organisation cannot rely on the founding entrepreneur and a few intrapreneurs. It has to become a 'learning organisation' (Pedler, Burgoyne and Boydell, 1991) in which the entire organisation learns both from its own experiences and good practice elsewhere, experiments with new ways of doing things, and adapts rapidly to changes in the external environment. Individual managers contribute to this through an *action learning cycle* (Figure 5-1) in which actions are followed by reflections on the outcomes, which in turn leads to learning about good practice for the future, and planning for new actions so that the cycle restarts again.

BP's corporate entrepreneurship model

From a troubled period at the end of the 1980s, BP has developed into a global energy company that has added renewable energies to its portfolio. It has addressed climate change issues by creating an innovation unit, BP Alternative Energy, to create new businesses from all types of low-carbon energy including solar and wind power.

In attempting to re-invent itself as a socially responsible supplier of all forms of energy BP has adopted a corporate entrepreneurship model with four key components that help guide and control entrepreneurial action:

■ *Direction* – the company's strategy, its goals, markets and overall positioning as a socially responsible corporation.

■ *Space* – the freedom given to business unit managers to deliver on their objectives including the freedom to experiment and innovate.

■ *Boundaries* – the legal and moral limits within which the company operates as laid down in policy documents or implicitly understood.

■ *Support* – information systems, training and work/life balance services to help the managers do their jobs.

The four elements are intended to create an organisational environment of controlled freedom in which individuals can act entrepreneurially within constraints determined by the company. If one element is missing or out of balance, the model breaks down – without space and support, entrepreneurial initiative is stifled, but without direction and boundaries it can get out of hand.

5.1.3 Problems and Issues in Developing an Entrepreneurial Culture
....

For every large enterprise that has managed to foster and sustain an entrepreneurial culture and corporate entrepreneurship, there are many more that have not. The barriers are considerable. Research by Wilson, Stokes and Athayde (2009) has highlighted a mismatch between corporate leaders who remain suspicious of entrepreneurs within their organisations and middle managers that nevertheless consider themselves to be entrepreneurial. The research found that over half of corporate managers considered themselves to be entrepreneurial and over 30 per cent did indeed act entrepreneurially. However, many corporate leaders believed that a much smaller percentage – sometimes as low as 1 per cent of their employees – were actually entrepreneurial. Some believed that there could only be one, true entrepreneur in the organisation, usually the founder. There was a general believe that entrepreneurs are difficult to manage although they were necessary in order to prevent stagnation. Thus the intrapreneur is regarded by many as a necessary evil who has to be given sufficient space to perform well but who needs watching carefully in case they take too many risks. It would seem there are still many dichotomies in the attitudes of leaders towards entrepreneurs in the corporate context.

5

Give us mavericks — just don't let them run anything

By Stefan Stern, *The Financial Times*

'It has been a very disappointing year so far for the cause of innovation and entrepreneurship.

Take the financial services industries. Doubtless it was innovative to lend billions of dollars to people who had no earthly prospect of ever paying the money back again. It was entrepreneurial to package up some of these loans into new securities, get them assigned a triple A rating and then sell them on to credulous investors. But, sadly, the consequences of all this nifty financing have been grim.... The only innovation we want from financiers right now are soundly based products and responsible decision-making. Business leaders wrestle constantly with this dilemma: how to encourage risk-taking and entrepreneurial flair without exposing the whole organisation to unquantifiable danger. It is one of the great paradoxes of leadership....

New research carried out by Kingston University's Entrepreneurship Centre confirms that employers still struggle to square this circle. Together with the executive search firm Cripps Sears & Partners, Kingston's team looked at 34 recent job descriptions and personal specifications for vacancies that had been filed by the search firm. Researchers also conducted focus groups with senior executives from client companies and with Cripps Sears headhunters themselves.

What emerged was a classic mismatch between what employers said they were looking for and what they were in fact comfortable with. The pressures of competition and the increasing commoditisation of goods and services, should encourage businesses to innovate and differentiate themselves. And yet, as the chief operating officer of a professional services firm observed: "A key challenge is reining in off-the-wall individuals." Kingston University's research highlighted that sense of otherness that employers often perceive in entrepreneurs. Their focus group of executives referred frequently to "these people", as in: "These people tend to have a lot of bad attributes but also some brilliant ones." There was also nervousness that entrepreneurs' drive and apparent fearlessness could conceal more worrying qualities. "You can easily confuse a bullshitter with an entrepreneur", said one....

Make no mistake, if you hire entrepreneurs you are inviting the awkward squad to join you at your table. Entrepreneurs are "very high maintenance people", one executive told Kingston's researchers. "They get angry and upset, so they go and step over the mark . . . life is actually easier if you get rid of them." And the punchline? "I'm not sure this is the right solution for the business."

5

Perhaps managers should be trying to encourage entrepreneurial behaviour, without necessarily hiring lots of hard-core entrepreneurs (if they would join them in the first place)…The most successful business leaders have a certain appetite for risk but they are not greedy for it.

Without entrepreneurs, there would be no businesses. But if we always put entrepreneurs in charge, there wouldn't be so many businesses left either. In his 1986 book *Innovation and Entrepreneurship,* Peter Drucker described an entrepreneur as someone who "always searches for change, responds to it, and exploits it as an opportunity".

I am all in favour of that sort of thing, provided it is kept rigidly under control.'

Do you agree with Stefan Stern the Financial Times correspondent who reported on this research into entrepreneurial behaviour? Should the financial crisis that developed from 2007, colour our views on the usefulness and dangers of entrepreneurs in corporate environments to the extent they should be branded as 'mavericks'?

© The Financial Times, 15 July 2009.

5.1.4 The Virtuous Circle of Corporate Entrepreneurship

Despite the problems experienced by intrapreneurs, entrepreneurial cultures do exist and thrive in the corporate environment. It is not only entrepreneurs who want to work in an entrepreneurial environment, but most employees who find that such environments give greater job satisfaction and rewards. The Kingston research found that executives were more likely to stay in an organisation that was entrepreneurially supportive, even if they did not claim to be entrepreneurs or acted entrepreneurially. A key factor in the development of an entrepreneurial culture would seem to be the employment of entrepreneurial people who in turn encourage other staff to thrive in this environment. This indicates that entrepreneurial activity can lead to a 'virtuous circle' as illustrated in Figure 5-2. This suggests that the development of an entrepreneurially supportive culture is itself contingent on the employment of entrepreneurial executives. The more entrepreneurially supportive the organisation the more likely the executives will display entrepreneurial behaviour and so on.

FIGURE 5-2   **Corporate entrepreneurship virtuous circle**

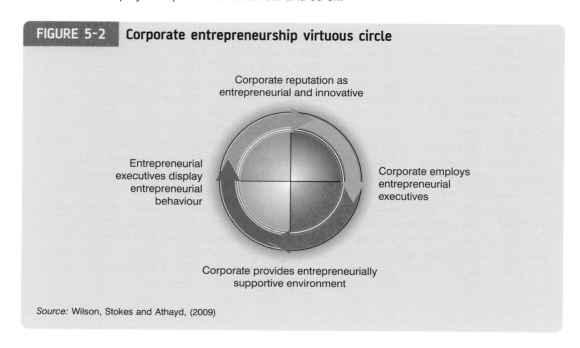

Source: Wilson, Stokes and Athayd, (2009)

5.2   SOCIAL ENTREPRENEURSHIP

Entrepreneurs are closely associated with making money but this is not the only way that they and society can benefit from their actions. Entrepreneurship can add value to individuals and to society in several different ways: it can help individuals to develop their personal confidence or *self-efficacy*; it is also increasingly used for social as well as monetary gain.

5.2.1   Self-Efficacy

Early on in the development of theories of entrepreneurship, Schumpeter (1934: 93–94) described a significant benefit of entrepreneurship as the personal growth of the individual involved who acquires 'the impulse to fight, to prove oneself superior to others, to succeed for the sake, not of the fruits of success, but of the success itself. From this aspect, economic action becomes akin to sport.'

There is now increasing evidence to support his claim. There seems to be a two-way linkage between self confidence – or *self-efficacy* – and the act of venture creation:

■ Someone who increases their levels of self-efficacy is more likely to become involved in new venture creation; and

■ An individual who creates a new venture is likely to improve their self-efficacy as a result (Lucas and Cooper, 2004).

Entrepreneurship involves having the confidence and vision to make things happen and to do things differently. In this sense, it can create value in a person through self-development – even if things go wrong. Entrepreneurs who have closed a business with financial losses still regard it as a positive learning experience (Stokes and Blackburn, 2002). The act of entrepreneurship itself has a social value in that it adds to the self-efficacy and personal effectiveness of those involved. (See Chapter 7 for more on the importance of self-efficacy in the personal development of an entrepreneur.)

5.2.2   Social Entrepreneurs

Many entrepreneurs take this a stage further in that they use entrepreneurial processes to add value to society by fulfilling the social or economic needs of others. 'Social entrepreneurs' act entrepreneurially in that they pursue opportunities without regard to the resources they currently control, but they do not have profit as their primary aim. Like entrepreneurs generally, social entrepreneurs operate in a variety of contexts. Some form ventures that have a social aim as their main purpose, and so form a 'social enterprise' – see below (5.2.3). Others run a private-sector, profit-making enterprise but with distinct social values and objectives. Whatever the context, social entrepreneurs make a positive difference to the lives of others by emphasising the social responsibility of their ventures before the need to maximise profits. They identify a social problem (which may or may not also be a business opportunity) and use entrepreneurial processes to create solutions to tackle the problem.

It has been argued that social entrepreneurs are no different from traditional entrepreneurs except that they do not prioritise the making of profits and put more emphasis on social rather than commercial results (Leadbetter, 1997). Research suggests that this also leads to different ways of operating: social entrepreneurs tend to have longer time horizons and they place more emphasis on resource acquisition as they often operate in fields where resources are scarce (Johnstone and Basso, 1999)

ENTREPRENEURSHIP IN ACTION

The social face of banking

Mohammed Yunis identified that a key problem for the poor of Bangladesh was to raise very small amounts of money for projects that would help them out of poverty. But the traditional banks were not interested in making tiny loans at reasonable interest rates to the poor due to high repayment risks and administration costs. Yunus set up the Grameen Bank (or 'Village Bank') for this very purpose, believing that the poor would repay the borrowed money given the chance. The success of his venture proved that 'microcredit' could be a viable business model. Not only was the bank commercially viable, but the social impact has been so great worldwide with the model copied in hundreds of countries that Yunis and his bank were awarded the Nobel Peace prize in 2006.

Source: http://www.grameen-info.org/

5.2.3 Social Enterprises

Many, but not all, social entrepreneurs create a 'social enterprise': that is 'a business with primarily social objectives whose surpluses are principally re-invested for that purpose in the business or in the community, rather than being driven by the need to maximise profit for shareholders and owners' (Department for Trade and Industry, 2005). This means that a social enterprise creates value of a non-financial kind, for example by regenerating local neighbourhoods, delivering public services such as healthcare, or providing employment to those disadvantaged by traditional job markets. The development of the green agenda has given social enterprise a new impetus as many have developed with aims to protect the environment. This has given rise to the 'triple bottom line' of social enterprise in which the three aims of profit, social good and environmental sustainability all feature.

Examples of social and green enterprises

- **Greyston Bakery** was founded by a Zen Bhuddist meditation group led by Bernard Glassman, in the Bronx, New York. It produces deserts and ice creams, including brownies for Ben & Jerry's ice cream. All profits go to the Greyston Foundation that supports local community projects including childcare. Their moto is: 'Do Goodies'.

- **Dayodaya Ethical Group (DEG)**, a cooperative organisation that works for animal rights in India, providing shelter to over 30,000 elderly cows, generating revenue by selling milk and producing bio-gas.

Township Trades in action in South Africa

- **Township Trades**, a not-for-profit business in South Africa where young adults, most of whom have lost parents to HIV/AIDS, can make soap that is sold at local markets. The business, based in the Khayelitsha township on the outskirts of Cape Town employs 16 locals who are trained to make soap from natural ingredients, which is then sold at market stalls.

- **Divine Chocolate** is a Fairtrade company that is co-owned by the cocoa farmers cooperative Kuapa Kokoo in Ghana. In order to increase their market share, the farmers' cooperative combined with other companies and institutions to manufacture and market their own range of chocolate bars – Divine. It now has sales of £11 million from its range of 25 products.

■ *Green-Works* is a recycling organisation that collects unwanted office furniture from businesses and redistributes it to schools, charities and community groups. The company achieves zero landfill, creates jobs for disadvantaged people and helps businesses to fulfil their corporate social responsibility (CSR) commitments. The company started with grants, but now generates 96 per cent of its own income, through fees charged to members for the collection and removal of their furniture, and the revenue received from the sale of the furniture (at 50 per cent of trade prices).

Social enterprises take on a number of different legal identities and business models, as illustrated in the examples of social and green enterprises. Some are for-profit companies that re-invest their surplus into foundations (e.g. Greyson Bakery). Others have a specific social purpose supported by income from a traditional activity (e.g. Township Trades). Others are cooperatives that are owned by their workers or suppliers (e.g. Divine Chocolate). Some develop both green and social agendas (e.g. Dayoda Ethical Group and Green Works).

Social enterprise has been a growth sector recently. In the UK, there are some 55,000 social enterprises, 5 per cent of all businesses with employees, with a combined turnover of £27 billion (Small Business Service, 2006). The UK has also developed a new legal form called the Community Interest Company (CIC), designed specifically for those wishing to operate for the benefit of the community rather than for the benefit of the owners of the company. This means that a CIC cannot be formed or used solely for the personal gain of a particular person, or group of people.[2]

The growth of the sector has led to the formation of national bodies in a number of countries to oversee and encourage social enterrpise.[3] In fact a number of social enterprises have formed to help others develop social enterprises including the School for Social Enterprise (SSE)[4] in the UK and Australia.

SIFE (Students in Free Enterprise) — a head for business, a heart for the world

SIFE is an international organisation that mobilises university students around the world to make a difference in their communities while developing the skills to become socially responsible business leaders. The students, guided by university and business advisers, form a student-led SIFE team to develop sustainable projects which create economic opportunity for others. Students take what they are learning in their classrooms about business and use it to solve real-world problems for real people. Business executives support the programme through corporate donations, personal contributions and the gift of their time.

The students are led by faculty advisers who challenge them to develop projects that specifically meet the unique needs of their communities. Their efforts help arising entrepreneurs, struggling business owners, low-income families and children experience success.

The SIFE programme concentrates on five areas: market economics, success skills, entrepreneurship, financial literacy and business ethics. Some examples include:

■ A team from the Technical University in Dreseden Germany helped to improve the marketing of a bike shop that had a workshop employing mentally disabled individuals.

■ The Unified Teaching Centre of Teresina in Brazil worked with a group of disadvantaged women to develop a handmade chocolate candies business.

> ■ The Beevelop programme helped families in Ghana establish beekeeping businesses, facilitated by students from the University of Nottingham.
>
> SIFE teams present the results of their community projects annually at regional, national and international competitions. Through SIFE, university students improve their community and experience profound personal growth.

5

5.3   PUBLIC SECTOR ENTREPRENEURSHIP

Public sector organisations are usually large[5] and exist to meet the needs of society rather than make a profit, so they take on many of the characteristics of corporate and social entrepreneurship. However they are owned by the state or general public and so have distinctive entrepreneurial characteristics and challenges.

5.3.1 The Need for Entrepreneurship in the Public Sector

Public sector organisations need to be innovative and entrepreneurial if they are to deliver high-quality services in a fast-changing environment (Kirby, 2003). The introduction of market forces into the public sector in many countries encouraged more entrepreneurial approaches in the delivery of services. Services such as education and health operate in environments that benefit from entrepreneurial activity:

- **Creativity and innovation** – health services are struggling from the combined effects of an ageing population, finite funding and the rapidly increasing costs of modern medicine. Innovative approaches are needed to deliver cost effective, sustainable health services available to all. Some governments have looked to the participation of the private sector to deliver this in private public partnerships (PPP).[6]

- **Resource acquisition** – state schools often struggle to find all the resources (books, sports facilities, musical instruments etc) they need so that the role of school managers in identifying and acquiring those resources at minimal cost is often crucial.

- **Networking** – many state educational establishments from nurseries to universities operate in competitive markets in which pupils and parents have an element of choice over which one to attend. The networking skills of teachers, academics and managers is particularly influential in this process because the recommendation of others is a key factor in the final decision (Stokes, 2002).

- **Small enterprise development** – although public sector institutions tend to be very large organisations in aggregate, some of the parts are small units. The budgets and staffing levels of a typical primary school are similar to many small businesses. Headteachers and small business owners share many common issues as a result (Stokes, 2002).

- **Risk taking** – taking risks is something not normally associated with public services and certainly in the delivery of many health and social services there are important procedures for the avoidance of risk in order to protect the well-being of end users. However the introduction of new services or better ways of delivering existing services, involves risk in terms of finding out what does and does not work. The public sector has become adept in piloting innovation at minimal risk to the end user and the public purse.

An entrepreneurial bureaucracy?

Bureaucracy or 'rule by office' may have had origins in Confusianism which has permeated Chinese life for centuries and includes compliance with authority as one of its guiding principles. It is often contrasted to entrepreneurship as bureaucracy provides structures, stability and specialisation whereas entrepreneurship tends to destabilise and operate outside of established organisational structures. In modern China, however, the bureaucracy has been supporting entrepreneurial ventures. Local government has played a significant role in encouraging Township and Village Enterprises (TVEs) which have been significant contributors to the growth of the Chinese economy and entrepreneurship.

5.3.2 Barriers to Entrepreneurship in the Public Sector

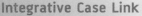
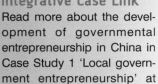

Integrative Case Link
Read more about the development of governmental entrepreneurship in China in Case Study 1 'Local government entrepreneurship' at the end of Part 1.

Despite the need for innovation and entrepreneurship in the delivery of publicly owned services, specific barriers and issues arise because of the distinctive nature of the public sector environment:

Restricted Markets Public services exist in markets subject to ongoing regulation and direction from one or more source, which restrict the freedom of action of potential entrepreneurs or intrapreneurs. For example, the educational programme delivered by schools is subject to the demands of a national curriculum that prescribes much of what happens in the classroom. Some public services are restrained from competing with the private sector on the grounds of preventing 'nationalisation by the backdoor' (Common *et al.*, 1993). However, market conditions of perfect competition rarely, if ever, exist even in the private sector.[7] Restricted markets may limit market entry by new competitors and therefore restrict the number of opportunities for entrepreneurial development in the public sector, but entrepreneurs are adept at using whatever environment exists to pursue new opportunities.

Multiple Constituencies Entrepreneurs who wish to innovate in the public sector will often find that progress is impeded by the complexities of the market relationships. More than one group of people can lay claim to being the 'customer' of public services because of the separation between those who pay for the service, those who choose it and those who use it. In education there is a clear split between those who ultimately pay for the service (taxpayers), agencies that control the purse-strings (central or local government bodies), people who decide the parameters of a service (education service, inspectors, teachers, governors), those who decide which particular institution to attend (perhaps a mixture of parents and pupils) and those who directly receive the service (pupils). Entrepreneurs have to address the needs of multiple groups such as these, often with conflicting interests, if they wish to develop an idea which is accepted in the public sector marketplace.

Open Access Entrepreneurs are adept at seeking opportunities in market niches, or highly targeted groups of customers with specialist needs. In principle, most public services are available to all and have to take account of the needs of a very diverse range of people. The opportunities for intrapreneurs within a public service to target services on niche segments of users may therefore be limited: health authorities have a responsibility to provide services ranging from emergency admissions to maternity care; the police and fire services have a duty to protect all citizens irrespective of location and socio-economic group.

Public Service Ethos The need for public services has been explained in terms of the need to atone for the failure of market forces to safeguard the public good by providing welfare to those disadvantaged by the interactions of the marketplace (Isaac-Henry *et al.*, 1993). This notion that a benevolent public realm is needed to compensate for the excesses of the private domain does not sit easily with the encouragement of entrepreneurial practices that are most commonly associated with the private sector. Some public sector managers resist entrepreneurship on the basis that it represents concepts which are alien to the ethos of their service.

Public Accountability and Scrutiny   Public services are overseen and scrutinised by the public or their political representatives in a way that does not exist in private sector entrepreneurial enterprises which are typically controlled by one person.[8] The speed and adaptability with which an entrepreneur can act can be severely restricted as a result. This can reduce initiatives in the public sector to cautious and inflexible activities in contrast to the creative, opportunistic processes typical in different entrepreneurial contexts.

Entrepreneurial headteachers

The Education Reform Act of 1988 gave headteachers in the UK considerably more autonomy in running all aspects of their schools. They were allocated a budget dependent largely on how many pupils attended their school, and they could decide how they spent the money providing they followed the stipulations of a new National Curriculum. For the first time, they had sufficient freedom to act entrepreneurially. Some seized this opportunity enthusiastically to raise more money by, for example, hiring out the school premises for community uses or seeking private sector sponsorship. A significant area for entrepreneurial activity was in pupil recruitment as a school's viability could be threatened by changes in levels of demand. Although some schools did adopt more traditional ways of advertising with glossy brochures and PR, there is evidence that many headteachers used entrepreneurial marketing methods to attract pupils (Stokes, 2002). Experienced headteachers knew that parents generally rely on word-of-mouth recommendations from other parents and friends in choosing a school. They therefore looked for ways of improving referrals and found that by developing deeper relationships with existing parents and involving them more in the life of the school, those parents would be more likely to recommend the school. This echoes the methods used by entrepreneurs running small businesses who rely extensively on recommendations to gain new customers and who use involvement with their business on a non-commercial basis as a key way of generating more favourable word-of-mouth communications. (*See Chapter 11 for more information on entrepreneurial marketing.*)

5.4   REGIONAL AND INTERNATIONAL COMMUNITIES OF ENTREPRENEURSHIP

So far, we have identified that entrepreneurship can develop in a variety of organisations with different aims and motives including large corporations, social enterprises and public services. The opportunities and challenges faced by the entrepreneur are strongly influenced by the nature of these varying contexts. A further important contextual influence is that of geography – where the entrepreneurial process takes place, the geographic reach of the enterprise and the cultural backgrounds of those that undertake it.

5.4.1   Clusters and Districts

In Chapter 3 we discussed how innovation is related to the size of the enterprise and that smaller units enjoy certain advantages in nurturing creativity and developing innovative opportunities. Smaller enterprises also have disadvantages in competing with larger organisations that have more resources, market power and economies of scale to reduce costs. In order to retain the benefits of fast-moving, flexible enterprises whilst overcoming some of the problems that arise from a small-scale operation, some entrepreneurs operate in 'clusters' or 'industrial districts'.[9] These are groupings of enterprises, often operating in the same sector, that cooperate and collaborate with each other in order to compete more effectively. Usually they operate in close geographic proximity to enhance this collaborative way of doing business. Well-known clusters include Silicon Valley in Northern California, the Emilio-Romagna region of Italy, and the science-based cluster around Cambridge in the UK. In some respects, these clusters are the reverse image of large corporations that are trying to retain the benefits of smallness by breaking their operations down into semi-autonomous small business units. In the case of clusters, smaller enterprises try to gain the benefits that larger corporations enjoy of several units working together for a common cause.

Porter (1998) applied his well-known model of competitive advantage[10] to regions and nations and highlighted the role that geographic groupings can play in encouraging innovation and economic development. McCann (2006) summarised the advantages of such groupings as:

- **Tacit knowledge**   Where businesses exist side-by-side, owners and employees share information and knowledge that allows them to build up a more complete picture of the market and external environment than they would have on their own.

- **Shared inputs and services**   Some services may be available to a group that are not so readily accessible by individual firms. For example, the growth of Silicon Valley was facilitated by the emergence of a dedicated venture capital industry from the 1970s, encouraged by the successful flotation of one of the resident companies, Apple Computer, for $1.3 billion in December 1980. Costs for specialists may be shared between the cluster giving them access to specialist services that they could not have afforded individually.

- **Specialised labour pool**   The geographic proximity of similar companies creates a workforce with shared and complementary skills. This not only ensures that the relevant skill sets are available but also gives individual firms more flexibility in adjusting the labour force up and down according to fluctuations in demand.

The success of high-profile clusters particularly associated with hi-tech industries has lead to their idealisation as a model of best practice. This so-called 'flexible specialisation' model has been put forward as the optimal environment in which entrepreneurs can create and develop new ventures, replacing older industrial estates more suited to manufacturing-based industries. In practice there are many types of clusters which tend to be suited to the business environment in which they operate. McCann (2006) identifies three main types:

- **The pure agglomeration**: small enterprises that share a common geographic space with no underpinning rationale for being co-located (e.g. businesses in the same urban area).

- **The industrial complex**: traditional industrial estate clustering found in industries such as steel and chemicals where manufacturers and suppliers group together to generate economies of scale.

- **The social network**: trading relationships develop into deeper forms of alliance such as joint ventures, joint lobbying and reciprocal arrangements. Trust is the most important ingredient in these newer forms of clustering.

Each type forms a different local environment in which entrepreneurs operate and can deliver specific benefits. However, there is little evidence to suggest that one model is superior to others in delivering an ideal spatial context for entrepreneurship (Curran and Blackburn, 1994).

5.4.2 Internationalisation and Globalisation

Entrepreneurship can be practised at a local, regional, national or international level. The international context is particularly challenging as trading across national boundaries usually requires additional investment and management skills (Buckley, 2006). Export sales inevitably carry greater risk and an increase in debtors as payments are slower. The external knowledge of entrepreneurs is usually limited to their immediate trading environment with little scanning of global markets. These added burdens lead to a traditional pattern of incremental selling overseas in which internationalisation comes gradually in stages. Sometimes the first stage is a chance order from an overseas customer that leads to further business in that territory. As entrepreneurs make extensive use of word-of-mouth recommendations through existing networks, their ability to sell into customer groups outside of those networks is limited (see Chapter 11 on Entrepreneurial Marketing). The advantage of incremental internationalisation is that it limits risk and allows entrepreneurs to build their knowledge of overseas markets gradually.

Globalisation   This traditional model of the internationalisation process of SMEs has been challenged by some firms that go global simultaneously in one 'big bang'. This has been labeled as *globalisation* and contrasted to the traditional, gradual *internationalisation* model (Buckley, 2006).

Globalisation has the advantage of exploiting an international opportunity quickly before competitors have time to react. It is usually made possible when foreign markets have many similarities to the home market. Many markets have become homogenised around the world as global communication tools such as the Internet align the aspirations and purchasing habits of consumers. The conditions for successful globalisation are therefore more common.

This has encouraged some entrepreneurs to go *'global at birth'*. They have no preference for a 'home market' but intend to sell internationally from the start-up of the firm. Software firms are typical of this new breed of global start-ups. They often use relationships with larger firms to piggy back their products into global markets more rapidly (Coviello and Munro, 1997). The development of *e-commerce* in which a business is set up to trade over the Internet means that many more firms are now potentially multi-national at birth. Providing that the product or service can be paid for and delivered electronically, then international trading can start from day one.

WHEN THINGS GO WRONG

A wave of born global entrepreneurial ventures took place during the so-called 'dot-com' bubble of the 1990s. From specialised applications in the public sector and industry, the Internet quickly emerged as an international communications tool that could be used by all. Many new business ideas were conceived and launched to take advantage of the new technology.

Unfortunately many of these did not have a viable business model – they had not worked out how to actually make money from an Internet company. Despite their global reach and potential to overcome traditional international distribution barriers, they could not generate the cash to sustain their business once the initial investment had run dry. For example, Pets.com was launched in 1998 to sell pet supplies and accessories over the web. It rapidly proved to be a highly popular site with nearly 1 million hits per day drawn by extensive advertising and its trademark sock puppet with button eyes that captured the attention of the market. In 2000 it successfully went public on a major stock exchange (NASDAQ) but the company was forced to close within nine months of the flotation never having made a profit. Consumers decided that purchasing bulky pet items on the Internet made no sense at a time when the logistics of such an operation was in its infancy.

5.4.3 Immigrant and Ethnic Minority Entrepreneurship

An important driver towards the globalisation of entrepreneurship is that it has become an increasingly mobile process. Entrepreneurial activities probably exist in every society on earth, but some systems of government encourage entrepreneurs whilst others discourage and suppress them. Many entrepreneurs therefore travel to more favourable environments to practise what they know best. Others who have emigrated are pushed into entrepreneurial activities because alternative forms of work are not available. These immigrant and ethnic minority entrepreneurs form an important sub-set of entrepreneurship, not least because they are often highly influential people. For example, Nathan Rothschild is cited as the 'most successful entrepreneur in history' (Godley, 2006: 601). He was born in a Jewish ghetto of Germany before moving to Manchester where he became a dominant figure in the global financial markets of the Victorian era.

From the earliest times there has been a strong relationship between migration and entrepreneurship. Regional or national economies that are thriving attract entrepreneurs who have an eye for an opportunity, and the early rise of industrialisation in the UK attracted many immigrant entrepreneurs. Marc Brunel escaped from the stifling economic environment of revolutionary France to England via the US not only to develop innovative methods of manufacturing and tunnelling, but also to father one of the greatest engineering entrepreneurs, Isambard Brunel. Sometimes the immigration is of groups of people who are seeking a better life, or sometimes just survival. For example, in the late nineteenth century the British government in India encouraged some of the Indian population to go to East Africa to develop the railways and commerce there. They had a major impact on the Kenyan economy especially in areas such as banking, textiles and retailing. In 1972 President Idi Amin expelled them, many fleeing to the UK where they also had a disproportionate effect on business creation.

Ethnic minorities tend to have higher rates of entrepreneurship, as measured by self-employment, and are more likely to own a business. However the rates of entrepreneurship are not uniform amongst all ethnic groups: in the UK, Chinese and Pakistanis have a higher self-employment rate than Bangladeshis and Indians who in turn have higher rates than the Black African and Caribbean population, although this has begun to change (Ram, Barrett and Jones, 2002). The increasing trend to global entrepreneurship favours ethnic minorities who are more likely to have international networks to take advantage of trading across borders.

Basu (2006) summarised the factors that 'push' or 'pull' ethnic minorities into entrepreneurship as follows:

■ Discrimination in the labour market may push some into self-employment as the only option.

■ Cultural heritage and family influences may pull others into starting a business, although there is inconsistency in the evidence for this; for example the Indian population in Silicon Valley has displayed greater entrepreneurial potential than those with similar backgrounds in other countries including India itself.

■ 'Ethnic enclaves' offer trading opportunities for specialist goods and services specific to a minority population – for example types of food and clothes.

■ Access to ethnic resources such as relatively inexpensive labour, finance, information and advice from within the local community, and access to external ethnic networks internationally.

The growth of the economies of the places of origin of immigrant entrepreneurs, especially in Asia, has lead to a worldwide circulation of entrepreneurial talent as some see opportunities in their home countries and return (Saxenian, 2000).

5

Silicon Valley's immigrant entrepreneurs

Silicon Valley in California where the integrated circuit, the microprocessor and the microcomputer were born, is perhaps the best known cluster of hi-tech companies in the world. The development of the Stanford Industrial Park by Stanford University was one of the catalysts, home for example to Hewlett Packard in its early days. The growth of high-technology industries in Silicon Valley coincided with a change in US immigration policies that allowed significant new immigration into the region. Between 1975 and 1990, Silicon Valley's hi-tech companies created more than 150,000 technically skilled jobs of which 30 per cent were filled by immigrants, mostly engineers from China and India. The new immigrants proved highly entrepreneurial. Jerry Yang was born in Taiwan and moved to California when he was eight years old, knowing only one word of English (shoe). Whilst studying at Stanford University in 1994, he and Gerry Filo set up a web portal that acted as a directory of Internet websites. Originally called 'Gerry's Guide to the World Wide Web', it was renamed Yahoo! of which Yang was the CEO until 2009. Sabeer Bhatia lived in India until he went to study at Stanford University in 1989. From there he joined Apple after which he and Jack Smith created an email system called HoTMaiL (the uppercase letters spelling HTML, the language of the webpage). Launched as a free service in 1994, it attracted over 1 million subscribers in six months. These two well-known success stories are only the tip of the iceberg. Around 50 of the largest, publicly quoted technology companies in Silicon Valley were started by Chinese or Indian immigrants and nearly one-quarter of private companies are also run by immigrants (Saxenian, 2000). There is evidence that they retain and develop ties back home, strengthening trading relationships between Silicon Valley and China and India in particular. The economic and social effects of this mobile entrepreneurship is global not just regional.

Jerry Yang. Co-founder and former CEO of Yahoo!

5.5   SUMMARY AND ACTIVITIES

The context of entrepreneurship is not limited to private sector start-ups. It exists in many organisational and geographic contexts.

Corporate entrepreneurship or **intrapreneurship** describes a large company's efforts at renewal through innovation and new business development through business venturing. It uses entrepreneurial processes but it is restorative rather than developmental. Intrapreneurs aim to restore innovation and counter stagnation in an existing organisation, which often involves overcoming a corporate culture that resists change.

To support corporate entrepreneurship a number of conditions are necessary including: tolerance of failure, availability of resources for new initiatives, suitable reward systems and support from the top management. However, although the need for intrapreneurs is widely recognised, there is a belief that they are mavericks that cannot be left to their own devices, a notion reinforced by the collapse of important banking institutions through the activities of rogue dealers. A virtuous circle of corporate entrepreneurship is put forward in which the employment of entrepreneurial executives in a supportive culture leads to entrepreneurial behaviour and a reputation for innovation that attracts entrepreneurial employees, and so the circle begins again.

Social entrepreneurship is designed to add value to individuals and society. **Social entrepreneurs** emphasise the social responsibility of their ventures before the need to maximise profits, identifying a social problem (which may or may not also be a business opportunity) and using entrepreneurial processes to create solutions. **Social enterprises** are 'businesses with primarily social objectives whose surpluses are principally reinvested for that purpose in the business or in the community, rather than being driven by the need to maximise profit for shareholders and owners'.

Public sector entrepreneurship responds particularly to the need for innovation, resource acquisition, networking and intelligent risk taking in the public sector. However there are significant barriers including: restricted markets, multiple constituencies (or clients), the need for open access, the public service ethos and public accountability and scrutiny.

The **geographic reach** of entrepreneurship is a further important contextual factor. Many entrepreneurial ventures operate in **clusters** or **industrial districts** to overcome some of the disadvantages of smallness. **International trading** for entrepreneurial ventures is challenging so that most entrepreneurs operate at a local level. However, technological developments such as e-commerce and the homogenisation of markets has facilitated a more rapid **globalisation** of new ventures, some of which go '**global at birth**'.

Entrepreneurship is a mobile process so that **immigrant and ethnic minority entrepreneurs** are a significant contextual factor. Entrepreneurs migrate to seek opportunities and immigrant populations are sometimes forced into entrepreneurship as the only way of finding work. Ethnic minorities are more likely to own a business although the rates of entrepreneurship are not uniform amongst all ethnic groups. The increasing trend to global entrepreneurship favours ethnic minorities who are more likely to have international networks to take advantage of trading across borders.

REVIEW QUESTIONS

1 What is an intrapreneur? Why are they necessary?

2 How would you encourage the development of entrepreneurship in a large organisation?

3 What are the problems in developing an entrepreneurial culture in a large organisation?

4 What is a social enterprise?

5 Name four different ways or business models that facilitate social objectives in an enterprise.

6 Why is entrepreneurship needed in the public sector?

7 What are the barriers to the development of an entrepreneurial culture in a publicly owned enterprise?

8 What are the advantages of enterprises operating in clusters or local communities?

9 What has made the globalisation of a new venture easier?

10 Why do ethnic minority groups tend to have higher rates of entrepreneurship?

5

'Without entrepreneurs, there would be no businesses. But if we always put entrepreneurs in charge, there wouldn't be so many businesses left either'.

Discuss this assertion in light of the international banking crisis that developed from 2008.

Preview case continued

The Maverick who turned his company upside down

When Ricardo Semler joined his father's business, Semco, in Sao Paulo, Brazil fresh from Harvard Business School, he tried hard to fit in. He bought a corporate suit and tie and moved into the office next to his father's. Tensions soon emerged between father and son as Ricardo found it hard to accept the traditional hierarchical lines on which the company was run. It was a difficult time for the company as the national economy moved into recession and the shipbuilding industry that Semco supplied with marine pumps was one of the hardest-hit sectors. When Ricardo threatened to leave, his father made a brave decision and handed control over to his inexperienced 21-year-old son. He took control by firing 60 per cent of Semco's top management and installing a new CEO. He dragged the company back from the brink of bankruptcy and made acquisitions to diversify the business away from its dependency on the declining ship building industry. But although he improved the company's performance and business processes, he did not change its style as a disciplined, hard-driven company run by aggressive managers armed with innumerable statistics.

This required him to work at a frenetic pace to maintain control by overseeing all aspects. When at the age of 25, he was diagnosed with very high levels of stress, he decided he had to make a complete change in the way that he and his employees worked. He began by considering his own quality of life and time-management, moving on from there to a complete redefinition of how he and his business would work.

Over several years he evolved innovative forms of business processes and management styles that aimed to introduce democracy into the workplace, believing that placing more trust in all employees would improve productivity and decision-making in the organisation. He effectively stood the business on its head by giving power to all and taking it away from top management. His innovative way of running a corporation has been guided by six principles:

1 *Forget about the top line*. Growth in sales for the sake of it, is misguided. Semco's focus is on generating sufficient cash and profits to survive and develop as they wish.

2 *Never stop being a start-up*. People working in small units can know and trust each other. Once a Semco business unit employs 150 people it is split in two, even if economies of scale are against such a move initially. Every six months each unit has to redefine its purpose, asking the question: 'if we didn't exist today, would we want to set it up?'

3 *Don't be a nanny*. Semler decided to treat his employees as adults, claiming that 'once they walk through the plant gates, companies transform them into children, forcing them to wear identification badges, stand in line for lunch,…and blindly follow instructions without asking any instructions'. Even

▶

though the unions objected, he abolished searches of people leaving the factories and replaced clocking-in with self-completed time cards. Factory committees elected from all levels are empowered to question all aspects of management and audit the books. Flexi-time has been extended even to factory workers. For major decisions, everyone is given a say. In order to relocate a factory, they showed all the workers possible new sites and then took a vote.

4 *Let talent find its place.* Semco allows employees to chose which project they work on, provided that can persuade the existing group that they can contribute. When a vacancy arises, a Semco employee who meets 70 per cent of the requirements is given preferential consideration over an outsider.

5 *Make decisions quickly and openly.* Semler changed the old 12 reporting levels arranged in a hierarchical pyramid into just three levels based on concentric circles. All employees have one of only four titles:
- Councillors who coordinate strategy;
- Partners who run business units;
- Coordinators who act as a first level of functional management in marketing, sales, production and engineering; and
- Associates – everybody else.

6 *Partner promiscuously.* Instead of doing business with outsiders, Semco helps their own employees to set up their own companies, leasing them equipment at favourable rates and offering business training. When Semco employees heard that their customers were complaining about the high costs charged by companies to maintain the cooling towers that Semco sold, they set up a new business themselves to service the towers. Another group of employees have set up a business to manage inventories using the Internet.

Democracy is the cornerstone of the Semco system. There is no organisation chart nor a human resources department. The business is based on trust and delegation which in turn generates peer-pressure and self-discipline to make it all work. Expansion has come from new ventures suggested by employees and a research group, the 'Nucleus of Technological Innovation' that is free of other responsibilities to invent new products or to improve processes and market strategies.

The most interesting point about this radical system is that it works. When Semler took over in 1982, the company employed 90 workers; now it has over 3000. Sales have increased from $4 million to $200 million. Perhaps a greater testament is how the company reacted in times of trouble. It is easier to set up experimental business models in good times, but they are severely tested when the economic climate changes. It happened in Brazil when President Fernando Collor de Mello imposed draconian restrictions on borrowing to counter hyper-inflation. Semco was in severe difficulties, and it was the workforce who came up with the solution. They offered to take a wage cut of 40 per cent provided that it applied to everyone including the managers, and they could increase their profit share to 39 per cent. The crisis gave employees a greater insight into the operations of the business so they were able to make improvements such as reducing the inventory by 65 per cent.

Ricardo Semler is now branching out into other ventures including the building of an eco-tourist resort. Naturally, the local inhabitants are deciding the design and participating in the building works.

Questions

1 *Although Semler claims his business has survived and thrived because of workplace democracy, few other organisations have followed his radical measures. Why is this?*

2 *Semler has said that: 'Rather than force our people to expand a business beyond its natural limits, we encourage them to start new businesses.' This implies that large*

▶

organisations cannot be entrepreneurial and innovative unless they are divided into a series of smaller units. Do you agree with this?

3 *Semco has an entrepreneurial business philosophy of giving people the freedom to do what they want, on the basis that their*

successes will outnumber their failures. Would it not be better to introduce systems to eliminate the failures? If not, why not?

4 *In what sense is Semco a social enterprise?*

© The Financial Times, 15 July 2009

5.6   NOTES, REFERENCES AND FURTHER READING

Notes and Further Information

1. Semler, R. (1993) *Maverick! The Success Behind the World's Most Unusual Workplace*, London: Century Random House. Ricardo Semler has also written *The Seven-Day Weekend: Changing the Way that Work Works*, Portfolio, 2004.

2. For a CIC, legislation caps the level of dividends payable at 35 per cent of profits and returns to individuals are capped at 4 per cent above the bank base rate. A CIC cannot be formed to support political activities and a company that is a charity cannot be a CIC, unless it gives up its charitable status. However, a charity may apply to register a CIC as a subsidiary company.

3. The national body for the social enterprise movement in Britain is the Social Enterprise Coalition (SEC) and this liaises with similar groups in the regions. In the USA there is the Social Enterprise Alliance (http://www.se-alliance.org). In Canada the Canadian Social Entrepreneurship Foundation (www.csef.ca) exists to develop education, mentoring, networking and resourcing in the field.

4. The School for Social Enterprise (SSE at http://www.sse.org.uk) 'exists to provide training and opportunities to enable people to use their creative and entreprenurial abilities more fully for social benefit'. It was founded in 1997 by social entrepreneur Michael Young who had previously launched the Consumer Association and the Open University. The SSE is supporting the establishment of local schools in the UK and since 2008 in Australia.

5. For example the National Health Service of the UK is the largest employer in Europe with nearly 100,000 employees.

6. A public–private partnership (PPP or P^3) is a government service or private business venture which is funded and operated through a partnership of government and one or more private sector enterprises. For example the International AIDS Vaccine Initiative was set up in 1996 to accelerate the development of a vaccine to prevent HIV infection. It is funded by governments and major private sector companies.

7. The economic condition of 'perfect competition' has five requirements:

   • The commodity must be supplied in sufficient quantity of similar units so that buyers can shift swiftly from one seller to another;

   • The market must be sufficiently organised and informed so that every unit sold at the same time is sold at the same price;

   • Sellers must be numerous and have a small market share; likewise buyers must be numerous and buy small percentages of total output;

   • Buyers and sellers must be independent and subject to neither public controls, nor private agreements;

   • The market price rises and falls in response to the changing conditions of supply and demand.

   Any serious departure from these conditions results in 'imperfect competition', which is the reality in most marketplaces. For example, an 'oligopoly' exists if sellers are few in number, as is the case for most mature, manufactured consumer products (e.g. motor cars). An 'oligopsony' exists if there are relatively few buyers, which is the situation in several important industrial markets (e.g. the aerospace market).

8. For example, even a very small school in the UK is legally required to appoint at least eight governors in contrast to equivalent-sized private sector enterprises which are controlled typically by one owner-manager.

9. See also Chapter 4 subsection 4.5.5 'Entrepreneurship in Italy' that gives more detail of Italy's industrial districts.

10. Porter's five forces model of competition analyses the structural forces in an industry that determine the competitive environment. These forces are: the power of buyers; the power of suppliers; the potential for new entry; the potential for substitutes; and the intensity of existing rivalry within the industry.

References

Basu, A. (2006) Ethnic minority entrepreneurship, in Casson, M. *et al.* (eds) *The Oxford Handbook of Entrepreneurship*, Oxford: Oxford University Press, pp. 580–600.

Buckley, P.J. (2006) International expansion: Foreign direct investment by small and medium-sized enterprises, in Casson, M. *et al.* (eds) *The Oxford Handbook of Entrepreneurship*, Oxford: Oxford University Press, pp. 671–693.

Burns, P. (2008) *Corporate Entrepreneurship*, 2nd edition, Basingstoke: Palgrave Macmillan.

Common, R., Flynn, N. and Mellon, E. (1993) *Managing Public Services: Competition and Decentralisation*, Oxford: Butterworth-Heinemann.

Coviello, N. and Munro H. (1997) Network relationships and the internationalisation process of small software firms, *International Business Review*, 6 (4): 361–386.

Curran, J. and Blackburn, R.A. (1994) *Small Business and Local Economic Networks*, London: PCP.

Department for Trade and Industry (2005) *Social Enterprise: a Strategy for Success,* London: DTI.

Gautam, V. and Verma, V. (1997) Corporate entrepreneurship: Changing perspectives, *The Journal of Entrepreneurship*, 6 (2).

Godley, A. (2006) Migration of entrepreneurs, in Casson, M. *et al.* (eds) *The Oxford Handbook of Entrepreneurship*, Oxford: Oxford University Press, pp. 601–610.

Hisrich, R.D. and Peters, M.P. (1995) *Entrepreneurship: Starting, Developing and Managing a New Enterprise,* third edition, Chicago: Irwin.

Isaac-Henry, K., Painter, C. and Barnes, C. (1993) *Management in the Public Sector*, London: Chapman and Hall.

Johnstone, H. and Basso, G. (1999) Social Entrepreneurs and Community Development, *Proceedings of the Atlantic Schools of Business Conference*, Halifax, Nova Scotia.

Kirby, D. (2003) *Entrepreneurship*, London: McGraw-Hill Education.

Leadbetter, C. (1997) *The Rise of the Social Entrepreneur*, London: Demos.

Lucas, W.A. and Cooper, S.Y. (2004) *Enhancing Self-efficacy to Enable Entrepreneurship: The Case of CMI's Connections*, MIT Sloan Working Paper No. 4489–04, May, MIT Sloan School of Management.

Macrae, N. (1976) The coming of the entrepreneurial revolution: A survey, *The Economist*, 25 December, p. 42.

Marvel, M.R., Griffin, A., Hebda, J. and Vojak, B. (2007) Examining the technical corporate entrepreneurs' motivation: Voices from the field, *Entrepreneurship Theory and Practice,* 31 (5): 753–768.

McCann, P. (2006) Regional development: Clusters and districts, in Casson, M. *et al.* (eds) *The Oxford Handbook of Entrepreneurship*, Oxford: Oxford University Press, pp. 671–693.

Morris, M.H. and Kuratko, D.F. (2002) *Corporate Entrepreneurship,* New York: Harcourt College Publishers.

Pedler, M. (1996) *Action Learning for Managers*, London: Lemos and Crane.

Pedler, M., Burgoyne, J.G. and Boydell, T. (1991) *The Learning Company: A Strategy for Sustainable Development*, London: McGraw-Hill.

Porter, M. (1998) Clusters and the economics of competition, *Harvard Business Review*, 76 (6): 77–90.

Ram, M., Barrett, G. and Jones, T. (2002) Ethnicity and entrepreneurship, in Carter, S. and Jones-Evans, D. (eds) *Enterprise and Small Business: Principles, Practice and Policy*, 2nd Edition, Harlow, Essex: Pearson Education.

Ramachandran, K., Devarajan, T.P. and Ray, S. (2006) Corporate entrepreneurship: How? *Working Papers Series, Indian School of Business* (http://www.isb.edu/faculty/Working Papers pdfs/Corporate Entrepreneurship.pdf).

Rieple, A. and Vyakarnam, S. (1994) Corporate entrepreneurship: A review, *The Journal of Entrepreneurship*, 3 (1):1–20.

Saxenian, A. (2000) *Silicon Valley's New Immigrant Workers*, Working Paper 15, May, The Center for Comparative Immigrant Studies, University of California, San Diego.

5

Schumpeter, J.A. (1934) *The Theory of Economic Development*, Cambridge, MA: Harvard University Press.

Small Business Service (2006) *Annual Survey of Small Businesses: UK 2005*, URN 06/389a, Brighton: Institute for Employment Studies.

Stokes D.R. (2002) Entrepreneurial marketing in the public sector: The lessons of head teachers as entrepreneurs, *Journal of Marketing Management*, 18 (3–4): 397–414.

Stokes, D.R. and Blackburn, R.A. (2002) Learning the hard way: The lessons of owner-managers who have closed their businesses, *Journal of Small Business and Enterprise Development*, Spring, 9 (1): 17–27.

Wilson, N., Stokes, D. and Athayde, R. (2009) *Entrepreneurs in the Corporate Workplace, A Report to Cripp Sears*, March, Kingston University Entrepreneurship Centre, Kingston upon Thames.

Recommended Further Reading

Burns, P. (2008) *Corporate Entrepreneurship*, 2nd edition, Basingstoke: Palgrave Macmillan.

Basu, A. (2006) Ethnic minority entrepreneurship, in Casson, M. *et al.* (eds) *The Oxford Handbook of Entrepreneurship*, Oxford: Oxford University Press, pp. 580–600.

Leadbetter, C. (1997) *The Rise of the Social Entrepreneur*, London: Demos.

Porter, M. (1998) Clusters and the economics of competition, *Harvard Business Review*, 76 (6): 77–90.

Ram, M., Barrett, G. and Jones, T. (2002) Ethnicity and entrepreneurship, in Carter, S. and Jones-Evans, D. (eds) *Enterprise and Small Business: Principles, Practice and Policy*, 2nd Edition, Harlow, Essex: Pearson Education.

CHAPTER 6

The Life Cycle of Entrepreneurship

LEARNING OBJECTIVES

After studying this chapter, the reader will be able to:

- Identify the phases in the development of an entrepreneurial venture from creation to closure
- Analyse the reasons for the high growth of some entrepreneurial ventures
- Analyse the reasons for business closure
- Understand what happens to an enterprise that closes
- Understand what happens to entrepreneurs who close a business
- Appreciate the nature of serial entrepreneurship.

INTRODUCTION

Entrepreneurship is closely associated with new venture creation, one of its key properties identified in Chapters 1 and 2. The idea of entrepreneurship as the 'identification, evaluation and exploitation of an opportunity', itself suggests a focus on the early stages of setting up a new enterprise. Much of the research and literature in entrepreneurship concentrates on this creative and developmental period of entrepreneurial activity. However, the entrepreneurship process encompasses the complete life-span of an enterprise and the career of an entrepreneur. Entrepreneurial ventures mimic the pattern of life on earth in that there is a beginning and there is an end. Businesses open and sooner or later they close. The only question is how long they will survive – at least in their current form. Therefore it is important to consider phases other than the start-up of an entrepreneurial venture, including its closure.

Similarly, individuals undertake entrepreneurial ventures at different stages of their lives and careers. There is also a cycle of entrepreneurship that relates to what the entrepreneur is doing – which may not coincide with what is happening to the enterprise. At one extreme, an enterprise may be thriving but the founding entrepreneur may wish to leave it for a variety of possible reasons; at the other end of the spectrum, the business may fail and close but the founder remains an entrepreneur by starting a new venture. This chapter investigates what typically happens to an enterprise as it develops and declines and also to the entrepreneur as they enter into and exit from an enterprise.

6

PREVIEW CASE

The successful entrepreneur who studied failure

Christopher Fogg addressed a group of students who were eager to learn from this successful portfolio entrepreneur. Not only had he developed and run his own businesses, he had helped countless others through his enterprise incubators.[1] To the students' surprise, Fogg began by claiming that he had had a string of business failures and that he wanted to talk about these rather than his success stories. He went on to describe ten business ventures he had been involved in that had not achieved their objectives and had closed down. These ranged from Chinese bicycles to 'ball ponds' for children and the sale of used aircraft.

Many entrepreneurs seem keen to talk about their successes. Why do you think Christopher Fogg wanted to talk first about his failures rather than invite the students to emulate his success? Do you think he is unusual in having been involved in several ventures, many of which have not worked out?

(Find out what he said in the case study 'Fogg's Failures' at the end of the chapter.)

Christopher Fogg, a portfolio entrepreneur

6.1   THE LIFE CYCLES OF AN ENTERPRISE

6.1.1 Life Cycle Models

Entrepreneurial ventures evolve over time through various stages from start-up, development and growth through to decline and closure. The enterprise changes its characteristics in each of these stages in a way that often requires different skills, structures and resources to manage them. A number of models – or ways of categorising and predicting these characteristics – have been put forward in order to conceptualise the life cycle of an enterprise from start to finish.

Greiner (1972) developed an early model of evolution and revolution in the growth of an organisation (see Figure 6-1). Greiner proposed that an organisation evolved through various stages but that movement from one stage to another was precipitated by a crisis that led to more revolutionary change. If the firm managed its way through this period it progressed to the next stage. For example, the first stage of 'growth through creativity' leads to a 'crisis of leadership'; once this is resolved the next stage of 'growth through direction' begins. By the fifth stage, a more collaborative management approach emphasises teamwork and matrix style organisational structures, but Greiner was unable to predict what crisis might precipitate the move into yet another phase.

Other models follow Greiner's five-stage approach but with different descriptors for each of the stages. Churchill and Lewis (1983) identified the stages of: existence; survival, success, take-off and maturity. Scott and Bruce (1987) described the five stages as: inception, survival, growth, expansion and maturity. In each of these stages, they suggest that the role of the top manager, the style of management and the organisational structure will change accordingly. Thus the management role moves from 'direct supervision' in stage 1 to 'decentralisation' by stage 5. The organisational structure evolves from 'unstructured' in stage 1 to 'decentralised' by stage 5. In the first stage of 'inception' the management style is assumed to be

FIGURE 6-1	**Greiner's model of organisational growth**

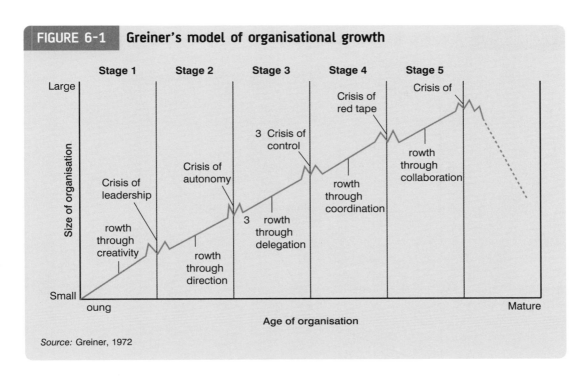

Source: Greiner, 1972

'entrepreneurial, individualistic'. By the fourth stage of 'expansion' this has changed to 'professional, administrative' and by the final fifth stage of 'maturity' the style has become that of 'watchdog'.

A common feature of these models is that they describe the management style of the entrepreneur and the key functional activities in each phase of development. A composite model by Stokes and Wilson (2006) described the five stages, shown in Figure 6-2, as follows:

- **Stage 1: Concept/test**

  Before a business is launched, it undergoes some form of conception and planning. This may involve a market test or running the business as a part-time operation, before the owner places complete dependence on it. Creative thinking, information gathering and networking are key activities in this stage.

- **Stage 2: Development/abort stage**

  The business is launched and either develops to a viable size, or it is aborted at an early stage. This will depend critically on whether sufficient customers in the marketplace adopt the product or service on offer, hence marketing linked to cash flow management are often the key functional activities. Typically an individual entrepreneur manages the enterprise in this stage largely through their own efforts. This is a particularly vulnerable stage for a business as statistics indicate that it is the smallest and youngest firms that have the highest rates of closure (more on this below in section 6.3).

- **Stage 3: Growth/decline stage**

  Some enterprises that have developed into a viable entity in the marketplace continue their growth quickly or, in some cases, more steadily. Such growth may place strains on the internal structure of the enterprise. The management of internal processes and people are often the critical functions. The one-person entrepreneurial management style may prove inadequate to fully sustain growth. A division of managerial tasks, the recruitment of non-owner-managers and the development of a functionally organised team are often prerequisites to take a business through this phase, without which it may struggle and close.

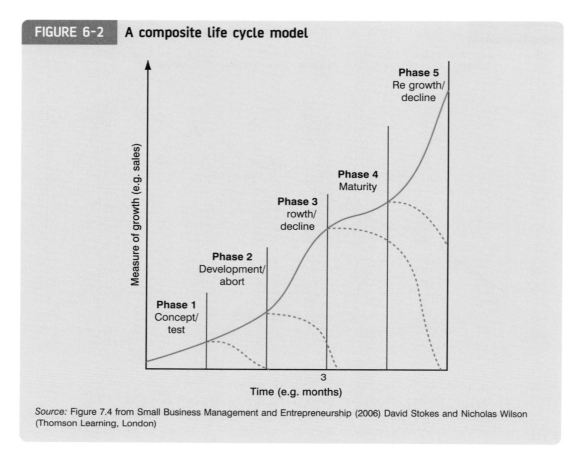

FIGURE 6-2   A composite life cycle model

Source: Figure 7.4 from Small Business Management and Entrepreneurship (2006) David Stokes and Nicholas Wilson (Thomson Learning, London)

■ **Stage 4: Maturity**

Most surviving business go through a period of stability, when growth flattens and the enterprise matures. It may at this stage lose its simple structure of centralised decision-making, use more sophisticated business processes and become more bureaucratic in its procedures. In other words, it takes on some of the characteristics of a larger organisation.

■ **Stage 5: Re-growth/decline**

Once an enterprise has established itself in the marketplace with a competitive advantage over its rivals, profits or external investment may be available to exploit further the successful business model. The so-called 's-curve hypothesis' suggests that such investment may trigger a second period of growth. Without this further period of growth, the maturity stage can turn into stagnation and decline, as competition intensifies from existing rivals or new entrants into the market.

6.1.2 Limitations of Life Cycle Models

Several commentators (Storey, 1994; Deakins, 1996) have pointed out that such stage models have considerable limitations as *predictors* of enterprise development and growth:

■ Growth is rarely as smooth as the curve of the graph suggests. It is more likely to represent spikes of growth and contraction rather than rounded peaks. For example many small businesses have relatively few customers, so that the addition of one new significant client will lead to a sudden growth spurt. Conversely, the loss of one large client can significantly shrink the size of the business.

■ The transition from one stage to another does not necessarily take place in the order predicted by the model. Economic or trade cycles outside the control of the firm may contribute substantially to the growth or decline of an enterprise at any time irrespective of the stage of development. The economic downturn of 2008/9 forced a large number of businesses to decline in size, whatever stage in their development they had reached.

■ The contention that the transition from one stage to the next is triggered by a particular kind of crisis has not been tested through empirical research. The development of an enterprise is likely to be subject to many different internal and external variables so that isolating one primary cause for the evolution of a firm from one stage to another is an over-simplification of a very complex process.

■ Many enterprises reach a stable size and never make the transition out of this phase. Once they have developed a business to a stage of survival, life-style entrepreneurs will have little motivation to grow it further. Some take deliberate steps to avoid growth which they see as threatening the very independence they sought when they created the enterprise (Stokes and Wilson, 2006).

The economic life cycles of nations

The economies of nation states exhibit cyclical phases like the many enterprises that make them up.[2] The competitiveness of one nation compared to others changes over time, sometimes gradually, sometimes more rapidly. National economies go through phases of evolution and revolution, just as the enterprises in Greiner's life cycle model develop gradually until a crisis precipitates more fundamental change.

The graph in Figure 6-3 shows the share of worldwide production of leading industrial nations from 1870 to 1938, a crucial period in the formation of modern states that began with the unification of Germany and ended with the Second World War. Industrialisation and the creation of modern capitalism has taken place in phases of development that have favoured different countries at different times. Great Britain led the first industrial revolution in which the traditional energy reliant on humans and animals was replaced by new sources of power derived from steam and coal. Visionary entrepreneurs such as Stephenson and Brunel created the transport and communication infrastructure of a commercial empire that represented 32 per cent of the world's output in 1870.

By then the advantages of being the first industrialised state were already slipping away. A second industrial revolution was underway that used new forms of power based on electricity and the internal combustion engine and new materials such as rayon and plastics. Entrepreneurs in the US such as Henry Ford and E.I. du Pont laid the foundations of an industrial nation that controlled over 40 per cent of the world's production by 1929.

FIGURE 6-3 **World's industrial production: percentage by country 1870–1938**

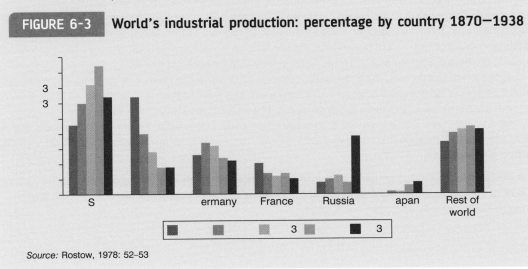

Source: Rostow, 1978: 52–53

When Germany became a unified state in 1871, it changed the economic balance of Europe and the world. By 1900 it had become a major economic force with 17 per cent of the global industrial production, challenging the UK's position and well ahead of its continental rivals, France and Russia. By 1913 it was the largest exporter of iron and steel goods, led by entrepreneurial dynasties such as the Thyssen and Krupp families.

The aftermath of the First World War and the economic problems of the 1930s saw a decline in the share of world production of the Western leaders and the rise of new stars in the East. Japan's first 'economic miracle' was underway including the transformation of its textile industry into the world's largest exporter of cotton goods by the late 1930s, helped by entrepreneurs such as Sakichi Toyoda who invented an automatic loom and his son Kiichiro Toyoda who diversified his father's company into cars under the Toyota name. (See below for more of this story).

Such economic cycles can only be viewed over relatively long periods and other examples of enterprise life cycles in this chapter take a more historical perspective for this reason. Today, the picture looks very different with the emergence of new world economies such as China and India and the continued decline in the share of global production of Western economies in North America and Europe.

Source: Rostow (1978: 52–53)

6.2 THE GROWTH OF AN ENTERPRISE

6.2.1 To Grow or Not to Grow

One of the key limitations of the life cycle models described in section 6.1 is the assumption that growth is a part of the natural order of business ventures. Entrepreneurial success is often linked to growing a new venture or small business into a much larger one. Examples of successful entrepreneurs and enterprises are usually taken from those that start small and grow into an international giant (for example, Steve Jobs and Apple; Richard Branson and Virgin; Rupert Murdoch and News Corporation). Much less attention is given to entrepreneurs who have succeeded in meeting their business objectives but remained relatively small (no examples, to prove the point that they would be unknown to most readers).

This narrow view of success does not take into account the vast majority of businesses and their owners. A few will grow quickly and in time become medium or large firms employing over 250 people with substantial turnovers. However such high-growth firms are very small in number as can be seen from the business population data: less than one per cent of enterprises in Europe qualify as medium or large, employing more than 50 people; only 40,000 of the 140 million enterprises in Europe are large, employing more than 250 people (Observatory of European SMEs, 2004). As a result, if the size distribution of the population of businesses is visualised as a triangle, the base of very small businesses is extremely broad and the apex of large firms is very small (see Figure 6-4).

If success means moving from the base to the tip of this triangle, then it is rare indeed: most very small businesses do not grow beyond their classification as a micro firm; only a few small firms grow to become medium-sized, and even fewer grow into the large companies of the future.

This has led some commentators to classify enterprises and entrepreneurs by their propensity to grow. Storey (1994) suggested three groups: *'failures'*, *'trundlers'* and *'flyers'*. Hisrich and Peters (1995) divided start-ups into:

- *A lifestyle firm* that exists primarily to support the owners. Privately owned, it achieves modest growth due to the nature of the business and/or the motives of the entrepreneur. These are typically micro business with up to ten employees.

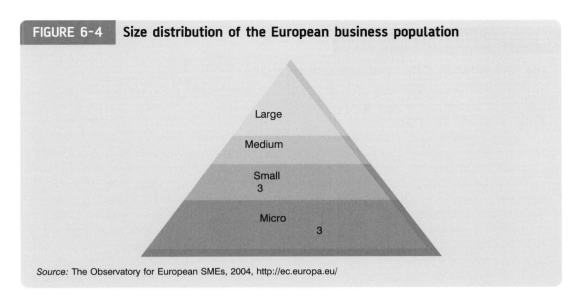

FIGURE 6-4 | **Size distribution of the European business population**

Source: The Observatory for European SMEs, 2004, http://ec.europa.eu/

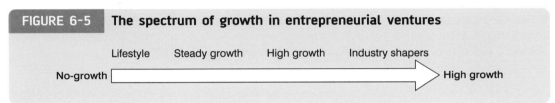

FIGURE 6-5 | **The spectrum of growth in entrepreneurial ventures**

- A *foundation company* is created from research and development and lays the foundation of a new industry. Its innovation changes the nature of an entire sector. This category includes companies like the Apple Corporation founded by Steven Jobs and Stephen Wozniak that turned computing from a specialised technology into a mass market.

- A *high-potential venture* achieves rapid growth because of its innovative product/service in a large market, and also receives greatest investment and public interest. For example, Rupert Murdoch's News Corporation has grown from a loss-making newspaper in Adelaide, Australia into the world's largest media conglomerate.

The complexity of entrepreneurial ventures makes it difficult to categorise business growth into so few types. The characteristics of an enterprise in relation to business growth can best be described as a spectrum with low growth, lifestyle enterprises at one end and rapid growth companies that change the shape of an industry at the other (Figure 6-5). In between there are many possible patterns of enterprise growth.

6.2.2 Factors Influencing the Growth of an Enterprise

Finding out what influences an enterprise to grow is obviously very important for policy-makers, investors and advisers as well as business owners themselves. Although there has been much research and commentary in this field, no single theory that adequately explains the interplay of all the factors influencing growth has been developed. The wide variety of different circumstances surrounding each individual enterprise, and the complex interactions of forces that influence them, has so far prevented the development of such a model. However the research does suggest a general framework of factors

ENTREPRENEURSHIP IN ACTION

The Toyoda family:[3] The 'first Japanese miracle'

In 1929, the economic life cycles of nations (described in subsection 6.2.1) indicate that Japan's share of global manufacturing was miniscule, although the country's first 'economic miracle' was already underway. The UK was still one of the world's largest producers but in decline. Symptomatic of these changing economic fortunes was a deal signed that year by Sakichi Toyoda, a Japanese inventor and entrepreneur, and Platt Brothers, the world's leading manufacturer of textile equipment (Bernstein,1997). The deal was a licensing agreement giving Platt Brothers the right to make and distribute Toyoda's automatic loom. That such an international company should agree to sell a Japanese innovation was a huge achievement for the entrepreneur behind it. His fast-growing business was a *foundation company* that helped transform the textile industry and enabled Japan to overtake the UK as the world's largest exporter of cotton goods. Toyoda achieved his success after many failed attempts. Trained as a carpenter, he built loom after loom from wood but when he set up in business to sell his patented invention he closed down his first business after only a couple of years. He persisted and began designing steam-powered looms but left the business that had been founded to make the product when sales fell. Benefiting from a textile boom during the First World War, he finally found the necessary investment and time to develop a loom that automatically replenished the yarn when it ran out and was thus more productive. By 1929 when he signed the deal with Platt, Toyoda had a large group of companies involved in textile manufacture that was an integral part of the fast-growing Japanese textile industry.

even if it cannot predict which will influence particular enterprises and entrepreneurs. As Burns (2001: 271) put it: 'we know the ingredients, but the precise recipe can vary from situation to situation'. Burns (2001) suggested that the important ingredients are: the *entrepreneurial character*; the *business culture*; *company strengths*; and *business decisions*. This overlooks the crucial influence of the external business environment, a factor that is taken into account in the framework presented by Smallbone and Wyer (2006) who modified a model first suggested by Storey (1994). This proposes that growth is influenced by: the characteristics of the entrepreneur and of the enterprise, the management strategy and the external business environment (as shown in Figure 6-6).

The Entrepreneur   The characteristics of the entrepreneur are widely accepted as *the* vital ingredient that influences growth (see Chapter 7 for a more detailed discussion of entrepreneurial characteristics). Research indicates that the particular characteristics of the entrepreneur that are associated with growth of the enterprise include:

■ *Motivation* – if the entrepreneur's reasons for starting the business originated in 'pull' or 'opportunity-driven' motives such as the desire to exploit a market opportunity, rather than 'push' or 'necessity-driven' motives such as unemployment, then the resulting enterprise is more likely to grow. The commitment of the entrepreneur to growth makes a considerable difference.

■ *Previous management experience* – prior experience of managing people and processes is valuable in maintaining growth.

■ *Demographics* of the entrepreneur – age and education can influence growth. Some research suggests that middle-aged founders benefiting from some experience yet still retaining the energy necessary to drive a business forward are more likely to grow their business. Entrepreneurs with higher educational qualifications are more likely to found high-tech and knowledge-based firms which tend to be linked with higher rates of growth.

FIGURE 6-6   A framework of influences on enterprise growth

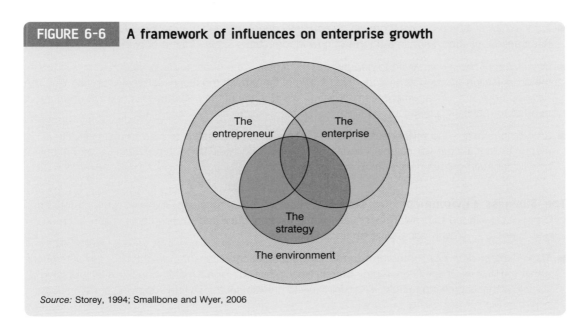

The entrepreneur

The enterprise

The strategy

The environment

Source: Storey, 1994; Smallbone and Wyer, 2006

■ *Number of entrepreneurs* involved – enterprises founded by a group of entrepreneurs are more likely to grow than one-person bands. Access to a wide range of skills, experiences and resources is important to growth, and an entrepreneurial team is more likely to possess the attributes needed than just one person.

Other characteristics of the entrepreneur have also been put forward as influencing growth including: family history; training and functional skills; gender; social marginality; and experience of the sector. However there is less evidence to support the influence of these factors (Storey, 1994).

Type of Enterprise   The characteristics of the enterprise also have an influence on its growth prospects:

■ *Legal form* – limited companies seem to grow more than sole traders or partnerships. This is probably associated with the number of entrepreneurs involved as there are likely to be more in a limited company. Limited companies may also lend greater credibility to an enterprise which can assist in attracting both the customers and resources needed for growth. The equity investment needed for growth is facilitated by incorporation into a limited company (see Chapter 15 on the types of entrepreneurial finance). It is also possible that as companies grow they adopt limited liability status so that the legal form is a result, rather than a cause, of growth.

■ *Firm age* – younger firms tend to grow more quickly than older ones, although this partly reflects the need for young firms to achieve a critical mass to survive in the marketplace.

■ *Firm size* – the very small firms find it hard to grow, partly because many entrepreneurs with micro firms do not wish to grow, and partly because of resource constraints and lack of competitiveness.

The Management Strategy   The management decisions and actions taken by the entrepreneur once trading has begun significantly influence growth:

■ *Market position* – the adoption of clearly defined niches and market segments is a key ingredient for growth.

■ *Introduction of new products* – growth companies cannot rely on a narrow product/service range so that continuous innovation in the form of new introductions is also key to growth.

■ *Devolution of decision-making to non-owning managers* – the change of management structures as the organisation grows was an important feature of the growth models described in section 6.1. The development of a management team to lessen the reliance of the enterprise on one entrepreneur is needed to maintain growth.

■ *Sharing of equity* – the willingness to include others in the ownership of the business attracts resources that aid growth including additional finance, innovation through partnerships and retention of the management team with share options.

The Business Environment Key factors outside of the internal environment of the enterprise influence its likelihood to grow. Enterprises exist in external business environments which are more or less favourable to growth depending on such factors as:

■ *Market sector or industry* – the growth rate of the market conditions the potential for the enterprises within it. However this influence may be relatively localised: for example, if one firm is supplying a company that is growing rapidly, it is more likely to grow faster than a firm supplying a more stagnant player in the same industry or trade.

■ *Competitive forces* – competitive conditions between direct and indirect rivals, and the relative power of suppliers and buyers in the market, represent forces largely outside of the control of an individual enterprise but which influence its growth prospects (Porter, 1980).

■ *Location* – the geographic location of an enterprise may affect its business environment depending on the market sector. For example, retail growth is dependent on the economic health of the local population.

Growth Factors Important to the Entrepreneur Research into the reasons for growth, and the factors that might curtail this, is important. But what lessons does it offer entrepreneurs who are attempting to grow their business? Some of the factors discussed above (such as the business environment and demographics of the enterprise owner) are outside the control of individual entrepreneurs. However, there are key messages for those who wish to grow an enterprise:

■ No growth is not a good long-term option as a very small firm is more likely to succumb to the vagaries of the external business environment.

■ The need to refresh the products or services on offer also indicates that an enterprise needs continuous development if it is to survive and grow.

■ The entrepreneur and the enterprise need a competitive edge derived from answering the following key questions about the market place:
  • Who are the customers – what is the target market or niche?
  • What benefits do these customers get from what the enterprise is offering?
  • Why will they buy from this enterprise and not another?

■ The organisation cannot depend totally on the skills and efforts of one entrepreneur if it is to continue to grow. An entrepreneurial team – both within and outside of the enterprise is needed (see Chapter 13, The entrepreneurial team).

ENTREPRENEURSHIP IN ACTION

The Toyoda family: The 'second Japanese miracle'

Sakichi Toyoda helped transform the Japanese textile industry, but he encouraged his son Kiichiro to follow his own dream. Kiichiro Toyoda wanted to make cars not looms, and in 1933 he established an automobile division within Toyoda Automatic Loom Works, Ltd. It was a risky diversification as the Japanese automobile market was small and dominated by Ford and General Motors. Changes to the market environment soon endorsed Kiichiro's decision however. In 1936, driven by military considerations, the Japanese government restricted motor manufacturing to domestic producers only, thereby removing all foreign competition. Kiichiro understood the changing market well enough to develop not only cars but trucks which the military needed. Kiichiro ran a competition to re-brand the car company. The winning entry was 'Toyota'.

During the Second World War the Japanese government converted most textile firms into armaments' producers whilst the need for trucks and buses boomed (Bernstein, 1997). Thus, Kiichiro's diversification proved a wise business decision and led to the emergence of a successful car company from the old textile conglomerate. After the war, the company became one of the great innovators of modern production techniques such as 'lean manufacturing'. By the 1980s, Japan had the highest productivity in the world, a key part of the 'second economic miracle'.

6

6.3   THE CLOSURE OF AN ENTERPRISE

6.3.1 The Churn of Entrepreneurial Ventures

The enterprise population is a dynamic and continuously changing one. The population of businesses in an economy may seem relatively stable at the macro level for considerable periods of time; for example, the UK business population was relatively stable around 3.5 million for the decade 1992–2002. But even in periods such as this when the total population is neither growing nor declining, there was turbulence beneath the surface. The total number of enterprises is affected by the number of new ventures being created on the one hand and the number of businesses that close down on the other. At any one time a large number of new ventures are in the process of being formed and others are being closed down.

This is happening in most economies at relatively high levels. In the UK, there were 425,000 start-ups (9.5 per cent of the total population) and 490,000 closures (10.9 per cent) in 2007 so that the business population contracted slightly during the year (Barclays Bank, 2008). Start-up and closure rates of around 10 per cent of the total population are fairly typical of developed economies in normal economic conditions. Some countries are higher particularly in Asia and Latin America. For example Australia recorded a 17 per cent start-up rate and a 15 per cent closure rate in 2007 in a total business population of 2 million.[4] The US has also exhibited a high start-up and closure rate of around 15 per cent (Headd, 2003). Several European countries, including Italy, Portugal, Finland and Sweden have had somewhat lower start-up rates of 6–7 per cent (Vale, 2006). The percentages may vary but it all adds up to a very large number of enterprises that start up and close down every year. The Global Entrepreneurship Monitor (Bosma et al., 2008) estimates that more than 50 million new businesses may start each year around the world and a similar number may close. (See Chapter 4 for more on the importance of enterprise creation in the global economy.)

This movement in and out of the business population is referred to as business '*churn*'. It is central to the process of entrepreneurship and the role of 'creative destruction' it plays in the economy, as described by Schumpeter (see Chapter 1).

Churn can be viewed in different ways:

■ At the micro level of the individual entrepreneur, high levels of churn indicate that a large number of businesses have closed which may mean personal and financial difficulties for some of the owners and a loss of jobs for employees. However not all closures can be considered 'failures' and it is important to distinguish between businesses that close leaving indebtedness and those that close for more positive reasons. This is a theme which is developed in section 6.4 below.

■ At the macro level of the regional and national economy, churn can generate benefits as it helps to renew and improve the competitiveness of the business stock. The competitive market system operates as a process of natural selection of enterprises. Some businesses take market share and customers away from other firms which may be forced to close as a consequence. Assuming that businesses survive based on their higher levels of efficiency, innovation and customer service, the result should be a more healthy population of high-performing enterprises and entrepreneurs. In this way, churn is desirable so that market mechanisms can motivate entrepreneurs and reward investors whilst detering those who are less productive and unwilling to change.

A low churn rate in an economy can be symptomatic of restricted competition, lack of incentives to innovate and high barriers to new business entry – an economy in need of more entrepreneurial activity. Conversely a high churn rate is usually indicative of an entrepreneurial economy in which new entrants with novel products and processes force out complacent competitors or stimulate them to improve and innovate in order to remain competitive. In this way, high rates of churn are often associated with stronger economic growth. An economy that is growing relatively quickly exhibits a higher start-up rate; more start-ups lead to more closures as many new ventures do not last very long and so churn is increased. For example, Australia exhibited relatively high rates of churn (over 15 per cent start-up and closure rates) at a time when its GDP was growing at 3–4 per cent per annum from 2003 to 2007 (Australian Bureau of Statistics, 2007). In times of economic downturn, closures continue at high rates or accelerate whilst start-ups slow down so that the total business population declines and economic growth is depressed further.

Iceland's meltdown

As we have seen, there is cyclical churn amongst the economies of nation states in that some rise as others fall in terms of economic output and wealth. Iceland has recently risen and fallen in spectacular fashion. From the 1990s, Icelandic entrepreneurs used a combination of favourable factors in the commercial environment to acquire business assets around the world. Backed by cash from fish quotas and a stock market based on stable pension funds, they found it easy to obtain international credit for rapid expansion through acquisition. For example, Johannes Jonsson and his son, Jon Asgeir Johannesson, founded 'Bonus', a cheap food store in Reykjavík in 1989 which developed rapidly into a national chain within a few years. Changing the name to Baugur (the 'Ring of Steel') after merging with another Icelandic chain in 1992, the new group provided the platform for a host of overseas acquisitions. They focused particularly on well known brands in the UK High Street such as the fashion chains Oasis, Karen Millen and Whistles, the toy store Hamleys, the department store House of Fraser, the tea company Whittard of Chelsea, the jeweler's Mappin and Webb and the supermarket chain Iceland (of course). This international expansion was good for the home economy and Iceland's small population enjoyed one of the highest incomes per capita in the world.

It all went badly wrong during the financial crisis in 2008 when Iceland's banks ran out of money. Iceland's currency devalued and inflation increased rapidly. Baugur's expansion was facilitated by leveraging debt on a large scale to buy stakes in companies around Europe. The international financial crisis left Iceland's three major banks particularly exposed and two were nationalised to avoid collapse. This effectively left part of Baugur's debts in the hands of the government. They considered selling off parts of their empire, asking for help from entrepreneurs such as Philip Green, owner of BHS and other UK retail chains, but found the deals unacceptable at first. In February 2009, Baugur's UK division were put into administration with the Chairman Johannesson complaining of 'British vultures' circling over his collapsed empire hoping to pick up bargains. In March the company was declared bankrupt. Johannesson had already set up his next venture, Tecamol, to buy different retail businesses in a more focused way.

6.3.2 Which Enterprises Close and When?

The data on business closures indicate that there are two groups of enterprises that are most vulnerable to closure (Observatory of European SMEs, 2006):

■ *Smaller enterprises* – the very small micro firms are most likely to close as closure rates are lower amongst medium-sized and larger firms. The largest numerical segment of SMEs – micro enterprises – are most at risk of closure. This indicates that standing still and staying small is not a good survival strategy even though many business owners do not want to grow.

■ *Younger enterprises* – the chances of survival improve as the business ages so that the most vulnerable are the very young, relatively new enterprises.

The message to the founding entrepreneur is clear: the longer you can keep going and the more you can grow your business, the greater chance you will have of survival.

Survival Rates   As the youngest enterprises are the most vulnerable it follows that survival rates are lower in the early years and improve as a firm ages. However, claims that a very high percentage of firms close in the first year of trading are unfounded. Phillips and Kirchhoff (1989) investigated the myth that nine out of ten new businesses close in their first year in the US and found that 76 per cent of firms were still trading after two years. More recent research by Headd (2003) indicated that 66 per cent had survived two years. In the UK, survival figures seem more optimistic with 80 per cent surviving two years (see Table 6-1), but this could be because the data are derived from VAT registered businesses that have a turnover above £60,000 (2005/6) and therefore have an above average size distribution (Office for National Statisitcs, 2008).

TABLE 6-1 Enterprise survival rates in the UK and US		
Percentage of firms still trading after	**US**	**UK**
1 year		96
2 years	66	80
3 years		65
4 years	50	54
5 years		45
6 years +	40	

Source: Headd (2003) and Office for National Statistics (2008)

The general picture seems to be that approximately one-third of start-ups close within three years, and one-half after five years.

6.3.3 What Happens to Businesses that Close?

At the macro-economic level, active churn amongst enterprises with a high level of business start-ups and closures is normally a sign of a healthy economy. However at the micro level, we tend to regard the closure of an individual business in a negative way, assuming that it has somehow failed. 'Business closure' and 'business failure' have come to be used as interchangeable, negative terms. Until relatively recently there was little research to contradict or support this gloomy picture but now there are insights into this final stage of the business life cycle.

There are clearly positive and negative reasons why an enterprise closes. Using financial criteria, business closures can be placed on a spectrum with large monetary gains for the owners at one end and significant losses at the other. In between many businesses are closed down because either they no longer meet the owners' objectives, or they have already done so. Even after a relatively short time, an enterprise may have met the objectives set by the founders. For example, ventures in the creative industries often have a natural, short existence to fulfil a particular project such as the making of a film or an advertisement. A new business entity is often set up to facilitate this objective and closed down when it is completed.

A research study by Kingston University (SBRC, 2002) examined the closure of over 300 businesses and classified their fate into four main groups: sold-on, reopened, closed down and declared insolvent (as shown in Figure 6-7).

At the positive end of possible financial outcomes, around one-third of businesses were sold on by their owners for a monetary gain, mainly for modest amounts as the well publicised multi-million pound deals are rare.

On the negative side of financial outcomes, up to 20 per cent of businesses that close do so with debts that are left unpaid. In the UK, there are approximately 40–50,000 liquidations of companies and bankruptcies of sole traders and partnerships in a typical year outside of an economic recession. This represents around 1 per cent of the total business population or 10 per cent of all the businesses that close. Although in the economic downturn of 2008/9 bankruptcies rose by over 25 per cent, this still represents less than 2 per cent of the total business stock. Financial insolvency is not very common therefore, although it can have profound effects on those involved.

Between these extremes of financial gain and pain, a large number of enterprises simply close down and stop trading. Some close because they no longer meet their owners' objectives. Others are undoubtedly ailing financially and are closed before they can cause too much damage. Some owners prefer to concentrate on a different idea for a business venture, or maybe they are attracted back into employment. A business may close for negative, non-financial reasons such as the breakdown in relationships between partners or the ill health of the owner. In many cases the 'business' or trade does

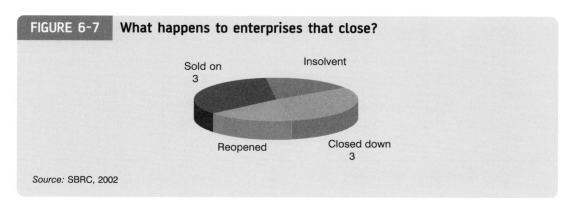

FIGURE 6-7 **What happens to enterprises that close?**

Sold on
3

Insolvent

Reopened

Closed down
3

Source: SBRC, 2002

WHEN THINGS GO WRONG

Brunel goes to prison

The rise of Britain as the leading economic nation in the world was not without many business casualties, some involving well known names. Isambard Kingdom Brunel is famous as one of the giants of the Victorian era, an engineer and entrepreneur who built the bridges, railways and ships at the heart of Britain's trading success in the nineteenth century. The achievements of his father Marc Brunel are less well known but also very significant. The Brunels[5] were in fact French, but Marc fled the excesses of the French Revolution to the US where he became chief engineer to the City of New York. He fell in love with an English woman, Sophia Kingdom and moved to England to marry her in 1799. As well as ensuring his famous son was English (rather than French or American), he was also partly responsible for the defeat of France through his entrepreneurial activities. A prolific inventor, he became aware of one of the British navy's greatest needs during the Napoleonic wars – pulley blocks that controlled the rigging ropes of the sails. Each year the fleet needed 100,000 of them and they could not get enough as they were made laboriously by hand from a solid block of oak. Marc Brunel designed a system using machines to do the work, one of the first examples of automated manufacturing replacing craft-based production. He also designed a production line process to make boots for the army, many of which were worn at the Battle of Waterloo when Napoleon's army was finally defeated. The end of the war also meant the end of a thriving business for Brunel as neither the navy nor the army needed his mass-produced products in viable quantities. The penalties for failing to pay off debts were severe in the nineteenth century, and when his enterprises could no longer meet the bills, he was sent to debtor's prison as his businesses collapsed. Fortunately the Duke of Wellington remembered the contribution of this French émigré to the English war effort and arranged for his release.

not really cease at all as it is passed on to another business entity. 'Technical closures' are often motivated by tax or legal reasons and one business entity takes over the trade of another – for example, when a sole trader or partnership is changed into a limited company.

These findings from UK research are broadly supported by studies in other countries. Headd (2003) examined a large dataset of businesses that had closed in the US and found that 34 per cent of those that closed within four years were considered 'successful'. He concluded that: 'potential entrepreneurs … have less to fear than is commonly believed. Their prospects of survival are reasonable, and if they close, their prospects for being successful at closure are reasonable' (Headd, 2003: 59).

6.4   THE LIFE CYCLE OF THE ENTREPRENEUR

6.4.1 What Happens to the Entrepreneurs Who Close a Business?

In the introduction to this chapter, we made the point that the life cycle of an enterprise might be very different from that of the career of the entrepreneur involved. So what does happen to entrepreneurs who close down their enterprise? There is still an assumption that most entrepreneurs that close down their business have been unsuccessful and may therefore give up the entrepreneurial trail, but this is not reflected in what entrepreneurs actually do when they exit from an enterprise. The majority of entrepreneurs who close one business become involved in another one. The SBRC (2002) study tracked what the owners of closed businesses had done on exit. The results are illustrated in Figure 6-8: The majority (60 per cent) continued as business owners by opening or buying a new or similar business to the one closed, or through the existing ownership of another business. Around 10 per cent

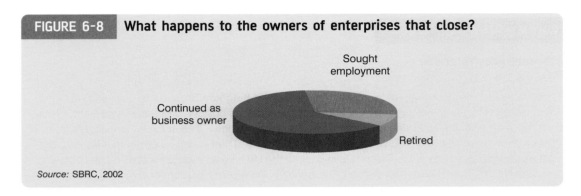

FIGURE 6-8   **What happens to the owners of enterprises that close?**

Source: SBRC, 2002

of owners retired from active involvement. Only 30 per cent dropped their entrepreneurial ambitions by returning to employment or becoming unemployed.

6.4.2 The Revolving Door of Enterprise Ownership

The way out of entrepreneurial ventures resembles a revolving door rather than a one-way exit. Most owners re-enter because they are sufficiently encouraged by their experiences the first time round. Even those who experience financial difficulties in one venture, try again. Figure 6-9 illustrates the outcomes as described by the entrepreneurs who had closed a business (SBRC, 2002). This classified entrepreneurs who leave a business according to:

■ how their business performed financially – positively or negatively; and

■ their future intentions and attitudes towards running a business – positive or negative.

This resulted in four categories as shown in Figure 6-9:

■ *Determined entrepreneurs* (45 per cent of those who close a business). Even though they experienced financial difficulties in their previous venture, they returned to business ownership determined to do better. They often regarded closure as a beneficial experience.

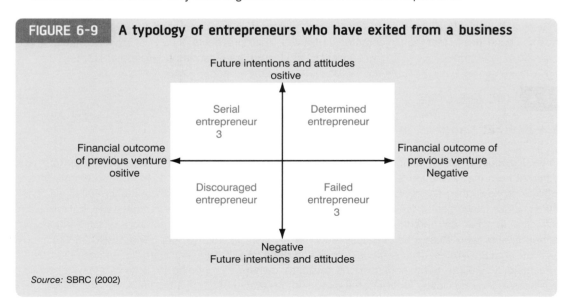

FIGURE 6-9   **A typology of entrepreneurs who have exited from a business**

Source: SBRC (2002)

■ *Serial entrepreneurs* (37 per cent). Having succeeded financially in a previous venture, this group returned to invest their human capital and other resources in a new business.

■ *Failed entrepreneurs* (13 per cent). The financial problems of a previous venture discouraged this relatively small group from re-entering into business ownership. They have 'failed' in that they have closed a business in financial difficulty, often leaving bad debts, and returned to employment, or unemployment.

■ *Discouraged entrepreneurs* (5 per cent). Although their previous business venture succeeded, they did not wish to repeat the experience. Often the strains of running a small business outweigh the financial rewards, so this relatively small group also withdraw from business ownership.

A number of studies in Europe (e.g. Stam, Audretsch and Meijaard, 2005; Metzger, 2006), the US (Headd, 2003; Henley, 2004) and Japan (Harada, 2005) have confirmed that entrepreneurs who exit one business tend to go back into business ownership and that people with experience of entrepreneurship, even if it has been problematic, are more likely to start new ventures.

Some entrepreneurs believe that coping with setbacks and crises is the best way to learn about entrepreneurship and running a business. When asked to rate their skills after closure compared to when they started, entrepreneurs cited a number of improvements including business planning, building a customer base and financial record keeping. However, they rated managing and motivating themselves through the changing fortunes of their venture as the most valuable learning experience (SBRC, 2002).

6

The start-up that never gave up

Julian Harris formed an IT company in 1989 with high growth ambitions. However it coincided with an economic recession that particularly affected technology companies and the company was moth-balled until 1993. It was re-born three years later and soon rated as one of the fastest-growing UK companies. By 2000 the cyclical nature of the IT industry caused problems again and Julian decided to restart as a new company, Smart421. After a period of high losses, the business turned round and Julian sold out in 2006.

6.4.3 Serial and Portfolio Entrepreneurs

The above analysis indicates that many entrepreneurs own more than one business. They can be classified according to whether they do this either concurrently or sequentially:

Integrative Case Link
Read more of Julian's roller coaster ride in Case Study 9 on Smart421 at the end of Part 3.

■ A *portfolio entrepreneur* owns more than one business at the same time;

■ A *serial entrepreneur* runs a business, sells it and moves on to another venture in a relatively short time.

Some portfolio entrepreneurs build up a series of ventures as a way of de-risking their investments. They are prepared to sacrifice the high growth or profitability of one venture by owning several businesses with lower growth and profitability that overall meet their financial and personal needs. Others are just very good at entrepreneurship and build up a series of successful enterprises.

Serial entrepreneurs often excel at the early stages of venture creation but are less motivated or able to build a business over a lengthy period of time. They thrive on the psychological reward of creating

ENTREPRENEURSHIP IN ACTION

The Thames Tunnel

Marc Brunel was typical of many entrepreneurs in that he was already planning his next venture whilst suffering the consequences of the first. When he was imprisoned for debt following the bankruptcy of his manufacturing businesses, he spent much of his time working on a problem that was threatening the supremacy of nineteenth-century London as the world's commercial centre – traffic congestion. As the city developed around the docks both north and south of the Thames, a major bottle-neck for carts and coaches developed on London Bridge, but other crossings could not be built downstream without impeding shipping using the docks. Brunel realised that the only alternative was to build a tunnel under the Thames, but under-water tunnelling was an undeveloped skill at the time. First he designed the 'Great Shield', a patented method that provides protection for workers who dig and build the walls at the same time. It was an innovation that formed the basis of modern tunnelling technology and was used during the construction of the Channel Tunnel that now links Brunel's country of birth with his country of adoption.

Next, he formed the Thames Tunnel Company, raised the necessary capital from private investors and began work in Rotherhithe in 1825 on a tunnel to Wapping, a quarter of a mile away on the north bank. He employed his son Isambard as one of the engineers. Three years later they had reached the middle of the Thames, but water burst through several times, precipitating a financial crisis that halted the work and temporarily closed the business. Marc Brunel had already demonstrated his resilience in the face of problems and five years later in 1836 he had raised new capital from the government to begin the project again. He was 73 years old when the Thames Tunnel[6] was finally completed in 1842, 17 years after he had begun the project.

something new but are less interested in the management and day-to-day running of an established business. They also tend to regard closure and even failure as an experience that will make them stronger to take on new challenges.

6.5   FACTORS INFLUENCING THE DECLINE AND CLOSURE OF AN ENTERPRISE

What are the problems and key issues that confront entrepreneurs and ultimately drive some out of business? Many researchers and practitioners have attempted to answer this question concerning the causes of the closure and failure of an enterprise. The earlier sections of this chapter have argued that many of the reasons for closure are positive: entrepreneurs may sell up or lose interest in their business for a whole variety of reasons that are not related necessarily to significant business problems. However, there are many business issues that cause significant problems and in some cases, the closure of the enterprise. These can be classified broadly into external and internal factors:

■ *External influences:* conditions in the macro-economy such as interest rates and overall levels of consumer demand have an influence on the fortunes of enterprises in general. However, it is likely that localised, micro-environmental factors will be more crucial in determining whether an enterprise will survive. Changes in demand within the local catchment area or industry sector can have a rapid and devastating effect. For example, the arrival of a superstore will often reduce the numbers of small, independent retailers in the neighbourhood. The demise of a large player within a particular industry will have an adverse effect on the many smaller companies that were dependent on it. As we have noted, young and very small firms are particularly vulnerable to these changes in the business environment as they tend to have fewer resources and less experience to deal with them. Much will depend on the entrepreneur's ability to adjust swiftly to changes in the business environment. Longitudinal research suggests that enterprises that are most active in making adjustments, particularly in relation to their products or services and the approach to the market, are more likely to survive (Storey, 1994).

■ *Internal factors.* We have already noted that the entrepreneur's characteristics and the decisions they take are crucial factors in the growth of an enterprise and they are equally important influences in whether it declines or closes. A number of studies have focused on the particular functions or areas of expertise that are most likely to influence entrepreneurial failure (Berryman, 1983; Cromie, 1991; Birley and Niktari, 1995; Stokes and Wilson, 2006). A composite list of internal functions and factors which have been found to have particular impact on survival include:
- Accounting
- Marketing
- Management of people
- Availability of finance
- Management capability and behaviour of the owner.

Such a list is rather broad and covers most of the functions of an enterprise except for manufacturing and business operations and processes. How to make things or the methods of delivering a service appear not to be a significant, survival issue for entrepreneurs. Whilst numerous studies of business closure have categorised the causes of failure in different ways, the one factor that is common throughout is the influence of the entrepreneur who remains central to whether or not the business survives. This influence will evolve as the nature of the enterprise changes. In the early days, the founding entrepreneur's judgement in selecting the type of business and their skills in creating a

ENTREPRENEURSHIP IN ACTION

A social entrepreneur who knew when to let go

Jamie Oliver is a social and a portfolio entrepreneur with chains of restaurants as well as publishing and television enterprises. 'Fifteen' is a good example of how he manages to keep all of his entrepreneurial ventures running successfully. Named after the first cohort of trainees, Fifteen is a high-class restaurant that doubles as a training programme for disadvantaged young people interested in becoming chefs. As a social enterprise it takes on trainees with backgrounds of crime, addictions or homelessness who are given a year-long work placement at the restaurant. Those who finish take work placements around the world or open their

Jamie Oliver, a social and a portfolio entrepreneur

own restaurants. Jamie Oliver set up the first restaurant in London, tracked by a very successful TV show *Jamie's Kitchen* and it now has spin-offs in Amsterdam, Cornwall and Melbourne. He now has only non-executive involvement, leaving the management to a CEO, Penny Newman, who used to run Cafédirect. Jamie has gone back to doing what he does best as a celebrity chef.

Source: http://www.fifteen.net

customer base will be crucial. As the business develops, financial influences and the cash flow become more significant. If the business continues to grow, the unwillingness or inability of the entrepreneur to draw others in to help with the management of the enterprise can cause closure. Drucker (1985) made one of the earliest summaries of what is required to keep an enterprise going through the various stages of its life cycle and it stills seems valid today. He proposed that the four key factors, in chronological order were likely to be:

1 Focus on the market

2 Financial foresight, especially planning cash needs

3 Building a management team – before it is needed

4 Finding an appropriate role for the founding entrepreneur in a developed enterprise.

6.6   SUMMARY AND ACTIVITIES

The entrepreneurship process encompasses the complete life-span of an enterprise and the career of an entrepreneur. This chapter has therefore considered what happens to businesses as they grow and decline, and also what happens to entrepreneurs as they enter into and exit from an enterprise.

Life cycle models of an enterprise from start to finish typically describe five stages:

■ Concept/test stage

■ Development/abort stage

■ Growth/decline stage

■ Maturity

■ Re-growth/decline.

Such models have limitations as growth is rarely smooth and does not necessarily take place in the order of the model; many enterprises reach a stable size and never grow out of this phase.

Enterprise growth is on a spectrum with low-growth, life-style enterprises at one end and rapid-growth companies that change the shape of an industry at the other, although the latter are relatively rare. In between there are many possible patterns.

Growth is **influenced** by:

■ The *entrepreneur* – their motivation, previous management experience, demographics (age and education) and the number of entrepreneurs involved in the enterprise;

■ The *enterprise* – the legal form, age and size of the business;

■ The management *strategy* – the market position, introduction of new products, devolution of management to non-owning managers, and sharing of equity;

■ The external *business environment* – the market sector or industry, competitive forces and location.

Business Closure   Business '*churn*' refers to movements in and out of the business population. In most economies this is at relatively high levels – typically 10 per cent of the business population close down and 10 per cent are new start-ups in any one year. At the *macro-economic level*, churn can generate benefits as it helps to renew and improve the competitiveness of the business stock. A low churn rate in an economy can be symptomatic of restricted competition, lack of incentives to innovate and high barriers to new business entry.

The two most vulnerable groups of enterprises to closure are: *smaller enterprises* and *younger enterprises* – the chances of survival improve as the business grows and ages. Approximately one-third of start-ups close after three years, and one-half after five years.

Not all closures can be considered 'failures' as there four main groups: sold-on for monetary gain; reopened in a different form; closed down with neither pain nor gain because it no longer meets owner's objectives; declared insolvent and closed down with unpaid debts (under 20 per cent of closures).

Entrepreneurs Who Close a Business A high proportion (60 per cent) of owners who close a business, continue as entrepreneurs by opening or buying a new or similar business to the one closed, or through the existing ownership of another business. Even entrepreneurs who suffer financial losses return to try again.

Many entrepreneurs own more than one business: A *portfolio entrepreneur* owns more than one business at the same time; a *serial entrepreneur* runs a business, sells it and moves onto another venture in a relatively short time.

Business issues that may **cause the closure** of the enterprise are:

■ *External influences:*
  ● Macro-economic influences such as interest rates and levels of consumer demand
  ● Localised, micro-environmental factors – changes in demand within the local catchment area or industry sector especially the loss of a major customer. Entrepreneurs who can adjust swiftly to changes in the business environment increase the chances of survival.

■ *Internal factors* found to have particular impact on survival include:
  ● Accounting
  ● Marketing
  ● Management of people
  ● Availability of finance
  ● Management capability and behaviour of the owner.

REVIEW QUESTIONS

1 Outline five possible stages in the life cycle of a business from its beginning to its closure.

2 What are some of the limitations to the usefulness of business life cycle models?

3 Name the four key influences on the growth of an enterprise.

4 What key factors in the character of the entrepreneur are likely to influence growth?

5 What advice based on research evidence would you give to an entrepreneur who wished to grow their business?

6 Why is business churn good for an economy?

7 What happens to businesses that close? Give both positive and negative outcomes.

8 What typically happens to entrepreneurs who exit from a business venture? Give a range of possible outcomes.

9 What is the difference between a serial entrepreneur and a portfolio entrepreneur?

10 What are the key internal factors that may cause a business to close? Give four strategies that help to minimise these problems.

6

SEMINAR TASK

Rudyard Kipling's view was that both success and failure were nothing more than different life experiences and should be treated equally as such. In his poem 'If', he described to his son the attitude of a man of character:

> If you can meet with Triumph and Disaster
>
> And treat those two impostors just the same

Consider how this advice might relate to running a business venture. *Can the success or failure of an enterprise be treated 'just the same'?*

Preview case continued

Fogg's Failures: The entrepreneur who studied unsuccessful ventures

Christopher Fogg was invited to address a group of students who were interested in developing their entrepreneurial capabilities. This is what he said:

'Since qualifying as a Chartered Accountant I have become a portfolio entrepreneur and have started over 50 businesses – alone and with others. But I am going to talk about my "failures" not my successes as I believe we can learn more from what doesn't work than from what does.

Recently I have set up a number of Business Incubators including an "Incubator Without Walls", based on Connect San Diego, which is regarded as the best private model to help entrepreneurs start and develop high growth businesses. This work involves assessing large numbers of new ventures. I have developed a simple methodology to help me carry out the first stage assessment based on "Four Anchors" (see Timmons, 1999) relating to the business itself and then a review of the business environment.

The **Four Anchors** are

1 *Value – does the business create or add value to a customer or end user?*

2 *Client's willingness to pay – is the customer or client likely to pay for this added value? Does the business solve a significant problem, or meet a want or need, for which someone is willing to pay a premium?*

3 *Money making characteristics – is the market large enough for sufficient money to be earned? Has it got high growth potential and early positive cash flow? Will it produce profits to satisfy investors? Will the rewards balance the risks?*

4 *People – is the business a good fit with the characteristics, knowledge and expertise of the founding entrepreneur and their management team?*

I recently asked myself whether my methodology would have helped predict my own failures. A review of my **"Top 10 business failures"** against these Four Anchors went as follows:

▶

Venture 1: Gambling with marbles

When I was 10 years old, I encouraged fellow students to roll their marbles towards holes that I had cut into a shoe box. If they didn't get through one of the holes, I kept the marble. It was perhaps the highest rated business I have ever had satisfying each and every one of the four anchors: it met a need – the excitement of gambling that clients were willing and able to pay for with their marbles. It had instant cash – or rather marble – flow, and I was the perfect entrepreneur with experience – I loved marbles and started gambling on horses with a postal tote service at a young age.

Why did it fail?

Children at my school quickly caught the gambling habit and soon began asking their parents for more money to buy marbles to replace the ones they had lost to me. I was reported to the headmistress who not only made me close my business but also return all the marbles I had won because I fell foul of the rules of gambling in schools. I learned that although a new venture might meet all the business criteria, it also has to be legal.

Venture 2: Reproduction MG sports cars

Whilst travelling in Brazil, I noticed absolutely brilliant reproductions of old MG sports cars, based on the structure of VW Beetles. I started to import the kits, but for UK safety regulations these had to be built on the base of used right-hand drive VW Beetles imported from Europe.

Why did it fail?

Clients did not want to take the risk of a car based on an old VW Beetle – even though it looked beautiful. The entrepreneur (me) had no knowledge or experience of the import and sale of specialist cars (Anchor 4).

Venture 3: Chinese bicycles

I was in China endeavouring to sell very large-scale capital equipment for the manufacture of paper. Selling to China is very difficult so I tried a different tack – bartering. I was dealing with a Chinese trading company that also sold Chinese bicycles and I made the gesture of buying 1000 of their bikes. Everyone was delighted and I received a lot of publicity for the first sale of Chinese bikes to the UK.

Why did it fail?

I overlooked one thing – when the bikes arrived in the UK I discovered that I had not bought finished bikes but components for 1000 bikes – which is a lot of components. By the time I had paid for the assembly of these, the profit margin was low, especially as I could hardly sell old fashioned Chinese bikes at a premium. Obviously, the entrepreneur (me) had no knowledge or experience of bicycle importing, manufacturing or marketing (Anchor 4).

Venture 4: Second-hand Jumbo Jets

I was running an international trading company and received an enquiry (from my local Bangladesh Restaurant) for three used Jumbo Jets for Bangladeshi Biman (the national airline). Having contacted other airlines and agents, I flew out for a meeting in Dhaka with a portfolio of eight used Jumbo Jets for sale in my briefcase. A group of about 20 people from government, banks, the air force and the airline grilled me with a barrage of technical, product and commercial questions.

Why did it fail?

I could not answer any of their questions! I was also very immature in understanding what "individual commissions" would have to be paid to secure the business. Once again the entrepreneur (me) had come up short as I had no knowledge or experience of the business of selling used aircraft (Anchor 4).

Venture 5: Siemens vacuum pumps

Siemens market a vast range of electrical and electronic products, including a mechanical pump for producing a vacuum that was technically superior to competitive products. Its sales were almost zero. We persuaded Siemens to let us market the product through a

6

network of 30 agents in the US. We poached engineers and salesmen from the brand leader and the business was an amazing success with sales in excess of our most optimistic projections. At the end of six years, Siemens advised that they would not continue our contract. They were using too many of their own resources to service our clients, and, even more critically, they deemed it too risky to continue as they could not control us.

Why did it fail?

The business was too successful. If our sales were more modest Siemens would have let us continue. (It met all four anchors but failed on barriers to entry.)

Venture 6: Hunt Wesson tomato products

On a visit to the US in connection with Siemens, I looked out of my hotel window and saw an enormous factory with a name on the side that I just did not recognise – Hunt Wesson. Intrigued, I found out they were the largest producers of tomato-based products in the US – bigger even than Heinz. I hadn't heard of them for the simple reason they did not sell to the UK. So I approached them for the UK marketing rights. To my surprise, they gave it to me on the spot for a trial period of 18 months.

Why did it fail?

It proved too difficult to get the product introduced to UK supermarkets without massive marketing budgets that Hunt Wesson expected us to fund. We did not have the financial resources to establish a new brand to compete with Heinz. The entrepreneur (me) had no knowledge or experience in selling products to supermarkets (Anchors 3 and 4).

Venture 7: Orville Redenbachers Gourmet Popping Corn

When Hunt Wesson acquired Orville Redenbacher's business I used my contacts there to negotiate the rights to sell their Gourmet Popping Corn in the UK. We had a massive launch at the UK Trade Centre and attracted a lot of PR.

Why did it fail?

We could not interest retailers in stocking up-market, highly priced popcorn. The consumer was just not ready to pay the premium for this specialised product (Anchor 2).

Venture 8: Honour snacks

This was another idea that I borrowed from the US. You leave a tray of snacks and sweets in offices with an honest box for payment. Each week you top up the tray and, in theory, collect the cash. Today in the UK this is a successful business model operated by "Snacks in the Bar" and a number of charities.

Why did it fail?

The trays and the cash boxes were both empty at the end of the week. At that time office workers in the UK were not willing to pay for the product (Anchor 2) – but happily took advantage of my 'gifts'.

Venture 9: Fortune teller balls

An entrepreneur approached me to help him to import glass fortune teller balls into the UK. I did identify the dangers of this business in advance, but I have included it here as it led to a much bigger opportunity.

Why did it fail?

The entrepreneur gave up as he did not sell enough balls. The market in terms of size and profit margins in cash was not big enough to sustain the business and the entrepreneur (Anchors 2 and 3).

Venture 10: Waterless swimming

A director of Trust House Forte went to Blackpool beach and had his fortune told. He asked the fortune teller where he could find a supplier of plastic balls that he had seen in an amusement centre in the US. The fortune teller said she did not know, but she gave him my details as I had supplied her fortune teller ball. I then received an enquiry for 100,000 plastic balls – which I took up immediately. The business was a massive success – I was even pictured in the *Financial Times* lying in a ball pond of balls.

These "Ball Ponds" – a tank or inflatable filled with 20,000 plastic balls – are still around today.

Why did it fail?

Once we had established the market, our supplier began to sell direct. If we had not been so successful, the ball manufacturer would have left us with the market. There were few barriers to entry so we lost the market and withdrew. (Met all the Anchors but failed through very low barriers to entry).

Should I have spotted my mistakes?

I believe my assessment methodology of the four Anchors would have identified eight out of ten of my failures. The other two (Siemens Pumps and Waterless Swimming) needed higher barriers to entry to make them into viable long-term businesses. Their success meant that competitors in the form of the manufacturers entered the market. But note that four of what I call failures led directly to other opportunities.

Today, one of my most important roles is to facilitate "good business failures". That is, I help entrepreneurs to know when to quit, so that they do not leave debts behind nor suffer other trauma, when one particular venture does not work out. Most importantly I encourage them to learn from what went wrong.'

Questions

1 What is the most likely cause of 'Fogg's Failures'?

2 Why does Chris Fogg believe that:
   a failure is an essential part of business success?
   b the study of failures is a very important part of learning about entrepreneurship?

3 Why does Chris Fogg have so many business ventures to his name? Should he have concentrated on researching just one of them to make it into a long-term success?

4 Check a successful business that you know about against Fogg's Four Anchors. For example, how would you assess the business of text messaging from mobile phone operators against each of the four criteria?

Source: http://www.connectlondon.org

6.7   NOTES, REFERENCES AND FURTHER READING

Notes and Further Information

1. Chris Fogg's current venture is 'Connect London' which obtains funding for technology and high-growth entrepreneurs and connects them to a network of like-minded business owners, mentors and supports (http://www.connectlondon.org).

2. For more on economic development life cycles see Chapter 4, section 4.3 'The nature of the relationship between entrepreneurship and the economy', which explores economic life cycles within phases of economic development. See also the Introduction to McCraw, T.K. (1997) *Creating Modern Capitalism: How Entrepreneurs, Companies, and Countries Triumphed in Three Industrial Revolutions,* Cambridge, Mass.: Harvard University Press. This gives not only some background to world economic development cycles but also examples of entrepreneurs who were influential in each stage.

3. The remarkable Toyoda/Toyota story is well documented. See for example Bernstien, J.R. (1997) Toyoda automatic looms and Toyota automobiles, in *Creating Modern Capitalism: How Entrepreneurs, Companies, and Countries Triumphed in Three Industrial Revolutions.* Cambridge, Mass.: Harvard University Press.

4. Most countries keep data on the business population including total numbers and indications of starts and finishes. The data here are taken from the Australian Bureau of Statistics (2007) *Counts of Australian Businesses,* including Entries and Exits 2003 – 2007 (www.abs.gov.au/AUSSTATS).

5. Both Marc and Isambard Brunel kept diaries and there are many books that document their lives. See for example: Brindle, S. (2006) *Brunel: The Man who Built the World*, London: Orion Books.

6. The Thames Tunnel is still in use today as part of the London transport network. There is a museum on the site which has an interesting website with educational material (http://www.brunel-museum.org.ik).

References

Barclays Bank (2008) *Business Customer Economic Focus*, Barclays Commercial, London (http://www.business.barclays.co.uk/BBB/A/Content/Files/EconomicFocus.pdf).

Berryman, J. (1983) Small business failure and bankruptcy: A survey of the literature, *European Small Business Journal*, 1 (4): 47–59.

Birley, S. and Niktari, N. (1995) *The Failure of Owner-Managed Businesses*, London: Institute of Chartered Accountants in England and Wales.

Bosma, N., Acs, Z.J., Autio, E., Coduras, A. and Levie, J. (2008) *Global Entrepreneurship Monitor 2008 Executive Report*, Babson College, Universidad del Desarrollo, London Business School, available at http://www.gemconsortium.org/download/1233669410187/GEM_Global_08.pdf.

Burns, P. (2001) *Entrepreneurship and Small Business*, Basingstoke: Palgrave.

Churchill, N.C. and Lewis, V.L. (1983) The five stages of small business growth, *Harvard Business Review,* 61 (3): 30–41.

Cromie, S. (1991) The problems experienced by young firms, *International Small Business Journal*, April–June, 9 (3): 43–61.

Deakins, D. (1996) *Entrepreneurship and Small Firms*, Maidenhead: McGraw-Hill.

Drucker, P.F. (1985) *Innovation and Entrepreneurship*, London:Heinemann.

DTI (2007) Survival Rates of VAT-Registered Enterprises, 1995-2004, DTI Small Business Service, February (http://stats.berr.gov.uk/ed/survival).

Greiner, L.E. (1972) Evolution and revolution as organisations grow, *Harvard Business Review,* 50, July–August 55–67.

Hall, G. (1995) *Surviving and Prospering in the Small Firm Sector*, London: Routledge.

Harada, N. (2005) *Which* firms exit and why? An analysis of small-firm exits in Japan, *Department of Social Systems and Management, Discussion Paper Series*, No. 1129, Tsukuba: University of Tsukuba.

Headd, B. (2003) Redefining business success: Distinguishing between closure and failure, *Small Business Economics*, 21: 51–61.

Henley, A. (2004) Self-employment status: The role of state dependence and initial circumstances, *Small Business Economics*, 22: 67–82.

Hisrich, R.D. and Peters, M.P. (1995) *Entrepreneurship: Starting, Developing and Managing a New Enterprise*, 3rd edition, Boston: Irwin Inc.

Metzger, G. (2006) Afterlife: Who takes heart for restart, *Centre for European Economic Research (ZEW)*, No. 06-038.

Observatory of European SMEs (2006) *SMEs in Europe, 2003*, European Commission 2003/7, Luxembourg.

Office for National Statistics (2008) *Business Demography 2007: Enterprise Births, Deaths and Survival*, November, Newport.

Phillips, B.D. and Kirchoff, B.A. (1989) Formation, growth, survival: Small firm dynamics in the US economy, *Small Business Economics*, 1: 65–74.

Porter, M.E. (1980) *Competitive Strategy: Techniques for Analyzing Industries and Competitors,* New York: The Free Press.

Rostow W.W. (1978) *The World Economy: History and Prospect*, Austin: University of Texas Press.

SBRC (2002) *Opening Up Business Closures: A Study of Businesses that Close and Owners' Exit Routes*, A Report to HSBC, Small Business Research Centre, Kingston University, Kingston upon Thames.

Scott, M. and Bruce, R. (1987) Five stages of growth in small business, *Long Range Planning*, 20 (3): 45–52.

Smallbone, D. and Wyer, P. (2006) Growth and development in the small business, in Carter, S. and Jones-Evans, D. (eds) *Enterprise and Small Business: Principles, Practice and Policy*, Harlow: Pearson Education.

Stam, E., Audretsch, D. and Meijaard, J. (2005) Entrepreneurial intentions subsequent to firm exit, *EIM Business and Policy Research,* SCALES-paper N200506.

Stokes, D. and Wilson, N. (2006) *Small Business Management and Entrepreneurship*, London: Thomson Learning.

Storey, D.J. (1994) *Understanding the Small Business Sector*, London: Routledge.

Timmons, J.A. (1999) *New Venture Creation*, New York: McGraw-Hill.

Vale, S. (2006) *The International Comparability of Business Start-up Rates Final Report*, OECD Statistics Working Paper Series, OECD Statistics Directorate (www.oecd.org/std/research).

Recommended Further Reading

Smallbone, D. and Wyer, P. (2006) Growth and development in the small business, in Carter, S. and Jones-Evans, D. (eds) *Enterprise and Small Business: Principles, Practice and Policy*, Harlow: Pearson Education.

Stokes, D. and Blackburn, R.A. (2002) Learning the hard way: The lessons of owner-managers who have closed their businesses, *Journal of Small Business and Enterprise Development*, Spring, 9 (1): 1462–6004.

Storey, D.J. (1994) *Understanding the Small Business Sector*, London: Routledge, Chapters 4 and 5.

6

Part 1 Integrative Case Studies

INTEGRATIVE Case Study 1

Local Government Entrepreneurship

BY DR JUN LI, *Entrepreneurship and Innovation Group, Essex Business School*

In China's recent path to growth and development, SMEs have been a major driving force in this country's 'economic miracle'. Township and village enterprises (TVEs) in particular can be seen as important contributors to the re-emergence of contemporary Chinese entrepreneurship. Additionally, local governments often played a crucial role in facilitating entrepreneurship, in general, and the development of TVEs, in particular. A number of generic terms have been used to describe this phenomenon, including: 'local state corporatism', 'local government entrepreneurship', 'developmental state', and 'governmental entrepreneurship'. These terms appear also to originate in the widely recognised model of 'developmental state' which is also characteristic of the development governance of other economies in East Asia.

Local government entrepreneurship in the Chinese context refers to a mode of public sector entrepreneurship in which empowered local governments invariably coordinated economic activities within their territory as if it was a diversified business corporation, with officials acting as the equivalent of a board of directors. Under this system, TVEs were seen to represent a form of public ownership not far remote from the large urban state sector, except that government has clearer incentives and a greater ability to monitor these firms and enforce their interests as owners.

FISCAL DECENTRALISATION AND LOCAL EMPOWERMENT

The transformation of the 'traditional local government' into an 'entrepreneurial local government' resulted from fiscal decentralisation and the corresponding local empowerment and this was set in motion by the implementation of the fiscal contracting system in economic reforms that took place during the 1980s. Fiscal reforms assigned to local government specific rights over increased income and served to clarify their ownership over the assets that they administer; these reforms had in effect reallocated property rights downward within the official hierarchy and in favour of local government; and decentralisation allowed freedom for local actors within resource constraints, and under pressure, to build real coalitions forcing synergy between political, social and economic goals. The fiscal contracting system thus provided a fertile economic foundation for rapid, local government-led economic growth, by giving officials both the incentive and the investment funds to become effective promoters of localised entrepreneurship.

RESOURCE MOBILISATION AND RISK-SHARING

Another distinct feature of local government entrepreneurship centred on its unique community-based mechanism for resource mobilisation and risk-sharing, underpinned by the community objectives of local government. Under this unique mechanism, local government was able to redistribute the profits of collective firms, shift the debt obligations of a specific firm to other firms, significantly influence the allocation of community capital, including loans from local banks and credit co-operatives, and bear most of the risks of debt financing which would otherwise be taken by banks or enterprises.

In terms of resource mobilisation, local governments largely internalised the capital market within its jurisdiction, thereby overcoming market imperfection that existed in rural areas of China during the 1980s. This reduced transaction costs and, more importantly, allocated scarce resource to better and more profitable use. First, local governments facilitated the flow of capital to TVEs, including the redistribution of TVE operating profits. Second, using their knowledge and information advantage about the enterprises they administered, local governments were able to evaluate and inform the most efficient (re)allocation of relevant bank loans. Similarly, there were inherent benefits in relation to start-up risks within the territories under their control. Third, local government served as guarantor for 'township enterprises' and effectively mobilised funds through the use of personal and professional connections for most major investments.

They were also in a position to support and control the operation of semi-private credit institutions within their jurisdiction. As a result of community-based resource mobilisation, enterprises were also able to take advantage of relatively abundant household savings. Consequently, profitable opportunities and acceptable risk levels in the rural small firm sector kept investment returns high and contributed to higher household saving rates.

In a business environment in which the institutional arrangements underpinning emergent markets remained relatively weak, local governments managed to reduce transaction costs of entrepreneurship. For example, in the absence of contractual laws and routine compliance and enforcement, TVEs needed political allies to help negotiate and enforce contractual arrangements, especially those involving dominant state agencies and enterprises. Furthermore, obtaining business contracts with local government backing may have also reduced transaction costs for state enterprises and foreign firms, mainly by providing official assurance that the terms set by the contract will be fulfilled in a timely manner.

It should be noted, however, that not all the effects of internalisation of markets were positive. Profit redistribution within the local community tended to weaken the financial strength of TVEs, leaving most of them over-dependent upon short-term debt and thus vulnerable to cyclical business changes and demand variations. In overcoming such problems, local state corporatism chose to rely upon its community-based risk-sharing facilities. Arguably, since local economies are invariably more diversified than individual enterprises, local governments were able to spread start-up risks, essentially by having the entire local community absorb the cost of failure. Thus, by underwriting a large proportion of entry risks, local governments reduced entry barriers and enabled most start-up firms to commence production on a larger scale, taking advantage not only of niche market opportunities but also of inherent economies of scale. Given their stricter budgetary constraints, these local governments were also keener to monitor enterprises and enforce their interests in a stronger financial performance. As a result, it appears that some public enterprises operating in smaller, budgetary constrained territories may have achieved many of the desirable features of successful private businesses.

Yet, the community-based risk-sharing mechanism should be examined in a much broader context, with particular attention to the interplay between the community economy (at micro level) and the regional and national economy (at macro level). For instance, when risk-sharing at the local level proved an insufficient cushion to absorb the total financial risk generated by local enterprises, part of it was channelled onto the wider economy, through a variety of bailing out provisions offered by organisations external to the community. Thus, a careful scrutiny of local government entrepreneurship reveals a number of key entrepreneurial support factors:

- The institutional capacity of the local government that served as the administrative foundation of community risk-sharing, allowing pooled profits to subsidise or bail out struggling firms;

- Local financial institutions which extended soft credit to both start-ups and growing businesses;

- A flexible labour market that provided a ready pool of experienced and well qualified employees; and

- The collective land system that afforded an added insurance function.

It should be recognised, however, that practices of local government entrepreneurship in China encountered some teething problems. For instance, local governments were superior to the prevailing principal-agent relationships, and able to coerce local banks in financing their priority projects regardless of the interests of these institutions. Wong (1987) highlighted the detrimental effects inherent in the allocative powers of local governments:

- The fragmentation of control tended to obstruct resource flows, and opposition could have slowed or even curtailed the development of local capital markets;

- Resource allocation was not necessarily following 'market regulations', as local governments were making the bulk of investment decisions; and

- Local governments reduced competition by shielding enterprises from market pressures and by intervening in interregional trade.

Overall, local government entrepreneurship in the Chinese context underscores four important aspects of entrepreneurship and regional development:

- Entrepreneurial behaviour is not solely the domain of private businesses.

- There is a close link between entrepreneurial behaviour and motivation, in both private and public organisations.

- Successful entrepreneurship and small business development often require entrepreneurial orientation and behaviour from most, if not all, the key stakeholders engaged at local, regional and national levels.

- The creation of 'bottom up' development capacities in growth-oriented entrepreneurial outlets should place key actors and stakeholders in leadership roles. Through empowerment, they can develop and implement new and/or innovative strategies, behaviours and organisational forms in an embedded 'way of doing things', to work together more efficiently and profitably.

QUESTIONS

1 Local governments in China appeared to have played a crucial role in facilitating entrepreneurship. What is local government entrepreneurship in the Chinese context, and how do you describe the distinct features of local government entrepreneurship in China?

2 What are the strengths and downsides of the Chinese model of local government entrepreneurship?

3 Why does this case study imply that entrepreneurial behaviour is not solely the domain of private businesses?

INTEGRATIVE Case Study 2

Global Entrepreneurship

Partner Logistics: Entrepreneurial Decisions in International Context

By STIJN VAN DEN HOOGEN, *Tilburg University*

HISTORY

At the end of the 1990s, Bram Hage had been working for a large Dutch logistic service provider. Bram had been involved in a project to do research for an automated warehousing solution. The project was done in order to win a tender for a leading producer of potato products. When the project was almost finished, Bram's employer decided to withdraw from the tender, fearing that there was not enough expertise to support the tender. Bram, however, thought differently. He had a huge amount of confidence in the proposed solution. So he decided to quit his job and continue the project he had been working on for such a long time. He founded his own company: Partner Logistics.

In cooperation with suppliers and informal investors, the newly founded firm managed to win the tender. Partner Logistics (PL) signed its first long-term contract for operating an automated cold store in 2000. This first site in Bergen op Zoom (the Netherlands) became operational just two years afterwards, in 2002. In the same year, a second site in Waalwijk (the Netherlands) became operational as well.

At this moment, Partner Logistics has an annual turnover of €35 million, operates ten warehouses in four countries, and Bram is now CEO and in charge of over 450 employees, making Partner Logistics one of the leading players in Europe.

CORE BUSINESS

In the past few years, Partner Logistics has become *the* specialist in operating highly automated warehouses with designing, building and implementing expertise available in-house. This means that Partner Logistics actually develops and finances the warehouses by itself. In return, those clients are prepared and willing to sign long-term contracts for the provision of the warehouse services, which is quite unique in the field of logistics.

Partner Logistics manages to realise service level improvements and cost advantages for its clients by implementing advanced – but proven – technology in the field of warehousing. The key to success lies in the linkage of systems and people.

MARKET

With the first site in Bergen op Zoom (BoZ), Partner Logistics had entered the market of cold stores for food producers. As Bram and his co-founders had limited experience with frozen warehousing, a Belgian cold store company was acquired, thus providing the entrepreneurs with the necessary know-how and people to successfully operate the new site.

At the same time, the Belgian acquisition meant the first international experience for PL. A second acquisition in Belgium introduced a new type of client: retailers. So from this moment, PL was active in two parts of the supply chain: both producers and retailers. Because of the dominant position in the supply chain, retailers are interesting parties to service. Having experience with servicing producers and retailers, PL becomes an interesting partner for all parties in optimising their supply chains. Because retailers often see the distribution centres as a part of their core business, it is very difficult to penetrate the market. The acquisition provided PL this opportunity and the specific know-how. Based on this experience PL has been able to attract new retail clients in the Netherlands and Russia.

Although PL's automated warehousing solutions can be developed for companies from various industries, in 2009 PL's clients are still mainly food producers and food retailers.

INTERNATIONAL EXPANSION

Thanks to the fast international expansion, since 2002 PL has developed into one of the leading logistics service providers in Europe in the field of operating automated warehouses.

Because the Benelux market is very competitive, PL decided to focus on entering markets with less competitive pressure. PL mainly looked at markets in which there are large volumes of business, but where the existing warehouse solutions are not state of the art. Another interesting opportunity lies in the fast-growing markets in which there is a large potential, but limited supply of any warehousing services.

Examples of the former are the UK, France and the US. Examples of the latter are Russia and India. In 2009 PL entered the UK market where two warehouses were built. In Russia the first warehouse is operational. And in both France and Russia additional warehouses are in the planning stage.

In addition to this international expansion, new projects in the Netherlands and Belgium were developed, and the Bergen op Zoom site was upgraded in 2009, now providing capacity for 126,000 pallets.

COUNTRY-SPECIFIC FACTORS

The search for growth, and seizing opportunities in new countries or markets may seem quite logical from a theoretical perspective, but in practice it is not so easy.

Besides the standard project risks, there are many threats to a smooth market entry that are not visible at first sight. Some of the challenges that PL has encountered are:

■ Limited sector-specific know-how available.

■ Receiving a permit to build a 33 meter high automated warehouse, or use of new technologies in the warehouse (e.g. oxygen reduction to prevent fires spreading in the high-bay warehouse).

■ Continuous and reliable availability of electricity (cold stores require a lot of electricity, and the automated systems too).

■ Availability of skilled employees.

■ Financing projects in risky environments.

■ Cultural differences (i.e. the power distance in Russia is much higher than in the Netherlands).

Some of the risk-mitigating measures that PL has taken when entering new markets are:

■ Acquire know-how by acquisition of a company, perform market research, hire know-how, specialists.

■ Form a partnership with a local company.

■ Follow a current client to a new market.

■ Have an own team of people to manage the entire project development process from first client contact to project implementation.

■ Train local people to operate automated warehouse in existing sites.

■ Work with long-term contracts only in order to secure long-lasting relationships with client and maintain cash flows.

■ Focus on spreading the PL culture when starting a new operation. For this reason with starting up there is at least one (expat) manager with PL-blood.

QUESTIONS

The growth of PL is limited by, among other factors, the resources of the in-house development department. For this reason PL focuses its resources on implementing the most attractive projects in terms of project risk and profitability.

1 Which new countries or sectors do you think offer good project opportunities for PL? Why is that?

2 Which risk factors should PL take into account when developing its business in this new market/these new markets?

3 What can PL do to mitigate these risks?

REFERENCES

www.partnerlogistics.eu

http://www.supplychaindigital.com/Partner-Logistics–Taking-care-of-business_13383.aspx

INTEGRATIVE Case Study 3

Social Entrepreneurship

TSiBA Education: 'Igniting Opportunity'

By Dr Retha Scheepers, *Stellenbosch University*

Pumla is very excited, despite getting up at four this morning and taking several trains and taxis to get to TSiBA (The Tertiary School in Business Administration) Education's Campus at Mupine in Pinelands, Cape Town, South Africa. The 18-year old knows that she is about to embark on the opportunity of a lifetime. Ahead of her lie four years of study. She has enrolled for TSiBA's enriched Bachelor in Business Administration (BBA) programme, focused on Entrepreneurial Leadership.

Had it not been for TSiBA, she would never have been able to enrol for tertiary studies. Her mother has been a domestic worker all her life, while Pumla's father left them when she was only eight years old. Even though Pumla worked very hard in school and her mother used most of her salary, as well as contributions by other family members to put her through school, she was not able to obtain a bursary. Without a tertiary qualification, prospects for employment were bleak in South Africa for a young, black girl from a very poor family, with only a Matric certificate! Pumla's thoughts are interrupted by the noise and activity around her. She is here, on the TSiBA campus.

She sees one large, multi-storey building, with several smaller buildings around, beautiful green lawns and a large parking area. She nervously walks towards the main campus building.

Pumla enters the main campus building, she is greeted by Thandeka, a final year student, and one of the volunteers showing first-year students around campus. Thandeka is very welcoming and excitedly explains the various facilities the TSiBA campus has to offer. The campus itself consists of seven large lecture rooms, accommodating between 200 to 250 students, a number of smaller tutorial venues and two information technology labs, with 40 computers each. Administrative and supportive staff utilise the ground floor and offices to perform the various support duties necessary. A full service library, with computers, a study area, canteen and function hall are also available on campus, as well as ample parking and security.

As they walk around campus, Thandeka goes on to explain that TSiBA not only offers educational programmes, but also has a very active Career Centre, which has networks with some of the most influential companies in the country. The Career Centre found a fantastic job for one of Thandeka's friends last year, Sisa. Sisa was busy with her internship, as part of her Business Communication and Career Management course, at Woolworths. Since she was such an efficient and passionate intern, they offered her a permanent job after graduation, with the option of continuing to work part-time for them until then. Pumla was impressed. She knew how difficult it was to find a good job.

Suddenly Thandeka stops in her tracks. She lets out a loud 'Whoooo...'

and runs towards a young man on the other side of campus. Pumla is uncertain, should she follow?

Then Thandeka calls her closer. 'This is Lizo Mgobozi,' she introduces the young, attractive man. 'But we call him MC. He started his own tourism company, called ProTeam SA and runs township tours.' MC looks very young to be having his own business.

It seems as if he can sense Pumla's disbelief and says: 'I started with the help of TSiBA's Entrepreneurship Centre. They helped me to see that I was focusing too much time on the operational aspects of my business and too little on the marketing side. Peter Kraan, the manager of the Entrepreneurship Centre, helped me to design an effective marketing campaign and encouraged me to register myself as a certified tour guide. We've redesigned brochures for the business and also revamped the website. I've also placed all my brochures in tourism offices and hotel lobbies across the Western Cape! The new website has also generated a lot of business. It's so cool!' Pumla is astounded; she doesn't really know what to say: 'That's great!' is all she can muster. 'Come on,' says Thandeka, 'we'd better go back to the main Hall where the Welcome and Orientation will be starting soon, or I'll get you into trouble on the first day for being late. Bye, MC, catch you later …'

They rush back to the main building and gather with many other first-year and senior students to enter the largest lecture room on campus. In front, the Director of Academic Programs, Mrs Adri Marais, of TSiBA Education is getting ready for the 'Welcome and Orientation' of the first-year students.

Pumla has butterflies in her stomach. She must make a success of this year; her whole family's hopes are pinned on her. Her grandmother would be so proud if her, when she becomes the first person in her family to earn a degree. She can just see it now …, but the rowdy students around Pumla bring her daydream to an abrupt end. She can see students all around her sitting in groups, and senior students are also around.

Adri Marais steps forward and starts to calm the group down. She explains that TSiBA Education is a private provider of Higher Education in business, which was established in 2004. Most students sitting in front of her are enrolled in TSiBA's unique Foundation Certificate in Business Administration and will follow the enriched Bachelor in Business Administration focused on Entrepreneurial Leadership; only a few of the senior students are in their final year. TSiBA specifically targets scholars and potential students who would otherwise not have access to tertiary level education, by offering successful applicants full tuition scholarships. Pumla realises that she definitely falls into this category.

All students at TSiBA are on scholarship; as such, TSiBA partners with corporate and individual funders who sponsor the operations and management of the institution. The TSiBA degree is fully registered and accredited by the South African (SA) Department of Education and the SA Council on Higher Education. Marais continues, for those students who did not know the name TSiBA, it means to jump, and this is their chance to jump at the opportunity of education. TSiBA's vision is therefore 'igniting opportunity', realised by means of their mission, 'to be an innovative and sustainable learning community that graduates business leaders who ignite opportunity within economically impoverished communities'.

Marais goes on to talk about TSiBA's philosophy of 'Pay it Forward'. Through this philosophy TSiBA strives to create an inspirational environment where they, the students, staff and volunteers can be the best they can be and engage in knowledge sharing within the context of their wider community. 'It is for this reason that the practices of leadership and self-development are integrated throughout the curriculum', she says, also 'all foundation year students, who sit in front of me today, will by the end of the week be involved in activities in and around the campus, helping out. By the time you are senior students you will be running enrichment programmes in your communities.'

Pumla has never heard of such a concept at university-level – she thought that she needed to concentrate solely on her studies this year. Although she is very involved in and around her home, she has never been expected to be involved in community activities at school. Marais says that students are involved through Imbizos, study groups, mentorship, syndicates and a dedicated Student Representative Council (SRC).

Marais then introduces the Registrar, Lisa Cloete. Despite her lack of sleep, Pumla tries to focus and concentrate on what Lisa Cloete is saying. Pumla knows that the registration process, and Rules and Regulations of TSiBA that Mrs Cloete will speak on may not be exciting, but if you don't listen to this stuff, you might be lost later on.

Before Mrs Cloete talks about which forms to fill in, where to go and the Rules and Regulations, she first explains where TSiBA came from and why there is a need for such an institution in South Africa.

According to Mrs Cloete, TSiBA is a university which meets the needs of the business world. She says: 'The need for experienced, work-ready graduates in South African business is great. Of the many challenges facing our country, unemployment and appropriate skills development are two of the most pressing. Their shadow sides, crime and poverty, complete what is becoming an ever-darker picture of the future, unless the state of education in South Africa changes fast.' She says that statistics show that only 1.4 per cent of South Africa's population studies at tertiary level and that 71 per cent of tertiary students who enrolled in 2000 had dropped out by 2004'. 'Wow' thinks Pumla 'those are scary figures. No wonder there's such a huge need for quality graduates.' Mrs Cloete goes on to explain that TSiBA has focused on the three key challenges historically disadvantaged students experience in their approach, namely access to education, retention and throughput, and work readiness.

TSiBA Education's solution to problem of access, lack of financial means and poor performance of historically disadvantaged learners is to actively recruit and identify untapped talent within communities that are impoverished, both academically and economically. Students who successfully pass the extensive application process are awarded a full tuition scholarship, thereby eliminating the financial burden which excludes many learners from studying at university level. Further, the TSiBA degree is structured to ensure that additional learner support is fully integrated into the curriculum.

Previous studies have also shown that although some black African students have the potential to enrol at higher educational institutions, they drop out at the end of their first and second year, due to financial difficulties, personal problems and lack of support at home. TSiBA aims to support their students by minimising class size, providing counselling, maximising face-to-face engagement between lecturers and students and integrating academic, personal and social development into the curriculum. Thereby, TSiBA is able to provide students with the support needed so that they can complete the full four year degree. Financial support over and above the provision of the scholarship is facilitated through part-time work which is sourced via the TSiBA Career Centre and the TSiBA Entrepreneurship Centre. In addition, TSiBA also recently started a loan scheme to provide students access to subsistence loans, where tuition support has not been enough.

Finally TSiBA also focuses on enhancing the work readiness of their students by providing additional career preparation, in terms of facilitation in class and internships. In the modern economy, the skills and qualities required for participation as professionals extend beyond the simplistic vocational sense. Employers want graduates who are work-ready and can demonstrate a strong array of analytical and problem-solving skills, and a solid grounding in writing, communication and presentation skills. Therefore TSiBA offers a wide variety of experiential learning opportunities through coordinated internship, mentorship, leadership, entrepreneurship and career management programmes that are core to the degree offering.

Pumla feels more grateful by the minute – she realises that she's been given the opportunity of a lifetime. Some of the senior students start handing out forms again. Pumla receives an information booklet and registration forms.

Adri Marais steps forward again and focuses the attention of all the students on page 3 of the booklet, detailing TSiBA's innovative education model.

A NEW MODEL OF EDUCATION

In the booklet information is provided on how TSiBA's model addresses the challenges in South Africa via two distinctive innovations:

Firstly, in terms of funding, TSiBA sources funding from private institutions, individuals, corporates and foundations so that students with potential do not need to pay TSiBA back for their scholarships. Rather their focus is on enabling their leadership impact but encouraging the philosophy of 'Pay it Forward', growing future leaders, who will return and work with their communities when they are successful. Secondly, in terms of the academic curriculum, TSiBA's highly practical and effective curriculum integrates knowledge, skills and attitude. They have conceived a 'Profile of Graduateness', which has been designed to match the needs of employers or the competencies needed to be a successful entrepreneur.

'What is a Profile of Graduateness?, What is she talking about?' Pumla wonders, but Marais goes on to explain: 'As you can see on page 4 of your information booklet, TSiBA Education believes that an effective graduate needs a wide array of competencies to succeed in today's competitive job market. We have examined the characteristics, values and knowledge which the business world requires. These competencies need to be developed by focusing on the development of knowledge, skills and the right attitude. The three aspects that TSiBA focuses on by developing the appropriate knowledge, skills and attitude, we call our *Profile of Graduateness*.' (See Figure 1.)

'While you will gain fundamental and business knowledge, while developing entrepreneurial leadership throughout your studies, we also

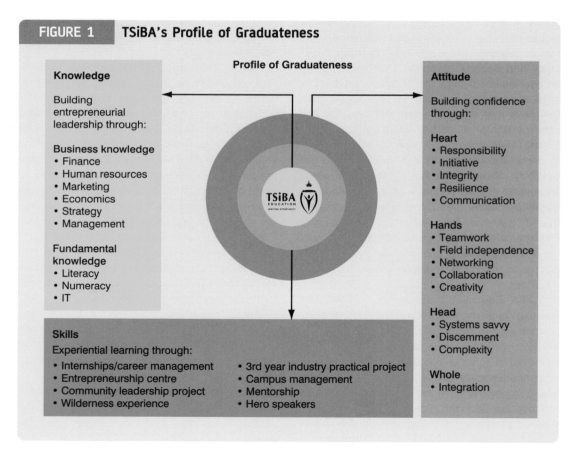

FIGURE 1   **TSiBA's Profile of Graduateness**

focus on each and every student's attitude. Your attitude is made up of your heart, head and hand, in other words what you feel, you know and what you do – all these aspects will be integrated in your learning and development here. Finally we also focus on experiential learning opportunities throughout your studies. In this way TSiBA is different from many mainstream universities and business schools in South Africa.'

Marais continues: 'In many other business administration courses offered in South Africa, undergraduate business degrees tend to process students in an insufficiently supported and 'sausage-machine like' way; and then expect those same sausages to be employed by businesses that are looking for up-and-running, business-savvy, hit-the-ground-, self-starting business graduates. TSiBA is different, since we specialise in producing the sort of graduate the business world is looking for. This saves businesses and graduates time, trouble and money; and begins the long haul of successfully bridging the ever-widening skills gap. Moreover, as most of our students come from poor backgrounds, which are almost exclusively black, we also help companies meet their affirmative action targets in a meaningful way, with qualified graduates. Last, but by no means least, comes the knock-on effect of income-earning graduates on the poverty of their families and the subsequent poverty alleviation's effect on levels of crime. The vicious circle becomes a virtuous one and everybody, not least the well-trained, well-assimilated students benefit.'

Pumla can't believe her luck. She has been blessed, beyond measure. She has truly found her starting point in the world. It seems like TSiBA's approach is comprehensive and will enable her to achieve her dreams. As she fills out the various registration forms, she can't wait to get started. The education she receives here will be the beginning of her and her family's chance to escape the poverty cycle. She fondly remembers her grandmother, quoting Nelson Mandela's words:

'Education is the great engine of personal development. It is through education that the daughter of a peasant can become a doctor, that a son of a mineworker can become the head of the mine; that a child of a farm worker can become the president of a country'.
Nelson Mandela

QUESTIONS

1 Can 'entrepreneurial leadership' be taught?

2 Can TSiBA Education be seen as a socially entrepreneurial organisation?

3 Compare the business model of TSiBA to that of a mainstream university.

4 Identify the opportunities and threats facing TSiBA within a developing country, such as South Africa.

5 Is the business model TSiBA Education is pursuing sustainable?

Part 2

....

IN SEARCH OF THE ENTREPRENEUR

....

Going in Search of the Entrepreneur

....

Jake looked at the email he had just received about the entrepreneurship competition.

'You can forget about the celebration. We didn't win', he said.

'What! I thought our idea was brilliant. Who would not want to support an enterprise that revolutionised the beekeeping business?' said Jasmine.

'It's a pity we could not get to speak to any real beekeepers as I'm sure that would have made our entry even more believable. The email says if we are still interested in developing our entrepreneurial potential we could go along to some talks that actual entrepreneurs are giving next week', read Jake.

'Well one thing I did learn from the people we spoke to is that entrepreneurs do not give up, so we had better go along and try again', said Jasmine

The following week, Jasmine and Jake listened to talks by two people who had started their own enterprises. They discussed the two speakers afterwards.

'Who do you think was the most entrepreneurial?' asked Jake.

'Well, the woman had lots of ideas and tried many of them out, but only one had really worked and is still running as a business. I am not sure you can really count her as an entrepreneur with so many failures', said Jasmine.

'But she said that's how she had learned how to be an entrepreneur – through her many different experiences that finally led her to what she does now. She is in the music business so she had to be creative and try different things. And she seems to know everyone in the business judging by all the names she dropped.' said Jake.

'I was more impressed with the second guy who had planned it all very carefully from the time he had the idea with his two friends, to when he tested it out and then launched it all round the country. He even wrote the business plan when he was still at university', argued Jasmine.

'Ok, but he just took the idea from America and brought it over here – so he wasn't very creative, was he? He was more like a manager than an entrepreneur I would say. The woman was much more creative and original', countered Jake.

'But he raised lots of money and took quite a risk. Do you have to be original to be an entrepreneur?' asked Jasmine.

What do you think are the important qualities that separate out entrepreneurs from the rest? Do they have to be original or just successful?

Learning Objectives and Structure of Part 2

The chapters in Part 1 investigated entrepreneurship as a *process* and how it exists or operates within organisations and society. However, entrepreneurship is more than a way of doing things and a social phenomenon. It is also about people. This section turns towards the individuals who are *entrepreneurs*, and considers what they are like, and what they do. It considers whether entrepreneurs are born or made, and examines some of the behaviours and activities typically ascribed to entrepreneurs. It also considers what key knowledge areas they share, and how these might be acquired.

By the end of Part 2, the reader should be able to:

■ Identify what entrepreneurs do and how they do it

■ Assess what entrepreneurs need to know and how they learn

■ Understand the nature of, and need for, the management of creativity

■ Evaluate the value of networks and how to access them

■ Develop decision-making and business planning skills.

There are four chapters that focus on these learning objectives:

Chapter 7   The search for the entrepreneur

Chapter 8   Entrepreneurs and managing creativity

Chapter 9   Entrepreneurial networking

Chapter 10 Entrepreneurial decision-making and planning

CHAPTER 7

The Search for the Entrepreneur

LEARNING OBJECTIVES

After studying this chapter, the reader will be able to:

- Evaluate whether entrepreneurs are born or made
- Identify typical entrepreneurial behaviours
- Understand the influences on the development of entrepreneurial characteristics
- Understand how entrepreneurs learn from positive and negative experiences and transform them into knowledge
- Appreciate the role of self-efficacy in fulfilling entrepreneurial potential
- Identify ways of improving their entrepreneurial capability and knowledge areas for entrepreneurship.

INTRODUCTION

This chapter provides an overview of the main theories relating to entrepreneurial capability and behaviour. The objective is to enable readers to focus on what entrepreneurs are like, how they learn to be entrepreneurial, and how they develop their businesses. If entrepreneurship is an important phenomenon in society, and entrepreneurial action is important to the growth of economies and societies, then the supply of entrepreneurs is also important. We need to develop ways of identifying what individual entrepreneurs are like and how they become entrepreneurial. If we can understand what makes entrepreneurs tick, we may be able to increase the level of entrepreneurship in society in general and advise individuals how to become more entrepreneurial.

Are entrepreneurs born, or made? Some people argue that being an entrepreneur is an innate trait, an aspect of a person's personality (for instance McClelland, 1961; Brockhaus, 1982). They point to the fact that some people start many businesses (often starting from a very young age), while others never even consider starting something new, as evidence that entrepreneurs are a certain type of person. According to this view, entrepreneurs are simply born that way, and others need not apply! Others disagree, arguing that entrepreneurs are made, not born. They argue that people learn to be entrepreneurs through their social context, through a formal education process, or through experience (for instance Chell, 2008).

PREVIEW CASE

Gareth and Mark: Contrasting starts to entrepreneurial careers

Gareth was a salesman in a financial services business, his wife a franchise holder of a successful beauty therapy business. Gareth was keen to develop his business knowledge, and decided to do an Executive MBA, on which he was part-sponsored by his employer. As part of the MBA, Gareth took a business start-up module, and produced a business plan for introducing a new product into the UK. The product was a baby hammock, which Gareth and his wife had discovered when they were looking for a way to help their baby to sleep better.

Mark Parry started his first businesses as a teenager, and by the age of 23 had started five, closed one and sold one. These were mostly in the IT industry, although there was also a mobile discotheque. Mark studied IT at university, and his more recent businesses all exploit the knowledge he gained there.

Why do you think that some people start businesses at a young age, while others wait to get started? How does their education influence these decisions?

Read more about Mark and Gareth at the end of this chapter.

7

This chapter builds on the debate begun in Chapter 1 about who entrepreneurs are and what they do by investigating some of the theory and evidence about what entrepreneurs are like. In particular it invites you to consider what constitutes entrepreneurial behaviour, and what skills appear to underpin this behaviour. What are entrepreneurs good at, and how do they behave? It also considers whether attitudes are an important aspect of entrepreneurship, and how entrepreneurs might learn about entrepreneurship and change and develop their attitudes.

7.1   WHAT IS AN ENTREPRENEUR?

Some questions draw researchers to them, like moths to a flame. Two questions that have attracted the attention of entrepreneurship researchers for many years are: Who can be described as an entrepreneur? Are they born that way, or can anyone learn how to be one? This body of work was introduced in Chapter 1 (section 1.3 'Dominant perspectives on entrepreneurship') and is summarised by Chell (2008) into some key areas that we will explore in more detail below:

■ the social and cultural background of entrepreneurs;

■ entrepreneurial traits or other personality theories;

■ the type of knowledge that entrepreneurs have in common;

■ the role of education for entrepreneurship.

7.1.1 Social, Cultural and Economic Influences

One of the challenges to the idea that entrepreneurs are born rather than made, comes from national and international studies of entrepreneurship. As discussed in earlier chapters (e.g. Chapter 4 'Entrepreneurship and the economy'), entrepreneurship levels and rates of new enterprise start-ups vary from country to country. Is it likely that different nations have a different genetic makeup relating to entrepreneurship?

Different societies show different levels of entrepreneurship, as identified by the rate of new venture start-ups. This implies that people may be influenced by cultural, societal and institutional settings, rather than simply being born entrepreneurs. The Global Entrepreneurship Monitor (GEM) studies entrepreneurship across 42 countries, and provides rich comparative data on national rates of entrepreneurial start-ups. The data show very different rates of enterprise start-up between countries (for instance Bosma, Jones, Autio and Levie, 2008).[1] Seeking explanations of these differences is an important strand in entrepreneurship research, as understanding them would help to develop policy interventions to encourage entrepreneurial activity.

Governmental interest in entrepreneurship as an engine for economic development is well established (see Chapter 4 for a full discussion of this area). Governments intervene to encourage entrepreneurial activity in many ways, including taxation, fiscal stimulation, regulations relating to international trade and the legal framework for protection of intellectual and other forms of property. These different incentives and controls are applied at the level of industries, regions, countries and international trade, for instance within the European Union (Minniti, 2008). However, which of these methods are most successful is not clear (Capelleras, Kevin, Greene and Storey, 2008).

The GEM researchers suggest a distinction between **opportunity driven** entrepreneurship and **necessity** entrepreneurship (Reynolds, Camp, Bygrave, Autio and Hay, 2001), particularly in countries with low employment levels. In less developed countries for instance, entrepreneurship levels are often higher than in more developed countries, because it is more difficult to find employment there. The distinction is between entrepreneurs on the one hand who say they have had different employment options open to them, but have chosen to pursue an entrepreneurial idea instead, and those on the other hand who have no option but to go into self-employment. There is, however, debate about whether the distinction between these two different drivers is clear-cut, and evidence that the notion of necessity entrepreneurship is not meaningful to those pursuing self-employment in these contexts (Rosa, Kodithuwakku and Balunywa, 2006). People may be consciously pursuing higher-status jobs or careers by entering self-employment, rather than doing so because of a complete absence of alternative work. So the availability of work which is perceived to be appropriate may be significant, rather than the total amount of work available (see also Chapter 4 subsection 4.3.2 'Economic conditions that support entrepreneurship').[2]

Culture is also suggested as a significant factor in forming entrepreneurs. Culture is essentially a set of widely shared norms, values, beliefs and behaviours, within a country, region or organisation (Hofstede, 1980). We learn culture and become socialised into our society continually, throughout our life, starting from the moment we are born. Perhaps some cultures are more attuned to entrepreneurship, enabling individuals to grow up with a better appreciation of and ability to undertake entrepreneurship. There are various challenges to this proposal. First, it is difficult to separate out levels of culture. Nations (which are the basic unit of data collection for the GEM studies, for instance) do not necessarily contain or represent a single culture. So the relative influence of culture and national institutions is not clear. There is evidence that national institutional arrangements are a more significant influence (Tan, 2002) than cultural influence. In addition, some research has begun establishing aspects of entrepreneurship which may be universal across cultures. In particular, there may be attitudes towards engaging in entrepreneurship which are universal (Mitchell *et al.*, 2002).

Education appears to be another factor which influences the number of entrepreneurs, particularly in more developed countries, which have high levels of employment. Studies have identified that people who have stayed in education longer are more likely to be self-employed, and to be successful in self-employment (Robinson and Sexton, 2002; Harding, 2007). For instance in the UK and US, people with more education in general and more enterprise education in particular are significantly more highly represented among entrepreneurs than others. People with access to enterprise education are twice as highly represented among entrepreneurs in the UK as those without such access (Harding, 2007). Thus more formal educational arrangements within a society seem to help to create entrepreneurs.

We conclude from these observations that entrepreneurs emerge from a context. Individually we experience a multi-faceted environment from our earliest days, and this environment may promote or hinder our ability to develop our entrepreneurial capability. This seems to be because individuals in different countries are presented with different barriers to starting an entrepreneurial venture such as institutional arrangements, laws, education and other practical difficulties. The GEM studies make a compelling case for improving the institutional arrangements nationally and internationally which support entrepreneurship.

Some of the influences already identified are culture, institutional support and arrangements, and education. Entrepreneurs in this view are not born, but made.

ENTREPRENEURSHIP IN ACTION

Rajasana Otiende: *Lifescape* magazine (www.lifescapemag.com)

Media Studies student Rajasana Otiende had a dream of starting a lifestyle magazine focused on well-being, ethical trade and natural products and services. The concept reflected her interests, beliefs and pastimes, and she felt there were many others who shared these with her. She decided to make her dream reality after she graduated, and founded *Lifescape* magazine, but it wasn't as easy as she thought. For her first editions, Rajasana did everything herself: writing, layout, purchasing print, editing, selling advertising, finding distribution channels. Supported by her husband, she funded the first edition personally, working on the assumption that the advertising sales and cover price of the magazine would cover her costs from the start. The first edition appeared in due course, but didn't cover the costs as she expected.

She got a quote for printing the magazine, and accepted it. After a few editions, she decided to get further quotes, and discovered that the charges from the first printer were rather higher than anyone else would have charged. She had several other disappointments among her suppliers, too; late deliveries were common.

Rajasana was organising distribution herself, and found that increasing sales volumes was difficult. The costs of the advertising campaigns that were needed to make an impact were high, but she and her husband supported them themselves. The slow growth of distribution affected the growth of advertising income too, so overall her income was much lower than she had expected, while costs were higher. After she started her business, she had two children. One of the things she likes about running a business was that she could work from home while she looked after them. The autonomy that being her own boss provided was a big positive factor.

Determined to make *Lifescape* a success, Rajasana decided she needed to know more about business, and went back to university. From her business degree she learned about business terminology, business planning and a little bit about finance. She also found mentors and other supporters in the entrepreneurship community there. The business didn't grow, however, and eventually both her home and her car were threatened. Still she continued with the magazine. She was supported in part by advertisers who liked the idea of the magazine and wanted it to succeed. They paid her more than market rates to advertise in the magazine because it matched their advertising needs so perfectly.

After six years, *Lifescape* started breaking even on an issue by issue basis. Rajasana was delighted – her dream was finally coming true!

7.1.2 Male and Female Entrepreneurs

The GEM studies also show differences in entrepreneurship rates between males and females (Harding *et al.*, 2008). But these differences are not consistent across countries. In most developed countries, including the UK, female rates of early stage entrepreneurship were only about half that of men. However in the US, it was 60 per cent; in Brazil, the rates were the same between men and women. There is some evidence that the numbers of female entrepreneurs have been under-reported. Women who co-own a business with a partner may be excluded from definitions of female-owned businesses, or their influence in running an enterprise may be hidden (Forson, 2006). Despite these regional differences and definitional issues, female entrepreneurs internationally exhibit distinct trends:

- Women still constitute a lower proportion of business owners than men;

- They are catching up, as females have been starting new ventures at a higher rate than men; and

- They tend to be owners of smaller, less high-growth firms than men (Morris, Nola, Craig and Coombes, 2006)

Does this mean that female entrepreneurs are intrinsically different from male entrepreneurs? Do we need a distinctive set of theories and conceptual models for female entrepreneurs compared to their male counterparts? According to Brush (2006) there are many similarities but also some interesting differences.

- **Similarities** include:

  - *Demographics* – gender differences are less important than other demographic variables such as ethnicity and social background.

  - *Motivations* – women become involved in entrepreneurial ventures for similar reasons to men such as the need for independence and achievement.

  - *Business issues* – female-owned enterprises seem to face similar issues to those of men, and have similar survival rates. Male- and female-owned businesses that grow substantially tend to end up with similar structures and practices.

- **Differences** include:

  - *Market sector* – female-owned enterprises tend to be concentrated in the retail and service sectors whilst male-owned firms are more widely spread.

  - *Entrepreneurial process* – there is some evidence that the lack of equal opportunities in employment may influence the way in which women approach entrepreneurship. If they are disadvantaged in gaining access to managerial posts and higher salaries whilst employed, women may have less human and financial capital when starting up their own ventures, which in turn may make them more cautious and less ambitious for the growth of their venture.

  - *Access to resources* – women tend to start up in business with less capital than men. Morever they are less likely to use equity finance. Whilst this can be partly explained by lower finance requirements of female owners because of the sectors they tend to concentrate on, there does seem to be a 'finance gap' in relation to female entrepreneurs (see also Chapter 15, section 15.4.2 'Market failure in the money markets').

Both liberal and social feminist perspectives explain these differences by reference to inequalities in the business and economic environment rather than to any inherent characteristics of female compared to male entrepreneurs. It is the uneven playing field, rather than the entrepreneurial potential of the players, that counts.

Gloria Serobe: Empowering women in South African society

Gloria Serobe is attempting to create more equal entrepreneurial opportunities for women in South Africa. She set up WIPHOLD (Women Investment Portfolio Holdings Ltd), an investment company with the aim of creating a critical mass of South African women in business. They invited women to invest money in the shares of the fund and 18,000 came forward, but they had to buy them out again when WIPHOLD ran into trouble.

7.1.3 Entrepreneurial Traits

The social and economic context affects the rate at which people undertake entrepreneurial ventures. Does this mean that there is an 'entrepreneurial stereotype', a particular type of person who is more likely to be entrepreneurial? If we can identify a typical entrepreneurial personality, it would help to identify potential entrepreneurs in the population and focus investment and support for new ventures on them. This so-called 'trait' or personality approach has generated much research, the importance and influence of which has fluctuated over time.

Integrative Case Link
Read more about Gloria Serobe and how she turned WIPHOLD round in Case Study 4 at the end of Part 2.

Research approaches to personality traits are derived from the observation of people and their behaviours. Traits are descriptors of people, in particular their habitual patterns of thought, behaviour or feeling. Traits can be measured, so that how much of a particular trait someone displays can be evaluated. This means that people can be compared, and norms for different groups of people (for instance people in different occupations) can be established. In this way it can be established if entrepreneurs are similar to one another and how or if they are different from other groups of people.

Various traits have been linked to entrepreneurship over many years of study, but three in particular stand out: the need for achievement, locus of control and risk taking.

■ The **need for achievement** describes the extent to which people need positive feedback for what they do (McClelland, 1961). It is argued that some people, including entrepreneurs, need to see results or positive outcomes from their activities more than others. People with a greater need for achievement also set high standards, and measure themselves by constantly seeking feedback. Positive feedback leads to further striving and attainment. In the field of entrepreneurship, this need for achievement translates in practice into the creation of new businesses.

■ The **locus of control** trait describes the extent to which an individual perceives themselves in control of circumstances, or believes that circumstances are outside of their control (Brockhaus, 1982). It is argued that entrepreneurs typically see themselves as being in control, so that they see themselves shaping circumstances. This empowers them to address and overcome situations that others might see either as too demanding, or within someone else's control.

■ The **risk-taking** trait describes the extent to which an individual takes risks. Although initially the suggestion was that entrepreneurs were invariably high risk-takers, research now indicates that entrepreneurs are moderate risk-takers (Brockhaus, 1980). Perceptions of risk are quite subjective, and dependent on individual knowledge and insight into a situation. Entrepreneurs are said to take risks which they are able to calculate and make sense of for themselves.

These three traits are sometimes expanded to include two more: the need for autonomy and a creative tendency (Caird, 1991).

■ A strong **creative tendency** links with the process of entrepreneurship, which involves the innovation or modification of a product or service, or the improvement of a process (as discussed in Chapter 3, Entrepreneurship and innovation). To introduce change and innovate, entrepreneurs need higher than average levels of creativity (Ward, 2004).

■ The **need for autonomy** is a further measure on which entrepreneurs are thought to score highly (Hornaday and Aboud, 1971). This measure is associated with a reluctance to work for others, and a need to work outside of formal structures. Starting an enterprise is a manifestation of this need for autonomy.

While some research (for instance Lee, 1996) has established that these factors may be important in entrepreneurs (particularly the need for achievement), the results of many studies have been inconsistent, creating uncertainty about their usefulness. Chell (2008) has also pointed out that there are methodological problems with the research which undermine its authority. A particularly telling criticism is that the research is inconclusive about cause and effect. Are people entrepreneurial because they have these traits, or does being an entrepreneur help to develop them? There is a lack of consensus on how these traits are developed. Is it by experience, education, or in some other way?

A trait provides a snapshot of what an entrepreneur is like, but like all snapshots, it is a static view. Entrepreneurship is a process of value creation, and it is enacted by people over time. Traits descriptions do not indicate what entrepreneurs do to develop value. If one objective is to increase the supply of entrepreneurs, it is not clear how an analysis of entrepreneurial traits would help.

7.1.4 Personality Types and Entrepreneurship

A similar approach is provided by the Myers-Briggs Type Indicator (MBTI) and its underlying theory, which are widely used in career and life counselling settings. The theory is that people are born with certain preferences in their personality, which they are able to exercise from a young age. However, although we have a natural preference (like being right- or left-handed), we can improve our skills in both the less-preferred and the more-preferred characteristics (Briggs Myers and McCaulley, 1985).

The MBTI preferences operate across four dimensions:

■ *Extraversion – Introversion*: whether the individual is oriented towards the external world of activity and objects, or to the internal world of ideas and feelings. Individuals gather their energy by preference from one or the other, and pay attention more easily to one or the other.

■ *Sensing – Intuition*: how the individual takes in information – via their senses, or via their intuition or pattern-making capability. In the case of sensing, we take in the world through the concrete reality presented by our senses. Using intuition, we see patterns, connections, symbols and possibilities rather than the concrete present.

■ *Thinking – Feeling*: how the individual makes decisions – via a logical and impersonal process, or via a more personal process which focuses centrally on the implications of decisions for people.

■ *Perception – Judging*: how individuals interact with the world around them – in an open manner, seeking new sensations or connections, or in a more decisive manner, making decisions and coming to conclusions.

These dimensions, and the interactions between them, enable a total of 16 different personality types to be identified. Many studies of employee and professional groups have identified that any particular job or role may attract certain personality types more than others. The original purpose behind the development of the MBTI test was in fact to help people to find roles and employment which suited their personality type.

The theory enables some hypotheses to be made relating to personality type and entrepreneurship, but there is only limited research that has done so and tested them. However, two Finnish studies, one of entrepreneurs (Routamaa and Miettinen, 2007) and one of business students and their aspirations (Jaalstrom, 2002), suggest that certain of these types can be considered more entrepreneurial than others, because they are more highly represented in the sample groups examined.

In particular, these studies suggest that individuals who are spontaneous and flexible in their interactions with the world (a perceiving rather than judging preference) are significantly more highly represented among entrepreneurs than other groups. The perceiving preference indicates flexibility and openness to change, as opposed to decisiveness and seeking closure. It can be linked to opportunity seeking, and also to adaptability to changing circumstances. This approach to the world would seem to fit with the needs of entrepreneurship in two ways:

- seeking the opportunity which forms the basis of any new venture, and

- being flexible and adaptive in developing that venture. In the face of a very competitive and changing market, the ability – indeed the desire – to adapt business models, marketing approaches and resource configurations in a venture may be an important attribute.[3]

The MBTI specifically maintains that some aspects of personality are innate. However, it provides a more dynamic view of personality than the traits theories described above, because it holds that while individuals have preferences, they can also develop their skills in using them. The types and preferences identified by the MBTI are not considered restrictive or limiting. Although people find it easier to work with and develop their preferences, they can develop their less preferred options too. For example, someone who does not favour perceiving, can nevertheless develop an open and perceptive approach to the world. Thus while the MBTI identifies preferred styles and approaches, it also points towards the potential for development and learning.

ENTJs

ENTJs in the Myers-Briggs Type Indicator show preferences of Extraversion, iNtuition, Thinking and Judgement. This means they are more likely to:

- feel motivated by their interaction with other people (E),

- focus their attention on strategic issues rather than day-to-day details (N),

- use logic in making decisions (T) and

- tend to plan their activities well in advance (J).

Relatively rare in the population, ENTJs can make good leadership material: they are thought to include three very influential political leaders, Napoleon Bonaparte, Franklin Roosevelt and Margaret Thatcher. More relevant to entrepreneurship, Microsoft's founder, Bill Gates, is also thought to be an ENTJ. He had the vision to see the importance of a common operating system for computers, and who grew and managed the company in a combative, domineering style from 1975 to 2008.

COURTESY OF MICROSOFT CORPORATIONS

Bill Gates, co-founder of Microsoft.

7.2 KNOWLEDGE AREAS FOR ENTREPRENEURSHIP

If we accept that entrepreneurship can be learned, we now need to consider what has to be learned in order to be more entrepreneurial. What is it that entrepreneurs know, or understand how to do?

7.2.1 Business Plans and Abstract Business Knowledge

Entrepreneurship education encompasses a wide range of information and many different styles of study. Most business schools have modules or courses on aspects of entrepreneurship, typically focused on developing a business plan for a new product or service. The business plan integrates various aspects of learning about enterprise development: the production of financial forecasts; consideration of sources of funding; market research and marketing plans; a discussion of the product, service, or change being proposed (see Chapter 10, Entrepreneurial decision-making and planning). These are certainly all useful knowledge areas, and an individual considering starting a business would be well advised to develop some understanding of them. The business plan also has the advantage that it encourages the individual to investigate, develop, and articulate their idea in a way which is coherent and able to be understood by someone else. Business planning has an educational value in relation to learning about entrepreneurship.

However, emphasis on the development of a business plan as the main preparation for starting an enterprise has been criticised (Sarasvathy, 2004). While plans help to clarify an idea and evaluate the conditions under which an idea might be successful, they also suffer from certain limitations:

- **Not dynamic**   Business plans present an idea and the argument for it in static terms. This is at odds with reality: situations and the business environment change continuously, competitors come up with and implement similar ideas, and partners and supporters often move on to different challenges. This often means gradual or radical adaptation of the idea and its implementation, and a move away from the predictions and promises of the plan.

- **Financial imperative**   Business plans are normally produced to satisfy a prospective funder – a banker, angel, or venture capitalist for instance. Funders need to justify providing funds to an individual, so they need to have documentary evidence to support their decision.

- **Optimistic**   Plans are prone to being overly optimistic in their forecasts, often because they are produced to woo or satisfy funders.

ENTREPRENEURSHIP IN ACTION

Clause Meyer has started several businesses in the food industry in Denmark. His first was a restaurant, which quickly established a reputation as the best in the country, winning many international awards. Inspired by French cuisine, he started the restaurant with a vision to change Danish perceptions and attitudes towards food, but with no clear plan. Despite his preference for improvisation over formalised plans, his vision has created international interest in Scandinavian food generally, and several highly successful businesses:

Clause Meyer

'This is something that just happened. I never worked with plans.'

7.2.2 Industry and Customer Knowledge

Integrative Case Link
Claus Meyer: see the full Case
Study 5 at the end of Part 2 in
this book.

While the integration of abstract business concepts into a business plan has its uses, entrepreneurs need to develop an understanding of practical issues relating to the industry in which they operate, and the particular types of customers they are serving.

An in-depth knowledge of an industry can provide an entrepreneur with many opportunities for innovation. Industries typically have their own competitive dynamics, which are made up of various factors:

- Number and relative size of suppliers, customers and producers in the industry

- Regulatory, legal and social constraints and changes in these

- Technology and changes to the technology

- Products and services available in the industry.

The definition of an industry changes over time. At one time many industries were national in scope, but with deregulation of international markets these may have become regional, international or global. Other redefinitions may incorporate technological change: the growth of the Internet, for instance, has redefined many industries by providing direct virtual shopping; in other markets the convergence of products and technologies has changed the way we buy services, for example in the telecoms and television industries.

The UK power industry – an industry transformed

The power (electricity) industry in the UK was for many years made up of suppliers and producers in the one country. British Coal supplied regional electricity generating companies who sold power into their local markets. Deregulation and international competition have changed this, however. Coal is supplied from producers in several countries, including Russia and Poland; power generating capacity is owned by French, Spanish and American companies; investment for new capacity, particularly nuclear capacity, is likely to come from many countries. Entrepreneurial activity in this industry has been focused on new payment schemes and packages linking electricity and gas customers together, on prospecting new customers in different countries, and on finding new sources of electricity. Technological innovation has focused on the development of wind, solar and water power products.

Knowledge of customers or particular groups can also be an important source of opportunity.[4] In-depth knowledge of consumer behaviour, or of the unfulfilled needs of a group, for instance, can trigger new ideas. This knowledge may come from various sources, for instance first-hand experience or the study of a particular group.

Many entrepreneurs identify and pursue opportunities in industries with which they are familiar in this way. The familiarity is increased with each opportunity investigated and pursued, which in turn increases knowledge and reveals further opportunities.

> ## ENTREPRENEURSHIP IN ACTION
>
> ### I need help ...
>
> Debbie Smith was a PhD student in psychology. She was studying young people who became parents while still teenagers. She noted that this group often failed to access the public services which were available to them to advise them on caring for their babies, on health issues and on housing and other needs they might have. She also noted that they used their mobile phones very frequently, particular the inexpensive text messaging option. So she devised a help service which was accessed via SMS text messaging. The young parents could contact and receive expert advice by their preferred communications channels. Knowledge of this particular group, their difficulties and their behaviour patterns came together.

> ### The Booking People
>
> Mark Parry's product, The Booking People, is a web-based reservations system for independent restaurants. Through it, prospective diners can book a table or tables in a restaurant in advance without phoning the restaurant. Mark developed the system in response to an identified need within the industry. He knew about the industry and its needs through his father, who had worked in the industry for some time. In addition to understanding the industry's needs, Mark also had insight into the way in which such a system might be distributed into the industry. His father distributed cash registers into the restaurant trade, and Mark designed his system so that it could be integrated into the information already held by the cash registers.
>
> (*See the case study at the end of this chapter for more about Mark's ventures.*)

7.2.3 Business Models or Types of Business

Every enterprise – social, public, or commercial – has an operating system or approach to the way it survives and thrives. The 'business model'[5] is the means by which value is drawn from a particular opportunity. For instance, a franchising business model is one by which a successful business is packaged into a common formula in its approach to the market and operating systems, and the right to this package is then sold to others who introduce it into new markets. This approach is particularly popular in the restaurant and retail trades, where famous names like Burger King, Pizza Express and Body Shop all have franchised outlets. This business model facilitates fast growth, as individuals wanting to start their own enterprise can do so by purchasing a franchise, and the entrepreneur who owns the original concept can expand their market coverage quickly by leveraging the efforts and finance of others.

The importance of business models was emphasised in the course of the advent and development of the Internet. One of the first models identified on the Internet was the merchant model in which a web-based shop sold directly to the customer. However, as the Internet has become more ubiquitous, web tools more sophisticated, computing power cheaper, and broadband telecoms more widely subscribed, the range of business models in use has multiplied. This in turn has allowed clearer thinking about business models more generally. Specialists in business models like consumer retailing, the subscription model, the metred usage model, or franchising are sometimes able to turn their knowledge into opportunities in industries or with products about which they know relatively little. Thus retailing experts move from shoes to groceries.

ENTREPRENEURSHIP IN ACTION

TopUp TV – expertise in a new venture

TopUp TV was founded by David Chance and Ian West, both formerly senior executives at BSkyB. The pair had more than 15 years' experience each in the industry, and extensive knowledge of its competitive platforms, its key players and its technologies. Their expertise also encompassed pay-TV business models, as they had developed BSkyB distribution through both direct-to-home satellite TV and cable TV. They had experimented over the years with many different types of pay-TV pricing and packaging, and had been key in establishing BSkyB's dominance of pay- TV in the UK.

(See the case study at the end of Chapter 13 for more about TopUp TV.)

7.2.4 Networking

There are other less theoretical or explicit knowledge areas which entrepreneurs may need to excel in as summarised by Gibb (2003).[6] These include the ability to network effectively.[7] Although some people may have a preference for extraversion, be more externally oriented and have a wide circle of people whom they call friends, this does not necessarily mean that they are effective networkers. Networking is a critical skill which successful entrepreneurs display. Through networking, entrepreneurs meet prospective partners, employees, customers and sponsors. They find resources, and work out how to bring them into their own enterprise. Networking is not a win–lose situation, as an important objective of networking is to find ways to build mutual success. Once again, this skill is not innate but can be learned.

Some key tips for successful networking are listed below. Entrepreneurs who network successfully make sure they:

1 Have something to say about themselves, their ideas and their venture. People want to hear about personal details.

2 Think about what they are looking for – whether it is partners, help, finances, information or customers.

3 Network with an open mind – they never know what will happen, who they will meet, or what they will discover.

4 Stay interested in other people – they are the source of ideas, money, resources and help of all sorts.

5 Think about what they have to offer – networking is a reciprocal activity, and people they help, give information to or otherwise support will be likely to help them in turn.

7.2.5 Opportunity Recognition

As we discussed in Chapter 2,[8] opportunity recognition is the starting point for entrepreneurial activity (Politis, 2005). An opportunity is a recognised need in the marketplace, to which an entrepreneur has a response or solution. Recognising the need, understanding it and coming up with a feasible means of dealing with it implies certain kinds of knowledge. This knowledge is likely to come partly from theoretical learning, but for entrepreneurs it often has its roots in the experience of accessing and evaluating previous opportunities.

> ## ENTREPRENEURSHIP IN ACTION
>
> ### Serial entrepreneurs – in the same industry
>
> Serial entrepreneurs often start their businesses in the same or a closely related industry. Dov and Arna Bar-Gera have established and sold a series of ventures in the telecoms industry in Switzerland. Following an MBA at Insead in France, they entered the telecoms industry, which was just deregulating in Switzerland in the 1990s. A series of ventures in the same industry enabled them to build experience and contacts, and to continually see opportunities as they arose. As new technologies emerged, expanding the telecoms industry, they found ways of implementing new services quickly. Each new venture was developed and sold quickly to more dominant players.
>
> *Source:* FT.com 23 June 2008

Handling the challenges or liabilities associated with creating something new is another area of knowledge that is learned once an opportunity has been identified and pursued. Some of these challenges include finding customers, building reputation, establishing positive cashflow and developing lasting competitive advantage. Again, these may be informed by theoretical learning, but the experience of actually undertaking these activities provides the substantive lessons on which entrepreneurs build their knowledge base.

7.3   ENTREPRENEURIAL LEARNING

One way of learning how to be an entrepreneur is to investigate how entrepreneurs themselves learn their trade, and imitate this process. To do this, we need to explore learning mechanisms in greater depth as entrepreneurs tend to learn in ways that are sometimes at odds with formal education systems.

7.3.1 Experiential Learning

One of the interesting aspects of entrepreneurship is the extent to which entrepreneurs learn from their experiences. Entrepreneurs often start many new businesses in their careers, and attribute some of their successes to the mistakes they made. Their ability to identify what went wrong (or right) and why is an important source of learning.

Evidence that entrepreneurs learn from experience comes from two sources in particular:

- The data on business start-ups and closures indicate that entrepreneurs are typically more successful with each venture they undertake. The majority of business owners who close a business start another one (SBRC, 2002) and those who do, have a greater chance of survival than novice entrepreneurs who are starting for the first time (Politis, 2005).

- Entrepreneurs themselves claim they learn more from their failures than from their success.[9] In the case study in Chapter 6 ('Fogg's Failures') Chris Fogg summarised the lessons he learned from ten business start-ups and claimed that:

    'I believe we can learn more from what doesn't work than from what does.'[10]

This is not a unique feature of entrepreneurship. We all learn from experience but entrepreneurs tend to learn from particular types of experience.

Experiential learning theory (Kolb, Boyatzis and Mainemetis, 2000) puts forward the concept that learning only occurs when *experience* is *transformed into knowledge*. The theory describes two means of acquiring experience:

■ **Concrete experience** – participation in, or observation of, a real event. For example, in order to learn how to drive a car we can simply sit behind the wheel, turn the key and try the controls, although this normally works better if accompanied by an instructor.

■ **Abstract conceptualisation** – information derived from the experience and knowledge of others. In learning to drive, we might read the car manual or the highway code.

These forms of experience can be transformed into knowledge in two ways:

■ **Reflective observation** – thinking about the experience. To improve our driving, we reflect on a journey we have made or remember points from a lesson we have had.

■ **Active experimentation** – testing out different ways of doing things. In a driving lesson, we might practise reversing into a parking space several times in order to learn the best way of doing it.

These four actions form the basis of a *learning cycle* in which knowledge is gained, as illustrated in Figure 7-1. Concrete experiences are the basis of observation and reflection. These reflections are distilled into abstract concepts from which new implications for action can be tested and serve as guides for new actions and experiences (Kolb, Boyatzis and Mainemetis, 2000).

A key point of this concept is that concrete or abstract experience is not enough on its own for knowledge to be acquired. A reflective or active transformation has to impact on the experience to turn it into knowledge. We can either learn from our experiences or continue to make the same mistakes. The majority of entrepreneurs do learn from their experiences, but many do not and repeat patterns that have caused similar problems in the past.

Intelligent Failures Experience can be of successful, unsuccessful, or neutral outcomes and positive learning can be gained from any of these. Kolb (1984) suggests that people have different learning preferences or styles, and notes that these correspond with the types described by the MBTI and other personality instruments. Entrepreneurs show a preference to learn from concrete experience transformed through active experimentation (Politis, 2005). They have little time for abstract theories and want to undertake practical tasks to learn. They also like to experiment and test their concepts in practice rather than reflect on them for very long. Rather than undertake detailed research before launching a new venture,

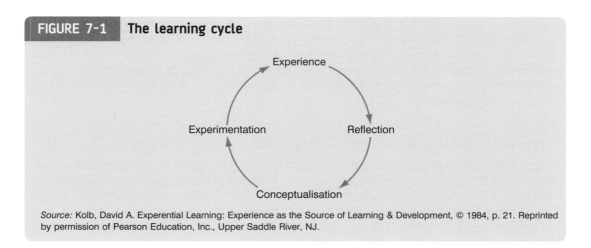

FIGURE 7-1   The learning cycle

Source: Kolb, David A. Experiential Learning: Experience as the Source of Learning & Development, © 1984, p. 21. Reprinted by permission of Pearson Education, Inc., Upper Saddle River, NJ.

WHEN THINGS GO WRONG

Dyson learns from experience in the construction industry

James Dyson is a prolific innovator who learned many lessons on his way to the successful exploitation of his range of vacuum cleaners and other household products. One of his early inventions was the 'Ballbarrow' that was born of his personal experience as a DIY builder whilst renovating an old farmhouse – a 'concrete experience' in more ways than one. Frustrated by his perceived limitations of the traditional metal builders' barrow, he created a more stable, lighter design out of plastic, replacing the wheel with a ball. His first mistake was to assume that the construction industry would share his enthusiasm for replacing their traditional barrow. They did not, but he reflected on the experience and concluded that 'the entrenched professional is always going to resist longer than the private consumer' (Dyson, 1997: 83). He therefore experimented with advertising directly to consumers in the newspapers and was astonished when he achieved a very good response. He built a successful business based on a direct appeal to household gardeners and DIY rather than professional builders.

7

many entrepreneurs follow their intuition, introduce their idea into the market and see what happens. Often, it does not succeed but the lessons learned are invaluable and lead to a more successful venture with suitable modifications, or sometimes an entirely new concept.

For this process of entrepreneurial trial and error to work most effectively, it is important for two conditions to prevail:

■ The experience needs to be significant enough to attract the entrepreneur's attention. We cannot learn from something we have not noticed.

■ The experience needs to be small enough to avoid negative reactions. If the experience is too traumatic, it may damage the entrepreneur's resources and confidence beyond repair.

This has been expressed as a need for 'intelligent failures' (Politis, 2005).

SME Experience   There are ways of learning through experience other than starting up new ventures repeatedly. The GEM studies indicated that people who have already worked in small enterprises are highly represented among those who start new ventures. This suggests that working in a small firm provides relevant experience for starting a new enterprise. Small firms typically provide close contact with an entrepreneur, so that it is possible to acquire knowledge through observing their work and personal learning experiences. In addition, working in a small firm provides rapid and direct experience of the many challenges and activities involved in running an enterprise. Such experience can provide new understanding of the entrepreneurial process. This view is supported by Gibb (2003) who cites an appreciation for the entrepreneurial lifestyle as a useful outcome from a good programme of entrepreneurship education.

Experiential learning within a formal programme

Some formal entrepreneurship programmes integrate experiential learning. The Young Enterprise programme (or 'Junior Achievement' programme in other countries), for instance, used in schools and some universities, enables students to start and run an enterprise for the period of the school or college year within a low-risk framework. Students work through the steps of starting, running and closing down a business. They select a product or service, develop it, raise funds, buy and sell, manage a board of directors, shut the business down, and pay taxes. These experiences can provide valuable knowledge, not only of the legal and financial routines of business, but also of the behaviours needed to work in a team and successfully develop and sell a product.

Some examples of businesses set up at Kingston University include a vintage clothing retailer, a web-design enterprise, and a company importing and selling USB memory sticks from China. The programme holds two market fairs each year, when all of the student companies have stands. In addition, students can sell around the university or in the town centre. Some also go to well-known markets like Camden Town and Portobello Road to sell their goods.

7.3.2 Peer Learning

Entrepreneurs also make extensive use of peer learning. This approach, which is linked to networking, identifies the benefits which entrepreneurs gain from talking and discussing common issues with one another. Meeting with other entrepreneurs and debating in this way enables them to access one another's experiences and interpretations of experience. Through peer learning, the experience of one entrepreneur can be regarded as a resource that can be leveraged by others.

ENTREPRENEURSHIP IN ACTION

Striding Out – a peer support network

Striding Out is an entrepreneurial network established in the UK by Heather Wilkinson, an entrepreneur and policy analyst. Heather realised that young entrepreneurs need the opportunity to learn from one another, and set up a social enterprise to enable this. There is a joining fee for the network, then monthly events with speakers who are entrepreneurs and experts in related entrepreneurial topics. The events provide networking opportunities, through which young entrepreneurs can find partners, customers, and new opportunities. In the first three years since Heather started Striding Out, it has expanded, starting local networks in seven towns in the UK. Many similar networks have been started by others with similar aims, for example Prowess,[11] which supports women entrepreneurs, and Project:Senso[12] in Singapore.

7.4 SELF-EFFICACY

The traits approach to discovering what makes an entrepreneur can be criticised for being insufficiently flexible to allow for personal growth through learning (as discussed above in section 7.3.2). Experiential learning theory takes an opposing view by placing experience at the centre of entrepreneurial learning, but it does accept that entrepreneurs have a preferred style of action-oriented learning. A further concept that synthesises some of the traits approach with the experiential learning perspective of how entrepreneurs develop is **self-efficacy** (Bandura, 1997). This links psychology with action.

The starting point for self-efficacy is that people share several fundamental capacities:

■ We can *symbolise* things – which enables us to make sense of our experience and provide structure and continuity for our lives. Symbols are the vehicles of our thoughts.

■ We can *learn from others* – by observing them doing things, by imitating them and by using them as role models.

- We can plan things ahead and develop strategies for doing things, which Bandura (1997) calls *forethought.*

- We can *self-regulate* – that is, we can keep track of how we are doing at something, judge our own performance against others and react in order to improve our performance.

- We can *reflect* – in order to compare, evaluate or learn.

These capacities mean that we can use our experience and our observations to learn and shape our futures.

We evaluate our own capability to do things successfully. Self-efficacy beliefs are 'people's judgements of their capabilities to organise and execute courses of action required to produce given attainments' (Bandura, 1997: 3). If we believe we have the capability to do things to achieve something we have identified, then we are said to have self-efficacy. Belief in our own capability is said to be an important contributor to our success.

There are several positive (and perhaps some negative) outcomes of self-efficacy. An individual's belief in their own abilities leads them to see things as challenging, rather than difficult, and to seek to meet and overcome the challenges, rather than just avoiding them. Indeed, high self-efficacy leads individuals to establish challenging goals and maintain their commitment to them. Commitment to the task is paralleled by high levels of interest in it. When things go wrong, and failure occurs, people who have self-efficacy will typically think that they have not worked hard enough at the problem, and will increase their commitment and effort. Psychological recovery from failure is swift.

Self-efficacy is said to be developed in several ways, most of which we have touched on already in the context of other learning theories. Experience of success and failure are both important. Success provides positive feedback, while failure which is overcome tends to enhance positive feelings of capability. Success and failure can be experienced through third parties. Seeing someone else being successful is a positive influence on self-efficacy. Self-efficacy can also be enhanced by positive evaluations from other people.

Self-efficacy emphasises that people can learn, and that they do so at least in part through experience. It draws together several of the foregoing areas. The contextualisation of learning into a living or working environment which is full of learning opportunities reflects the evidence of international studies that we learn from our surroundings. The notion of challenge, and that people need positive

WHEN THINGS GO WRONG

Dyson recovers from an IP error

James Dyson's Ballbarrow business (discussed earlier) grew so rapidly that he brought in external investors to fund increased manufacturing capacity and expansion into overseas markets. This diminished his own shareholding in the company to the point where he had only a third of the equity. After falling out with the other shareholders, he was amazed when one day they fired him. Although he was the innovator of the product, he was dispensable because he had made a crucial mistake: he had assigned the patent for the Ballbarrow to the company rather than to himself.

'I had no rights at all to the invention I had created and laboured over for so long. It was not a mistake I was ever to make again' (Dyson, 1997: 96).

As he said, he learned from this early error. He not only made sure that his next invention, the Dual Cyclone vacuum cleaner, was protected with strong patents that he has successfully defended in court, but he also ensured that he owns them in his own name.

Source: Dyson, 1997

feedback, recalls the need for achievement trait discussed earlier. The positive feedback earned from experience draws on experiential learning theory.

Many entrepreneurs set up new ventures repeatedly, and there is a possibility of failure and resulting losses each time. Entrepreneurs need self-efficacy in two areas: the personal conviction that their idea is right and the conviction that they know what to do to implement it. It can be lonely to be an entrepreneur; a positive attitude and self-confidence can help. Innovating or starting something new is also practically challenging, requiring continuous learning across a variety of knowledge areas. Self-efficacy encompasses both personal conviction that the individual knows what to do, and the skills and orientation to learn new things. For these reasons, it is a useful concept for entrepreneurs.

7.5   SUMMARY AND ACTIVITIES

This chapter has introduced the study of entrepreneurs themselves: who they are, how they become entrepreneurial and what they do that distinguishes them as entrepreneurs. We identified several important themes in entrepreneurship:

Entrepreneurs are not all born entrepreneurial. Many develop through a process which includes various **sources of learning** including national, social and cultural influences, the prevailing legal and economic environment and the available formal educational opportunities.

Descriptions of the **typical traits** of entrepreneurs help us to understand them, but explain neither how they develop, nor how to help them do so. Personality research generally provides very mixed evidence of what makes an entrepreneur.

Knowledge areas that assist entrepreneurship include theoretical understanding of business functions and how to integrate them into an enterprise. Entrepreneurs prefer not to learn through abstract concepts but through more direct action.

Understanding of a particular industry, type of business, or business model is a good precursor to starting a successful enterprise. However, such knowledge may be learned through repeated, sometimes unsuccessful, attempts to exploit opportunities.

Entrepreneurs learn from experience but according to **experiential learning** theory, understanding only occurs when experience is transformed into knowledge. There are two means of acquiring experience:

■ *Concrete experience* – participation in, or observation of, a real event.

■ *Abstract conceptualisation* – information derived from the experience and knowledge of others.

These forms of experience can be transformed into knowledge in two ways:

■ *Reflective observation* – thinking about the experience.

■ *Active experimentation* – testing out different ways of doing things

These four actions form the basis of a **learning cycle** in which knowledge is gained. As experiences are often negative, entrepreneurs can limit the damage through 'intelligent failures' that are big enough to notice but small enough to survive.

As well as learning from the experience of trying things out, entrepreneurs may **learn from their peers**, from **observing** others at work, and from **working** in entrepreneurial enterprises. These may provide motivation, examples and knowledge of how to get things done.

Opportunity recognition and dealing with the **risks and uncertainties** of new situations are the two important activities which entrepreneurs need to learn about.

Self-efficacy is a concept which unites various theories of learning in entrepreneurship. Self-efficacy entails having the self-confidence, knowledge and self-awareness to believe that you can do something. In the case of entrepreneurship, this may mean starting an enterprise or developing an entrepreneurial project.

7

REVIEW QUESTIONS

1   How do statistics on entrepreneurial ventures in different countries help us to understand entrepreneurs?

2   What is the impact of national culture and institutions on entrepreneurs?

3   What limits the rate of entrepreneurial start-ups among women?

4   What traits are commonly used to describe entrepreneurs?

5   What is meant by 'experiential learning'?

6   What are the four elements of Kolb's learning cycle, and how do they interact?

7   What are the key knowledge areas for entrepreneurship?

8   What are the main ways that entrepreneurs develop their knowledge?

9   What are the main elements of self-efficacy for entrepreneurship?

10 How do entrepreneurs develop self-efficacy?

SEMINAR TASK

Split into groups of about six people. Each group should identify at least three entrepreneurs, working across different domains of activity, including at least one social entrepreneur. Having identified these, consider what it is they are or do which helps to define them as entrepreneurs. What are the similarities between them? How did they become entrepreneurs, and what patterns of action can you identify?

Debrief to the plenary group. Identify commonalities between responses. Try to lay out a range of aspects of entrepreneurial behaviour or character.

Preview case continued

Gareth and Mark: Contrasting starts to entrepreneurial careers

Gareth was a salesman in a financial services business, and his wife a franchise holder of a beauty therapy business which was successful in the South East of England area where they lived. Gareth was keen to develop his business knowledge in order to accelerate his career, and decided to do an Executive MBA, on which he was part-sponsored by his employer. As part of the MBA, Gareth took a business start-up module, and produced a business plan for introducing a new product into the UK. While he was studying, his wife gave birth to Rosie. The rest of his course was punctuated by the sounds of Rosie not sleeping.

Whilst looking for a solution to their lovely, but non-sleeping, baby, Gareth discovered a product which they thought might help – a baby hammock. The hammock was said to

▶

encourage sleep, and when they purchased one from New Zealand, where it had originated, it did.

Gareth's MBA business plan envisaged him becoming the main distributor for the product in the UK. He entered his idea into the university's business ideas competition, and to his own amazement, he won one of the top prizes. As he later said, this encouraged him to continue developing his business proposal and investigating the opportunity.

Having secured the rights to the product for the UK, Gareth gave up his job in order to pursue the opportunity. He had the product redesigned to make it more attractive, and approached 60 manufacturers before finding one to make the new design in the UK. His path was fraught with difficulties and delays, and with each delay the opportunity seemed further away. Gareth took delivery of a prototype just before speaking at an entrepreneurship event for students at his own university, and discovered to his dismay that he couldn't assemble it easily. He had to have it substantially redesigned both for ease of production and simple home assembly.

Mark is what is often called a serial entrepreneur. He began starting enterprises when he was a teenager, finding ways of buying and selling things to other students at school in London.

Mark was lucky to be at a secondary school which participated in an enterprise education programme run by an organisation called Young Enterprise. Young Enterprise is a social enterprise which receives some corporate sponsorship as well as fees for its services to schools and young people. It is committed to the concept of experiential learning, and is focused on the knowledge area of how to set up and run enterprises. Its main programme, run in schools and universities, entails teams of young people setting up, running and closing down businesses.

The process is that teams develop a product or service, market and sell it, deal with customers, and keep accounts for a year before closing the business down. The team has to name a Board of Directors from within their group, establishing what each one will do. They produce a business plan, raise funds on the basis of their plan, and implement it. The programme provides experience and understanding of the legal and regulatory steps entailed in starting up a business, key business functions like marketing, accounting and operations, as well as the requirements of financial stakeholders.

Young Enterprise run a competition nationally between schools which participate in their programme. The winners of regional competitions go to semi-finals and national finals. Mark was the Managing Director of the firm, and took the team to the national finals of the associated business competition.

Separately, Mark started a mobile discotheque business, playing gigs at student parties, and family get-togethers like weddings and birthday parties. He continued this business into university, as a way of paying his university fees.

At university Mark studied IT, and as his degree unfolded, he became interested in businesses relating to the web. As he developed his knowledge in the field, he started another business, designing websites and providing web-based services for other organisations. Although at first he did all the development work himself, as the business grew he outsourced the software and webservice production to contractors in low-cost countries like Poland and India. He developed a network of contacts whom he could work with virtually in order to complete orders on time.

Mark's IT degree included a year's placement within a business. This placement, common in degree programmes in the UK, provides experience in a firm, helping students to apply their knowledge, and to see what it is like to work in an organisation. For those working in a smaller enterprise, it often provides exposure to the founders and their work ethic and lifestyles. It also provides

7

experience across functional areas, as in small businesses people have to do more than one thing. Mark worked with Acme Enterprises in IT, a medium-sized enterprise. The experience particularly helped him to learn about the realities of project management.

Before returning to the university for his final year, he participated in a five-day intensive programme in entrepreneurial skills development. He then decided to take an optional course in entrepreneurship as part of his final year. The entrepreneurship course was something of a disappointment to Mark. It focused on producing a business plan. The business that Mark chose to work on was something he had been considering for the last year or so – an online booking service for independent restaurants. Although there were similar systems for larger restaurants and chains, these were expensive and complicated to implement. Smaller restaurants which hadn't the resources to invest in an online system would benefit from Mark's simpler, more modern approach. The business plan helped him to explore and draw together his thinking about the idea, but as he indicated in an interview later, he made quite a lot of the figures up.

On graduation, Mark abandoned the discotheque business and went full-time into his IT business. His website development business, though somewhat labour intensive, was cash-positive and enabled him to finance other developments. His web-business took him into a new area providing IT solutions for restaurants within the exhibitions and events industry. He won a contract to supply the IT for all the catering outlets within Exel, a major exhibition centre in the East of London. His unique approach to these was to constantly provide them with new ideas for IT-related developments to keep their business format fresh. This in turn would help them to maintain their catering contracts, which are re-tendered periodically.

He sold his first business (the website development business) when he was 24, in order to focus most on his more profitable areas of activity. By this time, Mark has launched three further businesses, including installing wifi networks in blocks of flats.

Each of Mark's businesses and new products was developed with a different fellow-entrepreneur. His father and uncle were partners in his first web-based software. They themselves had an interest in the business area – restaurants – that was the target market of this business. They also therefore had an interest in the restaurant IT support business. A friend from university was a partner in the wifi venture. As things developed, Mark became more and more thinly spread, and he began hiring staff. His sister became his first employee, administering the businesses from a central hub.

A baby hammock

Discussion questions

1 *Identify the learning opportunities that Mark and Gareth have experienced. To what extent are they formal or informal?*

2 *Allocate the various learning experiences that Mark and Gareth have had to the different parts of Kolb's learning cycle.*

3 *What are the characteristics that you would say describe the two as entrepreneurs?*

7.6 NOTES, REFERENCES AND FURTHER READING

Notes and Further Information

1. Chapter 4 'Entrepreneurship and the economy' reviews the GEM studies as they have become important to our understanding of how entrepreneurship has different impacts on economic development in different countries. See www.gemconsortium.org for a complete list of publications.

2. For a discussion on the factors that pull or push ethnic minorities into self-employment see Basu (2006). See also Chapter 5, section 5.4 'Regional and international communities of entrepreneurship'.

3. See Smallbone and Wyer (2006) who emphasise that successful entrepreneurial ventures rely on adaptive strategies. This is discussed more fully in Chapter 6 section 6.2 'The growth of an enterprise'.

4. For a fuller discussion on the sources of business opportunities see Druker's seven sources of innovation (Drucker, 1985) as described in Chapter 3, subsection 3.6.1 'Where does innovation come from?'

5. Chapter 14 'Entrepreneurial business models and processes' covers the topic of business models in more detail.

6. Gibb's (2003) summary of knowledge areas needed for entrepreneurship are listed in Chapter 1 section 1.3 'Dominant perspectives on entrepreneurship'.

7. Networking is covered in Chapter 9 'Entrepreneurial networking'.

8. Opportunity recognition is covered more fully in Chapter 2 section 2.4 'Entrepreneurial projects and identifying the opportunity'.

9. A study of owners who had closed a business found that even those who had lost money through the venture claimed that it had been an invaluable learning experience (SBRC, 2002). The subject of learning from so-called 'failure' is covered in more detail in Chaper 6, subsection 6.4.1 'What happens to the entrepreneurs who close a business?'

10. Chris Fogg relates the story of his business failures and the lessons he learned from each in the case study at the end of Chapter 6, 'Fogg's Failures: The entrepreneur who studied unsuccessful ventures'.

11. Prowess is an association of organisations that support women who start and grow businesses (www.prowess.org.uk).

12. Project:Senso in Singapore, www.projectsenso.com.

References

Acs, Z.J., Arenius, P., Hay, M. and Minniti, M. (2005) *The Global Entrepreneurship Monitor, 2004 Executive Report*, London Business School and Babson College.

Bandura, A. (1997) *Self-Efficacy: The Exercise of Control,* New York: WH Freeman.

Basu, A. (2006) Ethnic minority entrepreneurship, in Casson, M. *et al.* (eds) *The Oxford Handbook of Entrepreneurship*, Oxford: Oxford University Press, pp. 580–600.

Bosma, N., Jones, K., Autio, E. and Levie. J. (2008) *Global Entrepreneurship Monitor 2007 Executive Report*, Babson Park: Babson College, and London: London Business School and GERA, published at www.gemconsortium.org.

Briggs Myers, I. and McCaulley, M.H. (1985) *Manual: A Guide to the Development and Use of the Myers-Briggs Type Indicator,* Palo Alto: Consulting Psychologists Press.

Brockhaus, R.H. (1980) The effect of job dissatisfaction on the decision to start a business, *Journal of Small Business Management,* 18 (1): 37–43.

Brockhaus, R.H. (1982) The psychology of the entrepreneur, in Kent, C.A., Sexton, D.L. and Vesper, K.H. (eds) *Encyclopedia of Entrepreneurship*, Englewood Cliffs, NJ: Prentice Hall, pp. 39–71.

Brush, C.G. (2006) Women entrepreneurs: A research overview, in Casson, M. *et al.* (eds) *The Oxford Handbook of Entrepreneurship*, Oxford: Oxford University Press, pp. 611–628.

Caird, S. (1991) Research on the enterprising tendency of occupational groups, *International Journal of Small Business*, 9 (4): 75–82.

Capelleras, J., Kevin, M., Greene, F. and Storey, D. (2008) Do more heavily regulated economies have poorer performing new ventures? Evidence from Britain and Spain, *Journal of International Business Studies*, 39 (4): 688–702.

Chell, E. (2008) *The Entrepreneurial Personality: A Social Construction*, 2nd edition, Hove: Routledge.

Drucker, P.F. (1985) *Innovation and Entrepreneurship*, London: Heinemann.

Dyson, J. (1997) *Against the Odds: An Autobiography*, London: Orion Publishing.

Forson, C. (2006) The strategic framework for women's enterprise: BME women at the margins, *Equal Opportunities International*, 25 (6): 418–432.

Gibb, A. (2003) Towards the Entrepreneurial University: Entrepreneurial Education as a Lever for Change, *NCGE Working Paper*, published at www.ncge.org.uk.

Harding, R. (2007) *Global Entrepreneurship Monitor 2006 UK Report,* London Business School and Babson.

Harding, R, Brooksbank, D., Hart, M., Jones-Evans, D., Levie, J., O'Reilly, M. and Walker, J. (2008) *Global Entrepreneurship Monitor: United Kingdom 2007*, London Business School and GERA.

Hayton, J.C., George, G. and Zahra, S.A. (2002) National culture and entrepreneurship: A review of behavioral research, *Entrepreneurship: Theory and Practice*, 26: 33–52.

Hofstede, G. (1980) *Culture's Consequences: International Differences in Work Related Values*, Beverly Hills, CA: Sage.

Hornaday, J. and Aboud, J. (1971) Characteristics of successful entrepreneurs, *Personnel Psychology*, 24: 55–60.

Jaalstrom, M. (2002) Organisational employment vs entrepreneurship: The personality approach to business students' career aspirations, *Journal of Business and Entrepreneurship*, 14 (1).

Kolb, D.A. (1984) *Experiential Learning: Experience as the Source of Learning and Development*, Engelwood Cliffs, NJ: Prentice-Hall.

Kolb, D.A., Boyatzis, R.E. and Mainemelis, C. (2000) Experiential learning theory: Previous research and new directions, in *Perspectives on Cognitive, Thinking and Learning Styles* (eds R.J. Sternberg and L.F. Zhang), New Jersey: Lawrence Erlbaum.

Lee, J. (1996) The motivation of women entrepreneurs in Singapore, *Women in Management Review*, 11 (2): 18–29.

McClelland, D.C. (1961) *The Achieving Society*, Princeton, NJ: Van Nostrand.

Minniti, M. (2008) The role of government policy on entrepreneurial activity: Productive unproductive, or destructive? *Entrepreneurship Theory and Practice*, 32 (5): 779–790.

Mitchell, R.K., Smith, J.B., Morse, E.A, Seawright, K.W., Peredo, A.M. and Mckenzie, B. (2002) Are entrepreneurial cognitions universal? Assessing entrepreneurial cognitions across cultures, *Entrepreneurship: Theory & Practice*, 26 (4): 9–33.

Morris, M.H., Nola, M.N., Craig, W.E. and Coombes, S.M. (2006) The dilemma of growth: Understanding venture size choices of women entrepreneurs, *Journal of Small Business Management*, 44 (2): 221–244.

Politis, D. (2005) The process of entrepreneurial learning: A conceptual framework, *Entrepreneurship: Theory and Practice*, 29 (4): 399–424.

Reynolds, P.D., Camp, S.M., Bygrave, W.D., Autio, E. and Hay, M. (2001) *The Global Entrepreneurship Monitor, 2001 Executive Report*, London Business School and Babson College.

Robinson, P.B. and Sexton, E.A. (2002) The effect of education and experience on self-employment success, *Journal of Business Venturing*, 9 (2): 141–156.

Rosa, P., Kodithuwakku, S. and Balunywa, W. (2006) *Reassessing Necessity Entrepreneurship in Developing Countries*, Cardiff: Institute for Small Business & Entrepreneurship Annual Conference.

Routamaa, V. and Miettinen, A. (2007) Awareness of Entrepreneurial Personalities: A Prerequisite for Entrepreneurial Education, *NCGE Working Paper 019*, published at www.ncge.org.uk.

Sarasvathy, S. (2004) Making it happen: Beyond theories of the firm to theories of firm design, *Entrepreneurship: Theory & Practice,* Winter, 28 (6): 519–531.

SBRC (2002) *Opening Up Business Closures: A Study of Businesses That Close and Owners' Exit Routes*, A Report to HSBC, Small Business Research Centre, Kingston University, Kingston upon Thames.

Smallbone, D. and Wyer, P. (2006) Growth and development in the small business, in Carter, S. and Jones-Evans, D. (eds) *Enterprise and Small Business: Principles, Practice and Policy*, Harlow: Pearson Education.

Tan, J. (2002) Culture, nation, and entrepreneurial strategic orientations: Implications for an emerging economy, *Entrepreneurship: Theory & Practice*, 26 (4): 95–112.

Ward, T.B. (2004) Cognition, creativity and entrepreneurship, *Journal of Business Venturing*, 19 (2): 173–218.

7

Recommended Further Reading

There are a large number of books written about or by individual entrepreneurs, and many of these provide valuable insight into their motivations and approaches. The following two books are examples of the genre, and it is worth looking for others.

Roddick, A. (2005) *Business as Unusual: My Entrepreneurial Journey, Profits with Principles*, London: Thorsons.

Branson, R. (1999) *Losing My Virginity: How I've Survived, Had Fun, and Made a Fortune Doing Business My Way*, New York: Three Rivers Press.

7

CHAPTER 8

Entrepreneurs and Managing Creativity

LEARNING OBJECTIVES

After studying this chapter, the reader will be able to:

- Appreciate the need for the entrepreneur to manage creativity successfully

- Recognise the dangers of stereotyping creativity according to particular activities or people, evaluating the extent to which creativity is a talent of 'special' individuals

- Understand key features of the cultural and creative industries and the particular challenges facing entrepreneurs working in this sector

- Evaluate the macro and micro-level conditions which enable the entrepreneur to promote creativity

- Recognise the key individual and organisational tensions involved in managing creativity successfully

- Understand the creative process and be able to apply key tools for creative thinking.

INTRODUCTION

Earlier on in this book we introduced the idea that creativity plays a crucial and central role in the entrepreneurship process. As human beings, we all have creative potential. Whether or not we employ our creative skills to innovate depends upon prevailing structural and cultural conditions, including macro-economic factors, and the choices we make about undertaking an entrepreneurial project. In this chapter we take a closer look at the concept of creativity and the challenges facing the entrepreneur as they seek to manage it.

PREVIEW CASE

Cadbury's 'Gorilla' – wild about chocolate

Advertising a well-known brand of chocolate by getting a gorilla to play the drums to the sound of an old Phil Collins classic, might sound like monkey business. For Cadbury and their advertising agency, Fallon London, however, this ability to manage and recognise creativity has proved hugely successful. In the case study at the end of this chapter we take a look at the context for Cadbury's Gorilla ad, and at some of the challenges and obstacles those involved were faced with, and review how these were overcome.

Albert Einstein, who surely knew a thing or two about creativity, said 'If at first, the idea is not absurd, then there is no hope for it.' *Can you think of some examples of absurd ideas that have gone on to be great examples of innovation and entrepreneurship?*

Source: The account on which this case study is based is available at CreativityWorks08 DANDAD, http://www.dandad.org/inspiration/creativityworks/08/pdf/Creativity_Works_Gorilla.pdf, accessed 5 April 2009

8.1 CREATIVITY – AN INITIAL WARNING

The link between creativity and entrepreneurship begins with our individual creative potential – our ability to generate and then exploit novel and valuable ideas. There is a problem, however, with what we actually mean when we refer to the term creativity, and whom we might include as 'creative' people.

> 'Stripped of any special significance by a generation of bureaucrats, civil servants, managers and politicians, lazily used as political margarine to spread approvingly and inclusively over any activity with a non-material element to it, the word 'creative' has become almost unusable.'
> John Tusa (Director of Barbican Centre, London), 2003: 5–6

There is a very real danger that creativity is seen as something 'special', and the preserve of the few. There are a number of problems with this 'exceptionalist' position which it is useful to highlight at the start of this chapter:

■ First, this viewpoint threatens to deny the birthright of creativity for each and every one of us. Creativity, at least in the form of creative potential, is a feature of all human beings. A genuinely creative society is comprised of creative people in all walks of life.

■ Second, by implicitly limiting creativity to those given some kind of sanction to be creative (i.e. of 'special significance') one is effectively increasing the difficulty in supporting creativity in the context of management (or any other field), where there is likely to be a backlash from two directions. The management mainstream may well think that creativity is the domain of the cultural sector and of artists, all too easily reducing it to something that just 'creatives' do. The arts establishment, for their part, may stand outraged that dreary managers are professing to have any interest, let alone right to creativity, as it is seen as their territory.

Context matters hugely when we are discussing creativity. There is clearly a big difference between a great performance of Shakespeare's *Hamlet* on the stage of London's National Theatre, the sometimes mundane reality of the entrepreneur's business plan, and the white-coated precision of the science lab experiment. There is a common thread, however, in the form of human beings' creative potential being realised in some way. As the psychologist Carl Rogers has noted, 'The mainspring of creativity appears to be . . . man's tendency to actualize himself, to become his potentialities' (Rogers, 1976: 298).

In devoting this chapter to looking at the relationship between entrepreneurs and managing creativity, therefore, we begin with something of a warning. Discussion of creativity is made difficult by

8

the extraordinarily entrenched nature of preconceived notions and stereotyping that surrounds the concept. This is not just an issue of academic interest, but also has very real practical consequences. If managers, entrepreneurs, politicians, scientists and others believe that creativity is somehow 'off limits', the preserve of specially talented musicians, artists, film-makers and so on, they are unlikely to see the benefit of developing their own creativity, or encouraging it in those around them.

8.2   UNDERSTANDING CREATIVITY

Notwithstanding the many different interpretations that surround the concept of creativity, we noted earlier that it depends upon two central characteristics (Bilton, 2007; Sternberg and Lubart, 1999), both of which are closely linked to entrepreneurship. The first of these is difference or novelty. Creativity can be understood as the generation of new ideas (Cox, 2005). The second characteristic is individual talent or vision which is expressed through creative individuals. Allied to this second characteristic is the notion that creativity produces not just 'new' ideas but valuable ones. Robinson (2001), for example, defines creativity as 'imaginative processes with outcomes in the public world that are original and of value'. We can point to a divergence between those (psychology-based) approaches (see, for example, Boden, 1994 and Weisberg, 1993) that equate novelty with innovation, therefore embracing innovation within the wider concept of creativity, and other (management) approaches which effectively reverse this relationship, embracing creativity within the wider concept of innovation.

There are further challenges, such as how one determines (a) what is novel – given that 'there is nothing new under the sun', and (b) what is valuable – given that value is a subjective phenomenon, and largely dependent upon who is doing the valuation. These are questions that matter to entrepreneurs but are typically resolved in the course of their taking a new product or service to market. 'Will it sell?' is the real question on the entrepreneur's mind.

8.2.1 Problems of Newness and Value

The dictionary defines creation as 'to bring into being or form out of nothing'. Philosophers and scientists have long battled with the implications of this perspective, noting the so-called *ex nihilo* paradox – the idea that on the one hand a new idea cannot have previously existed, whilst equally trying to explain how the new idea could exist out of nothing.

Creation and the giant tortoise

The theoretical physicist Stephen Hawking describes an amusing anecdote in his book *A Brief History of Time* that nicely captures the *ex nihilo* conundrum on an epic scale. He recounts how a well-known scientist once gave a public lecture on astronomy, during which he explained how the earth orbits around the sun and how the sun, in turn, orbits our galaxy. At the end of his talk, a little old lady at the back of the room got up and said: 'What you have told us is rubbish. The world is really a flat plate supported on the back of a giant tortoise.' The scientist gave a knowing smile before replying, 'What is the tortoise standing on?' 'You're very clever, young man, very clever,' said the old lady. 'But it's turtles all the way down!'

Source: A Brief History of Time by Stephen Hawking, published by Bantam Books. Reprinted by permission of the Random House Group Ltd.

The issue of what is accounted as 'valuable' and who does the accounting is also controversial. Margaret Boden (1994) distinguishes between two senses of creativity. One is psychological (P-creativity), and the other historical (H-creativity). Boden explains that a valuable idea is P-creative if the person having the idea could not have had it before. It doesn't matter how many times other people may have had the idea already. By contrast, a valuable idea is H-creative if no one else, in all human history, has ever had it before. All H-creative ideas are, by definition, P-creative as well. To illustrate this distinction we could point to the simple case of a child accidentally knocking a mug of coffee off a table and discovering that it spilled all over the carpet, much to the annoyance of mum and dad. For the child in question we could suppose that the idea 'if I knock a mug of coffee off the table it will spill all over the floor' is an example of P-creativity. It is related to both a novel experience (this was the first time for the child that this connection was made) and also a valuable one (they can learn not to do this again – so staying in their parents' good books). No one would suggest, however, that this was remotely valuable to society as a whole. Isaac Newton's ideas concerning gravity, published in his *Philosophiae Naturalis Principia Mathematica* in 1687 on the other hand, which also came about from observing an object in motion (this time an apple), represent H-creativity, a genuinely new idea in human history. Even this is to simplify a more complex story. It may well be that other people had indeed had the ideas about gravity that Newton articulated, but perhaps they did not recognise their importance, or communicate them with others. On this point there is a clear connection with entrepreneurship. Although well-known entrepreneurs such as Akio Morita, Anton Rupert, Bernard Arnault, Richard Branson and Vinod Khosla are now recognised for their often innovative business dealings, they would probably be the first to agree that other people had come up with similar ideas before them.

Percy and the cat's-eyes

The story of how Percy Shaw invented cat's-eyes in the 1930s is the stuff of legend – in fact several legends! One account has it that it was the demise of the tram-line, in favour of cars and buses that led to the invention. Percy noticed that motorists had come to rely on the steel tram-lines to reflect the car headlights in the dark. When the lines were taken up it was clear that some other night-time guide to traffic was needed. A more romantic version of the story tells how Percy was driving home in foggy conditions when he saw two shining objects ahead in the road. He stopped to see what it was and discovered it was a cat but also that he had left the road and was in danger of driving over a steep hillside. This inspired him to develop the concept of cat's-eyes embedded in roads to guide drivers.

Contrast this discovery with the endless experiments that others had to go through to create something new, e.g. Marconi's radio or Edison's commercially practical electric light.

In seeking to avoid over-romanticising the concept of creativity, science has tended towards a definition that is based on the 'novel combinations of old ideas'. A good new idea is very often two old ideas meeting for the first time (Stokes and Wilson, 2006). However, it is important to stress that novel combinations in themselves may not be terribly interesting or valuable. As Edward De Bono has remarked, wearing your hat upside down would be 'different' but not terribly useful. Theories of creativity that centre on combination tend to assume that we can associate similar ideas and recognise more distant analogies. In fact, history teaches us that it is the recognition of the novel analogy that is often very surprising. In presenting our emergent model of entrepreneurship we have purposefully drawn particular attention to the need to recognise creativity before the event (i.e. before it is proved to be valuable when it becomes innovation).

8.2.2 Creativity and the Genius Myth

Problems about novelty and value aside, there remains the issue of how to account for the role of 'special' individuals in the process of creativity. Creativity theorists 'have focused overwhelmingly on the individual as the main, and often only, contributor to creativity' (Ford and Gioia, 1995: xxi). This is despite the fact that the analysis of creative people and creative objects has demonstrated that most scientific and artistic innovations emerge from joint thinking, passionate conversations and shared struggles among different people, emphasising the importance of the social dimension of creativity (John-Steiner, 2000; Fischer, 2005).

The dominant individualistic model of creativity perpetuates the notion that creativity is the exclusive property of a particular type of talented person. This notion is tremendously enduring. However, research by Weisberg (1993) has persuasively debunked much of the rhetoric about creativity in what he refers to as the 'genius myth'. His research indicates how Mozart, Picasso and others we might readily refer to as geniuses accomplished much of their work through logical progressions, memory, training, opportunity and sheer hard work. Research suggests that in many domains it is common for there to be at least 10 years or 10,000 hours of deliberate practice before achieving real expertise. It would seem that creativity, rather like entrepreneurship, demands perspiration as well as inspiration.

8.2.3 Creativity, Duality and Paradox

The concept of creativity is marked out by duality and paradox. For example, whilst creativity is sustained by exceptional individuals, it is more likely to be achieved through networks and systems; whilst creativity is an ubiquitous characteristic of human beings there are many people (one might suggest most) who don't think of themselves as being 'creative'; although creativity is thought of as generating 'new' ideas, it is equally about the combination of two or more existing ones; and so on.

This notion of duality is central to our increasing scientific understanding of how individuals act creatively. Neurologists have highlighted dualism in the creative process between left brain and right brain. It has been shown that the two different sides (or hemispheres) of the brain control two different 'modes' of thinking (see Table 8-1). Furthermore, each of us tends to have a dominant mode (though this is a preference not an absolute).

Whilst left-brain academic subjects in school and university might focus on logical thinking, analysis and accuracy, right-brained subjects, on the other hand, focus more on aesthetics, feelings and creativity. Some argue that there is clearly scope for our education system to become more 'whole-brained' in its orientation.[1] This would be of particular value to nascent entrepreneurs whose business it will be to develop innovative products and services (requiring them to call on all their powers of analysis and imagination).

McMullan (1976) suggests that the creative individual has got to be able to manage a set of tensions or paradoxes (see Figure 8-1), holding them in balance. Try mapping your own ability to hold these tensions in check. How consistently do you manage to do this (or maybe you have good and bad days)?

Artists (like entrepreneurs) possess an ability to tolerate complexity and contradiction.[2] Koestler noted that the creative act always 'operates on more than one plane' (1964), introducing the notion of divergent thinking as important. There has been some interesting work on divergent thinking showing

TABLE 8-1	Left and right-brain thinking
Left hemisphere functions	**Right hemisphere functions**
Rational	Intuitive
Analytical	Holistic
Sequential	Synthesising
Logical	Random
Verbal	Prosodic (rhythm/stress)
Objective	Subjective
Language (grammar/vocabulary)	Language (intonation/accentuation)

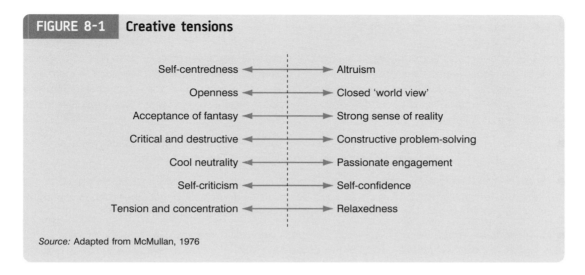

FIGURE 8-1   **Creative tensions**

Self-centredness ←——————→ Altruism

Openness ←——————→ Closed 'world view'

Acceptance of fantasy ←——————→ Strong sense of reality

Critical and destructive ←——————→ Constructive problem-solving

Cool neutrality ←——————→ Passionate engagement

Self-criticism ←——————→ Self-confidence

Tension and concentration ←——————→ Relaxedness

Source: Adapted from McMullan, 1976

that our capacity for this skill is very much with us as children, but that we seem to get less and less good at it as we get older. If you want to see how good you are at divergent thinking then try the Divergent Thinking Test.

Divergent Thinking Test

Give yourself 1 minute to come up with as many different uses for a paper-clip.

Tip: You're doing very well if you can come up with 80–100. Good luck.

Creativity is something of a multidimensional process that requires a combination of thinking styles and a tolerance for contradiction and paradox. Note that this is a far cry from the view that creativity comes from a lack of thought and from being in a very relaxed state (though these can help in terms of restoring balance for new ideas to emerge). There is a state of tension that exists between times of conscious and subconscious thought. The challenge must be to find a way of being that can allow this tension to be managed and not to become overwhelmed with the inevitable stresses and strains of the new venture. Central to this process is the balance to be achieved between illusion (imaginative thinking about 'What if?') and reality ('What can I afford?').

WHEN THINGS GO WRONG

'Little Mary's' message

The Oscar-winning film star Mary Pickford, who starred in 52 features, many of them as her own producer, and who co-founded United Artists together with Charlie Chaplin and Douglas Fairbanks, once said: 'You may have a fresh start any moment you choose, for this thing we call failure is not the falling down, but the staying down.' Individuals the world over will recognise the truth in Pickford's remark. Though she was born in an altogether different era, and though she was talking about her experiences of working in the film industry, her words are just as applicable now to those undertaking entrepreneurship.

8.2.4 Creativity as Discovery

One way to get round some of the philosophical problems associated with a definition of creativity founded on novelty and value (and the need to recognise creativity) is to consider it in terms of discovery instead. Martin (2007) has put forward a conception of creativity which is based on the human potential to make discoveries about the world. The key implications of this realist conceptualisation of creativity are as follows:

■ Creativity exists as a universal human attribute. We all (creatives and 'others') possess what might be thought of as creative potential – the power to make discoveries about the world.

■ Whether or not this creative potential is actualised (i.e. a discovery is made) is dependent upon our interaction with a myriad of other powers and potentials (including, amongst others, those relating to other people, ideas, arts, sciences, management, education and policy interventions).

■ Creativity is an emergent property, arising from the necessary interaction of humans across boundaries (whether naturally occurring or of their own making). This emergent interaction may or may not be recognised at the level of individuals, organisations, disciplines or society in general.

■ Creativity is fundamentally a social process resulting from the interaction of human beings, their ideas and beliefs, through the undertaking and realisation of particular projects.

The implications of this perspective are that the social context in which creativity is undertaken, matters.

8

8.3   CREATIVITY IN CONTEXT

A recurring theme in the course of this part of the book is the ability and necessity of entrepreneurs to act proactively, whether it is to spot opportunities, network with key people, make critical decisions or leverage vital resources. Entrepreneurship is very much about doing things. Similarly, there is no creativity without thought and action (and thought and action are never context-free). The particular context for our discussion is entrepreneurship that itself takes place in a wide variety of contexts and environments ranging from lifestyle start-ups to large public sector organisations (see Chapter 5). Common to each of these cases, however, is the ability to create value (whether financial, cultural, aesthetic, political or environmental). The process of value creation will be appropriate to the particular context involved, and will be understood in different ways, depending upon the internal workplace culture, and the external social and economic conditions within which enterprises operate. Creativity is a socially embedded process.

Although creativity and entrepreneurship happen across many and varied industrial sectors, there is one in particular in which creativity is held to operate at a premium. This is within the cultural or creative industries.

8.3.1 The Cultural and Creative Industries

The UK government has branded the cultural industries, including those activities which we traditionally associate with the arts, as well as TV and broadcasting, design-related and computing software enterprises, as the 'creative industries'. The government's Department for Culture, Media and Sport (DCMS) has defined the creative industries in terms of the following:

> Those activities which have their origin in individual creativity, skill, talent, and which have the potential for wealth and job creation through the generation and exploitation of intellectual property.

> DCMS, 1998; 2001

In focusing attention on the inputs and outputs of creativity, this definition places particular emphasis on the role of the individual, on the one hand, which we might see as reinforcing a notion of creatives as 'different' to the rest of us, and on the other hand, on the importance of symbolic goods – ideas, images and experiences. The definition used brings together 13 industries where individual creativity and the communication of symbolic goods or 'texts' (see Hesmondhalgh, 2007) is paramount. These have been taken to be comprised of the following sectors:

Advertising; architecture; art and antiques; crafts; design; designer fashion; film; interactive leisure software; music; performing arts; publishing; software; television and radio.

Together these areas of economic activity account for a large part of the national output.

Creative industries in the UK

Between 2009 and 2013 the UK creative industries are set to grow by 4 per cent (more than double the rate of the rest of the economy). This places the creative industries firmly at the heart of the country's economy and sees them as integral in recovery from recession. By 2013, there may be as many as 180,000 creative businesses in the sector, compared to the current number of 148,000; the sector is expected to contribute as much as £85 billion to UK value added, up from £57 billion; the sector is also forecast to employ more people than those who work in the financial sector. A key reason for this growth in jobs and opportunities is the potential impact of innovative digital technologies.

Source: NESTA[3]

8

8.3.2 Characteristics of the Creative Industries and Creative Products

Although the cultural and creative industries comprise a very broad spread of activities, we can distinguish a range of particular features which make up a distinctive environment for the creative industries entrepreneur:

■ Many of the enterprises operating in the creative industries are both young and very small (micro-businesses). Often the entrepreneur running the business will have been working in the industry for many years.

■ Some creative industries (e.g. film, music) are dominated by a few 'major' businesses. In the music business, for example, four music businesses – EMI; Sony Music Entertainment; Warner Music Group; and Universal Music Group together hold an estimated 80 per cent share of the world music market. Overall, the shape of the creative sector is that of an hour-glass (see Figure 8-2), with many small 'independent' businesses, some very powerful large enterprises and relatively few middle-sized businesses. The reason for bringing attention to this shape is to highlight the apparent difficulty (and rarity) of growing small firms into larger ones. Despite the high level of creativity which characterises many smaller creative industries businesses, there remain very few that will see growth comparable with the likes of Google, Microsoft, Amazon or Infosys.

■ Many businesses in the creative industries are focused on the short-term (so-called 'chart' businesses) and are run by (and for) creatives. Such businesses are often very good at producing for novelty, resulting in a range of different organisational structures and models emerging to suit 'local solutions'.

■ The role of intermediaries can be crucial in the development of the creative industries. For example, in the music industry the agent or the A&R (artist and repertoire) representative is crucial in acting as a filter and establishing where the best talent lies. This filter is needed because strange though it might sound, it can actually be difficult to know just how good any given creative product actually is. Many creative products are distinguished by this characteristic of 'quality uncertainty'.

FIGURE 8-2   **The shape of the creative sector**

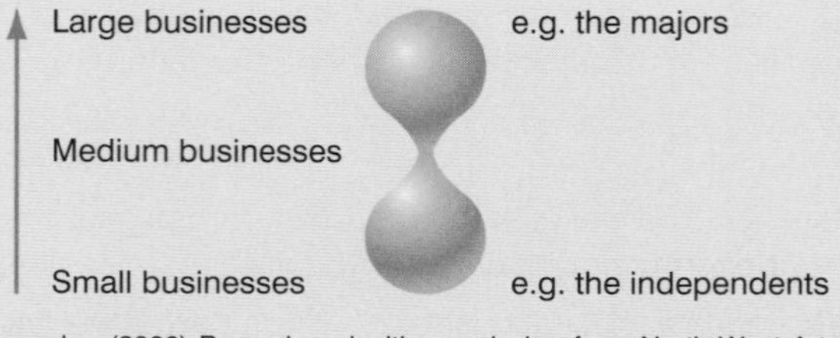

Large businesses   e.g. the majors

Medium businesses

Small businesses   e.g. the independents

Source: K. Hackett and P. Ramsden (2000) Reproduced with permission from North West Arts Board, Manchester.

Technological innovations have encouraged considerable interest in the possibility of 'disintermediation' – the idea that somehow these industries could cut out the 'middle-man'. For example, in the 1990s music online business 'peoplesound.com' sought to topple the monopoly of the major record companies by providing a service whereby the public could vote for their favourite artists who could then go on to secure lucrative publishing or recording deals. However, so far, there seems little firm evidence that disintermediation is happening on a significant level (peoplesound.com went into partnership with EMI in 2000).

■ There is typically fierce competition in the creative industries, with many independent operators scraping for work in niche areas. A feature of creative products is what is termed 'over-supply'. There are typically more singers, musicians, actors, authors, designers and other creative 'wanna-be's' than there are opportunities for fame and fortune. There is a perception that highly successful creative workers can and do rise to the top without working up a career ladder or through undertaking conventional education and training. This 'just do it' approach to work (which arguably is being reinforced through media interest in reality stars) is making the creative industries an ever-more popular career destination.

I dreamed a dream – and it came true!

The Scottish singer Susan Boyle appeared on the third series of the talent show *Britain's Got Talent* in April 2009. Singing 'I dreamed a dream' from the musical *Les Misérables* in the opening round, she stole the show and the hearts of the audience. It is estimated that within nine days of her television debut, Boyle had been watched on the Internet more than 100 million times. A record contract and a film are amongst the deals alleged to be being discussed in the wake of her appearance.

■ The creative industries are characterised by a high level of project-work. Many of the creative industries have very short life cycles with people coming together for relatively brief periods of time and then disbanding again once the project is finished (see Blair, 2001, for example, for a detailed account of this environment in the film industry).

■ The role of networking is particularly important for those working in the creative industries (as it is for entrepreneurship in general – see Chapter 9). There are also interesting network effects which arise from the fast-pace of change. For example, the fashion industry is built on relatively few individuals' assessments of what styles, materials, textiles, colours and so on are 'in' for a given season.

■ There is a considerable level of short-term, albeit highly skilled employment within the cultural sector. The competition and over-supply of creative and cultural workers means payment can be very low, or even non-existent in a lot of cases (such as unpaid work in festivals and event management).

8.3.3 **Macro-Level Context – the Creative Economy**

The underlying premise of our creative age is that for the first time in history, knowledge and creative individuals' new ideas are the primary source of economic productivity (Seltzer and Bentley, 1999; Florida, 2003). There has been a shift from manual work to 'thinking' jobs that emphasise a whole new range of skills. According to John Howkins (2002), 'creativity is not new and neither is economics, but what is new is the nature and extent of the relationship between them, and how they combine to create extraordinary value and wealth' (p. 8). The creative economy embraces sweeping economic and social change whilst ensuring that the individual and their creativity remain firmly at the centre of the picture. The UK government has led the way in developing a series of creative industries and entrepreneurship policies which see individual creativity and talent as key drivers of wealth and job creation (BERR, 2008a, 2008b).

The rhetoric of the creative economy provides an important backdrop to both interest and activity in the area of managing creativity. Although critics have questioned the potential dominance of the 'creative class' at the expense of more traditional types of industrial activity (including manufacturing), digital technology is enabling individuals in all sorts of contexts to work creatively, generating new ideas, concepts, information and understanding. It would be wrong to equate creativity solely with those information-related activities which are supported or enabled by the Internet, however. Arguably, the real money in the creative industries comes from 'value added' in the manipulation and development of content into marketable commodities.

8.3.4 **Micro-Level Context – Creative Conditions**

Turning now to the micro-level context we can see that there are some important internal factors which promote creativity. The psychologist Carl Rogers notes that our openness to experience is the first key factor in this respect. Being open to new situations and to learning new skills represents a critical first step for the entrepreneur. Without keeping eyes and ears open, and without being open to new situations, it is unlikely that we will be able to spot entrepreneurial opportunities when they arise.

> We have the potential to find creative boundaries anywhere; we just need to put ourselves in the mindset of noticing them, because they are all around us. We are how we are, and we do what we do, mostly because it serves us fine and we have got into the habit. We do not have the desire to make things different. Although we could . . .
>
> Piers Ibbotson, 2008

Linked to this openness is the ability to judge whether or not our experience is valuable. It helps to have a strong internal locus of evaluation. The third key factor which can promote creativity is effectively the ability to play – to toy with elements and concepts. As we saw earlier, this ability for divergent thinking as well as having fun and enjoying what you do is a key determinant in creativity.

How do you *feel* about creativity?

Read through the selection of quotations below and reflect on the degree to which your ability to come up with new and valuable ideas is founded on a rational and logical thought-process, or whether you are more likely to rely on your feelings, intuition and gut-feel. *How many of the great entrepreneurial businesses you can think of started with little more than a 'hunch'?*

'The heart has its reasons that reason cannot know.'

B. Pascal

'The artist is not a man who describes but a man who feels.'

E.E. Cummings

'Conditions for creativity are to be puzzled; to concentrate; to accept conflict and tension; to be born everyday; to feel a sense of self.'

E. Fromm

'In creative work, imagination is more important than knowledge.'

A. Einstein

'Art is a lie that makes us realize the truth'.

Picasso

'I can't prove it, but I'm pretty sure that people gain a selective advantage from believing in things they can't prove.'

R. Nesse

Source: 2005 Edge question

When we talk of the micro-context for creativity we should not ignore the physical surroundings we are working in, whether this is the workplace, at home, the classroom or just out and about. After all, as many observers have discussed, our surroundings can make a huge difference to how creative we feel.

8

Context matters – the Googleplex

One of the world's leading and most creative businesses is the Internet search engine Google, which has established a particular environment for its staff. While not all Google offices around the globe are equally well-stocked, these are some of the essential elements that define a Google workspace:

- **Lobby décor** – Piano, lava lamps and live projection of current search queries from around the world.

- **Hallway décor** – Bicycles and large rubber exercise balls on the floors, press clippings from around the world posted on bulletin boards everywhere.

- **Googler offices** – Googlers work in high-density clusters – reflecting their server set-up – with three or four staff members sharing spaces with sofas and dogs. This improves information flow and saves on heating bills.

- **Equipment** – Most Googlers have high-powered Linux OS workstations on their desktops. In Google's earliest days, desks were wooden doors mounted on two sawhorses. Some of these are still in use within the engineering group.

© GOOGLE

Life's a beach for Google employees

- **Recreation facilities** – Gym with weights and rowing machine, locker rooms, washers and dryers, massage room, assorted video games, football, baby grand piano, pool table, ping pong, roller hockey twice a week in the car park.

■ **Google café** – Healthy lunches and dinners for all staff. Stations include 'Charlie's Grill', 'Back to Albuquerque', 'East Meets West' and 'Vegheads'. Outdoor seating for sunshine daydreaming.

■ **Snack rooms** – Bins packed with various cereals, gummi bears, M&Ms, toffee, liquorice, cashew nuts, yoghurt, carrots, fresh fruit and other snacks. Dozens of different drinks including fresh juice, carbonated drinks and make-your-own cappuccino.[4]

Source: This detail is listed on Google's website, available at http://www.google.co.uk/corporate/culture.html, accessed on 2 April 2009

8.4 UNDERSTANDING CREATIVITY IN A MANAGEMENT CONTEXT

As we discussed at the beginning of this chapter, there is something of a self-reinforcing mythology that surrounds both creativity and management, and which serves to sustain differences between those labelled as either 'creative' or 'manager'. That we are referring to mythology rather than genuine characteristic features of each group can be inferred by the fact that not all creatives are solitary beings possessed of some divine madness, nor do all management structures operate with the clinical and dispassionate efficiency of a machine-driven bureaucracy. Just as creative artists are far better managers than they are prepared to admit, so too managers are required to be creative, especially as they confront increasingly complex organisations and unpredictable markets (see Bilton, 2007).

The inevitable stereotyping of artists as 'creatives' and managers as 'suits' is more than a convenient way of labelling different occupational roles (though this labelling is certainly alive and well in some quarters – e.g. advertising agencies). There is an interesting irony here in that many artists, designers, film-makers and musicians would shudder at the thought of being labelled creative, and the lingering suspicion that anyone who includes 'creative' in their job title probably isn't very (unfortunate for one of the authors of this book!).

Creatives and managers do work alongside each other, of course. Typically, they do so in what has been referred to as 'hybrid and emergent organisational spaces' (Jeffcutt and Pratt, 2002: 231) where multiple stakeholders interact. The challenge of coordinating such a diverse set of individuals with different skills (also referred to as the 'motley crew' – Caves, 2000) is often held up as what makes the complex, ambivalent and contested context (Hesmondhalgh, 2007) of the creative industries so distinctive.

8.4.1 Managing Creativity

Given what has been said already about creativity, the key question is whether it can be 'managed'. Management all too easily implies a lack of freedom when it comes to new ideas. It is useful to look more closely at what management actually is. Tsoukas (2000: 39) has defined management in terms of the following three abilities:

1 The ability to control the transformation of labour power of subordinates to actual labour (i.e. getting work done).

2 The ability to elicit active cooperation from subordinate members through the provision of material and symbolic rewards (e.g. pay, benefits and reputational advantage).

3 The ability to manage the drive towards efficiency and effectiveness.

Clearly the power of management to 'control' those working in the organisation is a central feature of the relationship between managers and creatives. However, in many creative businesses it is the creative that holds the senior management position, and it is their very creativity which legitimises their position 'in charge'. Nevertheless, there is an inherent tension between being efficient and effective (keeping costs down) on the one hand, and encouraging creativity, new ideas and new approaches, with the risk that this entails, on the other. Andriopoulos (2003) has highlighted six related paradoxes in managing creativity which when harnessed appropriately capture the dynamic qualities of good management:

- Paradox 1: Support employees' passions, but achieve financial goals.

- Paradox 2: Challenge employees, but build their confidence.

- Paradox 3: Encourage personal initiative, but maintain a shared vision.

- Paradox 4: Encourage diversity, but build cohesive work teams.

- Paradox 5: Learn from the past, but seek new areas of knowledge.

- Paradox 6: Take incremental risks, but break new grounds.

From the earlier analysis of micro-conditions which enable creativity, it is clear that for creativity to flourish, the individual needs a supportive environment in which their potential worth and their creative abilities is accepted and nurtured in an empathetic climate that is not overly judgemental (i.e. where an external locus of evaluation dominates).

8.4.2 Creative Organisations

A key issue in the effective management of creativity is the level of control or constraint that is perceived by creative staff in the organisation. As Charles Handy has noted,[5] organisations don't need to have all the people in the same place at the same time in order to get things done. Many of them can be anywhere, and can work at any time that suits them. Organisations can increasingly pay people for work delivered rather than for the time they spend in the workplace. Workers can be treated as providers, with wages being replaced by fees. The resulting relationship can be beneficial if both sides feel that they have achieved their objective. Handy goes on to note the potential impact this kind of outsourcing relationship could have on creativity. In particular, he observes that the ownership of an idea is critical to creativity. By encouraging this kind of outsourcing approach, managers can bring out the best in staff, whilst still empowering them to act on initiative and be creative. Handy describes what he terms the 'doughnut principle', in which the organisation can be visualised as an inverted doughnut or what we suggest you might think of as a fried egg.

The solid core in the middle (the yolk) represents the essential job requirements, or the things that have to be done within the organisation. The white space is the opportunity for initiative and creativity. This is where people go beyond the expected (as outlined on a typical job description) and achieve extra value. However, there remains a boundary which represents a limit to discretion, beyond which one should not go. One might liken the managers' challenge to cooking the perfect egg 'sunny side-up' (and making sure it doesn't break before serving it to a hungry customer).

8.5 THE CREATIVE PROCESS

There is, of course, no *one* model of the creative process which can account for its steps or stages in any given context. As any film producer, record producer or first-time author knows, there is no simple correlation between inputs and outputs in the creative industries. Processes are unpredictable and

FIGURE 8-3   **The creative process**

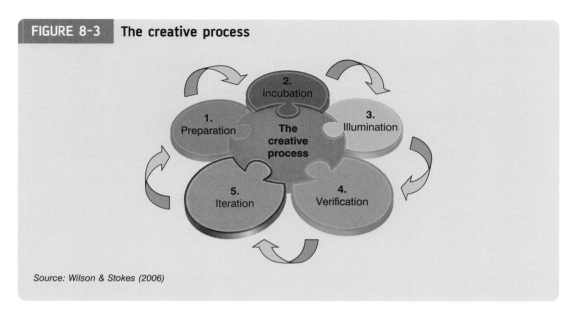

Source: Wilson & Stokes (2006)

discontinuous. What works in one case may well be altogether hopeless in another context or at another time. Nevertheless, commentators have long tried to capture some of the key stages or steps of the creative process. Amongst the most well known of these is the model put forward by the late nineteenth-century mathematician Henri Poincaré. This breaks the creative process down into four distinct stages – preparation, incubation, illumination and verification.

In the first stage the problem or issue is defined and analysed. The second stage involves a period of incubation when the subconscious mind works upon the problem. The 'eureka' moment, or creative breakthrough, typically follows in the third stage of illumination. In the final phase of verification the new solution is tested. We present this process in Figure 8-3, adding an additional fifth stage of 'iteration', highlighting the sense in which the creative process typically works through a number of these cycles before the final creative product or service or outcome is achieved.

Lest this model of the creative process looks too formulaic or mechanical, we should remember that Poincaré himself noted 'It is by logic that we prove, but by intuition that we discover' (quoted in Root-Bernstein and Root-Bernstein, 2001).

8.6   CREATIVE THINKING TOOLS

There are hundreds of techniques that can be applied to the structured problem-solving process. Probably the biggest barrier to successful creativity at the personal level is fear. As Susan Jeffers wrote (1987: 3) 'Fear seems to be epidemic in our society. We fear beginnings; we fear endings. We fear changing; we fear "staying stuck". We fear success; we fear failure. We fear living; we fear dying.' With such a comprehensive list of fears it is perhaps not surprising if being creative, doing something different, can present individuals with something of a challenge.

Five truths about fear

1   The fear will never go away as long as I continue to grow.

2   The only way to get rid of the fear of doing something is to go out… and do it.

3 The only way to feel better about myself is to go out ... and do it.

4 Not only am I going to experience fear whenever I'm on unfamiliar territory, but so is everyone else.

5 Pushing through fear is less frightening than living with the underlying fear that comes from a feeling of helplessness.

Source: Jeffers, 1987

Fear, of course, represents an emotional barrier to activity (entrepreneurial or otherwise). Usually emotions represent something of a no-go area within the organisational context. Opportunities for overcoming emotional barriers such as fear are seldom provided, save by a small number of enlightened employers. However, in recent years there has been an increasing awareness of the role played by emotions in thought, decision-making and individual success. The concept of 'emotional intelligence' (see Goleman, 1996), for example, has gained particular recognition within the business training arena. Attributes such as self-awareness, impulse control, persistence, zeal and motivation, empathy and social deftness are seen as marking those people that excel (some of whom are entrepreneurs). The good news is that emotional intelligence (EI) can be nurtured and strengthened in all of us. Daniel Goleman's book on emotional intelligence[6] provides a very good introduction to this often overlooked subject in business. Elsewhere, Timothy Gallwey, author of the *Inner Game* series,[7] has brought attention to the possibility of improving performance by decreasing the level of interference (of getting in the way) that we find ourselves doing habitually.

Emotions aside, the process of coming up with new ideas demands effective thinking. Here again, we can improve our thinking and sharpen our intellect. As Edward de Bono has remarked 'Thinking is the ultimate human resource. Yet we can never be satisfied with our most important skill. No matter how good we become, we should always want to be better' (1985: 2). He goes on to add 'The main difficulty of thinking is confusion. We try to do too much at once. Emotions, information, logic, hope and creativity all crowd in on us. It is like juggling with too many balls.' As a result de Bono has put forward various approaches which aim to separate emotion from logic, creativity from information, and so on. Most famously, he also introduced the concept of lateral thinking. Lateral thinking and thinking 'outside the box' are often put forward as the means by which we will come up with new ideas.

ENTREPRENEURSHIP IN ACTION

Scooby-doo – the birth of a Warner 'brand'

Iwao Takamoto created Scooby-Doo after talking to someone who looked after Great Danes. The dog breeder showed him pictures and 'talked about the important points of a Great Dane, like a straight back, straight legs, small chin and such', Mr Takamoto explained.

'I decided to go the opposite [way] and gave him a hump back, bowed legs, big chin and such. Even his colour is wrong.' This example of what might be seen as utilising the 'playing' and 'transformation' tools, gave rise to a cartoon legend which continues to enchant and delight, providing a very sizeable revenue stream for Warners to this day.

Source: The story on which this is based is available at the BBC: http://news.bbc.co.uk/1/hi/entertainment/6243717.stm, accessed on 9 January 2007

FIGURE 8-4	13 creative thinking tools

Imaging

Modelling

Transforming

Recognising patterns

Abstracting

Synthesising

Analogising

Dimensional thinking

Playing

Empathising

Observing

Forming patterns

Body thinking

Source: Based on SPARKS OF GENIUS: The 13 Thinking Tools by Robert and Michele Root Bernstein (2001) Mariner Books.

8

Root-Bernstein and Root-Bernstein (2001) have highlighted what they term 'tools for thinking', such as emotional feelings, visual images, bodily sensations, recognisable patterns and analogues. They suggest that scientists, musicians, artists, mathematicians, sculptors (even entrepreneurs) all use a common set of these tools – highlighting 13 particular types (Figure 8-4).

Your creativity journal

■ When you face a 'problem', what is your first reaction?

■ Thinking back, when do you feel most creative?

■ How do you motivate others to be creative?

■ Taking creative risks leads to successes and failures. How do you turn 'failures' into learning experiences?

A range of creative thinking tools and structured problem-solving techniques and useful website links are included on the website accompanying this book. These include tests and exercises relating to Myers-Briggs; Edward DeBono's 'Six Hats', as well as access to free mind-mapping software.[8]

Structured problem-solving stages

A. Problem finding

1 Making tacit knowledge more explicit as the problem is explored. Here the emphasis is on divergence and opening up the issues and feelings. Extensive use of metaphors at this stage.

2 Making sense of the issues through systematic efforts to clarify and argue different perspectives and beliefs.

3 Data gathering where information both inside and outside the group and or organisation is gathered.

4 Data analysed and shaped to suit the context in which the problem is being presented and addressed.

5 Statements of the problem are formulated and models are tested against the perceptions of the group.

6 A first version of the problem statement is made and agreed, with exception statements by group members being noted.

B. Idea and solution finding

7. A range of alternative ways of responding to the problem statement are listed.

8. The most favoured and attractive ideas are selected.

9. Criteria for selecting the ideas with which to go forward are listed. These would include features that will be important when attempting to implement the ideas and will recognise the benefits being sought and timescales.

10. Ideas tested against the criteria and also submitted for comment to sponsoring groups or stakeholders.

C. Acceptance and implementation testing

11. Support and assistance to the implementation of the idea checked for availability and understanding.

12. Plans for implementation created and submitted for sign-off by those responsible for the outcomes and delivery of the benefits.

Examples of some approaches to problem-solving (including problem boundary definitions; brainstorming; reframing a problem; mapping and diagramming; systematic inventive thinking) can be found in the accompanying website.[9]

Source: Isaksen and Treffinger (1985)

8.7 ENTREPRENEURS AND LETTING CREATIVITY 'FLOW'

Creativity is central to the process of entrepreneurship. For the entrepreneur the ability to handle our fundamental state of uncertainty, to 'live by ear', and to be able to take crucial decisions about the allocation of resources before 'knowing' what will happen, all demand the ability to manage creativity.

Allan Gibb (2005) has suggested that the dominant 'Frankenstein-like' model of entrepreneurial education is all too often founded on the metaphor of 'rational, reductive, objective, corporate, information processing brain', as opposed to what he advocates in terms of an entrepreneurial vision and feel or 'way of life'. This is characterised by an ability to tolerate (even enjoy) uncertainty and ambiguity. Gibb draws particular attention to the ability of the entrepreneur to learn from doing and from enjoying and being stimulated by the process. In the creativity literature this relates closely to the concept of 'flow'. Mikhail Csikszentmihalyi (2002) draws attention to our ability to take control over the contents of our consciousness. He suggests that many of our best moments happen when we accomplish something difficult and worthwhile. The implications of this are that we should transform jobs into 'flow producing activities', which happen under certain conditions:

1   When we confront tasks we have a chance of completing

2   When we are able to concentrate on what we are doing

3   When the task has clear goals

4   When the task provides immediate feedback

5   When we have deep but effortless involvement

6   When we have a sense of control over our actions

7   When our search for the self disappears (but paradoxically 'self' emerges stronger)

8   When our sense of duration of time is altered.

Clearly there are implications for the entrepreneur here. Ask yourself how this relates to entrepreneurial goals. Are they flow-producing? To what extent do you think the 'extrinsic' goal of making money impacts the entrepreneur's ability to get into the flow? As Ken Robinson has observed (2009) in order to maximise creativity you need to be in control of your medium (whether this is clay, paint, a piano, technology or the world of ideas), be able to play and take risks (having learned the basics), and keep an acute sense of what will work (critical judgement). The message for the entrepreneur is that they need to find their particular 'element' – the expression of their particular talents and interests – and ensure that their entrepreneurial projects are ones which can draw on this fully.

8.8   SUMMARY AND ACTIVITIES

Discussion of **creativity** is often hampered by preconceived notions and **stereotyping** that treats it as a quality or phenomenon associated with 'specially' talented individuals. Creativity is an ubiquitous feature of all human beings. However, there are **conditions** which enable (and constrain) how we all develop our creative potential. For the entrepreneur the ability to maximise their creativity and to successfully manage the creativity of others represents core competences.

Creativity involves both **novelty** and **value creation**. The task of **recognising** creativity as both novel and valuable is particularly important for the entrepreneur, since they must make decisions on the allocation of resources and without firm proof, based on this assessment. Creativity is closely associated with **dualism** and **paradox**. At a personal level, creativity requires being able to manage creative tensions and hold on to apparently opposing ideas, in what is referred to as **divergent thinking**.

The **cultural and creative industries** represent a set of 13 sectors in which creativity is valued at a premium. Technological breakthroughs in digitisation and the storage and communication of information have had a sizeable impact on the types of jobs people do (with the rise of the so-called '**creative class**' who generate new ideas) and the types of organisation we work for in today's **creative economy**. At an individual level, we can see that our ability to stay **open** to experience, **self-critical** and willing to **play** with ideas will have an important bearing on our capacity for creativity. The **physical conditions** in which we work and play also affect our creativity.

In the context of management, there is a likelihood of dividing people into either '**T-shirts**' (creatives) or '**suits**' (managers), with the danger that this results in poor communication holding back the overall level of creativity within an organisation. A business climate that is supportive to individuals whilst also being able to harness the **six paradoxes** of managing creativity requires that senior management gives sufficient freedom for individual initiative and creativity to flourish.

Though creativity defies any single formula or recipe, commentators have put forward a number of models of the **creative process** which share common attributes. These highlight a mix of rational analytical thinking and the space for the subconscious mind to work through problems before a breakthrough is achieved. Within the creative process it may be useful to draw on one of many **problem-solving techniques** which can be helpful in managing the duality of illusion and reality – in other words, coming up with new ideas which are novel and valuable but also achievable. This can be supported by undertaking **flow-producing activities**, or those that allow the entrepreneur to live and work productively and fully in their **element**.

REVIEW QUESTIONS

1   What is meant by the term 'the genius myth'?

2   Explain what is meant by H-creativity and P-creativity.

3   Creativity is often referred to as being a dualistic phenomenon. What does this mean?

4   Individuals with right-brain dominance tend not to be very rational or logical. True or False?

5   Explain what is meant by divergent thinking.

6   List three conditions which tend to enable creativity.

7   How many industries are there in the 'creative industries'?

   (a) 3   (b) 13   (c) 33

8   What is meant by the term 'quality uncertainty' and why is this an issue for the creative industries?

9   Outline the key stages in the creative process.

10   Describe what you would think as flow-producing activities.

SEMINAR TASK

YouTube is well known for providing an exciting and interactive forum for sharing film, music, video, cartoons and stories with family, friends and people everywhere. Now the online organisation has gone a stage further in coordinating the activities of musicians from across the globe to form the world's first Internet symphony orchestra – the YouTube Symphony Orchestra. The coordinating role of YouTube, and its ability to extend its reach so widely, is hoped to bring a new take on musical creativity.

Inspired by this example, working in small groups, identify a novel and valuable combination of ideas that (a) involves people from at least three continents; (b) targets children; (c) focuses on things that children do best; and (d) can be supported by one (or more) of the following organisations:

YouTube

Flickr

Apple iTunes

BBC

Google

Wikipedia

Use the creative process and problem-solving ideas in this book and on the website to help you. Be sure to discuss the creative and commercial challenges that would need to be faced in managing creativity in your chosen project.

Preview case continued

Cadbury's 'Gorilla' – wild about chocolate

IMAGE COURTESY OF THE ADVERTISING ARCHIVES

Entrepreneurship can be defined as the emergent process of recognising and communicating creativity such that the resulting economic value can be appropriated by those involved. In making this explicit link between entrepreneurship, creativity and value creation attention is cast on the difficulty of 'knowing' whether what seems a good idea will turn out to be a genuine business opportunity. Cadbury's Gorilla advertisement provides an interesting

example of how an entrepreneurial advertising business managed the process of creativity.

Cadbury's Dairy Milk is a brand of chocolate that has enjoyed strong demand in the UK and elsewhere for over a century. However, the company had begun to notice that people responded to the brand in an increasingly passive way. As the director of marketing for block chocolate and beverages, Lee Rolston put it, 'It's a bit like the comfy sweater you keep at the back of the wardrobe that you'll never throw out but you start wearing less and less'. Cadbury therefore approached their advertising agency Fallon London with a clear brief to 'get the love back'. With crucial marketing deadlines pending, however, Fallon were given just one week to come up with something. As Chris Willingham, account handler for Fallon London recalls, 'Obviously, we jump at those opportunities, so we put a couple of creative teams, plus Juan Cabral, on the brief'. Sure enough, a week later, the creatives had come up with the umbrella concept for the brand 'Glass and a Half Full Productions' which represented a kind of holding production company 'where smiles are made'. Cabral had also worked up an advert idea involving a gorilla playing the drums to the sound of Phil Collins. This was to become the critically acclaimed Cadbury's 'Gorilla' advert.

On the face of it, a drum-playing gorilla has little to do with chocolate. The creatives were naturally anxious that this would be just too far for

▶

8

Cadbury to go from where they were at that point. As Willingham recalls 'We expected them to be completely nonplussed but, to their credit, their faces lit up when we read the script and played the music'. Getting the advert past Rolston and his colleagues was one thing, but they then had to sell it up through Cadbury's senior management. This involved an awful lot more research to convince everyone that this was the right idea at the right time. There followed several stages when it looked like the idea wasn't going to make it. A key factor in its subsequent success was the enduring belief in the idea that the key players in both Fallon and Cadbury clung on to. 'They fought and risked their jobs for it, I think it would be fair to say' says Willingham.

The ongoing challenge of bringing the advert to market involved some interesting practical obstacles. Finding the very best gorilla suit (operated by no less than three people) proved difficult – but it was eventually tracked down and sourced from Los Angeles, having been used for such Hollywood blockbusters as *Gorillas in the Mist* and *Congo*. Teaching the person in the suit to play the drums convincingly, having never touched the drums before, presented another challenge, especially because it was only possible to wear the suit for around three minutes before succumbing to heat exhaustion.

As an innovative new product, the Gorilla advert broke new ground by utterly moving away from traditional category conventions. For example, there was no chocolate in the ad at all. There were also no people demonstrating their experience of the product. Another innovation involved advertising the launch of the Gorilla advert in newspapers and online. Advertising the ad included posting it on YouTube on the night of the Big Brother reality TV programme final, with over 100,000 hits in the first 24 hours (this has grown now to well over 12 million).

The success of the campaign is undeniable with a rise of about 9 per cent in the short term and a gradual and consistent build in sales of the Cadbury's brand subsequently. Looking back, the very tight creative constraint of one week proved to galvanise all concerned, including the client. 'There was a sense that we were doing something together at high speed that was against the odds and I think that created an immediate sense of togetherness and partnership' observes Willingham. To this Rolston adds 'We've learned about the power of irrational creativity. Sometimes you can't rationalise why something works or what people take from it. It just feels like the right thing to do.' Sound advice, but unlike the chocolate perhaps, not always that easy for businesses to swallow.

Discussion questions

1 *Creativity is defined in terms of novelty and value. What methods did Willingham and Rolston employ to assess the value of their creative ideas?*

2 *What macro and micro-level conditions enabled and constrained the creativity described in this case study?*

3 *Imagine you were the one to come up with this idea. How would you have sold it to your senior management?*

8.9   NOTES, REFERENCES AND FURTHER READING

Notes and Further Information

1. For a critique of Western education and the dominance of the 'productivity' model see Robinson, 2001.

2. The power to hold on to two opposing ideas simultaneously (known as Janusian thinking – after the Roman God, Janus, often depicted as having two faces looking in opposite directions, who gives January its name as he represents the threshold from the old year into the new) has long been associated with creativity.

3. These statistics are from a NESTA article available at http://www.nesta.org.uk/uk-creative-industry-to-drive-significant-growth-in-uk-economy/ downloaded on 10 March 2009. NESTA (the National Endowment for Science, Technology and the Arts) have produced a range of excellent research reports on the creative industries and entrepreneurship. For more details visit their website.

4. For an interesting take on the role of 'space' in enabling creativity see Baroness Susan Greenfield's idea essay at 'space for ideas', available at http://www.spaceforideas.uk.com/IsolatedStorage/5f544d60-45d1-46fe-865d-76726a3ed822/ContentAssets/Documents/greenfield.pdf.

5. Charles Handy outlines this approach in his idea essay at 'space for ideas', available at http://www.spaceforideas.uk.com/rpmServer/zSpace4Ideas/pdf/Charles%20Handy%20Paper.pdf.

6. See Goleman, D. (1996) *Emotional Intelligence – Why It Can Matter More Than IQ*, London: Bloomsbury Publishing.

7. See, for example, Green, B. and Gallwey, W.T. (1986) *The Inner Game of Music*, London: Pan Books.

8. See, for example, Myers and Briggs MBTI Personality Type (http://www.myersbriggs.org/); Edward De Bono creative thinking tools (http://www.edwdebono.com/); Tony Buzan's mind mapping (http://www.buzanworld.com/); free mind-mapping tools (http://www.snapfiles.com/get/freemind.html).

9. See, for example, brain-storming tools (http://www.mindtools.com/brainstm.html); Ishikawa diagrams (http://www.isixsigma.com/tt/cause_and_effect/).

References

Andriopoulos, C. (2003) Six paradoxes in managing creativity: An embracing act, *Long Range Planning*, 36 (4): 375–388.

BERR (2008a) *Creative Britain: New Talents For the New Economy*, London: Department for Business Enterprise and Regulatory Reform.

BERR (2008b) *Enterprise: Unlocking the UK's Talent*, Strategy document, London: Department for Business Enterprise and Regulatory Reform. URL: http://www.berr.gov.uk/bbf/enterprise-smes/enterprise-framework/index.html [accessed on 16 March 2009].

Bilton, C. (2007) *Management and Creativity*, Oxford: Blackwell Publishing.

Blair, H. (2001) You're only as good as your last job: The labour process and labour market in the British film industry, *Work Employment & Society*, 15 (1).

Boden, M.A. (1994) *Dimensions of Creativity*, Cambridge, MA: Massachusetts Institute of Technology.

Caves, R.E. (2000) *Creative Industries: Contracts Between Art and Commerce*, Boston: Harvard University Press.

Cox, G. (2005) *Cox Review of Creativity in Business*, London: HM Treasury.

Csikszentmihalyi, M. (2002) *Flow: The Classic Work on How to Achieve Happiness*, London: Rider.

DCMS (1998 and 2001) *Creative Industries Mapping Document*, London: Department for Culture, Media and Sport.

De Bono, E. (1985) *Six Thinking Hats*, London: Penguin Books.

Fischer, G. (2005) Social creativity: Making all voices heard, Paper at University of Colorado, Center for LifeLong Learning and Design (L3D), Department of Computer Science, Boulder, CO, available at http://l3d.cs.colorado.edu/~gerhard/papers/social-creativity-hcii-2005.pdf.

Florida, R. (2003) *The Rise of the Creative Class*, London: Basic Books.

Ford, C.M. and Gioia, D.A. (eds) (1995) *Creative Action in Organisations,* Thousand Oaks, CA: Sage.

Gibb, A.A. (2005) Towards the entrepreneurial: University entrepreneurship education as a lever for change, *National Council for Graduate Entrepreneurship Policy Paper 3*, available at: http://www.ncge.org.uk/downloads/policy/Towards_the_Entrepreneurial_University.pdf.

Goleman, D. (1996) *Emotional Intelligence – Why It Can Matter More Than IQ*, London: Bloomsbury Publishing.

Green, B. and Gallwey, W.T. (1986) *The Inner Game of Music*, London: Pan Books.

Hackett, K. and Ramsden, P. (2000) *The Employment and Enterprise Characteristics of the Cultural Sector in Europe,* A report for Banking on Culture, Manchester: North West Arts Board.

Hawking, S, (1988) *A Brief History of Time*, London: Bantam Books.

Hesmondhalgh, D. (2007) *The Cultural Industries*, 2nd edn, London: Sage.

Howkins, J. (2002) *The Creative Economy: How People Make Money from Ideas*, London: Penguin.

8

Ibbotson, P. (2008) *The Illusion of Leadership*, London: Palgrave Macmillan.

Isaksen, S.G. and Treffinger, D.J. (1985) *Creative Problem Solving,* Buffalo: Brearly.

Jeffcutt, P. and Pratt, A.C. (2002) Managing creativity in the cultural industries, *Creativity and Innovation Management*, 11(4): 225–233.

Jeffers, S. (1987) *Feel the Fear and Do it Anyway*, London: Arrow Books.

John-Steiner, V. (2000) *Creative Collaboration*, New York: Oxford University Press.

Koestler, A. (1964/1976) *The Act of Creation*, London: Hutchison.

Kretschmer, M., Klimis, G. and Choi, C.J. (1999) Increasing returns and social contagion in cultural industries, *British Journal of Management*, 10, S61–S72.

Leadbeater, C. and Oakley, K. (1999) *The Independents*, London: Demos.

Martin, L. (2007) An augmented conceptual framework for creativity studies, in *Unpublished doctoral thesis*, Department of Organisation, Work and Technology, Lancaster: Lancaster University.

McMullan, W.E. (1976) Creative individuals: Paradoxical personages, *The Journal of Creative Behaviour*, 10 (4): 265–275.

Poincaré, H. (1982) *The Foundations of Science*, Washington, DC: University Press of America.

Robinson, K. (2001) *Out of Our Minds: Learning To Be Creative*, London: Capstone.

Robinson, K. (2009) *The Element. How Finding Your Passion Changes Everything*, London: Penguin.

Rogers, C.R. (1976) Toward a theory of creativity, in Rothenberg, A. and Hausman, C.R. (eds) *The Creativity Question*, Durham, NC: Duke University Press, pp. 296–305.

Root-Bernstein, R. and Root-Bernstein, M. (2001) *Sparks of Genius: The 13 Thinking Tools*, US: Mariner Books.

Seltzer, K. and Bentley, T. (1999) *The Creative Age: Knowledge and Skills for the New Economy*, London: Demos.

Sternberg, R.J. and Lubart, T.I. (1999) The concept of creativity: Prospects and paradigms, in R.J. Sternberg (ed.) *Handbook of Creativity*, Cambridge: Cambridge University Press.

Stokes, D. and Wilson, N. (2006) *Small Business Management and Entrepreneurship*, London: Thomson Learning.

Tsoukas, H. (2000) What is management?, in S. Ackroyd and S. Fleetwood (eds) *Realist Perspectives on Management and Organisations,* London: Routledge, pp. 26–44.

Tusa, J. (2003) *On Creativity: Interviews Exploring the Process,* London: Methuen.

Weisberg, R.W. (1993) *Creativity: Beyond the Myth of Genius*, New York: W.H. Freeman.

Recommended Further Reading

Baronet, J. (2003) Creativity in action, paper available at: http://www.sbaer.uca.edu/research/usasbe/2003/pdffiles/papers/13.pdf.

Bourdieu, P. (2002) *Distinction. A Social Critique of the Judgement of Taste*, London: Routledge. This is the definitive work on the subject of 'taste'.

Davis, H. and Scase, R. (2000) *Managing Creativity*, Milton Keynes: The Open University Press.

Henry, J. (1991) *Creative Management,* London: Sage Publications. This is a very good edited collection of papers on creativity, creative management, creative processes, creative development and the creative future.

Sternberg, R.J. (ed) (1998) *Handbook of Creativity*, Cambridge: Cambridge University Press.

West, M.A. and Farr, J.L. (1990) *Innovation and Creativity at Work*, London: Wiley.

CHAPTER 9

Entrepreneurial Networking

LEARNING OBJECTIVES

After studying this chapter, the reader will be able to:

- Understand what a network is, and how it can be defined or mapped
- Understand some aspects of the theory of social networks
- Have an understanding of different types of network, and be able to analyse and evaluate a network
- Have a better awareness of the networks and networking tools which already exist around you
- Have access to some networking skills, and suggestions about how to continue developing them.

INTRODUCTION

No man is an island, entire of itself . . .

John Donne, Meditation XVII, 1624

John Donne's meditation on mortality identifies the interconnectedness of individuals, and the extent to which meaning in our lives is created by other people. Although written almost 400 years ago, the sentiment of the passage is as alive and relevant today as then.

Today, we talk, write and act both consciously and unconsciously within a highly networked world. Some important products which facilitate networking include inexpensive and powerful computers and high-capacity mobile and fixed communications infrastructure. These have created greater opportunity to connect more people at greater distances than ever before. This chapter considers what we mean by networks and networking, and what the implications are for entrepreneurship. It provides an introduction to social network theory and some practical suggestions about how you can develop your networking capability and your networks.

For entrepreneurs and entrepreneurial firms, networking is an important tool. Networking helps to create or identify opportunities, gather resources, and find partners and employees. In this chapter we investigate:

- What networks are;
- Examples of different types of network;
- How entrepreneurs use them;

- Approaches and skills entrepreneurs use in networking;

- How to develop and use networks to advantage; and

- The barriers to effective networking.

Finally, it considers the pitch, a key instrument for communicating our ideas.

A student entrepreneur develops her networks

Yuliana is a Russian student studying in England. She initially found little to engage her enthusiasm outside of her studies, but one day happened on an advertisement for a three-day entrepreneurship boot camp. Her participation introduced her to a network of other students with entrepreneurial interests, and to the infrastructure for enterprise support in and around her university. She has since helped to establish an Entrepreneurs' Society at two universities. She and a core group have developed the contacts of those networks by entering enterprise competitions, running educational and social events, fundraising and tapping into the local and national support programmes. The societies many competitive successes have given them exposure to employers and enterprise funders, and helped them to develop their networks of students to their current strength of 900 members.

Have you joined any entrepreneurial networks like those that Yuliana developed? Are there any that are available to you? Read more about Yuliana in the case study at the end of the chapter.

9.1 WHAT IS A NETWORK?

A network is a collection of connected points. The points are known as *nodes*, while the connections are known as *ties* (Figure 9-1).

Networks may be large or small, dense or sparse, open or closed. The nodes may be very active, or very passive. The ties may be strong or weak.

FIGURE 9-1 **A typical network diagram showing nodes and ties between them**

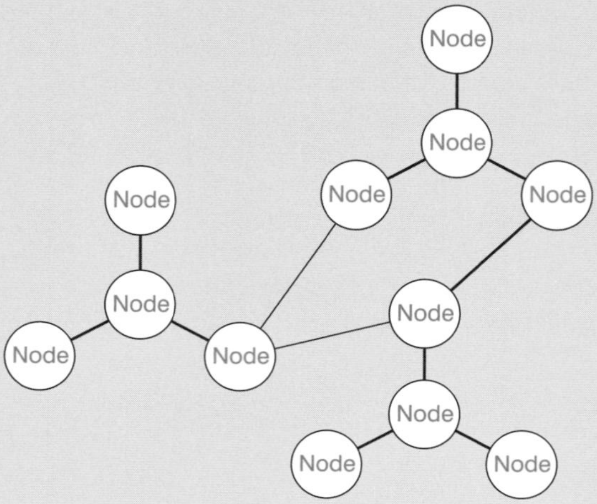

Facebook — the world's largest network?

Facebook[1] is a very large global network whose members communicate through the Internet for social and other purposes. Founded by Mark Zuckerberg in 2004, it has grown rapidly to more than 200 million users. These are divided into nodes, or 'friends', according to the contacts of an individual or the common interests of specific groups. The ties between the friends may be family relations, friendships, backgrounds such as a common school or region, or shared concerns such as social causes or clubs. Some nodes are highly active, communicating with one another frequently; others register but then let their usage lapse. Ties range in strength from close friends sending messages to one another regularly to infrequent contact between members of an alumni group.

Facebook is open to anyone to use, although registration is required at first, and access to networks can be controlled by nodes. For instance, nodes can decide they have to accept you as a 'friend' before you gain access to their particular network. It has also been closed in several countries in the past including Syria and Iran.

The network concept, though drawn from technical and scientific domains, has been widely applied in the social sciences, particularly in business and entrepreneurship research. The social sciences application stems from Mitchell (1969) who articulated that society is made up of networks, and identified various aspects of networks which helped to describe their interactions. However, this social analysis was not initially applied to economics and business so the use of network theory is more recent within the domain of entrepreneurship education. It draws on the work of Granovetter (1985, 1992), who argued that economic activity occurs and is embedded in relationships between people. Previously, economic theory applied to business made the case for only two types of economic organisation, namely markets and hierarchies, while Granovetter's work argued for the addition of a third type, namely networks. While social theorists like Mitchell identified that society is made up of actors communicating with one another and operating individually and in groups, Granovetter (1985, 1992) moved the analysis into the economic domain by providing a social analysis of how economic value is created. He argued that economic activity can be understood only by seeing it within the social context of individuals and organisations connected by a variety of ties.

Conceptually, the idea of a network is neither positive nor negative. The concept simply provides a means of analysing and discussing some social and economic phenomena. However, networks can have either positive effects such as business development, or negative outcomes such as people involved in organised crime. It is the purposes to which networks are put that creates or destroys value.

In entrepreneurship, networks are thought to be extremely important and add value in several ways, as they are:

■ a source of ideas, and of ideas evaluation;

■ a route to resources in the form of money and other assets;

■ a key means of finding customers, partners, distribution channels and other collaborators.

A corollary of this is that the ability to develop and use networks is an important skill for entrepreneurs.

9.1.1 Individuals or Organisations?

Networks may be made up of individuals or organisations. If they are made up of individuals, they are generally considered to be personal or *social networks*. If they are made up of organisations, they are known as *inter-organisational networks*. In the area of entrepreneurship, research has evaluated both types of network (O'Donnell, Gilmore, Cummins and Carson, 2001). Various aspects of the social networks of individual entrepreneurs are considered to be factors leading to their success in establishing viable enterprises. The networks that entrepreneurial organisations enter into are also of interest, and show differing levels of intensity of interaction (Curran and Blackburn, 1994).[2]

This chapter considers both individuals and their personal networks, and organisations and their networks. It is important to remember that a preponderance of enterprises have only a single employee who is also the owner. In the UK alone, for instance, approximately 75 per cent of its 4 million plus enterprises have only the owner as employee (BERR, 2007).[3] They may be marketing their own expertise, creativity, talent or skills, for instance as freelance artists and musicians, or as builders and decorators. They may also own a specific piece of intellectual property such as a trade mark, patent, design, or copyright materials which they can exploit through other firms. In all of these cases the owner is intimately connected with the brand, idea or skill which they have developed and the line between individual and organisation is very blurred. However, they are linked – both formally and informally – in networks with many other individuals who are similarly identified with their organisations.

9.1.2 Sources and Types of Network

Networks can be found in all types of human activity. Such social groupings may of course overlap, for instance as we count colleagues among our friends, and as we work in specialist contexts like a particular sport. Table 9-1 shows examples of the content or source of more common networks.

A starting point for thinking about developing networks is to identify the ones to which we already belong. Most people will be able to identify that they are a part of one or more of these types of network.

TABLE 9-1	Network content
Type of content	**Examples**
Employment	Employees in the same firm Employees in similar roles across an industry
Family ties	Brothers, sisters, cousins Tribe or clan
Friendship	School or college Neighbours
Common social interest	Social clubs Sports clubs
Professional interest	Medical or legal specialists Product specialists
Business interactions	Buying or selling Providing complementary resources Partnership

Mapping these, and identifying the knowledge and other resources which they might be able to make available to use, is a useful starting point for developing a network.

9.1.3 Spatial Distance Within a Network

The members of networks might be physically close together or far apart. For instance, a group of entrepreneurs with offices or desk space in an incubator or business hub specially developed for the purpose may be considered a network. Their physical proximity enables largely informal, but quite intensive and frequent interactions, for instance at the coffee machine or water fountain. They may act as clients and suppliers to one another, but just as importantly they may help one another identify new customers or opportunities, act as sounding boards for one another, and help motivate one another when times are tough. Immediacy of contact may create special benefits.

A more physically dispersed network example might be a network of people with common professional or business interests who connect together via the Internet from around the world to share scientific, operational and market information. Once again, the contact may be formal or informal.

A hive of beekeepers

A beekeepers network, Apimondia[4] acts as a central node for beekeepers and beekeeping associations around the world. It holds information on bees, beekeeping and the markets for bee products. By linking far-flung beekeepers together, it allows them to access scientific, product and market information which they might individually be unable to find easily. It also allows them to make contacts directly with one another. However, the website itself has little functionality for networking online (at the time of writing) so that although the website initiates the introduction, it is up to the associations and individuals to pursue developing the contacts.

Search on the Internet for international beekeepers networks, and see what you find. Consider the purpose and scope of any networks you identify. How many members are there, and how far apart are they physically? What is the nature of their interaction?

Regional networks sit between the extremes of very local and very global or dispersed networks. The strength and importance of these will vary with local conditions as well as with the type of enterprise which is involved. The density of creative industry entrepreneurs and enterprises in London, England, for instance, reflects the individualistic nature of many of such enterprises – the individual is the artist or creative talent, and freelance work is common. The availability of such talent also attracts further talent and work into the area.

Pinewood Studios Group – a creative force?

Making films and TV programmes is a very intense collaborative process. It requires a large number of skills and resources to be brought together. The Pinewood Studios Group encompasses three famous film studios: Pinewood, Shepperton and Teddington. All three studios are located on the outskirts of London, England. The studio group is both a film production business and a property business. In the latter guise, the group brings together over 280 specialist firms which support film production. These include transport and catering, special effects, post-production, theatres and set-makers to name just a few. This cluster of businesses brings high levels of expertise together, aiming to attract film-makers from around the world. Their competition includes Cinecitta in Italy, and studios in the United States.

9.1.4 Network Boundaries and Perspectives

Networks vary in how open or closed they are to members. If a network is flexible and open to new members, it is likely to attract new ideas, activities and resources. If it is more closed, for instance like a group of close friends who do many things together, then the members know so much about one another that they are less likely to acquire new ideas and resources. For entrepreneurs, larger and more diverse networks are shown to be valuable to firm growth (Zhao and Aram, 1995; Aldrich, Rosen and Woodward, 1987; Hansen, 1995). A large size of network implies that there are more sources of information and resources at the disposal of the entrepreneur (Singh, Hybels, and Ellis, 2000). A more diverse network implies more opportunity to find out and combine different resources and opportunities in new ways.

There are two main ways of representing or graphically illustrating a network:

■ A representation of the network as a whole, and the connections between the nodes. Figure 9-1 'A typical network diagram showing nodes and ties between them' is an example of this kind;

■ A representation of the network as centred on a single individual or organisation, with consideration of how many and which people that individual knows directly (Figure 9-2).

This approach can also help to reveal the significance of an individual in a context, by showing the extent to which they are connected to particular types of people. So for instance a network map of European royal families might be centred on the British Queen Elizabeth II, who is the most connected individual. For an individual interested in entrepreneurship and just beginning to think about and map their networks, this approach is a good way to start, with themselves in the middle, and different groups of contacts arranged around them. Thus family, friends and professional contacts might lead off in different directions, into different networks.

Integrative Case Link

For more on the boundaries and focus of networks, consider the case of Gloria Serobe, Case Study 4 at the end of Part 2.

It is not just who you know, but who you may have access to indirectly that matters. Networking creates the possibility of finding people who know other people, and being able to make introductions or pass information and opportunities along. The boundary of a network is continually changing, as new people are introduced or lost from the network, and these changes create new opportunities for interaction and sharing.

FIGURE 9-2   **A network diagram focused on a single node**

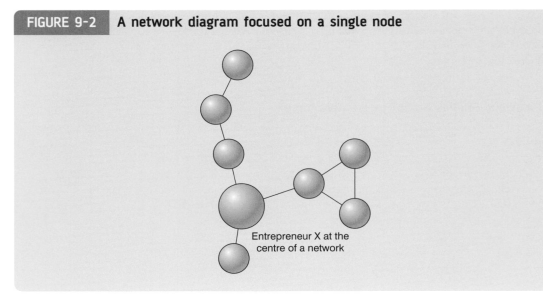

Entrepreneur X at the centre of a network

9.1.5 **Formality of Ties**

Network nodes may be individuals (entrepreneurs) or organisations (as discussed in subsection 9.1.1 above). The ties which connect them may be informal or formal. Table 9-2 indicates some of the types of link which can be found in entrepreneurial networks.

Less formal links are typically created by and for the purpose of information-sharing, learning, mutual support and collaboration. These may have no explicit contractual content as there may be no formal contract within the connection. Networks between individuals are often of this nature. More formal links are more thoroughly articulated or described, and more highly contractualised. Organisations networked with one another to buy and supply products and services, or to work together to create new projects, products or services will typically have contracts which record and govern the relationships.

The nature of the ties between individuals and organisations may well change over time. Ties that begin informally may become formalised as a business relationship develops. Indeed, the contacts between organisations of any size are between people, and the first contact is therefore inevitably informal.

TABLE 9-2	Types of link in entrepreneurial networks	
Increasing formality of links	Individual to individual	Family Friend Colleagues Collaborators Business partners
	Organisation to individual	Client Supplier Consultant Partner
	Organisation to organisation	Supplier Client Partner Joint venture Co-branders

Benetton production and supply chain ties

Benetton[5] became a retail empire selling branded goods in airports, shopping malls and High Streets around the world through the 1970s and 1980s. The family-owned firm originated in an area of Northern Italy which has a long tradition of small manufacturing firms producing clothing. As a knitwear firm, it developed an approach to manufacture in which a substantial proportion of the work was outsourced to smaller local firms. These firms produced orders of standard designs or part designs for assembly by other firms, which were then finished and packaged elsewhere, often in Benetton facilities. At the retail end of the production chain, Benetton used a franchising approach. Individuals acquired the rights to develop Benetton shops as long they exclusively presented Benetton merchandise. These approaches provided Benetton with flexibility: the outsourced production resulted in flexible capacity which could be brought on-stream or taken off-stream to suit market conditions; outsourcing production and franchising the retail network also meant that Benetton itself could grow its total output with a smaller financial investment in fixed costs.

The small firms which made up Benetton's outsourced capacity were managed in a variety of ways, some informal, some formal. Perhaps the most important nodes were the individual agents who managed the sub-contractors and retailers. They effectively developed and controlled the networks, ensuring an efficient production and retail distribution process. These nodes interacted intensively with both sub-contractors and the family firm.

9.2   TRUST

We have described how networks have complex structures with different origins, flexible boundaries and different strengths and intensity of ties between members. So how do individuals cope with all of this complexity and change? While sociologists provide a range of answers, the concept of trust is a key factor.

A family business network

Trust in a strong internal network is a key factor in the success of family businesses as a form of enterprise. If defined as any business that employs more than one family member, they account for three-quarters of all businesses and are particularly prevalent amongst small enterprises. Why is this form so common? A recent survey of owners of family businesses claimed that they were more likely to survive the economic downturn because of several inherent strengths: the strong support network of family members; shared values and trust; and the ability to take a long-term view (Barclays Wealth, 2009). Family businesses also share common issues that are not typical of other enterprises including: coaching and encouraging the next generation of owners, coping with family politics within a business context and making arrangements for inheritance and gift taxes. These issues are mostly ignored by general business networks. To fill the gap, the Family Business Network[6] was set up in 1990. It has rapidly spread to over 50 countries that cover North America, Latin America, Asia and Europe, with a current membership of more than 3200 family business leaders. The network offers regional and global contacts, events, advice and support to its members. Its mission statement summarises what many networks are all about:

The Family Business Network (FBN) is about:

■ *sharing best practice and knowledge within our worldwide network;*

■ *supporting the next generation (aged 18–40) of business-owning families; and*

■ *promoting the case for family business to governments and tax decision-makers.*

Source: http://www.fbn-i.org/fbn/web.nsf

When we trust someone, we make ourselves vulnerable to them. We have certain expectations of them – for instance that they will do something (or not do something) even though we cannot control them directly. If we mistrust someone, we tend to be more reluctant to either share information or to develop a deeper relationship with them.

Trust is therefore a way of dealing with complexity and uncertainty. We decide to trust someone based on what we know of them and their behaviour. As our networks get bigger and more diverse, it becomes more difficult to make that judgement on an individual basis. Networks are a way of developing trust. Because we meet people through a social context, we make judgements about them based on this context – who they know that we know (the nodes), and what they do or share with us (the ties).

ENTREPRENEURSHIP IN ACTION

Avedis Zildjian Co. - developing trust for 400 years

Avedis Zildjian[7] set up a family business in Constantinople in 1623 that has survived in the US to this day, and is currently run by 14th-generation descendant, Craigie Zildjian, its first woman CEO. The orignal founder discovered a mix of base metals that he used to craft cymbals that had such unique sound qualities that the Sultan gave him the name 'Zildjian', meaning the 'family of cymbal smiths'.

When the family brought their business to America in 1929, it was not only the sound quality that helped them succeed, it was the close relationships they developed with the great jazz drummers of the day. They continued to forge close links with music networks; in 1964, demand soared when the Beatles appeared on the Ed Sullivan show with Ringo Starr's drum kit prominently displaying the Zildjian name. Today close ties with networks have made their cymbals the first choice of musicians from the Israeli Symphony Orchestra to the Clash, who all know they can trust the quality of products that have been made by the same family for nearly 400 years.

What information we are prepared to share, and the extent to which we will develop a relationship will depend on our understanding of their social context.

9.3   SOCIAL NETWORKING ON THE WEB

Some important aspects of the world today which facilitate networking include inexpensive and powerful computers and high-capacity mobile and fixed communications infrastructures. These have created greater opportunity to connect more people at greater distances than ever before. Web 2.0 applications have particularly enabled new means of networking people together.

The key to the success of these applications is that they enable user-generated content to be incorporated cheaply and easily. Individuals create and input their own content to the site of their choice. The functionality of the sites then allows the creator to edit the content, and other users to access it, use it, comment upon it, and in many cases edit or change it in some way. Computing power and communications capacity mean that this content can be of many kinds: written, audio, video or visual. Individuals have the opportunity to present themselves and their ideas across media in a public forum.

Typically, social networking websites have targeted purposes which determine the nature of the functionality which is enabled. So the information that an individual can add will be restricted by the original concept of the purpose. Table 9-3 provides some examples.

Most sites have commercial objectives although the business models that they use to make money vary from one site to the next. They also change and develop over time, as the competitive context changes and the capability of the technology changes. However, a common theme is that they need very high levels of use or traffic in order to be successful. This not only means that many visitors need to use the sites but also that the intensity and regularity of use must also be relatively high. Shared information which is out of date is of little use.

There are many opportunities to use these sites for entrepreneurial purposes. For instance, eBay allows you to set up an online retail outlet, at very low cost. This can provide you with fast market feedback as well as sales. LinkedIn can provide you with introductions to relevant potential buyers and clients. Facebook groups provide entrepreneurs with forums for sharing information, contacts, or ideas.

9

TABLE 9-3	Some examples of social networking sites[8]	
Website	**Purpose**	**Typical content**
LinkedIn	Professional networking site for job seeking, career development and employee recruitment purposes	Career profiles, expertise, resumes and CVs
Facebook	Casual social interaction and information-sharing between friends	Greetings, current photos, information about current pastimes, states of mind and activities
YouTube	Sharing of videos, music and photos	Videos, music, audio files for sale or for free download
Friends Reunited	Re-establishing connections between old friends and acquaintances	Social information related to groups from particular contexts, for instance schools, workplaces, clubs or other social groupings
eBay	Bringing together people and organisations to buy and sell goods through auctions	Goods and services for sale

9

WHEN THINGS GO WRONG

Friends Reunited — a failing network?

Friends Reunited was launched in 2001 and quickly developed a large customer base. It fulfilled a need which was un-served at the time – helping people to connect with friends, colleagues and relations whom they hadn't seen for a long time. It very quickly reached a million customers. However, the application was overtaken by newer applications (Facebook, Plaxo), which became much larger very quickly. These were made available on a free basis, and Friends had to drop its charges completely to compete. (*More on Friends Reunited in Chapter 13.*)

Entrepreneurs start up on eBay

According to *The Sunday Times* (2004) 'eBay has become the fastest-growing forum for start-ups in Britain. . . . More than 23,000 enterprises are trading through the online auction site, with an estimated three-quarters of them using it as the sole way of conducting their business. The site's attractions — virtually no set-up costs, little red tape and minimal overheads — have made it an ideal forum for start-ups. And eBay has moved quickly to establish a sellers' support network in order to sustain the growth in new businesses.

© ROBERT GALBRAITH/REUTERS/CORBIS

eBay – a Key Start-up forum

'Wilmamae Ward, 36, is typical of the new breed of eBay entrepreneur. The former public-relations executive began using the site to satisfy her tastes in vintage and designer clothes.

'"After one particular buying spree I realised I had more clothes than I could wear in a lifetime so I started selling them," she said.

'Last June, three months after her first sale, she opened her own eBay shop, The Gathering Goddess, went full-time and now turns over about £5,000 a month.

'"As you build up your business, you realise there is a science to eBaying," said Ward. "It's all about the key words you use to sell a particular item. You have 88 characters and you soon learn which words work and which don't."

'As a registered eBay "power seller", Ward gets online support and a telephone helpline. There is also a power-seller conference — the first being held in London in the summer — as part of eBay's ambition to build a community of sellers.'

Each of these commercial sites has different trust-enabling mechanisms built into it. So for instance, the eBay community works on the basis of feedback for buyers and sellers. Each time you buy or sell something, you are requested to provide feedback, and buyers and sellers are subject to a rating system. With Facebook, you can determine who can see your profile, and what information you provide. However, individuals are surprisingly open about what information they provide, implying that there is a high level of trust in the site and other users. LinkedIn is an explicit networking system, where individuals recommend one another for jobs and other opportunities.

While the sites mentioned here are open to anyone to use, there are others which are private and can be joined by invitation only. Some of these are corporate sites, like Sabre Town, established by Sabre to bring together and encourage trust, information-sharing and problem-solving between their employees who are located around the world. Another private site is aSmallWorld,[9] which although commercial in its objectives, targets wealthy individuals who travel extensively. This site can be joined by invitation only, which provides a reason to trust other members as well as the site owners.

9.4   HOW TO IMPROVE NETWORKING ABILITIES

This section is designed to help the reader to build confidence in networking with direct advice on how to develop networking skills. It provides some tips and suggestions on how to join networks and how to behave when you do. The important action to take away from this section is that you need to engage with people in order to build your networks – to be proactive at finding opportunities to meet new people and expand the range of people with whom you interact.

9.4.1 Identifying Networks

You are very likely to be already a part of several networks, made up for instance of your extended family, your friends and fellow students, colleagues and employers in your place of work, staff in your college or university. A starting point for networking is to identify and explore these networks. Try to make explicit how you interact within them, what you bring to them, and what they bring to you. Think about how often you interact with them, and what you interact about. If you have an entrepreneurial idea, what information, advice or other resources could each of them bring to you? What do you offer them?

Many people reading this book will be studying at a college or university, and most of these have student-run clubs and societies which organise events, introduce members to enterprises outside of the university, or simply do interesting things. Some will be sporting clubs and societies, some perhaps more intellectually oriented, like the entrepreneurs' society or the chess society. However, all of them will help you to meet new people who will have different information and resources to share, so a further source of networks will be these clubs and societies, most of which you can join.

Wherever you live, your college or university, local Chamber of Commerce or government development agency will provide networking opportunities. These often take the form of events and talks, which enable you to meet people, share ideas and find out about resources. Some organisations like Chambers of Commerce are specifically established to encourage networking between entrepreneurs and organisations.

Kingston Chambers of Commerce

Do a search on the web for a Chamber of Commerce in your area. Depending on the size of your community, and on the particular arrangement of government structures, you may find that your relevant Chamber is a national, regional or local organisation. For instance a web-search for Kingston Chamber of Commerce threw up the following results (Table 9-4) (Kingston is a relatively common name for a town). Each of these Chambers is slightly different to the others, with some being member-driven, some more governmentally driven. They all run or promote events at which business owners and managers can meet one another.

TABLE 9-4	Kingston Chambers of Commerce
Kingston, Ontario, Canada	Small city served by a single Chamber of Commerce
Kingston upon Thames, London, England	Part of the large (c. 8 million inhabitants) city of London. One of several chambers of commerce there
Kingston, Jamaica	Jamaica Chamber of Commerce is located in Kingston Jamaica
Kingston, Washington, USA	A smaller, more rural community with a Chamber of Commerce

9.4.2 Barriers and Challenges

It can be challenging to engage with people you do not already know, or who are from a different educational, social or economic background than you. This reluctance stems from many sources and may be represented by any of the following statements:

■ 'Don't like talking to strangers' – perhaps a long-standing, acquired belief that strangers may be in some way dangerous, or that someone you do not know who is simply different, is unable therefore to be reached.

■ 'Don't feel comfortable introducing myself or talking about myself' – often this is the result of shyness, social discomfort or lack of confidence. We are often trained, and sometimes simply unable, to talk about ourselves. In many contexts and cultures it is considered inappropriate or rude to talk about one's self. In addition, individuals may not immediately see how to talk about themselves, or know what to say.

■ 'Don't like asking for favours' – in some contexts, and for some individuals, networking in order to seek – or trade – resources seems to be the same as seeking favours. However, assets and resources need to be used and traded in order to create value. Offering to exchange or trade assets is not the same as asking for favours.

■ 'Don't know what to say' – conversations at networking events vary according to the purpose of the event, the people who are there and the circumstances around the event.

9.4.3 Overcoming Barriers

Working with the concept of reciprocity – give and take – is an important starting point. The ties between people and organisations are two-way. Both parties give and both get something. They may be quite different things; for instance, one party may get access to a brand name, while the other might get access to expertise in a particular product area. Whatever the level or nature of what each party gets, they make a social investment in the relationship, and they both get something from it. In some cases, the payoff from the investment may be delayed for one or both parties.

This concept of reciprocity helps overcome some of the barriers identified above (see Table 9-5).

9

TABLE 9-5	Overcoming barriers – some approaches
Barrier	**Possible action**
Talking to 'strangers'	■ Seek an introduction to the individual ■ Attend events which are specifically labelled as opportunities to network – others will be there for the same purpose ■ Seek common ground in conversation ■ Remember that you are also a 'stranger' to them – they may also be nervous of you
Introducing and talking about myself	■ Identify a small number of things that you can say about yourself, your ideas, or your enterprise ideas – be prepared to talk about them ■ Remember that you are an interesting person – because of where you are from, what you have done, what you want to do, and many other factors. ■ Once again, networking events and opportunities are reciprocal, and others are interested to hear about you

TABLE 9-5	Overcoming barriers – some approaches *(Continued)*
Barrier	**Possible action**
Asking for favours	■ Identify the things you have to offer or give to establish reciprocity, so that you are *not* asking for favours ■ Remember that you do not have to 'get' or 'give' immediately – under reciprocity, payoffs for either or both parties may be delayed ■ Listen to what the other party is indicating they need – it may not be what you expect. You may be able to offer something to them that you hadn't considered before
Don't know what to say	■ Be prepared with something to say, topics to discuss, and opportunities to follow-up on ■ Consider what you are looking for to develop your idea or your enterprise, and be prepared to explain this ■ Practise asking questions of others. What do you need to find out, and what questions would you ask to do so?

9.5 THE PITCH

The enterprise pitch is the brief summary of your enterprise opportunity, accompanied by a request for help of some kind. Delivering the enterprise pitch is an important way to gather critique and support for your ideas, resources to help develop them, and the clients and partners an enterprise needs in order to grow. Entrepreneurs may have to pitch their idea in a wide variety of circumstances, including to funding panels, bank managers and customers.[10]

It is often called an elevator pitch, which means that it should take no more to say it than it takes to get from one floor to the next in an elevator (usually about two minutes). This encapsulates the idea that the pitch needs to be brief and to the point, and it also needs to be ready prepared, so that it can be delivered unexpectedly – as when you encounter a potential funder or partner in a lift. Both of these factors – speed and surprise – create a genuine requirement for discipline and preparation in getting the pitch ready.

ENTREPRENEURSHIP IN ACTION

Kathy Jones – networks of steel

Kathy Jones set up a craft company when she was at university that makes individual items in steel. She relies on work that is commissioned, and so has to use all of her networks to keep orders flowing. She has learnt the importance of word-of-mouth recommendations and networking and is prepared to promote herself at every opportunity. She has joined local art and business groups and is always prepared to pitch for new commissions when the opportunities arise.

The content of a two-minute pitch is summarised in Table 9-6. While here we are principally concerned with entrepreneurial ideas, you may also want to develop a pitch about yourself in order to get a job or placement, find a mentor, or join a graduate school. The pitch in these circumstances would be focused on your personal skills and capabilities, and how these might help an enterprise.

Integrative Case Link

Read more about Kathy and her business in Case Study 8 'Formed Steel' at the end of Part 3.

TABLE 9-6	Key elements of the pitch
Content	**Example pitch**
What is the problem being addressed?	A construction project typically produces 250 formal documents per million pounds of expenditure, and these documents are shared between as many as 50 discrete firms working on the project. This creates extreme challenges for the companies managing large projects – of version control, sharing knowledge and contractual management. It also produces large volumes of paper.
What is the solution?	My networked software system allows your documents to be held on a server and accessed by the various participants in a construction project with a full audit trail of users, versions and access. Regular reports will show who has accessed which documents when, and how they have done so. It also alerts all users to changes, updates and red-flag issues.
Why is this solution better than others?	This solution gets rid of paper from the process, while providing a reliable audit trail of all user activity. It outsources the hosting of the service, enabling you to implement it more cheaply than other, similar systems.
What is the business model for the solution?	We install the software free of charge. Each user firm buys the number of access licences which is appropriate to the likely extent of their usage – this can be adapted if their demand changes. In addition, each transaction on the database attracts a fee of 10 cents. The document manager is paid for within overall project costs.
What help do I need?	I'm looking for my first client for this system. Your firm has the largest number of construction starts planned for the next year. I would like to work with you to identify a project on which you could pilot my system.

9

9.6   SUMMARY AND ACTIVITIES

Social network theory suggests that society can be analysed and described as a set or collection of **actors** who interact in various ways to **create meaning and value**. Social ties can be created through any human activity. Applied to the domain of business and enterprise, organisations are made up of **networks of individuals**, and the economy is made up of **networks of organisations** and individuals.

Networks are made up of **nodes** linked together with **ties**. The nodes are individuals or organisations, and are connected by ties of various sorts. Ties may be **informal** between individuals, or more **formal** and **contractual** as between organisations or organisations and individuals. The **intensity of ties** varies too, with some having very little traffic, and some being used very intensively.

Networks are particularly important to entrepreneurs because they **bring together** people and their resources, including **information**, **money**, **talent**, **physical plant and intellectual property**. The high number of enterprises which have only the owner or founder as employee makes networks particularly important. To grow their businesses, entrepreneurs need to build **relationships** with other entrepreneurs and organisations.

Trust is a basic concept in networking. Trust is risky, because someone you trust may let you down. Building trust requires **reciprocity**, or give and take. Getting something out of a relationship requires putting something in. Sometimes considerable investment is required before you get something back.

Attitudes towards and **skills** in networking can be developed and practised to improve entrepreneurial opportunities. For instance, it is possible to learn **verbal communications skills** like asking questions, listening and being able to talk about oneself, one's ideas and one's enterprise. It is also possible to learn **practical aspects** of networking like looking for networking opportunities, gathering and keeping track of the details of people you meet, and finding ways of staying in contact with them.

There are many **opportunities to build networks**, including:

- Joining professional networks which are locally based, like chambers of commerce and attending meetings

- Joining professional networks which are based on a relevant profession or industry

- Joining social networks like clubs and societies

- Attending events which are relevant to your interests

- Starting your own networks, for instance virtually through Facebook or another social networking service, or physically, by starting a local enterprise club.

The **elevator pitch** is a brief verbal communication which sells an individual, idea, product or organisation. It is the initial vehicle used for communicating about yourself and your enterprise to potential supporters, particularly those you meet for the first time. Delivery of a pitch is an important part of networking – you should **be prepared** to deliver a pitch at any time, if the right person walks through the door.

REVIEW QUESTIONS

1 What are the main principles of social network theory?

2 What are the elements of a social network, and what do they do?

3 How can social networks be mapped?

4 What are some of the benefits of networks and networking?

5 What are the key elements of an elevator pitch?

6 What are some of the ways to develop a network?

7 Identify the various networks you are a part of, and analyse them for the skills and resources they contain.

8 What are some of the skills of networking?

9 How do organisations network together?

10 Explain the concept of trust.

9

SEMINAR TASK

Write your own pitch about either an enterprise idea which you want to raise funds or find other support for, or about yourself for a job or placement. Make sure your pitch covers the five key areas. Practise your pitch, one to one, with the people in your study or seminar group. You should aim to deliver your pitch at least 10 times, and expect to listen to at least 10 pitches. For every pitch you hear, provide at least one suggestion for how to improve it. Write the suggestion down on a notepad or sheet of paper, and give it to the person who has done the pitch.

At the end of the pitching session, identify at least three key learning points for yourself from the feedback you received, and from your own feelings about the exercise.

Preview case continued

Yuliana Topazly — student entrepreneur

Yuliana is a student entrepreneur with an extensive network among her peers, and within the business community. She originally went to England on a mission for her father, an entrepreneur in St Petersburg. She was to source new equipment for the family business, which re-processes scrap metal, capturing high-grade metals into ingots for re-use. She decided to stay in Britain to study business and develop her knowledge of English. Like many students studying abroad, she initially found her new social context very challenging, partly because she was still learning English, and partly because of her unfamiliarity with British cultural routines and systems. Without her normal family friends and student networks from her home city, it was also challenging to find people who shared her interests. It was as though she was starting from scratch.

While studying she saw a five-day entrepreneurship boot camp advertised, and decided to see what it was all about. During the course she met another 50 students who shared her interest in entrepreneurship. Together some of them began developing some new product ideas. The friends she met on the course became colleagues working together to develop new businesses. One of the product ideas that they developed was a special scarf. In order to develop it, she had to commission a design, locate suppliers in China, develop a brief for them, and raise the finance to fund and order. She achieved all of this through her entrepreneurial contacts. She was put into contact with appropriate manufacturers through a Chinese friend that she had met at a networking event. A design student was commissioned to do the design of the scarf. She found the finance by entering and winning an ideas competition with the idea. As a result of this project, Yuliana had contacts in China, the experience of developing a brief and commissioning manufacture and a product ready to sell.

The enterprise course also introduced Yuliana to some of the support systems available to young entrepreneurs in the UK generally. She also met university staff whose aim was to help entrepreneurs get started. Yuliana began volunteering with these contacts in the university to promote the opportunities they had on offer to new students. Through this work, she met more students committed to developing new enterprises. She also met further mentors among staff in the university. One of these offered her a paid internship working with student entrepreneurs while undertaking a Master's degree.

In deciding what to do a Master's thesis on, Yuliana drew on her experience with entrepreneurs in Russia, and with cultural differences

▶

between Russia and the UK. Her subject was trust. What was the attitude towards trust of Russian entrepreneurs, emerging from the controls of the Soviet era? How did Russian organisations establish trusting relationships with other organisations at home and abroad? How had things changed? She chose entrepreneurship in the Kaliningrad area of Russia as the context of a study. As a border area, and Russia's port on the Baltic, Kaliningrad was likely to have more contact with European countries than many other areas.

She used contacts among her friends and family to find entrepreneurs operating in the area who would be interviewed. Yuliana's findings were that entrepreneurs thought personal trust was very important as a foundation for business trust. A typical comment was 'I deal with the person, not with the company'. Russian entrepreneurs had used this approach as they emerged from the Soviet era because the confusion and complexity of the legal system there were intense. They had bad experiences in dealing with other Russian companies. Personal relationships were very important. Russian entrepreneurs continued to maintain this approach as they emerged into the European business domain. This was true among Russian entrepreneurs when they were dealing with other Russian companies, and remained so when they expanded their businesses to work with non-Russian companies. Although work with European companies used more legal systems and contracts than personal contact, personal contact was still important to the entrepreneurs. European companies, used to operating with a more established and reliable legal system, also found personal contact important in dealing with Russian entrepreneurs, as it gave them reassurance that they knew with whom they were dealing.

Interestingly, one of the limitations on business development for Russian firms was the fact that their businesses grew through personal contact. This became a limiting factor as a company's aspirations grew. They could only manage so many contacts at a time, and depending on referrals to meet new business partners was a slower process than they wanted.

During her internship, Yuliana helped to found an Entrepreneurs' Society at the university where she worked. Their objectives were to build a sustainable student society which created opportunities for members and also brought existing opportunities into the university. She and a core group of students from that society entered numerous entrepreneurship competitions in order to win enough money to fund future club activities. The society raised over £10,000 from competition successes in one year, raising awareness of their work and of the university among competition sponsors. Each competition introduced the club to new people, and gave them the opportunity to pitch their ideas and aspirations to new audiences. They discovered that the competitions were often sponsored by employers looking for entrepreneurial students to join them on graduation, and as they honed their pitching skills, they found that they were being offered jobs and internships in these firms.

The members' list grew to over 500 students, who were regularly provided with information and opportunities to develop their ideas, their skills and their contacts. Several projects were developed during this period, which provided opportunities for students to work with the local community, develop skills and earn money. These included a project in Ethiopia helping to train new entrepreneurs, a project bringing entrepreneurship training into local schools in London, and a project working with a teacher training college in London. Each of these projects was found through friends and colleagues.

Yuliana has had several successes, and also a few failures. One failure was a trading website which she commissioned through which she was planning to sell jewellery and other craft items made by her friends. She commissioned the website from an IT student

9

whom she knew, but it was never delivered. The student had underestimated the complexity of building the site, and overestimated their ability to produce it! In this case, the trust she had invested in had been seriously let down.

As well as the student entrepreneurs in Yuliana's network, there were also a large number of graduate entrepreneurs and mentors from organisations which support enterprise nationally. Yuliana's personal contacts list expanded to over 600 people. She developed profiles on six different web-based social networking sites, looking for opportunities for herself and her colleagues and for partners to work with.

Some key benefits that Yuliana cites when discussing her networking experiences are: a large number of contacts whom she feels comfortable asking for information and advice; the self-confidence to ask questions of people whom she doesn't know well; a better understanding of entrepreneurial processes; greater awareness of different work contexts that she might explore in the longer run. Although she has now worked in several enterprise projects, she has yet to find one which will support her financially in the long run. But with an extensive network in two countries, she feels bound to find something!

Discussion questions

1   *Identify some of the networks that Yuliana has accessed. How did she join them?*

2   *What are the objectives of the networks which Yuliana is involved with, and what benefits has she gained from them?*

3   *How do your own networks compare to Yuliana's?*

4   *How would you go about establishing or building an Entrepreneurs' Society in your context?*

5   *What is your experience of establishing trust in your enterprise context?*

9.7   NOTES, REFERENCES AND FURTHER READING

Notes and Further Information

1. See www.Facebook.com, their website which describes the network as a 'social utility'.

2. See also Chapter 5, subsection 5.4.1 'Clusters and districts' that describes how smaller enterprises attempt to retain the benefits of fast-moving, flexible enterprises whilst overcoming some of the problems that arise from a small-scale operation, by operating in 'clusters' or 'industrial districts'.

3. See also Chapter 4, section 4.4 'The role of small firms in the economy' for a fuller explanation of how economic activity is organised in national states.

4. Apimondia's web address is http://www.beekeeping.com/apimondia, according to which they 'exist to promote scientific, ecological, social and economic apicultural development in all countries and the cooperation of beekeepers' associations, scientific bodies and of individuals involved in apiculture worldwide'.

5. See http://www.benettongroup.com for an overview of the Benetton company and its history.

6. See http://www.fbn-i.org/fbn/web.nsf for details of the Family Business Network.

7. See http://www.zildjian.com for Zildjian's company background, history and products.

8. The web addresses and aims of these sites are as follows:

> LinkedIn (www.linkedIn.com) 'strengthens and extends your existing network of trusted contacts'.
>
> Facebook (www.facebook.com) 'a social utility that connects people with friends and others who work, study and live around them'.
>
> YouTube (www.youtube.com) – 'broadcast yourself. Share your videos with friends, family, and the world'.
>
> Friends Reunited (www.friendsreunited.co.uk) 'Find, reunite, contact old friends from school, work, college, university, neighbours, armed forces, expats'.
>
> eBay (ebay.co.uk) – 'the online market place'.

For a map showing the development of different social networking sites around the world, see: http://www.oxyweb.co.uk/blog/socialnetworkmapoftheworld.php.

9. ASMALLWORLD is 'a private international community of culturally influential people who are connected by three degrees' (www.asmallworld.net).

10. For outlines of pitches, see websites like http://bplans.typepad.com/uk/2007/04/writing_a_winni.html.

References

Aldrich, H.E., Rosen, B. and Woodward, W. (1987) The impact of social networks on business foundings and profit: A longitudinal study, *Frontiers in Entrepreneurship Research*, 7: 154–168.

Barclays Wealth (2009) *Family Business in Safe Hands?* Wealth Insights Volume 8., March, Barclays Wealth and the Economist Intelligence Unit (at http://www.barclayswealth.com/research-insight/insight/insight_4786.htm April 2009).

(BERR) Department for Business, Enterprise and Regulatory Reform (2007) Small and Medium Size Enterprise Statistics for the UK and the Regions, accessed at http://stats.berr.gov.uk/ed/sme/ 17 November 2008.

Curran, J. and Blackburn, R.A. (1994) *Small Firms and Local Economic Networks: The Death of the Local Economy*, London: Paul Chapman Publishing.

Curran, J., Jarvis, R., Blackburn, R.A. and Black, S. (1993) Networks and small firms: Constructs, methodological strategies and some findings, *Small Business Journal*, 11 (13).

Granovetter, M. (1985) Economic action and social structure: The problem of embeddedness, *American Journal of Sociology*, 91 (3): 481–510.

Granovetter, M. (1992) The social structure of competition, in Nohria, N. and Eccles, R. (eds) *Networks and Organisations*, Cambridge, MA: Harvard Business School Press, pp. 25–56.

Hansen, E.L. (1995) Entrepreneurial networks and new organisation growth, *Entrepreneurship Theory and Practice*, 19 (4): 7–19.

Mitchell, J.C. (1969) The concept and use of social networks, in Mitchell, J.C. (ed) *Social Networks in Urban Situations*, Manchester: Manchester University Press, pp 1–50.

O'Donnell, A., Gilmore, A., Cummins, D. and Carson, D. (2001) The network construct in entrepreneurship research: A review and critique, *Management Decision*, 39 (9): 749–760.

Singh, R.P., Hybels, R.C. and Hills, G.E. (2000) Examining the role of social network size and structural holes, *New England Journal of Entrepreneurship*, 3 (2): 47–60.

The Sunday Times (2004) Entrepreneurs start up on eBay, *TimesOnline*, 5 December 2004, written by Christopher Price, http://business.timesonline.co.uk/tol/business/article398925.ece.

Zhao, L. and Aram, J.D. (1995) Networking and growth of young technology-intensive ventures in China, *Journal of Business Venturing*, 10: 349–370.

Recommended Further Reading

Fernandez Perez, P. and Rose, M. (eds) (2009) *Innovation and Entrepreneurial Networks in Europe*, Routledge.

Gold, T., Guthrie, D. and Wank, D. (eds) (2005) *Social Connections in China: Institutions, Culture, and the Changing Nature of Guanxi*, Cambridge: Cambridge University Press.

Freeman, L.C. (2004) *The Development of Social Network Analysis: A Study in the Sociology of Science*, BookSurge.

CHAPTER 10

Entrepreneurial Decision-Making and Planning

LEARNING OBJECTIVES

After studying this chapter, the reader will be able to:

- Understand the concepts of uncertainty and risk
- Analyse how entrepreneurs manage the problems presented by risk and uncertainty
- Understand the concept of effectuation
- Evaluate the business planning process
- Develop the parameters of a business plan.

INTRODUCTION

Organisations move forward by making decisions. Indeed, one way of thinking about management activity is as a series of decisions. These decisions are answers to questions like:

- What products shall we make?
- How will we package them?
- What markets should we target?
- How can we reach that market most effectively?
- What should we charge?
- Whom do we need on the team?

The answers to these questions are the strategic choices which managers make. Strategic choices define the organisation, how it operates and what its objectives are. Some choices are long-term, some more short-term (Wilson, 2003).

The area of decision-making has been widely researched and debated (Eisenhardt, 1999). In searching for entrepreneurship, we need to ask if all strategic decisions and choices are the same for all organisations, and whether there are differences between the way entrepreneurs make decisions and the way other managers do. Entrepreneurs operate in the context of considerable uncertainty, and as individuals or small groups develop organisations from nothing to a very large scale. What difference does this make?

PREVIEW CASE

Rescue in the Little Serengeti

Dr Laurie Marker is a scientist whose passion for cheetahs led her to establish a research centre and charitable trust, the Cheetah Conservation Fund, in Namibia. The road to the research centre was a long and winding one. An American, Dr Marker worked initially at several scientific institutes in the US, including running a cheetah breeding programme there. Concerned at the level at which cheetahs were being killed by Namibian farmers who saw cheetahs as the enemy of their livestock, she initially tried to work on the problem from the United States. This proved fruitless, however, so she moved to Namibia, and travelled across the country, work-

Dr. Laurie Marker with her cheetah Chewbakka Namibia.

ing to convince people that farmers and their animals could co-exist with the increasingly rare cats. This mobile approach of moving from area to area had some success, but eventually Dr Marker decided to establish a base, a ranch which could be both a research centre and an exemplar to others. Gradually, to encourage visitors and make her programmes more sustainable, Dr Marker developed some tourism facilities too. In addition to running the farm, she travels the world to raise awareness about nature conservancy, and the funds to support efforts to preserve rare animals and environments.[1]

Dr Marker's decision was a life-changing one. What factors other than her concern for cheetahs may have influenced her decision? Thinking of a life-changing decision that you made, how did you go about it?

Read more about the enterprise to rescue cheetahs in the case study at the end of this chapter.

We also need to consider how entrepreneurs research their decisions and choices. What processes and steps are important? Finally, this chapter will consider how these choices are often communicated through the medium of the business plan.

10.1   STRATEGIC CHOICES AND DECISIONS

Managers make decisions that influence the futures of organisations, despite the constraints placed upon them by factors in the external business environment like government policies and trade cycles, and specific local factors such as the culture or resources of their organisations.

How managers make such decisions has been the subject of considerable debate over many years. Reviewing the research into this area, Eisenhardt and Zharacki (1992) noted three paradigms or main approaches, explored over the preceding 15 years, which attempted to describe the nature of strategic decision-making:

■ **Rationality or bounded rationality**: rational actors gather information, analyse it without bias, and make decisions aimed at known goals like profitability;

ENTREPRENEURSHIP IN ACTION

EasyJet and Ryanair - two entrepreneurial airline start-ups

Stelios Haji-Ioannou who founded EasyJet and Tony Ryan who co-founded Ryanair, chose to enter a crowded industry of many well-established airlines with a new proposition – low-cost flights. Having decided that low-cost flights would meet demand that was not already satisfied, they then made certain choices about what routes to fly, what airports to use and which planes to purchase. These decisions led to quite different competitive positions from those adopted by more traditional airlines such as British Airways, Swissair or Lufthansa that offered a comprehensive range of services to and from major hubs. The success of these new airlines resulted in others doing the same thing, and budget airlines have sprung up across the world as a result. Their success also severely hit the profitability of the established competitors, forcing the management of long-established airlines like British Airways, to investigate new options and to enter a price and service war to continue to compete successfully.

- **Politics and power**: managers pursue their own interests, or the interests of coalitions, in order to make decisions; rationality is subjugated to the individual needs of powerful people;

- **Garbage can**: chance – for instance, who showed up at any given meeting – has a significant impact on decisions.

They concluded that no one of these models could claim to be the single way in which managers make decisions. In practice, the evidence suggests that all of these paradigms co-exist, often in the same organisation. There are lessons to be learned about each one. Perhaps the reality of decision-making processes could be best unravelled if they are understood as the product of political processes combined with rational methods of decision-making (Butler, 2002).

An associated issue is the extent to which managers (or entrepreneurs) have the freedom to select between options and make decisions. Some researchers see managers as fundamentally constrained – by for instance their mental processes and biases, the limitations of the information to which they have access, or the political and social contexts in which they operate (Eden and Ackermann, 2002). The external environment of competing enterprises, governments and consumers are often also seen as factors to which managers are merely responding. Thus the extent to which managers can control resources and events is unclear. Some authors see managers as being very much in charge and leading events and change; others see them as responding to events that are outside of their control (Whittington, 2000).

The founders of the budget airlines did not control the industry in general, or oil prices and regulators, or their competitors or customers. In setting up their airlines, they were not simply responding to events and the actions of incumbents. They appear to have identified opportunities, made choices and invested at the outset in order to progress their ideas. So what theory will describe how entrepreneurs make choices?

10.2   UNCERTAINTY, RISK AND HEURISTICS

10.2.1 Uncertainty and Risk

The statement 'the future is uncertain' is an obvious one – of course it is! In management we cannot know what is going to happen, or when, or what the impact of it will be. We can gather information and analyse it to try to understand better what might happen and what the consequences might be, but we

10

The world financial crisis of 2008

Between 2001 and 2008, some analysts observed that the property market in the US and the UK were overheated, house prices higher than they should have been, and credit more freely available than it should be. They predicted that a major market correction (or crash) would eventually occur. However, regulators, governments, managers and many entrepreneurs continued with the same strategies and activities. They saw the future differently: they chose to believe either that the problem would gradually dissipate and a crash would not happen, or that a crash if it happened would not be too severe, or that it would not affect them personally or their businesses. In the event, the crash was enormous, impacting on financial organisations, the people who work in them, their customers, businesses and entrepreneurial ventures – in fact most people around the world. The future was certainly uncertain!

can never know for sure. This fact is both a reason why managers are constrained, and a reason which they might use to justify their actions.

Risk is a concept through which we try to quantify future uncertainty. It uses probability theory and associated statistics to determine and express *how likely* to occur possible future events are. So for instance, if we drop a stone, we can say there is a 100 per cent probability that the stone will fall to earth. This assessment is based on our knowledge of the law of gravity. Such immutable laws do not exist in entrepreneurship, however; we have to accept that there is no guarantee that what we hope will happen actually will.

Outside of the immutable laws of nature, the assessment of risk may be based on a variety of factors. In general, however, it is based on past experience. In the world of insurance, actuaries calculate life expectancies based on known information about death rates within different groups of people (for instance people living in a particular country, men or women, or people who smoke). The calculation might for instance show a probability of surviving for five years once a diagnosis of lung cancer has been made. Such a calculation would be made based on the best available information about actual deaths over time among those diagnosed with lung cancer groups. Thus probabilistic prediction of the future depends on careful observation of the past.

While risk analysis provides us with a way of quantifying the future, there are problems associated with it:

■ Not all events or activities have a historic pattern that has been observed or recorded. Many new technological developments, for instance, have no historic precedent on which to base predictions;

■ Information is only as good as the methods used to collect it. These are often flawed, which makes the assignment of probability based on the information flawed in turn;

■ The fact that something has been assigned a probability that it will happen does not mean that it will actually happen – ever;

■ Changing circumstances may have an impact on the likelihood that something will happen. For instance, a smoker may stop smoking and improve his chances of surviving longer, or an antidote to the damage which smoking causes might be found;

■ The statistics underlying probability have certain rules and constraints, which limit their applicability.

For these reasons, risk analysis, though at times useful for providing quantified estimates of future activity, needs to be treated with some caution.

10

ENTREPRENEURSHIP IN ACTION

Pharmacy2U – a risky start

Daniel Lee and Julian Harrison started Pharmacy2U in 1999. The firm enables patients to order their subscription drugs on the Internet, and delivers them direct to people's homes. Unfortunately, the odds were stacked against the entrepreneurs, for a few reasons:

■ The evidence is that many firms never develop into anything substantial. About 10 per cent of firms in the UK close every year, and millions don't grow beyond the founder as employee (source BERR).

■ The business was illegal. The rules for prescription drug sales are determined by the Royal Pharmaceutical Society of Great Britain (RPS), and ordering through the Internet was not allowed.

■ The National Health Service pays for most prescription drugs in the UK, and is therefore the main customer for the service. However, only 16 per cent of government contracts are awarded to SMEs. So the probability of a new start-up getting an order was extremely small.

These factors made the probability of success seem low, but the founders persevered. The RPS changed its rules, and in order to improve his chances of gaining the NHS as a customer Daniel enrolled on an MBA programme that was funded by the NHS. The NHS employees on the course were helpful in explaining how the giant organisation worked.

Source: Financial Times, 15/16 March 2009

The concept of risk is also used to evaluate the possible financial returns that may result from an action or investment. Not only is the probability of something happening estimated, but also a value is placed on the possible outcome. The idea is that a very risky decision (i.e. a decision which has a low probability of being successful) is only undertaken if the potential returns are very high. Correspondingly, a decision which is not very risky is unlikely to make a high return (Figure 10-1).

10

FIGURE 10-1   Risk and return trade-off

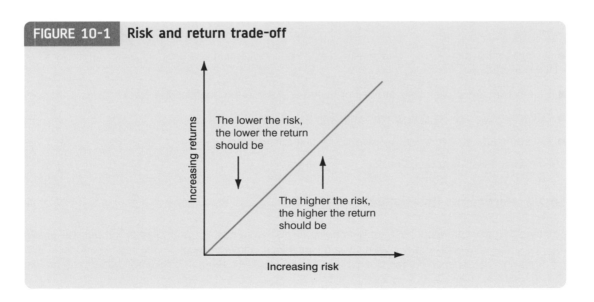

FIGURE 10-2	A continuum of pay-offs from entrepreneurial ventures	
Quality of result	**Commercial enterprise**	**Social enterprise – the Cheetah Conservation Fund**
Very good	I'm rich!	I've saved the cheetah and several other species from extinction!
	I'm making a good living	I've saved the cheetah and secured its future
	I'm barely breaking even	Things are the same as before – the cheetah is still endangered
Very poor	I've lost my investment and have new debts	There are fewer cheetahs than ever, and environmental campaigners have been banned from the area

Entrepreneurial decisions such as the decision to start a new enterprise usually require the investment of money, time and other resources that need a return to make them worthwhile. But there is a risk that the investor will get nothing in return, or even be worse off than before. There is a continuum of possible outcomes ranging from extremely positive with a very high return to extremely negative with substantial losses (Figure 10-2).

Entrepreneurial activity is inherently risky, and quantifying the outcome is fraught with difficulties. In the face of an unknown future, and the risks of investment, there are many choices to make, and much may be at stake. How do entrepreneurs make decisions in this environment? How do they make choices such as whether to launch their venture or not?

Propositions which might help answer these questions include:

■ Entrepreneurs are heroic (or foolish) people who take inordinate risks because they have an appetite for risk.

■ Risk is a relative concept – what is very risky to an individual in one situation is not very risky to someone else.

■ Entrepreneurs use heuristics or rules of thumb to cut through uncertainty and get things done.

■ Entrepreneurs use intuition to make decisions.

■ Entrepreneurs moderate risk by developing enterprises gradually.

The next sections will address each of these in turn.

10.2.2 Heroes, or Relativists?

The idea that entrepreneurs have a big appetite for risk is sometimes promoted in the popular press. After all, entrepreneurial activity involves trying new things, and entrepreneurs risk money and their time (and possible career developments) to pursue a new idea (Bird, 1989). It is common for entrepreneurial ventures to achieve only moderate or poor financial success, so entrepreneurs must appreciate that their chances of substantial financial rewards are small. They go ahead despite the evidence that they have only a small probability of being successful. By implication, they must be hungry for risk.

However convincing this argument may seem, it is not supported by empirical research (Busenitz, 1999). Studies of entrepreneurs have not shown that they have a greater appetite for risks than others, so there must be some other explanation.

Internet start-ups – a changing context

In the late 1990s, the Internet was in its infancy as a commercial medium. New start-ups that were dedicated to selling through the Internet, such as Boo.com, received large tranches of investment capital. The capital was needed to build a trading platform, delivery networks and a brand. However, with few exceptions they did not survive for long. Boo.com famously spent $135 million in the space of 18 months. While by 2009 starting an Internet trading company still carried high risks of failure, the financial investment needed had changed substantially. Improved Internet tools, lower set-up costs, more widespread usage of the Internet, and powerful search engines like Google had changed the start-up context. Internet start-ups could be undertaken incrementally or tested out using trading platforms like eBay, Etsi or Amazon. The nature of the risk has changed, so entrepreneurs starting an enterprise in 2009 can get started with substantially less investment.

Risk is a relative concept, and what is risky in one context is not so risky in another. The entrepreneurial environment is dynamic as circumstances and conditions change continuously. As the context changes, so do the risks involved in doing something. New technologies and changing customer interests and needs, for instance, lower the risks in starting a web-based retailing system. We learn how to do things in new ways.

In addition, the resources available to people make them see risks in different ways. Organisations see opportunities through the lens of the constraints of their resources, their current enterprises and their interests. The landscape of opportunity looks different from different places: for one organisation, an Internet start-up might seem extremely high risk, because they have no experience or knowledge of this type of enterprise; for another it may seem rather lower risk, because they already have activities or knowledge in that arena. Entrepreneurs see new things as less risky because they believe they know how to make them work.

10.2.3 Heuristics or Rules of Thumb

Heuristics are 'mental shortcuts that are used to reduce information overload, and yield quick decisions' (Wadeson, 2006: 92). These are also known as 'rules of thumb', short-cuts or biases. They help to cut through the innumerable uncertainties with which we are faced when making decisions. We work with biases all the time, and one suggestion is that entrepreneurs use these to help them to make decisions. In particular, two biases have been shown to be used more by entrepreneurs in new organisations than by managers in large ones: representativeness and overconfidence (Busenitz, 1999).

Representativeness bias is the practice of generalising from small samples. For instance, a tourist went to a city for the first time, and whilst there, they were robbed. They decided that the city was dangerous, and resolved never to visit it again, even though crime statistics show it to be no more dangerous than the city where they lived. They used a single experience to represent the city, rather than the more extensive and thorough information that might be available to them.

Overconfidence bias is the habit of assessing things from the outset in a more positive light than the evidence suggests. Having made the initial assessment, the bias then slows down re-assessment of the situation as new information is provided. The entrepreneur who uses this bias will tend to enter into new situations with more confidence than is warranted, and to only revise their optimistic view reluctantly when evidence becomes overwhelming.

The use of heuristics in organisational decision-making is generally considered to create dangers. Business planning processes are designed to help entrepreneurs to overcome their biases and look at things more thoroughly, by conducting research, and investigating scenarios and variations in possible outcomes. Risk assessments are intended to illustrate the possible down-sides of a particular course of action. Management teams should gather and apply evidence, consider many options, have a good debate about substantive issues, and therefore enter into new situations with solid risk assessments (Eisenhardt, 1989).

But perhaps entrepreneurs starting something new have to use rules of thumb, in order to get going. New enterprises are often set up by individuals or small teams; there is a lot of work to do, and many decisions to be made; decision-making can be nerve-wracking. Heuristics in this context may be helpful, as they cut through the uncertainty and the volume of work that needs to be done.

10.2.4 Intuition

In the theory underlying the MBTI (Myers-Briggs Type Indicator as introduced in Chapter 7 subsection 7.1.4 'Personality types and entrepreneurship'), intuition is one of two ways that we perceive the world, the other being sensing. Intuition is a style of perception which takes in the world through patterns, meanings, relationships and possibilities (Myers and McCaulley, 1985), rather than through facts. This style of perceiving typically is oriented to the future and its possibilities, rather than the present and its realities. In this theory, anyone can use their intuition, but some people use it more readily than others.

Intuition is a possible answer to the question of how entrepreneurs make decisions. Many entrepreneurial ideas come from an individual making a new connection between disparate or familiar things, or seeing a need or a possibility that no-one else has noticed. This use of intuition in the 'ideation' process is linked to creativity.

In addition, an entrepreneur faced with conflicting and uncertain information, may use their intuition, calling it a 'hunch'. The hunch may surface from their subconscious quite suddenly (Myers and McCaulley, 1985), or over a longer period of time (Mintzberg and Westley, 2001). Intuition use in this way is developed through mulling over data and issues over time. It becomes easier to make decisions about things when you are deeply familiar with them, and this familiarity takes effort to build up. Empirical evidence suggests

ENTREPRENEURSHIP IN ACTION

Partner Logistics

Bram Hage left his firm when it decided not to pursue a logistics solution that Bram had been working on for some time. The firm felt that they didn't have the expertise to support the particular application. Based on his in-depth understanding of the solution, Bram believed that he could make it work. He raised the capital to implement the solution, and started an enterprise which has grown substantially over the years. This combination of intense expertise and optimism helped Bram to decide to establish something new.

that entrepreneurial teams working closely with the facts are able to make fast decisions because they understand situations well and have considered a variety of different possibilities (Eisenhardt, 1989). Experienced entrepreneurs who understand an industry, context, or technology well, may be operating on hunches which are based on their in-depth understanding.

Integrative Case Link
Read more about Bram Hage's business Partner Logistics in Case Study 2 at the end of Part 1.

10.3 EFFECTUATION

Entrepreneurs and entrepreneurial teams start new things. This means that they are trying to invent a future for their products and services, sometimes in uncharted territory (as was the case for Apple's IPod), sometimes in the face of an existing industry structure and well-established brands (as was the case in the budget airline sector). Many entrepreneurs have no clear goals, partly because it is so difficult to predict outcomes, and partly because they start with very few resources. Did Stelios Haji-Ioannou of EasyJet and Tony Ryan of Ryanair have in their minds exactly what they were going to do, and how, from the outset?

The theory of effectuation (Sarasvathy, 2004) addresses these issues, as discussed briefly in Chapter 2. Effectuation has three key dimensions: uncertainty, ambiguity and enactment. The future is uncertain, goals are not clear and entrepreneurs are action oriented. The theory is that entrepreneurs start with an idea and a few resources, and create a new enterprise by doing things.

In trying to invent a future, there are many possibilities and options that could arise. Different individuals starting with the same idea, are starting from different places, standpoints and perspectives; they are likely end up in different places. It is difficult to set goals at the outset, because of the uncertainties associated with the unknown, so they are not pursuing a specified goal. As they progress through the entrepreneurial process, options open up or become clear. There are usually several pathways to follow, and some will be dead ends. Choices are made which are dependent on the availability of resources and stakeholders. Practical options manifest themselves only gradually as circumstances unfold, and the entrepreneur gathers resources and shapes situations.

A critical part of progress towards success is gathering stakeholders and their commitment. Stakeholders might for instance be investors, customers, partners or suppliers. Their commitment might come in various forms, but they will normally have a financial dimension. Which stakeholders come on board when, and what they bring with them, will determine what can be done next. In this view, entrepreneurs stay firmly in the present. Once they have resources, they are able to move forward. The resources that come with stakeholders enable them to design the future, as well as constraining future developments.

ENTREPRENEURSHIP IN ACTION

Claus Meyer, food entrepreneur

Claus Meyer is not a chef, yet his idea to change attitudes in Denmark towards food has made him into the country's most successful restauranteur and food entrepreneur. He says he did not (and does not) follow a plan – he wasn't sure what to do first, and started with an MBA. Then he was offered a large warehouse in Central Copenhagen, and developed his first offering there. Over 15 years he has built a group of companies associated with food, but not dependent only on restaurants. He approaches entrepreneurship as he approaches cuisine – with ingredients, but no recipe.

10

Effectuation helps to explain how many entrepreneurs develop their enterprises in the face of uncertainty and unclear objectives. They stay in the present, working with the resources they have available. The landscape of opportunity not only looks different to different people, but also changes its appearance as the entrepreneur moves through it. In addition, entrepreneurs shape the environment through the options they create and the choices they make.

Integrative Case Link
See Case Study 5 'Claus Meyer: An improvising serial entrepreneur in the quality food business' at the end of Part 2.

10.4   BUSINESS PLANS AND PLANNING

10.4.1 The Business Plan

The development of business plans represents an alternative to the serendipitous approach implied in the theories of effectuation. The business plan presents objectives, and proposes the means and the time horizons for achieving those. It presents a prediction about the future, given a certain resource investment. It makes assumptions and forecasts about many different aspects of an entrepreneurial venture including the size and nature of the market, the costs of producing and delivering certain products and services and the scope and potential responses of competitors and alternatives to the venture.

The business plan is not just designed to guide the entrepreneur; it is also designed to convince investors and bankers whether to invest or lend money. Business plans have certain benefits for this purpose:

■ They quantify the enterprise proposal, providing numbers to show possible inputs and outcomes. This provides a view of the size of the proposed enterprise, which may range from sales of £1 billion to sales of £100,000.

■ They provide information about the team and their track record, which contributes to an evaluation of their capability to deliver the objectives of the enterprise. Discussion of the plan will also enable a potential funder to investigate this further.

■ They provide some reassurance that the team or individual presenting the plan has thought about the markets and their likely responses to the new enterprise. The plan will require justification via market research and financial sensitivity analyses, which will show that the team has considered different scenarios.

■ They provide reassurance that the team has considered how to go about implementing their idea. The plan will explain in some detail how the enterprise will operate.

■ They provide a benchmark for evaluating progress in the future – if the enterprise develops significantly different from the plan, it will give a benchmark for questions about the validity of the predictions and the effectiveness of the team.

These are all areas that can be debated and questioned. In this sense, the business plan is a rhetorical device, an argument for a certain view of the future. The argument can be questioned, further clarification or information sought, and outcomes monitored and measured.

10.4.2 Elements of a Business Plan

Most business plans have approximately the same table of contents (Figure 10-3). Business plan templates and examples are readily available on the Internet.[2] The sections are designed not only to

FIGURE 10-3   Sections of a business plan

1 Executive summary

2 The team
   a Who is in the team, what knowledge and resources do they bring together?
   b What makes them the right team to develop the idea?

3 Objectives and goals
   a What are the objectives of the proposed enterprise?

4 The business model
   a What is the proposed business model?

5 The problem or need being addressed
   a What is the nature of the problem?
   b How widespread is it?
   c How serious or important is it?

6 Description of the product or service (or combination of the two)
   a How will it address the identified need?
   b How will it be developed and produced?
   c What intellectual property is inherent in it or needed to create it?

7 Description of the market
   a Who is the end user, and what are they like?
   b If they are different, who are the customers who are between the producer and the user, and what are their characteristics?
   c What are the channels through which the customer is likely to purchase and how will they be accessed?
   d How many / much of the product or service will be bought?

8 Competitor analysis
   a How are the needs identified already being addressed?
   b How is what you are proposing significantly different to what is already available?
   c What might be the response of competitors to the launch of this new product or service?

9 Financial predictions and analyses
   a What are the predicted costs of developing the product and introducing it to the market?
   b What are the predicted sales?
   c When will breakeven occur?
   d What cash flow and profits are predicted, over what time period?
   e How much investment and working capital is needed?
   f What will the return on investment be?

10 Contingencies and sensitivities
   a What happens if the market is smaller or larger than predicted?
   b What happens if costs are higher or lower?
   c What happens if competitors respond in a different way?

10

provide the reassurances that prospective investors seek, but also to create the rhetorical argument that will convince the entrepreneurs themselves of the wisdom of their choices.

Figure 10-3 lays out the essential parts of the business plan, and the questions which the sections aim to answer. These should provide a thorough review of the characteristics of the entrepreneurial team, and the approach they are taking to the opportunity they have identified. It should provide the basis for discussion, evaluation and investment appraisal. Prospective funders are aware of the dangers of the overconfidence and generalisation heuristics. They want evidence that the team has moved beyond these and taken a hard look at their own proposals, and gathered substantial evidence that they will work.

10.4.3 Researching the Plan

Researching the plan involves finding things out about markets, products, and competitors. The more you find out, the closer you come to the in-depth understanding which is so important to entrepreneurial success. There are many different sorts of help and support available to most entrepreneurs:

Networks are a good source of information and ideas. Personal and professional networks can be found on the web, in local communities and among professional organisations.[3]

Websites have become an outstanding source of information. Product and price comparison sites can illustrate the range of solutions to a particular need, as well as the range of prices at which they are available. Finding potential suppliers and getting quotes from them is relatively easy on the web, too. Blogs and consumer reviews are readily available and help to provide feedback from the market.

Government provides services to small businesses, including mentoring and advisory schemes, incubators, and grants and awards. Government-run websites (e.g. www.businesslink.gov) provide help and information as well as drawing together the strands of support that are available in the community.

10

ENTREPRENEURSHIP IN ACTION

Selling trees online

Gareth Mitchell set up his business selling trees knowing that he had plenty of competition from other online tree retailers. He analysed the market and decided he could offer something different: trees as gifts. His company adds value by personalising the gift of a tree with plaques and cards. He found it hard to raise start-up finance although he did write a business plan. His advice to anyone starting up an enterprise is: 'Conduct research and develop the idea. Write a plan because it is a tool that guides your research and development. It is like a simulation game.'

COURTESY OF TREE2MYDOOR.COM

10.4.4 Planning vs. The Plan

Integrative Case Link
Read more about Gareth's business Tree2mydoor.com in Case 6 at the end of Part 2.

While the communications value of the business plan is undeniable, it has another key purpose: to encourage the team to plan.

US President Dwight Eisenhower, the former Supreme Commander of Allied Forces in Europe during the Second World War, once commented:

> *Plans are worthless, but planning is everything.* There is a very great distinction because when you are planning for an emergency you must start with this one thing: the very definition of 'emergency' is that it is unexpected, therefore it is not going to happen the way you are planning.[4]

This observation can be applied as much to enterprise development as to emergencies. There is no certainty about what is going to happen next, but a planning process may help to identify more possibilities than would otherwise have been uncovered. Thinking through these possibilities at least gives the team a chance to address them if and when they occur.

Although incremental or effectual development of the enterprise is the reality of most entrepreneurs' existence, developing a plan may encourage them to investigate and reflect upon aspects of their proposal which are outside of their usual thinking, and improve the enterprise's likelihood of success.

ENTREPRENEURSHIP IN ACTION

Andre Campbell and Yuliana Topazly, Enfuse Youth

Andre and Yuliana started Enfuse Youth as a social project while still at university. They piloted providing enterprise education to young people in a local school through a series of workshops. The pilot was a success, and on graduation Andre decided to try to earn a living from it. The social enterprise Enfuse Youth was officially launched in November 2009.

The pair had to write a business plan in order to attract funding from various social enterprise funds. Initially, they saw producing a business plan as a bit of a chore, but they needed it to provide funders with the evidence that they were serious about their enterprise. Eventually they decided the process of writing things down had another positive side, as it pushed them to clarify their goals and their methods of achieving them.

Write the Plan

'At the beginning, I knew we needed a business plan but saw it more as a document for other people than as something to help us to make Enfuse Youth work. But if I started something new tomorrow I would write one much more willingly. The plan brings various benefits – from helping to secure finance to keeping focused on goals.

'We got help from our university mentors, and found examples on the web which described similar enterprises. Our bank also provided a template which helped with a framework. We mixed and matched bits from these different sources to produce an approach which was relevant to us. For example, because we were proposing a social enterprise, we needed to think through how to treat any surpluses we generated – which was different from most of the ones available on the web.'

Using the Plan

'We used our business plan to set out our strategic and financial goals, and our estimates of our cash needs, both in the short and longer term. We track our progress on an annual basis against what we said in the plan. We also go back to it whenever there has been a significant change in the business environment.

10

'Our business plan has also helped us to pace our expansion. Early on, we were offered quite a bit of work in different environment and different parts of the country. This seemed great but when we looked at our business plan – and particularly our cash flow forecasts – we realised that if took on everything we were offered we would be overstretched. We decided it was important to establish a core service locally before taking on work elsewhere.'

This suggestion is at the heart of normative business literature (for instance Grant, 2007). Some studies show systematic business planning has positive links to performance (for instance Dean and Sharfman, 1996), but most studies about planning have been conducted within multinationals or multi-divisional organisations. Evidence to support the idea that planning *per se* helps new enterprises to develop is somewhat scarce. However, given the strong link between business plans and funders, a business that needs investment in order to grow will be hard-pressed to progress without a plan.

For students of entrepreneurship or aspiring entrepreneurs, the discipline of developing a business plan has further value. It is a useful vehicle for learning how enterprises are put together, and for working out the inter-relationships between different aspects of an enterprise. It is also useful for learning to make a case – putting together an argument which holds water, and expressing it with conviction.

There is a distinction drawn between two different types of thinking about entrepreneurial activity and starting new enterprises. In the effectuation approach, entrepreneurs start with a set of resources but no clear goals. Through action, they gradually create and explore options and gain resources. The design of the enterprise unfolds gradually. In a goals-driven approach, entrepreneurs start with goals and then decide how they are going to get there. They set about planning how to achieve those goals, decide what resources they will need, and set out on the journey towards them. Business plans have the benefit of pushing entrepreneurs to try to envisage the future they are creating – not always an easy task. There is a contrast between effectual thinking, where the entrepreneur cannot specify goals, and goal-driven thinking, where goals are set and the means of achieving them decided at the outset of a new enterprise. Business plans operate from a goal-driven approach, and push the entrepreneur to consider specific paths towards their goal.

10.4.5 Limitations

In theory, a business plan should acknowledge areas of uncertainty, and make clear the research and decision-making heuristics which may be embedded within it. But a business plan is a rhetorical device, which may not reveal all of the salient information or intentions of its authors. In addition, substantial parts of the plan are based on predictions of the future. The key predictions[6] and assumptions are:

- That people will want the product or service, and decide either to switch from what they use already, or to add to what they use already;

- That enough people will be prepared to pay enough money to be able to build and sustain the enterprise over time;

- That the costs of production are known and predictable;

- That there will be competitor responses to the introduction of the product;

- That the relevant conditions of the business environmental in which the enterprise will operate are known and understood.

Market research and analysis are typically used to confirm or disconfirm these assumptions and predictions. However, market research which relates to the future is often flawed, specifically because the future cannot be fully known.

ENTREPRENEURSHIP IN ACTION

Flawed predictions and market research

The British inventor and entrepreneur Sir James Dyson produced a highly different and fully patented design for a new type of vacuum cleaner, whose key new characteristic was that it did not need a bag in which to collect dust. He tried to license his design to existing players in the vacuum industry, and they conducted market research to investigate its potential. Their customers said they would not switch to a bagless vacuum cleaner, so they turned Dyson down. Dyson eventually set up his own company to produce and sell machines himself. The Dyson vacuum cleaners were a hit, and changed the industry. Other manufacturers eventually changed their designs to mimic his innovation, once their market share was being eroded.

© ADRIAN SHERRATT/ALAMY

Sir James Dyson

Despite the flaws and limitations of business plans, they are useful vehicles for communicating an idea. They are also a requirement for most lenders or investors, who themselves have clear goals (return on investment), and want to know that the entrepreneur has considered their aims and how to achieve them. The practice of planning is also potentially beneficial for entrepreneurs, who may be aided in seeing aspects of their proposal which they had not considered before.

10

10.5 SUMMARY AND ACTIVITIES

All organisations **face choices** and **make decisions**. The organisation and its future success depends on those decisions. Starting something new requires a great many decisions to be made encompassing customers, suppliers, facilities, finances and the team.

The future is by definition **uncertain**; past experience does not necessarily provide a good guide to the future. **Prediction** is difficult; this means that new enterprises may have little to go on when they are planning for the future.

Risk analysis is a technique used to **quantify** that uncertainty. Based on **statistics**, risk analysis is itself problematic. It assumes that good **historic information** is available, and that it will continue to be relevant in the future.

Entrepreneurs use **heuristics** or **rules of thumb** to help them to make decisions; this helps them to deal with the uncertainty surrounding the many decisions that have to be made. In particular they tend to be **overconfident** about their chances of success, and to use small samples of experience to **represent** the world at large.

Effectuation is a theory which tries to explain how entrepreneurs develop enterprises in the face of high levels of uncertainty and without clear goals. Effectual reasoning starts with what resources are available, and gradually shapes a new enterprise. **Options gradually reveal themselves**, and choices are made which depend on what is already known and available.

Entrepreneurial managers can **moderate** the dangers of decision-making in various ways, including by using **intensive research** and debate; this does not necessarily slow down decision-making.

The **business plan** is a device used by prospective investors to help them in their decision-making about new enterprises. Conversely, researching and producing a business plan helps entrepreneurs to think through aspects of their activities which they might otherwise ignore. The **planning process** is hence very valuable.

REVIEW QUESTIONS

1 What are some of the problems associated with making decisions in organisations?

2 What is risk?

3 How do people cope with uncertainty and risk?

4 What are heuristics?

5 What is meant by effectuation?

6 What are the benefits of business planning?

7 Identify some of the characteristics generally attributed to good decision-making processes.

8 What approaches can be used to convince stakeholders to support a new venture?

9 What are the main elements of a business plan?

10 Why do financiers want to see business plans?

SEMINAR TASK

Pick an entrepreneurial venture which you are familiar with, or which you would like to research. Investigate how it got started. Try to answer the following questions:

1 Was there a plan in place from the outset, or was a plan produced at some later stage?

2 Who were the key stakeholders in the venture, and how did their involvement change the way the venture developed?

3 What biases do you think the start-up team used in order to get going?

4 What resources did the founder(s) have at the outset, and when and how were these increased?

Compare your research to someone else's in your seminar. What different approaches to decision-making can you find?

Preview case continued

Rescue in the Little Serengeti

By Teresa Levonian Cole

Dr Laurie Marker, 54, is a conservation scientist and an authority on cheetahs. She was born in Michigan, US, and has lived in California, Oregon, Washington and Oxford, UK. She moved to Namibia 18 years ago and set up the Future Farmers of Africa programme, aimed at educating schoolchildren and adult farmers in livestock and wildlife management. She is co-founder and executive director of the Cheetah Conservation Fund (CCF) and the chairman of the Conservancy Association of Namibia.

It was cheetahs that first took me to Namibia. The year was 1977 and I had been working at The Wildlife Safari in Oregon for three years, running a cheetah breeding programme there. I decided to take Khayam, a cheetah that I had hand-reared in the US, to Namibia to see how she would survive in the wild. I had to teach her to hunt. After three months we went back to the US but I returned many times to Namibia in the coming years to continue my research.

I made the move to Namibia in 1990. With 800–900 cheetahs being shot by farmers there every year, and having tried talking to anybody that would listen, it dawned on me that if I wanted to save the species I would have to do something myself. And the timing was right: Namibia had just gained her independence. On principle, I could not have contemplated living there before because I believe in freedom, especially in education. By 1990, I was working at the Smithsonian in Washington, where I met several Namibians in exile, who were later to become leaders of their country. Links with the [country's] new government proved very helpful, as they are strong supporters of our conservation projects.

So I sold up and, with two dogs, a (now ex-) husband, $15,000 and 14 trunks of research equipment, I arrived in Windhoek. At first we stayed with friends, then drove all round the northern part of Namibia – cheetah territory, an area about the size of the UK. I visited farmers door-to-door, getting to know them, studying demographics, learning about farmers' problems, suggesting alternative solutions that did not involve shooting cheetahs. We stayed in abandoned farmhouses wherever we could find them, then moved on again when our work in that area was done.

Conditions were very basic. Often there was no electricity and little water. The telephone system was eccentric. Phone calls, for example, had to be made through the operator and the entire village could listen in. But we were working so hard that there was no time to worry about such things. We just made do. I had no illusions that things would be easy. My previous visits had given me an idea as to the challenges that lay ahead.

But the real challenges I faced were less practical than cultural ones. I was a woman, white, and American, which made me, initially, an object of suspicion among the Afrikaaner farmers. But they were also fascinated by this crazy woman who brought cheetahs – like coals to Newcastle. They considered them to be vermin that killed their livestock. It didn't help that I was trying to persuade them to change their way of doing things and to find ways of co-existing with wildlife rather than killing it. I rocked the boat.

Children would look at me with sad eyes and say: 'Nobody likes you.' But I listened and eventually was able to blend into the community through my practical knowledge and ability to solve problems. I wasn't just a sentimental bunny-hugger – I could speak the farmers' language and persuade them scientifically. Gradually they came to trust me. We now work together but the first ten years were really uphill.

In 1994 I bought the 12,000-acre ranch where I now live with my partner, Bruce Brewer, a population geneticist. Farmers would say: 'You're not a farmer, you don't understand', so

10

▶

I decided to prove that I did. Our nearest town, Otjiwarongo, is a 45-minute drive away; a bumpy 30 miles along a dirt track frequented by kudu and warthogs. There was an old farmhouse on the property which was . . . funky. It didn't rain often but when it did water would rise to waist height. We had to drill holes in the walls to allow the water to drain and bail out with buckets. Because of the climate, floors are of cement and roofs are of tin. We had very little furniture – just beds and a few trunks. You can't have wood anywhere, because the termites are voracious.

Water was the biggest priority. I had to learn about bore holes. We had pumps but you couldn't pump for more than an hour a day or you dried up the well and burnt out the pump. Generators were vital and they kept breaking down. Diesel for them had to be brought all the way from Otjiwarongo.

My parents, who are now in their 80s, come and visit us. My father installed the computers and helped with building work. My mother, who claims to be 64, is extraordinary, a real lady. She used to send me food parcels and was the organisational force on the ground. She has managed to instil ladylike tendencies in me, so I always try to dress properly even in the bush.

We rebuilt the farm in 1998, with help from a benefactor who said: 'Your research is wonderful but your facility looks horrible.' We expanded the clinic and developed an educational museum and visitor centre, as well as dorms for volunteers who come to help us. Before, we conducted world-class research in an area the size of a bathroom. We have just won an award for our project to convert invasive thorn bush into a clean-burning, alternative fuel and are now looking at ways to make electricity from this biomass. To help finance our ventures we recently built a very small luxury lodge for guests.

We have achieved a model farm, where we practise what we preach. There is so much wildlife on our land that it's known as the Little Serengeti. We have 50 rescued cheetahs on the reserve, as well as livestock and game. We breed Kangals, a 600-year-old breed of Anatolian shepherd dog that we use to guard our livestock and which we donate to farmers to persuade them to do the same. It's all about ecological balance – man living in harmony with nature, livestock with wildlife. And it works. There's a great photo of two cheetah cubs curled on our bed, surrounded by our Kangal and his friend the goat.

There isn't really any social life. But I am quite self-contained and focused on my work. Every evening we have dinner with our team. There can be 35 of us tucking into barbecued oryx, from our land. It's like a big convivial family. If there is anything I miss about the States I suppose it is that in a bigger pool of people – you are more likely to find those who are like-minded, visionary.

My work requires me to travel around the world for about four months a year: fundraising, lecturing, meeting with scientists. When I'm abroad I catch up on the theatre, go to the dentist and stock up with maple syrup. But I would be much happier just staying here and having people come to us. Seeing is worth a million words.

Discussion questions

1 *Identify the decision-making processes which Dr Marker has gone through over the years. What were the key decision points?*

2 *What resources did Dr Marker acquire along the way, and how did these help to develop the organisation?*

3 *What were the risks that were faced by Dr Marker, and how did she approach these?*

4 *When she set out on her entrepreneurial journey, what do you think might have been in her business plan?*

© The Financial Times, 14/15 January 2009

10.6   NOTES, REFERENCES AND FURTHER READING

Notes and Further Information

1. The information for this vignette was drawn from an article in the *Financial Times*, 14 February 2009 (available at: http://www.ft.com/cms/s/0/088ec3ac-fa38-11dd-9daa-000077b07658.html?nclick_check=1>) and from the website of the Cheetah Conservation Fund (www.cheetah.org).

2. For instance, www.businesslink.gov.uk.

3. See Chapter 9 for an extensive discussion of networks.

4. Speech to the National Defense Executive Reserve Conference in Washington, DC 14 November 1957.

5. This case is copied from the website www.businesslink.gov.uk, accessed on 21 April 2009.

6. Chapter 15 covers the topic of financial predictions and forecasts in subsection 15.5.4 'Financial forecasts'.

References

Bird, B. (1989) *Entrepreneurial Behaviour*, Glenview, IL: Scott, Foresman & Co.

Busenitz, L.W. (1999) Entrepreneurial risk and strategic decision making: It's a matter of perspective, *Journal of Applied Behavioral Science*, 35: 325.

Butler, R. (2002) Decision making, in Sorge, A (ed) *Organisation,* London: Thomson Learning, 224–251.

Dean, J. and Sharfman, M. (1996) Does decision process matter? A study of strategic decision-making effectiveness, *Academy of Management Journal*, 39 (2): 368–396.

Eden, C. and Ackermann, F. (2002) A mapping framework for strategy making, in Huff, AS. and Jenkins, M. *Mapping Strategic Knowledge*, London: Sage, 173–195.

Eisenhardt, K.M. (1989) Making fast strategic decisions in high velocity environments, *Academy of Management Journal*, 32 (3): 543–576.

Eisenhardt, K.M. (1999) Strategy as strategic decision making, *Sloan Management Review*, Spring, 40 (3).

Eisenhardt, K. and Zharacki, M. (1992) Strategic decision making, *Strategic Management Journal*, 13: 17–37.

Grant, R. (2007) *Contemporary Strategy Analysis: Concepts, Techniques, Applications*, 6th Edition, Oxford: Blackwell.

Mintzberg, H. and Westley, F. (2001) Decision making: It's not what you think, *Sloan Management Review*, Spring: 89–93.

Myers, I.B. and McCaulley, M.H. (1985) *Manual: A Guide to the Development and Use of the Myers-Briggs Type Indicator*, Palo Alto, CA: Consulting Psychologists Press.

Sarasvathy, S. (2004) Making it happen: Beyond theories of the firm to theories of firm design, *Entrepreneurship: Theory & Practice*, Winter, 28 (6): 519–531.

Wadeson, N.S. (2006) Cognitive aspects of entrepreneurship: Decision-making and attitudes to risk, in Casson, M. *et al.* (eds) *The Oxford Handbook of Entrepreneurship*, Oxford: Oxford University Press. pp. 91–114.

Whittington, R. (2000) *What is Strategy – And Does it Matter?*, 2nd edn, International Thomson.

Wilson, D. (2003) Strategy as decision making, in Cummings, S. and Wilson, D. (eds) *Images of Strategy,* Oxford: Blackwell, pp. 383–410.

10

Recommended Further Reading

Eden, C. (1992) Strategy development as a social process', *Journal of Management Studies*, 29 (6): 799–8l2.

Elbana, S. (2006) Strategic decision making – Process perspectives, *International Journal of Management Reviews*, 8 (1): 1–20.

Hendry, J. (2000) Strategic decision making, discourse, and strategy as social practice, *Journal of Management Studies*, 37 (7): 955–977.

Jarzabkowski, P. and Wilson, D.C. (2006) Actionable strategy knowledge: A practice perspective, *European Management Journal*, 24 (5): 348–367.

Papadakis, V.M. and Barwise, P. (eds) (1997) *Strategic Decisions,* London: Kluwer, pp. 267–287.

Part 2 Integrative Case Studies

INTEGRATIVE Case Study 4

Female Entrepreneurship

Gloria Serobe: Empowering Women in South African Society

By Dr Retha Scheepers, *Stellenbosch University*

BACKGROUND AND HISTORY OF ACHIEVEMENTS OF GLORIA SEROBE

Gloria Serobe is regarded as a formidable force in frontier capitalism and financial services in South Africa. If a list of women, who have played a significant role in empowering and inspiring women in South Africa, is drawn up, Gloria's name would be among the top five. Co-founder of a successful women investment company – Women Investment Portfolio Holdings Ltd (WIPHOLD) – Gloria commands a reputation that dwarfs that of many other businesswomen, despite her small stature of a little over five foot.

Gloria and her business partner, Louisa Mojela, have a dream of empowering women in a world still very much dominated by men. They have enjoyed considerable success in making this dream come true and have had a significant influence on involving and empowering ordinary South African women into the economic mainstream, through their company, WIPHOLD. Their success has not gone unnoticed. Both Louisa and Gloria were finalists in the Ernst Young World Entrepreneur awards in 2006, Gloria was also crowned the Businesswomen's Association Businesswoman of the Year in 2006, she was named among the twenty most influential women in South Africa in 2004, by a leading business journal the *Financial Mail* and she serves on numerous boards, including that of the Johannesburg Securities Exchange, the University of Cape Town Graduate School of Business, Alliance Capital Southern African Fund, Old Mutual, Nedcor and others. Her need for achievement and work ethic has propelled her forward, since a very young age.

WORK ETHIC AND NEED FOR ACHIEVEMENT

From her childhood Gloria has had experience of what it is to rise above your circumstances. Gloria was one of seven daughters and three sons born in Cape Town to a Xhosa family with deep roots in Ndabeni, a township near the docks which was dismantled by the apartheid government. 'We were scattered all over the place – to Langa and Guguletu – when the land was taken away from us and turned into an industrial area', she says.

Despite the harshness of the apartheid era and her surroundings in Gugulethu, Gloria grew up in a relatively sheltered, close-knit community environment. Her parents were her first role models as entrepreneurs. Both her mother and father owned shops in the community and she learnt values of perseverance and hard work from them, needed to be successful in life. She credits her grandfather, Rev John Zamile Ndaliso, as the person who had the greatest formative influence in her life. He was a highly respected member of the Gugulethu community and gave her an important and priceless gift: self-belief. 'He always made me feel important', she says. 'My school report was even read out in church, so there was always pressure on me to perform. He also had great leadership qualities and was such an inspiration to me', she remembers fondly.

Showing promise from an early age, Gloria was one of the first five girls to attend St John's boys' school in Umtata, Transkei. She was sent there because schools for black children were better in the Eastern Cape. Much to her grandfather's delight, she performed well in school and went on to earn her BComm degree from the University of Transkei. Thereafter she won the highly sought after Fullbright Scholarship that enabled her to attain her MBA degree at Rutgers University in New Jersey.

CAREER AND WORK EXPERIENCE

After completing her MBA, she worked for Exxon as a trainee accountant in the United States of America, before returning to South Africa. This first job enabled her to obtain accounting positions at Premier Group's Epic Oils and Munich Reinsurance, but accounting held limited appeal for her. When the opportunity arose to move into investment and merchant banking at Standard Corporate & Merchant Bank (SCMB), she took a salary cut and leapt at the opportunity. Although she comments: 'I was really already too old, at 32, for a career change, and my bosses were all younger than me. But I wanted to be in an environment that wasn't industry-specific and that threw everything at you, from corporate and project finance to mergers and acquisitions. And Jacko Maree was a fantastic Managing Director and always had time for even the most junior of staff.'

At SCMB she learnt about corporate and project finance, and mergers and acquisitions. The move was also significant, because here she met one of her future business partners – Louisa Mojela. The two of them quickly became a formidable team and kept contact, even after

she secured the opportunity to work as Transnet's Executive Financial Director, a large South African parastatal. Gloria is described as determined, feisty, assertive and has a reputation in the corporate world of being competent and tough. Johannesburg Securities Exchange (JSE) CEO Russell Loubser, who has watched her at close hand on the JSE board, says Serobe is 'an entrepreneur. And that's why she's a valuable and effective board member. She's also fun, enjoys a good joke, a prank or two, and always makes her presence felt.'

Of herself she says: 'I'm not bright, I'm just hardworking and ambitious' (Stafford, 2005).

Her experiences in the corporate world, linked to her background and the opportunities in the South African economy in the 1990s, motivated Gloria and three-like minded women to address the inequalities women faced in the South African economy.

FOUNDING OF WIPHOLD

Wendy Luhabe, Louisa Mojela, Nomhle Canca and Gloria Serobe founded Wiphold Capital as an organisation dedicated to women's empowerment fifteen years ago. 'We reasoned that women, while the largest contributors to the economy, both as providers of labour and as consumers, have been the most disadvantaged. We believed that financial independence represented a powerful tool for helping women redirect their lives. So, we set up an organisation which, among other things, could galvanise women into investment opportunities that would deliver value for them', says Gloria.

The 'Wip' four put their heads together and decided to launch an investment company, in line with their experience, which could take advantage of the new economic opportunities in South Africa. Together they raised R500,000 in seed capital (in investment terms a meagre amount) and set about the apparently overwhelming task of launching such a company. However, from its inception, the 'Wip' founders thought about more than just opportunity for themselves. They wanted to be part of an investment company that brought wealth, not only to the four founders, but also to the vast number of SA women – black and white – who were then still excluded from the mainstream economy. 'We had a dream of creating a critical mass of women in business, as opposed to each one doing their own thing. We knew if we succeeded we would be rich, but we thought it would be so much nicer if we were surrounded by other rich women', says Gloria.

For this reason they decided to do an initial public offer / private placement to women only. After two years of doing their homework and preparation, which included touring the country to assemble and fire up potential women investors and developing a portfolio of business into which they could buy, their dream became a reality. In 1997 the fund was launched with an Initial Public Offer to women throughout SA of R25 million. The response, says Gloria, was incredible. Eighteen thousand women took up the invitation to become part of the dream and bought shares. Some of them were individuals, other were groups of women drawn from all nine provinces of the country, urban and rural. The arrival of WIPHOLD on the financial scene was greeted with great enthusiasm. WIPHOLD was the first Black Economic Empowerment (BEE) company to establish a permanent broad-based shareholding – long before the governmental BEE rules shifted in that direction.

At this point Gloria was trying to juggle a number of balls in the air. While working at Transnet, as their Chief Financial Director, she continued to be involved in WIPHOLD, helping it with its rights offer to women (R76 million) in 1998 and private placements worth R424 million in 1999, as well as assisting with listing the company on the JSE that same year.

PHILOSOPHY AND BATTLE TO CREATE SPACE FOR BLACK WOMEN IN HALLS OF CAPITALISM

The founders' dream of advancing and empowering women economically coincided with the emphasis the South African government placed in their policies to facilitate the inclusion of women in economic activity. Apart from the original 18,000 individual investors, other beneficiaries include women- and children-focused organisations such as the National Baptist Church, People Opposing Women Abuse and the Young Women's Christian Association. Strategic NGOs include the SA Democratic Teachers' Union (women's chapter) and the Democratic Nursing Organisation of SA.

One of the original investors is former Eastern Cape legislature member Sally Moiloa-Nqodi, who says: 'It has been wonderful being part of WIPHOLD and seeing women becoming part of the mainstream economy. And though it's had its ups and downs – and I haven't exactly made a fortune yet – I think WIPHOLD is entering an even more exciting, second phase.'

Nomvulo De Jesus, records manager at the Lesedi (Heidelberg) municipality, was also an early investor. 'It's been great being part of an initiative that puts women into the economy', she says. 'And I've made a nice sum of money out of my dividends.'

However, it has not been plain sailing for WIPHOLD, they've experienced an almost-failure and had to turn the company around.

TOUGH TIMES, ALMOST-FAILURE AND TURNAROUND

Many of the women's empowerment companies that were founded after 1994 no longer exist. WIPHOLD is one of the biggest survivors, even though it too came close to collapse. After its listing WIPHOLD experienced problems. The reasons for these problems were, among others, the market's weariness of empowerment investment trusts, the dilution of WIPHOLD's BEE profile by institutional shareholders, and a shake-out in the financial services sector. By 2000 WIPHOLD had fallen into what Gloria describes as a 'state of paralysis'. By 2001 it became clear that WIPHOLD needed more than her peripheral involvement.

She decided to join WIPHOLD permanently in August 2001 after her five-year contract at Transnet came to an end, because she wasn't prepared to let the company fail. 'If WIPHOLD had failed, it would have been a blow not only for me and my co-founders, but also for women in the wider sense.' She adds 'the burden of being a pioneer is that you can't afford to fail', she says. 'You find that you have attracted and become an inspiration and a role model. You become anxious to succeed, not only for your own sake, but also for your followers.'

As part of the turnaround strategy, one of the first things they did was to establish Wipcapital as a wholly owned financial services subsidiary of WIPHOLD, which allowed them to adopt a more operational focus. Gloria became its CEO. 'From 2001 to 2003, we really paid our school fees', she says. 'We went underground, avoided the press, and restructured the company. We delisted as a R1.5 billion company and, with backing from Old Mutual, bought out all our shareholders.' She adds that 'it was no secret that we were looking for a white knight and [Old Mutual SA MD] Roddy Sparks always believed in us and encouraged us'. Even the original 18,000 women investors were bought out, but they were brought back in again through the Wiphold Investment Trust. 'We felt that with listing, we could no longer control who bought shares, and our ideology of being a women-owned company was being eroded', she says. 'Now just over 60 per cent of the company is again owned by women, which is the way we like it.'

After they became more operationally involved and restructured, they went from strength to strength. In 2005 WIPHOLD announced that it had secured stakes in the local and London-listed insurance giant Old Mutual – as well as in subsidiaries Nedbank and Mutual & Federal. This deal was worth R7.2 billion, and attracted a lot of media attention, since it was one of the biggest BEE deals in SA at the time, and also the first substantial transaction to be driven by women. Later that same year, WIPHOLD also concluded a significant BEE deal worth R396 million with Distell and acquired a 1.12 per cent stake in Telkom. More recently WIPHOLD and Sasol Mining announced a transaction (valued at R1.9 billion) that has seen thousands of rural and per-urban women participating in a BEE transaction for the first time. WIPHOLD, through a new entity called WIPCoal Investments, became the BEE partner to Sasol Mining.

Today, almost fifteen years later, WIPHOLD represents over 300,000 women investors, and over 50 per cent of their shareholders are black. Although it has been bigger, it employs a stable workforce of 60 employees.

Gloria views the fact that they are an operational company and not just a portfolio-holding company as one of their secrets of success. 'For the transactions we conclude, we use our own authoritative investment time in-house, we don't have outside advisors', she says. Their ability to function independently, with technical expertise and operational capabilities, adds to their standing in the market, since BEE deals are often viewed with scepticism. Their obsession with not falling into a 'culture of entitlement', but to earn their credentials in the market shows signs of success. The remarkable turnaround of WIPHOLD, led by Gloria and co-founder Louisa Mojela (CEO of WIPHOLD), brought the company from the verge of collapse back to become one of the top-performing investment companies in South Africa.

LESSONS TO BE LEARNED

When asked to reflect, Gloria argues that the pressure to succeed is intense for women in leadership roles. 'For so long it has been said that women can't pull off big deals in business. I've always wanted to prove they can. And I have.' She fiercely believes in the credentials and ideals of WIPHOLD, as a vehicle to empower and enrich women.

However, Gloria is not just all work, and no play. She believes that hard work should be balanced with a good share of fun. For example their strategy sessions are 'about 30 per cent intense working and 70 per cent fun', she says, adding to make sure of the fun, they tend to go away somewhere for these annual sessions. In 2008, they went to in Kenya, in time to watch the annual game migrations, and in 2007 they went to Mauritius.

Besides her business interests, Gloria is also a wife and mother. She is married to Guar Serobe, and they have raised two boys. Despite her avid advocacy of women's rights, she believes in family and home values with a passion. 'I think marriage and home life play a vital role. Given the loneliness you experience in the boardroom, it is nice to know there is something at home for you', she says. She believes that women need good support networks and should turn their mother-in-laws into their allies. Her mother-in-law understands the difficulties of being a working woman and is committed to the happiness of her son and grandsons. The other key to keeping both spheres of life in harmony, says Gloria, is making sure that you are honest and that there are no surprises for anyone.

 ### CURRENT SITUATION AND FUTURE CHALLENGES

Gloria and Louisa are satisfied with where they are currently, but realise that WIPHOLD is in for tough economic times. They have prepared for the economic storm ahead in two major ways:

■ They have diversified business interests, the purpose being that if one sector does not do well, they still have investments in other sectors.

■ They also have confidence in their people. 'A good team, hard work and excellence have always been non-negotiables in this company. There is no substitute for superb performance and we balance our investments with enough conservatism', she says.

With these fundamentals in place, they are confident that WIPHOLD will continue to empower disadvantaged women, ensuring

greater economic equity in South Africa. These shareholders should see their investments growing exponentially over time and although Gloria and Louisa remark: 'We will never be billionaires because there are so many of us, but we will never be miserable either.'

Gloria has her own ubuntu opinions about empowering young women. She says: 'In Africa we believe that those who come after us must be better than us. If they are not, we have not done our job well. It is our responsibility to help them. They must transcend us. We must enable them to do so, because that is the only way to preserve the growth of our societies and ensure that these young women are better prepared for the challenges of the twenty-first century and beyond.'

QUESTIONS

1 Does Gloria display the characteristics of a 'typical entrepreneur'?

2 How are women entrepreneurs different from male entrepreneurs? Are these differences evident in the case?

3 Remark on the social and economic mission of WIPHOLD; is this economically sustainable over the long-term?

4 Would you view the social mission, reflected in this case, typical of African entrepreneurs?

5 Comment on the turnaround strategy followed in this case.

Serial Entrepreneurship

Claus Meyer: An Improvising Serial Entrepreneur in the Quality Food Business

By Prof. Torben Bager and Suna Løwe Nielsen *of the International Danish Entrepreneurship Academy*

'I never wanted to have a big company. I wanted big victories but I never wanted many employees or a huge turnover or having 7–8 companies … This is something that just happened. I never worked with plans, and until a few years ago I never worked with budgets, and the idea of having a Board is only four years ago. We never took loans in the bank. I have only tried that once and it was not a success (…).'

This is how Claus Meyer introduces his improvising and passion-driven approach to entrepreneurship at a speech at Copenhagen Business School. Since he was a student at that school about 15 years ago, he has built a quality food empire in Denmark, starting a series of small companies in quality food niches – and influencing the food and nutrition policy agenda in Denmark and other countries. In 2008, the Meyer Group consisted of eight food companies in Denmark which altogether employ more than 300 people (www. clausmeyer.dk).

It all begins in his childhood in a provincial town in Denmark. It is at a time in history when many women have left the kitchen in favour of the labour market.

Danish households at this time are dominated by frozen vegetables, minced meat, margarine and other types of food which are supposed to make everyday life easier and keep the expenses down – often at the expense of the quality of the food and the food experience. As a young man, Claus has no specific interest in food until one day he finds himself working as a servant for a famous chef in the Southern part of France. After that experience with high-quality food, his mission in life becomes evident for him. He will change and improve the Danish/ Nordic food culture. The roots, the soul, the quality and the sincerity should be brought back to Nordic food, but how? Claus has no plans about how he can possibly realise his mission.

Other people would perhaps have taken a chef training course, but not Claus. He begins to study at the Copenhagen Business School. Denmark's probably most famous chef today never gets any chef training. Instead Claus initiates his first entrepreneurial project from his study apartment while he is still studying at the Copenhagen Business School: 'Food out of the house'. Later on, the vice-chancellor of the Copenhagen Business School offers him the opportunity to take over the canteen. That is the beginning of a long and entrepreneurial journey. Many new

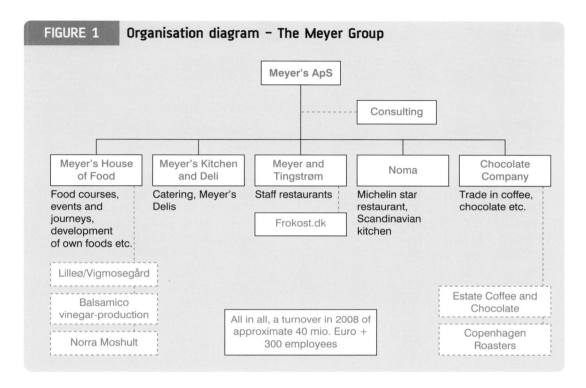

FIGURE 1 — Organisation diagram – The Meyer Group

businesses get started (The Chocolate Company, Meyer and Tingstrøm staff restaurants, luxurious company trips/teambuilding, fruit growing, restaurant Noma, Meyer's Deli, etc.). Figure 1 offers an overview of the businesses belonging to the Meyer Group in 2008.

CLAUS MEYER'S BEST IDEA

'The best idea of my life came to me approximately four years ago. The idea synchronised the last fifteen years of my life. I did not intend to enter the restaurant business, but I got a tempting offer … a lovely place … an old store-house in Central Copenhagen. My idea was to build a Nordic gourmet restaurant.'

His colleagues in the food sector laugh. Nordic food is not fine – not worthy of a gourmet restaurant. The colleagues scoff at the restaurant and call it 'The whale restaurant'. But Claus establishes together with his partner Rene Redzepi who has experiences with the gourmet business, the restaurant Noma – an abbreviation of 'Nordisk Mad' (in English: Nordic Food). They build the restaurant around the unique history, taste and originality of Nordic food production, vegetation and wildlife. Nobody has considered that before. We all know the Thai, the French and the Indian kitchen. But what is a Nordic kitchen? They wanted to explore that question – and do something about it.

None of the two entrepreneurs dream about creating an enormous economic success. Their dreams are about something bigger than that. Like Claus's mission in life, their overall success criterion is to develop and define the Nordic kitchen and to create a shared mission among Nordic farmers, small and big food companies, citizens, politicians, etc. towards promoting Nordic food of a high quality.

Everything turns out to be an enormous success. In 2008, two Michelin stars decorate Noma which is also ranked the fifteenth best restaurant in the world – the finest position a Nordic restaurant has ever achieved.

THE START-UP PROCESS

The establishment of Noma involves a lot of different people and in particular Claus's partner Rene Redzepi. Claus's role is primarily to back up Rene by using his experience as a serial entrepreneur:

> 'I facilitated him and helped with funding, building up a homepage, recruited staff members, created the first menus, chose the graphic designer, took care of contractual relations to the owners of the premises but the most important, I involved the entire Nordic food intelligence ... ministers from Norway and Denmark, etc. Even people from the Nordic food industry ... in order to discuss how everybody could share our vision.'

In order to get the Nordic Food concept off the ground – and create a supportive environment for Noma – Claus decides to invite ministers, managers from the Nordic food industry, journalists and famous chefs to a symposium in order to explain the idea about the Nordic kitchen. The participating chefs are asked to define a manifesto for the new Nordic kitchen, formulated as ten commandments.

The manifesto becomes the starting signal for a completely new movement – a movement with many different actors (chefs, consumers, politicians and business people from the five Nordic countries). The movement is gathered in order to promote Nordic food culture and the words of the manifesto. The Nordic ministers of food also become part of the movement since they, on the basis of the manifesto, formulate a 'New Nordic Food Programme'. This programme provides funding to entrepreneurs who aim to develop, produce or market products in accordance with the manifesto.

Consequently, a restaurant and its business idea has in reality turned into a movement. Through the movement, Claus succeeds with his mission of creating a platform for a quality oriented Nordic food culture that is no longer about frozen vegetables, minced meat and margarine: a food culture which promotes the unique quality, tastes and roots of Nordic food.

TO DANCE AROUND

During the lecture at Copenhagen Business School, Claus was asked whether he sees a connection between how he cooks and creates his businesses – and he gave an interesting answer:

> 'How will I compare cooking with entrepreneurship? There are many similarities. The way I love to cook is without a recipe and without any fixed plan. I love to come to some place, in Hungary or whereever, and see which vegetables do we have, what is grown in the garden, what meat is available and what is in the fridge? Then I dance a little, wondering what I can do and what I know. A kind of interfering with the surroundings and that is also the way in which I do business. I listen to people, I talk to my employees. If I have a dish washer who is good at flowers, then I should be dead if I did not ask him to do the flowers. If I meet someone in my life who wants to build a dairy, and if we did it together, it could be greater, then I would be attracted. So the way in which I build businesses is similar to the way in which I cook. I dance around, I see what happens and try to feel the energy.'

A PROFESSIONAL BOARD OF DIRECTORS

Over the years Claus creates his businesses without an overall plan for how they should look in the future. He acts and sees what happens. But as the companies start growing and the Meyer Group gets more complex, Claus experiences a growing need to professionalise and systematise the way he is running his businesses. He sets up a professional Board of Directors which, however, mostly is supposed to function as inspiration. He himself likes to have control:

> 'The Board supports me in developing a well organised company with the right competences at the right positions in accordance with what we want to do.

Who should be the leader of whom? (…)
I do not have much experience in building
up big companies. I never aimed for a big
organisation but now I have one (…). I
just hope that I am a good clergyman and
visionary person and that all the employees wish to follow my footprint. But I am
not the classical manager.'

QUESTIONS

1 Looking at this case, discuss under what
conditions and for what purposes a business
plan is an appropriate tool.

2 What is the particular approach and methodology this entrepreneur uses when he sets up
new firms?

3 What distinguishes an entrepreneur from a
manager?

*Video clips of Claus Meyer lectures and additional
interviews are available at www.idea-tool
box.dk*

INTEGRATIVE Case Study 6

Graduate Entrepreneurship and Sustainable Entrepreneurship

Tree2mydoor.com

By Dr Fernando Lourenço, *Manchester Metropolitan University*

INTRODUCTION: THE CONCEPT

Tree2mydoor is an award-winning sustainable gift company, based in Manchester, UK. This for-profit, sustainable gift company offers meaningful gifts to consumers whilst contributing to environmental protection and support. Twenty-three-year-old Gareth Mitchell initially created Tree2mydoor.com in 2002 as a sole trader business. By 2003, Gareth had founded Tree2mydoor Limited and launched the new company during the National Tree Week. Tree2mydoor specialises in the sale of high-quality natural gifts, including native and ornamental trees and wildflower gifts. Gareth explains, 'We sell over 30 tree species of all shapes and sizes. Each tree is individually packed with a personalised greetings card into an eco-friendly gift box before being mailed directly to our customers' chosen recipients.'

Gareth is aware that he is in the gift business and knows that he has a lot of competition. Direct competitors are, for example, tree-shop.co.uk, treesdirect.co.uk, treesbypost.co.uk, chewvalleytrees.co.uk, mailordertrees.co.uk, www.ornamental-trees.co.uk, store.ashridge-trees.co.uk and trees-online.co.uk. But nevertheless, one of the key strategies for differentiation is innovation through product design and value creation. He explains, 'Do my competitors sell trees? Yes. Do they provide a wide range of trees and plant species? Yes. Do they deliver to people's door? Yes. Do they protect the environment and support conservation projects? Yes. But one thing that they don't do is to add value to the act of giving a tree as something meaningful to both the giver and receiver.' For this reason, Tree2mydoor has three gift options: tree gifts, conservation gifts and occasion gifts. The first two options are the common products that are available at most tree gift companies. However, the product innovation is built in the occasion gift option. A tree gift is packed with personalised greeting cards or engraved pewter plaque, to celebrate birthdays, births, weddings, Valentine's day, memorials, Father's and Mother's day, and many more special occasions. One of Gareth's campaigns is based on the following concept and he asks: 'How long does love last? One night? One week? One month? Ten years? A lifetime? If we were to buy a gift for someone to represent our love, it should not last for a week like cut flowers or one fashion season like a handbag. If we buy a gift for a loved one, this gift should represent our love and it should last for a lifetime. Therefore, buying and planting a tree is the perfect gift that grows and lasts for a lifetime. This represents the idea of long-lasting love.' This concept adds value to

Tree2mydoor products and differentiates the company from competitors who only sell and deliver trees. This example indicates the importance of value creation and low-cost product innovation that became a marketing strategy and competitive advantage.

On the other hand, to overcome indirect competition such as the general gifts companies, Gareth said that apart from delivering meaningful gifts to people's door, 'Tree2mydoor provides tree gifts and wild flower gifts as an eco-friendly alternative for special occasions.' Tree2mydoor also provides a corporate gifts section that offers creative eco-friendly gift solutions for UK business. Moreover, 'Tree2mydoor also operate a unique gift service, such as a "dedicate a tree" scheme which directly supports conservation projects in the UK and around the world. The profit from this particular product is donated to conservation project managers.' Particularly in the corporate section, Tree2mydoor provides an alternative option to giving wasteful corporate gifts (e.g., pens, mugs, calendars) whilst allowing corporate organisations to be socially responsible. In 2008, Tree2mydoor Ltd had a turnover of £250,000. Despite the recession, for the first quarter of 2009, the company topped record sales.

THE PROCESS OF BUSINESS START-UP

Gareth was born in 1978 and grew up in rural Northern Ireland before moving to England to further his education and establish his career. During his early years, he learned many different species of local plants and wildlife from his grandfather. This upbringing built an attitude and fuelled a desire for conservation and environmental protection. During his GCSEs, Gareth developed an appetite for entrepreneurship. In brief, Gareth produced a range of handmade jewellery for his School Art project. Although most pupils kept their artwork at home, Gareth sold his pieces at school and made himself some extra money. He said, 'This made me realise that I could create things. By finding customers and selling what I create, I make money. This was my first lesson of entrepreneurship and business.'

Later on, Gareth completed a degree in BA (Hons) Design Marketing. He said, 'The best thing about this course was a project where I had to research a particular market, develop a product and market it. This built my behaviour of thinking and searching for opportunities and product innovation.' Subsequent to his graduation, he had a number of temporary jobs working in bars, telesales and publishing. Through these jobs, he learned a lot about life and business. His last employment was working in a charity as a Marketing Advisor and Environmental Marketing Executive based in Manchester. This work experience taught him many lessons. For example, he learned how to manage projects and picked up on the different aspects of business.

In 2000, the idea of selling trees as gifts struck Gareth. He wanted to buy a fruit tree for his parents and have it sent to their home in Northern Ireland. He said, 'I searched around the web but was unable to find a company that would deliver a tree as a gift. I realised this was my opportunity.' Subsequently he funded his own project with £3,000 to creat www.tree2mydoor.com as a sole trader. This website offered a Christmas tree delivery and collection service to customers in the Greater Manchester area. His initial target was to sell enough trees to fund his development of a tree gifts company. He said, 'I thought that I would start making money straight away, buying a new car and a big house and having lots of parties.' Despite a lot of efforts being put into marketing in Manchester City Centre, the company only sold 34 Christmas trees in 2002. Therefore, he learned that running a business was not easy. A lot of preparation and planning is needed. Just at the right moment, Gareth discovered and enrolled on a free business start-up programme called the New Entrepreneurs Scholarship (NES). Here he learnt about business start-up and management. Throughout this period, Gareth researched and developed his business, expanded his network with like-minded individuals, wrote a business plan, formed a limited company and raised capital to launch his Tree2mydoor Ltd in September 2003.

But nevertheless, Gareth found that being a young entrepreneur was not easy in terms of seeking start-up capital. He has been to a number of banks with his business plan. Gareth said, 'They all rejected my proposal and told me that I lack any experience. They did not understand the concept and they gave me the impression that they thought it was a stupid idea. I was young and I needed more experience. But I was very determined. I found a way to fund my business start-up by accumulating capital through small grants.' With his business plan, Gareth managed to accumulate £10,000 from the NES grant, The Prince's Trust and from some other small grants available through his local council. With an additional £4,000 from his personal savings, Tree2mydoor Ltd was launched in September 2003.

LESSONS LEARNED

Gareth said, 'My mother always wanted me to find a stable job. She did not like my idea of starting my own business, but now is proud of my actions.' He found his journey of business start-up extremely fruitful and fulfilling. The best thing about it is that he has created his own job and makes a living by doing what he has a passion for. Nevertheless, running a business can be very stressful. He said that it is important to have tolerance to uncertainty because no one knows exactly what will happen tomorrow. For example, he found it very hard to make enough profit to survive the early years of his business. But with determination and passion, and of course, with research, development and planning, he took the risk of starting and continuing his business. He said, 'Risks were assessed and calculated, therefore I took the risk.' Risk-taking is a calculated and planned action. Gareth also learned that making good decisions is a practice that can be developed by making mistakes along the way. Failure is just a lesson that will inform future practices. Value creation is another key aspect that Gareth learned. He said, 'A product is neutral. You give life to a product by giving it a meaning. This meaning creates a value. Customers pay for values. I have learned that value creation is a low-cost strategy for product innovation. All you need is time to think, research, creative thinking to generate ideas

and logical thinking to make it happen.' He also emphasised that networking is important as ideas can be developed through communication and networks represent resources that can be tapped into. Nonetheless, he said that everyone has their own opinions and ideas. There is no right or wrong answer. The ideas and information given by others are only ingredients that can be exploited for his business.

To sum-up his lessons, he emphasised his wisdom: 'Conduct your research and develop the idea. Write a business plan because it is a tool that guides your research and development. It is like a simulation game.' He thinks that it is important to gain some work experience prior to business start-up. He said, 'Students can have an unrealistic view of the reality and the world of work and business.' Therefore, it is important to gain some work experience as part of the process of becoming an entrepreneur. He said, 'If you have an idea and remain passionate enough about it after your graduation, what you should do is to treat it as a part-time project, you may have to work on it during the evening and at weekends. You need to do your research, plan and develop it. It is hard to start straight after university without a good understanding of the real world.' To conclude, he said 'I am making money, I am a businessman, but at the same time, I have positive impact on the society. I am directly and indirectly educating consumers, reducing carbon emissions by growing new trees and giving advice on how to live the sustainable way. I have learned a lot about myself, and the world around me. I found my role in today's society and am happy that my role is a positive one.'

QUESTIONS

1 Gareth's wisdom is 'Conduct your research, develop the idea. Write a business plan because it is a tool that guides your research and development. It is like a simulation game.' What do you think about this?

2 Doing good while doing well. In other words, run a profitable business while supporting

social well-being and environmental protection. What do you think about this?

3   Is it better to start up a business after your graduation or work for a while to gain experience prior to business start-up?

REFERENCES

Bessant, J. and Tidd, J. (2007) *Innovation and Entrepreneurship*, West Sussex: John Wiley & Sons Ltd.

Brinckmann, J., Grichnik, D. and Kapsa, D. (In Press) Should entrepreneurs plan or just storm the castle? A meta-analysis on contextual factors impacting the business planning–performance relationship in small firms, *Journal of Business Venturing*, corrected proof available online 29 November 2008.

Cohen, B. and Winn, M.I. (2007) Market imperfections, opportunity and sustainable entrepreneurship, *Journal of Business Venturing*, 22 (1): 29–49.

Dean, T.J. and McMullen, J.S. (2007) Toward a theory of sustainable entrepreneurship: Reducing environmental degradation through entrepreneurial action, *Journal of Business Venturing*, 22 (1): 50–76.

Walley, L., Taylor, D. and Greig, K. (2008) Beyond the visionary champion: Testing a typology of green entrepreneurs in Schaper, M. (ed) *Making Ecopreneurs: Developing Sustainable Entrepreneurship*, 2nd edn, London: Ashgate.

Westhead, P. and Wright, M. (1998) Novice, portfolio, and serial founders: Are they different? *Journal of Business Venturing*, 13 (3): 173–204.

Westhead, P., Ucbasaran, D., Wright, M. and Binks, M. (2005a) Novice, serial and portfolio entrepreneur behaviour and contributions, *Small Business Economics*, 25: 109–132.

Westhead, P., Ucbasaran, D. and Wrigth, M. (2005b) Decisions, actions, and performance: Do novice, serial and portfolio entrepreneurs differ? *Journal of Small Business Management*, 43 (4): 393–417.

Part 3

IN SEARCH OF ENTERPRISE VALUE

Going in Search of an Enterprise with Value

Jasmine and Jake had decided to join a programme that encouraged entrepreneurship by allowing students to set up a pilot business venture in a safe environment with mentors and other help. They met to discuss what type of business to set up and how to go about it.

'The guidelines say we should start an enterprise that has the potential to create value for either us or society, or preferably both. It suggests we should start by thinking of a well-known, successful business and work out why it is valuable', read Jake.

Jasmine had opened up her laptop. 'How about Google?' she said looking at the name on her home page. 'That's a pretty successful business. Everyone knows the name and millions of people must use it, so that's of value.'

'Yes but just how does it make any money? Everything is free to use. They don't really have a product that you can buy', said Jake.

'Maybe not, but I have just googled their financial results and it looks as though they made over $4 billion profit on sales of $22 billion in 2008. So financially they are doing something right. And they employ over 20,000 people worldwide so that is quite a team. There must be value in that', said Jasmine.

'And the name has a little ™ next to it which means no-one else can use it', said Jake, looking over Jasmine's shoulder at the Google image on her computer screen. 'I'm still not sure how they do it but we could do worse than set up a business like that.'

Why do you think that Google is such a valuable enterprise? What are the key ingredients that have created this value for Google and other entrepreneurial ventures?

Learning Objectives and Structure of Part 3

Entrepreneurship creates value from which both individuals and society benefit. To achieve this, entrepreneurs take an opportunity through progressive stages from identification and evaluation to creating and realising value. This section looks at five aspects that have been identified as crucial to the creation of lasting value in an enterprise: customer base and market position; knowledge base and intellectual property; the entrepreneurial team; the business model and processes; and cash flow and profits. The five chapters deal with each of these in turn.

By the end of Part 3, the reader should be able to:

■ Identify five factors that add value to a business

■ Understand how marketing works in an entrepreneurial environment

■ Assess the importance of protecting knowledge and intellectual property

■ Evaluate the importance of teams in an entrepreneurial venture

■ Analyse the ingredients of a successful business model

■ Understand how entrepreneurs raise and manage finance.

There are five chapters that focus on these learning objectives:

Chapter 11   Entrepreneurial marketing

Chapter 12   The creation and protection of knowledge

Chapter 13   The entrepreneurial team

Chapter 14   Entrepreneurial business models and processes

Chapter 15   Entrepreneurial finance

CHAPTER 11

Entrepreneurial Marketing

LEARNING OBJECTIVES

After studying this chapter, the reader will be able to:

- Explain the key areas of traditional marketing and its evolution
- Understand how entrepreneurial marketing differs from traditional marketing
- Assess the importance of word-of-mouth marketing to entrepreneurs
- Evaluate the processes of word-of-mouth marketing, including modern variants such as 'viral' and 'buzz' marketing
- Formulate an entrepreneurial marketing strategy.

INTRODUCTION

The purpose of this chapter is to understand how entrepreneurs interact with the marketplace – how they find customers and develop relationships with them. They do this through *marketing*, the business function that establishes and maintains the interface with the marketplace. However, entrepreneurs tend not to follow traditional principles when undertaking marketing activities. As a result, 'entrepreneurial marketing' is different in many respects to the traditional marketing as developed originally by larger corporations. The basic philosophy of marketing is that all the strategies and activities of an organisation should focus on meeting customer needs. Whilst entrepreneurs would not argue with this fundamental concept, they adopt very different strategies and methods to classical marketers whilst still ultimately fulfilling customer needs. Some differences exist because those setting up new ventures or running small enterprises simply do not have the resources to mount the extensive branding and promotional campaigns typical of traditional marketing strategies. Entrepreneurial marketing uses the time, energy and creativity of entrepreneurs instead of money. But it is not only a question of resources. Even entrepreneurs with well-resourced ventures do marketing differently. The preference of the entrepreneur does not lie in mass marketing campaigns orchestrated by formalised market research. They tend to use marketing methods that interact on a more personal basis with customers, based on informal assessments of the marketplace.

What is entrepreneurial marketing? Entrepreneurial marketing is the *business function of attracting and retaining customers, carried out in an entrepreneurial context*. It is marketing carried out by successful entrepreneurs and therefore takes key elements of the entrepreneurship process (such as opportunity recognition, innovation,

An Australian who gave a XXXX for anything else

The Australian beer market is dominated by two large companies, Fosters and Lion Nathan that supply over 90 per cent of the national market with brands such as Castlemaine XXXX, Fosters and Toheeys. Unlike Europe and the US where many micro-breweries compete with the big companies, Australia has a poor supply chain and distribution channels to support smaller brewers. A local entrepreneur, Liam Mulhall, wanted to upset this duopoly and enter the market with a new beer. He had experience of sales but not of marketing and insufficient funding for any extensive promotional campaign. In fact he didn't even have a product as he had yet to fully develop his beer. That was 2002. Now his company Brewtopia is thriving in a niche market for beers and marketed with virtually no promotional budget.[1]

If you were to launch a new beer product in such a market what would you do?
(Find out what Liam did in the case study at the end of the chapter.)

networking, resource leveraging and adding value) and applies them in the marketplace to build the optimum customer base. This is reflected in the following definition of entrepreneurial marketing:

> Entrepreneurial marketing is the proactive identification and exploitation of opportunities for acquiring and retaining profitable customers through innovative approaches to risk management, resource leveraging and value creation.

(Morris, Schindehutte and LaForge, 2002: 2)

However, this does not fully explain the difference between traditional marketing and entrepreneurial marketing in practice. To do this we need first to understand what we mean by traditional marketing and how it has developed in recent times.

11.1 TRADITIONAL MARKETING

11.1.1 The Four Key Areas of Traditional Marketing

Marketing is a widely used term that covers many business activities from research to advertising and selling. Traditionally, marketing theories relate to four key areas:

- The overall marketing concept of adopting a *market orientation* so that the business is focused on the needs of potential customers;

- The research and information that forms *the market intelligence* required to understand what customers need and to track the impact of marketing activities;

- The *marketing strategy* used to segment and target customers in the marketplace; and

- The *marketing mix* of methods used to win and keep customers.

A traditional marketing planning process[2] systematically follows these four areas as illustrated in Figure 11-1. Formalised market research is used to identify market needs; products or services are then developed in line with these findings. The strategy to market the product or service segments the market into groups of customers with similar buying characteristics, then identifies specific market segments that will be targeted, and finally positions the products/services in line with the characteristics of the target market. Elements of the marketing mix, often summarised as the '4 Ps' of product, price,

11

FIGURE 11-1 The traditional marketing process

promotion and place (or distribution) are used to ensure the product/service reaches the target markets. The process is completed when feedback from the performance of the product/service is monitored to provide market intelligence to identify further market needs.

This has been summarised into a definition of marketing as: 'the management process responsible for identifying, anticipating and satisfying customer requirements profitably' (UK Chartered Institute of Marketing).

11.1.2 The Evolution of Marketing

Marketing probably originated with the beginnings of trade itself, but it was not until relatively modern times that it developed into the formalised management concept described above. Since the 1950s, the principles of marketing have been gradually adopted throughout all sectors of the economy. As it has spread, it has also evolved to suit the particular contexts in which it has been practised:

- *Consumer goods* were the first to be marketed using modern techniques. Unilever, Proctor and Gamble and Mars were amongst the earliest companies to see the benefit of marketing their fast-moving consumer goods such as cereals, soap powders and confectionery. Consumer durables such as washing machines, record players, cameras and television sets soon followed, marketed by companies like Hoover, Electrolux and Philips. The emphasis was on developing a strong *brand* through *mass marketing* techniques.

- *Industrial products*, particularly in office equipment and supplies, became more widely marketed in the 1960s as companies such as Xerox and 3M followed the principles developed by the consumer marketers and offered differentiated, branded products in business-to-business markets. As products were often presented directly by a salesperson, this lead to an increased emphasis on *field marketing* such as exhibitions and hospitality events.

- *Consumer services* adopted marketing principles as their role in the economy grew and competition increased. Banks and insurance companies have fundamentally changed their services to be more in line with consumer demand. Marketing has adapted to suit the context of intangible products. As theories of *relationship marketing* emerged during the 1980s/90s, services marketing focused more on the development of longer-term relationships with customers rather than immediate transactions.

■ *The not-for-profit and public sectors* have also adopted marketing strategies. For example, charitable organisations have long been recognised as leading exponents of *direct marketing* in their appeals for funds. Political parties use market research such as *focus groups* to guide their policies and election planning.

■ *Small businesses* have become an increasingly significant part of developed economies. Whilst understanding the need for customer focus, many owners of smaller firms have neither the inclination nor the resources for formalised, mass campaigns typical of traditional marketing. Instead, they have developed an entrepreneurial style of marketing in which personal contact and *word-of-mouth recommendations* play an important part.

■ *The Internet* has created new opportunities for marketing in all industries and market sectors. It has spawned a new sector of companies that trade online. It has given existing businesses fresh ways of communicating with customers via websites or email. In an age of large, global markets, it has enabled organisations to become more accessible to individual customers. Whilst much of the publicity surrounding the Internet has involved consumer marketing organisations such as Amazon and eBay, the most rapid development of Internet applications has been in business-to-business markets. Entrepreneurs have been actively involved in using the Internet to enable new forms of word-of-mouth communications such as *viral marketing*.

Marketing at a Cross-Roads? In summary, marketing theory and practice has evolved over the past half-century or so from its roots in large companies selling fast-moving consumer goods to an instrument that can be used at a very individual level using modern communications technology. The adoption of marketing concepts and methods in different sectors and the advent of the Internet has led to significant modifications in the marketing methods that are employed. There is increasing evidence that traditional marketing campaigns based on mass media advertising are less effective than they used to be and the return on investment in them is diminishing (Zyman, 2002).[3]

Entrepreneurs have been an instrument of change in the evolution of marketing. Small business owners have long since rejected mass marketing approaches. Entrepreneurs have pioneered the marketing of goods and services immediately and inexpensively to an international audience via the Internet. They are making increasing use of the new forms of marketing that are emerging, including 'viral' and 'buzz' marketing that have developed ways of making word-of-mouth communications work even better (see section 11.4.2. below).

Does all of this add up to a fundamental redefinition of marketing principles for entrepreneurs? The justification for considering entrepreneurial marketing as different from traditional marketing arises from the behaviours of entrepreneurs when they successfully undertake marketing activities. Therefore, we will first explore the four key marketing concepts of market orientation, market intelligence, strategy and the marketing mix described above, to better understand what entrepreneurs do in each of these areas.

11

11.2 ENTREPRENEURIAL MARKETING VS. TRADITIONAL MARKETING

11.2.1 Market Orientation: Intuitive Innovation vs. Customer Needs

The key assumption of marketing theory is that the customer should be central to the entire enterprise and the focus of all its endeavours. Thus a detailed understanding of customer needs has to come before the development of any new products or services, the conception of marketing strategies or the implementation of promotional campaigns.

Customer Needs Through Intuition Entrepreneurial behaviour has characteristics which can be in conflict with this concept. Entrepreneurs tend to use heuristic decision-making relying on intuition – the gut feel of the entrepreneur.[4] This may happily coincide with the notion of market orientation if the entrepreneur can always truly put themselves in the position of the customer and feel empathy with their needs. A characteristic of many entrepreneurs is that they do have an intuitive feel for what their customers want, which has been described as 'an antenna into the market place' that never fails them. However, many entrepreneurs have shown that their intuition is not always a reliable indicator of customer demand. The ability to make rapid changes to what they do is also a key characteristic of entrepreneurs partly because they do misunderstand the nature of the marketplace and therefore have to make adjustments to compensate for misjudgements of customer needs and other decisions.[5]

In this sense 'entrepreneurial marketing' does differ from the traditional marketing concept in that entrepreneurs tend to understand customer needs by intuition, and then trial and error if they get it wrong. Entrepreneurs do not regard this as a potential weakness. Rather they emphasise the need to be flexible and adapt quickly to changes to market demand that may be slowed by the use of formalised research. They see this ability to adapt quickly as a competitive advantage over non-entrepreneurial companies.

Many entrepreneurs who have successfully launched new products/services into the marketplace have started first with *the idea, based on an intuitive feel* that it has market potential. This is often tested after only minimal research by trying it out in the marketplace and adapting rapidly to feedback from customers. The *innovation* that emerges is therefore based on an idea that finds market acceptance, rather than research into market needs that specifies a new product or service.

11.2.2 Market Intelligence: Informal Networking vs. Formal Research

Traditional marketing emphasises the need for structured market intelligence in order to understand customer needs including formal research and information-gathering activities. Entrepreneurs place a low value on formal market research. A key characteristic of entrepreneurs is that they maintain an 'external focus' through a network of personal contacts that keeps them alert to events and trends in the business environment – all part of their intuitive feel for customer needs. This is used as an informal intelligence-gathering process that replaces or diminishes the need for market research. Entrepreneurs have a rich network of contacts active in the marketplace that keeps them informed of developments. The entrepreneurial process of networking[6] modifies the traditional marketing process of formalised intelligence-gathering.

There are a number of reasons for this:

- Formalised research is seen as *slowing down the speed of reaction* needed in order to adapt to changes in the market.

- Research is regarded as *too expensive* for the results generated.

- Research *does not come up with breakthrough innovations* that change the nature of markets and industries that supply them.

The Role of Research in Innovation   The last reason is perhaps the most important for entrepreneurs who seek to develop radical innovations. Market research among potential consumers is unlikely to have come up with many of the breakthrough inventions in telecommunications that have shaped our modern world because they were unimaginable before they were invented. Often customers cannot describe to researchers what they need because they do not know what is possible; they cannot specify new products in areas where they have neither the vision nor the technological competence necessary to understand what is possible. They tend to be guided by what is already available so that research and development based only on customer preferences is likely to lead to modifications to existing products rather than radically different concepts.

This tendency towards modified rather than radical new products helps to explain why many key innovations come from outside of the main industry players that devote large budgets to research their market. If their research and development are based only on customer preferences, they are likely to be risk-free and lead to modifications to existing products rather than radically different concepts. The leading dot.com consumer marketing companies such as eBay and Amazon have not been developed by the existing retail giants. Existing organisations do become over-focused on the way things are, rather than on the way things could be.

No bites of the Apple

The world of IT in the early 1970s was dominated by large main-frame computers that used so much power and generated so much heat that they were isolated in air-conditioned rooms and serviced by teams of engineers in white coats. But two technical innovations made the development of much smaller personal computers possible: the integrated circuit (IC) which was developed in 1959 and the microprocessor which appeared in 1971. The IC enabled the memory circuits of computers to become miniaturised and the microprocessor reduced the size of a computer's central processing unit (CPU) to the size of a single silicon chip. These two developments meant that the potential existed for developing a small, separate system that could function as a complete microcomputer.

Xerox, a US corporation that had grown into an international giant by pioneering the use of plain paper copying machines, saw the potential and established the Palo Alto Research Centre (PARC) to develop its digital capability. By 1973 it had developed 'Alto', a computer designed for the use of one person. Senior managers were unconvinced of the product's viability and it was never marketed. In 1975 Xerox wrote off over $1 billion on its R&D and left the computer business.

A year later two Californian entrepreneurs, Steve Wozniak and Steve Jobs designed and built their first computer kit aimed at hobbyists who liked electronic gadgets. In 1977 they founded a new venture, Apple Computer, Inc., and introduced the Apple II, the world's first personal computer retailing for $1290. Within six years Apple had grown into one of the top 500 companies in the USA.

Xerox was not the only large corporation in the industry to miss the opportunity. Atari, Commodore Business Machines and Hewlett Packard all turned down opportunities to acquire Apple in its early days.

11.2.3 Marketing Strategy: 'Bottom-Up' Identification of Niches, vs. 'Top-Down' Segmentation, Targeting and Positioning

Traditional marketing strategy defines how an organisation competes in the marketplace through the three stages of market segmentation, targeting and positioning:

- First, the marketplace is divided through research and analysis into market segments – groups of customers who have different needs.

- Secondly, one (or more) of these segments is chosen as the most appropriate target for marketing effort.

- Thirdly, a product or service is offered to this target market that is positioned appropriately to appeal to the target customers.

This can be described as a 'top-down' process in that an overview of the market and how it can be divided into buyer groups or segments precedes the choice of which segment to target, which in turn leads to the relevant positioning strategy.

For example, a producer may segment the luxury clothes goods market into male and female buyers of different age groups and lifestyle aspirations before choosing professional female buyers from 35 to 55 as the target market for their range of suits for office wear. These are positioned for sale in upmarket retailers with glossy magazine advertising and an expensive price tag. In order to arrive at this strategy, extensive market research is used to test the aspirations and requirements of the segments and likely demand for potential products.

Bottom-Up, Entrepreneurial Targeting   Many entrepreneurial ventures succeed because they are highly targeted on specific customers by occupying a 'niche' in the market. This is a small segment or sub-segment of a marketplace that needs specialised products or services that are often price insensitive because competitive pressures are low due to the particular skills and resources required to meet demand. For example, within the general clothing market there are niches for particular products that do not achieve a mass market appeal; made-to-order hats for special occasions represent a niche market that require specialist skills in a limited although relatively price-insensitive market. Such niche markets tend to be occupied by entrepreneurs and small business owners.

In this and other ways, successful entrepreneurs do seem to follow the marketing principle of carefully targeting certain customers. However the processes they use in order to achieve this do not usually conform to the three stages of traditional marketing strategy formation described earlier. Evidence suggests that entrepreneurs practice a *'bottom-up' targeting process* rather than a *top-down process* of segmentation and targeting. Entrepreneurs first target a small market that they think likely to take their product/service and then expand the base gradually as experience and resources allow. Research into 'niche' marketing approaches indicates that targeting is achieved by attracting an initial customer base and then looking for more of the same (Dalgic and Leeuw, 1994). Instead of segmentation, targeting and positioning, the *three stages of entrepreneurial targeting* are:

- *Identification of a market opportunity*. An idea is developed into an opportunity by trial and error testing in the marketplace. The entrepreneur identifies the initial target market of customers based on their intuitive expectations which are sometimes, but not often, backed by some form of research.

- *Attraction of an initial customer base*. An initial group of customers are attracted to the service or product. These may or may not represent the target market and customer profile anticipated by the entrepreneur. As the entrepreneur is in regular contact with these customers, they get to know their preferences and needs.

- *Expansion through more of the same*. The entrepreneur seeks to expand the initial customer base by looking for more customers of the same profile. This is usually an informal process as it is the initial customers who recommend the business to others with similar needs to their own. A target customer group emerges and grows, through a process of self-selection with some encouragement from the entrepreneur, rather than through formal research and deliberate targeting.

This process has *advantages* over the top-down, traditional marketing approach:

- It is more flexible and adaptable to implement. In a sense the target market finds itself.

- Demand can be managed as it tends to build up more slowly.

- It uses fewer resources as it does not require extensive research and advertising.

It also has *disadvantages*:

- It is less certain of success as it is possible there is not a target market large enough to sustain the business.

- It can take longer to penetrate the market to full potential as it relies on informal communications.

- The business is likely to have a small customer base as it will be dependent on personal contacts.

ENTREPRENEURSHIP IN ACTION

Hat in the Ring

Ellery May loved making clothes, especially hats. She had a flair for the unusual in headgear and many of her friends asked her to make them a hat for a special occasion. When she was told that her office job was relocating to a call centre in Delhi, she decided it was time to make the break into self-employment. She launched her company 'Hat in the Ring' with weddings in mind as the name implies. She took advertisements in wedding magazines and went to wedding fairs, and waited for orders for her bespoke hats to arrive. A few trickled in but the mother of the bride proved a reluctant customer.

Another type of enquiry arrived in greater numbers. One of her friends was a horse racing enthusiast and caused quite a stir at a point-to-point meeting wearing one of Ellery's natty hats, modelled on the male 'cheese-cutter'. Friends of her friend were soon queuing up to order the exciting new headgear from Hats in the Ring which they assumed alluded to the horse ring rather than the wedding variety. The business branched out into other forms of clothing and headwear for men and women but all focused on the horse lovers market.

What happened to the wedding market? She asked a few customers why they thought this market was slow to take off and they confessed to doubts about buying one of her striking hat designs for a wedding in case they were seen to compete with the bride for the attention of the guests – which would not do at all. Competing with horses for attention was another matter.

11.2.4 The Marketing Mix: Interactive Word-of-Mouth vs. the Four Ps

Marketing strategies are implemented through a combination of methods and techniques designed to attract and retain the target customer. These include activities relating to product/service development, pricing, promotions and distribution channels. These are elements in the 'marketing mix', commonly summarised in traditional marketing texts as the four 'Ps' of product, pricing, promotion and place.[7]

Entrepreneurs' Interpretations of the Marketing Mix   Entrepreneurs are more comfortable with marketing defined at this level of meaning as they tend to see it in terms of tactics to attract new business and often equate marketing with selling and promoting only (Carson *et al.*, 1995; Stokes, Fitchew and Blackburn, 1997). This does not necessarily mean that they overlook other aspects of marketing, only that they are unaware of the terminology. Some entrepreneurs suggest that 'they do not have to do any marketing' because their customers come from recommendations. Entrepreneurs commonly cite *word-of-mouth recommendations* from customers as their number-one way of attracting customers. However, this reliance on recommendations is not necessarily an indication of minimal marketing effort, as such recommendations are often hard won. Entrepreneurs devote much of their time to building relationships with satisfied customers who then recommend the business to others. In other words, they spend considerable time and resources on marketing, but they call it by another name.

The preference for word-of-mouth communications to attract customers is indicative of the marketing methods preferred by entrepreneurs. They have preferences for direct contact with customers rather than impersonal marketing through mass promotions. They tend to seek interactive relationships in which they can listen to, and respond to, the voice of the customer, rather than undertake formal market research to understand the marketplace. Their personal contact with customers often represents the unique selling point of their enterprise as they are seen as the face of the business – their name is in effect their brand. Entrepreneurs stress the importance of personal relationships in developing a

11

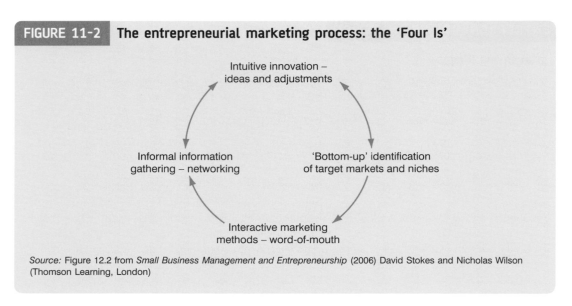

FIGURE 11-2 The entrepreneurial marketing process: the 'Four Is'

Intuitive innovation –
ideas and adjustments

Informal information
gathering – networking

'Bottom-up' identification
of target markets and niches

Interactive marketing
methods – word-of-mouth

Source: Figure 12.2 from *Small Business Management and Entrepreneurship* (2006) David Stokes and Nicholas Wilson (Thomson Learning, London)

customer base, and many express regret that the growth of their business reduces their opportunities for direct customer contact.

11.2.5 A Model of Entrepreneurial Marketing

In summary, entrepreneurs tend to use different marketing processes from those proposed by traditional marketing theory. They develop ideas into *innovations* through intuitive understanding of what may be needed in the marketplace, and rapidly adapt if they get it wrong or if the market changes. They *identify target markets* (especially niches) through grass roots, 'bottom-up' experience in the market, rather than top-down segmentation, targeting and positioning approaches. They attract and retain customers through *interactive methods especially word-of-mouth recommendations* rather than mass marketing promotions. This process is underpinned, not by formalised market research but by *informal information-gathering* through networking. This can be conceptualised as the 'four I's' of entrepreneurial marketing as shown in Figure 11-2.

This is a simplistic model that does not always take account of particular contexts and circumstances, but it does illustrate the marketing processes that many successful entrepreneurs have followed. It represents a further stage in the evolution of marketing away from its roots in large corporations and into a form that is more suited to today's entrepreneurial business environment. Recent research into the field of entrepreneurial marketing indicates differences of emphasis and sometimes of principle that does provide a contrast with much of the theory and practice of traditional marketing. Some of these differences are illustrated in Table 11-1.

11.3   WORD-OF-MOUTH MARKETING PROCESSES

11.3.1 The Importance of Word-of-Mouth Recommendations to Entrepreneurs

Studies show that the number-one source of new customers for small firms and entrepreneurial ventures is *word-of-mouth recommendations* from customers, suppliers or other referral groups (Barclays Review, 1997; Blankson and Stokes, 2003). One study of 300+ owner-managers (Stokes, Fitchew and

TABLE 11-1 Traditional vs. entrepreneurial marketing	
Traditional marketing	**Entrepreneurial marketing**
Slow response to changes in customer preference	Speedy reaction to shifts in customer preference
Focus on large markets	Exploit smaller market niches
Customer knowledge based on market research and expert knowledge	Customer knowledge based on market immersion/interaction
Marketing tactics are typically unidirectional	Marketing tactics are often two-way with customers
Planning is used to set goals and budgets	Planning, or lack thereof, is done in short, incremental steps
Vision and strategy guide marketing plans	Vision and strategy are driven by tactical successes
Marketing is separated from personalities	Founder and other personalities are central to marketing
Major marketing decisions made without frequent customer contact	Marketing decisions based on daily customer contact and networks
Formal market research is common	Formal market research is rare
Reliance on strategic analysis and planning	Reliance on intuition and experience
Product development processes are systematic stage gates	Product/venture development is interactive, incremental, informal with little research/analysis
An objective dispassionate science	A role for passion, zeal and commitment
Marketing follows customers	Marketing strives to lead customers
Maintain status quo with modest change in products and strategy	Innovation in products/services and strategies
Management of a balanced marketing mix	Heavy focus on selling and promotion

Source: Hills G.E, Hultman C, Morris M, and Carson D. (2005)

11

Blackburn, 1997) found that over 90 per cent of owner-managers of small businesses used word-of-mouth communications as their primary way of transmitting marketing messages. Recommendations from existing customers were the most frequently claimed type of promotional activity. Moreover the second most popular method of customer acquisition was recommendations from other sources (i.e. non-customers). This is not just lifestyle owner-managers who have little ambition to grow. In a study of established firms, nearly two-thirds of the companies identified as high growth claimed recommendations to be the most effective way of attracting customers (Blackburn and Stokes, 2003). Entrepreneurs seem to prefer direct interaction with their client base as face-to-face selling is often the next preferred method of customer acquisition to word-of-mouth.

Selling to the sellers

Brent Malik, the owner-manager of an electronics manufacturer never kept visiting salespeople waiting, nor did he discourage their calls. In fact he positively encouraged their visits in the early days of his business. But when he agreed to see someone, his golden rule on each sales call was that *he* presented to the salesperson first. His aims were clear: before they could sell to him, he wanted to sell the capabilities of his business to them. He knew that when they called on other potential customers they might also be potential clients for him. So it turned out to be. His first important client was introduced to him by Dee Chan, a component sales representative who knew of a company developing a new range of products. She wanted to get her electronic component locked into the design of the new products and so approached Brent to tender for the prototypes using her components. Brent got the contract with Dee's help and the two companies continue to support each other from different perspectives of the electronics industry supply chain.

The Impact of the Internet   Today 'word-of-mouth' communication is a misnomer. Although many recommendations are still made orally in face-to-face encounters, they often take place without personal contact because of developments in communication technologies. The use of the Internet by entrepreneurs has increased the usage of recommendations as the Internet has become a huge source of referral for products and services especially since the advent of 'Web 2.0' that invites interactive participation from Internet users. Emails, blogs and social networks such as Facebook offer opportunities to instantly pass on comments and advice about products and services to an international audience. Most Internet retail sites ask for customer comments on the products and services they sell which stand as recommendations to potential customers – an opportunity for the entrepreneurial seller to encourage favourable postings.

Recommendations or Referrals?   The terms 'recommendation' and 'referral' are often used interchangeably as though they have the same meaning. In fact it is useful to distinguish between them:

- *A recommendation* is an unsolicited opinion about a product or service given independently of the provider of the product or service.

- *A referral* is a recommendation for a product or service given independently *but solicited* by the provider of the product or service.

Recommendations just happen. Referrals can be positively encouraged and form part of a proactive word-of-mouth marketing campaign.

11.3.2 Word-of-Mouth Communications in Practice

Research into word-of-mouth communications spanning over 50 years has revealed aspects of how it works which are important to entrepreneurs.

The Power of Impartiality   The power of word-of-mouth communications stems from their assumed impartiality. We are naturally resistant to accepting information that we believe to be part of a selling process. Independent but amateur advice from friends is more trusted than expert recommendations from those in the business. There is evidence that we are more likely to believe what we overhear rather than what we are told directly as there is less chance of an ulterior motive in the communication. If the basic condition of impartiality is not fulfilled, the effectiveness of the recommendation is reduced. This poses a dilemma for those entrepreneurs who wish to give incentives to customers for recommending their service to others. However, if handled carefully, promotions that encourage word-of-mouth have been shown to work and good advertising can also stimulate recommendations.

Positive and Negative Recommendations Recommendations can be either positive or negative as we can either praise or complain about a product or service. However, customers are more likely to complain about disappointing experiences than to praise exceptional service. Often the complaint is to a friend or acquaintance and not directly to the product or service provider, so that entrepreneurs do not necessarily hear the negative comments about their business. Research has indicated that customers are less likely to spread negative word-of-mouth if complaining to the business is made relatively easy, or if efforts are made to put things right quickly (Blodgett, Granbois and Walters, 1993). Hence it is important to have procedures in place that can draw out complaints and make rapid compensation for any problems.

The Role of Opinion Leaders Consumers listen particularly to the recommendations of opinion leaders whose views they respect. There is evidence that the opinions of a small percentage (typically 10 per cent) of potential customers will strongly influence the behaviour of the rest of the market (i.e. the other 90 per cent) (Weimann, 1994). Opinion leaders owe their influence to:

■ *Who they are* – e.g. endorsements from trusted friends or admired celebrities

■ *What they know* – e.g. advice from an 'expert' source

■ *Who they know* – they are the hub of extensive personal networks in which they both obtain and communicate information about products and services.

Particularly during the launch of new ventures, it is important to ensure that opinion leaders in the industry are prepared to endorse the product or service as they heavily influence the take-up in the marketplace. Unfortunately it is difficult to identify opinion leaders. They have no general demographic characteristics in common and they are usually different people for different types of products and services. Their only common trait is their level of *involvement* with the product or service category – it represents an important feature of their life for professional or social reasons.

11

Finding opinion leaders

Marketing agencies recognise the importance of opinion leaders ('Hubs' or 'Alphas' as they are sometimes designated), and spend considerable effort in finding them. These are some of their techniques (Kirby and Marsden, 2006):

■ Ask existing customers to fill out a short questionnaire asking if they are considered a good source of advice by friends of the product/service category and if they offer such advice.

■ Ask others to designate opinion leaders – particularly used in business-to-business markets.

■ Assume certain job titles indicate likely opinion leaders, e.g. PAs to senior managers.

■ Search online networks, forums, discussion groups and blogs for frequently active participants.

Which Customers are Most Likely to Recommend a Business? Few entrepreneurs know exactly which customers are actively recommending their business, although many believe it is their loyal, long-standing customers who recommend them most. The 'ladder of customer loyalty', a key concept in relationship-marketing theory, supports this. It suggests that 'prospects' and one-off customers on the bottom rung can be encouraged through relationship building to climb the ladder and become 'clients', who order more than once, 'supporters', who think positively about the business, and 'advocates', who act positively about the business by recommending it to others. This implies that as the customer relationship progresses up the ladder over time, the potential for recommending or 'advocacy' also increases. However, a number of studies found that recommending behaviour actually *declined* as relationships matured (East, Lomax and Narain, 2000; Stokes, Ali Syed and Lomax, 2002). *Recent* customers were more likely to recommend a service than longer-term clients because they were more enthusiastic and prone to discuss new experiences than longer-standing relationships. This suggests that recently acquired customers may be better targets for word-of-mouth campaigns than loyal clients.

When are Recommendations Triggered? This is probably the most important and most difficult question to answer – what triggers a customer to make a recommendation and what might stimulate them to make them more often? One key is the level of *involvement* a customer feels with the owners and employees of a particular enterprise or business. Research indicates that those who have relationships with a business that go beyond basic commercial transactions are more likely to recommend it. This could be a passing acquaintance: for example, one study on the legal profession concluded that increased face-to-face contact between lawyer and client led to more referrals (File, Judd and Prince, 1992). It could be a more in-depth involvement such as giving advice or help: for example, research indicated that parents who were more involved with their school through raising money or helping in the classroom had a higher rate of recommending than other parents (Stokes, 2002). Telling stories and giving news about an enterprise through newsletters and articles may also stimulate recommendations. Visual aids such as free gifts have also been found to act in a similar way (Stokes and Lomax, 2002).

Tips on cultivating referrals

1 Directly ask for referrals from your contacts. Make it easy for them – draft a letter/email they themselves can send to their acquaintances recommending your services.

2 Encourage multiple referrals. It is better to be recommended by more than one source.

3 Develop more colourful clients as these are more likely to provide interesting stories and applications of your product or service.

4 Use competitors as sources of referrals. Competitors may be happy to recommend you if an enquiry is outside their core competences or if they are just too busy.

5 Use suppliers and sub-contractors as sources of referrals and recommendations. Supply chains in many industries have become flatter so that your suppliers may also be selling to potential customers for your business.

6 Reward those that make referrals with care as they may consider it inappropriate and it may invalidate the power of their recommendation.

7 Involve customers in your enterprise through personal contact, hospitality and other non-commercial activities.

8 Identify opinion leaders in your market and ensure they know about your product/service – ask them to sample it.

9 Give away interesting visual aids that remind people of your business and stimulate them to talk about it.

10 Publicise interesting stories and facts about your business through newsletters, blogs, trade press and conferences.

11 Find out *who* is recommending you and *what* they are saying about your business.

12 Find out *when* they are likely to recommend – what triggers it and how can it be prompted to happen more often.

11.4 INTERACTIVE WORD-OF-MOUTH MARKETING PROGRAMMES

It is not possible to control what people say about a business in the way that an advertising agency can be briefed to promote a business. Recommendations are essentially uncontrollable, but they can be encouraged. From the particular characteristics of word-of-mouth detailed above, it is possible to create effective interactive marketing programmes.

11.4.1 Seeding Trials

'Seeding trials' are a method of combining the power of *opinion leaders* and the *involvement* of potential customers in the actual development of new products and ventures to generate word-of-mouth recommendations. The idea is to identify a number of opinion leaders and involve them in the development of a new product or service. This involvement is designed to turn the opinion leaders into strong advocates of the new product.

ENTREPRENEURSHIP IN ACTION

The trial of Innocent

Three Cambridge graduates – Richard Reed, Adam Balon and Jon Wright were keen to set up their own business but were unsure of which idea to pursue. They were advised that before launching any business they should really understand their target audience – the people who would potentially buy their products. With their limited resources, they recognised that the only people they understood well were themselves and one of their problems was to stay healthy in today's fast-moving urban environment. They therefore decided to test the concept of fruit smoothies – a healthy drink made from

The Innocent Drinks founders

© INNOCENT SMOOTHIES

pure fruit that could be consumed quickly and easily. To do this they set up a stall at a music festival in London. People were asked to put their empty bottles in a 'yes' or 'no' bin depending on

11

whether they thought the three should quit their jobs to make smoothies. At the end of the festival the 'Yes' bin was relatively full, so they quit their jobs and set up Innocent.

They used the audience of the music festival to test their product idea because it attracted young people with similar lifestyles to themselves. The publicity which this trial stimulated is still generating word-of-mouth communications over ten years later through people relaying this story about how the company started. According to seeding trial theory, it is likely that the original 'yes' voters were amongst the first advocates of the new company when it launched as they would have felt a sense of involvement in its progress (although this has not been researched).

The following steps illustrate how to use seeding trails as part of a marketing programme (Marsden, 2006):

■ Identify enough opinion leaders in the target market to make an impact.

■ Sample, or trial, the new product or service so that influential members of the potential market feel involved in its development. This technique works best if opinion leaders can be offered a free trial, sample, download or preview of some kind.

■ Give those who take part in the trial a say or a vote in the future development or marketing of the product or business. This creates the feeling of involvement or ownership that generates word-of-mouth recommendations. This may be as little as an online vote on an advertising concept or as much as a selection of the brand name or features of the product (or whether to launch the business at all as in the case of the Innocent founders).

11.4.2 Viral Marketing

The digital media, particularly Internet-enabled communications including blogs, social networks, chat rooms, forums and instant messaging, have changed the nature of word-of-mouth marketing. It has dramatically increased the speed and reach of messages that can now be spread about a product or service:

■ *Face-to-face* communications tend to work in *local networks* and build appreciation of a new service relatively *slowly*. The use of word-of-mouth campaigns was therefore presumed to be for slow-growth, lifestyle entrepreneurs only.

■ *Viral marketing* is a relatively new term that describes how *marketing messages can be passed on by individuals in a way that can create exponential growth*. Like a virus, the message multiplies rapidly by being passed on in a way that allows for rapid duplication. The key difference between viral and normal word-of-mouth communications is that it allows for *rapid uptake* of the message, partly because it is the *marketing message* not a product recommendation that is passed on.

11.4.3 Buzz Marketing

'Buzz marketing' in some respects is word-of-mouth marketing by a different name in that it is being used to describe the creation of lots of rapid interest in a new product or service. But it is different in its deliberate intent to use consumers or paid professionals to spread a particular message about a product. Buzz marketing invites volunteers to try products, then encourages them to become 'buzz

The Hotmail virus

Hotmail was launched by Jack Smith and Sabeer Bhatia in 1996 making it one of the first free web mail services. It gained popularity rapidly mainly through the message 'Get your free email at http://hotmail.com' that was attached to the bottom of every email sent, thereby turning existing users into advocates for the service. It rapidly grew to over 10 million users and was acquired in 1997 by Microsoft for an estimated $400 million.

Other Internet services have copied the Hotmail technique. Social networks such as Facebook have expanded rapidly because members have asked for their friends to be invited to join.

agents' by talking up their experiences with the people they meet in their daily lives. *Live buzz marketing* makes use of an actual event or performance to create word-of-mouth (Foxton, 2006). The performance may involve ordinary consumers or paid actors to create an impact in order to generate comment. This may be covert in that the audience may not be aware that it is a pre-planned event, or overt in that they are fully understanding of the marketing that is going on.

Films that buzz – *The Blair Witch Project*

It has long been known that word-of-mouth recommendations from both friends and opinion leading critics play a leading part in the success or failure of films. Distributors are now using buzz marketing techniques to promote the new releases, particularly following the unexpected success of *The Blair Witch Project*. This became the most successful independent film made with box office receipts of $248 million worldwide despite a low-cost budget for both production and marketing. It was marketed using buzz marketing techniques to generate interest through speculation over whether the film was real or not. The poster for the film deliberately encouraged people to think the film was an actual documentary, and that the three main characters had really disappeared in the woods. A fake documentary, 'Curse of the Blair Witch', investigated the 'legend' surrounding the film just before its release, containing interviews with friends of the missing students, paranormal experts and local historians (all acted). The three main actors were listed for a short time as 'missing, presumed dead' partly because the producers put up missing posters of the three stars of the film during the Cannes Film Festival.

11

11.4.4 Creating a Word-of-Mouth Marketing Campaign

In order to benefit from these relatively new techniques it is necessary to fulfil one well-established condition: to offer a consistently high level of service and product quality. Once this is in place, there are three further steps to developing a word-of-mouth marketing campaign.

1 *Find out how the word-of-mouth communications' process takes place in the relevant market or industry*. In particular, investigate:

   ▪ *Who* is most likely to make recommendations – is it most recent or most loyal customers. Who are the opinion leaders? How can they be contacted?

   ▪ *What* exactly are they are saying about the business, product or service? It is important to know exactly what is being recommended about a business if only to ensure that this positive factor is not jeopardised in some way. Positive comments may not be in line with the expectations of the entrepreneur who may be unaware of the particular plus point of the business. If there are positive aspects of the business that are not being mentioned then maybe these need to be prompted by highlighting them in communications such as newsletters.

- *When* they are prompted to do it. As customers' perceived involvement with a business venture is likely to prompt recommendations, how is this to be encouraged?

2 *Intervene to influence the recommending process.* Devise a marketing campaign to increase referral rates either through explicit requests for referrals, or communications that create a discussion point. What role can newsletters and visual aids play in this? Can interventions through free trials, live events or performances create a 'buzz' about the product?

3 *Defuse potential complaints.* Ensure processes are in place to uncover potential negative communications and deal with complaints in an effective and generous way. Effective complaint handling not only limits the damage but can potentially generate referrals through a positive experience.

11.5   SUMMARY AND ACTIVITIES

Entrepreneurs find customers and develop relationships through entrepreneurial marketing strategies and methods.

    Entrepreneurial marketing is different from **traditional marketing** in four areas:

- Entrepreneurs tend to develop ideas into **innovations** through intuitive understanding of what may be needed in the marketplace, and rapidly adapt if they get it wrong or if the market changes. Traditional marketing uses formalised market research to identify market needs and develop products or services in line with these findings.

- Entrepreneurs **identify target markets** (especially niches) through grass-roots, 'bottom-up' experience in the market, rather than the top-down segmentation, targeting and positioning approaches of traditional marketing.

- Entrepreneurs attract and retain customers through **interactive methods especially word-of-mouth recommendations** rather than traditional mass marketing and promotions.

- This process is underpinned, not by the formalised market intelligence of traditional marketing but by **informal information-gathering** through networking.

This can be conceptualised as the **'Four I's' of entrepreneurial marketing**.

    The number-one source of new customers for entrepreneurial ventures is **word-of-mouth recommendations** from customers, suppliers or other referral groups. Important aspects of word-of-mouth communications include:

- **Internet usage** has increased these communications as it has become a huge source of referrals of different types.

- **The power** of word-of-mouth communications stems from their assumed impartiality.

- **Opinion leaders** – a small percentage of potential customers – strongly influence the behaviour of the rest of the market.

- **Negative word-of-mouth** spreads more quickly then positive recommendations.

- **Involvement** or a feeling of commitment to a business and its owner-managers triggers more word-of-mouth recommendations.

- **Seeding trials** identify opinion leaders and involve them in the development of a new product or service. This involvement is designed to turn them into strong advocates of the new product.

■ **Viral marketing** creates marketing messages that can be passed on by individuals over the Internet to generate exponential growth.

■ **Buzz marketing** aims to develop rapid interest in a new product or service by deliberately using consumers or paid professionals to spread stories about a product. **Live buzz marketing** uses actual events or performances to create word-of-mouth.

Developing an entrepreneurial marketing campaign:

■ Find out how how communications work in the relevant market:
  ■ Who are the opinion leaders?
  ■ What exactly are they are saying about the business?
  ■ When are they prompted to do it?

■ Intervene to influence the recommending process:
  ■ Involve customers in the business
  ■ Increase referral rates through requests or stories
  ■ Create a 'buzz' through free trials, live events or performances.

■ Defuse potential complaints by encouraging them.

REVIEW QUESTIONS

1 How would you define traditional marketing?

2 How would you define entrepreneurial marketing?

3 What are the four stages in an entrepreneurial marketing process?

4 Why is formalised market research not often used by entrepreneurs to develop and launch new ideas?

5 What is a niche market?

6 Describe how some entrepreneurs find their customers through a 'bottom-up' targeting approach.

7 What are the two key ingredients that make word-of-mouth marketing so powerful?

8 What is a 'seeding trial' and how does it work?

9 Define 'viral' marketing with an example of how it has worked.

10 What is buzz marketing? Give some examples.

11

SEMINAR TASK

Select an industry or market that is dominated by a few large companies. For example, in the UK this could be the banking market or the newspaper industry. Develop an outline plan of how you could use customers to first develop a new product or service and secondly market it through word-of-mouth techniques. (*Use the Brewtopia case study as an example of how this worked in the brewing industry in Australia.*)

Preview case continued

An Australian who gave a XXXX for anything else: A case of Brewtopia

As described in the introduction, the Australian beer market is effectively controlled by a duopoly of two giant companies, Fosters and Lion Nathan, that have acquired most of the successful breweries over the years. So how would you go about setting up in competition with them taking account of the poor distribution channels to drinks outlets available to smaller breweries?

That was the question that Liam Mulhall tried to answer in 2002 when he decided to quit his IT job and set up a brewery. His first idea was to buy a pub and put a small brewery into it. He did not know much about the beer industry and he soon found out that this simple concept was unlikely to work as it was almost impossible to put enough beer in front of consumers to get the economies of scale to make it work. However, he took inspiration from two different business models:

- From his career in IT sales, he was aware that many software products come into existence *after* they had been marketed to customers – so-called 'vaporware' that is not fully developed until sufficient customers are placing orders for it. Development time for software can be relatively quick but is very expensive, so it is a way of saving unneccessary R&D expenditure until the demand is cetain. He decided this could be the way to enter the monopolistic beer market in Australia.

- He was also aware of the concept of involving potential customers in a new product as a way of generating awareness and buzz around the product before it was launched. It was the early years of 'Big Brother' and other TV reality shows that gained audience participation and loyalty through voting for participants in the programmes. He decided to see if this could work in the context of the beer market by using the power of word-of-mouth

recommendations from friends in order to compete with the large marketing budgets of the big breweries.

The launch campaign

He combined these two ideas into a new business concept. First he invited about 150 friends and family to register on a website where they would get the opportunity to vote on the development and marketing of a new beer business. They were asked to vote on important aspects such as the name, style and taste of the beer, the type of bottle, pricing and sales outlets. He found it was important to give voters only two choices so that they felt really able to influence the decision. Secondly, he offered shares in the company for every vote cast, for buying the product and for referring friends. He felt that the physical involvement of owning shares would strengthen their emotional ties to the business and lead to more word-of-mouth communications.

The brewery was named 'Brewtopia' and the first beer product 'Blowfly' was launched in January 2003. The initial plan was to market the beer direct to consumers via Internet mail order, and then to expand into outlets such as pubs, restaurants and alcohol retailers once there was sufficient brand recognition to pull sales through the distribution. Liam believed that marketing Blowfly should not be about the beer but about entertainment and story-telling. The company generated plenty of press and other interest through its unorthodox approach, particularly the offer of shares. It even tried to create 'buzz' from the delivery of its beer. Instead of delivering to licensed premises at off-peak times to minimise disruption, Blowfly was offloaded when the bars were full by delivery men in lab coats who arrived in a van disguised as an ambulence with siren wailing. The website on which the products were sold direct to consumers was equally controversial. It featured stories that challenged the mystique generated by the advertising of the big brands

11

with claims that beer was easier to make than bread as it only had four ingredients, and it published the actual costs of brewing.

Changing the strategy

Liam Mulhall admits that 90 per cent of what they tried did not work. What did work was what he calls their 'stick-at-it-ness' – they kept on trying new things until sufficient worked to represent a viable business. That business is not the one envisioned in the original plan. The business model that worked is 'mass customisation' in that corporate or individual buyers can customise their own bottle of beer, wine or water by creating a personalised label and choosing from a variety of bottle sizes and product types. They stopped attempting to sell standardised beer such as Blowfly through retail outlets and focused more on the corporate and hospitality markets with customers such as Toyota and Sony. They sell own-brand products to restaurants and hotels. The products are retailed online aiming at the gift market with own-labelling or tribute beers such as 'Dudweiser' or 'Pooheys'.

Excerpts from www.blowfly.com.au

'Since 2002, we've dedicated our tiny minds to customising Beer, Water & Wines online. You can now even create your own labels for delivery Worldwide. We have no minimum order, no setup charges and 100% money back guarantee on all products. This is not your average company. In Australia in 2002 we created a beer built on an Open Source concept we dubbed "Viral Equity", which involved thousands of people in dozens of countries, helping us develop a brand new beer over the Internet, by voting on every aspect of its development. Crazy? Yes. Doomed to fail? Yes. But it didn't. And the result? A European Style lager brewed using the same recipe as our convict forebears but each with its own custom brand – and unique ingredient – YOU!

Of course since then, we have expanded into other beverages and focused much of our attention on the corporate and hospitality sectors.'

Questions

1 *Describe how this case study illustrates each of the four stages of 'the entrepreneurial marketing process' (the 'Four I's') – see Figure 11-2.*

2 *Which types of word-of-mouth marketing methods did the company employ and how?*

3 *Could these methods work in other markets to compete with dominant, established players? For example, how could you use some of the methods to enter the financial services market?*

11

11.6 NOTES, REFERENCES AND FURTHER READING

Notes and Further Information

1. Brewtopia charts its history and business philosophy on its website (http://brewtopia.com.au), on YouTube (http://www.youtube.com), and in other interviews and publicly available material many of which are listed on their website. They feature in several books including:

   McConnell, B., and Huba, J. (2004) *Testify! How Remarkable Organisations are Creating Customer Evangelists*, http://creatingcustomerevangelists.com/testify

   Kirby, J. and Marsden, P. (2006) *Connected Marketing: The Viral, Buzz and Word-of-Mouth Revolution,* Oxford: Butterworth-Heinemann.

2. For more detail of the concepts of marketing see for example: Stokes, D. and Lomax, W. (2008) *Marketing: A Brief Introduction*, London: Thomson Learning. Chapter 12 'Marketing Decisions and Planning' explains the stages of the marketing planning process as presented here.

3. A graphic history of marketing that illustrates this turning point in the evolution of advertising and promotions is available on YouTube: 'Short-history-of-marketing', http://www.youtube.com/watch?v=3GaAuuOLMyl.

4. Chapter 10 explores the role of heuristics and intuition in entrepreneurial decision-making. Subsection 10.2.3 'Heuristics or rules of thumb' defines heuristics as 'mental shortcuts to reduce information overload, and yield quick decisions'. Subsection 10.2.4 describes intuition as a style of perception which takes in the world through patterns, meanings, relationships and possibilities, rather than through facts.

5. For a summary of research into the importance of making adjustments to original plans particularly those relating to the marketplace see Stokes, D. and Wilson, N. (2006) *Small Business Management and Entrepreneurship*, Thomson Learning, p. 85. This lists the following areas as important to keep under review for possible change: market development; production processes; employment process; ownership and location.

6. The role of networking in this and other aspects of entrepreneurship is discussed in Chapter 9 'Entrepreneurial networking'.

7. The four P's are commonly extended to seven in services marketing theory by the addition of 'physical evidence, people and process'. See most marketing textbooks, e.g. Brassington, F. and Pettitt, S. (2006) *Principles of Marketing*, 4th Edition, Harlow: Pearson Education.

References

Barclays Review (1997) *Marketing and the Small Firm*, May, London: Barclays Bank.

Blackburn, R. and Stokes, D. (2003) *Who Are the Entrepreneurs? A Survey of the Owners of Small and Medium Sized Enterprises*, Report to Kingston Smith, September, SBRC, Kingston upon Thames: Kingston University.

Blankson, C. and Stokes, D. (2003) Marketing practices in the UK small business sector, *Marketing Intelligence and Planning*, 20 (1): 49–61.

Blodgett, J.G., Granbois, D.H. and Walters, R.G. (1993) The effects of perceived justice on complainants' negative word-of-mouth behavior and repatronage intentions, *Journal of Retailing*, 69: 399–428.

Carson, D., Cromie, S., McGowan, P. and Hill, J. (1995) *Marketing and Entrepreneurship in SMEs*, London: Prentice Hall.

Clancey, K. and Stone, R. (2005) Don't blame the metrics, *Harvard Business Review,* June, 83 (6).

Dalgic, T, and Leeuw, M. (1994) Niche marketing revisited: Concept, applications and some European cases, *European Journal of Marketing*, 20 (1): 39–55.

East, R., Lomax, W. and Narain, R. (2000) *Customer Tenure, Recommendation and Switching,* Kingston Business School Occasional Papers.

File, K. M., Judd, B.B. and Prince, R. A. (1992) Interactive marketing: The influence of participation on positive word of mouth and referrals, *Journal of Services Marketing*, 6 (4): 5–14.

Foxton, J. (2006) Live buzz marketing, in Kirby, J. and Marsden, P. (eds) *Connected Marketing: The Viral, Buzz and Word-of-Mouth Revolution*, Oxford: Butterworth-Heinemann.

Hills G.E., Hultman C., Morris M., and Carson D. (2005) Marketing, entrepreneurship and SMEs: Knowledge and education revisited, proceedings of the 10th Annual Research Symposium of the Academy of Marketing Special Interest Group on Entrepreneurial and SME Marketing, Southampton University.

Kirby, J. and Marsden, P. (2006) *Connected Marketing: The Viral, Buzz and Word of Mouth Revolution*, Oxford: Butterworth-Heinemann.

Marsden, P. (2006) Seed to spread: How seeding trials ignite epidemics of demand, in Kirby, J. and Marsden, P. (eds) *Connected Marketing: The Viral, Buzz and Word-of-Mouth Revolution*, Oxford: Butterworth-Heinemann.

Morris, M.H., Schindehutte, M. and LaForge, R.W. (2002) Entrepreneurial marketing: A construct for emerging entrepreneurship and marketing perspectives, *Journal of Marketing Theory and Practice*, 10 (4): 1–19.

Stokes D. R. (2002) Entrepreneurial marketing in the public sector: The lessons of headteachers as entrepreneurs, *Journal of Marketing Management*, 1, Spring.

Stokes, D.R., Ali Syed, S. and Lomax, W. (2002) Shaping up word-of-mouth marketing strategy: The case of an independent health club, *Journal of Research in Marketing and Entrepreneurship*, 4 (2): 119–133.

Stokes, D.R., Fitchew, S. and Blackburn, R. (1997) *Marketing in Small Firms: A Conceptual Approach*, Report to the Royal Mail, Small Business Research Centre, July, Kingston upon Thames: Kingston University.

Stokes, D.R. and Lomax, W. (2002) Taking control of entrepreneurial marketing: The case of an entrepreneurial hotelier, *Journal of Small Business and Enterprise Development*, 9 (4): 349–357.

Stokes, D.R. and Wilson, N. (2006) *Small Business Management and Entrepreneurship*, fifth edition, London: Thomson Publishing.

Weimann, G. (1994) *The Influentials: People Who Influence People*, New York: New York University Press.

Zyman, S. (2002) *The End of Advertising As We Know It*, Hobroken, NJ: Wiley.

Recommended Further Reading

Hills G.E., Hultman C., Morris M., and Carson D. (2005) Marketing, entrepreneurship and SMEs: Knowledge and education revisited, proceedings of the 10th Annual Research Symposium of the Academy of Marketing Special Interest Group on Entrepreneurial and SME Marketing, Southampton University.

Kirby J. and Marsden, P. (2006) *Connected Marketing: The Viral, Buzz and Word of Mouth Revolution*, Oxford: Butterworth-Heinemann.

Stokes, D.R. and Lomax W. (2002) Taking control of entrepreneurial marketing: The case of an entrepreneurial hotelier, *Journal of Small Business and Enterprise Development*, 9 (4): 349–357.

11

CHAPTER 12

The Creation and Protection of Knowledge

LEARNING OBJECTIVES

After studying this chapter, the reader will be able to:

- Evaluate how knowledge creation operates within an enterprise
- Distinguish between the main forms of intellectual property
- Understand know-how and the laws of confidentiality
- Consider patents as a form of knowledge protection
- Consider copyright and design right as a form of knowledge protection
- Evaluate trade marks and business names
- Develop a branding strategy.

INTRODUCTION

In Chapter 11 we explored how entrepreneurs can add value and longevity to their businesses by developing external relationships in the marketplace. In this chapter we turn our attention to the internal environment of an enterprise and evaluate how entrepreneurs can add value through the knowledge and expertise inherent in their products, services and processes. An entrepreneur can only establish a viable enterprise if they have knowledge of how to offer something that is of value to others. This knowledge may be how to make a particular product or how to offer a service. It may relate to the design of the product or the systems involved in the delivery of a service. It can also be about sourcing something that is made or offered by others, as entrepreneurs often act as go-betweens. This was the role played by medieval merchants as they had the knowledge of where to source the textiles and spices needed by others who had the wealth to buy them. They also had the knowledge of how to transport them, often through many hostile environments, to where the customers lived. Today this type of knowledge that helps potential customers to source products or services is a key role that many new Internet businesses are playing.

Entrepreneurs derive advantages over their competitors from these different types of knowledge so it is important to recognise and protect this essential resource. This chapter explores the nature of this knowledge and how it can be protected from others and enhanced so that the owner can gain maximum advantage.

PREVIEW CASE

Contrasting fortunes from the steam revolution

A technical innovation in the eighteenth century enabled human and animal muscle power to be supplemented and substituted for the first time (Botticelli, 1997). The new source of power was steam. Steam power was used in an increasingly wide variety of applications: in factories to drive the looms; in fields to turn the threshing machines; in coal mines to drain out water. Most revolutionary of all, it was used to power the first mass transport systems based on the rail locomotive. Many inventors contributed to the development of this technology. One was a famous Scot, who modified an earlier steam engine and made his fortune from it. Another was a relatively unknown Cornishman who contributed many inventions including the first steam locomotive to run on rails, but who died a pauper.

Who were these two innovators who contributed so significantly to the steam revolution? Why do you think they enjoyed such different fortunes in that one became rich and famous and the other obscure and impoverished? (See the case study, 'Inventing a revolutionary system of power and transport' at the end of the chapter.)

12.1   COMMERCIAL KNOWLEDGE AND INTELLECTUAL PROPERTY

12.1.1   What is Knowledge?

There has been considerable philosophical debate going back to Plato in Ancient Greece about the nature of knowledge without an agreed definition of what constitutes 'knowledge', or any prospect of one (Blackburn, 2003). There is a large grey area between what is 'opinion' and what is 'knowledge' so that absolute certainties in our understanding of the world around us are often not as common as we would like to think.

Knowledge can exist on a number of different levels. For example:

■ *Formalised group knowledge* – the sum total of what is known about a particular field or subject area, usually recorded in a variety of ways and publicly available. Examples include: business techniques as summarised on a management course; how to make a cake as written in countless different recipes.

■ *Informal knowledge* – shared by a discreet number of individuals about a particular topic and often not recorded. Examples include: how to securely lock up a particular factory; a local route using off-track paths and passage ways.

■ *Personal knowledge* – the expertise or skills of an individual acquired through experience and education. Examples include: an entrepreneur's knowledge of how to run a restaurant; an umpire's knowledge of the rules of the game.

Commercial knowledge is the understanding or expertise that relates to all aspects of business and enterprise development. As it can exist on all of the above levels, it may relate to general, group or individual knowledge that exists both formally and informally. Thus the knowledge that exists in a single enterprise derives from generally understood business principles, the collective knowledge of those involved about certain aspects of the business, and the particular expertise of the individuals involved in the enterprise. All of these types of knowledge have potential value depending on how widely available the knowledge is and its potential impact on the viability and profitability of the business.

12

The Knowledge

Licensed taxi drivers in London must have a detailed knowledge of roads and places of interest in London – known as 'The Knowledge'. To acquire the 'Green Badge' licence, drivers need a detailed knowledge of a circular area within a six-mile radius of Charing Cross containing 320 main routes, plus all the places of interest and important landmarks.

As it normally takes between two to four years to learn and pass the 'All London Knowledge' test, this provides a barrier to entry to new drivers and thus protects the earnings of the existing cabbies. Some drivers have other knowledge vital to their business. For example, they will know where and when likely customers will appear, the congestion bottlenecks to avoid and short cuts for faster journeys. This information is partly shared with other taxi-driving friends and partly kept secret to maximise personal earnings.

12.1.2 Knowledge Transfer

How is knowledge acquired? Experience and education are the normal sources of personal and group knowledge but there are others. The entrepreneurship process is concerned with the development of new forms of knowledge that flow from creative ideas and innovations. This creative process (discussed in detail in Chapter 3) usually combines different types of knowledge from various sources to form 'new knowledge' or an innovation that represents something of value that was not known about before, even though the component parts were.

Drawing together information and knowledge from disparate areas that are not normally connected and combining them in a unique way is a key entrepreneurial ability. In an increasingly complex world this is a difficult trick to pull off as it requires knowledge of different disciplines or sciences, in order to know how to combine them in a useful way.

In recognition of this difficulty, centres of knowledge such as universities or research establishments are today encouraged to share their knowledge with entrepreneurs in ways that may produce innovative products or processes. This is often referred to as **knowledge transfer** in that research information or academic expertise is made available to an enterprise from a knowledge base such as a university or a public sector research organisation (PSRO). To facilitate this, many universities have developed processes and policies to discover, protect and exploit IP rights.[1] As a result universities have increasingly commercialised their IP through licensing, joint ventures and 'spin-out' companies.

KTPs

Knowledge Transfer Partnerships (KTPs) claims to be 'Europe's leading programme helping businesses to improve their competitiveness and productivity through the better use of technology and skills that reside within the UK knowledge base' (www.ktponline.org.uk). It is a partnership between an enterprise, a university and a graduate. The enterprise benefits from a qualified graduate working as part of the business for up to two years on a project that will have a strategic impact. They are supported by a team of professors, senior lecturers or researchers, who bring technical expertise, research and innovation to the company. The graduate (Associate) is employed by the university but spends the majority of their time working in the company.

For example, a KTP between Kingston University and the Workspace Group plc sought to reduce the carbon footprint of the properties in the Workspace portfolio As the leading provider of premises to small businesses in London, Workspace have over 4000 SME tenants who together could have a substantial environmental impact. The aim of the project was to reduce the amounts of water, energy and waste used in the properties, introducing facilities to encourage tenants to go greener and refurbishing properties in an environmentally friendly way. As a result of the programme Workspace was one of the highest-rated companies in the capital for its sustainability programmes.

Source: http://www.workspacegroup.co.uk/sustainability/

12.1.3 What is Intellectual Property?

The knowledge that arises in the development of an enterprise can form 'intellectual property' (IP) that can be protected through legal processes to become intellectual property rights (IPR). This includes ideas, inventions, designs, processes, know-how or skills that are particular to an enterprise and its owners. IP also extends to the names that are given to the business or individual products or services. Intellectual property allows people to own the work and innovations they create in the same way that they can own physical property (Blackburn, 2003).

'Property' in this sense means something which is capable of exclusive ownership, use and disposal. If a particular object such as a bicycle or a book is your property then you can use it, sell it or do with it what you wish within legal limits. This is an exclusive right so that you can prevent others borrowing or taking your property without your permission. Intellectual property works the same way. Aspects of your work such as your ideas, creations and designs are your property for you to use to the exclusion of others, providing you have taken the necessary steps to protect them (Pearson and Miller, 1990).

However, it should be noted that there is often a difference in the ownership of the intellectual property and the physical item that may contain it. You may claim a book as your property because you have purchased it, but the intellectual property it contains usually belongs to the author or the publisher in the form of copyright. This prevents you from copying the book and passing it on to others even though the book belongs to you.

Intellectual property rights are not absolute. There are limits including:

- Time – patents are usually granted for 20 years and copyright in Europe lasts for the lifetime of the author plus 70 years.

- Public good – basic scientific inventions and methods for treating disease cannot be protected.

- Common names – generic names for objects (e.g. bicycles) cannot be claimed as protectable trademarks.

The ownership and rights to protect intellectual property are sometimes awarded automatically without any registration or application as soon as there is a record of what has been created (e.g. copyright). In other cases, intellectual property is not an automatic right and cannot be protected unless it has been applied for and granted (e.g. patents and trade marks).

The main ways of creating and protecting intellectual property are through:

- *Confidentiality* imposed on secrets and commercial and technical know-how.

- *Patents* for new and improved products and processes that are capable of industrial application.

- *Copyright* for material such as books, music, films, sound recordings and broadcasts, including software.

12

■ *Designs* that specify the appearance of a product, such as its shape, texture or ornamentation.

■ *Trade marks* that identify a product or service as a brand that can be differentiated from other offerings.

Each of these will be explored in the following sections.

12.2 CONFIDENTIALITY AND KNOW-HOW

Most businesses contain confidential information about what they do that would be extremely useful to competitive organisations. This may be a 'secret' (such as a food or drink recipe), or it may be commercial information (such as a list of customers and their rates of purchase). This is sometimes referred to as **know-how** – closely held information in the form of unpatented inventions, formulae, designs, drawings, procedures and methods, which together with the accumulated skills and experience of the owners of this know-how give potential value to an enterprise.

Australian sports know-how

Why do some countries do better than others at the Olympic games? Obviously size of population has something to do with it, with larger countries like the US, China and Russia all doing well in recent Games. But Australia has always been amongst the top medal winners despite a substantially smaller population than many competitors. One of the reasons is know-how. In many sports, only hundredths of seconds separate gold from fourth place and sports science know-how can provide that winning edge. It can help athletes to ensure their performance peaks at the right time. It can improve rest and recovery, and inform new hydration and cooling measures, important in hotter climates such as Beijing. The use of high-tech performance analysis systems to perfect the starts and turns in swimming relays is a good example of sport know-how. The Australian Institute of Sport (AIS) is widely acknowledged as a world best practice model for elite athlete development with world class facilities and support services. It has an Applied Research Centre to find new know-how across all the areas in sports science and medicine.

It would of course like to keep these developments to itself but other countries notably Britain have substantially increased their expenditure on the Olympics, 'buying' some of the coaches and their secrets from around the world. In contrast, South Africa with a strong tradition in many sports only managed one medal in Beijing but only spent a fraction as much as Australia and Britain on buying coaching know-how and preparation.

TABLE 12-1 Medal table for the last three Olympics

No of medals	Sydney	Athens	Beijing
AUSTRALIA	58	49	46
BRITAIN	28	30	47
CANADA	14	12	18
NEW ZEALAND	4	5	9
SOUTH AFRICA	5	6	1

The laws of confidentiality give some protection to the owners of know-how and confidential information against its misuse by others. There are limitations, however, as the control of information is a sensitive area. In practice, an individual has to acknowledge the obligation to keep something secret or confidential for this protection to work. This is commonly done in contracts of employment which stipulate the confidentiality requirements of an enterprise on its employees. In other cases, information is only revealed to someone once they have signed an agreement to keep the information confidential. These are commonly called **Confidential Disclosure Agreements (CDAs)** or **Non-Disclosure Agreements (NDAs).**

In summary, in order to obtain protection under laws of confidentiality it is normally necessary to have information which is:

- identified as confidential;

- not publicly known; and

- subject to an obligation on someone to keep it confidential.

British medal success in Beijing, 2008

This means that to enforce confidentiality it is wise to keep written records of what has been disclosed to whom and when, and if necessary sign CDAs or NDAs with the other party. Laws of confidentiality vary from country to country and unlike other forms of intellectual property there are no international conventions to simplify or harmonise them.

Top secrets

The formulae of some food and drink products are so secret that the companies go to extraordinary lengths to protect them. Although Coca-Cola is drunk daily by literally billions of people, only 3 or 4 company executives know how it is made. The formula contains 17 or 18 mostly common ingredients and it is kept locked in a secret bank vault. Similarly, the formula for KFC's chicken is closely guarded, known by only a handful of people who are contractually obliged to strict confidentiality. To ensure it stays that way the secret blend of eleven herbs and spices is mixed at two separate places and then combined in a third location.

12

12.3   PATENTS

12.3.1 What is a Patent?

During the early research and development phase of an invention it is possible to keep it secret provided that reasonable confidentiality precautions are taken as described above. But what about later stages when a new product or service is ready for launch into the marketplace? In a small number of cases the commercial secret can remain undetected by others (for example in the case of the recipe for Coca-Cola described above). However, in most cases it will be possible for others to copy the invention as the laws of confidentiality will not apply once the invention is in the public domain. Patents were introduced to provide protection in this situation.

A patent is 'a deal between an inventor and the state in which the inventor is allowed a short term monopoly in return for allowing the invention to be made public' (Intellectual Property Office[2]). A patent gives temporary protection to a new idea provided that it is accepted as superior to what went before and it has a useful, practical application. A patent is a monopoly right as it gives the inventor the power to prevent anyone else from making or selling their invention without a licence for a defined period of time, usually 20 years.

Crazy Patents Some registered patents contain inventions which are highly creative but which may seem wildly impracticable to many. For example in 1986 a US patent was granted to Anguita Waldemar for a greenhouse helmet which consists of a dome containing plants that fits over a person's head so that they can breathe the oxygen from the plants.

12.3.2 The Criteria for Obtaining a Patent

In order to be considered for a patent, ideas and inventions have to conform to the following criteria:

- *The invention must contain something that it is new and not already known about.* Prior to the filing of the patent, there can be no information about it available to the public anywhere in the world, even if it is from the inventors themselves. Making an idea public includes using, demonstrating or verbally describing it to others as well as publication through traditional methods such as journals and papers. To safeguard against prior knowledge of an idea, inventors need to ensure that anyone told about or shown an invention should sign an NDA (non-disclosure agreement) that ensures that the demonstration does not constitute a public disclosure.

- *The idea must involve an 'inventive step'.* As well as being new, the invention must represent a development that would not be obvious to anyone with a good knowledge of the relevant technology. If it is obvious, it cannot be said to be inventive or amount to a conceptual advance. It has to represent a genuine improvement or breakthrough rather than an obvious modification to existing products or processes.

- *The invention must be capable of an industrial or commercial application.* The idea has to have the potential to be made or used in some kind of industry in the practical form of a device, product, material, process or method of operation, whether for individual or social gain.

- *The invention must not be within an excluded area.* Under most jurisdictions, these include methods of medical treatment, scientific theory, mathematical methods, literary, artistic or aesthetic creations, methods for doing business or playing a game, the presentation of information and computer programmes.

Under the general categories of these exclusions, there may still be ways of creating valid patents. For example, a practical application of a new scientific theory can be patented, although the theory cannot be considered. New drugs are patentable as new 'methods of medical treatment' are limited to surgery and therapy. Although the rules of a new game cannot be patented, any new items involved in playing it can be protected.

> **Brazil bypasses patent on AIDS drug**
>
> Although there are now international agreements on patent protection, health-related IP still causes controversy. For example, in 2007, the President of Brazil authorised his country to break the patent on Efavirenz, an AIDS drug made by Merck & Co. This was done in order to acquire cheaper drugs for its AIDS prevention programme, a step also recently taken by Thailand. Under World Trade Organisation rules, countries can issue a 'compulsory licence' to manufacture or buy

generic versions of patented drugs deemed critical to public health. Talks with Merck broke down over the price of the drug when Brazil's health ministry rejected the company's offer to cut its $1.59 per pill price by 30 per cent. Brazil wanted to pay $0.65 per pill – what Merck charges Thailand. Drug makers often reduce prices to keep countries as clients and avoid compulsory licensing but Merck claimed most middle-income countries like Brazil paid $1.80 per pill. Merck also claimed that the decision would stifle research.

Brazil plans to import a generic version of Efavirenz from India, paying about 45 cents per pill, and may also start making its own copy of the drug. The government provides free universal access to AIDS drugs and distributes condoms and syringes free, a prevention programme that has helped Brazil slow infection rates to about 0.6 per cent of adults – similar to the United States. Importing the generic drug from India will save $237 million by 2012.

Source: Reuters, May 2007 (http://www.alertnet.org/thenews/newsdesk/N04351721.htm)

12.3.3 How to Obtain a Patent

In most countries, there are two main stages in the patent application process:

1 *The inventor files an initial patent application at the Patent Office or equivalent institution in the country in which they are resident.*[3] This first step is important as it is usually the first person to apply who will own the patent, even in other countries. The *'priority date'* of a patent is the date on which the very first application is made anywhere in the world. Even if the applicant applies for a patent in only one country at this time, the priority date is applied to subsequent applications in other countries,[4] effectively backdating those applications to the very first date the patent is applied for. This right does not last forever as international applications must normally be made within 12 months of the priority date.

Note also that the inventor normally has to make the first application to the patent office in their country of residence. In fact it is a criminal offence under the Patent Act 1977[5] for any one resident in the UK to make an application for a patent outside the UK without first having applied to the UK Patent Office. The reason for this is to maintain control over patent applications which could be prejudicial to national defence (Pearson and Miller, 1990: 60).

The term 'patent pending' can be used in relation to the invention once this initial application is filed. Inventors can now disclose their inventions publicly as from the priority date they have precedence over subsequent patent applications for similar inventions. They are free to explore the commercial potential and viability of the invention, before going to the time and expense of the full application.

2 *The inventor must begin a full application normally within 12 months or the application lapses.* This involves a full description of the invention, and a set of 'claims' to define the scope of the protection, followed by a patent search and detailed examination of the invention by the relevant patent authority. This often involves considerable costs: patent office fees and advice from an agent could be well over £1000 per application in the UK. It also takes time: the whole process takes around two and a half years or more in the UK, unless you chose the 'fast track' method which can reduce the process to less than 18 months.[6]

12.3.4 The Benefits and Pitfalls of Patents

Patents can add considerable value to a business as they offer the following benefits:

■ Protected by a patent, inventors can freely discuss their inventions with others with a view to setting up a business or some other form of commercial exploitation.

Howard Head's two big hits

When Howard Head tried out skiing, he found it a difficult sport and blamed the heavy wooden skis that were used at that time. As an aeronautical engineer who was designing airplanes, he was aware of new, lighter metals with properties that could make skiing a lot easier for novices like him. He began work on a metal ski, quitting his job and surviving financially by playing poker. Over several years he developed a new type of ski using honeycombed metal that revolutionised the industry. He later added rubber to absorb the vibrations caused by downhill skiing. Although he took out patents for his inventions, Head found that this did not prevent numerous competitors and imitators entering the market. However, the Head name became the leading brand and it was this and endorsement by skiers such as French world champion Jean Claude Killy that made the company successful.

He sold the Head Ski Company in 1971 and turned his attention to tennis. Once again, he was not a natural at this sport and blamed the rackets as difficult to use. He believed the 'sweet spot' – the area of the racket where the ball is hit most efficiently – was too small. As Chairman of the Prince Tennis Racquets company, he patented an oversized metal racquet, with over four times the total hitting area of a conventional racquet, and a sweet spot that was twice as big. Learning from his ski products, he secured patents on numerous oversized racquets designs, extracting royalties from many rival tennis manufacturers who wished to enter the expanding oversized racquet market.

- Patents give protection from competitors for up to 20 years. The existence of a patent is often enough to stop others from copying it.
- Patents have commercial value as they can be:
  - sold as a package including the invention
  - licensed to others in return for payment whilst the IP is retained by the inventor.

There are potential pitfalls surrounding patents that need careful consideration before the process of application is undertaken, including:

- Costs involved can be substantial, not just in the application process but also in maintaining patents as there are ongoing annual fees.
- Patents have to be defended against infringement which can be a costly and time-consuming process. Once a potential infringement is identified, a legal opinion is normally required to validate the infringement. Actions taken can be expensive if the infringement is disputed although costs may be recovered if the legal action is successful.
- A patent gives the owner the right to manufacture or sell only within a national territory. There are some international treaties such as the European Patent Convention (EPC)[7] and the Patent Cooperation Treaty (PCT),[8] which simplify the procedure for getting a patent in more than one country. But there is still no single European-wide or worldwide patent. As infringement is increasingly a global issue for many patents, this is a clear weakness in the system.

12.4 COPYRIGHT AND DESIGN RIGHT

Innovative ideas are not limited to physical products and tangible inventions. Many involve music, works of art and literature, fictional characters, films and computer software. These too can be protected from copying by others but not necessarily through the patent system. Similarly the form or appearance of a

12

product may contribute to its uniqueness and potential value so it is also important to be able to protect the design of objects and items. Protection in this area of the form and appearance of innovative ideas is covered by the laws of copyright and design right, two complementary and sometimes overlapping forms of intellectual property.

12.4.1 Copyright

Copyright recognises particular creative types of intellectual property and gives the authors exclusive rights over how they can be used, published, sold, distributed or altered. In short, copyright allows authors to profit from their creations and to control their use (Pearson and Miller, 1990). Thus it offers two types of protection:

■ Authors have financial rights over the copying or use of their material;

■ They also have 'moral rights' to be identified as the creator and they can object if it is distorted or changed in a detrimental way.

With the rapid growth of the creative industries in many economies, copyright has become an important business consideration for those enterprises operating in the creative economy. As many such enterprises operate globally, copyright has been increasingly standardised internationally through acceptance of the Berne Convention for the protection of Literary and Artistic Works.[9]

There are two particularly important considerations in the use of copyright:

1 *Copyright applies automatically to original works.*
    Unlike patents, you do not need to apply or register for copyright. However it is usually denoted by the international copyright symbol © followed by the name of the copyright owner and year of publication. Although this is not a requirement to obtain copyright, it is useful in warning others not to copy and as evidence in any infringement proceedings. In the case of a dispute, it may be necessary to prove authorship and the date of origination. Ways of doing this include: deposit a copy with a bank or solicitor; send a copy to yourself by a method that clearly dates the delivery, e.g. registered post.

2 *Copyright is limited by time.*
    Copyright does not last forever, but it does last longer than patents. Depending on the country of origin and type of work, it lasts between 50 and 100 years from the death of the author. In the European Union and the US it is 70 years.

12

What is Covered? Copyright protects an original artistic or literary work, according to the Berne Convention. This can cover almost any creative production including books, articles, plays, paintings, photographs, music, films, sound broadcasts and cable programmes. It also covers computer programmes, although there is some lack of clarity around this as it is an emerging field of interpretation. Protection covers most media in which materials can be published, including the Internet.

What is Not Covered? Although copyright protects original works of various types, it does not protect the idea behind it. Nor does it protect names or titles which are better protected as trademarks. The logo of a business or product name may be protected under copyright as an artistic creation, so it is possible that trade marks may also be covered by copyright.

> ### The trials of Procol Harem
>
> 'A Whiter Shade of Pale', the debut single of the band Procol Harem, became an international hit in 1967. But court proceedings to clarify ownership of the copyright to the music were finalised over 40 years later. The song was written by lead singer Gary Brooker who at first enjoyed full royalty rights until 2006. Then the band's organist Matthew Fisher claimed he had written the distinctive keyboard organ melody that introduces the song. He was awarded 40 per cent of the royalties but this was overturned on appeal in 2008. The Court of Appeal agreed that Fisher had contributed the organ theme but ruled that he should receive no money from past or future royalties as the judge said he was 'guilty of excessive and inexcusable delay in his claim to assert joint title to a joint interest in the work'.
>
> *Source:* Adapted from BBC News, 2008

12.4.2 Design Right

The design of a product or an article for sale can be an important asset to a business and may be synonymous with its image. If a particular design is recorded in a document, then that document can be protected by copyright so that it cannot be copied or sold to others without the author's permission. But copyright law does not stop someone from making a product using the design specified in the document in most cases.[10] The concept of 'design right' was introduced to provide such protection. As long as the design is original and not commonplace, design right protects the design of the:

■ shape and configuration of an article – internal or external, usually three not two-dimensional aspects;

■ the whole or any part of an article, other than surface decoration.

'Design' in this context refers to the appearance of a product – especially its shape, colours, texture or materials. Like other intellectual property, design right can be sold or licensed to third parties.

Like copyright, design right is an automatic right. However, designs can also be registered to formalise the protection.

Design registration gives the owner the right for a limited period to prevent a product to which the design has been applied, being sold without permission. You need to register a design with the appropriate body, usually the national patent office. In the UK it also gives more protection than unregistered design right; for example, it extends to two-dimensional as well as three-dimensional designs. It lasts for different periods according to country. From 2002/3 it became possible to secure European-wide design protection through the European Community Designs Regulations which established a Registered Community Design (RCD).[11] The scope and longevity of the European and UK design rights are summarised in Table 12-2.

12.5 TRADE MARKS AND BRANDS

In many cases, the intellectual property of an enterprise is encapsulated in a well-known word or two – the name or brand of the company or product. The name of a product, and symbols associated with it, can be more significant in determining customer choice than what goes into the product itself. Coca-Cola's secret formula would be worthless if we did not recognise the name and associate it with the

TABLE 12-2	Design rights in Europe			
	What does it protect?	**When does the right arise?**	**Is it a monopoly right?**	**How long does it last?**
UK Registered Design	Protects 2-D and 3-D designs across all sectors. Protects the appearance of the whole or part of a product resulting from features of, in particular, the lines, contours, colours, shape, texture, materials, of the product or its ornamentation (includes 'surface decoration'). There is no longer a need to limit a design to a specific product or article, so would protect things like typefaces and designs for cars.	On registration (application must be made within 12 months of first being made available to the public).	Yes – it protects the use of third party designs created entirely independently.	Initial 5 year term is renewable every 5 years, up to a maximum of 25 years.
UK Unregistered Design	Protects any aspect of the shape or configuration of a purely functional product. Applies to the whole or part of the product, and applies whether the aspect is visible from the outside, or is an internal component.	Automatically on creation.	No – it only protects against direct copying.	Either 10 or 15 years, depending on when the product is first made available for sale or hire.
Community Registered Design	Broadly the same as UK Registered Design, but extends across entire European Union.	On registration (application must be made within 12 months of first being made available to the public).	Yes – it protects the use of third party designs created entirely independently.	Initial 5 year term is renewable every 5 years, up to a maximum of 25 years.
Community Unregistered Design	The same as Community Registered Design.	Automatically when product first made available to the public.	No – it only protects against direct copying.	Maximum of 3 years.

Source: Pinsent Masons: http://www.out-law.com/page-7088; and OHIM (http://oami.europa.eu/ows/rw/pages/RCD/communityDesign.en.do)

12

WHEN THINGS GO WRONG

Laundry balls

Enforcement of design right has become increasingly important as the creative economy grows. Many infringements cross national borders which led to the establishment of a European office (OHIM) to regulate design affairs within the European Community. This has resulted in many cases. For example, Karen Miller the fashion chain successfully prevented Dunnes Stores in Ireland from selling a black knit top, a blue striped shirt and a brown striped shirt which they claimed copied their designs (Karen Millen Ltd vs. Dunnes Stores & Anor., Dec. 2007: http://oami. europa.eu/pdf/design/cdcourts/Ireland.pdf).

Other examples take on a more comic note including the case of Green Lane Products Ltd who make 'Dryerballs', spiky plastic balls for use in tumble driers which apparently help soften fabrics and reduce drying time by lifting and separating the laundry as it tumbles. Green Lane registered the design of its Dryerballs as Community Registered Designs (CRDs). They claimed infringement against PMS International Group Ltd who market spiky plastic balls which were originally sold as massage balls, not as laundry balls. In 2006, PMS decided to sell its balls (of exactly the same design as its massage balls) for other purposes too. One of these purposes is as a laundry ball, but other packages are marked 'Massage, Hand Exerciser, Easy-Catch Toy, Dog Trainer'. 'Green Lane claimed PMS infringed its CRDs if they continued to sell their product for anything other than use as a massage ball. PMS said the CRDs are invalid by reason of their prior sale of their massage balls. The judge threw out the case likening the facts to a 'student moot'.

Source: http://www.bailii.org/ew/cases/EWCAQ/Civ?2008/358.html

taste of those confidential ingredients. Thus the name or *brand* of a business is a crucial commercial decision as it is important to choose a name that is memorable and tells potential customers what is on offer. It is also crucial for legal reasons as it is important to protect the name once it becomes established in the marketplace.

Products have been branded from the earliest days. Ancient potters put a mark on their wares to denote the place of origin and the term 'brand' originates from burning a mark onto an animal to establish ownership. The rapid increase in economic activity in the nineteenth and twentieth centuries was accompanied by the rapid development of branded products. Many of the brands developed in those early years still predominate in their markets today. Kodak film, Wrigley chewing gum, Gillette razors, Coca-Cola, Campbell's soup, Goodyear tyres, Guinness ale and Burberry coats all became established brands in the late nineteenth or early twentieth century.

12.5.1 Trade Marks, Business and Domain Names

Although the choice of name should be based primarily on commercial grounds, there are legal restrictions to prevent others adopting a name that is already in use.

Trade Marks   A trade mark is a sign or a distinctive mark associated with a product or service. This might be words, logos, colours, slogans, three-dimensional shapes and sometimes even sounds and gestures. It tells the customer that this product or service comes from a particular source.

Trade marks have to be registered and for this they need to be represented graphically in words and/ or pictures. If you wish to protect your mark in particular individual countries, you should apply to the Intellectual Property Office for that country.

The 'Community Trade Mark' (CTM) was introduced in 1996 to cover the whole of the European Union and is valid in all member states. It is available through the Office for Harmonisation in the Internal Market (www.oami.eu.it).

Imitation of registered trade marks is a criminal offence. Even where names are not registered, attempts to pass off other goods for the real thing are also illegal.

Company Names   The name of a limited company can be registered provided it is not identical to an existing company, nor can it be considered offensive or illegal. In the UK certain words, about 80 in total, such as Royal, Windsor, National, British, University, Chemist, Trust, can only be used with the approval of the Secretary of State.[12] Sole traders and partnerships can use their own names without consent. If they choose, however, to operate under a name other than their own, they are legally required to disclose their names on business letters, invoices, receipts and other stationery.

Domain Names   A domain name, or website address, has become an important asset to a business. A domain name identifies a business on the Internet, and allows potential customers to find it by entering the name into the browser address box or through a search engine such as Google. Most countries now maintain a registry of domain names.[13]

12.5.2 **Branding Strategies**

A *brand* is a combination of name, symbol and design that clearly identifies one product from another. The *brand name* is the word(s) used to distinguish the brand (Mars Bar, Kellogg's, Rolls-Royce, Apple Macintosh). The *brand mark* or *logo* is a distinctive symbol or form of lettering which is always associated with the brand (the red lettering of Mars, Kellogg's K, the RR of Rolls Royce, and Macintosh's multi-coloured apple with a bite out of it).

If in doubt about which particular product to purchase, customers tend to choose established brands before unknown ones. The sale of products at low cost on the Internet was initially seen as a threat to the domination of branded goods. But e-commerce still has unknowns, especially in the areas of payment and quality, and in many cases, consumers have opted for what they already know – the established brands.

As an enterprise develops, the entrepreneur is often faced with a key decision in the development of a branding strategy. Should the same name be used for all products or should products be individually branded and left to develop their individual following? Both strategies are possible.

'Umbrella' Branding   Umbrella branding makes the maximum use of a well-established brand name by using it on all the organisation's products. This strategy has two main variants:

■ Use of the company name on all products, often with more descriptive, individual product names. For example, Kellogg's have kept the name of their founder Will Kellogg on all of their products – Kellogg's Frosties, Kellogg's Rice Crispies and Kellogg's Fruit 'n' Fibre. This has the advantage of a simple focused approach and maximises the use of the brand.

■ Use of one brand name for all products or a group of products which is different from the company name. For example, Marks and Spencer used the St. Michael label for their own products.

12

When is a Virgin not a Virgin?

'Virgin' has become one of the best known entrepreneurial brand names. Richard Branson used it for his first company that sold music by mail order in the 1970s because he and his partners were 'virgins in business'. Now the Virgin Group Ltd is a venture capital organisation that has created more than 200 branded companies with diverse products and worldwide coverage including health clubs (Virgin Active South Africa), space flights (Virgin Galactic), music festivals (Virgin Festival Canada), home loans (Virgin Money Australia), Media (Virgin Radio India) and shopping (Virgin Megastore USA). It also includes social enterprises such as Virgin Earth which is offering a prize of $25 million for a commercially viable design which removes greenhouse gases 'so as to contribute materially to the stability of the earth's climate'.

But Branson did once drop his famous brand name. In 1987 he decided to promote condoms to young adults at low prices as part of an HIV and AIDS awareness campaign. The Virgin brand did not seem appropriate so he used the name 'Mates' instead.

'Portfolio' of Brands   Some organisations are involved in diverse markets that require different brand names. For example, Reckitt Benckiser (formerly Reckitt and Coleman) market a wide variety of household products under many individual brands, many of which have their own variants. They range from health products such as Lemsip and Disprin to cleaning products such as Vanish, Mr. Sheen and Dettol. It would be difficult to see how their products – as diverse as Coleman's mustard and Harpic toilet cleaner – could be marketed under the same brand.

12.6   SUMMARY AND ACTIVITIES

Knowledge creation – The entrepreneurship process is concerned with the development of new forms of knowledge that flow from creative ideas and innovations. This creative process usually combines different types of knowledge from various sources to form 'new knowledge' or an innovation that represents something of value that was not known about before, even though the component parts were.

Formalised **knowledge transfer** is sometimes used in this process in that research information or academic expertise is made available to an enterprise from a knowledge base such as a university or a research organisation.

Intellectual property knowledge that arises in the development of an enterprise can form **'intellectual property' (IP)** that can be protected through legal processes to become **intellectual property rights (IPR)**. This includes ideas, inventions, designs, processes, know-how and the names that are given to the business or individual products. Intellectual property allows people to own the work and innovations they create in the same way that they can own physical property. There are several different forms of IPR.

Know-how is closely held information in the form of unpatented inventions, formulae, designs, drawings, procedures and methods, which give potential value to an enterprise. This can be protected by the laws of confidentiality but individuals need to be told of the need to keep something confidential, for example by a contract of employment or a **Confidential Disclosure Agreement (CDA)** or **Non-Disclosure Agreement (NDA)**.

A **patent** is 'a deal between an inventor and the state in which the inventor is allowed a short term monopoly in return for allowing the invention to be made public' (Intellectual Property Office). It is a monopoly right as it gives the inventor the power to prevent anyone else from making or selling their invention without a licence for a defined period of time, usually 20 years. A patent will be awarded only if the invention:

■ contains something that it is new and not already known about;

■ involves an 'inventive step' and is not obvious;

■ has a practical application;

■ is not in an excluded area such as medical treatment, mathematical theory and methods of doing business or playing games.

Patents offer the **benefits** to an inventor of: freedom to discuss their inventions with others; protection from competitors for up to 20 years; commercial value as they can be sold or licensed to others.

Problems around patenting include: costs of applying for and maintaining patents; time-consuming and costly defence against infringement; protection is only within a national territory as there is no single European-wide or worldwide patent.

Copyright protects an original artistic or literary work including books, articles, plays, paintings, photographs, music, films, sound broadcasts, cable programmes and computer software. It is an automatic right for the lifetime of the author plus 50 to 100 years. It gives authors financial rights and control over how the works are used.

Design right protects the shape, colour, texture or materials of an article. It is an automatic right but design registration offers more protection. It last from 3 to 25 years.

A trade mark is a sign or a distinctive mark associated with a product or service – words, logos, colours, slogans, three-dimensional shapes, even sounds and gestures. They have to be registered by applying to the Intellectual Property Office of each country. The **'Community Trade Mark'** (CTM) covers all of the European Union.

A brand is a combination of name, symbol and design that clearly identifies one product from another. When in doubt customers tend to opt for established brands.

REVIEW QUESTIONS

1 How is 'new knowledge' usually formed?

2 What is 'intellectual property'?

3 Name four types of intellectual property rights.

4 What is 'know-how' and how can it be protected?

5 What is a patent and how long does it normally last?

6 Name four important criteria for the granting of a patent.

7 What is copyright? How can it be obtained?

8 What is design right? How can it be obtained?

9 What is a trade mark? How can it be obtained?

10 Describe two different types of branding strategies that an enterprise can adopt.

12

SEMINAR TASK

Inspired by the cartoonist, the Rube Goldberg Contest challenges college students in the US to design a machine that uses the most complex process to complete a simple task (e.g. put a stamp on an envelope, screw in a light bulb, make a cup of coffee) in 20 or more steps. (See the website http://news.uns.purdue.edu/UNS/rube/rube.index.html for details of past competitions and winners.)

Try your hand at this inventive process by sketching a design to complete the following task in more than 20 steps: *squeeze the juice from an orange and then pour the juice into a glass.*

When you have completed your design, decide which intellectual property rights could apply to your work.

Preview case study continued

Inventing a revolutionary system of power and transport

When we think of the 'railway' today, we have in mind trains, carriages and trucks that run on rails. This particular form of transport in fact evolved from three separate discoveries in different areas of knowledge: the wheel, the rail and power. The wheel has been used by man to assist in transporting goods and people for many thousands of years. Wheels running on rails can do more work and require less energy to move them than wheels running on ordinary ground. This secret may have been discovered by the Romans and was certainly known in medieval times. It was not exploited much, however, until the rapid increase in coal mining from the seventeenth century. Coal initially used the widespread network of water-ways on canals, rivers and seas, but, as the mines developed away from this network, coal had to be carried to the waterways in wagons. Horse-drawn wagon-ways using wooden tracks soon criss-crossed the land between collieries and water-ways. Thus by the end of the seventeenth century the wheel and the rail were widely used, but still only using the power of animals and humans.

The development of steam power was the next step that revolutionised this system. The name most widely associated with the develop-ment of the steam engine is James Watt, who is often cited as the inventor of the first steam-powered unit. But Watt only improved earlier steam engines and it has been argued that he actually stifled innovation because of the 25-year patent that he enjoyed for his own engine (Marsden, 2002: 2). One of the earliest machines was patented by Thomas Savery in 1698 with the intended application of pumping water from the tin and copper mines in Corn-wall, but although the machine did work it was never up to its intended job. He was granted a catch-all patent so that when steam power was finally harnessed to draw water from the mines by Thomas Newcomen, he had to go into partnership with Savery. Newcomen's first machine (called the so-called 'atmospheric engine' because it used a partial vacuum created by condensing steam) went to work in a coal mine in 1712, protected by patent until 1733. Although the Newcomen engine and derivatives became a relatively common sight in the coal mines of Europe, its application was limited as it used a lot of coal and was uneconomic for applications outside of the pits.

This is where James Watt came in. He developed a steam engine which was much more economical on coal through the use of a separate condensing unit. Watt teamed up with a Birmingham-based manufacturer Matthew Boulton and together they were granted a patent in 1775 that was to run until 1800. Boulton and Watt not only had an effective monopoly on early steam power but they also developed a business model that made the

12

▶

take-up of their equipment easier. Instead of selling a rather expensive machine, they created a form of lease in which the user paid them one-third of the savings in the cost of fuel that their engine produced over the earlier Newcomen machines. It proved a lucrative business especially in Cornwall where there was no cheap, local coal. It was also difficult to control especially when several local Cornish inventors claimed to have come up with more efficient engines that they were prevented from exploiting by the Boulton and Watt patent.

The most prolific and energetic of these was Richard Trevithick, a headstrong Cornishman who created many inventions. He developed engines that worked with high-pressure steam, rather than the low pressure of Boulton and Watt's engines, but their introduction was slow until the expiry of Watt's patents. Boulton and Watt's machines were big with large boilers to generate sufficient power from low-pressure steam. At first steam engines were used as stationary units positioned on top of a hill to winch wagons up and lower them down the other side. Trevithick's engines used 'strong steam' under higher pressure and thus enabled the development of much smaller, lighter units which could power themselves along. Watt criticised this development as dangerous, pouring scorn on the whole idea of 'propelling a carriage with an explosive kettle' (Weightman, 2007: 58). But this proved to be a vital breakthrough equivalent to the transformation in computer design when the original, large processors using valve technology were replaced with compact machines using microchips. The smaller steam engines did indeed have the capacity not only to pull other objects but also to power themselves along at the same time. It was Trevithick, not George Stephenson as many suppose, who created the first full-sized steam engine which could power itself along on rails – the breakthrough invention that was to revolutionise transport systems around the world.

Trevithick's first prototype had an eventful but short life. Although the engine worked well travelling up a steep hill in 1801, it tipped over on its next outing because of its rudimentary steering. Trevithick and his companions retired to a nearby inn to consider what to do next, forgetting to extinguish the fire in the boiler. When the water finally evaporated, the engine caught fire and the first locomotive was destroyed. Undeterred, Trevithick built other locomotives to run on rails, including one that he took to London where he demonstrated it on a circular track in 1808. Naming his attraction 'Catch me who can', he charged one shilling admission to the enclosure including a ride on the engine for anyone who dared. Unfortunately the wooden track was not strong enough for the engine and the demonstration was regarded as the work of an eccentric rather than the forerunner of a transport revolution. When his locomotive was not taken up quickly, Trevithick moved onto other things including a steam hammer and a barge with paddle wheels driven by steam. It was left to George Stephenson to take forward his locomotive invention and apply it, first to hauling coal from the mines and secondly carrying passengers as well as freight on the world's first public railway to use steam locomotives – the Stockton and Darlington Railway that opened in 1825.

Richard Trevithick, British inventor and mining engineer.

12

Questions

1 The first locomotive came from three separate discoveries in different areas of knowledge: the wheel, the rail and steam power. What types of discoveries in different areas of knowledge led to the following transport revolutions?
   a the automobile
   b the airplane
   c space travel.

2 Did patents help or hinder the development of the industrial revolution in the eighteenth and nineteenth centuries?

3 What other forms of intellectual property might apply today to these developments in steam power?

4 Why did Watt make a fortune on his patent of a steam engine whilst Trevithick died a pauper? Which of these two contributed more to the industrial revolution?

12.7 NOTES, REFERENCES AND FURTHER READING

Notes and Further Information

1. There are many organisations that support knowledge transfer including:
   - Association of University Transfer Managers (AUTM) in the USA (www.autm.net);
   - The Institute of Knowledge Transfer (IKT) in the UK (http://www.ikt.org.uk);
   - Association of European Science and Technology Transfer Professionals in Europe (www.astp.net), who have provided a conduit for knowledge transfer professionals across the public and private sectors to identify best practice and develop effective tools and techniques for the management of PSRO/college produced IP;
   - The Global Innovation Network, an online group for knowledge transfer practitioners (www.autm.net).

2. The Intellectual Property Office is an operating name of the UK Patent Office. Their website at www.ipo.gov.uk provides a valuable source of information on the criteria, benefits, costs and timeline on applying for a patent and other types of intellectual property. It also provides the facility for online applications.

3. Other national Patent Offices usually have good websites that offer information and advice on all aspects of intellectual property. For example:
   - Australia: IP Australia – http://www.ipaustralia.gov.au
   - Canada: CIPO – http://www.cipo.gc.ca
   - France: INPI – http://www.inpi.fr
   - Germany: DPMA – http://www.dpma.de/
   - Italy: UIBM – http://www.ipi.it
   - New Zealand: IPONZ – http://www.iponz.govt.nz
   - Sweden: PRV – http://www.prv.se
   - S. Africa: CIPRO – http://www.cipro.co.za.

4. Patents are normally granted on a national basis but there are international conventions that recognise the 'priority date' of applications for a year or sometimes more: the European Patent Convention (EPC) of 1973 that has led to the establishment of a European Community system for common patent applications; the Patent Cooperation Treaty (PCT) of 1970 which set up a system for international patent searches and evaluation before a patent is handled in the country of origin.

5. In the UK, the Patents Act 1977 is the main legislation currently covering patents. This superseded the Patents Act 1949, although many of the provisions are the same. The Copyright, Designs and Patents Act 1988 deals mainly with Copyright and Design Right.

6. The Intellectual Property Office provides a full list of possible fees chargeable in the UK including: processing fee £200; £30 preliminary examination; £100 per search; £70 per substantive examination (http://www.ipo.gov.uk/types/patent/p-applying/p-cost.htm, November, 2008). Patent agents and advisers normally provide a free initial consultation and estimate of future costs.

7. See note 2 above. The EPV led to the setting up of the European Patent Office (see www.epo.org) which does provide a uniform application procedure for patents applied for in the 38 European member states.

8. See note 4 above on the PCT. There is also the World Intellectual Property Organisation (WIPO) of the United Nations which promotes international protection of intellectual property (www.wipo.int).

9. The Berne Convention for the Protection of Literary and Artistic Works of 1886 first established the principle that copyright protection should be granted automatically and specifically forbids that a member country can require any formal application to acquire copyright. The US did not sign up to the Berne Convention until 1989, before which it operated a registration system. The Berne Convention also made copyright an international protection as it recognised the rights of authors in all the member states. There are now 164 countries signed up to the Convention.

10. Copyright does protect some designs. For example if the design is for something which itself is an artistic work then copyright applies. It also applies if the design is for a new typeface.

11. OHIM (the Office of Harmonisation of Internal Markets) is the official European Agency responsible for registering trade marks and designs in all countries of the EU. See their website: www.oami.eu.it.

12. A register of company names is kept at Companies House in the UK (www.companieshouse.gov.uk). Similar registers exist in other countries.

13. Nominet.UK (www.nic.uk) holds a database of domain registrations and provides neutral advice on registering and maintaining a name. Some sites carry international directories of domain registries (for example, www.norid.no/domreg.html).

References

Blackburn, R.A. (2003) *Intellectual Property and Innovation Management in Small Firms*, London: Routledge.

Botticelli, P. (1997) British capitalism and the three industrial revolutions, in McGraw, T. (ed) *Creating Modern Capitalism*, Cambridge, Mass.: Harvard University Press.

Intellectual Property Office, www.ipo.gov.uk.

Marsden, B. (2002) *Watt's Perfect Engine: Steam and the Age of Invention*, Icon Books UK.

Pearson, H. and Miller, C. (1990) *Commercial Exploitation of Intellectual Property*, London: Blackstone Press.

Weightman, G. (2007) *The Industrial Revolutionaries: The Creators of the Modern World 1776–1914*, London: Atlantic Books.

Recommended Further Reading

The Intellectual Property Office website in your country (e.g. IPO.org.uk for the UK Patent Office) (see note 3 above for a list). These are usually full of practical advice and information.

Bainbridge, D. (2008) *Intellectual Property*, London: Pearson Education (comprehensive textbook on intellectual property law from a UK perspective).

12

http://www.gadgets-gizmos-inventions.com. This is a great website that both informs and amuses about the world of inventions and intellectual property. It has a section on wacky inventions as well as more serious sections on patentability (from a US perspective).

Weightman, G. (2007) *The Industrial Revolutionaries: The Creators of the Modern World 1776–1914,* London: Atlantic Books. If the case study of the development of steam power fires your imagination, then read this excellent history of the many innovators who underpinned the industrial revolution. It is more appropriate to entrepreneurship than many industrial history texts as it describes the entrepreneurs behind the inventions.

12

CHAPTER 13

The Entrepreneurial Team

LEARNING OBJECTIVES

After studying this chapter, the reader will be able to:

- Understand the importance of teams to entrepreneurship
- Identify members of their own team, and understand their roles in helping them to develop their enterprises
- Evaluate some of the factors which require teams to change
- Analyse some of the characteristics of team members to take into consideration in developing a team.

INTRODUCTION

Publications about entrepreneurship often focus on the entrepreneur, as a lone individual who establishes an enterprise or enterprising project through their own creativity, determination and grit. This focus on individuals rather than teams is as common in the popular press as it is in the academic literature. The likes of Steve Jobs, Anita Roddick and Richard Branson who became famous because of their success have been acclaimed as celebrities. Although they have been extremely significant in the success of the organisations which they co-founded, each one has also been part of a high-performing team. Steve Jobs needed the support of Steve Wozniack and Mike Markkula; Anita Roddick partnered with her husband Gordon and a financial angel whose investment enabled Body Shop to grow; Richard Branson works with a close circle of relatives and friends, and places management teams in each of his new brand extensions.

PREVIEW CASE

TopUp TV

David Chance and Ian West worked together at BSkyB and spotted an opportunity to develop a new service. Together they set up TopUp TV, a pay-to-view service that piggy-backed on the main TV providers. Once they had established the service, they brought in a new management team to run the company, and moved on to new challenges.

Why did these two entrepreneurs decide not to manage the new venture they had set up? Have you ever played a role in starting something and then quickly moved on to something new?

Read more about David Chance and Ian West in the case study at the end of this chapter.

IMAGE COURTESY OF TOPUPTV.COM

The Body Shop – not just a famous face!

The Body Shop is an internationally known cosmetic company. It has retail outlets in many countries around the world, selling its own brand of cosmetics. It was founded by a husband and wife entrepreneurial team, Anita and Gordon Roddick. Although Anita until her death in 2007 was the spokesperson and face of the organisation, her husband Gordon was also central to the organisation. As Finance Director and co-chairman, he oversaw the financial development of the organisation, and was crucial to its successful development. A third member of the team was a business angel, who provided the company with the capital it needed at a very early stage, in exchange for a substantial shareholding in the company. The Roddicks have acknowledged the importance of his support from the earliest days of the company.

13

The narrative of the individual entrepreneur, often heroic in nature, is common, but flawed. It downplays the importance of supporters and teams, and is therefore an inaccurate representation of entrepreneurial activity. Fast-growth ventures are more likely to have been started by teams than solo entrepreneurs (Cooney, 2005; Timmons, 1994)[1] and many entrepreneurial projects are started by groups of two or more people working closely together for common goals.

In most enterprises, whether new or established, some form of group or teamwork is normal. Although individuals and their characteristics and behaviours are important, organisations are by their nature collections of people, and their outputs or results derive from the activities of many people working together. A key source of value in any organisation is the people – their knowledge, how they work together, their relationships with one another and with customers, partners and suppliers.

However, just as human interactions in general create challenges as well as opportunities, so do teams. Teams may be more or less successful in achieving their aims, and considerable research has gone into trying to understand what factors influence success or failure. The results of this research are mixed: there is no simple recipe for success, but researchers have identified various issues which are important to improving team performance.

The areas which researchers have investigated fall broadly into these key themes:

■ Dynamics of team development – as tasks and priorities change, new resources are needed and members develop their working relationships.

■ Composition of teams – who's in, who's out, and why?

■ Individual vs. team work – entrepreneurs have different orientations which affect how they behave in teams, and these may clash.

■ Improving teamwork – working in teams presents challenges but our teamwork can be improved.

13.1 TEAM DEFINITIONS

We tend to have a perception of what a team is, when we think of a sports team for instance, but it's worth considering what the difference is between a group of people who happen to be together, and what we would consider to be a team. People are put together in groups in many different contexts, for instance in focus groups, on a bus, in a seminar or workshop, or on a tour, but often they are not perceived to be a team.

One way of thinking about entrepreneurial teams is to consider teams in a different context. What are the characteristics of a winning or a losing sports team – football, or hockey for instance? Some considerations and characteristics that may be identified to be important include:

■ Key skills – e.g. ball or stick handling, running, tackling

■ Clear and effective playing in each position or role

■ Good strategy for particular games and opposing teams

■ Good coaching (skills and strategy development)

■ Good captaining (marshalling forces and motivation during the game)

■ Effective equipment

■ Effective working together to complete plays

■ Shared commitment to winning.

These considerations can be translated quite easily into the sphere of entrepreneurship and management in general. Teams in these contexts also need the right skills, clarity about roles, effective strategies, good coaching and leadership, the right equipment and a shared commitment to particular goals. Crucially, we can distinguish a team from a group of people who are brought together more randomly through their joint purpose, common direction and interdependence.

Teams in different contexts have different purposes. For instance, a venture capital investment team may have a specific remit to investigate the rate of return and undertake due diligence enquiries on any potential client company. An enterprise support team may have the purpose of identifying and helping young entrepreneurs start up in business. Entrepreneurial musicians may have the objective of developing a distinctive brand through their style of music.

Teams are both a collection of individuals, who bring particular skills, knowledge and contacts to the team, and a collective unit which operates more or less effectively together. The individuals are resources, as is the team itself. Social network theory (as discussed in Chapter 9, 'Entrepreneurial networking') notes that individuals and their connections create and find resources as well as representing a resource themselves. The entire unit is a resource which combines resources and delivers performance.

In searching for entrepreneurship, we have identified that it has a strong focus on seeking, evaluating and exploiting opportunities, often by creating an enterprise of some kind. Perhaps because of the focus on individuals rather than teams in both the popular press and the academic entrepreneurship literature, specific definitions of entrepreneurial teams are relatively undeveloped. Cooney (2005: 229) has offered this definition of an entrepreneurial team:

> 'two or more individuals who have a significant financial interest and participate actively in the development of the enterprise'.

Given the endless variety of organisations, people and situations which can be called entrepreneurial, Cooney emphasises the areas of flexibility built into this definition:

- The *number of team members* may be small or large.

- The size of the *financial interest* of the individuals is relative to the specific organisation, as some organisations are started on a shoe-string, others with substantial cash injection.

- The *financial interest* may represent cash, labour or other types of in-kind investment.

- *Participation* implies the action orientation which is so important to entrepreneurial ventures, and which effectively excludes silent financial partners.

- *Development* reflects the changing nature of organisations as they grow or shrink, develop their products and services, hire or fire new people.

Although this definition is particularly focused on teams which are starting new enterprises, there are many other entrepreneurial contexts in which it might be applied. For example, innovation teams in established organisations often have a personal investment in their innovations, which pays off through bonuses or promotion. Elsewhere, creative collaborations such as musicians working in bands or ensembles work together to compose music, and this collaboration between specialists produces work which is often jointly owned: the Beatles' Lennon and McCartney are a famous example of a successful composition team, as are Lerner and Loewe, librettist and composer of *My Fair Lady*, *Gigi* and *Camelot* among other Broadway hits.

13.2   RESOURCES AND TEAMS

13.2.1   The Resource-Based View of Strategy

The resource-based view of organisations (Grant, 1991; Barney, 1991) argues that organisations are bundles of resources (human, financial or physical; tangible or intangible). These are combined in different ways to create the great diversity of enterprises which we can observe around us. The resource-based concept considers that a successful enterprise strategy involves competing for and winning resources and then developing and deploying them in unique ways. Following this model, the strategic choices open to entrepreneurs are therefore dependent on having or building new resources. Choices are constrained by the availability, quality or style of resources within the enterprise and its environment. They are also constrained by previous decisions to use and build resources into particular configurations. It can become difficult to reconfigure resources in order to change organisational direction.

Difficulties and opportunities in reconfiguring resources

British Telecom (BT) was the monopoly telecoms provider in the UK. With a few small exceptions, it owned the network of cables, wires, stations and sub-stations, it sold subscriptions to telephone services, and it also for many years sold the equipment which households and businesses needed to use the network (for instance switchboards, exchanges, telephones). When the telecoms industry was deregulated, allowing new competition to be introduced to the market, BT had substantial difficulties in learning to do new things. The networks were an enormous asset, but extremely difficult to modernise. Ownership of the wires meant that it had an enormous cadre of engineers whose role was to maintain these. Options to do new things were extremely limited, because of their existing resource configurations.

Entrepreneurs thrive on such situations, and many who entered the market after deregulation had neither large employee bases, nor physical networks; they had greater flexibility to install new technology, to outsource labour and to try different business models. For example, Denis O'Brien (who has been described as the Richard Branson of Ireland) founded Esat Telecom which was granted a telecommunications licence to use the existing Irish networks to become the first domestic competitor to T Eireann (now Eircom). His controversial use of 'autodiallers' to route calls onto his new network was upheld by the European regulators and he expanded the business into mobile phone and Internet applications. The enterprise was so successful that BT acquired it in 2000 for £1.5 billion. O'Brien now runs Digicel, a successful mobile phone business and has radio interests across Europe.

Earlier (in Chapter 10, 'Entrepreneurial decision-making and planning') the contrast between effectuation and planning approaches to decision-making was discussed (Sarasvathy, 2004). Entrepreneurs often start with a few resources, an idea and determination and gradually accrue and develop resources over time, designing an enterprise around what they have available and what they gradually leverage from the environment. Alternatively, they may start with goals and a view of the resources

> **Integrative Case Link**
> For more on team development and motivation, see the case of Gloria Serobe, Case 4 at the end of Part 2.

they require to achieve them, and specifically seek these resources in order to proceed. The resource-based view of enterprises underpins both of these approaches. The entrepreneurial team brings together a bundle of resources in a particular way to create something new. The team begins with resources which are mostly human – the founders, their knowledge and their networks – to explore and develop an idea or ideas. In order to compete and survive, they build enterprises which have unique assets, or which deploy resources in unique ways.

13.2.2 Team Members as Resources

Enterprises are started by individuals and teams whose key resources are often just themselves, their knowledge and skills. Establishing what resources are needed to get a venture going also means establishing who is needed on the venture team. Researchers have investigated what the characteristics of individuals within successful teams are, with inconclusive results. However, some interesting issues have emerged as significant: industry experience, work experience and experience of various functional backgrounds; size of team and time or experience together; social networks (Vyakarnam and Handelberg, 2005); demographic mix (Hambrick and Mason, 1984).

Experience and Knowledge As noted in Chapter 7,[2] 'The search for the entrepreneur', entrepreneurial learning is experiential, combining action, reflection, observation and the use of abstract theory. There is evidence that knowledge developed through these different types of learning is important to successful entrepreneurial teams. These include:

■ Marketing and technology: experience in these areas within the same industry (Cooper and Bruno, 1977)

■ General management: running a company or having general management experience within the same industry (Stuart and Abetti, 1986)

■ Varied functional experience (Timmons, 1994).

Although each of these may be important, some also argue that the team needs to be complete, which means that it needs to have members with experience of all of the functional areas, and with industry experience, in order to be successful (Timmons, 1994; Roure and Keeley, 1990).

Working in an entrepreneurial firm to develop experience

There are many schemes which encourage students and recent graduates to work in smaller firms. These have positive outcomes for both the enterprises and the individuals. For the enterprises, the recently acquired knowledge of the student or graduate can contribute to solving strategic problems or introducing new approaches and technologies. For the student or graduate, the exposure to the realities of working with a small firm is invaluable. The student sees at first hand the long hours that entrepreneurs put into their enterprises, and the motivation they have to continue. They also get experience in several different domains of management – for instance marketing, operations management, team building. This approach is thought to be so valuable that the European Union (EU) in 2009 introduced Erasmus for Entrepreneurs, a scheme for young entrepreneurs to work with established entrepreneurs in other European countries, again for exposure to the entrepreneurial process and mindset, and to build networks between young and more established enterprises.[3]

In some cases, knowledge can be purchased; in others, it is central to the enterprise development process itself. Many university spin-outs for example are formed around the advanced knowledge of a researcher or inventor who is indispensable to the enterprise. Although the intellectual property developed by the researcher may belong to the institution where it was developed, the knowledge of the intellectual context in which it was developed will be central to its development.

Size of Team and Time Together The effort of starting a new venture is taxing as there is both a large number of things to do, and a wide variety of different things required. Having more people on the team would seem to be an effective means of dealing with these issues, and is associated with faster growth (Eisenhardt and Schoonhoven, 1990). A larger team may bring in more and wider experience and ideas. However, larger teams create problems of their own, requiring more time to be spent on communication, and increasing the likelihood of conflict (Bales and Borgatta, 1966). A simple illustration (Figure 13-1) shows the difference in number of communications channels between a small and a larger team.

Ensuring that discussions explore the ideas of the entire team will be time-consuming because of the number of different channels. In addition, a more diverse group across different dimensions (for instance knowledge, motivation, beliefs, social background), will require more intense communication to achieve agreement.

It has also been suggested that the length of time which entrepreneurs have spent working together, either in previous ventures, or in the new venture, is significant (Eisenhardt and Schoonhoven, 1990). Familiarity through longer association leads to trust, shared values and therefore faster decision-making, which is important in rapidly changing markets (Eisenhardt, 1989). However, teams can also become set in their ways, blinkered, and reduce their innovative capacity when they have worked together for a long time (Katz, 1982).

FIGURE 13-1   Team size and communications complexity

Team of 3 – Team members A, B, and C each have 2 people to communicate with, making 3 communications channels.

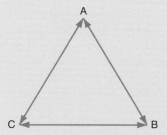

Team of 6 – A similar diagram shows the possible communications channels between a team of 6, whose members are known as A, B, C, D, E & F – a total of 15 different lines of communication.

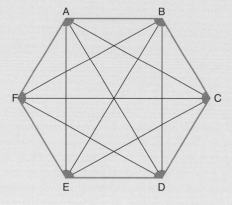

Social Networks   Finally, key entrepreneurial resources (as discussed in Chapter 9, 'Entrepreneurial networking') are the social and professional networks which individuals develop and invest in over time. These are resources in themselves, and a means of finding and bringing together resources. Individuals within a team bring their networks with them to their ventures, and this may enhance its value (Matlay and Westhead, 2005).

Demographic Diversity   Since the mid-1980s, many researchers have considered the composition of top management teams. This research was initiated by Hambrick and Mason (1984) who argued that if decision-making is a process, and process is affected by behavioural factors, then the behaviour of top managers is important to understanding the strategic decision-making process. This behaviour is at least in part derived from the characteristics of the individuals at the top of the enterprise. In keeping with the view that strategic decisions are made by the enterprise's most senior managers, many authors have explored the actions and composition of top managers and management teams, and the effects of these on strategic decisions (e.g. Vyakarnam and Handelberg, 2005). As the 'top managers' in entrepreneurial ventures are usually the entrepreneurs themselves, these concepts are relevant to the development of entrepreneurial teams.

Human diversity has many aspects including ethnic background, educational status, age, gender and social networks. Whilst teams may be considered to benefit from such diversity, research shows that team selection tends to favour *homogeneity*: we tend to build teams among people we know, to hire people who are rather like us and to limit our searches for people to the networks which are readily available to us. In common parlance, *birds of a feather flock together.*

13

ENTREPRENEURSHIP IN ACTION

Knomo Bags[4] – a developing team

The Knomo team has grown since the executive bags brand was started in 2004. The idea that a new style of bag was needed in the market came to Howard Harrison initially when he was on a business trip, and he found he didn't care for the latest ranges from existing firms. He started working from his bedroom, developed the brand name and found a designer to develop an initial range. Needing help with his first trade show, Harrison turned to an old friend, Benoit Ruscoe. The two had known one another at university in Durban, and both were living and working in London. They met another South African in London who was working for a Chinese leather factory, and his introduction to Chinese manufacturers got their sample production started. The addition of Alistair Hops, another university friend and finance specialist completed the initial team. The need to expand into the large US market meant finding team members who knew that market. They met, hired as a consultant and subsequently secured investment from Charlie Clifford, who had founded the TUMI leather goods brand. Working with this new partner presented the team with new challenges. The Americans had different views of the product and its likely impact in the United States. According to Harrison:

> 'We did a huge amount of homework before launching into the US . . . If we hadn't had Charlie involved, we would have probably done it much quicker, but then we also probably wouldn't have done it the right way.'

While this approach may have the benefit of seeming to be comfortable, it may also limit our ability to perform in a diverse and changing world. In general, theories about teams at work suggest that it is better for teams to have greater *heterogeneity* (i.e. that the members be different from one another across various dimensions), because this will tend to support the introduction of more points of view, greater searches for information and more extensive investigation of situations and possibilities (Amason, 1996).

In practice, research in this area which tries to link diversity with performance has provided equivocal results, with different studies showing positive and negative effects for both homogeneity and heterogeneity (for instance Smith *et al.*, 1994; Papadakis and Barwise, 1995; Miller, Burke and Glick; 1998; and Keck, 1997). Demographic diversity may be significant to particular teams in particular contexts. But they are not the only issue which influences team performance. Conclusions from these studies suggest that diversity of individual characteristics of members of the team may require a team building or team management process which enables them to integrate effectively.

An entrepreneurial team of academics

At Boise State University, a decision was made to establish a creative team to investigate starting a new Executive MBA programme. The Associate Dean created a team along the following criteria: 'four were chosen because of their diversity along a perceived creativity dimension, a shared lack of personal agendas, and their willingness to look at a program that would benefit the college and not necessarily their own disciplines. A fifth faculty member brought prior experience in delivering an EMBA program at another institution ... The faculty members were diverse in disciplines ... as well as in thinking patterns'.

Source: Napier *et al.*, 2009: 67

The research on team members and teams as resources provides a wide range of findings. These point to important issues, but do not provide a clear recipe for creating a team.

13

13.3 TASKS AND PRIORITIES: THE CHANGING NATURE OF THE WORK OF TEAMS

The evolutionary nature of entrepreneurial ventures as they change and develop over time has been conceptualised into life cycle stages, as discussed in Chapter 6.[5] Each stage represents a major shift in the typical objectives and activities undertaken by an entrepreneurial venture and models of this life cycle approach have become a standard way of understanding firm growth and management behaviour (Stokes and Wilson, 2006).

The needs of the organisation change through the different stages, in terms of knowledge, skills, access to finance, facilities and other resources. The tasks of developing a new product, testing it and protecting intellectual property associated with it are inherently different from the tasks of expanding into new markets, developing supply and distribution infrastructures and managing customer relationships (see Table 13-1).

TABLE 13-1	Typical stages of development, activities and resource needs	
Stage of development	**Key activities**	**Typical resource needs**
Concept / Test	■ Developing and protecting intellectual property ■ Market research and trials ■ Exploring business models ■ Building prototypes	■ Creativity and ideas ■ Flexibility ■ Understanding of business / industry ■ Networks ■ Intellectual property
Development and growth	■ Building market access and brand awareness ■ Building relationships with manufacturers and suppliers ■ Enhancing products and services ■ Managing customer relationships	■ Knowledge of customers and customer relationships ■ Routines and systems for managing activities ■ Money and financial expertise ■ Competitor knowledge
Maturity	■ Maintaining competitive position ■ Efficient management of resources ■ Shareholder management	■ Routines and systems for managing activities ■ Market and industry intelligence ■ Financial skills
Enterprise re-growth	■ Investigation of new products, markets, technologies, systems ■ Management of change and restructuring	■ Knowledge of products and markets ■ Creativity and ideas ■ Product and market development knowledge
Enterprise decline or closure	■ Efficient management of resources ■ Closure of particular operations and or markets ■ Re-orientation into most lucrative activities	■ Analytic financial skills ■ Knowledge of change management ■ Asset valuation skills

13

These different tasks or stages of development require different skills and knowledge of the entrepreneurial team. While an existing team may learn these, it is more likely that the team membership will need to change to address the new requirements, problems or opportunities that have arisen. In most cases, early phases of enterprise start-up require the team to grow – to bring in new knowledge and resources, and quite simply to do all the work that is required.

WHEN THINGS GO WRONG

Friends Reunited – a team too far?

Friends Reunited[6] is a social networking website which started from an idea in 1999. Julie Pankhurst was wondering what her old school friends were doing, and whether they, like her, were in the process of starting families. As there was no easy way to find old friends, the concept of an Internet membership organisation through which people could find one another was born. The first market was old friends from school, college or work.

Julie didn't have the IT skills to develop a suitable site, and after working on the idea for some time she eventually convinced her husband Steve and his associate Jason, who both worked in IT, to write the application in their spare time. Once the site was launched in July 2000, its popularity grew very quickly and within a year it had a million members. Julie, Steve, Jason and his wife Ann spent all their spare time looking after it. Further companion websites designed to bring like-minded people together for different reasons (for instance Genes Reunited) were added, and the business continued to grow very quickly for the next 18 months.

The founders wanted to spend more time with their families, and decided to rethink what would secure the profitable future of the site. They did not have the business and media experience to capitalise on this type of growth, nor the knowledge of financial and legal aspects of selling a business, which seemed a sensible goal. A management team was brought in with operational, marketing and financial experience, in exchange for equity in the business. This team was led by Michael Murphy, former Chief Operating Officer of the *Financial Times,* who had been looking for an entrepreneurial project to invest in which would use his experience and skills. This new expertise enabled the founders to back away from day-to-day management, while still maintaining a financial interest.

In 2005, the business was sold to ITV, a UK television broadcaster, for £120 million as part of its online and interactive business. The founders sold their share of the company, whilst the management team they had brought in remained in place on a three-year earn-out. In 2008, the management team withdrew, having successfully met their targets and a new team from ITV took over running the business.

However, since 2005 competitive social networks such as Facebook have developed their applications much more quickly than Friends, which has lost market share and income as a result. The onset of a severe global recession in 2008 hit advertising expenditure hard, and created difficulties for ITV in its core television business as well as in its online business. As a result, ITV has decided to sell Friends Reunited. Estimates vary, but it is thought that the business is likely to fetch less than £50 million if it is sold in 2009 as it is unclear who can now create further value from the concept.

13.4 DIFFERENT TEAM TYPES

13.4.1 Large Organisations and Innovation

As enterprises change and face new tasks as they develop, the requirements on teams are also likely to change. Even within an organisation which has a strong orientation towards learning and managing change, entrepreneurial teams may be hard pressed to keep pace. The specialisms which enterprises develop as they grow, and the structures they develop may inhibit intrapreneurial teams.

Larger or well-established organisations are often divided into either functionally specific areas (marketing, operations, finance) or into geographically specific areas (Europe, Middle East, Africa, Asia) or into product-specific areas. Such structural arrangements are appropriate means of organising expertise and activity. However, at the same time they may reduce or impede innovative activity because they stop people talking to one another, sharing information and insight, and challenging one another's thinking. It also impedes the creative bringing together of ideas into new constellations and arrangements (see Table 13-2).

As technologies and demographics change, the need to change the organisation of knowledge and activity may also change within an organisation. For most organisations, and larger ones in particular, such change is both time-consuming and difficult to achieve. One of the approaches which organisations adopt for achieving change is to turn to innovation teams.

13.4.2 Innovation Teams

Innovation is at the heart of much entrepreneurial activity (as discussed in Chapter 3, 'Entrepreneurship and innovation'). Large organisations need to innovate – develop new products and services, deliver them in new ways, find new markets – in order to survive and grow. They also need to find and implement innovative ways of reducing costs, reshaping their organisation to meet changing market needs, and providing improved solutions to manufacturing problems.

The pros and cons of the different ways of organising large firms, and the challenges of developing new ideas in a rapidly moving context has led some firms to find new ways to innovate, including the encouragement and establishment of formal and informal innovation teams. Cross-disciplinary problem-solving or innovation teams are also a means of addressing the challenge of change. Cross-disciplinary teams are particularly used in areas like product development, engineering and construction management. They bring together different professional and knowledge perspectives, approaches to problem-solving and experience to address particular identified problems.

More informally, some organisations have become known for creating opportunities for employees to mix and develop ideas in an *ad hoc* fashion. High-tech enterprises from California's Silicon Valley have become particularly known for this approach. Following in the footsteps of Google, the web-search organisation, which has particularly become known for this, they design their office space to be flexible and encourage interaction away from desks. Offices feature coffee rooms, cafeterias and meeting pods where employees are encouraged to network. Food and drink are free, and the design of the offices encourages people to move around in all directions, to meet new people, develop new teams and problem-solve together.

13

TABLE 13-2	Organisational structure themes, their pros and cons	
Structural theme	Possible pros	Possible cons
Functional	Strong professional orientation, based on knowledge of function: marketing, finance, sales	Producer orientation, lack of shared focus on either the customer and their needs, or the potential of technologies and ideas which cross functions
Geographic	Strong knowledge of particular geographic markets and their needs, particularly distribution channels	Lack of comparative needs analysis, lack of knowledge of market segments which transcend geographic boundaries
Product-based	Knowledge of particular products or services, and how to extend their functionality, style or attractiveness in other ways	Lack of awareness of the potential of packaging combinations, or new product development for different needs
Technology- or platform-based	Leverage of value from particular technologies or platforms by deploying them across products and markets	Over-commitment to platforms and technologies; lack of search for alternative approaches or ways of leveraging benefit from different platforms
Matrix-based	Brings together different sorts of expertise and activity from across the organisation to drive cross-functional working	Complex and potentially expensive to manage; individual functions or areas may still have different objectives and not derive benefit
Task-based	Organisations work on specific projects which typically have a fixed time horizon for delivery, and clear remit for what to do.	May not be able to integrate new approaches successfully, because the project teams work in isolation from one another, and the members disperse when the task is complete

13

Interdisciplinary problem: Presenting a palace display

Hampton Court Palace on the outskirts of London was once a home to royalty, but it is now a cultural centre and museum, its extensive landscaped grounds, architecture and collections exhibiting rich aspects of material design and production, and its educational programmes and curating providing insight into the past, present and possible futures of aspects of British culture. The palace's exhibitions have many different focuses, and different areas of the palace, which has nearly 1000 rooms, provide different insights and opportunities for visiting. One area, a series of apartments which were until recently lived in by elderly people who had retired in the service of the state (from the civil, diplomatic or armed services for instance), has been converted to provide exhibition space devoted to explaining these lives. This exhibition has not, however, been successful at attracting visitors. Its themes are not as high profile as the royal themes which are exhibited elsewhere in the palace, and the area itself is less accessible because of its location within the palace. In order to try to remedy the situation, the palace managers brought together a mixed team to address the problem, including marketing and operations managers, historians and designers. The team worked intensively over four days on the problem, considering it from different angles. Their diversity brought fresh insights into the problem, and resulted in a relaunch of the area with a new advertising campaign and approach to its presentation.

13.4.3 Virtual Teams

The advent of the Internet and its associated communications technologies has created the potential for virtual entrepreneurial teams to be formed (Isenberg, 2008). These teams are often international in scope, with members operating from bases in different countries, and in operation, with production and sales occurring in different places from their inception (Matlay and Westhead, 2005).

ENTREPRENEURSHIP IN ACTION

WildChina – a Chinese-American venture

WildChina is a travel company based in Beijing. It offers distinctive guided trips within China, promising superior access to locations and to expertise in the country. The company was established in 2000 by Mei Zhang, a Harvard MBA and native of Yunnan in China. She was inspired by a difficult trip that she had taken herself to a remote and beautiful spot in Tibet, and realised that a company providing support to adventurous travellers was needed. Three years after founding the company, she brought Jim Stent, an American with a love for Chinese culture and history, into her team. In 2004, Zhang moved to the United States, leaving her colleague in Beijing as Chief Executive. Zhang continued as chairperson of the company, despite operating from a different continent. The team has since expanded, drawing in local and international expertise, and continues to work over a geographically dispersed area.

Source: Isenberg, 2008; www.wildchina.com

13

TABLE 13-3	Advantages and disadvantages of virtual teams of e-entrepreneurs
Advantages	**Disadvantages**
Availability of quality data and information	Limitations in terms of ownership status
Reliability of 'information advantage'	Curtailment of individual business styles
Cost advantages in data testing and transmission	Restricted freedom of action
Pool of human, financial and knowledge resources	Complexity of cross-team interactions
Team-wide task-related support	Rigidity of virtual team structure
Continuous technical and linguistic support	Concentration of decision-making processes
Sustainable pan-European e-customer base	Extended working hours
Multinational niche market benefits	Lack of conflict resolution mechanisms
Strong sense of virtual community	
High levels of virtual trust	

Source: Matlay and Westhead (2005) Reproduced by permission of SAGE.

Such international enterprises create interesting new challenges and opportunities for their teams. Matlay and Westhead (2005) studied a group of 15 European teams and identified that entrepreneurs who joined these teams saw a series of advantages and disadvantages (Table 13-3).

These teams also split into core and more peripheral members. The peripheral members were brought in and out of the team on an *ad hoc* basis, and the core members had greater privileges, rights and control within the team.

13.5 CHANGE, CONFLICT AND TEAM PROCESS

13.5.1 Team Change and Development

Teams change over time. People come and go, their personal circumstances change and their evaluation of their needs change. Major life changes, like parenthood and marriage, change their perception of priorities. Combined with changes in organisational tasks, such changes can be challenging to understand and address, and potentially very disruptive to the continued development of an entrepreneurial organisation.

Sometimes change means that teams become more effective, at other times, less so. One very influential framework (Tuckman, 1965) describes stages in team development, using rhyming words to make it more easily remembered: forming, storming, norming and performing.

Forming When teams first get together (for example, a group of proto-entrepreneurs first establishing a venture), typically members are somewhat uncertain about the goals of the group, roles and responsibilities, how they will be able to contribute, and anxious about how their contributions will be received. This uncertainty and anxiety means that good interaction can be blocked. There is a stronger focus on politeness and formality than on openness and shared communications. Team members are 'scoping out' one another.

Storming As the group gets going on its task or project (for example, they begin to research or test a new venture concept), dissatisfaction often crops up, as individuals gain confidence without yet being able to communicate effectively. Responsibility, power and authority are established gradually or acquired by individual team members. The extent of individual commitment to the group and the task or project is explored. These areas often create conflict, as some people become more respected or liked, show more commitment or greater skill at particular tasks and so on. In this phase, arguments are a means for people to express their differences and find a common way forward.

Norming In this phase (which may, for example, occur when an entrepreneurial team first test launch their new service), the group establishes rules for working together, based on mutual understanding of expectations and needs. The focus moves from individual to common goals, and the team can operate more effectively. Improved understanding and listening between members lead to a greater possibility of trying new things. As people feel more secure in themselves and their roles, they are more able to air and address personal issues individually and together.

Performing In this stage (which hopefully comes at least by the time the team are fully commercialising their idea in the marketplace), relationships are working well, objectives are clear and goals are being achieved. The team is open to change of operating procedures and problem-solving processes if need be. Efficiency (the cost of getting things done) and effectiveness (the appropriateness of what gets done) are both addressed. This is characterised by trust and openness between members.

It is important to note that these stages do not all necessarily occur: for instance, sometimes a team begins to perform very quickly because perhaps the members know one another already, or because the task is relatively clear and straightforward. Or perhaps the team never reaches a point where it is truly performing well, because of time constraints, changes imposed from the outside, or because of differences which are never fully addressed. Equally, although the stages are broadly sequential, a team may go 'backwards' in its development and have to go through stages more than once. Again, changes to the task, introduction of new team members, or perhaps new external time pressures may cause this kind of cycling between stages of development.

> **Integrative Case Link**
> For more on the impact of change on teams and their role in managing change, see Case 7 at the end of Part 3, on Donegal China.

13

13.5.2 Conflict

While the membership of a team and its suitability to particular tasks and structures all have some impact on the likely success of a venture, a further issue which crosses each of these is that of process and conflict. How the team behaves, how it problem-solves, how it interacts, what it does is significant to the success of the team (McGrath, 1964). This is a rich area of investigation and of potential for teams of all sorts. Team processes are complex, specific to the enterprise context, and arise from a variety of circumstances (Matlay and Westhead, 2005). This *situated* nature of team processes creates challenges for researchers, entrepreneurs and managers alike (Pettigrew, 1992).

It is difficult to determine what works best for different entrepreneurial teams. A smaller group may be able to air their ideas and have a debate with less difficulty, because it is smaller and there are fewer viewpoints to express. However, the fact that there are fewer viewpoints may in itself be problematic.

WHEN THINGS GO WRONG

A fledgling team cracks up

As part of a course within their undergraduate degree, teams of students set up and run businesses for a year, closing them down at the end. The teams often find this a challenge, as they have to establish team norms of behaviour and activity as well as running an enterprise. One team was working on an idea for a new type of online business directory. The idea was brought to the team by one student, James, and the others decided to support the idea. However, tensions cropped up. Some of the team felt that they were working for James, rather than with him, and it became clear that any financial benefits were unlikely to be shared. The team was just beginning to address these issues when the originator of the idea had a family bereavement and disappeared from the course. The rest of the team progressed the idea, but when James returned he rejected their work. This provoked angry protests from the rest of the team, and after a vote some of the team decided to start something different. The team split meant that two new enterprises were being developed. Each of the new, smaller teams was able to progress their idea separately.

Conversely, a larger or more diverse team may have difficulty establishing good working relationships between its members, as there are so many viewpoints, attitudes, personalities and approaches to consider and integrate. More physically dispersed teams may have different needs and problems than those which are co-located.

Examining ideas and possibilities for their viability is a central part of entrepreneurial activity in established organisations as well as in new ones. Part of this examination involves being able to have a good debate about the pros and cons, feasibility and acceptability of a particular strategy or choice. One challenge faced by teams is how to do this without falling out with one another, or being destructive of the team and the organisation.

Conflict can generally be categorised into two types – affective and cognitive (Amason,1996). *Affective conflict* is emotional, and personal, and considered dysfunctional – it results in poorer decisions. When people are either pursuing their private political agendas or criticising people rather than their ideas or the information available about a problem or an opportunity, they tend to leave substantive issues under-discussed. This means that the team will not have a shared and thorough understanding of the problem, information or opportunity, and may make poorer decisions as a result. *Cognitive conflict* is impersonal and about ideas and issues that are independent of the people involved. Cognitive conflict examines impersonal issues – markets, costs, processes and how to develop and manage IP, for instance – more thoroughly, resulting in more reasoned, better understood decisions. Eisenhardt, Kahwajy and Bourgeois (1997) conclude that conflict: 'reflects a continuously evolving understanding of the world that is gained through interaction with others around alternative viewpoints' (p. 60).

Eisenhardt *et al.* (1997) make some suggestions for 'How managers can have a good fight'. Their research was conducted in firms operating in the very dynamic and entrepreneurial environment of Silicon Valley in the 1990s. Their research showed successful teams shared certain approaches to decisions:

'Team members:

■ worked with more, rather than less, information and debated on the basis of facts;

■ developed multiple alternatives to enrich the level of debate;

- shared commonly agreed-upon goals;

- injected humour into the decision process;

- maintained a balanced power structure;

- resolved issues without forcing consensus' (p. 78).

This research is helpful in identifying how entrepreneurial teams can function effectively, despite different points of view and high volumes of information and uncertainty about the future.

13.6 IMPROVING ENTREPRENEURIAL TEAMWORK

Having a repertoire or collection of concepts about effective entrepreneurial teamwork is an important starting point for improving performance, but there is often a gap between understanding concepts and actual behaviour. Effective team behaviour can be developed by recognising and practising skills and eliciting and acting upon feedback. Some of the skills which are important to address include:

Listening

- Giving people time and space in a conversation to share their thoughts and ideas

- Considering their contributions seriously rather than rejecting them out of hand or indeed accepting them without evaluation

- Considering the motivations and needs of others in a conversation, to ensure they are met for the benefit of the team.

Questioning

- Showing genuine interest in people, their ideas and objectives

- Asking open questions (beginning with how, what, where, when, why, who) to allow them to give more extensive answers than simple yes or no

- Providing information in response to questions of a similar quality to what you are looking for.

Balancing

- Checking that people, task and ideas are all being addressed in group work; drawing attention to gaps in the team's orientation

- Working across roles in order to provide the team with roles that it wouldn't otherwise have.

13

13.7 SUMMARY AND ACTIVITIES

This chapter has introduced some perspectives on entrepreneurial teams and the challenges and opportunities associated with them.

Teams are at the heart of most human activity. Despite stories about hero entrepreneurs, new enterprises are often started by teams of two or more people. An entrepreneurial team is defined as 'two or more individuals who have a significant financial interest and participate actively in the development of the enterprise' (Cooney, 2005: 229).

The **resource-based view of strategy** sees enterprises as bundles of resources. Enterprises compete *for* resources and compete *with* resources. To compete successfully and create value, enterprises need to develop unique resources or deploy them in novel ways.

As entrepreneurial teams gather and deploy resources, they shape their enterprises. This helps to define direction, and creates constraints on what can be done in the future. Well-established organisations have extensive resource constraints, and this creates new entrepreneurial opportunities for others.

Teams and their members are resources which enable enterprises to grow. **Knowledge** and experience, **networks**, team **size** and **diversity** are all aspects of entrepreneurial teams which are thought to be significant to success. However, there is no simple recipe for which of these factors are most significant.

Increasing diversity of knowledge and social networks which the enterprise can access are important reasons for increasing the size of the team, and criteria for consideration as the team grows. The size of the team and its diversity can also hinder a team by creating communications problems.

Large organisations may struggle to be entrepreneurial because their teams are specialised into locations or roles. Cross-disciplinary innovation teams are a means of overcoming this.

Conflict in teams is common, and has many sources. Two main types of conflict – affective and cognitive – can be identified. **Affective** conflict is personal and destructive in a team. **Cognitive** conflict is about ideas, is impersonal, and is good for teams because when aired it helps to improve ideas and solutions.

REVIEW QUESTIONS

1 What are the main characteristics of a successful team?

2 Define an entrepreneurial team.

3 What is the resource-based view of strategy?

4 Identify the main resources that come together in an entrepreneurial team.

5 How does team size affect a team?

6 What are the different stages in team development?

7 How do teams need to change as organisations grow?

8 How do larger organisations encourage intrapreneurship?

9 Suggest some ways of dealing with team conflict.

10 Identify the pros and cons of conflict.

13

SEMINAR TASK

Identify a team of which you are a member. Who are the members, and what roles do they play? Why did they come into existence, and how have they changed? What problems have they had, and how have you dealt with these?

Discuss what would be your 'dream team'. Who would be on it, and why?

Finally, identify an entrepreneurial team of which you are not a member. What are its main characteristics? What are its strengths and weaknesses?

Preview case continued

TopUp TV – an experienced entrepreneurial team

The UK television broadcasting industry has developed substantially since the late 1980s. By 2008, there were three competing technological platforms for distributing television signals. Terrestrial broadcasting was the first of these. Satellite distribution was led by BSkyB, whose digital services required a satellite dish to be received. Cable TV required a connection to a cable network. These all sold overlapping packages of television channels and other services at competitive subscription prices. Only the terrestrial service, Freeserve, had no charge associated with it.

TopUp TV is a pay-TV service in the UK which operates by piggy-backing on the free digital terrestrial television broadcasting platform. Subscribers pay a monthly charge to receive a package of channels through the Freeserve platform in addition to the normal 40+ Freeserve channels. The channels are downloaded to a digital recorder which is an enhanced version of the normal Freeserve reception box. The TopUp Box is slightly more expensive to purchase than the normal Freeserve box, but creates the opportunity for the viewer to subscribe to these additional channels.

TopUp TV was founded by David Chance and Ian West, two highly experienced entrepreneurial managers from the pay-TV industry. They had both worked for several years at BSkyB, the satellite broadcaster which dominates pay-TV in the UK. David had started as Marketing Manager there, but eventually became Deputy Managing Director. He had been a key player in the introduction of major sporting events to BSkyB, which resulted in the creation of the English Premier League, and the professionalisation of Rugby Union in the UK. After leaving BSkyB, David pursued different entrepreneurial opportunities. First, he and a colleague, Sam Chisholm, the former Managing Director of BSkyB, established a consultancy business to help sports organisations to negotiate sales of their intellectual property. This endeavour met with mixed success, and Chisholm moved back to his native New Zealand.

Subsequently Chance and another colleague, Ian West, joined forces. Ian had various roles at BSkyB, including network development, and latterly as Managing Director of Sky Entertainment, when he was responsible for the introduction of Sky's digital service. Together, they had extensive knowledge of programming, relevant technologies, competitor organisations and people within the industry.

David and Ian both joined the board of Intertrust, a technology start-up in the US which owned extensive patents in the digital rights management field. They brought their experience and networks to the management team there, and helped Intertrust to sell their intellectual property to a consortium of technology producers in 2002 for over $450 million.

After the sale of Intertrust, the pair turned to developing TopUp TV from scratch. This involved negotiating the technology, programming, and access to distribution channels – namely the Freeserve platform. Having established the service, they brought in a new management team to run the company, and themselves moved on to developing new challenges and opportunities.

Questions

1 *Teams bring together various resources. What resources come together at TopUp TV?*

2 *Describe the social networks brought together at TopUp TV. How are they valuable?*

3 *What would you expect the next team change to be at TopUp TV?*

13

13.8   NOTES, REFERENCES AND FURTHER READING

Notes and Further Information

1. This reference is from a special edition on entrepreneurial teams published in the *International Small Business Journal*, 22 (3) in 2005.

2. Chapter 7, section 7.3 'Entrepreneurial learning' investigates how entrepreneurs learn. Subsection 7.3.1 covers 'Experiential learning' or how entrepreneurs learn from their experiences.

3. Erasmus for entrepreneurs helps students and graduates to do placements in SMEs in different parts of Europe, with the objective of sharing experience and encouraging the establishment of new networks; www.erasmus-entrepreneurs.eu.

4. This case is based on an article in *The Financial Times*, 14/15 March 2009, 'Knomo Bags', by Hugo Greenhalgh.

5. Life cycle models applied to both enterprises and entrepreneurs are discussed more fully in Chapter 6, 'The Life Cycle of Entrepreneurship'.

6. The account on which this case is based is sourced from *The Scotsman*, 7 December 2005, at: http://news.scotsman.com/friendsreunited/Friends-Reunited-founders-net-30m.2684403.jp; and http://www.friendsreunited.co.uk/press/history.htm both accessed on 15 April 2009.

References

Amason, A.C. (1996) 'Distinguishing the effects of functional and dysfunctional conflict on strategic decision making: Resolving a paradox for top management teams', *Academy of Management Journal*, Briarcliff Manor, 39 (1): 123–149.

Bales, R.F. and Borgatta, E.F. (1966) Bridging the boundary: External process and performance in organisational teams, *Administrative Science Quarterly*, 37: 527–548.

Barney, J.B. (1991) Firm resources and sustained competitive advantage, *Journal of Management*, 17(1): 99–120.

Cooney, T.M. (2005) Editorial: 'What is an entrepreneurial team?' *International Small Business Journal*, 23 (3): 226–235.

Cooper, A.C. and Bruno, A.V. (1977) Success among high-technology firms, *Business Horizons*, April: 16–20.

Eisenhardt, K.M. (1989) Making fast strategic decisions in high velocity environments, *Academy of Management Journal*, 32 (3): 543–576.

Eisenhardt, K.M, Kahwajy, J.L. and Bourgeois, L.J. (1997) How management teams can have a good fight, *Harvard Business Review*, July–August.

Eisenhardt, K.M. and Schoonhoven, C.B. (1990) Organisational growth: Linking founding team, strategy, environment, and growth among U.S. semiconductor ventures, 1978-1988, *Administrative Science Quarterly*, 35 (3): 504–529.

Grant, R.M. (1991) The resource-based theory of competitive advantage: Implications for strategy formulation, *California Management Review*, 33 (3): 114–135.

Greenhalgh, H. (2009) *Financial Times*, 14/15 March, London: Pearson.

Hambrick, D.C. and Mason, P.A. (1984) Upper echelons: The organisation as a reflection of its top managers, *Academy of Management Review*, 9 (2): 193–206.

Isenberg, D.J. (2008) The global entrepreneur, *Harvard Business Review*, December.

Katz, R. (1982) The effects of group longevity on project communication and performance, *Administrative Science Quarterly*, 27: 81–104.

Keck, S.L. (1997) Top management team structure: Different effects by environmental context, *Organisation Science*, 8 (2): 143–156.

Matlay, H. and Westhead, P. (2005) Virtual teams and the rise of e-entrepreneurship in Europe, *International Small Business Journal*, 23 (3): 279–302.

McGrath, J. (1964) *Social Psychology – A Brief Introduction*, New York: Holt.

Miller, C., Burke, L. and Glick, W. (1998) Cognitive diversity among upper-echelon executives: Implications for strategic decision processes, *Strategic Management Journal*, 19: 39–58.

Mueller, D.C. (1972) *A Life Cycle Theory of the Firm*, Oxford: Blackwell.

13

Napier, N.K., Bahnson, P.R., Glen, R., Maille, C.J., Smith, K. and White, H. (2009) When 'Aha moments' make all the difference, *Journal of Management Inquiry*, 18 (1): 64–76.

Papadakis, V.M. and Barwise, P. (1995) Top management characteristics & strategic decision processes, paper presented at the British Academy of Management Conference.

Pettigrew, A. (1992) On studying managerial elites, *Strategic Management Journal*, 13: 163–182.

Roure, J.B. and Keely, R.H. (1990) Predictors of success in new technology based ventures, *Journal of Business Venturing*, 5 (4): 201–20.

Sarasvathy, S. (2004) Making it happen: Beyond theories of the firm to theories of firm design, *Entrepreneurship: Theory & Practice*, Winter 28 (6): 519–531.

Smith, K.G., Smith, K.A., Olian, J.D., Sims, H.P., O'Bannon, P. and Scully, J.A. (1994) Top management team demography and process: The role of social integration and communication, *Administrative Science Quarterly*, 39 (3): 412–439.

Stokes, D. and Wilson, N. (2006) *Small Business Management and Entrepreneurship*, London: Thomson Learning.

Stuart, R.W. and Abetti, P.A. (1986) Impact of entrepreneurial and management experience on early performance, *Journal of Business Venturing*, 5 (3): 151–162.

Timmons, J.A. (1994) *New Venture Creation: Entrepreneurship for the 21st Century*, 4th edn, Homewood, IL: Irwin.

Tuckman, B.W. (1965) Developmental sequence in small groups, *Psychological Bulletin*, 63: 384–399. The article was reprinted in *Group Facilitation: A Research and Applications Journal* – Number 3, Spring 2001.

Tyson, S. and Jackson T. (1992) *The Essence of Organisational Behaviour*, New York: Prentice-Hall.

Vyakarnam, S. and Handelberg, J. (2005) Four themes of the impact of management teams on organisational performance: Implications for future research of entrepreneurial teams, *International Small Business Journal*, 23 (3): 236–256.

Recommended Further Reading

International Small Business Journal (2005) Special Issue: Entrepreneurial Teams and Small Firms, 23 (3) June. This contains four articles and an editorial on entrepreneurial teams, including papers on technology-based and virtual teams.

Belbin, R.M. (1981) *Management Teams – Why They Succeed or Fail*, Butterworth-Heinemann.

13

CHAPTER 14

Entrepreneurial Business Models and Processes

LEARNING OBJECTIVES

After studying this chapter, the reader will be able to:

- Understand what business models are, and their key elements
- Evaluate the key differences between different types of business model
- Analyse the key drivers for value in business processes and models
- Assess different business processes, and how to design them
- Understand the links between business processes, business models and enterprise value.

INTRODUCTION

This chapter considers how to structure and organise the enterprise's activities most effectively in order for it to become viable and valuable. The road from the formation of an enterprise idea to the creation of a viable enterprise is usually a long and winding one. The initial stages of the journey involve clarifying how an idea may become viable, and how the enterprise should be designed to maximise its value. Market research and pilot tests will help to inform these decisions. Later stages of the journey require the acquisition of appropriate resources, and the design and building of processes which will deliver customer service efficiently. Even those enterprises that are begun with a clear idea of how they will be structured and developed will be subject to alteration to match changes in the competitive environment, and in customer expectations and needs.

This chapter will look particularly at two areas of this process of value creation: business models and business processes. These two areas are closely linked, as they both describe and enact the structure and systems which define the enterprise.

PREVIEW CASE

El Bulli, a model restaurant[1]

Internationally famous for its innovative cuisine, El Bulli in northern Spain is often referred to as the best restaurant in the world. With many more potential customers than it can cater for, it is only open for six months in the year or less, only some days in the week, and rarely for lunch.

How can such an enterprise survive and prosper as it does? What is the business model that it follows?

Read more about this fascinating business in the case study at the end of the chapter.

14.1 DEFINITIONS OF BUSINESS MODELS

14.1.1 What Are Business Models?

There is still some debate over what constitutes a business model and the concept, which was developed initially among consultants and industry commentators rather than academics, has not been fully accepted into the academic literature (Zott and Amit, 2008). The topic came to the fore in the late 1990s when the development of the Internet allowed many new web-based businesses to be launched that had uncertain potential to create value and become commercially viable. Although much of the developing analytical discussion of business models continues to relate to web-based enterprises, the Internet revolution has in fact highlighted the importance of the concept to enterprises in general (Hedman and Kalling, 2003).

Every enterprise begins with a business idea which encapsulates an opportunity, a robust solution to a clearly identified customer problem. Once the business idea is articulated, the entrepreneur must find a way to turn it into a successful economic entity. A business model is the means by which the enterprise does this. Amit and Zott (2001: 511) provide this definition:

> 'A business model depicts the content, structure, and governance of transactions designed so as to increase value through the exploitation of business opportunities.'

More simply put, it is *the system through which the entrepreneur captures the value inherent in the business idea* (Hedman and Kalling, 2003). All enterprises operate a business model, including social and public enterprises. They use resources to provide services and products for customers and attract revenues, which can be represented or measured in terms of money.[2]

Enterprises seek to create competitive advantage (Porter, 1980, 1985). They do this through positioning products and services in markets (Porter, 1980) and through building and deploying unique resources and competences (Peteraf, 1993). Business models also have the potential to create advantage, as they can be the source of entrepreneurial 'creative disruption' (Schumpeter, 1934). They may for instance change the way in which consumers purchase, resources are bundled together or transactions take place (Amit and Zott, 2001). These may lead to higher profits through greater efficiency or through differentiation from competitors.

14.1.2 Integration Through the Business Model

The concept of the business model is integrative of various business concepts and activities. The model is the 'story' which explains how the enterprise works, and the story has two parts: the narrative and the profit and loss account (Magretta, 2002). The narrative brings together customers, markets and

14

products, identifying the customer's motivation to buy, or the value proposition. The profit and loss account considers resources, technology and production, summarising the economic logic by which the company will deliver or the means of production, delivery and charging (Amit and Zott, 2001; Chesbrough and Rosenbloom, 2002; Morris, Schindehutte and Allen, 2005; Magretta, 2002).

Because it draws together the main value-creating elements of the enterprise, and explains how it will make money, the business model is at the heart of any business plan, and the search for a business model which is sustainable and profitable is at the centre of entrepreneurial activity.

14.1.3 Increasing Complexity – Value Chains and the Value Web

Industries are made up of suppliers and customers who come together in chains of value-adding organisations. The *value system* of an industry includes all of the suppliers who are linked together to create value for an end customer (Porter, 1985). This concept, developed particularly with manufacturing industries in mind, is useful for highlighting how different organisations in a vertical system that link raw materials through manufacture and delivery to the end customer, add value in different ways. However some industries, for instance creative industries like film-making, seem to defy such simple analysis. They create a *value web*, an image which better describes how many participants, connected through lateral as well as vertical connections, contribute to creating value (Cartwright and Oliver, 2000).

Pinewood Studios and Sohonet

Pinewood Studios Group operates three film and TV production studios in London, England. These bring together about 250 entrepreneurial firms on the production lot, specialising in all aspects of production and providing support services during the production period. The dense network of firms reflects the collaborative and project or task-based nature of the industry. Each project needs different expertise combined for different periods of time. The presence of these services and the standard of their skills are part of the attraction of the Pinewood Studios to producers. As digital content has become more significant to production, it has become possible for long-distance interaction to take place, and these enterprises interact with many others in London and around the world.

The collaborative and geographically dispersed nature of media projects has created interesting entrepreneurial opportunities. Sohonet is a private broadband company which provides communication services for digital production companies. It provides media sharing and collaboration facilities tailored to the digital industry's needs. Given the value of the materials being shared and distributed, security and trust are key attributes which Sohonet provides. Pinewood and Sohonet co-promote one another on their respective websites, recognising their importance to one another and to maintaining London's strength in these industries.

14

This type of formation is particularly common in e-commerce enterprises. The universality and ease of use of the Internet has enabled organisations to come together in novel ways to create new value (Cartwright and Oliver, 2000). In particular, the boundary-spanning potential of the Internet has facilitated these new networks and webs (Amit and Zott, 2001). As so many businesses have intangible infrastructures and operations, there are fewer physical boundaries and associated barriers and these are therefore less relevant. Firms can collaborate more easily, drawing together their intellectual property and other resources in new ways. Business models which create and exploit webs in this way may be particularly valuable sources of innovation.

TABLE 14-1	Elements of business models and design questions
Key elements	**Design questions**
Customer	Who is the customer, what is the need being addressed, and how does the customer get value from the proposed solution?
Product and service offering	What is the offering?
Operations	What are the processes which implement the business concept, and connect the business to its customers?
Costs	What are the costs of producing and delivering the product or service?
Revenues	How will revenues be generated, and what will they be?

14.1.4 Elements of Business Models

The key elements and questions to consider in developing a business model are shown in Table 14-1. During the formation of an enterprise, key decisions are taken which influence the relationships between each of these elements. For example, the amount of resources dedicated to sales and marketing in a new enterprise will influence the time it takes to build revenues and will also affect the level of costs. Many start-ups increase their sales gradually so that they can simultaneously build the appropriate resource and cost base. Other businesses attract sufficient resources to be 'born-global' and launch on an international scale from the beginning.[3]

Business models explain the interactions of these elements, and how they work together to create economic value. To create value in an enterprise, the entrepreneur works out what drives revenues, how to best use resources and optimise costs in order to maximise profits.

14.2 CUSTOMERS AND THE PRODUCT OFFERING

14.2.1 What Do They Pay For?

Identifying what creates value for a customer is a central issue when considering business models. Enterprises create value by using expertise and resources in different ways according to their particular business model. For example, Table 14-2 describes how operators within the property industry use their skills and other assets to contribute to the value chain.

Clearly identifying the customer and their specific needs is at the heart of any business proposal. Enterprises create value for customers in various ways, and it is the sum of this value which is important: the value proposition.

Entrepreneurs need first to establish what they are offering in terms of expertise and resources that add value to buyers in the target market. The next issue is to provide this in a manner which is competitive with other individuals or enterprises with similar knowledge, skills and resources. In the crowded marketplace of the modern economy, new ventures need to provide a differentiated value proposition to succeed.

14

TABLE 14-2	The property industry – roles and value creators
Property developer	Uses knowledge of property and access to finance to spot property opportunities, purchase properties and commission building on the property. May do this speculatively, or on commission from a client looking for a property. Sells the improved property, or may keep it and rent it to users.
Architect	Uses creativity, technical design knowledge and knowledge of planning to provide advice and design service to the property developer. May use knowledge of construction processes to supervise the construction of the project.
Builder	Uses knowledge of construction trades and skills, and access to manual and skilled labour to construct the building according to the architect's plans.
Real estate agent	Brings buyers and sellers together, typically receiving revenue (commission) from sellers. Values properties on behalf of sellers and advertises in local newspapers, websites and retail outlets. Knowledge of a particular geographic and specialist (e.g. commercial or domestic) market is critical.
Mortgage consultant	Advises buyers on best form of finance for property acquisition and guides them through the application process. Receives revenue (commission) from mortgage companies and banks.

ENTREPRENEURSHIP IN ACTION

Rank Xerox and the free machine

In the late 1950s, Rank Xerox brought to market a new form of photocopying. Whereas previous copiers had been used mostly in industrial applications because of the poor quality of the copies, the new machines delivered a much higher quality of copy. They were, however, very expensive to make, and it was uncertain who would buy them. Was there an office copying market out there waiting to be found? Xerox presented the customer with a very strong value proposition for the new model, in order to get it into the market. They leased the machines at a monthly rate instead of selling them, and charged per copy only after a threshold level of copying was reached. This gave firms a very low-cost way of acquiring the technology. In addition, the lease could be cancelled with just a month's notice, so firms had low switching costs if they decided it wasn't worth having. The value proposition was therefore high-quality copies in the office at a low risk, variable cost rate. Firms found that they passed the threshold very quickly, resulting in a very substantial revenue stream from the beginning.

Source: Chesbrough and Rosenbloom, 2002

14.2.2 **Product and Service Offering**

Products and services are often combined in interesting ways to create value for the customer. The business model needs to clarify what this bundle includes.

■ *Products* are tangible objects. Very often products come with services like insurance, after-purchase maintenance, usage advice and instruction. This may facilitate the use of the product, or enhance the usage.

■ *Services* are intangible. Services can also be bundled together, or enhanced with products to make them more useful, immediate or personal.

Mobile telephony, laptops and netbooks

Mobile telephony has spawned a large number of service and product bundles to suit different customer needs as technology and usage have developed. At the most basic level, the telephone is the product, the network is the service. One approach is to offer phones for sale and for the service to be provided on an occasional, 'pay as you go' basis. This model has the advantage of flexibility for the customer who only wants to use the phone occasionally. Another approach is to offer a network subscription which reflects the type and frequency of usage required with a free or heavily discounted phone. The advent of netbooks has introduced a new product / service combination of a subscription to broadband mobile Internet services, which comes with a free netbook. Apple have innovated in bundling together a novel high-performing phone with video, music and Internet services.

Finding a unique means of bundling products and services is a possible source of competitive advantage. To maintain such an advantage in a marketplace is challenging however, unless the bundle is protected by, for instance, patents or by the uniqueness of know-how and resources within the enterprise.

14.3   OPERATIONS AND PROCESSES

14.3.1 **Gaining Competitive Advantage Through Processes**

Operations and processes are the means by which enterprises produce and deliver products and services. They include the activities, equipment and buildings through which products and services are designed, produced and delivered. Depending on the enterprise, the objective of operations may be to collect, deliver, change, make, transform or look after goods, information or people (see Table 14-3).

The objective collectively is to create enterprise value and this encompasses all organisational activities including marketing, manufacturing and managing people, and relationships with suppliers and partners. Figure 14-1 indicates the main focus areas for enterprise processes. As already noted, the ideas of the value chain and the value web are useful in considering how enterprises add value. Both of these activities imply boundary-spanning activities. The figure shows a generalised schema of the different generic types of boundary-spanning processes. These may be facilitated by electronic capability, but they may also be largely physical in nature.

14

TABLE 14-3	Some examples of operations and their focus
Type of operation	**Focus**
Taxi	Movement of people from one place to another
Factory	Manufacture of goods from parts or raw materials
Price comparison website	Collection and analysis of information online
Medical practice	Personalised knowledge-based professional services to make people well
Office cleaning	Deploying people and machinery to change the condition of an office from dirty to clean

FIGURE 14-1 A generalised view of boundary-spanning enterprise processes

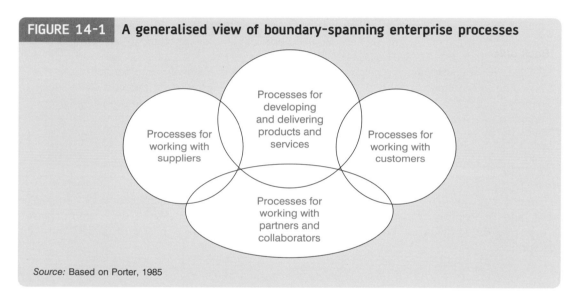

Source: Based on Porter, 1985

ENTREPRENEURSHIP IN ACTION

Calyx and Corolla: Using alliances to deliver flowers

C&C is a flower delivery company in the United States. As an entrepreneurial start-up, the firm re-engineered boundary-spanning activities. The enterprise features more exotic flowers made up into bouquets and arrangements, telephone ordering from a catalogue and next day delivery.

Flowers were mostly grown in the United States, rather than overseas, and the company established close links with growers to ensure they grew the flowers the enterprise wanted. Rather than delivering flowers to a warehouse to be made into bouquets there, the growers are incentivised to make the bouquets to specification themselves, and to package them for home delivery. C&C established a strategic relationship with UPS, who handle all deliveries. UPS brought their delivery vans to the growers' farms where the completed bouquets were loaded, enabling faster turnaround, less damage to bouquets and lower warehousing costs.

C&C also established promotional alliances with product manufacturers, whereby combination purchases were possible. For instance, a promotional campaign with a crystal vase manufacturer meant that a bouquet would be delivered the day after a vase purchase.

14

Boundary spanning through technology, logistics and supply chain innovations can be a source of advantage, and there are many other such sources from the operations field. They include the type of environment in which the service is offered, the intensity of contact with service providers and machines, and the competence and reliability with which a promised benefit is delivered (Parasuraman, Berry and Zeithaml, 1985).

Processes can be categorised into two distinct areas:

- the front office / back office divide in operations; and

- the analysis of volume and variety.

14.3.2 **Front Office / Back Office**

Front office operations are customer-facing and interact directly with end users and customers. For instance, in a restaurant staff greet guests, take them to a table, take an order and serve the dinner. All of this takes place with the involvement of the customer. The customer sits in a service environment which is designed to create a particular atmosphere.

Back office operations take place behind the scenes, without direct customer involvement. For example, restaurants' processes which are invisible to the diners including purchasing, preparing and cooking the food, training waiters and kitchen staff, managing accounts and devising marketing strategies. The customer is normally unaware that they are taking place (except for those 'closed for staff training' notices).

Process innovation may happen as a result of playing with the division between the back and front office.

>
> **Integrative Case Link**
> For an example of a firm based on back office processes, see Smart421, Case Study 9 at the end of Part 3.

Front office / back office innovation in restaurants

Some restaurants have pioneered unusual forms of interaction with customers, and made these a value-creating feature which helps to define the brand of the restaurant.

Sapporo Teppanyaki is a restaurant chain in which food is cooked in front of the customers. Customers sit around three sides of a large hotplate, and the chef works in front of them. Cooking is made a piece of theatre, with chefs juggling food and implements in order to impress the customers. Customers join in together and encourage the chef, making a party atmosphere.[4]

McDonald's, the worldwide chain of burger restaurants, has been highly successful at standardising their food and their dining experience on the key value adding issues of speed and reliability at a low price. Customers approach a counter and order their food from a limited menu shown on the wall. The food is produced very quickly, and the kitchen is visible through equipment panels. Customers pay at the point that the food is delivered, and carry their meal to a table. They have to unwrap their choices, and eventually clear their own table, putting used packaging and unconsumed food in the bin themselves. The customer thus does most of the front office work.

Yo! Sushi is a chain of Japanese sushi restaurants, in which the food is prepared in the customer area of the restaurants. Unlike most restaurants, however, the food is carried around the restaurant on a narrow conveyor belt which passes by all of the tables. Diners watch the conveyor belt and decide what to eat as it goes by. They pick up the food, then stack the empty dishes on their table. Once they have had enough, an employee counts up the number of empty dishes, and prepares a bill.[5]

14.3.3 Volume and Variety

Processes can be further classified according to the volume and variety of products produced or customer transactions completed.

The **volume** of demand is the quantity of goods and services wanted or purchased. Measures of volume answer the questions *how much* or *how many*. How many shoes, meals, cars or music downloads will customers want? How much electricity, wood, or lettuce will they purchase? How many people will join Facebook, and how many times per day or week will they look at it?

Variety of demand refers to the range of different things that are required, and answers the question, *what sort* or *which*. This may include different items, or different means of delivering products or services. For instance, how many different sizes or colours of a product, or what different delivery times, ordering methods, or combinations and packages of goods and services?

The combination of volume and variety helps to focus on the main issues of concern in developing and managing processes and operations (Figure 14-2).

Low Volume, High Variety Demand of this type is usually relatively expensive to respond to. Producing a small number of very different things implies designing and making to order, or perhaps pursuing a special artistic activity like high-quality sculpture or other visual art forms. The reproduction of original works of art through mechanical methods – photographs and prints of paintings, or castings of sculptures – is common, in order to squeeze further value from the original, unique work of art.

Low Volume, Low Variety Occasional demand for a narrow range of products and services implies that the product or service is produced on demand, often on a project basis – for example the project management of disaster relief. Although each natural or man-made disaster may be different, there are certain key issues to resolve – clean water, food, shelter and medical care. Organisations like Médecins Sans Frontières, the medical relief charity, have core, standardised approaches which are tailored to different situations.

High Volume, High Variety Demand of this type is complex to manage and organise. Keeping track of many different things, or providing a wide range of different services is difficult. A large retail store such as Selfridge's in London's Oxford Street or the online store Amazon carry large volumes of diverse stock to satisfy many different needs. In order to handle the complexity thus created, they both have a

FIGURE 14-2	Volume and variety combinations	
High Variety	**Low Volume, High Variety**	**High Volume, High Variety**
	Artists and craftspeople working on distinctive pieces like Damien Hirst. Additional value can be created by using duplicating technology like print-making	Large retail stores like Selfridge's in London, or online stores like Amazon
Low Variety	**Low Volume, Low Variety**	**High Volume, Low Variety**
	Disaster relief services and other occasional services	Facebook, Bebo and other mass services. Steel and electricity production and distribution
	Low Volume	**High Volume**

single delivery mechanism: a large shop in the first case, and a single web portal, ordering and delivery system in the second.

High Volume, Low Variety Demand of this type is typically for commodities – products and services that are little differentiated from one another. The operation will be large and routinised, with as much mechanisation as possible. Electricity and steel are typical examples, and so too are call centres responding to repeated questions. Facebook and other online community services are also in this category. They are used for a relatively limited range of transactions, but by a very high volume of people.

These different types of demand and operation require different types of resources: a manufacturing business or a utility (e.g. a water or electricity company) focuses on fixed assets and equipment; a retail model places a major focus on premises in the right place, whether physical or virtual; service business models such as 'infomediaries' (e.g. market research agencies) are often people intensive. An entrepreneur needs to decide which resources are most critical to their particular business model and prioritise expenditure and management time on them.

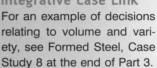

Integrative Case Link
For an example of decisions relating to volume and variety, see Formed Steel, Case Study 8 at the end of Part 3.

ENTREPRENEURSHIP IN ACTION

Adele Fashions

Adele is a Johannesburg-based fashion entrepreneur. She has worked in the industry for 25 years, and has extensive knowledge of the industry (designers and producers) and the market (retailers and end consumers). She sells women's fashion ranges to retail chains in South Africa. To create these ranges, she examines trends in the European fashion market, and produces ranges of clothing based on these trends, but adapted for the South African market. Her business model uses her knowledge, experience and contacts to draw together resources from around the world to produce her clothing range. Her business model uses outsourced labour in London, South Africa and China in the following sequence of events:

- A consultant in London identifies trends that they think are important in the mainstream retail market, and buys samples which show off these trends. Photographs of these samples are emailed to Adele for consideration. The samples she thinks will work best in South Africa are then couriered to her;

- A designer in South Africa produces designs which are based on the trends in London, but tailored to South African habits, climate and price range;

- Adele shows the designs to her retail contacts, and agrees a price and volume;

- A manufacturer in China produces the goods to Adele's specification, and ships directly to the retailer;

- The retailer sells the clothing under their brand name, handling all promotion and display of the product.

Adele creates value by identifying international fashion design trends that can be adapted to suit needs in South Africa quickly and cheaply. Designs based on the latest trends in London can appear in South Africa for the next season, making her service particularly attractive to retailers. She employs sub-contractors on a job-by-job basis, keeping her costs and risks low, and enabling other entrepreneurs to develop businesses of their own to support hers.

14

Finding novel ways of dealing with demand across these dimensions can create advantage and value in an enterprise, particularly when they deal with previously unidentified or unmet customer needs.

14.4 THE COSTS OF CREATING VALUE

Costs are incurred in several fundamental ways, sometimes to invest in resources, sometimes through activities:

Premises: For a small enterprise, a lease on premises or land is often the single largest liability that it will have on its balance sheet. This has three main implications: minimising these costs will be important for a new enterprise; the revenues required from an enterprise which holds them will be higher; and the acquisition of such assets may increase the risk inherent in a new entrepreneurial venture. For this reason, many new ventures are started in the entrepreneurs' home until the scale of the enterprise justifies separate premises.[6]

Employees: costs incurred include not just salaries and bonuses but also insurance, pension, travel and training costs. In many countries, the legal framework of employment constrains firms from letting staff go cheaply – so there can be substantial costs involved in redundancy. For firms of all sizes, an important decision will be whether to hire people as direct employees, or whether to purchase services from another enterprise which employs the people instead.

Equipment and other fixed assets. Some businesses require substantial investments in equipment and machinery so that the business model requires more revenue to make them viable. For example, manufacturers typically need more sales to reach break-even point[7] than service companies.

Activity generates costs: each action such as a sales call made, a letter posted or a phone discussion incurs a cost to the enterprise.

Finance: indebtedness requires interest payments and share capital comes at the cost of an expectation of a return on investment.

A business model considers the interaction between the costs of resources and the value they create for the enterprise. It is not only the absolute cost of an item which is important, but the extent to which any item adds value to the enterprise. For instance, the fact that people are expensive should lead not to an entrepreneur deciding against hiring anyone, but to a careful consideration of the knowledge and skills that are the most effective at adding value within the adopted business model that has been developed, and the best way to acquire those skills for the enterprise.

14

WHEN THINGS GO WRONG

Boo.com

Boo.com is one of many online businesses set up in the 1990s to take advantage of the emerging medium of the Internet. It was a fashion business selling directly to consumers. However, the costs incurred in establishing the trading platform, branding and logistics systems were so large that it failed very quickly, leaving the venture capitalists who had funded it stranded.

ENTREPRENEURSHIP IN ACTION

David Beckham, international football star

Football teams have revenues from several sources: winning competitions, selling seats at matches, selling television and other media rights, sponsorship and advertising, branded merchandise sales and hospitality and catering. The resources needed to generate revenues include a stadium, a team, a manager and support staff, and a carefully managed brand name. Individual players are not only a key playing resource but also contribute to the development of the brand value and merchandising revenues.

David Beckham has been one of the most valuable resources in the football world. During his time playing for Manchester United, the team became the most financially successful in the world because it won competitions, and also because of the star quality of this unusual player. In particular, it earned more money from merchandise sales than any other team. When Beckham left to join Real Madrid in Spain, his new team substantially improved their merchandise sales. He then moved to the US, and his celebrity status contributed to popularising his team and the sport more generally there. Although past the peak of his playing career, Beckham continues to draw new money into the teams which hire his skills and his star quality, including Milan in Italy.

© WWD/CONDÉ NAST/CORBIS

David and Victoria Beckham

Unusually among football players, Beckham's star quality has been carefully managed alongside that of his wife Victoria – a former pop singer. The two are co-branded, wearing clothes by the same designers and employing stylists to ensure they look compatible. They share a similar fan base, including many people who have little interest in football!

While the Internet and its associated technologies have created virtual environments and businesses which have become familiar, the virtual firm is a long-standing business model. In these flexible enterprises, the entrepreneurial team or founder develops an enterprise around relatively small investments, using their expertise, contacts or other resources to run the business. This model has the advantage of being relatively low risk in terms of investment. It can also flex its capacity to suit changing economic circumstances and customer needs.

For many firms, acquiring resources may mean simply acquiring access to them, rather than owning them outright. It may be more effective for the enterprise to sub-contract some activities to another firm and manage the contract and relationship with that firm, than to directly employ people to create products and services. The labour force in an international call centre is an example of a resource that is acquired without being owned. Licences to use the intellectual property of other entrepreneurs such as patents and copyright, or a franchise contract to use a pre-existing business idea are common ways to acquire the use of valuable resources.

14

Outsourced call centres

Improved international communications allowed entrepreneurs to develop and utilise outsourced telephone call centres. Firms which take high volumes of telephone calls in order to provide service elect to hire another enterprise to run this activity for them. Often, this activity is moved from high wage to lower wage areas or economies. Regions or countries with lower wages compete to attract this business in order to create employment and develop a new skills base. This has had several benefits for the enterprises involved, including moving wages off their payroll and lowering the risks associated with possible future restructuring of their businesses. In lower wage areas and economies, many new enterprises have been created to handle this work, creating new employment and opportunities for more people there.

14.5   SOURCES OF REVENUE

There are many potential sources of revenue available to an entrepreneurial venture, and the choice of business model determines which type of revenue will be most important to the enterprise and how the finances will be structured. There are two key questions which relate to this:

- Who is going to pay?
- How are they going to pay?

14.5.1   Who Is Going to Pay?

Customers come in many forms. There are dozens of words in English which indicate the person or group who receives or uses a service or product, including: subscriber, patient, client, parishioner, annuitant, user, viewer, sponsor. Customers may be private individuals (in retail, or business-to-consumer marketing), or enterprises (wholesale, or business-to-business marketing). Usually an organisation will focus on one type of customer, and one type of marketing and selling. This helps to simplify the business model, and therefore the activities and processes of the organisation.

Normally, we think of the customer as the person or organisation which uses the service or product. However, this is not always the case. Often the person who uses the product is not the person who pays for it. Table 14-4 shows some different cases of who pays.

TABLE 14-4	Who pays for what? Some examples	
Case	**Who pays**	**Description**
Food retailing supermarket	End user	Retailer provides a range of goods, in a certain location (a shop), where consumers come to select and purchase food
UK medical services (NHS)	Government (not patients)	Hospitals, clinics and most other healthcare is funded by the government; care is free to patients when they use it
eBay online auction site	Sellers (not buyers)	Reliable and secure auction and payment systems attract millions of buyers; the sellers pay commission to eBay for access to these potential customers
Facebook social networking website	Advertisers (not users or content providers)	Easy and free information exchange attracts millions of people; advertisers pay Facebook to access these users

The value web introduces interesting complexities in who pays whom for the value created by web members, which in turn creates innovation.

14.5.2 How Are They Going to Pay?

Revenue models come in many different forms, the key parameters being the frequency of payment, and what is being paid for. For instance, payments may be made for items purchased, delivery, usage, or for service delivered, and they may be one-off payments, subscriptions based on time, or pay as you go. These different approaches will depend on a mixture of factors, including competitive positioning, the relationship with customers and the type of value being paid for.

The Booking People – an evolving payment model

Internet-based restaurant booking service The Booking People targets small independent restaurants. It provides restaurants with an outlet on the Internet so that customers can book tables online. The restaurant can also insert bookings themselves when customers phone or drop by to book rather than doing it online. At any point, the restaurant can see how many people have booked, and use this information for planning and marketing. The system is paid for in two ways: the restaurants pay a small monthly subscription, and online bookers pay a small fee per seat booked at the time of the booking.

Although the system was accepted by some restaurants, in due course the subscription charge to the restaurant had to be dropped, as the restaurants were uncertain about the value the website created for them. The only way to penetrate the market was to offer the system for free.

Although restaurant sign-ups increased, The Booking People struggled to attract traffic and thus revenue to its website. A major competitor in the industry, Top Table, had a similar product. This was more cumbersome and expensive for a restaurant to use, yet Top Table's marketing muscle enabled it to capture larger restaurants, chains and hotels as customers, and attracted more bookers to its system. In due course The Booking People made a deal with Top Table, so that customers could book through either system. This gave The Booking People's restaurants access to Top Table's larger market potential.

From a revenue perspective, the new deal had positives as well as negatives for The Booking People. Although more people were likely to use the system, revenues that came via the Top Table system would have to be shared with Top Table. Thus The Booking People paid for access to the market which Top Table had created. Splitting the fee meant that The Booking People had to raise its prices, or there wouldn't be enough left over to cover costs.

(Read more about The Booking People and the entrepreneur who devised it in Chapter 7, 'The search for the entrepreneur'.)

14

14.6 TYPES OF BUSINESS MODELS

Having considered the many components of business models, and the ways in which these can be flexed or traded off against one another, we now consider complete business models in more depth.

14.6.1 Innovation Through the Business Model

Enterprises create value for their customers or end users. For every problem or customer need, there may be a number of possible solutions. Not only may a particular problem elicit different solutions but each of these may be implemented in different ways or through a variety of business models.

One form of innovation is to experiment with a different model for dealing with a common problem. Some enterprise opportunities use new technology to enable this type of innovation.

How to mend a broken heart

Services aimed at curing a broken heart abound, and include social as well as commercial enterprises. As most people experience a broken heart (or a lonely heart) at some time or other, there are many different approaches taken to helping them: different solutions to the problem. Each of these solutions can in turn be implemented through several different business models or approaches.

Solution 1: The talking cure

One solution for dealing with this real problem is a counseling service – a one-to-one service for helping people by enabling them to talk about their problems and receive advice or sympathy. This one idea can be implemented through various business models. For instance: a priest may offer advice as part of their ministry, paid for by the church which employs them; a psychologist can offer help on an individual fee for service basis, with individuals paying for a specific counselling session; a telephone helpline can be set up to provide fast access, with many operatives available to talk or listen to the broken-hearted, the service being paid for through sponsorship or donations; an online community for the broken-hearted can be developed, with revenues provided either by subscription or by advertising.

Solution 2: The matchmaking service

A second solution to the problem is a matchmaking or dating service, which can be implemented in different ways such as: through the Internet with online profiling; through more discreet agencies where an agent works with the individual to create a profile and to match people together; or through running speed dating events which individuals pay to attend with an expectation of meeting a number of people at each event.

Each of these solutions presents different resource requirements and economic opportunities to the enterprise owners and represents a particular business model. Each makes different assumptions about the nature of the need, the number of people who will be helped, the particular skills and resources required to deliver the service, and how it will be paid for.

Successful and innovative business models have the capacity to change industries. Prompted by the development of the Internet, a wide range of business models has emerged, some of them highly innovative.

eBay – the ancient art of the auction online

One of the most successful of web-based enterprises has been eBay. Founded in 1995 in the US, it has auction sites based in dozens of countries. Although auctions have been around for thousands of years, eBay has re-invented the traditional format thanks to some of the unique characteristics of the Internet, and to some innovative approaches which it pioneered.

The business model is to provide an online platform where buyers and sellers can engage in commerce. EBay charges sellers a listing fee and a small percentage of their income from each transaction; it charges them to use Skype and for payment processing through Paypal; it also sells advertising within the site. The business model relies on high usage levels being generated by several factors:

■ A robust and trustworthy technology platform;

■ An efficient, transparent and well-policed commercial system;

■ Universal availability within the national markets where the company has launched;

■ A relatively low transaction cost for buyers and sellers;

■ A genuine need for a marketplace existing.

These factors attract high volumes of traffic from both buyers and sellers, which are necessary to generate high revenues (the website reported $100 million revenue in Q2 of 2005) from what are often very small financial transactions.

The appeal of the commercial platform to both buyers and sellers has created new entrepreneurial opportunities, with sellers using it to set up shops, rather than simply auctioning a few items now and then. The company estimates there are approximately 178,000 enterprises running through the platform. This is a new industry of small traders able to start a shop and access a large potential customer base with minimal capital outlay.

However, many of the early Internet businesses did *not* create value, and as in the physical economy, there continue to be successful and unsuccessful web-based enterprises. It has also become clear with the exploration of the business model concept that many e-businesses replicate models that already exist in the non-web economy.

14.6.2 Taxonomies of Business Models

Taxonomies or lists of different business models have been developed and continue to evolve, as new models are developed.[8] Categorising enterprises by type of business model in this way helps to focus on how each model works. Table 14-5 lists some common business models which are available both online and in the physical world.

These models are not necessarily mutually exclusive or 'pure'. In fact, many enterprises combine models in order to maximise revenues from a target market. Business models also evolve over time, as industries, markets and economic conditions change. The process of effectuation may involve starting with one business model, testing it out and changing it to fit circumstances which most effectively captures the value of the idea (Chesbrough and Rosenbloom, 2002; Magretta, 2002).

14

TABLE 14-5	Some business models available both in the physical and virtual worlds	
Business model	**Key activity**	**Examples**
Brokerage	Brings buyers and sellers together	Real estate agents
Advertising	Provides a medium which advertisers use to reach their target audience	Free newspapers
Infomediary	Collects, digests and sells information, particularly about audiences and markets	Market and media research agencies
Merchant	Sells goods	Retail outlet
Manufacturer (direct)	Sells directly to target market, rather than through wholesale or retail channels	Any manufacturer with direct sales
Affiliate	Links providers together to share performance	Television channel
Community	Provides space for interaction between users	Community arts centre Social networking sites
Subscription	Sells access to a service for a time-based (monthly, weekly) fee	Magazines or telephone connections
Utility	Users pay per usage	Electricity, water, telephone services

Source: Michael Rappa, www.digitalenterprise.org

Friends Reunited – an evolving business model

Friends Reunited started using a hybrid subscription and advertising business model. Basic access was free, enabling users to post information about themselves on the site. This attracted traffic, as people began looking for old friends who had posted their details there, and Friends rapidly became *the* place to search for friends and family. However, to begin contacting people through the site a subscription had to be paid. This model had the benefit of creating a growing revenue stream from the outset. In addition, the company sold some advertising on the site, taking advantage of the large number of users.

In due course, other social networking sites like Bebo, MySpace and Facebook established themselves and provided free mail services to end users. They used a pure advertising model. This new competition meant that Friends Reunited users could switch to other providers for free.

ITV, the television network which bought Friends Reunited in 2005 similarly uses an advertising model. It decided in 2008 that Friends Reunited should drop its paywall and become purely advertising supported. At the same time, new features were launched targeting the over-30s users who were more likely to want to track old friends.

However, from 2008, an extreme decline in advertising income in both the television and the online markets hit. It remains to be seen whether the pure advertising business model will continue to be successful for social networking sites.

14.6.3 Franchising: A Popular Business Model for Rapid Growth

Franchising is a business model which allows rapid growth for established enterprises, and creates opportunities for entrepreneurs to establish a new enterprise with relatively low risk. A 'franchisor' sets up an enterprise, works out standardised systems and processes that enable it to be replicated and then sells the right to operate that business to 'franchisees'. In this way, franchising provides a useful means for entrepreneurial businesses to expand their business quickly, and for new entrepreneurs to enter markets as franchisees.

Franchise operations are usually location specific. A franchise offers a licence to use a business concept that has already been proven in a particular location. The concept being replicated typically includes business processes, supplies, a successful brand name, know-how and marketing support (Clarkin and Rosa, 2005). Retailing and restaurants are common franchise opportunities. To expand a retail or restaurant chain, an entrepreneur will need to replicate the original business concept in many locations; this is time-consuming and requires substantial capital investment. Through franchising, the founding entrepreneurs recruit a team of other entrepreneurs who bring in capital, time and energy to set up outlets.

Many well-known restaurant chains such as Pizza Hut and McDonald's and retail brands like Body Shop and Benetton developed through franchising. However, franchises can be developed for many different products and services, and many lesser-known enterprises in business and domestic services have also expanded in this way (see Table 14-6). An Internet search will show that franchises are available in many different countries, and that there are directories of franchises available which can be searched to find opportunities.[9]

ENTREPRENEURSHIP IN ACTION

The Big Issue – franchising the homeless

The Big Issue is a novel franchise devised by Gordon Roddick and A. John Bird. It is a weekly newspaper which is exclusively sold on the street across Britain by homeless people. In order to become a Big Issue vendor an individual must prove that they are homeless or vulnerably housed, undergo an induction process and sign up to a code of conduct. Once they have done so they are allocated a fixed location to sell from and issued with five free copies of the magazine (ten in London). Once they have sold these magazines they can purchase further copies, which they buy for 70 pence and sell for £1.50, thereby making 80 pence per copy.

The Big Issue is a social enterprise, and any profits made go into a trust which supports the homeless and campaigns for social change.

Source: www.bigissue.com

John Bird

14

TABLE 14-6	Some interesting franchise opportunities
Name of franchise	**Main business**
ChipsAway	Car paint chip repair operation
EmbroidMe	Embroidery and promotional products
Tutor Doctor	Private tutoring for school children
Pals4Pets	Professional pet care services
AlphaJuice	Smoothie franchise
TransitFast	Same-day freight and courier service
JaniKing	Commercial cleaning service

Source: Rappa, M. (2009) www.digitalenterprise.org

14.7   SUMMARY AND ACTIVITIES

Every enterprise has a **business model**. Although academic definitions of business models vary, they are essentially the system through which the entrepreneur captures the value inherent in the business idea. It encompasses the value proposition, the main activities and systems through which this is delivered, and the means through which money is collected from the customer.

The study of business models has come to the fore since the advent of the Internet in the late 1990s. Although the Internet has brought a welcome focus to the study of business models, many of those identified are pre-existing models from the physical world. Analysts have provided **taxonomies** of business models.

The **value chain** is the vertical chain of organisations from extraction or production of raw materials through to consumers of end products. Value chain analysis shows where value and cost are added through the chain. The **value web** concept captures the complexity of collaborations within network-based industries, or created through the Internet.

The business model concept is **integrative** in several senses. It integrates different theoretical perspectives about enterprises; it expresses the integration of the enterprise's activities; it brings together the narrative of the enterprise with the profit and loss account.

The components of a business model are customers and the value proposition for them, the product and service offering, operations, costs and revenues. These are integrated into the business model in order to create value.

The business model should describe the market, its needs, and how the particular product and service satisfies these. It should also identify the main operational parameters and the costs of developing and operating these. Finally, it should encompass what is being paid for, and how it is being paid for.

Business models are sources of innovation when they reconfigure an industry in order to create new sources of value. They may for instance create new routes to customers or suppliers, bring together new combinations of resources, or create new configurations of enterprises.

Franchising is a common business model adopted for rapid expansion of location-specific businesses. The franchising model brings in revenues from franchisees to a business concept which has been proven in a market. The franchisor owns and develops the business concept, and markets it to gain new franchisees.

14

REVIEW QUESTIONS

1 What is a business model?

2 What are the main components of business models?

3 What is meant by 'value proposition'?

4 What is meant by value chain and value web?

5 How do entrepreneurs determine what business model to use?

6 Identify the factors which lead enterprises to change their business models.

7 Identify at least five different business models and enterprises which use them.

8 What role do costs play in determining the business model?

9 Discuss the pros and cons of franchising as a business model.

10 What are the characteristics of successful and unsuccessful business models?

SEMINAR TASK

Imagine you are establishing a new enterprise to produce T-shirts. Discuss the possible business models which you could develop for the business to be a success. Take at least two of these and develop them further. What would be the main factors which would ensure their success?

Preview case continued

El Bulli – a model restaurant

Restaurants are extremely varied in their approach to food, drink and service. The variation is partly due to different ethnic traditions of cuisine, and partly to the range of preferences among customers in terms of price, style of eating, access and other dimensions. In some parts of Europe, cooking and restaurants have been elevated to an art form, and certain chefs are regarded as stars and cultural icons. Many of these chefs have established restaurants of their own with distinctive styles; some have behaved as entrepreneurs, turning themselves and their skill in the kitchen into well-known brand names through television, books, food products and often chains of restaurants or serial restaurant openings. In these cases, it is sometimes the chef who is the brand name, sometimes the restaurant. For example, Jamie Oliver has helped set up a number of chains including Jamie's Italian and a franchised social enterprise chain – 15.

At the expensive end of the restaurant market are restaurants which are highly rated by the famous Michelin Guides – a well-established brand name in the restaurant and tourist guide market in Europe. El Bulli, in the

14

Costa Brava area of north-east Spain, is often referred to as the best restaurant in the world and is considered by food writers to be in a class of its own. The food is unique and extraordinary, and its chef and owner, Ferran Adria, hailed as a genius. The cuisine is extraordinary not only because it is of the highest quality, but also because it uses cultural references, language jokes and visual puns combined with unusual ingredients and tastes presented in a distinctive way so that diners do not know what to expect when they eat something. Adria has put in place highly distinctive working processes to deliver this extraordinary cuisine.

The food itself is not the only unusual thing about El Bulli. The restaurant's location is part of its charm, being in a converted farmhouse on a somewhat remote hill an hour's drive from Barcelona. The restaurant operates in a highly unusual manner. First, despite becoming famous across the world, the restaurant is only open for six months in the year or less, only some days in the week, and rarely for lunch. Bookings are taken by email, and all places are allocated within a few days of opening the booking period in December or January of each year. The restaurant is quite small (just 54 covers), so the total number of diners who experience this cuisine is relatively small. The restaurant is so famous that it allegedly receives 1,000,000 requests for meals each year, but in total can only accommodate approximately 8000.

Second, in the months when the restaurant is closed, the chef and his team work in laboratories in Barcelona, inventing new dishes. They use scientific and experimental approaches to rethink ingredients so that they can be presented in the unusual combinations and forms for which they are famous. The process of inventing completely new dishes is unusual enough, but at El Bulli, the number of such dishes produced every year (about 120) is unprecedented.

A further difference between El Bulli and its main competitors among the very best restaurants in the world is the variety of dishes which each diner experiences. Nicholas Lander of the *Financial Times* estimates[10] that in the course of a meal, each diner will experience about 45 different dishes (many of them single mouthfuls), resulting in over 2000 dishes being produced for each sitting. This contrasts with other restaurants of the highest class, in which each customer might be served 10 different dishes. In addition, each table will have a different combination of dishes, so although low volume, this is a high variety operation. Producing each dish at the right moment, at the correct temperature with the required appearance requires a large, labour intensive back room operation in a European country with relatively high employment costs.

The business model and operations strategy of the restaurant are counter-intuitive. Given the cost of running a laboratory for several months of the year, and the unusually complex kitchen and serving operations within the restaurant, the organisation's costs are very high compared to its competitors in the high-quality end of the restaurant market. A normal approach to this would be to increase capacity, or perhaps to franchise the concept, but the restaurant remains small, and is open only for part of the year, thus being able to serve only a limited number. The high demand for places might encourage the restaurant to charge extremely high prices, but in fact its prices are in line with other famous restaurants in Europe. Given high costs, small capacity, and average prices for its class of restaurant, it seems unlikely that the restaurant itself is profitable. So how does Adria make money?

The brand names of the chef and his restaurant are highly valuable assets, as are the techniques and recipes which he has created. Other operations in different domains leverage value from this intellectual property. A look at the website (www.elbulli.com) helps to explain how this is done. Videos and books explaining the philosophy and techniques of the master chef are available for sale, as well as food, kitchen equipment, tableware and decorative products. A small number of associated hotels are advertised, as are links with educational organisations and seminars. These other activities contribute significantly to the profits of the organisation. If the claim that the restaurant receives 1,000,000 requests per year for bookings is true, then sales of merchandise through the website are likely to be substantial. Indeed, the first page that opens on the website is the merchandise sales page, indicating that this is the most important page – the one that most customers want to use.

The management of merchandising, including the selection of sub-contrators and the design and production of products, is a major operation in its own right. So too is the management of online sales including the administrative operations of holding stock, managing packaging and delivery and clearing payments. These non-culinary activities employ many people and absorb considerable time and energy within the organisation. Decisions about whether to outsource these activities, and how to manage partnerships with suppliers, are important to the brand. Standing as it does for constant innovation and excellence, the brand is unusual and the merchandise and the sales methods reflect these qualities. The website is visually edgy, conveying some of the surprise and excitement of the eating experience. The designers and their products are carefully selected for their avant garde credentials and the equipment for sale is mainly the unusual items that are needed to create Adria's inventive food.

The business model is therefore one in which developing intellectual property, a resource that can be used and sold in many ways, is more important than the actual restaurant operations. The R&D laboratory creates the IP in recipes and techniques, while the restaurant provides the evidence that these work and are extraordinary. The brand names of the chef / owner and his restaurant are leveraged to reap economic value from many other applications. The restaurant is thus like the tip of an iceberg – the visible part of something much larger underneath.

Questions

1 *You and an entrepreneurial team have decided to replicate El Bulli's business model in another country. How would you go about this? What problems would you foresee?*

2 *What core skills would you expect the leader of such an operation to possess? How do you measure the success of such a business?*

3 *You have been called in as a consultant to sell the business of El Bulli to the highest bidder. Summarise a potential sales prospectus for the business that outlines its key assets and selling points.*

Source: El Bulli website, www.elbulli.com

14.8   NOTES, REFERENCES AND FURTHER READING

Notes and Further Information

1. The El Bulli website is at www.elbulli.com, and contains information about products, philosophy and the restaurant.

2. For a detailed discussion of the role of entrepreneurship in the economy, see Chapter 4. In particular section 4.3 investigates the nature of the relationship between entrepreneurship and the economy.

3. Chapter 5, 'Entrepreneurship in context' discusses the internationalisation of new enterprise in more detail under section 5.4 'Regional and international communities of entrepreneurship'.

4. For a video demonstration of this experience at a Sapporo restaurant, see www.sapporo.co.uk.

5. For a more detailed description of the operation see www.yosushi.com.

6. For a case study example of a business that started literally on the kitchen table and then progressed to separate premises as it grew, see the case study near the end of Chapter 15, 'Boogles adds up'.

7. For a definition of the break-even point and a discussion of other important revenue–cost relationships see Chapter 15, section 15.5 'Financial management and forecasting'.

8. Professor Michael Rappa of the University of North Carolina, US runs a website www.digitalenterprise.org which is a particularly useful resource in discussing business models. He provides a list of business models on the web, and continually updates the list as new models are developed. However, the models he discusses are equally likely to be available in the physical world.

9. Franchise directories provide useful market information for entrepreneurs wishing to set up a new business even if they do not wish to use the franchise model. By using the directories, they can check to see if there are any services or products similar to their idea already on offer. Similar services being offered as franchises may mean that the business idea they have spotted could represent a genuine opportunity but it also could mean that there is potentially stiff competition in the offing. Some examples of franchise directories include:

   - Australia: http://www.franchisebusiness.com.au – directory of the Franchise Council of Australia.

   - India: http://www.franchisebusiness.in – an online directory published in association with the Franchise Association of India.

   - UK: www.franchiseinfo.co.uk.

10. As reported in the *Financial Times* on 11 October 2008 (www.ft.com).

References

Amit, R. and Zott, C. (2001) Value creation in e-business, *Strategic Management Journal*, 22 (6/7): 493–520.

Barney, J. (1991) Firm resources and sustained competitive advantage, *Journal of Management*, 17: 99–120.

Cartwright, S.D. and Oliver, R.W. (2000) Untangling the value web, *Journal of Business Strategy*, 21 (1): 22–27.

Chesbrough, H. and Rosenbloom, R.S. (2002) The role of the business model in capturing value from innovation: Evidence from Xerox Corporation's technology spinoff companies, *Industrial and Corporate Change*, 11 (3): 529–555.

Clarkin, J.E. and Rosa, P.J. (2005) Entrepreneurial teams within franchise firms, *International Small Business Journal*, 23 (3): 303–334.

Fiet, J.O. and Patel, P. (2008) Forgiving business models for new ventures, *Entrepreneurship: Theory & Practice*, 32 (4): 749–761.

Hedman, J. and T. Kalling, T. (2003) The business model concept: Theoretical underpinnings and empirical illustrations, *European Journal of Information Systems*, 12: 42–59.

Magretta, J. (2002) Why business models matter, *Harvard Business Review*, May.

Morris, M., Schindehutte, M. and Allan, J. (2005) The entrepreneur's business model: Toward a unified perspective, *Journal of Business Research*, 58 (6): 726–735.

Parasuraman, A., Berry, L.L. and Zeithaml, V.A. (1985) A conceptual model of service quality and its implications for future research, *Journal of Marketing*, 49: 41–50.

Peteraf, M.A.(1993) The cornerstones of competitive advantage: A resource-based view, *Strategic Management Journal*, 14 (3): 179–191.

Porter, M. (1980) *Competitive Strategy*, New York: Free Press.

Porter, M.E. (1985) *Competitive Advantage*, New York: Free Press.

Porter, M.E. (1991) Towards a dynamic theory of strategy, *Strategic Management Journal*, 12 (S): 95–119.

Rappa, M. (2002) *Business Models on the Web*, http://digitalenterprise.org/models/models.html.

14

Schumpeter, J.A. (1934) *The Theory of Economic Development: An Inquiry into Profits, Capital, Credit, Interest and the Business Cycle*, tr. R. Opie, Cambridge, MA: Harvard University Press.

Shafer, S.M., Smith, H.J. and Linder, J.C. (2005) The power of business models, *Business Horizons*, 48 (3): 199–207.

Zott, C. and Amit, R. (2008) The fit between product market strategy and business model: Implications for firm performance, *Strategic Management Journal*, 29: 1–26.

Recommended Further Reading

Chesbrough, H.W. (2006) *Open Business Models: How to Thrive in the New Innovation Landscape*, Boston, MA: Harvard Business School Press.

Magretta, J. (2002) *What Management Is: How it Works and Why it's Everyone's Business*, New York: Free Press.

14

CHAPTER 15

Entrepreneurial Finance

LEARNING OBJECTIVES

After studying this chapter, the reader will be able to:

- Understand the impact of the entrepreneurial environment on financial management
- Analyse the main sources of debt funding for entrepreneurial ventures
- Analyse the main sources of equity funding for entrepreneurial ventures
- Evaluate which type of funding is needed for a particular purpose
- Analyse the main types of financial reporting used by an enterprise
- Understand how to undertake a financial forecast for an entrepreneurial venture.

INTRODUCTION

In Part 3 of this book we have so far considered four of the components that add value to an entrepreneurial venture:

- The customer base and market position (Chapter 11);
- The embedded knowledge and the intellectual property rights which might protect it (Chapter 12);
- The team of people involved in running the enterprise (Chapter 13); and
- The business model and processes used to operate the enterprise (Chapter 14).

In this chapter we consider the role of finance in the development of an entrepreneurial venture. Finance has been likened to the life-blood of an enterprise: it flows through the various operating areas of an enterprise and provides them with the sustenance to keep going. It is also the most common way of measuring the health of an enterprise. Financial measurements such as cash flow and profits tell us whether the four factors above are working well and if the enterprise is actually increasing in value. This chapter considers answers to three commonly asked questions about an entrepreneurial venture:

1 What sources of finance are available to entrepreneurial ventures from debt and equity sources?

2 How much money does an enterprise need, now and in the future?

3 What financial management controls are required to maximise the cash flow and profits of an enterprise?

PREVIEW CASE

Boogles adds up

Lisa Newton started Boogles Ltd, a bookkeeping service, as soon as she finished at university. She claims that, with just £150 to invest in the business, she had the advantage of becoming an entrepreneur whilst 'still in student mode.'

What do you think she means by this?

Read more about how Lisa set up her business in the case study at the end of this chapter.

Lisa Newton, founder of Boogles Ltd.

15.1 THE FINANCIAL ISSUES OF ENTREPRENEURIAL VENTURES

15.1.1 Why 'Entrepreneurial' Finance?

Much of the material on entrepreneurial finance may seem similar to traditional financial management texts. In some respects it is: raising and managing finance is a core discipline in any business whether or not it is entrepreneurial. However, important aspects of entrepreneurship make raising and managing finance different in this context:

■ The uncertainty of outcomes in an entrepreneurial venture increases the degree of risk to investors and therefore the difficulties in raising finance.

■ In entrepreneurial ventures, investors and the management of the enterprise are usually more intertwined than shareholders and management in large organisations. Entrepreneurs are commonly both the manager and the owner of their enterprise, raising finance from a variety of sources. In larger organisations, particularly publicly quoted ones, there is a clear separation between investors who are shareholders and those who run the business (Jarvis, 2006).

■ The financial markets available to entrepreneurs are more limited than those open to corporations and large institutions. Entrepreneurial ventures often have to appeal to private investors rather than stock markets to raise funds and shortages of funding opportunities are a problem for some enterprises.

■ The opportunist nature of entrepreneurial ventures, often operating with little precise knowledge of the environment, makes forecasting the financial needs of an enterprise problematic.

■ The small scale of an entrepreneurial venture at start up, and the need to make rapid adjustments as it develops, make uncertainty in the management of finance more likely.

■ The personal characteristics of entrepreneurs, including their resource acquisition skills and intuitive decision-making, introduce further uncertainty in financial planning and influence the type of finance acquired and the methods used to manage it.

15

- The financial statements required by statute for small businesses are usually less rigorous than the statutory reports published by large public companies.[1]

- Entrepreneurs tend to make less use of financial statements and controls than corporate managers (Collis, Jarvis and Skerratt, 2004).

15.1.2 Overview of the Financial Issues Faced by Entrepreneurial Ventures

These differences in the way that entrepreneurs raise money and control their finances give rise to a number of particular financial issues. These are not necessarily static issues that exist at all times as they tend to change with the development of the enterprise through its life cycle.

In the early stages, many nascent entrepreneurs begin their new venture journey by seeking sources of finance with an inadequate knowledge of how much money they actually require in the various stages of launching the venture. One venture capital organisation[2] claimed that entrepreneurs invariably overestimate the initial finance required to test the viability of the idea and then underestimate the amount required to launch it in the marketplace. If assessing the finance required is the first hurdle, raising the finance is often regarded as the most daunting task, although there are a wide variety of funds available in most developed economies to test innovative products, processes and services.

As an enterprise progresses there are further financial difficulties, often more serious. The second tranche of finance required to commercialise the idea fully is likely to be more substantial than that required for initial prototyping and market testing, and the sources of finance become a greater problem. Control of costs can also be overlooked in the rush to get in early sales. As a new venture takes off and moves into a growth stage, it can trade beyond its financial resources and run out of cash even though its sales are booming.

As the business matures, owners and investors seek a return on their investment which may cause a financial burden on the enterprise and disagreement between investors on the optimal rates of return. As the industry becomes more competitive, the likelihood of a customer defaulting on payment increases. In the final stages, some of the sources of finance may be withdrawn as investors seek an exit route.

An illustration of these key issues in the five stages in the life cycle of an entrepreneurial venture are shown in Table 15-1.

TABLE 15-1	Financial issues in life cycle stages
Life cycle stage of the enterprise	**Financial issues**
Concept/test stage	Need for seed investment. Lack of reliable forecasts
Development	Under-capitalisation – inability to raise enough finance. Ineffective cost controls
Growth	Working capital crisis from over-trading. Equity gap causes second phase funding issues
Maturity	Return on investment required by investors. Bad debts more likely
Decline	Exit routes for investors and lenders. Tax issues on exit

15

KAT's financial life cycle

KAT was started over 20 years ago to manufacture electronic products in niche markets by three shareholders (yes their names did begin with K, A and T): two technical specialists to run it and one to act as a non-executive business adviser. The non-executive partner contributed £60,000 of the £80,000 share capital for 40 per cent of the shares. The two executive partners each received 30 per cent of the shares but put in only £10,000 each as they did not have much cash to invest and they would be contributing 110 per cent of their time. They also negotiated a £30,000 bank overdraft based on personal guarantees given by the three directors. Their initial purchase of equipment and machinery was funded partly by a government grant for innovative enterprises and partly by hire purchase.

It took longer than their original estimates to get the business to a break-even point and for a while the partners thought they would use up all of their original investment before the cash flow became positive. But on the last day of the eleventh month a cheque arrived just in time to save them from breaching their overdraft limit and during the following months they traded profitably.

A further three years of profitable trading helped them to make further investments in new equipment and to expand their sales. Then they lost one large customer as a recessionary period in the industry deepened, sufficient to turn profits into losses and the cash flow negative. Unable to secure any further support from the bank, two of the partners decided to invest more money themselves. The third partner had been working in the business and when he decided not to invest further he pulled out of the day-to-day running of the company and asked the other shareholders to buy him out. They refused and their new investment in the business watered down his original shareholding to under 10 per cent.

Fifteen years on the business has survived and is profitable, giving a reasonable return to the shareholders. But the problem remains of one disgruntled shareholder whose original investment was diluted but who still has not found a satisfactory exit route.

Can you categorise each of KAT's financial problems according to the financial issues of the life cycle stages illustrated in Table 15.1?

15.1.3 Matching Sources with Uses of Finance

The life cycle analysis illustrates that almost all entrepreneurial ventures need finance at some time. However, the reasons for this funding vary greatly from long-term capital equipment investments at one end of the spectrum to short-term working capital to pay for office supplies until trading begins, at the other end. It is important to match these diverse uses of finance with appropriate sources as different types of money should be used for different purposes (Burns, 2001). However, not all businesses have access to all types of funds so this is a further factor to consider when matching the sources and use of funds. In summary the matching process of funding has to take account of:

■ **The type of enterprise**: some forms of enterprise have limited or no ability to raise external equity finance from shareholders. Sole traders and partnerships do not have shareholders and so the equity route is closed although they can attract loans. Social enterprise is normally funded by grants and donations rather than shares. Some cooperatives can only raise limited amounts of share capital.

■ **The risk/reward relationship**: the relationship between the risk involved in funding a venture and the likely rewards influences the types of funds available. If the risks are great but the rewards equally large, equity funding from investors prepared to take the risk is the usual route. If the risks are small and the rewards less, debt finance through loans and bank overdrafts are more appropriate. The

15

stage of development of the venture is a key factor in this balance: early stage ventures involve more risk and possibly offer more reward so that share capital is more likely to be involved at this time. More mature businesses are less likely to raise money through shares unless they have a major requirement as they can meet most needs through bank finance.

■ **Assets acquired** as part of the funding: if funding is required to purchase specific items such as equipment, property or vehicles, specialist forms of funding are available to match the type of asset.

15.2   TYPES OF ENTREPRENEURIAL FINANCE: DEBT FUNDING

15.2.1 Debt vs. Equity Funding

There is a primary divide in the types of funding available to an enterprise between *debt* and *equity* finance.

■ **Debt** is money that is borrowed with the intent to pay it back on certain terms and conditions. Debt finance requires the borrower to pay back the amount borrowed within a certain time (the 'term' of the loan) plus a fee usually expressed as an interest rate. Typically it might be a bank loan or overdraft. The amount borrowed is normally paid back from the income accruing to the business. An important advantage of debt finance is that the entrepreneur does not have to give away any ownership of the business to obtain it. The key disadvantage (over equity finance) is that there is a payment schedule that has to be maintained whatever the state of the business.

■ **Equity** is money that is invested in an enterprise in return for a share in the ownership of the enterprise. The investor shares in the profits of the business, but is not normally repaid until the business is sold. The advantages and disadvantages are the reverse of debt finance: a key advantage of equity finance is that there is no fixed repayment plan for investors who are only rewarded when the business can afford it; the disadvantage to the entrepreneur is that they have to give away a percentage of ownership in the business. Types of equity funding are explored in the next section.

As entrepreneurs typically value control of their own destiny above other considerations, they do not like to give away part-ownership of their business. They therefore tend to favour debt over equity finance with bank finance accounting for over 60 per cent of the external finance of small firms in the UK (Cosh and Hughes, 2000).

There is a further primary divide between **internal** and **external** funding that needs to be considered for both debt and equity finance.

■ **Internal funds** are generated within the business or from the founders. Entrepreneurs usually invest some of their own money into their enterprise. Once running, the venture can generate cash which can be ploughed back to sustain and expand the business.

■ **External funds** are generated from outside of the business. Friends and family form an important source of funds for new ventures. Their investment can be in the form of loans or equity, but loans are often the preferred route as the founding entrepreneur does not have to dilute ownership, and loans can be repaid more easily than investments in the form of shares. Banks and venture capitalists are further examples of external funders, as described in the sections below.

15.2.2 Bank Finance

Entrepreneurial ventures use banks more than any other source of external funding, typically with a combination of overdraft and loan finance (see Table 15-2).

TABLE 15-2 Types of debt finance used by SMEs		
Type of external finance	% of SMEs using that type of finance	% of SMEs for which that type is largest external source
Overdraft	24	14
Loan	40	29
Commercial mortgage	7	5
Leasing/HP	44	19
Invoice finance	8	4
Other	17	9
Don't know	16	18

Source: Bank of England, 2003: 11

Bank Overdrafts An overdraft is a short-term loan in which the bank grants the customer the right to overdraw on their account by a certain amount for a certain period of time. It is intended to finance the *working capital* requirements of a business: that is the fluctuations in the amounts of cash coming in and going out that is caused by the trading cycle rather than the underlying performance of the business. It is not intended to finance longer-term needs such as losses in the business or the purchase of assets.

Bank Loans Although today term loans are the most common form of bank lending in most countries, this was not always the case (Jarvis, 2006). Prior to the 1990s, loans accounted for approximately half of small business indebtedness to the clearing banks in the UK. By the end of the 1990s this had shifted to a ratio of two-thirds loans and one-third overdrafts (Bank of England, 2004). The reasons for the shift towards loans was twofold: first the banks encouraged the move by those businesses that had a fixed element of overdraft that did not fluctuate and therefore did not represent genuine working capital needs; secondly, business owners found that loans were a more secure form of borrowing as they could not be withdrawn provided that payments were maintained, whereas overdrafts could be stopped at very short notice (Jarvis, 2006). In times when the economic environment is less favourable, this is an important consideration as banks are prone to withdraw overdraft facilities when credit tightens.

Debt Factoring and Invoice Discounting Banks and other lenders like to have security in case the borrower defaults on debt repayments. Overdrafts and bank loans are often secured on the assets of the entrepreneur (such as their house) or the assets of the business (such as equipment or debtors). After legal challenges and bad publicity in relation to the use of personal property to secure loans, the clearing banks have begun to favour more direct security for their borrowing. One way of achieving this is through lending based on the value of unpaid invoices to customers or *debt factoring*. This works by giving the business a prepayment against the value of sales invoices yet to be paid. The factoring bank agrees to pay a percentage – up to 85 per cent – of the value of invoices as they are issued to customers. The bank then effectively owns this invoice until it is paid so that the risk is secured against it. Although this effectively transfers the risk from the business borrowing the money to its customer base, it does spread the risk across a greater number of businesses. To maintain this spread, the bank normally limits the amount that can be secured against any one customer with a large share of the turnover of the business. In some forms of factoring the bank actually takes over the sales ledger of the company, collecting monies owed directly and chasing up slow payers and bad debts.

15

Invoice discounting is an increasingly popular form as the business keeps control of its sales ledger and deals directly with their own customer base for the collection of money. However, it is normally only available to established businesses with a track record of dealing with their sales ledger and this limits take-up by entrepreneurs to under 10 per cent of debt finance (see Table 15-2).

The advantages[3] of this form of borrowing over normal overdrafts for entrepreneurial ventures are:

■ Borrowing is linked to sales so that as a business grows it automatically can borrow more if the need arises;

■ Credit control is thorough as it is a pre-condition of the system;

■ Cash is released as soon as the invoice is issued rather than when it is paid, thus improving the cash flow of the business.

The disadvantages are:

■ If sales decline, the amount of finance available also decreases;

■ A business loses an element of control over its customer base in some forms of factoring, although much less so in invoice discounting;

■ Factoring was originally set up to help companies already in financial difficulties and so a stigma of desperation may still be attached to it. This should not apply to invoice discounting as the customer is normally unaware that this arrangement is in place.

Discounting at KAT

When they first launched KAT, the directors negotiated a bank overdraft of £50,000 with the bank, secured by their own personal guarantees. After three years of trading, the debtors' ledger had grown to an average of £100,000, and the directors successfully asked the bank to release their personal guarantees in favour of a security against the debtors of the business. When sales flattened off a few years later, they managed to keep within the overdraft limit but it was fully used for most of the time. The bank insisted that they convert some of the facility into a loan, describing some of the overdraft as 'hard debt'.

A successful sales campaign led to a rapid increase in sales a few years later, which placed a cash strain on the business as it had to buy more stocks and the debtors almost doubled. The bank manager recommended they switch to invoice discounting as this effectively gave them an overdraft limit that grew with their sales. This did indeed solve the cash problem, until the recession hit their industry hard. As their sales declined so did their debtors, and hence their facility with the bank shrank with their order book. The directors were forced to take out a loan guaranteed by a government scheme to compensate for the lack of credit.

15

15.2.3 Other Forms of Debt Finance

Factoring and invoice discounting are types of **asset finance** in that an asset – in this case an invoice – is used as specific security against a debt. More tangible assets in the form of buildings, plant, machinery and vehicles can be funded by asset finance of various types:

■ **Commercial mortgages** provide business owners with the opportunity to buy the premises from which their business operates. They work rather like domestic mortgages in that the amount borrowed is secured against the property although the loan-to-value ratios and the repayment term of the loan are typically less than for a house purchase. The volatility of commercial property prices and the need to focus finance on the core business of the enterprise has kept the uptake of commercial mortgages low.

- **Leasing** gives the entrepreneur use of equipment, machinery or vehicles without actually owning them. Ownership is retained by the leasing company, although in many cases there is a purchase option at the end of the lease period.

- **Hire purchase** gives the entrepreneur use of the asset and also ownership of it, provided that payments according to the agreement are made.

The usage of these types of debt finance by SMEs is shown in Table 15-2. Although HP/leasing and loans are the most popular forms of finance with over 40 per cent of firms using both types, loans represent the largest external source for 29 per cent of firms compared to 19 per cent for HP/leasing, indicating that loans are typically for larger amounts of money.

International Trade Finance International trading creates an additional burden on cash flow. Currency fluctuations, lengthy payment terms and security of payment all give rise to the need for some kind of specialist or export finance.

- *Letters of credit* or *documentary credit* is a fixed assurance from the buyer's bank that payment will be made.

- *Export specialists* offer a wide range of services to exporters including finance.

15.3 TYPES OF ENTREPRENEURIAL FINANCE: EQUITY FUNDING

Sources of equity funding can be sub-divided into internal and external sources:

15.3.1 Internal Equity

Internal equity is the finance contributed by the founding owners of the enterprise – usually the entrepreneurs who do the work of setting up and running the new venture. It is used to refer to the finance provided by them whether the enterprise is a limited company, sole trader or partnership, even though technically sole traders and partnerships do not issue shares. Whether for shares or not, equity finance acts as permanent capital in that it is not repaid or serviced as an investment until the venture can afford it. An investment in equity is rewarded by dividends from profits, or a capital gain when shares are sold. Unlike a loan, equity finance does not have an automatic right to some of the cash flow of the enterprise because the entrepreneur/investor accepts that returns are not automatic, but only made from surpluses. It is used to finance the initial, one-off costs of starting an enterprise, or any major new developments such as innovative new products that come later in the business life cycle. In some cases, a business owner has to refinance a firm that has run into such significant problems that the required finance is not available externally. An entrepreneur may also provide equity finance to buy out the shares of a partner.

The amount of equity invested depends on the circumstances of the entrepreneur and the business, but research suggests that typically it represents about 30 per cent of the capital structure of a new venture (Jarvis, 2006).

15

15.3.2 External Equity Finance

External equity comes from two main sources:

- **Private equity** or **venture capital (VC) funding** is provided either by specialist companies or by high-net-worth individuals also known as 'business angels'. Venture capital investment consists in the purchase of shares of young ventures (typically less than five years old) primarily for capital gain rather than dividends (Cressy, 2006). The gain normally comes from a trade sale or an *Initial Public Offering (IPO)* in which the company is floated on a public stock exchange for the first time.

- **Public equity funds** are provided through stock markets specialising in fast growth, smaller companies such as NASDAQ in the US or the Alternative Investment Market (AIM) in the UK. AIM was launched in 1995 with less regulation and restrictions on size of company than the London Stock Exchange in order to attract smaller businesses. In 2009, AIM formed an Asian incubator stock market 'Tokyo AIM'. Although most European countries have their own stock exchanges, there is no pan-European market focused on small companies, which may be a barrier to the development of venture capital as there is no clear exit route for investors.

Equity finance makes up only 3 per cent of the external finance of SMEs in the UK, and therefore represents only a small part of the funding accessed by entrepreneurs (Bank of England, 2003). It is associated with well-publicised, high-risk investments in innovative, high-tech firms, some of which go on to become household names, such as Apple and Amazon. Even though they are small in number compared to the total business population, these young, high-growth companies contribute significantly to economic growth and external equity investment plays a crucial role in their development. Their finance needs are normally outside of the parameters and scale of bank lending as typically they do not have a profitable track record, nor a product that is easy to understand, and they require significant sums of money. The average investment is over £1 million, an indication that without venture capital at an early stage, these companies would find rapid expansion on a global scale very difficult (Cressy, 2006). For founding entrepreneurs, the major disadvantage of this type of investment is that the venture capitalist will require a high proportion – often a majority – of the shares, to ensure an adequate return for a high-risk investment. If the business does not meet certain predetermined milestones, the entrepreneur also finds that their control diminishes further and if problems persist they are forced out of the business.

15.3.3 Venture Capital (VC) Funds

Venture capital funds provide finance from pooled investments of third-party investors. They are typically managed by partners who recommend and manage investments in growing businesses. They tend to be very selective, investing only in a very small percentage of the opportunities presented to them. They obtain investment funds from a variety of sources, including pension funds, insurance companies, investment trusts, regional development agencies and private individuals (British Venture Capital Association, 2008).

Several different stages of funding are considered by VCs including:

- Seed funds: small amounts of finance needed to test a new idea. This is usually provided by specialist funds, government grants or business angels;

- Start-up: early stage finance for product development and marketing;

- First-round: funds for early sales growth and manufacturing;

■ Second-round: working capital for the early stages of companies that are launched but not yet making a profit;

■ Third-round: also called 'mezzanine financing', this is funding for the expansion of a newly profitable company;

■ Fourth-round: also known as 'bridge financing', as it is needed for the expenses of a public flotation.

Venture capitalists particularly look for a sound, detailed business plan, an enthusiastic, qualified management team who have also invested in the venture and, very importantly, a defined exit route to realise their investment. As venture capital is risk finance, the target rates of return for investors are high – typically 40 per cent per annum. Levels of share ownership normally start at less than 50 per cent (typically 30 to 40 per cent) with a seat on the board of directors to maintain a close watching brief.

The structure of an investment deal may include different types of shares including preference shares that rank ahead of ordinary shares; for example they may give the VC rights to fixed dividends or conversion into ordinary shares if performance targets are not met so that the VC can take control of the company (British Venture Capital Association, 2004[4]). These requirements generally restrict formal venture capital investments to established, high-growth ventures rather than start-ups. Management buy-outs (MBOs), in which the existing managers of a company buy the business from its current owners, have been a particular target of the VC industry.

VC Around the World   The US has the most developed VC industry in the world. In 2008, it invested $283 billion in 3800 ventures (NVCA, 2009). According to the British Venture Capital Association (2008), there are over 200 VC funds based in the UK that invested £31.6 billion in 1680 businesses during 2007. More investments were made in continental Europe and the US than the UK itself as the industry is not restricted to national markets, substantiating the BVCA's claim that the UK has the most developed venture capital industry in Europe, although still behind the US in world rankings. Over 60 per cent of the funds were invested in MBO type deals, with 4 per cent in early stage companies. The number of early stage companies, however, represented 35 per cent of the total number of businesses receiving investment as the amount of funds required were smaller. The largest investors in the VC funds were pension funds followed by banks, insurance companies and government agencies (British Venture Capital Association, 2008).

The VC industry has grown quickly in most developed economies. Australia has 60 VC companies with AUS$10 billion invested; the China Venture Capital Association based in Hong Kong has over 150 VC members with over US$100 billion invested; South Africa's private equity industry has R86.6 billion invested.[5]

Table 15-3 indicates a country ranking by VC investments in 2006/7, showing that smaller economies such as Sweden, South Africa and Singapore still have significant VC activity.

The industry was hard hit by the banking crisis that unravelled during 2008 as investors sought to de-risk their portfolios. European VC investments fell 20 per cent compared to 2007 (EVCA, 2009). However, there are still entrepreneurial opportunities even in times of financial crisis as investments in some sectors have increased, notably in energy and environmental technologies. For example, in the US, VC investments in total fell by 8 per cent in 2008 compared to 2007 but investments in the 'clean technology' sector grew by 50 per cent (NVCA, 2009).

15

Sequoia Capital

Sequoia Capital provides venture capital funding 'to founders of startups who want to turn business ideas into companies' (www.sequoiacap.com). Although based principally in China, it is active internationally with offices in India, the US and Israel. They invest in very high-growth companies principally in technology fields where 'sudden change promotes fresh growth'. They list their investment stages as:

Seed stage	$100K – $1M
Early stage	$1M – $10M
Growth stage	$10M – $50M

It has a wide range of investments in China in companies ranging from Great Dreams, a leading animation company to China Linong that produces vegetables and agricultural products. It has made substantial investments in the US and claims to have been the first venture capital partner in companies that make up 10 per cent of NASDAQ's value. Unusually they like being directly involved in start-ups and even house some of them in their own premises. The VC is making investments in India such as start-ups like Guruji that launched a localised Internet search engine aimed at the Indian web consumer.

Source: www.sequoiacap.com

TABLE 15-3   VC investment activity 2006/7 (US$bn)

Country	Investments
USA	440.8
UK	51.2
France	12.6
Japan	8.0
China	7.4
Sweden	5.3
India	5.0
Singapore	4.4
Germany	4.4
Italy	4.3
South Africa	3.7
Spain	3.5
Netherlands	3.0
Australia	2.3
Korea	2.1
Brazil	1.3
Canada	1.2
Belgium	1.2
Switzerland	1.0
New Zealand	0.8

Source: KPMG and SAVCA, 2008

15.3.4 Business Angels

Informal venture capital from so-called 'business angels' provides an alternative type of investment to the venture capital provided by formal funds and investment companies. Business angels have been defined as 'high net-worth individuals who invest their own money directly in unquoted companies in which they have no family connection in the hope of financial gain and typically play a hands-on role in the business in which they invest' (Mason, 2006: 363). This informal venture capital market is somewhat invisible but a number of business angel networks (BANs) exist to provide an introduction service for owners seeking money and business angels willing to invest.[6]

Business angel investments are an important source of equity finance as they tend to target an area of perceived difficulty in raising funds, the so-called equity gap of smaller investments from £50,000 to £1 million (see section 15.4.2 for more on the equity gap). Business angels tend to make investments of £50,000 to £250,000, smaller amounts than most VC funds, and they are prepared to finance earlier stages of the entrepreneurship process including seed, start-up and first stage funding.

According to Mason (2006) a typical angel profile is:

■ Male – 95 per cent are male;

■ Cashed-out entrepreneurs – most have had their own business and invest the proceeds in other businesses;

■ 45–65 years old – reflecting the time to build sufficient wealth to invest and having some energy left to be involved in other ventures.

The European Business Angel Network estimates that there were 75,000 business angels in Europe who invested a total of €3 billion in 2006 (EBAN, 2008). This may be an underestimate as earlier research estimated that there were 20,000 to 40,000 business angels in the UK alone, who invested between £500 million and £1 billion per annum in around 3000 to 6000 businesses, or an average of just over £150,000 per investment (Mason and Harrison, 2000). In the US, business angels invested $26 billion in over 57,000 entrepreneurial ventures during 2007 (Center for Venture Research, 2008). Business angels also work in collaboration with other angels and VC funds, spreading their risks through joint investments.

They achieve a wide range of outcomes from their investments. A study of over 500 US angels indicated that just over half (52 per cent) of investments lost money whilst 7 per cent achieved returns of ten times the money invested (Wiltbank and Boeker, 2007). Factors that positively influenced the success of the investments were:

■ *Due diligence time* – how much time the angel spent on investigating the investment before it was made;

■ *Experience* – the angel's expertise in the industry in which the investment is made;

■ *Participation* – the angel's level of involvement in the business post-investment as a mentor of the entrepreneurs and a monitor of their performance.

Angels help monitor energy usage

Thames Valley Investment Network (TVIN) members invested £250,000 in energy-efficiency monitor developers Green Energy Options, as part of an £800,000 funding round. This investment was matched by an investment of £250,000 from the Bank of Scotland Corporate's Growth Capital team. TVIN is a business angel network of high-net-worth individuals that helps growing companies to raise funding. Green Energy Options (GEO) has developed sophisticated monitoring devices that make energy use visible. Their products can provide real-time meaningful information about energy use that clearly demonstrates where and when people are spending most on their energy. The company has a number of products that are aimed at the home, business and school markets. The new funding round will allow GEO to invest in its supply chain and further develop routes to market for all its products.

Source: British Business Angels Association, http://www.bbaa.org.uk/index.php?id=232

15.4   KEY ISSUES IN ENTREPRENEURIAL FINANCE

15.4.1 Relationship with Banks

Entrepreneurs and the High Street banks have often been uneasy partners, with a relationship that is considerably affected by general economic conditions. In times when the economy is doing well, the banks have been accused of irresponsible lending by extending too much credit to business owners who are encouraged to take too many risks and become highly geared. When the economic climate worsens, banks are believed to be letting down entrepreneurial ventures by turning off credit and charging them very high levels of interest.

In 2009 small businesses across Europe faced difficult trading conditions with declining demand as economic growth diminished. Governments launched initiatives to support businesses and interest rates were heavily cut. But there were complaints that the banks were creating barriers that prevented the help getting through to SMEs. In Spain 200,000 SMEs were reported to have problems securing finance (Jones, 2009). A survey by the Federation of Small Businesses in the UK found that one-third of small businesses had suffered from increasing bank charges or more onerous borrowing conditions (Federation of Small Businesses, 2009). It was claimed that these problems were threatening to offset the benefits of the many initiatives by governments to help small firms such as the Enterprise Finance Guarantee.[7] A particular concern in relation to this scheme was that although the government was guaranteeing 75 per cent of the loan, banks were still demanding 100 per cent personal guarantees from business owners (Bridge, 2009).

Although these issues tend to be cyclical, with problems magnified by the particular strains of a recessionary economy, they do indicate an uneasy relationship between large bureaucratic organisations such as banks and their entrepreneurial customers. Entrepreneurs learn from experience and their distrust of banks in the past may have encouraged them to save more. Since the 1990s, small business bank deposits have grown steadily and although entrepreneurs have high levels of borrowing with banks, they also have equally high levels of deposits with overall savings of the SME sector as high as its indebtedness (Bank of England, 2004).

Irish small firms face tough competition for bank funding

'The announcement of a new €300 million loan package for small businesses from the European Investment Bank (EIB) came as welcome news for Ireland's hard-pressed SME sector ... Such initiatives provide a welcome good news story in bank lending for small business, but access to funding remains a problem for some customers.

Finance for working capital and extension and/or renewal of facilities such as overdrafts remains a problem, according to Mark Fielding of ISME, which carries out regular surveys of bank lending to the sector. Fielding said that his latest figures, covering the period up to the end of February showed refusal rates of 48 per cent on lending applications but admitted that this was an improvement on the high point at the end of last year of 58 per cent. The comparable figure for last summer was 24 per cent, he said. Fielding also said his members had reported instances where banks had asked firms to reduce their existing overdraft facilities within 60–90 days and, in general, banks were being more active and critical in reviewing facilities than they had been in the past.

Felix O'Regan, of the Irish Bankers Federation, agreed that banks were being much more proactive in managing the accounts of small business. "There's a lot more bankers back at the coalface. Relationship management is now a big issue for the banks again so there are a lot more conversations taking place than you had during the boom years", he says.

Banks are also making greater use of behavioural scoring, also known as customer or predictive scoring, which rates customers on the way they operate their financial affairs, based on the pattern of activity observed by banks on existing customer accounts, O'Regan explains. Behavioural scoring is typically used where customers have been with a bank for a period of time. This information is used to consider credit applications, and for the ongoing management of account facilities, as it builds up a picture of how a customer manages their money. An example of a negative indicator might be where cheques or other items have been returned unpaid.

Lending is clearly more selective now, with a bias towards low risk, but there are alternatives to traditional bank finance. "It is fair to say that problems of the banking sector have meant that access to credit has been problematic but a combination of equity and debt is very much accessible for SMEs with growth potential", says Norbert Gallagher of Equity Environmental Assets Ireland, which invests in green projects.'

Source: http://www.irishtimes.com/newspaper/innovation/2009/0330/1224243687981.html, excerpts from an article in the *Irish Times*, 30 March 2009 by Frank Dillon

15.4.2 Market Failure in the Money Markets

The financial markets do not always provide entrepreneurs with the finance they need, even though they may have a viable business proposition. This is caused by **market failure** – an inability of the supply side of the financial markets to meet the demand for finance from certain types of enterprise, also known as 'hard capital rationing'. There has been considerable debate in the literature as to the extent of this market failure in relation to both debt and equity funding, going back to the 1931 Macmillan Committee that reported that small firms were not well served by financial institutions (Jarvis, 2006).

The possible causes of market failure include:

- **Information asymmetry** – This arises when one side in a potential relationship or deal has better information than the other. In assessing the creditworthiness of a small firm, a bank is likely to have less information than the entrepreneur and this uncertainty may make the bank wary of lending what the entrepreneur claims to need. This is less likely to arise with larger companies because there is more publicly available information including evaluations of the businesses by outsiders such as stock market analysts.

- **Requirement to provide collateral or guarantees for loans** – This has been a particular problem in the UK where banks have tended to advance loans on the basis of the security provided against the indebtedness, whereas US and continental European banks tend to lend on the basis of the business's ability to repay the debt from future earnings – the 'going concern' basis (Berry, Grant and Jarvis, 2003). This issue was recognised by the British government when they introduced the Small

15

Business Loan Guarantee Scheme in 1981 that effectively gave a state guarantee on loans that business owners could not cover with sufficient security.

■ **Fixed costs of providing finance** – The costs of investigating the suitability of an investment or a loan for any venture, small or large, have a number of fixed elements so that they are similar for small or large amounts of finance required. For example, the costs of the process of due diligence and contract preparation for investigating a relatively unknown venture requesting a small amount of capital are not very different to the costs of investigating a better known business that is asking for a substantial sum. Although the costs may be similar, the profits from a larger investment or loan are considerably more, hence the bank or VC are more likely to favour larger rather than smaller deals.

■ **Lack of investment readiness** – Many entrepreneurs are reluctant to spend the time to make a well-presented case for investment because they believe it may come to nothing. They perceive the costs of obtaining equity finance as high and they are reluctant to seek it because it may lead to a loss of control.

There is no real evidence for the widespread existence of a finance or equity 'gap'. There are specific problems for a minority of high-growth start-ups that require equity funding in the range of £100,000 to £500,000 but there is little evidence of unmet demand for debt finance (Cruickshank, 2000). To some extent, business angels exist in order to fulfil the required lower range of equity funding (£50,000 to £250,000).

However, finance gaps do exist for particular groups that find it harder to raise money. Women setting up an enterprise achieve one-third of the funding of men starting up a business (Jarvis, 2006). Although this is partly explained by the fact that female start-ups tend to require less capital, it still remains an issue. Securing finance is also an issue for ethnic minority business owners as evidenced by research in Europe and North America (Ram, Barrett and Jones, 2006).

The banking crisis of 2008 has led to a rationing of credit in all financial markets including business, although the underlying problem is a decline in demand for products and services which in turn has increased the need for finance to support business losses and restructuring.

15.5   FINANCIAL MANAGEMENT AND FORECASTING

Financial reports provide key information both to the financial institutions advancing funds to entrepreneurial ventures and to the entrepreneurs who run them. Although banks and venture capitalists make frequent use of such reports, entrepreneurs often misunderstand their meaning or make insufficient use of them (Jarvis, 2006). It is crucial to regularly measure the financial performance of an enterprise for two main reasons:

■ It indicates the strengths and weaknesses in the ongoing operations of the enterprise.

■ It is the basis for forecasting and monitoring the future financial needs and health of the enterprise.

A number of financial statements act as key indicators of business performance, including cash flow, profit and loss and balance sheet reports. They also form a key part of the forecasts required in a business plan.

15.5.1 Cash Flow

Cash flow records the **receipts** or actual cash received into a business from sales and investments, and the **payments** or the cash that goes out of a business to employees and suppliers. Total receipts less total payments represent the cash flow in any given period, and it can be either positive (i.e. receipts exceed payments) or negative (i.e. where receipts are less than payments). Bank account statements are often a good proxy for cash flow reports if receipts and payments are made through a single account.

Entrepreneurial financial management starts with the management of cash flow. Cash is critical to survival and most entrepreneurial ventures are short of it, especially in the early months when investments in the necessary equipment, premises and working capital need to be made and sales have to be built up from zero. This is a period of **cash burn** when sufficient start-up capital has to be available to cover the outgoings of the business before these can be covered from sales revenue. In some business models this period is short; in others it is a much longer period. For example, a new restaurant has a short period of high investment as the premises are fitted out and staff trained, but as soon as the doors are open for business, customers pay to eat there, so immediate cash is generated. An Internet business often has a longer period without cash receipts because the website has to be developed and sufficient traffic driven to it before it can justify revenues from advertising and other sources. The important factor is to know how much cash is required to develop the business to a **break-even point** when sales receipts at least equal payments made out of the business.

As an enterprise grows, an increasing amount of cash tends to become tied up in unproductive areas, particularly debtors, work-in-progress and finished stock. A key function of the financial management of an enterprise is to minimise the cash locked up in these areas by shortening the time it takes to collect money from customers and improving the turnover time of stock.

15.5.2 Profit and Loss Statements

Profits and cash flow are not the same. Profits measure the amount of money that is made on any particular transaction, representing the difference between the sales income for an item and the costs of producing and delivering the item to the customer. A **profit and loss account (P&L)** is a statement of all the sales made and all the costs incurred by the business over a period of time. Unlike the cash flow, this is a notional summary because at any one time there are sales and costs that have been invoiced, but not yet paid for. Although these are recorded in the P&L, they have yet to affect the cash flow as this only considers the income received from sales invoices and the actual payments made against purchase invoices. The costs of assets such as plant and machinery are also depreciated over their useful lifetime in the P&L which may not be the same as the period over which they are paid for.

Normally, profits eventually translate into cash unless:

■ a customer does not pay their bill and the bad debt is deducted from sales;

■ stocks, debtors and other working capital requirements increase to absorb the cash;

■ investments are made in equipment or new business ventures.

Profits are an important measure of the health of a business at various levels. **Gross profit** is the difference between the sales value of a product or service and the direct costs to make or deliver it. For example, the gross profit of a particular model of car to a dealer is the sales price achieved for the car from the end user who buys it, less the costs paid for the car to the manufacturer or supplier. This can be expressed as a percentage of the costs of the product (mark-up), or as a percentage of the sales price (gross margin). These are important indicators of the underlying profitability of the business, but do not take account of the other indirect costs of running the business such as premises and administration. When all costs are deducted from the sales revenue this represents the **net profit** (or loss) of the business.

15

Motorize profit statement

Motorize, a car dealer, sold 20 cars in a month for a total revenue of £300,000. On each car, the dealer made an average gross profit margin of one-third of the sales value. The total costs of running the business in terms of its overheads of people, premises, marketing and other costs was £75,000 per month. A simple statement of profits for the month are shown below:

	£000s	Percentage of sales value
Total sales	300	100.0
Direct costs	200	66.7
Gross profit	100	33.3
Indirect costs – Overheads	75	25.0
Net profit before tax	25	8.3

The use of these numbers helped the dealer to maintain a basic financial control of their business. They knew that the average gross profit on each car sold was £5,000 (33.3 per cent of the selling price). They also knew that the fixed overheads of the business did not change much at £75,000 per month. So to cover this overhead and make neither profit nor loss for the month (i.e. break-even), they had to sell 15 cars (£75,000 divided by £5000). Once they had achieved break-even point, every additional car sale added £5000 to the net profit. In this particular month they sold 20 cars – 5 more than break-even so the net profit was £25,000. Awareness of the break-even point focused their sales targets to at least make this figure and reward their sales staff when it was achieved.

Some types of business produce good profits but less cash because they require constant re-investment to survive. For example, manufacturers in a competitive sector such as the car industry need to reinvest most of the cash they generate in the next generation of products.

15.5.3 Balance Sheet

The balance sheet is a third type of financial statement that shows different aspects of the health of the business. It is a snapshot at a given moment in time, usually the end of a financial period such as a month or a year. It summarises two key aspects of the business:

■ The uses of funds – what the money in the business has been spent on; and

■ The sources of funds in the business (where the money came from, or who is funding the business).

The total amount of funds used should equal the total amount of the sources of funds put into business – hence the term 'balance sheet'.

The use of funds on the balance sheet include:

■ Fixed assets – plant machinery, equipment and premises fixtures and fittings

■ Stocks and work in progress

■ Debtors – money owed to the business by customers

■ Cash still in the business.

The sources of funds include:

■ Share capital – money introduced by shareholders

■ Trade creditors – money owed to suppliers

■ Bank overdraft and loans

■ Hire purchase and leases

■ Retained earnings – profits kept in the business.

Some of these items such as debtors and stocks are particularly important to the cash flow of a business.

Debtors Debtors are particularly important to track carefully, not only in terms of the total amount owed by customers to an enterprise but also in terms of the **age of debtors**. The older the debt, the more likely it will go unpaid. During recessionary times, the risk of bad debts increases and the impact on small, entrepreneurial ventures of even one unpaid invoice can sometimes be terminal. The management of debtors is a key entrepreneurial skill including analysing debtors by age and taking regular action to remind slow payers.

Stocks The management of stocks and work in progress is a particularly difficult balancing act between ensuring that goods are always on hand when customers need them, whilst minimising the cash tied up in slow-selling items. The consequences of running out of stock are often more serious than the costs of over-stocking so entrepreneurial ventures frequently carry too much stock.

Liquidity Some balance sheet items represent relatively long-term commitments, such as fixed assets and share capital. Others are more short-term assets or liabilities such as debtors, creditors and overdrafts. When assessing the health of a business it is important to consider the **liquidity** that is shown by the balance sheet – that is a measure of how quickly items can be turned into cash. For example, current stocks, debtors and money in the bank are all **liquid assets** in that they can be turned into cash relatively quickly compared to longer-term assets such as machinery and equipment. Offsetting these assets are liabilities or sums that the business has to pay either in the short term (**current liabilities** such as trade creditors), or in the longer term (hire purchase and bank loans). If current liabilities exceed liquid assets then the venture is likely to be experiencing cash flow problems.

Motorize runs into cash problems

Motorize was making profits but when the owner looked at the balance sheet, he realised he had cash problems. He had decided to shift old stock before new models came in and did so by offering customers discounts and extended credit of two months before they had to pay. This put his sales up, but meant he had no cash coming in to pay suppliers for his stock of cars and other creditors such as the Inland Revenue. By looking at the amounts of current assets and liabilities on the balance sheet, he realised that a short-term liquidity problem of £100,000 was just around the corner.

Current (liquid) assets	£000s
Stock – vehicles and parts	200
Debtors – credit to customers	600
Total current assets	800

15

Current liabilities	
Car suppliers	600
Other creditors (Inland Revenue, etc)	100
Bank overdraft	100
Total current liabilities	900
Total current assets less liabilities	−100

15.5.4 Financial Forecasts

Predicting the financial future is a difficult but necessary entrepreneurial skill. The ability to see financial problems before they arrive allows more time for adjustments and corrective action to be taken. A key ingredient in forecasting is historical records. An enterprise that has a well-documented financial history is better placed to look for trends and learn from the past.

But what if there is no history on which to base forecasts? This is the question that faces most would-be entrepreneurs as they contemplate making a profit and loss and cash flow forecast as part of the business planning process for a new venture. The increase in uncertainty in estimating for a new venture makes the use of **triangulation** of a number of different points of view important (Allen, 2009). Triangulation involves bringing together different types of evidence to bear on a particular problem so that the issue can be looked at from a number of different angles before a conclusion is reached. For example, in order to diagnose what is wrong with patients, doctors triangulate a number of sources of evidence: first they ask the patient to describe what is wrong; next they make a physical examination themselves; thirdly they send for specific analysis such as X-ray or blood samples. A similar process can be adopted in financial forecasting by using a number of different starting points and arriving at a consensus between them. Types of evidence used in financial forecasts include:

Bottom-Up Forecast Based on Costs Costs are usually easier to estimate then revenues. Sales of a new product or service are an unknown quantity before an enterprise is launched but the costs of doing business are derived from existing activities that can be estimated. It is not difficult to find out the costs of equipment, premises, staff and other overheads. A first step in considering the financial future of a new venture is therefore to look at the likely cost base of making and delivering the product or service. From this a break-even point of the sales revenue that has to be generated to cover the cost base can be calculated. Comparing this break-even calculation with other estimates of sales gives a picture of how hard (or easy) it will be to make profits. The time it takes to achieve this break-even point is the cash burn period of a start-up and strongly influences the funding requirements of a new venture.

Top-Down Forecast Based on Market Potential Secondary data on the size of the total market is often available from market research reports. In other cases, industry information is available from trade bodies and associations or government statistical offices.[8] These tend to give information on large-scale markets and do not always have detailed reports on the niche markets typical of new ventures. However they can give indications of trends and the potential total market for a new product or service, and therefore form an important part of the triangulation of evidence for demand.

Comparative Forecast Based on Other Market Players The demand for comparable products and services can form the basis of a further estimate of sales. This is especially relevant if the new product is an extension or modification of an existing product, or if it has a direct competitor. Where the venture is based upon a break-through innovation, this is more difficult but estimates can be based on substitute products or services already in the marketplace.

Market Research and Tests Taking soundings in the market place is an essential part of forecasting the future of an entrepreneurial venture, however it is done. It can be done through qualitative interviews and focus groups or quantitatively through larger-scale surveys. Entrepreneurs, even those that launch high-growth companies, often shy away from formalised primary research as they feel it is not reliable and only serves to slow down the innovation process (Hills and Hultman, 2005). They prefer informal research by talking to experts within the marketplace and networking with potential customer groups.

An important way to take some of the risk out of a new venture is to undertake a market test in which the new product or service is launched in a limited area to test the reactions and take-up of the marketplace (Allen, 2009). This then forms an important piece of evidence on which to base forecasts for the roll-out of the venture to a larger market.

A forecasting puzzle

An entrepreneurial student developed a new product, inspired by visiting his grandfather who had Alzheimer's disease. He found that his grandfather enjoyed doing jigsaw puzzles but that conventional puzzles were inappropriate to his attention span and problem-solving abilities. So he developed a range of puzzles adapted to his specific needs. These proved so popular in his grandfather's care home that he decided to market his new product more widely. But how many should he produce? How many could he expect to sell in a limited market such as this?

He based his estimates on a number of different enquiries. First he found out what it would cost to produce the puzzles in various quantities from manufacturers. This indicated that a volume of at least 250 puzzles was needed to keep costs at a realistic level. Next he found out how many people suffered from Alzheimer's regionally, nationally and internationally. He also found out how many homes specialised in dementia conditions in his local region. This gave him a picture of the total market potential. He also found out that other products such as large print books with rich imagery were available for such patients and looked at the financial accounts of a company that sold these products. This told him that there was a small but profitable niche market for such activities. Finally he undertook a market test, by producing a small batch of puzzles and taking them into a number of homes and gauging the reactions of both patients and staff. He also enquired what level of budgets the homes had for buying such products. From this triangulation of evidence he was able to build up his first forecast of sales and costs to make and sell his product.

Ben Atkinson-Willes and his puzzle

15

15.6 SUMMARY AND ACTIVITIES

Financial management in entrepreneurial contexts is different because the uncertainty of outcomes and characteristics of the entrepreneur makes raising finance more difficult, forecasting less accurate and managing cash more crucial. Different types of money should be used for different purposes. Entrepreneurs favour **debt** over **equity** funding because they prefer to remain in control and banks are the most popular source for this.

Loans have become more used than **overdrafts** because of the increased security of lending. **Invoice discounting** is also more popular for established businesses because the facility automatically increases as the enterprise grows. Commercial mortgages, leasing, hire purchase and international trade finance are also used.

Private equity or **venture capital (VC)** funding is provided either by specialist companies or by high-net-worth individuals also known as **business angels**. Venture capital funds provide finance from pooled investments of third-party investors and it is available in different stages of the development of an enterprise from seed funding to finance for an **Initial Public Offering (IPO)**. Most countries have an active VC industry, with the US and the UK the most developed. Business angel investments are an important source of equity finance as they tend to target an area of perceived difficulty in raising funds from £50,000 to £1 million.

Relationships with banks are affected by the economic cycle. During the recent downturn banks have been accused of not doing enough to help small businesses. The so-called **finance gap** does arise for funding between £100,000 to £500,000. Women and ethnic minority entrepreneurs also have particular problems securing finance.

Cash flow tracks the movements of money in and out of the business. It is different to a **profit and loss** account that records the difference between sales revenues and costs. The **balance sheet** shows the sources and uses of funds in a business at any one time. Debtors and stock levels particularly affect the **liquidity**, or cash available to a business.

Forecasting finance is made more accurate by **triangulation** of different sources of information including: the cost base; market potential; competition; and market research and tests.

REVIEW QUESTIONS

1 Which factors make raising and managing finance in an entrepreneurial environment different from other contexts?

2 Name five types of debt finance and their principal uses.

3 What is the difference between equity and debt finance?

4 Name six stages of venture capital funding and its usage.

5 Give an example of a Public Equity Fund. What is an IPO?

6 What is a 'business angel'? Why are they important to entrepreneurial ventures?

7 What causes market failure in meeting the demands of entrepreneurial ventures for finance?

8 What is the difference between the cash flow and profitability of an enterprise?

9   What do the two sides of a balance sheet represent? Name some key headings that the owner of a growing business should watch particularly carefully.

10   'Reliable financial forecasts depend on triangulation'. What is meant by triangulation? How would you use this to produce a financial forecast for a new venture?

SEMINAR TASK

Governments around the world are being asked to ensure that new ventures and small businesses receive the finance they need. However, banks are often reluctant to take the risks of funding entrepreneurial businesses, and venture capital is not readily available in the small amounts that entrepreneurs frequently need.

You have been asked to advise government on this important issue and in particular whether to intervene or allow market forces to prevail. Summarise the arguments on both sides and present your recommendations.

Preview case continued

Boogles adds up

COURTESY OF BOOGLE LTD.

Lisa Newton started Boogles Ltd at the age of 23, in the month she finished her Master's degree in investment management, with just £150. Never having had a full-time job in her life, Lisa's transition from full-time education to full-time entrepreneur was perhaps made slightly easier as she was (in her own words) 'still in student mode'. With so little start-up capital, there were no flashy offices, only a back bedroom and a kitchen table. Some businesses (including online businesses) are easier to start this way: Michael Dell began his computer company in his university dorm, Henry Ford started in a garage, and Facebook launched from a college campus. So Boogles are in good company although it was natural for them to keep a keen eye on the figures – they are bookkeepers who keep the accounts for other companies.

Lisa has stuck to being frugal and budgeting carefully. She decided that the clients' premises were the best place to carry out the work as it reduced the outlay on premises costs. This was important as they initially operated in Nottingham and London, where rents are not cheap.

The £150 was made up of £100 of Lisa's personal overdraft and a £50 investment from her mum. It takes personal sacrifice to begin a business in this way, but Lisa saw this as part of the challenge of entrepreneurship:

> 'I did not really miss having a regular pay cheque as I had never worked full-time before. You don't need money to start a business. You just need passion and an idea, and other people will be drawn to help you on your mission.

15

▶

Entrepreneurial finance is different in that often the first people an entrepreneur will seek funds from are friends and family. They often raid their own resources before approaching the bank, and on the whole, women tend to be more cautious than men.'

The banks were not keen to take a risk with Boogles until it had proved itself. With a young entrepreneur at the helm who had no track record of even working in a full-time job, they were very restrictive. Lisa used credit cards, constantly transferring the balances to get those offering nought per cent interest rates. Initially she did this in her own name, but as the business established a track record, banks become more willing to lend finance to the company, although a director's guarantee always had to be signed. The first bank account was with the Bank of Scotland, but they would not give Boogles an overdraft, only a £500 credit limit on a credit card. After three years of struggling, Lisa switched to HSBC where she had had a personal account since her student days. HSBC immediately approved a loan of £10,000, an overdraft facility of £8500 and a credit card limit of £1500.

With so little start-up finance, Boogles experienced severe growing pains. In the first five years, turnover doubled year on year, and each time they had to find the money through careful juggling to pay the new staff as they came on board. Initially, Boogles would invoice clients monthly on 28-day payment terms, and pay staff weekly. As the business grew, this become less and less feasible, so Lisa switched it around. Staff are now paid monthly, and clients are invoiced fortnightly on 7-day payment terms (extended to 14 days if they pay by direct debit). Expenses were paid by credit card, fully utilising the credit terms on nought per cent finance wherever possible. Lisa explains the difficulties that she, and other entrepreneurs in these circumstances, experience:

'Cash flow is crucial to small businesses particularly those under

funded from the offset. A growing business *needs* to have money spent and reinvested. Setting up staff contracts, client terms of business, the website, trademarks – all need to be paid for initially. And then some costs like new product development are constant. Despite being profitable, I have always had to manage the cashflow carefully, because the costs continue to rise through expansion. Having enough cash helps a business to grow more easily. It's like having enough blood in your body. The blood which is there has to pump around your system faster to keep all the organs functioning … and you can't do too much as you don't have the funds for it. As the business grew, it got too big for just me and the kitchen table so I had to take on an administrator and premises – all fixed costs, which have to be met each month. The good thing is that businesses like Boogles don't waste money. They can't afford to. As long as a business remains lean and efficient, it will be profitable and in good order. When companies employ lots of staff, there is more room for them to hide and skive off.'

Boogles opted for debt finance all the way. As they have grown and made money, they have paid back debt … and then borrowed more, and then paid it back, and then borrowed more. Undoubtedly, the Boogles brand and business is worth more now than the original £150 investment, so Lisa believes she was right not to seek an outside investor:

'Interest payments on loans can be written off as an expense. But had I been funded by equity and not nought per cent credit card debt, then paying to buy out that investor would've been much more difficult and expensive because the value of the asset "Boogles" would have

▶

increased over all the years we've been trading. And then I would still have to find the money to pay them out. So, using equity investment such as a dragon or an angel has its price. As the sole director, I have far more influence on the direction of my company, and perhaps an investor would not have agreed with me (rightly or wrongly).'

Boogles has constantly added new products and services since it began in 2004 as a bookkeeping service for small businesses and charities. Lisa soon added a division solely dedicated to solicitor's accounts and legal bookkeeping. She has also developed other income streams such as short courses on accounting software and weekend money courses for women.

She was keen not to limit the brand to just bookkeeping but to establish her core theme as numbers and money. Through customer feedback, she recognised that there was a fun and child-friendly element to their brand name, and so added two other things to the product mix: the Boogles kids club aimed at helping young people to understand the value of money, and a maths game called 'Making Numbers Fun!' aimed at 5–11-year-olds. Boogles now have a series of books, CDs and other products available from their online shop. Lisa has managed to fund this constant product development with partnerships, not cash:

> 'Sometimes entrepreneurial businesses don't need the money, they need the ability to get a job done. For example, I had students to illustrate my books. Sweat equity if you like but in return, they get their name in print. So, forming win-win partnerships that exchange no cash, is one way in which entrepreneurial businesses can get a job done plus generate goodwill in their local community by providing jobs for work experience.'

A new short story written by Lisa Newton that illustrates the steep learning curve when starting up a business.

With a degree in accounting and marketing, Lisa not only had the finance skills but she also understood how to attract customers and keep them happy. She realised the importance of having a good brand and has always tried to develop its value. Again, she has managed to do this without the investment of much cash. Boogles has benefited from free PR through winning various awards. Lisa won 'Young Entrepreneur of the Year Award' in 2007, and in the following year Boogles won an 'Enterprising Business Award' plus £1000 for new product development (which they used to get their maths game created). Through free publicity she has raised awareness of her business which has helped her raise funds from the bank. As Lisa says: 'Sometimes it's not "cash funding" that you need, but the end result in publicity, raised awareness, or an end product, which you can then sell and raise cash, and invest that money back into the business.'

15

Boogles' latest project is to develop the bookkeeping service as a franchise. They were awarded funding of £3000 to test the feasibility of this as a business proposition. Lisa sees this initiative as a way of financing the business using other people's money:

> 'Franchising a business model brings income into the business which is reinvested to build the brand name and extend it further across the franchised territories. Plus, you get great, competent people who want to push the name further for you. And arguably, a franchisee will work much harder than any employee. So, using other people's money and other people's time is how many entrepreneurs grow their business, regardless of whether they start out with cash or not.'

(To find out more about Boogles visit: www.boogles.co.uk.)

Questions

1 *Boogles shows us that it is possible to start from nothing and make something out of it.*

But would Lisa have benefited from raising more money from external equity either at the beginning or as the business grew?

2 *Were the banks right not to give Lisa an overdraft or loan when she first started when she had a convincing business idea and seemed well qualified to develop it?*

3 *Are there sources of funding for her business that Lisa has overlooked?*

4 *Lisa has followed a policy of constant innovation, funded from reciprocal arrangements, grants and, most recently, franchisees who pay to set up a Boogles branch. Instead, Lisa could have concentrated on one core service until it became cash positive, and then used this cash to expand the business in different directions. Evaluate the advantages and disadvantages of these alternative approaches, and offer Lisa your advice on future strategy.*

15.7 NOTES, REFERENCES AND FURTHER READING

Notes and Further Information

1. For example, in the UK sole traders and partnerships are not required to publish a profit and loss account and balance sheet, but limited companies are.

2. Chris Fogg of Kingston Innovation Centre said that he always asked entrepreneurs seeking investment why they needed this amount of money, and usually found that they could only justify a smaller amount in the early stages.

3. For a summary of advantages and disadavantages as applied to the UK market see Business Link's website at http://www.businesslink.gov.uk.

4. The BVCA's booklet on private equity (British Venture Capital Association, 2004) is an excellent guide to the industry for those seeking investment. It is available on their website (www.bvca.co.uk).

5. Most developed economies have an active private equity sector with national and regional associations that provide information on the industry. For example:

   - The Australian Private Equity and Venture Capital Association Limited (www.avcal.com.au)
   - China Venture Capital Association (CVCA) based in Hong Kong (www.cvca.com)

15

- European Private Equity and Venture Capital Association (EVCA) (www.evca.eu)
- National Venture Capital Association of the US (www.nvca.org)
- South African Venture Capital Association (www.savca.co.za).

6. A number of associations of business angels represents a good starting point for either investors or entrepreneurs to make contact with business angels. For example:

   - British Business Angels Association (BBAA) – successor to the National Business Angel Network (NBAN) – www.bbaa.org.uk.
   - EBAN is the European Trade Association for Business Angels and Early Stage Investors, an independent and non-profit association representing the interests of business angels networks and early stage venture capital funds and other entities involved in bridging the equity gap in Europe. EBAN was established with the collaboration of the European Commission in 1999 – www.eban.org.

7. The Enterprise Finance Guarantee was introduced in the UK in January 2009 in response to the economic downturn, replacing the Small Firms Loan Guarantee Scheme. The £1.3 billion scheme supports bank lending between £1000 and £1 million to businesses with a turnover of up to £25 million with a government guarantee of up to 75 per cent of the loan. The decision on whether or not to use it for any specific loan was however fully delegated to the lenders, that is the banks.

8. A summary of the sources of information for entrepreneurs, particularly focused on the UK market, is given in Stokes, D. and Wilson, N. (2006) *Small Business and Entrepreneurship*, 5th edition, London: Thomson Learning, p. 1771.

References

Allen, K.R. (2009) *Launching New Ventures*, 5th edition, Boston: Houghton Mifflin.

Bank of England (2003) *Finance for Small Firms – A Tenth Report*, April, London: Bank of England.

Bank of England (2004) *Finance for Small Firms – An Eleventh Report*, April, London: Bank of England.

Berry, A., Grant, P. and Jarvis, R. (2003) *Can European Banks Plug the Finance Gap for UK SMEs?* ACCA Report No. 81, Certified Accountants Educational Trust, London.

Bridge, R. (2009) Banks demand total security, *The Sunday Times*, 8 March.

British Venture Capital Association (2004) *A Guide to Private Equity*, October, BVCA and Price Water House Coopers, London.

British Venture Capital Association (2008) *Private Equity and Venture Capital Report on Investment Activity 2007*, July, BVCA and PricewaterhouseCoopers, London.

Burns, P. (2001) *Entrepreneurship and Small Business*, Basingstoke: Palgrave.

Center for Venture Research (2008) *2007 Angel Market Analysis Report*, Whittemore School of Business, University of New Hampshire, Durham, www.unh.edu/news.

Collis, J., Jarvis, R. and Skerratt, L. (2004) The demand for the audit in small companies in the UK, *Accounting & Business Research*, 34 (2): 87–100.

Cosh, A. and Hughes, A. (2000) *British Enterprise in Transition*, ESRC Centre of Business Research, University of Cambridge.

Cressy, R. (2006) Venture capital, in Casson, M. *et al.* (eds) *The Oxford Handbook of Entrepreneurship*, Oxford: Oxford University Press, pp. 580–600.

Cruickshank, D. (2000) *Competition in UK Banking: A Report to the Chancellor of the Exchequer*, HMSO.

EBAN (2008) *Special Issue 8th EBAN Annual Congress 2008 – Matchme*, 14-15 April, Arnhem, Netherlands.

EVCA (2009) Private equity activity slows during 2008, Press Release from *EVCA Investors Forum* 2009, 12 March, Geneva, www.evca.eu.

Federation of Small Businesses (2009) *Putting the Economy Back on Track: Business Support and Finance*, London: FSB.

Hills, G.E. and Hultman, C.M. (2005) Marketing, entrepreneurship and SMEs: Knowledge and education revisited, *Proceedings of the 10th Annual Research Symposium of the Academy of Marketing Special Interest Group on Entrepreneurial and SME Marketing*, Southampton University, 6-7 January 2005.

15

Jones, R. (2009) Credit crunch imperils small businesses in Europe, *International Herald Tribune*, 12 March.

Jarvis, R. (2006) Finance and the small business, in Carter, S. and Jones-Evans, D. (eds) *Enterprise and Small Business: Principles, Practice and Policy*, 2nd edition, Harlow, Essex: Pearson Education, pp. 338–356.

KPMG and SAVCA (2008) *Venture Capital and Private Industry Performance 2007*, May, KPMG South Africa.

Mason, C. (2006) Venture capital and the small business, in Carter, S. and Jones-Evans, D. (eds) *Enterprise and Small Business: Principles, Practice and Policy*, 2nd edition, Harlow, Essex: Pearson Education, pp. 357–384.

Mason, C. and Harrison, R. (2000) The size of the informal venture capital market in the UK, *Small Business Economics*, 15 (2): 137–148.

National Venture Capital Association (2009) *Venture Capital Investments by Q4 and Full Year 2008 – National Data*, NVCA, US (availailable at www.nvca.org).

Ram, M., Barrett, G. and Jones, T. (2006) Ethnicity and entrepreneurship, in Carter, S. and Jones-Evans, D. (eds) *Enterprise and Small Business: Principles, Practice and Policy*, 2nd edition, Harlow, Essex: Pearson Education, pp. 192–208.

Wiltbank, R. and Boeker, W. (2007) *Returns to Angel Investors in Groups*, Ewing Marion Kauffman Foundation, Missouri (available at www. http://www.eban.org/download/Angel_groups).

Recommended Further Reading

Cressy, R. (2006) Venture capital, in Casson, M. *et al.* (eds) *The Oxford Handbook of Entrepreneurship*, Oxford: Oxford University Press, pp. 580–600.

Jarvis, R. (2006) Finance and the small business, in Carter, S. and Jones-Evans, D. (eds) *Enterprise and Small Business: Principles, Practice and Policy*, 2nd edition, Harlow, Essex: Pearson Education, pp. 338–356.

Mason, C. (2006) Venture capital and the small business, in Carter, S. and Jones-Evans, D. (eds) *Enterprise and Small Business: Principles, Practice and Policy*, 2nd edition, Harlow, Essex: Pearson Education, pp. 357–384.

15

Part 3 Integrative Case Studies

INTEGRATIVE Case Study 7

Exit/Closures

Breaking the Mould: A Study of Donegal China

By Dermot Breslin, *University of Sheffield*

Donegal China was founded in Ballyshannon, Ireland in 1985 by entrepreneur Danny Breslin, then in his forties. Danny's inspiration for setting up a business derived from his experience of growing up in Derry, where he observed the successes of many small business owners 'despite the weaknesses that they possessed'. From an early age he was intent upon creating a new venture as soon as a suitable opportunity presented itself. Whilst working as a management accountant for the long-established porcelain company Belleek China, Danny recalled a conversation with the managing director, which sparked the idea to create a porcelain business to exploit the growing giftware market in Ireland and overseas.

Whilst Danny was an experienced management accountant, he lacked the necessary production and sales expertise to run a successful porcelain company and he convinced a number of individuals from a rival porcelain company to start the business with him. To differentiate their product from that of major rivals, Donegal China made their product designs simpler and lighter, and exploited the use of transfers as opposed to hand painting the china. Following start-up the company's sales rapidly expanded both within Ireland and beyond to North America and the UK. Danny noted that in these initial years customers wanted Donegal China because they perceived it to be cheaper,

more modern and better quality. Danny took responsibility for the marketing operation and lacking experience in this area learnt the skills needed through experimentation and trial and error.

Danny recalled how he drove both himself and the team within the growing business to continually 'be better' than their competitors. On one occasion following start-up, he noticed that the weight of the products being made by the production team resembled that offered by competitors. Danny felt that this similarity stemmed from the strong entrenchment of the rival company's practices within his colleagues, and was determined to make them view the product and the production process from a different perspective. In a discussion with the production directors, Danny told them that 'everything that you have made that is that weight will be destroyed today', and together all three destroyed every piece of porcelain that had been made in the previous three weeks. Danny pointed out that this action was necessary in order to change the mentality of the team, and he stressed to them that their existing approach would not differentiate the product enough in the marketplace. Danny felt that Donegal China not only had to break the link with the conventional view of hand-painted porcelain, but break the behavioural mould that had shaped the team's way of operating and viewing the market. Danny's drive to 'be better' drove the company's growth and development in the first ten years following start-up as the firm grew from 10 to 100 employees (mainly in the production department) and to a turnover of £2 million per annum.

The company's growth during this period was principally through retail sales to gift shops and department stores throughout Ireland and overseas. Danny's drive to 'be better' continued to open up a number of lucrative markets for the company. For example, during this period the company opened a state-of-the-art visitor's centre complete with catering facilities, showrooms and audio-visual rooms, located on the main road into the North West region of Ireland, with a view to increasing sales margins by selling china direct to customers thereby exploiting the growing tourist trade in the region. Upon discovering this opportunity, Danny embarked upon a series of public relations exercises to attract visitors to the factory, and negotiated with regional coach operators, hoteliers and tourist centres to put Donegal China firmly on the map as a tourist destination. As a result of this expansion, the company recruited staff to deal with the provision of services to visiting tourists including caterers, retail sales, coach valeting services and the increasingly popular factory tours. As a result of these moves, the company gained a reputation as an innovative dynamic business both building upon and adding to the growing tourism trade within the North West region.

However, ten years after start-up in the mid-1990s, sales at the company started to plateau, as both rival businesses and new entrants started to erode Donegal China's rapid growth in an increasingly competitive market. In light of these challenges facing the company, Danny decided to broaden the management team and recruit a professional marketing director. When the marketing director arrived at Donegal China in 1997, he commented on the company's disjointed approach to marketing which had resulted in a lack of co-ordination and planning with regard to the firm's strategic marketing direction. He therefore made a number of recommendations to the management team which included the establishment of a more consistent and efficient approach

to marketing, and a call for a radical change in the design of the porcelain. The new arrival felt that Donegal China's product designs were no longer in line with the changing demands of the Irish consumer. These changing habits and tastes of the Irish consumer were being driven by major economic and cultural shifts in the 1990s. In light of these changes, the ethnic giftware which accounted for up to 40 per cent of Donegal China's product range was no longer desirable. As Danny himself later noted, the 'days when people have glass cases full of giftware were gone'. Despite this realisation, Danny recalled how few of the recommendations made by the marketing director were followed up by the business.

Whilst the marketing director called for Donegal China to develop a more contemporary range of products to suit this changing marketplace, the production team resisted any attempt to change the existing product range which might have implications on the way the china was made and in particular the mould design. As a result the company's response to these recommendations was to continue to innovate in a piecemeal fashion using existing mould and transfer designs. During the late 1990s Donegal China replaced up to 30 per cent of their product range in an attempt to introduce new designs and increase sales. However, the firm's sales continued to fall, as major retailers demanded discounts from products that were selling poorly. The arrival of the marketing director created tension within the existing management team who viewed him as 'lacking in pragmatism'. Indeed, the new arrival commented on the strong production and financial bias in the company and called for a stronger orientation towards marketing to deal with the changing marketplace and customer tastes. These comments further aggravated existing tensions not only within the production team but with Danny himself who up to that point had assumed complete control of the marketing operation. The existing team felt that the new arrival was poorly placed to make these comments given his lack of experience within the industry. Moreover, the team felt that their existing approach had been proven in the marketplace given the success of the business over the previous 12 years. Ironically, the behavioural mould that Danny had so passionately broken in the early days of Donegal China had become resistant to any further attempt to change. This resistance was manifest not only in the company's product design but the practices and approaches adopted by the entire management team.

These difficulties resulted in the marketing director's failure to become assimilated into the existing management team, who continued to view his approach as 'hands-off' and lacking any understanding of the design/production process. A further consequence of this division was the polarisation of opinions on how Donegal China should adapt the product range, and the entrenchment of the existing view of what that product range consisted of. The team never resolved their differences and the marketing director left in 1998. Following the departure of the marketing director, Danny recalled how he 'saw the writing on the wall', and convinced the management team that they look for a buyer for the business. 'Giftware as we made it, and as it was known as a collectible, was no longer a collectible'. Danny believed that the only viable future for the company in the changing marketplace was to downsize to a much smaller scale and sell exclusively direct to customers. This option, however, could not have sustained the company at its existing size. Therefore, Danny together with the management team decided to sell the business to Belleek China in 2000.

QUESTIONS

1 How did changes in the Irish giftware market in the 1990s influence the decision to sell the business?

2 How did the growth of Donegal China constrain its ability to adapt to changes in the marketplace towards the late 1990s?

3 To what extent did Donegal China balance its management team to both exploit existing knowledge and continue to explore market opportunities as the company grew?

Rural/Craft Enterprise

Formed Steel

By Prof. Mike Clements, *Staffordshire University* and Prof. Chris Birch, *Thames Valley University*

Kathy Jones was born in Kenya and brought up in Swaziland. She grew up in a family involved in 'making things' for sale in the local craft tourist industry. From an early age she had shown a delight in working with materials, some of which she had made for sale to friends and family. Friends and associates alike consider her a person of determination and self-belief in her ability to succeed at whatever she applies herself to. With a pleasant but steely personality, at the age of nineteen she travelled alone to England to undertake a 3D Design Craft degree at Staffordshire University, graduating with a First Class Honours degree. As part of her degree studies she found herself with a particular skill and love of working with metals, in particular iron and steel, winning whilst a student a number of local awards and featuring in the local newspapers. Her work drew considerable attention at the year-end exhibition of student work, where she was able to sell a number of her items. Though receiving encouragement from her tutor to continue her academic studies, she decided instead to enrol on the University's one year Enterprise Fellowship Scheme aimed at helping graduates start their own businesses. She has been on this programme, which includes provision of premises and access to specialised equipment, intensive business training and external mentor support, for almost a year and will soon be facing the prospect of 'going-it alone'.

Like most new craft-based firms, she has no predetermined product mix, rather responding to what enquiries she has received where she feels confident enough that these enquiries will generate satisfactory income. She is not afraid to reject commissions that do not appear to make her money, though where she feels her prestige might be increased by taking the commission she will give consideration even though it will not make her a profit. In her first year of trading she has produced sculptures, candlesticks and garden furniture.

These are tailor-made (bespoke items) to order, each individually hand-made in steel. Her love in what she does is the challenge of the next product; as she says 'I like the immediacy of working with steel. With lots of crafts it can take a long time to see the finished product, but with forged steel it is almost immediate.' Her studies have introduced her to the rudiments of pricing and costing. She is aware as a new artist that her commissions will not command high prices until she is established and thought highly of in the market. She has, however, been working to a simple model where she will cost an enquiry against the time she estimates it will take her to complete it and the amount of materials required, apportion a percentage to that amount to

cover her overheads and then add what she sees as a reasonable profit for the job, conscious that the final price needs to fall within the expectations of the client. To date that has worked well for her. She is no accountant, she tells you. She is satisfied with the income generated over the first year and the repeat business it has produced, though she feels at times it would be 'wonderful to have a holiday once in a while'.

From time to time she has considered the idea of taking on some help, but worries that she would not be able to provide them with a steady income to reflect their skills. She has never employed anyone before and worries about recruiting a 'suitable person'. She knows she is a perfectionist with her work and worries that she might not be a good employer.

She has a clear vision of her market segments. She supplies her products to what she calls 'affluent people' prepared to pay for something out of the ordinary in their gardens or homes. She has found that even in times of economic downturn, this market continues to thrive. Her other market has been what she calls 'public art', working on commissions from local councils and community projects. Being based in a craft/equestrian centre with over 20,000 visitors to the centre and the equestrian events it hosts every year, she finds visitors enquire and commission her work or visit her on the recommendation of others. She intends to continue working out of these premises for the foreseeable future. To date, unlike some of her contemporaries, she has chosen not to sell her work through (art) galleries. She feels they can be unkind to new artists, promoting works of more established artists whenever possible and because of the principle of sale-or-return operated by the galleries and, as she puts it, the 'immoral prices' they charge the client she is disinclined to use them as a sales outlet.

Her marketing and promotion relies entirely upon her own efforts. She has learnt the importance of word-of-mouth and networking for a small company and is pleased at how well she is now prepared to promote herself and her company at every opportunity. She has joined local art/artist and business groups as well as featuring in a number of promotional brochures produced by the local council. Her work has meant sometimes local public bodies will now approach her, but otherwise she is always prepared to pitch for new commissioned work as and when the opportunities arise.

She has engaged a friend to construct a website for her. She has great plans for this website but at present is little more than letting people know she exists.

She admits her financial system consists of a shoe box for receipts and invoices aided by a simple financial spreadsheet she produced whilst on the EFS Scheme, but she maintains 'it works'. She has been able, using the opportunities of the scholarship, to incur a minimum of start-up costs, financing her business to date from funding and the commissions she has achieved. She is not too keen on the idea of taking on significant debt to support the company. She realises there may be times when there will be shortfalls between income and expenditure but hopes the local bank manager will be sympathetic with her existing small overdraft facility.

Overall she feels the year where she has had the opportunity to start up her business using the university scholarship has been a most satisfying experience. She is even more determined than before that she wants to succeed as a commercial artist running her own company. She is equally excited about her forthcoming marriage and plans to start a family in the not too distant future.

As closure to the Enterprise Fellowship Scheme she is eligible to a counselling session with a qualified business adviser, who will provide impartial advice as to the opportunities ahead for her. You are asked to consider yourself in the role that role of that adviser.

QUESTIONS

1 Given the difficulty for new firms to survive beyond their first two years of operation, what do you believe should be her priorities for the next 12 months?

2 She has asked you to help her develop an outline business plan to cover this period.

3 With her marriage approaching and her plans to start a family soon after, identify what might be the impact upon both her business and her family and her current work/life balance.

Smart421

The Start-Up That Never Gave Up

By Steve Barnes, *University Campus Suffolk*

A new company was born in 1989 in the UK, called Salmon, and Julian Harris was one of the five directors appointed with a mission to be the Number 1 PacBase consultancy in the UK. Pacbase is a COBOL code generator that is developed and maintained by IBM, and it runs on a mainframe computer. The applications that are produced by this structured programming language are big, and would typically be used for complex enterprise solutions like council tax, utility billing systems, and other public service applications.

Things started well, the client base started with a few large 'blue chip' customers, the pipeline grew and work seemed secure. Julian admitted that he didn't know the first thing about how to run a business, and didn't really think about an exit strategy either. He was just enjoying the buzz of trying to create the best computer company in the world.

Just three months after Julian joined the company, they ran out of work, as customers stopped spending money and the country had to cope with the first of a number of technology recessions. This recession was deep and long-lasting, and it is only by looking back that we can see how serious it was. A recession that is severe by recent historical standards lasts around two years (Schmitt and Baker, 2008); the 1989 recession lasted longer with unemployment reaching a peak in 1989, and not recovering until after 1992 (ibid.).

Prospects were bad, directors drifted off, and Julian took to contracting in the City of London, to make ends meet. It looked like the dream had come to a very quick end, and for the next few years the company struggled.

In 1993, work started to pick up for Salmon as the country recovered, and as income started to grow again. From 1993 until 1999, revenue was doubling every year and this was noticed by industry analysts. It was rated 31st-fastest growing company in the UK by *Sunday Times Fast-track* and by the year 2000 it had posted revenues of £22 milion, with a staff of 350. The boom times had come it seemed, for Salmon and many other technology and 'dot-com' companies. Stock values raced ahead as speculators bought into the technology sector, and company values soared.

Then, on 13 March 2000 the NASDAQ saw its largest fall in stock prices that year, and once again Salmon, along with many other technology companies, would have to fight for its life as the recession started to develop. This time Salmon was much larger and so had further to fall, and business life was stressful and sometimes unpleasant. Julian and his equal shareholder and joint CEO had to make the decision whether to sell the company on the open market, demerge it, or to sell his share to the other directors.

Julian decided to restart, and in June 2000 started a new company, called Smart421: Smart solutions for the

21st Century. This time it was aimed at providing complex, multi-channel solutions to blue-chip clients. The company had to rebrand, reposition, and in many ways start again. It was a very creative time, and many new small companies were formed by the Smart421 group: Oakington, GUTS, SmartIntegrator, and others. On reflection this was a creative, hugely enjoyable, but costly exercise, and the company started to lose focus, customers and lots of money.

The combination of the dotBomb in the early 2000s and loss of focus was painful. On one day Julian had to sack 50 people! The overdraft was growing, and at one point Julian had to secure their £1 million overdraft against invoices for work carried out, but which was falling in value month by month. Pay cuts started to bite, and staff became demoralised. Times were hard and getting harder. The company had missed its exit window because the falling value of the company and the tough financial environment just wouldn't allow a company sale.

In 2003, Smart421 was again restructured, repositioned and started to try to recover. It was now selling high-end complex solutions with niche software toolsets like IBM Webshare. Other changes were brought in as they closed their non-core business, and Julian began the process of building the company value to meet the exit strategy of selling it to the highest bidder. This time he wasn't going to miss the exit window. In 2003 they worked out that to build real value for an exit, they needed to increase the forward order book, and the key decision that was made was to provide clients with more outsourced, managed services work, rather than just short-term consultancy, which then allowed them to lock in customers to three-year deals.

The exit process started in September 2005, and took 12 months of careful management and patience waiting for the right market timing and for income figures to recover. The process was clear: firstly, Julian set up a beauty parade of M&A consultancies who specialised in the IT sector. Working with these they built the Information Memorandum for the company, i.e. their sales document.

Finally, an invitation to tender went out to 30 targets and after short listing a blind auction ran on a select few. Four weeks were taken to complete due diligence, before final selections took place. On 29 September 2006 Kingston communications acquired smart421 for £24.24 million.

So what were the keys to success?

The company It had valuable underlying business with blue-chip clients, a strong management team and revenues of over £10 million. It had high profitability with 15 per cent+ margins, it had an order book with a pipeline, and an inventory of high-end skills by its employees.

The Process Revenues were grown through the whole of the deal-forming period, and negotiations were well managed. The timing of the sale with market behaviour was good and, most importantly, the process was managed *not* by the acquirer, so there were always choices.

Lessons from the process Don't underestimate the strain on the underlying business, and mentally prepare staff for the ups and the downs that will inevitably occur. Don't underestimate the petty stuff, e.g. photocopy maintenance, etc. Remember, it's an emotional time for all in the company, but with the right attitude it can be fun! Get good advisers but make your own decisions.

PERSONAL LESSONS FOR THE CEO

Decide what you are: lifestyle or growth, and then plan your exit, but plan it at the beginning – when, who, how much, terms. Determine share ownership and structure at the beginning and make sure all stakeholders have the same vision. Understand the value drivers of your industry. **What** do you have and **who** would pay **what** for it, e.g. IPR, customers, order book, etc. 'Get big, get niche or get out'.

WHY DID HE KEEP TRYING?

'You have to be single-minded, and I believed that I could pull us through. In any case I had invested too much to lose and I had other livelihoods relying on me. It would have been pretty hard to work for someone else once I had made the leap to run my own show'.

WHERE IS HE NOW?

Julian now lives with his family in Sydney and has started a new technology company (www.first-servis.com.au) and sits on the board of an environmental NPF (www.ozgreen.org.au).

QUESTIONS

1 Julian Harris has listed his reasons for success. Can you add any others from the information you have?

2 Why didn't Julian go to a VC to get the money he needed to continue rather than fight on his own?

3 Julian chose 'sale' as an exit strategy. What others could he have chosen, and with what benefits?

REFERENCES

Schmitt, J. and Baker, D. (2008) *What We're In For: Projected Economic Impact of the Next Recession*, Washington, DC: Center for Economic and Policy Research.

GLOSSARY OF TERMS

Action learning an approach to learning that emphasizes *experience* as a possible source of learning

Asset anything of worth owned by the business, including *tangible assets* such as cash, property, equipment and stocks, and *intangible assets* such as image and customer goodwill

Asset parsimony using the minimum possible amount of assets to deliver the organization's outputs

Banner advertising advertising through promotional messages on web sites

Base rate also called the Repo (repurchase transaction) rate, this is the borrowing and lending rate set by the Bank of England

Benevolent autocracy management style that combines a firm but friendly control

Big Five personality dimensions five traits that have been put forward as important influences in entrepreneurship: need for achievement, need for autonomy, locus of control, risk-taking and self-efficacy

Branding strategy to clearly identify one product from another and develop positive associations with the brand name

Break-even the level of sales required to cover the ongoing costs of doing business

Business angel a wealthy individual who contributes personal funds and expertise, usually at an early stage of business development

Business closure the closure of a business entity

Business exit the exit of an owner from a business

Business failure the closure of a business that has substantially failed to meet the owner's objectives, usually leaving financial problems

Business model the means by which an enterprise opportunity is turned into a viable, value creating enterprise

Business plan a written document that identifies a business's goals and objectives and outlines how the firm intends to achieve these

Buy-out purchase of a business by its existing management

Buzz marketing word of mouth marketing communications prompted through provocative or amusing stories and events, usually created deliberately by the suppliers

Cash flow the movement of cash into and out of the business

Churn movements in and out of the business population through start-ups and closures

Competitive advantage a firm's relative market position and potential to differentiate what it sells from competitors' offerings

Confidential Disclosure Agreement (CDA) or Non-disclosure Agreement (NDA) legal contract that allows two or more parties to share confidential information whilst restricting the access of third parties

Copyright grant to the originator of a literary, musical, dramatic, or artistic work, the exclusive rights of publication, production, sale, or distribution

Core Competence the skills that enable a firm to deliver a fundamental customer benefit

Corporate entrepreneurship the venturing and innovation activities of companies, particularly larger ones

Customer relationship management (CRM) integrated information system used to plan and control all aspects of dealing with customers, and prospective customers

Domain name web site address

Dominant design a design of product or service that achieves some dominance in the market, usually after a period of competitive activity between new entrants (e.g. the QWERTY keyboard)

Dynamic capability a learned and stable pattern of collective activity through which the organization systematically generates and modifies its operating routines in pursuit of improved effectiveness

EC European Community: an economic and political organization formed in 1967. Its members are the same as those of the European Economic Community

Economy of scale significant cost reduction resulting from the high level of output in an industry

Effectuation an emergent approach to developing an enterprise, which emphasizes current resources and the present, rather than objectives in the future

Electronic commerce transactions in which products, services, and/or information is bought, sold, transferred or exchanged via computer networks, including the Internet

Enterprise culture a way of thinking or philosophy that values and fosters the entrepreneurial spirit

Entrepreneur/entrepreneurial team an individual or group who mediates the process of entrepreneurship

Entrepreneurial alertness the ability to scan the external environment for opportunity

Entrepreneurial marketing marketing carried out in an entrepreneurial context

Entrepreneurship dynamic the role of teams or individuals who work collectively, either formally or informally, to found new organizations and to create innovations

Equity gap funding gap held to be between approximately £250,000 and £2 million which results from a combination of supply-side and demand-side issues, including information asymmetry and a lack of investment readiness

EU an economic and political union established in 1993 after the ratification of the Maastricht Treaty by members of the European Community, which forms its core. In establishing the European Union, the treaty expanded the political scope of the European Community, especially in the area of foreign and security policy, and provided for the creation of a central European bank and the adoption of a common currency by the end of the twentieth century

Finance gap unwillingness on the part of suppliers of finance (often banks) to supply it on the terms and conditions required by small businesses

Flexible specialization gives priority to value maximization and product differentiation in contrast to mass production of standardized goods that emphasizes cost minimization. Enabled by subcontracting, collaboration and inter-firm networks

Flotation when a company first sells its stock to the general public, through a stock market

Free market a market economy based on supply and demand with little or no government control

GDP Gross Domestic Product. GDP is the grand total of all the consumer and government spending, investments and exports minus the value of imports

Gearing the percentage of borrowing compared to the percentage of assets. The gearing ratio measures the percentage of capital employed that is financed by debt and long-term finance. The higher the gearing, the higher the dependence on borrowings, and the higher the level of financial risk due to the increased volatility of profits

Goodwill arises when more is paid for a business than the value of its tangible assets. Includes the reputation, customers and skill base of a business

Incubator organization that supports businesses with a range of services including provision of space, management coaching, business planning, administrative services and sources of financing

Industry the firms that produce and sell products and services that are close substitutes for one another (i.e. sellers)

Initial Public Offering (IPO) making shares in a business available to the general public, usually through a stock exchange flotation

Innovation the successful exploitation of a new idea

Intellectual property rights (IPR) ideas, inventions, designs, know-how and names associated with the business form intellectual property (IP) that can be protected to become intellectual property rights

Intrapreneurship Term for Corporate Entrepreneurshipo

Investment readiness refers to an entrepreneur's understanding of the motivations, needs and information requirements of potential investors

Know-how information that gives potential value to an enterprise, often in the form of unprotected inventions, processes and formulae

Knowledge transfer making available the knowledge and expertise of an institution such as a university to business and other enterprises

Liability of newness refers to the difficulties experienced by new firms simply as a result of being 'new'

Life Cycle changes in an enterprise over time

Limited company a business that is organized in such a way as to give its owners limited liability

Liquidation when a business is terminated or bankrupt, its assets are sold, the proceeds paid to creditors and anything left is distributed to shareholders

Locus of control the belief that we can influence the environment in which we find ourselves

Macroenvironment consists of factors which have an impact on firms nationally and Internationally

Manufacturer innovation when the developer expects to benefit by selling it

Market existing or potential customers for a given product or service (i.e. buyers)

Market information information about customers and competitors

Market intelligence information on customers, competitors, and trends in the business environment

Market orientation business philosophy that puts customer needs at the centre of all decision-making

Marketing mix the marketing methods used by a business including product development, pricing, promotions and distribution

Microenvironment local factors which influence firms operating in particular markets and competing in certain industries

National systems of innovation the particular endowment of resources, technologies and capabilities that influence the potential of businesses to innovate in any country

Necessity-based entrepreneurship where individuals participate in entrepreneurial activities because all other employment options are either absent or unsatisfactory

Networking key management behaviour that produces a chain of interconnected persons and enables entrepreneurship

Opinion leaders people who strongly influence the perceptions of others including the customers in a particular market

Opportunity-based entrepreneurship where individuals participate in entrepreneurial activities in order to exploit a perceived business opportunity

Patent   grant that confers upon the creator of an invention the right to prevent others from making or selling the invention without license for a defined period

Path dependence   where an organization can only develop as fast as its past (and current) position, paths and processes allow

Portfolio entrepreneur   entrepreneur owning more than one business at the same time

Positioning   how a business or product/service is perceived in the marketplace in relation to its competitors

Product/service benefit   the value of a product or service to a customer

Profit and loss account   shows how a business is doing in terms of sales and costs - and the difference between them of profit or losses

Push and pull influences   motivations for becoming self-employed

Recession   a decline in the economy: if there is a decline for two quarters in succession, then it is officially a recession. A severe recession is a depression

Resource-based view of the firm   the approach that sees the firm's resources as the foundation for firm strategy

Resource-leveraging   key entrepreneurial management behaviour based on the premise of 'more for less'

Seeding trials   market tests that involve potential customers in the development of a product or service with the aim of enlisting them as advocates of the new product

Segmentation   categorizing customers and consumers into groups with similar needs and expectations from their purchases

Self-efficacy   an individual's belief in their ability to undertake and accomplish some particular task or activity

Serial entrepreneur   entrepreneur who owns more than one business sequentially, owning and selling each business in a relatively short time

SME   small and medium-sized enterprise

Social enterprise   a business with primarily social objectives whose surpluses are principally reinvested for that purpose in the business or in the community, rather than being driven by the need to maximize profit for shareholders and owners

Social entrepreneur   someone who works in an entrepreneurial manner, but for public or social benefit, rather than to make money

Social network   a network of individuals connected together by common interests, location, background, or activity and who may be resources to one another

Sole trader   business owned and controlled by one person who is solely liable for its obligations

Strategy   a plan, pattern, ploy, perspective, or position relating to how a business is going to compete, what its objectives are, and how these are to be achieved

Supply chain   the suppliers (both individuals and organizations) who provide goods and services to other organizations or enterprises in a sequence or chain all the way to the consumer

Technology   the combination of people, ideas, and objects to achieve a particular goal. Alternatively, it is the mix of physical appliances and human ways of doing things

User innovation   when the developer expects to benefit by using it

Venture capitalist   a person (usually working for a venture capital company) who invests money into risky but potentially very profitable businesses

Viral marketing   communication of marketing messages and opinions over the internet to generate exponential growth

Word of mouth marketing (WOM)   positive or negative recommendations for a product/service made through person-to-person communications perceived to be independent of the provider of the product/service

INDEX